Marriage in Ireland, 1660–1925

What were the laws on marriage in Ireland, and did the church and state differ in their interpretation? How did men and women meet and arrange to marry? How important was patriarchy and a husband's control over his wife? And what were the options available to Irish men and women who wished to leave an unhappy marriage? This first comprehensive history of marriage in Ireland across three centuries looks below the level of elite society for a multi-faceted exploration of how marriage was perceived, negotiated and controlled by the church and state, as well as by individual men and women within Irish society. Making extensive use of new and under-utilised primary sources, Maria Luddy and Mary O'Dowd explain the laws and customs around marriage in Ireland. Revising current understandings of marital law and relations, *Marriage in Ireland, 1660–1925* represents a major new contribution to Irish historical studies.

MARIA LUDDY is Emeritus Professor of Modern Irish History at the University of Warwick and a Fellow of the Royal Historical Society. Her book *Women and Philanthropy in Nineteenth-Century Ireland* (1995) was awarded the James S. Donnelly Sr Prize for best book in Irish history in 1996. She has published extensively on Irish social history, writing on unmarried mothers, nuns and the history of Irish childhood. Her most recent publications include *Prostitution and Irish Society, 1800–1940* (2007) and the co-edited collection *Children, Childhood and Irish Society, 1700 to the Present* (with James M. Smith, 2014).

MARY O'DOWD is Emeritus Professor of Gender History at Queen's University Belfast and a Member of the Royal Irish Academy. She has published extensively on women and gender in Irish history. Her most recent publications include *Reading the Irish Woman: Studies in Cultural Encounters and Exchange, 1714–1960* (co-authored with Gerardine Meaney and Bernadette Whelan, 2014) and *A History of the Girl: Formation, Education and Identity* (2018), which she co-edited with June Purvis.

Marriage in Ireland, 1660–1925

Maria Luddy
University of Warwick

Mary O'Dowd
Queen's University Belfast

CAMBRIDGE
UNIVERSITY PRESS

CAMBRIDGE
UNIVERSITY PRESS

University Printing House, Cambridge CB2 8BS, United Kingdom

One Liberty Plaza, 20th Floor, New York, NY 10006, USA

477 Williamstown Road, Port Melbourne, VIC 3207, Australia

314–321, 3rd Floor, Plot 3, Splendor Forum, Jasola District Centre, New Delhi – 110025, India

79 Anson Road, #06–04/06, Singapore 079906

Cambridge University Press is part of the University of Cambridge.

It furthers the University's mission by disseminating knowledge in the pursuit of education, learning, and research at the highest international levels of excellence.

www.cambridge.org
Information on this title: www.cambridge.org/9781108486170
DOI: 10.1017/9781108645164

© Maria Luddy and Mary O'Dowd 2020

First published 2020

Printed in the United Kingdom by TJ International Ltd, Padstow Cornwall

A catalogue record for this publication is available from the British Library.

Library of Congress Cataloging-in-Publication Data
Names: O'Dowd, Mary, author. | Luddy, Maria, author.
Title: Marriage in Ireland, 1660–1925 / Maria Luddy, University of Warwick, Mary O'Dowd, Queen's University Belfast.
Description: Cambridge, United Kingdom ; New York, NY : Cambridge University Press, 2020. | Includes bibliographical references and index.
Identifiers: LCCN 2019036968 (print) | LCCN 2019036969 (ebook) | ISBN 9781108486170 (hardback) | ISBN 9781108731904 (paperback) | ISBN 9781108645164 (epub)
Subjects: LCSH: Marriage–Ireland–History.
Classification: LCC HQ619 .O36 2020 (print) | LCC HQ619 (ebook) | DDC 306.8109417–dc23
LC record available at https://lccn.loc.gov/2019036968
LC ebook record available at https://lccn.loc.gov/2019036969

ISBN 978-1-108-48617-0 Hardback
ISBN 978-1-108-73190-4 Paperback

For Mary Cullen and Margaret MacCurtain who began it all

Contents

Figures

Illustrations

Tables

Acknowledgements

We gratefully acknowledge the Arts and Humanities Research Council for funding this project. This funding supported two wonderful research assistants, Dr Katie Barclay and Dr John Bergin. We are most thankful to them for their hard work, valuable insights and burrowings in the archives. We are also grateful to Dr Leanne Calvert for her work on the project and for generously sharing some of her own research on Presbyterian marriage. Many other individuals assisted with research over the years, in particular: Dr Antonina Kalinina, Dr Georgina Laragy, Dr Sean Lucey, Andrew Lyall, Dr Ruth Thorpe, Dr Alexandra Tierney and Dr Rachel Wilson. We thank too all those who attended the workshops organised under the auspices of the project, with special thanks for their contributions to Professor Joanna Begiato, Professor Catherine Clinton, Dr Elizabeth Foyster, Dr Claudia Kinmonth and Professor Rebecca Probert. Maria Luddy would like to thank Dr David Durnin in particular for his research expertise. Many colleagues generously provided us with research leads and information from their own work, which was much appreciated. We especially thank Dr Marie Coleman, Dr Elaine Farrell, the late Professor Ruth-Ann Harris, Dr Niamh Howlin, Dr Georgina Laragy, Dr Heather Laird, Dr John Logan, Máire Mac Conghail, Dr Des Marnane, Mary Mackey, Dr Anne O'Dowd, Rosemary Raughter, Professor Diane Urquhart and Professor Bernadette Whelan. Dr Claudia Kinmonth, Louisa Costelloe, the late Dr Vivienne Pollock and Dr Audrey Whitty provided helpful assistance on illustrations.

We also thank the staff of the many libraries and archives that we and our postdoctoral fellows used for our research: the British Library; Lambeth Palace Library; the Library of the Society of Friends, Dublin; the Linenhall Library, Belfast; the National Archives of Ireland; The National Archives, Kew; the National Library of Ireland; the Presbyterian Historical Society of Ireland, Belfast; the Public Record Office of Northern Ireland; the Royal Irish Academy and University College Dublin Archives. Libraries in Tralee and Tipperary also provided us with substantial support while we were engaged in research on the project. We would like particularly to thank the ever-helpful Deirdre

Wildy and the staff in the Special Collections Library at Queen's University Belfast. We are also grateful to the General Register Office, Ireland, for facilitating access to the marriage register of Johann Georg Schulz; and Irish Genealogy.ie for access to its database.

We visited a number of Catholic diocesan archives, the most welcoming of which were those of the Cork and Ross Diocesan Archives, Dublin Diocesan Archives, Kildare Diocesan Archives and the Galway Diocesan Archives. Unfortunately, a number of diocesan archives were closed, either because they had no archivist or did not wish to make their records available to researchers. Our visits to some ecclesiastical archives were limited by a refusal to allow us to look at cases related to marriage, even those going back over two hundred years.

Maria Luddy would like to thank the Department of History at Warwick University for its support of this project over the years. She is indebted to Robert Horton for all his help with figures and illustrations and his 'tiffing' expertise. She is also grateful for the use of the library facilities at Boston College, which has made online research a feasible option, and she is grateful to Dr Christian Dupont, director of the Burns Library, for continuing access to this resource. Mary O'Dowd acknowledges her gratitude to the history students at Queen's with whom she discussed her research on gender, family and marriage over many years. She also notes the financial support for research provided by Queen's University Belfast.

Our first readers were Professors Virginia Crossman and Bernadette Whelan. They made many wise suggestions for change, most of which we took on board. We also thank the anonymous reviewer of the manuscript for Cambridge University Press for a very supportive and helpful report.

The dedication reflects our admiration and respect for the work of two pioneering Irish women historians. Since the 1970s they have paved the way for all of us who engage with Irish gender history.

Abbreviations

BL	British Library, London
CIF	Criminal Index Files
CRF	Convict Reference Files
CSO/RP	Chief Secretary's Office, Registered Papers
DDA	Dublin Diocesan Archives
DIB	*Dictionary of Irish Biography*
DMP	Dublin Metropolitan Police
KL	Kildare and Leighlin Diocesan Archives
NAI	National Archives of Ireland
NLI	National Library of Ireland
ODNB	*Oxford Dictionary of National Biography*
PHSIB	Presbyterian Historical Society of Ireland, Belfast
PRONI	Public Record Office of Northern Ireland
TNA	The National Archives, Kew

Introduction

Marriage is one of the oldest institutions in Ireland. The earliest legal codes in Irish history incorporated a detailed set of regulations on the rights and responsibilities of husbands and wives. In the medieval period, marriage was at the core of the conflict between Gaelic and English customs and social practices. Marital alliances were also an essential element in sixteenth- and seventeenth-century political and economic networks. The continuing significance of family connections is also evident in eighteenth-century Irish political life. In the nineteenth century, the financial arrangements for marriage were an important factor in the economic structure of rural society. Marriage also set the parameters for the sexual moral code that prevailed in twentieth-century Irish society.

In this book we set out to write an extended study of the history of heterosexual marriage on the island of Ireland from 1660 to 1925. The time frame begins with the Restoration of Charles II as king of Ireland and ends with the parliamentary debate on divorce in the Irish Free State. The starting date of 1660 was partly determined by the availability of source material but the Restoration also marks the beginning of the legislative structure and the political divisions that were to frame the history of Ireland over the following two hundred and sixty years. We chose 1925 as our concluding year because the Oireachtas[1] debate on divorce marked a significant turning point in evolving attitudes to marriage in the Irish Free State and Northern Ireland. The public controversy provoked by the debate silenced parliamentary discussion on the possible introduction of divorce in the Irish Free State. The 1937 constitutional ban on divorce continued the reluctance of the Irish state to countenance legislation on marital dissolution and remarriage until compelled to do so in the 1990s. 1925 was also an important year in the history of divorce in Northern Ireland. By contrast with the Irish Free

---

[1] The Oireachtas refers to the two houses of the Irish legislature (the Dáil, lower house and Seanad, upper house).

1

State, the newly established parliament in Belfast agreed in 1921 to accept petitions for divorce and the first petition was read in the Northern Ireland House of Commons in 1925. Thereafter, marriage law in Northern Ireland was gradually brought into line with that in England. In 1939, divorce was transferred from the jurisdiction of the parliament to the High Court of Northern Ireland, a move that emphasised the increasing legal divergence of the two parts of the island.[2]

Irish Historiography on Marriage

The primary focus of this book is the logistics of marriage among the social classes below the level of wealthy landowning families: exploring how marriage was perceived, negotiated and controlled by church and state as well as by individual men and women. Despite the importance of marriage in Irish history, only a handful of historians have analysed it in depth. A number of significant publications have appeared on marriage in elite families. Anthony Malcomson has led the field with his research on the importance of heiresses in the survival of aristocratic families. Deborah Wilson elaborated on this theme to explore the property arrangements of married women in landed families and, in particular, the role of widows in the late eighteenth and early nineteenth centuries. More recently, Rachel Wilson has documented the marital and domestic arrangements of women in wealthy families for an earlier period while Maeve O'Riordan has explored similar issues for a later generation of women in Munster in the years between 1860 and 1914.[3]

Surprisingly little has been published on the history of marriage among the 'middling' and lower social classes in rural or urban society. There are scattered studies on individual marriages and marriage law but there is no major or extended study of the history of marriage in Ireland for any period of time. In the 1950s, K. H. Connell was the first historian to utilise parliamentary papers and contemporary literature to understand what he called 'peasant' marriage patterns in nineteenth-century Ireland.[4] Connell's conclusions on the prevalence of marriage at a young

---

[2] See Diane Urquhart, *Irish Divorce: A History* (Cambridge, 2020), chapter 5.
[3] A. P. W. Malcomson, *The Pursuit of the Heiress: Aristocratic Marriage in Ireland 1740–1840* (2nd ed., Belfast, 2006); Deborah Wilson, *Women, Marriage and Property in Wealthy Landed Families in Ireland, 1750–1850* (Manchester, 2009); Rachel Wilson, *Elite Women in Ascendancy Ireland, 1690–1745: Imitation and Innovation* (Woodbridge, Sussex, 2015). Maeve O'Riordan, *Women of the Country House in Ireland, 1860–1914* (Liverpool, 2018).
[4] K. H. Connell, 'Peasant marriage in Ireland after the Great Famine', *Past and Present*, 12 (1957), 76–91; 'Peasant marriage in Ireland: Its structure and development since the famine', *Economic History Review*, 14, 3 (1962), 502–23.

age in pre-Famine Ireland have been critiqued by a subsequent generation of historians searching for explanations for the rapid rise in the Irish population after 1750. Few scholars, however, have developed Connell's more general analysis on marriage in rural Ireland before and after the Great Famine (1845–1850). In 1985, Art Cosgrove edited a collection of essays entitled *Marriage in Ireland*. Directed at a general readership, the volume provided the first study of the ecclesiastical and, to a lesser extent, the civil law on marriage from the early Christian period through to the twentieth century.[5] Like Connell's work, the challenges and questions posed by the individual chapters in this volume have not been explored in any detail in the thirty years since its publication. In this book, we aimed to take a fresh look at the themes in this collection and, through the use of a wider range of sources, to write a more in-depth study of the history of marriage in Ireland between 1660 and 1925.

Although there is no general history of marriage with which we could engage in our study, demographic and legal historians have made significant contributions to the field. There has been a considerable amount of work published on the fluctuating demography of Ireland, particularly in the eighteenth and nineteenth centuries. Cormac Ó Grada, Mary E. Daly, Leslie Clarkson, Liam Kennedy and others have explored marital age and fertility and offered explanations for the decline in rates of marriage in late-nineteenth-century Ireland and the relatively large size of families of couples who did marry.[6] Although not specifically focussed on the history of marriage, we have drawn on this literature, particularly in Chapters 3 and 8 when we examine age at marriage and, in a more cursory manner, marriage fertility in the nineteenth and twentieth centuries.

In *Marriage in Ireland*, Art Cosgrove, Margaret MacCurtain and P. J. Corish provided an outline of medieval and early-modern Irish civil and

---

[5] Art Cosgrove (ed.), *Marriage in Ireland* (Dublin, 1985). Rudolph Thurneysen *et al.*, *Studies in Early Irish Law* (Dublin, 1936) was a pioneering collection of essays that focussed on the earliest Irish law codes, particularly as they related to women and marriage. For a more recent study see Fergus Kelly, *A Guide to Early Irish Law* (Dublin, 1988). See also Salvador Ryan (ed.), *Marriage and the Irish: A Miscellany* (Dublin, 2019).

[6] Mary E. Daly, 'Marriage, fertility and women's lives in twentieth-century Ireland (*c.* 1900–*c.* 1970)', *Women's History Review*, 15, 4 (2006), 571–85; Cormac Ó Grada, *Ireland: A New Economic History, 1780–1939* (Oxford, 1995); Liam Kennedy, Kerby A. Miller and Brian Gurrin, 'People and population change, 1600–1914' in Liam Kennedy and Philip Ollerenshaw (eds.), *Ulster Since 1600: Politics, Economy, and Society* (Oxford, 2013), pp. 65–66. Eugenio F. Biagini and Mary E. Daly (eds.), *The Cambridge Social History of Modern Ireland* (Cambridge, 2017) is the best guide to recent writing on Irish social history.

ecclesiastical marriage law.[7] This has been developed in more recent years, especially in the collection of essays edited by Niamh Howlin and Kevin Costello entitled *Law and the Family in Ireland 1800–1950*. The volume, part of an inter-disciplinary series of seminars, included innovative studies on a range of issues related to the history of marriage law. We have made use of this stimulating work throughout our work.[8] Diane Urquhart, who is a contributor to the Howlin and Costello collection, has also published a more detailed history of divorce in Ireland, which traces the evolution of the laws on divorce from the eighteenth through to the twentieth century.[9] Our book is also a history of marriage law, but we wanted in addition to integrate a study of the law with an account of the lived experiences of married couples and the ways in which they conformed to or ignored legal imperatives, whether of church or state.

The history of marriage in Ireland has also attracted the attention of scholars in disciplines other than history. Linda Ballard's *Forgetting Frolic: Marriage Traditions in Ireland*, documented the material culture associated with marriage customs and practices. This is a rich area of research and we have only had space to point to themes, some of which are noted by Ballard, that merit further exploration. In particular, the commercialisation of weddings and the development of a consumer culture around wedding dresses, engagement rings, printed invitations, hotel rooms for hire and wedding breakfasts are worthy of much more research.[10]

A major theme running through this book is that of sexuality. In his 1982 book, *Priests and People in Pre-famine Ireland, 1780–1845*, Sean Connolly devoted a chapter to marriage and sexual behaviour. This was a pioneering and wide-ranging survey of marriage practices, notably in rural Ireland. Connolly identified the central role of the family in arranged marriages observing that 'the pattern of marriage in pre-Famine

---

[7] Art Cosgrove, 'Marriage in medieval Ireland' in Art Cosgrove (ed.), *Marriage in Ireland*, pp. 25–50; Margaret MacCurtain, 'Marriage in Tudor Ireland' in Art Cosgrove (ed.), *Marriage in Ireland*, pp. 51–66; Patrick J. Corish, 'Catholic marriage under the penal code' in Art Cosgrove (ed.), *Marriage in Ireland*, pp. 67–77. See also Patrick J. Corish, *The Irish Catholic Experience: A Historical Survey* (Dublin, 1985); Art Cosgrove, 'Marrying and marriage litigation in medieval Ireland' in Philip L. Reynolds and John Witte, Jr. (eds.), *To Have and to Hold: Marrying and Its Documentation in Western Christendom, 400–1600* (Cambridge, 2007), pp. 332–59.

[8] Niamh Howlin and Kevin Costello (eds.), *Law and the Family in Ireland, 1800–1950* (London, 2017).

[9] See Urquhart, *Irish Divorce: A History*. This pioneering study appeared too late for us to engage with its findings. See also David Fitzpatrick, 'Divorce and separation in modern Irish history', *Past and Present*, 114 (1987), 172–196.

[10] Linda Ballard, *Forgetting Frolic: Marriage Traditions in Ireland* (Belfast, 1998).

Ireland subordinated the interests of the individual to those of the family'.[11] Our book builds on Connolly's work on courtship and marriage in the period between 1780 and 1845. By extending the time period and drawing on a wider range of sources we provide a more detailed understanding of men's and women's experience of courtship, marriage and marital discord. We trace in particular the ways in which people devised means to subvert ecclesiastical and civil law, thereby undermining family expectations of spousal choice.

Historians of Irish Presbyterianism have also explored sexual activity and morality in the north of Ireland. The work of Paul Gray, Andrew Holmes and Leanne Calvert, especially, has expanded our knowledge of attempts by Presbyterian church leaders to control the marriages and the sexual behaviour of their congregations.[12] In Chapter 3, we engage with this research and problematise further the denominational distinctions that are assumed to have existed in pre-nuptial sexual practices.

Scholarship on the history of sexuality in Ireland has expanded considerably in the last ten years. Building on research into women's and gender history, historians have investigated, among other issues, prostitution, the problems associated with pregnancy outside marriage, infanticide, abortion, celibacy and same sex relations.[13] This research has questioned popular assumptions about Irish society in the past and the

[11] S. J. Connolly, *Priests and People in Pre-famine Ireland, 1780–1845* (Dublin, 1982); 'Marriage in pre-Famine Ireland', Cosgrove, *Marriage in Ireland*, pp. 78–98.

[12] Andrew Blaikie and Paul Gray, 'Archives of abuse and discontent? Presbyterianism and sexual behaviour during the eighteenth and nineteenth centuries' in R. J. Morris and Liam Kennedy (eds.), *Ireland and Scotland: Order and Disorder, 1600–2000* (Edinburgh, 2005), pp. 61–84; Andrew R. Holmes, *The Shaping of Ulster Presbyterian Belief and Practice, 1770–1840* (Oxford, 2006); Leanne Calvert, '"Do not forget your bitwife": Marriage and the negotiation of patriarchy in Irish Presbyterian marriages, c. 1780–1850', *Women's History Review*, 26, 3 (2017), 433–54; '"He came to her bed pretending courtship": Sex, courtship and the making of marriage in Ulster, 1750–1844', *Irish Historical Studies*, 42 (162) (2018), 244–64.

[13] See for example, Maria Luddy, *Prostitution and Irish Society, 1800–1940* (Cambridge, 2007); Diarmaid Ferriter, *Occasions of Sin: Sex and Society in Modern Ireland* (London, 2009); Leanne McCormick, *Regulating Sexuality: Women in Twentieth-Century Northern Ireland* (Manchester, 2009); Cliona Rattigan, '*What Else Could I Do?': Single Mothers and Infanticide. Ireland 1900–1950* (Dublin, 2012); Elaine Farrell (ed.), '*She Said She Was in the Family Way': Pregnancy and Infancy in Modern Ireland* (London, 2012); Elaine Farrell, '*A Most Diabolical Deed': Infanticide and Irish Society, 1850–1900* (Manchester, 2013); Virginia Crossman, *Poverty and the Poor Law in Ireland, 1850–1914* (Liverpool, 2013); Jennifer Redmond, Sonja Tiernan, Sandra McAvoy and Mary McAuliffe (eds.), *Sexual Politics in Modern Ireland* (Dublin, 2015); Cara Delay, 'Girls, the body, and sexual knowledge in modern Ireland' in Christina Brophy and Cara Delay (eds.), *Women, Reform, and Resistance in Ireland, 1850–1950* (London, 2015), pp. 163–84; Lindsey Earner-Byrne and Diane Urquhart, *The Irish Abortion Journey, 1920–2018* (London, 2019). See also James Kelly, 'Infanticide in eighteenth-century Ireland', *Irish Economic and Social History*, 19 (1992), 5–26.

presumed sexual innocence of Irish men and women. Our study adds to this history by examining further the level of non-conformity in sexual matters amongst individuals and couples over a long time period. We see sexual non-conformity, for instance, in cohabitation, adultery, the keeping of mistresses and the advantage taken of women servants in households. We also explore women's consensual sexual behaviour as witnessed in breach of promise to marry cases and seduction. We observe the blurring of public/private distinctions when, for example, cases of criminal conversation come to court. Newspaper reporting of such cases investigated people's private sexual relationships and exposed their domestic arrangements to public scrutiny.

Outline

The book is structured around four main themes: the laws on marriage; the formation of marriage through courtship and financial arrangements; marital relations and what could lead to conflict, particularly of a violent kind, between husbands and wives; and finally the breakdown of marriage and the processes involved in desertion, separation and divorce.

In Chapters 1 and 2, we analyse how the state and the different religious denominations defined a legally valid marriage and the complexities that arose when these definitions clashed. The nineteenth-century insistence on public registration of marriages was aimed at the standardisation of the religious and civil process, but throughout the period the Catholic church successfully maintained a detached attitude to state law on marriage. This was, as we indicate at different stages in the book, of mixed benefit to the Catholic church and its adherents. All the churches, however, converged on their disapproval of private marriage ceremonies, known variously as 'clandestine' or 'irregular' marriages, particularly those conducted by clergymen with no formal affiliation to a church, commonly known as couple beggars. The figure of the couple beggar was often depicted in comical terms as an alcoholic, dishevelled man who presided over drunken unions in a public house or fair (see Illustration 2.1). Yet, the reality was more complex and we examine the reasons why large numbers of people opted for a marriage celebrated by a couple beggar or a degraded minister.

In Part II, we ask how marriages were arranged, how couples met and at what age they married. A major theme of the book is an examination of how and why particular marriage partners were chosen. Religious belief was only one element in choosing a partner. Individuals and families were also influenced by other criteria including, most importantly, the economic and social status of the potential partner. We also focus attention on the process of courtship, and the extent to which parental and family approval took precedence over individual wishes. Documenting the financial arrangements for individual marriages is challenging as few of the families that we examine left written explanations. Newspaper reporting of court trials, particularly for breach of promise to marry, enable us to provide some context for the negotiations over dowries and the role that different family members played in them. In Chapter 3, we suggest that marriage ages differed across economic classes as well as regions. The age at which people married was often related to the economic prospects of the couple. It is also important to remember that before the mid-nineteenth century many people did not know how old they were and ages were often guessed or assessed by physical attributes rather than chronological years.

Despite the importance of financial arrangements in marriage negotiations, there were, especially among the middling groups in society, agreed forms of courtship behaviour. The failure of men, in particular, to observe them might lead to the breakdown of the courtship either by the woman or by a member of her family. Courtship practices for the middling sorts are evident in letters and diaries and through evidence presented in legal disputes concerning a range of marital issues. Many breach of promise cases, for example, begin with a preliminary overview of how couples met and provide an understanding of what was considered acceptable behaviour in terms of class and respectability. The places in which people courted, whether or not they were chaperoned and the gifts and love tokens they gave each other all had a class component. Couples from a middle-class background, in urban and rural areas, were monitored more closely by their families than those from further down the social scale. It is, however, worth noting that there is very little evidence of the 'traditional match-maker', a popular figure in the Irish imagination, before the twentieth century. There were matches, certainly, but they were usually arranged by the families involved or by a male relative or family friend. Witnesses in court cases claimed never to have come across a 'match-maker'. For their part, barristers and judges in the late nineteenth and early twentieth centuries, often presented a marriage arranged by a 'match' as an antiquated and ancient phenomenon that had no place in modern society.

The transition to marriage for romantic love and young people having the freedom to marry the partner of their choice reached the towns before the rural parts of Ireland. Within the realm of courtship, social rules dictated that people did not interact without an introduction, but in urban society, men and women might mix socially and more informally. The emergence of new cultural activities in which both sexes participated also facilitated social interaction between strangers outside the family circle or network. The two worlds could also, of course, overlap. Rural women, working in towns or cities, might meet men independently but as the courtship progressed, they returned home to enable the more formal negotiation of marriage to take place.

The rules for courtship behaviour did not include pre-marital sex but it is clear that many couples did have sex before they married. Some did so with the tolerance, if not the approval, of the local community. The elders at local sessions of the Presbyterian church, for example, administered public punishments to those who admitted to engaging in sex before marriage. They were, however, more forgiving of the offence if the couple subsequently married. In Catholic and Protestant communities, a pregnant bride was less scandalous than an unmarried mother. Not all sex before marriage was, however, consensual. As we document in Chapter 6, the violent abduction of young single women was common among the lower classes in rural Ireland until the middle decades of the nineteenth century. The aim was to force the woman or her family to consent to marriage. The seduction of single women could also involve rape, as their stories in court often revealed.

Courtships could also break down and not result in a happy union. In Chapter 5, we look at what could go wrong in the arrangements for marriage. Promises to marry were, sometimes, broken if a better offer materialised. Reneging on what was perceived as a binding commitment was considered a serious offence by all the church authorities. Until 1818, the church courts had the power, at least in theory, to compel anyone who made a promise to marry to fulfil that promise. Furthermore, from the late eighteenth century, men and women could sue the reneging partner for a breach of a promise to marry in the civil courts. Breach of promise cases that came before the Irish courts can tell us a great deal about attitudes to courtship and marriage.

In Part III of the volume, we move on to the wedding ceremony and its aftermath. We look at relationships of husbands and wives and the different ways in which patriarchy was manifest in marriage. Generalisations based on the personal and emotional bonds between men and women are difficult. Some men were more domineering figures in the home than others, while women too could exercise emotional pressure on their husbands. Economic co-dependence also mitigated against the worst excesses of the patriarchy embodied in the legal system. External developments, particularly, in relation to women's ability to access paid employment outside the home and new laws on women's property rights gave married women greater control over their lives by the late nineteenth century.

As Chapter 10 graphically demonstrates, however, domestic violence remained a common feature of marital relations throughout the two hundred and sixty-five years covered by the volume. The chapter looks not only at issues of assault in marital relationships but also at the extent of spousal murder over the period. Such violence occurred at all social levels, but was less acceptable and less visible at higher social levels. It is difficult, however, to estimate how common domestic abuse actually was. There was some level of social acceptance of mild domestic violence but families and neighbours tended to intervene when matters become too serious. By the nineteenth century, cases involving domestic violence were considered in the lower courts on a weekly basis. The women who reported their husbands to the authorities mainly requested that they be bound to the peace, rather than punished. How effective this was as a means of controlling violence is open to question. There was also a considerable level of other intra-familial violence, including violence against children, parents, in-laws, siblings and other relatives. Access to land and family resources, disputes over relationships and the irritability caused by the close proximity of extended families living in small spaces could all lead to violent conflict. Documenting the prevalence of domestic violence can only, however, provide a partial record of the reality of married life for some couples.

In the final part, we focus on the breakup of marriage: the reasons for it and the available processes for separation. The 1857 Act, which opened up divorce proceedings to the middle classes in England was not enacted in Ireland. The omission of Ireland from the Act did not create any significant opposition. The barristers and judges in the Irish courts increasingly argued that divorce was not natural to Irish society and they urged Irish juries not to condone the dissolution of the marriage bonds. Yet, from the early eighteenth century, it was possible for men (and later, women) to petition parliament for a dissolution of their marriage. It was a complicated legal process and only available to those who could afford it. In 1922, it was initially assumed that petitions for divorce would be heard by the new legislature of the Irish Free State, but under pressure from the Catholic hierarchy this assumption was quietly dropped. The lack of access to divorce led many people to devise their own solutions to unhappy marriages. Men and women deserted wives and husbands, cohabited with new partners or committed bigamy by marrying them. As we document in Chapters 11 and 12, the ecclesiastical and common law courts imposed financial penalties on men who deserted their wives but it proved difficult to implement such judgments. In the middle decades of the nineteenth century, new maintenance legislation, however, strengthened the ability of the courts to chase deserting husbands.

Historical Context

A constant contextual theme throughout the period is the impoverishment of Irish society. Many travellers to pre-Famine Ireland were struck by the poverty that they witnessed in the form of the numbers of beggars they encountered, or the extent of the 'hovels' in which people lived. The size and shape of domestic dwelling is, of course, an important consideration in examining marital relations. In the 1770s Arthur Young described how wandering families in Ireland constructed their habitations 'with a few sticks, furze, fern, etc. [they] make up a hovel much worse than an English pigstie, support themselves how they can, by work, begging and stealing, if the neighbourhood wants hands, or takes no notice of them. The hovel grows into a cabbin'.[14] In 1841, the census commissioners divided the houses of the country into four classes. Over 600,000 families lived in fourth-class housing, or one-roomed houses. The third class of house consisted of dwellings, including cottages built of mud, but having two to four rooms and windows. Classes three and four made up about 77 per cent of the housing available in the country.

As many historians have documented, the living conditions of the poor in Irish cities were also cramped and unhealthy. In 1841 in Dublin, 20,097 families lived in 8,289 second-class houses (five to nine rooms with windows). By the early years of the twentieth century, the city contained some of the worst slums in Europe. By contrast, in rural Ireland, standards in housing rose steadily after the Famine and by 1891 more than half of Irish rural families lived in dwellings with at least four rooms. In particular, the provision of labourers' cottages improved standards for the poorest of rural workers in Ireland. What is evident from the 1850s onwards, therefore, is the development of a greater level of private space within households. This is particularly clear in the provision of separate bedrooms for parents and children.[15]

---

[14] Arthur Young, *A Tour in Ireland with General Observations on the Present State of That Kingdom Made in the Years 1776,1777, and 1778, and Brought Down to the End of 1779* (2 vols., Dublin, 1780), ii, pp. 269–70.

[15] T. W. Freeman, *Pre-famine Ireland: A Study in Historical Geography* (Manchester, 1957), pp. 146–52; Barry O'Reilly, 'Hearth and home: The vernacular house in Ireland from c.1800', *Proceedings of the Royal Irish Academy*, Section C, 3 (2011), 193–215; Frank Cullen, 'The provision of working- and lower-middle-class housing in late nineteenth-century urban Ireland', *Proceedings of the Royal Irish Academy*, Section C, 3 (2011), 217–51; Caitriona Crowe, *Dublin 1911* (Dublin, 2011); Jacinta Prunty, *Dublin Slums, 1800–1925: A Study in Urban Geography* (Dublin, 1998); Ellen Rowley, 'Housing in Ireland, 1740–2016' in Biagini and Daly (eds.), *Cambridge Social History*, pp. 212–32; Angela Bourke, *The Burning of Bridget Cleary: A True Story* (London, 1999), pp. 46–7.

Eighteenth- and early nineteenth-century Ireland is also remarkable for dramatic demographic change as the size of the population rose from less than 2 million people in 1660 to over 8 million in 1841. Between 1730 and 1800 the population rose from about 2 million to 5 million. The hearth-money collectors suggest a population of about 2.544 million in 1767. The 1821 census returned a population of 6.8 million people. By 1841 the population had reached 8.2 million. While there were similar population increases in other countries, Ireland's increase differed in that it was an expansion in a rural, rather than an urban and industrialising, population.[16]

In 1807 one commentator observed that in Ireland 'an unmarried man ... or a woman ... is rarely to be met in the country parts.'[17] Before the Famine only a small proportion of the population did not marry: 8–12 per cent of men over fifty-five and 12–15 per cent of women over fifty-five.[18] The catastrophe of the Great Famine ushered in considerable changes in Irish demography. Marriage patterns changed and emigration became commonplace. Between 1846 and 1855 more than 1 million Irish people died of starvation and its associated diseases. At the same time over two million Irish people emigrated and a high level of sustained emigration remained the norm in Ireland until the 1960s.[19] As we discuss in Chapter 3, such demographic disruption had a profound effect on marriage patterns.

The 1821 census recorded that just over 6 per cent of the population of the country lived in the major cities of Belfast, Cork, Dublin, Limerick and Waterford. By 1841 about 20 per cent of the population lived in towns and villages. For the census records a village meant an area where there were defined groups of twenty of more houses.[20] There was no industrial revolution in Ireland, except perhaps in the north east of Ulster. By the 1870s Belfast had overtaken Dublin as the largest and most industrialised city in the country with a population of more than 400,000. The Irish road, railway and canal systems were relatively well developed by the mid-nineteenth century, allowing for the transport of goods and people and improved mobility for those seeking employment in different parts of the country. Despite the growth of towns and cities, Ireland remained a predominantly rural society until the 1960s.

---

[16] Ó Grada, *Ireland: A New Economic History*, pp. 3–5.
[17] T. J. Rawson, *The Statistical Survey of the County of Kildare* (Dublin, 1807), p. 23.
[18] T. W. Freeman, 'Land and people, c.1841' in W. E. Vaughan (ed.), *A New History of Ireland: Ireland under the Union, 1801–70* (Oxford, 1989), p. 260.
[19] Kevin Kenny, 'Irish emigrations in comparative perspective' in Biagini and Daly (eds.), *Cambridge Social History*, pp. 405–22.
[20] T. W. Freeman, *Ireland: A General and Regional Geography* (London, 1965), p. 129.

The Great Famine changed the social structure of rural Ireland as the labouring class was drastically reduced in numbers. The middling and large tenant farmers and commercial class in the towns were less severely affected by the Famine and began to dominate politically and socially in post-Famine Ireland. It was members of this class, too, who were most likely to observe the rules of their respective churches on marriage. It was also families in this social group that provided the priests and nuns who serviced the expanding infrastructure of the Catholic church in post-Famine society and supervised the adherence to a stricter sexual morality than had prevailed in an earlier period.

The 1834 Commission of Public Instruction in Ireland was the first official report to provide detailed information on the religious composition of Ireland. It calculated that at that time about 81 per cent of the population was Catholic, with 10.7 per cent members of the Church of Ireland while just over 8 per cent were Presbyterian. By 1861, the first national census to take account of religious affiliation revealed that the Catholic population of the country had declined to 77.7 per cent, with Church of Ireland members making up 12 per cent and Presbyterians 9.9 per cent.[21] After the Famine the reconstruction and renewal of the Catholic church proceeded more rapidly. Tony Fahy has estimated that in 1800 there were 1,850 priests, an astonishingly low number of men who could not possibly have monitored the marital or sexual practices of their parishioners. By 1900, while the population of Ireland had halved in size, the number of priests had nearly doubled to 3,500. More importantly, perhaps, in terms of instilling observance of a strict code of morality in young people through their widespread involvement in education, the number of nuns in Ireland rose from 1,500 in 1851 to 9,000 in 1911.[22]

Increased urbanisation, migration and emigration also had an impact on social and moral customs and practices. Desertion of a spouse, cohabiting without marriage and bigamy were all easier to get away with in the expanding cities of Belfast and Dublin. Bigamous relations and cohabitation, for example, seem to have been tolerated among the migrant workers of inner-city Belfast in the late nineteenth and early twentieth century.[23] Emigration and migration provided accessible solutions for unhappy marriages in a society where divorce and remarriage

[21] Sean Connolly, *Religion and Society in Nineteenth-Century Ireland: Studies in Irish Economic and Social History* (Dundalk, 1985), p. 3.
[22] Tony Fahy, 'Catholicism and industrial society in Ireland', *Proceedings of the British Academy*, 79 (1992), 249–50.
[23] See Chapter 9.

were not available to the majority of the population. Living and working away from home also, as we have noted already, gave young men and women greater independence in their choice of marriage partner. The necessity to acquire family approval of a prospective spouse was less evident among city workers by the end of the nineteenth century.

Another important social change that had an impact on attitudes to marriage was the increase in literacy rates and the availability of formal education through the national schools for even the poorest levels of society. Literacy in English coincided with a decline in the number of people who spoke Irish. By 1901, only 14 per cent of the population could speak Irish, with the majority living in the west of Ireland.[24] By contrast, in 1841, according to the census of that year, more than half of the population was illiterate but by 1901 that figure had declined to 16 per cent.[25] Literacy in English not only facilitated better employment opportunities, it also enabled more people to read the newspapers that began to proliferate from the mid-nineteenth century in Ireland. As will become clear in the course of this volume, many regional and national newspapers filled their pages with law reports of trials in Ireland and England for various marital-related offences including breach of promise, seduction, bigamy, domestic violence and divorce. Newspapers were, therefore, an important medium through which men and women became aware of the sexual misdemeanours occurring in Irish society.

A final context that we have considered in the course of research for the volume is the changing and evolving legal system. In the medieval and early modern period, most disputes concerning marriage were dealt with in the ecclesiastical courts. There were twenty-five consistory courts but this number was reduced to twelve in 1864.[26] The ecclesiastical courts were abolished in 1870, but long before that civil courts had begun to hear more and more disputes involving marriage. This was mainly the work of innovative lawyers who endeavoured to stretch the interpretations of existing legislation on personal injury and contract to enable suits for

---

[24] Niall Ó Ciosáin, 'Gaelic culture and language shift' in L. Geary and M. Kelleher (eds.), *Nineteenth-Century Ireland: A Research Guide* (Dublin, 1995), pp. 136–52; Garrett Fitzgerald, 'Estimates for baronies of minimum level of Irish speaking among successive decennial cohorts: 1771–1781 to 1861–1871', *Proceedings of the Royal Irish Academy*, Section C, 84 (1984), 117–55; Aidan Doyle, *A History of the Irish Language* (Oxford, 2015).

[25] Mary E. Daly, *Social and Economic History of Ireland since 1800* (Dublin, 1981).

[26] R. B. McDowell, 'Ireland in 1800' in T. W. Moody and W. E. Vaughan (eds.), *A New History of Ireland: Eighteenth-Century Ireland 1691–1800* (Oxford, 1986), p. 708; R. B. McDowell, *The Irish Administration* (London, 1964), p. 120.

divorce, breach of promise and seduction to be heard. The secularisation of marriage law was, therefore, well under way before the establishment of the Court for Matrimonial Causes and Matters in 1870.

Legal disputes relating to marriage came before a range of courts, the lowest of these were the petty sessions. More serious crimes were dealt with in the quarter sessions and above these courts were the assizes. Justices of the peace and resident magistrates presided over the local legal system.[27] The correspondence from resident magistrates to the Dublin administration, dating from the eighteenth century allowed us to track the marital behaviour of individuals in Ireland, particularly in instances of abduction, sexual assault and bigamy. Important changes in the court system included the extension of the petty sessions from 1828. Petty sessions were the lowest courts in Ireland and there were about 600 in operation from the mid-nineteenth century. They were held on a regular basis throughout the country and were presided over by magistrates who aimed to resolve less serious local grievances. As Chapter 11 indicates, the petty session courts were much used by the poorer classes of society, particularly poor women seeking relief from abusive husbands. The petty sessions, along with the police service, had a role in maintaining social order at a community level.[28] Working-class people also used the courts and the legal system as an extension of the community, as an arena in which to carry on disputes with neighbours and as a check on behaviour considered unwelcome in the community (see Illustration 11.1). Greater access to the courts, such as petty sessions, assisted women in seizing the initiative to deter abusive husbands, secure their property and ensure the welfare of their children. Beyond the quarter and petty sessions, more serious cases involving murder or rape were brought before the county assizes where professional judges presided and juries settled the verdicts.[29] The courtroom structured the stories that individuals wanted to tell and the newspapers that reported those cases were an extension of the courts, broadening the court audience. The courts both reflected and helped to transform the behavioural expectations of men and women in marriage. Courts were often surprisingly flexible when it came to dealing with unhappy or assaulted wives, the payment of maintenance or a couple's desire for separation.

---

[27] McDowell, 'Ireland in 1800', p. 709; McDowell, *Irish Administration*, pp. 112–9.
[28] On the establishment of the police service see Brian Griffin, *The Bulkies: Police and Crime in Belfast, 1800–1865* (Dublin, 1962); Galen Broeker, *Rural Disorder and Police Reform in Ireland, 1812–36* (London, 1970).
[29] On the Irish jury system see Niamh Howlin, *Juries in Ireland: Laypersons and Law in the Long Nineteenth Century* (Dublin, 2017).

Sources

Newspapers proved a key source for this study and the digitisation of national and regional newspapers has considerably aided our research and enabled us to trace reporting of legal cases and the individuals involved across time as well as in different localities.[30] As the Select Bibliography makes clear, we have explored a wide range of other sources in manuscript and printed forms. We have drawn on ecclesiastical sources from the Catholic church, the Church of Ireland, the Presbyterian church and the Society of Friends. The kirk-session and Presbytery records preserved in the archive of the Presbyterian Historical Society of Ireland, Belfast and elsewhere and the diocesan records of the Catholic church were particularly useful. Unfortunately, we were only given access to a selected range of material in the latter, and during the research period a number of important diocesan archives were closed to researchers. We have also made use of contemporary printed literature that appeared throughout the two hundred and sixty-five years examined in the book, and government reports and statistical compilations that are particularly rich for the nineteenth century. We endeavoured also to identify relevant personal and private archives in the form of diaries, correspondence and memoirs. This latter type of source is not as abundant as we would have liked, mainly because men and women from the social classes below the level of the very wealthy were less likely to keep written records of their activities. By the middle decades of the nineteenth century, many in the middling group of society were, however, making wills and drawing up private deeds of settlement for marriage and separation. Although a large number of relevant records was destroyed in the burning of the Public Record Office of Ireland in 1922, we have, with the aid of our postdoctoral researchers, Dr Katie Barclay and Dr John Bergin, uncovered a wealth of miscellaneous manuscript material. The loss of archives, particularly court records, did, however, shape how we could write about many aspects of marriage, especially in the seventeenth and eighteenth centuries. For instance, in our chapter on marital violence we originally sought to explore the persistence of domestic violence over time and space, as well as to examine any changes in attitudes towards such violence within families, the local community and through the legal system. However, such aims were not always feasible given the lack of consistent documentary evidence. We have few surviving

---

[30] We have made use of the British Newspapers Archive (www.britishnewspaperarchive .co.uk) and the Irish Newspaper Archive (http://archive.irishnewsarchive.com).

consistory or matrimonial court records, while assize court records are also rare even for the nineteenth century before the 1870s. Consequently, we had to rely heavily on contemporary newspaper accounts for records of spousal violence and murder. Petty sessions records are available from 1828, but are again regionally sporadic and survive more extensively from the late nineteenth century. The newspapers of the eighteenth century did report cases of non-lethal and murderous violence between spouses, but they provide little detail and often noted only extreme cases. Cases of spousal violence were reported more frequently in the nineteenth and twentieth century press, but even in the early nineteenth century it is not always easy to discover the outcome of a trial. Unfortunately, judicial and criminal statistics did not distinguish between various types of murders, except for those associated with agrarian crime. Nor do they identify different forms of assaults.[31] The loss of records is to be lamented, and a reliance on newspaper reports has its own dangers, notably the need for an awareness of the political stance of the papers. Many crimes were given political motivations where none really existed. Also reports, particularly in the eighteenth- and early nineteenth-century press, were often brief and the information not necessarily accurate. The papers also fed and possibly led the reading public's interest in the salacious details of cases such as criminal conversation, bigamy and breach of promise to marry. Journalists were adept at finding entertainment in the courts. They judged some individuals, particularly men who took breach of promise to marry cases against women, as particularly feeble and unmanly. They commented on how men and women presented themselves in court and often ridiculed complainants and, thereby, elicited sympathy for one side or the other. Nonetheless, newspaper reports also provide an insight into the lives of the individuals who appear before the courts: their marital dilemmas, their desire to manage their own marital affairs and their stories of fortune and misfortune.

In the introduction to his study on *The Family, Sex and Marriage in England 1500–1800,* Lawrence Stone commented on the dilemma confronting the historian of the family: 'how best to interweave fact and theory, anecdote and analysis'.[32] He opted to draw on both 'analysis which tries to explain, and anecdote which tries to teach'. In our methodology for this book, we have followed a similar approach in an

---

[31] For an excellent analysis of the difficulties faced by historians using these kinds of statistics see W. E. Vaughan, *Murder Trials in Ireland, 1836–1914* (Dublin, 2009), chapter 1.

[32] Lawrence Stone, *Family, Sex and Marriage in England, 1500–1800* (London, 1977), p. 16.

endeavour to tell the stories of men's and women's experiences of marriage and its related issues and to integrate our analysis into and around those stories. Inevitably, there are questions about the typicality and the unevenness of the source material. Those who appear in a court trial may not necessarily be representative of a general trend, while the authors of correspondence, diaries and memoirs tend to come from one particular class and, frequently, one religious denomination. There is, for example, a dearth of memoirs and correspondence from the Catholic middle classes. Generalisations are always a particularly complex challenge in the history of the family and marriage. As Stone noted, conclusions are often open ended and we can never be sure if the examples cited are typical.[33] In our analysis, we have aimed as far as was possible to draw on supporting but different types of evidence, which has enabled us to identify general trends while also recognising that they might not necessarily apply to all the stories of individual men and women.

---

[33] Ibid., p. 17. See also Lawrence Stone, *Uncertain Unions: Marriage in England, 1660–1753* (Oxford, 1992) and *Broken Lives: Separation and Divorce in England, 1660–1857* (Oxford, 1993).

Part I

What Is a Marriage?

1   A Legal Marriage?

Early in the summer of 1724, Elizabeth Leeson met William Fitzmaurice. Leeson was a young widow of twenty-eight years of age with two children. She had a respectable annual widow's jointure of about £50. Fitzmaurice was a little older at thirty and was heir to his father, the earl of Kerry, whose estate was valued at £5,000 per year. He had served as a soldier and, according to one account, 'pursued the usual pleasures of a soldier, being … too fond of wine and addicted to promiscuous love'.[1] Fitzmaurice was not a good-looking man. Smallpox had damaged his face and he had suffered what appeared to be a stroke, which impeded his speech and made him walk with a limp.[2]

Leeson was clearly, however, attracted to Fitzmaurice and she permitted him to visit her at her home in Duke Street, Dublin. The relationship became intimate very quickly and, according to Leeson, on 23 June 1724, she and Fitzmaurice swore an oath on a Bible that they would 'marry one another, and never marry anyone else, during our Joint Lives'.[3] Shortly after this, Fitzmaurice left Dublin for his family home in Kerry but the couple maintained a correspondence in which both repeated their attraction to each other but no specific reference was made to their marriage.[4] When Fitzmaurice returned to the city for the winter, the couple, according to Leeson, read the marriage service in the Book of Common Prayer and, subsequently, consummated their union. The

---

[1] *Love without Artifice: Or, the Disappointed Peer. A History of the Amour between Lord Mauritio and Emilia. Being the Case of Elizabeth Fitz-Maurice, Alias Leeson, and the Lord William Fitz-Maurice, Relating to a Marriage-Contract between Them; Which Was Confirmed by a Court of Delegates, in the Lady's Behalf, on Wednesday, March 14th 1732–3, at Serjeant's-Inn, in Chancery-Lane* (London, 1733), p. 3.

[2] Ibid.

[3] *Observations on the Case of the Right Honourable the Lord Fitzmaurice, and Mrs Elizabeth Leeson, Concerning a Pretended Contract of Marriage* (London, 1733), p. 6.

[4] Edward Spencer Dix, *The Case of Regina v Millis et Regina v Carroll, in the Queen's Bench in Ireland in Easter and Trinity Term, 1842* (Dublin, 1842), p. 14.

ceremony, which took place in Leeson's house, was witnessed by her domestic servant.[5]

The relationship was kept secret, although Leeson's family were aware of the liaison. Fitzmaurice's mother appears to have heard about it through rumours circulating in Dublin, which were particularly strong in the summer of 1725 when Leeson was pregnant.[6] The countess of Kerry was unhappy about her son's indiscretions as the family were involved in the process of negotiating a more suitable match for him with the daughter of a wealthy family. These discussions proceeded despite Leeson's evident dismay. In 1726, when the marriage was publicly announced, Leeson submitted a legal caveat to the Dublin ecclesiastical court to prevent the marriage, asserting that Fitzmaurice was already contracted to marry her. The judge was not impressed by Leeson's evidence that a promise of marriage had been made by Fitzmaurice and dismissed the case. Leeson, however, persisted and appealed the decision through the London court of delegates, which reversed the Dublin court's verdict and declared that Fitzmaurice had made a valid promise of marriage to Leeson and was, therefore, obliged to marry her.[7] The marriage does not, however, appear to have been formally solemnised.[8]

The *Fitzmaurice v Fitzmaurice* case became a *cause célèbre* in London and Dublin, partly because it pitted a woman from a middling social rank against a future peer of the realm and partly because in the course of the legal proceedings, the correspondence of the couple was read into the court record. Leeson's letters to Fitzmaurice were published in three separate pamphlets along with a commentary as to her intent in her relationship with Fitzmaurice.[9] The popular titillation implicit in these publications was, as we shall see later in the volume, a precursor to the subsequent publication of legal proceedings in breach of promise, divorce and seduction cases.[10]

---

[5] *Observations on the Case of the Right Honourable the Lord Fitzmaurice, and Mrs Elizabeth Leeson*, p. 7.

[6] Ibid., pp. 14–20   [7] *Love Without Artifice*, pp. 44–5.

[8] Fitzmaurice went to France following the verdict against him. There is no record of him meeting again with Leeson, who died in 1737. Fitzmaurice married another woman in 1738. For a more detailed analysis of the case see Mary O'Dowd, 'Women litigants in early eighteenth-century Ireland' in Deborah Youngs and Teresa Phipps (eds.), *Litigating Women* (forthcoming, 2020). For the details of the proceedings in the London court of delegates see The National Archives, DEL 2/27.

[9] *Observations on the Case of the Right Honourable the Lord Fitzmaurice, and Mrs Elizabeth Leeson; Love Without Artifice*; a new edition entitled *Love and Artifice…* was published in London in 1734. See also *Arches-Court Law. Being Some Late Proceedings Therein, Argued and Adjudged. Containing Three Remarkable Cases …* (London, 1735).

[10] See Chapters 5 and 12.

Legally, the case is significant because it affirmed the importance of the marriage vow in the definition of a legal, valid marriage. Promises to marry either in the present (*per verba de presenti*) or the future tense (*per verba de future*) were the foundation on which marriage law was based. Until 1818, the Irish ecclesiastical courts had the power to compel anyone making such a promise to solemnise the marriage in the presence of a minister (*in facie ecclesiae*).[11] This was the basis on which the London court made its decision directing Fitzmaurice to marry Leeson.

Church and State Laws on the Validity of Marriage

The Leeson–Fitzmaurice case also assumed significance because it was later cited in relation to legal discussions on what constituted a valid marriage. Was it the private promise between the man and the woman in the present or in the future tense or was it the religious ceremony performed by a minister in a church in front of witnesses?[12] The legal confusion over the answer to this question had its origins in early medieval canon law, which deemed a promise to marry in the present tense as constituting a marriage and a promise in the future tense as binding on both parties. Neither a formal nor a public service was required as validation. The marriage was legally perceived to have existed when the couple made a promise to marry either in the present or in the future. Sexual consummation was not necessary nor was the presence of a priest or of witnesses required to make the marriage valid. In the course of the late middle ages, the church authorities began to exert greater control over the marriage contract. Marriage was deemed a sacrament from the thirteenth century and the church also insisted on witnesses, evidence of the willing consent of both partners and their parents, if they were under age, and that the promise be made in a church or, at least, in the presence of a priest. The marriage service, church guidelines also asserted, should be publicised through the proclamation of church banns in advance to allow for the presentation of possible reasons why the marriage should not proceed.[13] None of these requirements was, however, necessary

---

[11] An Act for Extending to That Part of the United Kingdom Called Ireland, Certain Provisions of the Parliament of Great Britain, in Relation to Executors under the Age of Twenty-One Years and to Matrimonial Contracts, 58 Geo. III c.81. 1818 abolished the power of the ecclesiastical courts to compel the celebration of marriage following a pre-contract.

[12] See, in particular, Edward Spencer Dix, *The Case of Regina v Millis et Regina v Carroll, in the Queen's Bench in Ireland in Easter and Trinity Term, 1842*, pp. 14, 116, 206–7, 235.

[13] Philip L. Reynolds, 'Marrying and its documentation in pre-modern Europe: Consent, celebration and property' in Philip L. Reynolds and John Witte, Jr. (eds.), *To Have and to*

under canon law, and a private promise of marriage was deemed sufficient for a canonically valid, if irregular union, into the post-Reformation period. There was a long tradition in Ireland of private marriages but it is unclear from the surviving evidence when the ecclesiastical or the common law courts began to insist on the presence of a minister to validate the union.[14] There could be practical reasons why couples did not have their union sanctioned by a priest. The annual reports of the Jesuit order in seventeenth century Ireland regularly listed the lax observance of Catholic canon law among the laity. The author of the 1662 report noted that in the west of Ireland, 'many couples, who, because they were far from priests, had performed marriages themselves'.[15] By the eighteenth century, if not before, the ecclesiastical courts appear to have deemed a marriage valid only if it had been solemnised in the presence of a minister. In the legal dispute concerning the validity of marriages solemnised by Presbyterian ministers in the 1830s and 1840s, some members of the Irish bar and judiciary and legal authorities argued that a private promise of marriage was a valid marriage under common law even if it was not recognised as valid in the ecclesiastical courts. As Sir Thomas Staples noted in the famous case of *Regina v Millis* in 1842:

I have been in cases in the Ecclesiastical Court, where that Court refused to give to parties married without religious ceremonies, rights to which they would have been entitled if the marriage had been regularly celebrated. It clearly appears that legitimate marriage, means marriage by contract alone, whilst *ratum*, or ratified marriage, means marriage regularly celebrated.[16]

The distinction between common and ecclesiastical law is an important one when considering legal issues relating to marriage. Before 1844, the regulation of marriage in Ireland was primarily the business of the consistory courts. Legal validation of marriages was within their

---

Hold: *Marrying and Its Documentation in Western Christendom, 400–1600* (Cambridge, 2007), pp. 1–42.

[14] Art Cosgrove, 'Marrying and marriage litigation in medieval Ireland' in Reynolds and Witte (eds.), *To Have and to Hold*, pp. 332–59; Alison Forrestal, *Catholic Synods in Ireland, 1600–1690* (Dublin, 1998), pp. 18–20; Mary O'Dowd, 'Men, women, children and the family, 1550–1730' in Jane Ohlmeyer (ed.), *Cambridge History of Ireland* (Cambridge, 2017), ii, pp. 337–63.

[15] Vera Moynes (ed.), *Irish Jesuit Annual Letters 1604–1674* (2 vols., Dublin, 2019), i, p. 882.

[16] Dix, *Report of the Cases of Regina v Millis, et Regina v Carroll, in the Queen's Bench in Ireland, in Easter and Trinity Terms, 1842*, p. 112; see also the arguments in *Regina v Smith* (1841) in George Crawford and Edward Spencer Dix, *Reports of Cases Argued and Ruled in the Circuits, in Ireland: During the Years 1839–1846. Together with Cases Decided at the Nisi Prius Sittings, and in the Courts of Criminal Jurisdiction at Dublin* (3 vols., Dublin, 1841–47), ii, pp. 318–46.

jurisdiction as were applications for divorce and separation. Wills were also proven and probated in the consistory courts, a process that could lead to investigations into the legitimacy of heirs and the validity of the marriages of their parents or other antecedents. If the marriage was not celebrated according to the laws observed by the ecclesiastical court, then a widow could be refused access to dower from her husband's estate and children of the marriage might be deemed illegitimate.

There was an ecclesiastical court in each diocese and appeals from the diocesan court could be made to the metropolitan consistory court of the archdiocese.[17] The decisions of the latter might be queried through the Irish court of delegates, which was an occasional court summoned by the Irish chancellor to review particular cases.[18] Appeals, as Elizabeth Leeson discovered, could also be made to the English court of delegates. Few records of any of the Irish ecclesiastical courts survive. Until the early nineteenth century, the Dublin consistory court and the prerogative court were held in a number of different locations including the home of the presiding judge. Not surprisingly, record keeping was haphazard even before the destruction of court records in the Public Record Office in 1922.[19] A small scattering of ecclesiastical court documentation exists for the dioceses of Dublin, Tuam and Killaloe but it is not sufficient to analyse the activities of the courts in any satisfactory detail.[20] It remains difficult, in particular, to discern changes over time.

In determining issues relating to marriage, the judges in the ecclesiastical courts relied on a combination of the code of canon law inherited from the medieval church and the statutory laws on marriage passed following the introduction of the Protestant Reformation in the sixteenth century. The latter took precedence over the former but on issues for which there was no statute law, the consistory courts referred back to pre-Reformation canon law.

---

[17] In the case of Dublin, the consistory court also served as the prerogative court in Ireland. See also Arthur Browne, *A Compendious View of the Ecclesiastical Law of Ireland: Being the Substance of a Course of Lectures Read in the University of Dublin. To Which Is Added, a Sketch of the Practice of the Ecclesiastical Courts, with Some Cases Determined Therein, in Ireland* (Dublin, 1803). The number of consistory courts was reduced in 1864.

[18] See P. A. Howell's review of G. I. O. Duncan, *The High Court of Delegates* (Cambridge, 1971), *Historical Journal*, 16, 1 (March 1973), 191–2.

[19] C. R. Milward, *Reports of Cases Argued and Determined in the Court of Prerogative in Ireland, and in the Consistory Court of Dublin. During the Time of the Right Honourable John Radcliff, LL. D.* (Dublin, 1847), p. vii.

[20] Dublin Consistory Court Cause Papers (NAI, 4/271/37); Killaloe Court and Register book 1707–1868 (NAI, 4/201/31); Tuam Consistory Court Book, 1740–42 (NAI, M 6833); Miscellaneous Papers of the Consistory Court and Diocese of Killaloe, 1671–1824 (BL, Add MSS 31881–2).

The ecclesiastical courts recognised the laws and regulations of the Church of Ireland only if they had been incorporated into statute law. The rules of the established church in relation to marriage were laid out in Canons 46–55 of 1634 and Canon 5 of 1711. They closely followed the guidelines of the pre-Reformation church. The 1634 regulations specified that the marriage should be celebrated in the parish church of one of the partners between eight and twelve in the morning. The couple should be of age, but if they were minors the marriage could take place if parental consent was forthcoming. The intended marriage should be advertised through the pronouncement of banns on three Sundays or Holy Days in the three-month period before the marriage took place. This requirement could be dispensed with on application for a licence from the appropriate diocesan official. Canon 47 forbade marriages between persons related within the forbidden degrees and directed that a table of these should be publicly on view in each parish church. In 1711, an additional canon condemned the practice of marrying without banns or 'in any other form, than that which is prescribed by the Church of Ireland' and threatened anyone who did so with public penance. They were also obliged 'under pain of excommunication' to name the minister who had married them.[21]

In 1753, the Act for the Better Preventing of Clandestine Marriage was passed in Westminster. It incorporated the Anglican canons on marriage into English statute law. Thereafter, only marriages that followed the procedure laid out in the Act were deemed legally valid.[22] The Act, which is often referred to as Lord Hardwicke's Marriage Act, did not apply in Ireland nor was there any equivalent legislation passed in the Irish parliament.[23] The canons of the Church of Ireland in relation to marriage never formed part of Irish statute law. Consequently, the Irish consistorial court considered the rules of the Church of Ireland as binding on the clergy who performed the marriage service but not on

---

[21] *Constitutions and Canons Ecclesiastical, Treated upon by the Archbishops and Bishops and the Rest of the Clergy of Ireland: and Agreed by the King's Majesty's License in Their Synod, Begun and Holden at Dublin, Anno Domini, 1634. To Which Is Added Constitutions and Canons Ecclesiastical, Treated upon by the Archbishops and Bishops, and the Rest of the Clergy of Ireland: And Agreed upon by the Queen's Majesty's License in Their Synod, Begun and Holden at Dublin, Anno Domini, 1711 …* (Dublin, 1767).

[22] Rebecca Probert, 'The impact of the Marriage Act of 1753: Was it really "A most cruel law for the fair sex"?', *Eighteenth-Century Studies*, 38, 2 (2005), 247–62; *Marriage Law and Practice in the Long Eighteenth Century: A Reassessment* (Cambridge, 2009).

[23] The Act was introduced to parliament by Philip Yorke, 1st Earl of Hardwicke who was Lord Chancellor in Great Britain, 1737–1756.

the couple who were being married.[24] Ministers could be punished for presiding over an irregular service but this did not invalidate the marriage.

Prior to the Marriages (Ireland) Act 1844, Irish statute law relating to the marriage service was, therefore, far more limited than was the case in England after 1753. Marriages did not require witnesses nor the proclamation of banns to validate them. As John Radcliff, the judge in the Dublin consistory court, noted in 1832:

> There being no statutable requisitives in Ireland to validate marriages of adult persons, the secrecy and irregularity cannot impeach it, though the priest or parties might have been canonically censured for the irregularity ... all that is necessary ... for a valid marriage is a contract by words of the present tense between parties able to contract, with the intervention of a priest in orders.[25]

In other words, in the absence of statute law, the consistory court relied on medieval canon law for its definition of a legally binding marriage: a promise in the present tense in the presence of a clergyman.

The absence of statute law regulating the marriage service also meant that record keeping of marriages was lax and, in many cases, nonexistent. Before the legislation of 1844, the Irish ecclesiastical courts did not always insist on a marriage certificate or record to prove a marriage.[26] Margaret Steadman worked as a lady's maid in the household of the duchess of Rutland in the 1780s. She travelled with the duchess to Ireland when the duke of Rutland was appointed lord lieutenant in 1784. Steadman became pregnant in 1786 and it 'was rumoured' that the father was James Powell, an *aide-de-camp* in the service of the duke. On hearing the news, the duchess of Rutland insisted that the couple marry or they would both be dismissed from the viceregal household. The couple claimed that they had married privately and that they had 'acknowledged each other as husband and wife'. Steadman was referred to as 'Mrs Powell' and was 'universally reputed' to be the wife of James Powell. The couple separated some years before Steadman died in 1820. Prior to her death, Steadman, in an attempt to prevent her husband inheriting her considerable savings accumulated in the service of the duchess, alleged that she had not been validly married to Powell

---

[24] Edward Bullinbrooke, *Ecclesiastical Law: or, the Statutes, Constitutions, Canons, Rubricks, and Articles, of the Church of Ireland Methodically Digested under Proper Heads. With a Commentary, Historical and Juridical* (2 vols., Dublin, 1770), i, pp. iii–vi.

[25] Milward, *Reports of Cases Argued and Determined in the Court of Prerogative in Ireland*, p. 291. See also W. Harris Faloon, *The Marriage Law of Ireland: With an Introduction and Notes* (Dublin, 1881), pp. 6–9.

[26] For a list of extant marriage registers, 1660–1925 see John Grenham, *Tracing Your Irish Ancestors* (4th ed., Dublin, 2012).

and that she was, therefore, a single woman. She made a will bequeathing her savings to her brother. Powell queried her right to do this as she was a married woman. There were no witnesses to the marriage and the clergyman who had officiated was not known. The London judge who heard the case decided in favour of Powell arguing that in Ireland, as in England prior to the 1753 Act, marriages were provable by circumstantial evidence.[27] Judge John Radcliff made a similar statement in the Dublin consistory court:

The law of Ireland imposing no statutable forms or ceremonies in order to a marriage, it is not essential to prove the fact of marriage by direct evidence to the point; it is sufficient to prove it circumstantially and strict proof is not to be expected in a country where marriage registries are disregarded and the law is so loose.[28]

Ecclesiastical law not only required that a clergyman be present at a marriage but it had to be a particular type of minister: 'a priest in orders'. In canon law, a 'priest in orders' meant a priest who had been ordained by a bishop. Ministers in the Church of Ireland and in the Roman Catholic church were ordained and both groups were recognised by the ecclesiastical court. Despite the introduction of the Protestant reformation and the legal prosecution of Catholic priests in Ireland in the late seventeenth and early eighteenth century, the marriage of Catholics by a Catholic priest continued to be recognised as valid by the state. From 1697 to 1871, statute law prohibited Catholic priests from solemnising the marriages of two Protestants and, until 1793, a Protestant and Catholic but it did not hinder them marrying two Catholics.

The most important consequence of the fact that only marriage services witnessed by ordained ministers were recognised by the ecclesiastical courts was that a marriage solemnised in the presence of a Presbyterian minister was deemed invalid because Presbyterian clergymen were not ordained by a bishop. The questioning of the legal validity of marriages conducted by Presbyterian ministers was most severe in the 1690s and early decades of the eighteenth century. In 1738, legislation was passed by the Irish parliament that partly remedied the situation. The law defined Presbyterian marriages as 'marriage contracts' that had

---

[27] Edward D. Ingram (ed.), *Reports of Cases Argued and Determined in the English Ecclesiastical Courts, with Tables of the Cases and Principal Matters* (Philadelphia, 1831), ii, pp. 29–30.

[28] Milward, *Reports of Cases Argued and Determined in the Court of Prerogative in Ireland, and in the Consistory Court of Dublin...*, pp. 292–3.

not been solemnised by a recognised clergyman, but at the same time it exempted Presbyterians from prosecution in the ecclesiastical courts.[29]

In 1782, the law went one step further although it still did not recognise Presbyterian ministers as quite equal to an ordained minister of the Church of Ireland or of the Roman Catholic church.[30] Under the Act, marriages between Protestant dissenters solemnised by Protestant dissenting ministers were legally sanctioned 'as if the marriage had been celebrated by a clergyman of the Church of Ireland'. The Act did not legalise marriages by Presbyterian ministers involving members of the established church or Roman Catholics but the fact that it did not specifically invalidate such marriages was to become an important legal issue in the following decades.[31]

Despite the restrictions imposed on Presbyterian ministers in solemnising marriages, the regulation of marriage within the Presbyterian community was very similar to that of the Church of Ireland and, as we shall see, the Catholic church. Marriage was to be solemnised by a minister in the church or the 'place appointed … for publick worship' and before other witnesses. The marriage contract was also to be publicised three Sundays in advance of the ceremony in the place where each partner lived. The consent of the parents of both partners was considered desirable but not essential.[32]

Although the guidelines of the Presbyterian Church followed the format of the Church of Ireland, Presbyterian views on marriage adhered more closely to early canon law, which defined marriage as a private promise between a man and a woman. The *Directory for the Publicke Worship of God* stated clearly that marriage was not a sacrament and although it was to be solemnised in front of a minister, the marriage was validated through the verbal promise by each of the partners rather than through the actions of the minister.[33] *The Assembly's Shorter Catechism Explained*, which was published in several editions in Belfast, answered in response to the question 'what is necessary to constitute a

---

[29] J. C. Beckett, *Protestant Dissent in Ireland, 1687–1780* (London, 1948), pp. 116–23.

[30] An Act for the Relief of Protestant Dissenters, in Certain Matters Therein Contained, 21 & 22 George III c.21. 1782.

[31] Ibid.

[32] *The Humble Advice of the Assembly of Divines, Now by Authority of Parliament Sitting at Westminster, Concerning a Confession of Faith, Presented by Them Lately to Both Houses of Parliament* (London, 1647), pp. 43–4; *A Directory for the Publicke Worship of God Throughout the Three Kingdoms of Scotland, England and Ireland* (Edinburgh, 1645), pp. 47–9.

[33] Ibid.

marriage?' that it was 'the voluntary and mutual consent of both parties' and provided the Biblical reference to Genesis, 24, 58, 67, which is the account of Rebekah, daughter of Abraham, promising to marry Isaac and of the couple marrying privately without reference to a religious ceremony.[34]

In 1701, in his famous *A Vindication of Marriage*, John McBride summed up the tension in the Presbyterian definition of marriage between the private and the public:

> We believe marriage sacred, yet we know it is no sacrament. Nor do we look on the presence and prayer of a minister, as absolutely necessary to the being of this relation; for the first was good, tho' no priest was present, God himself joining them.[35]

Although acknowledging that 'the want of ministerial benediction can never make it [i.e. a marriage] void', McBride also emphasised that it was 'highly expedient a minister of the word be present' and that marriages should be publicly celebrated in accordance with the guidelines outlined in the *Directory for the Publicke Worship of God*.[36]

Andrew Holmes has cautioned against generalising about eighteenth-century Ulster Presbyterianism, as theological disputes and the separation of congregations led to divergences in beliefs and practices with some congregations adhering more strictly to what was perceived to be the orthodoxy of the 1647 foundation document of the *Westminster Confession of Faith*.[37] Holmes' assertion might also apply to marriage practices and, more particularly, to ideas about what constituted a valid marriage, with some more willing to accept the sufficiency of a private avowal than others. The minutes of the Seceder congregation of Cahans in County Monaghan in the second half of the eighteenth century, for example, reveal an awareness among members of the congregation of the distinction between a private promise of marriage and the solemnisation of the marriage by a minister. In 1777, Thomas Irvine submitted a complaint to the Cahans session that described how he and Rossanna Lister 'married ourselves privately in the words of the Confession of Faith and afterwards, bedded sundry nights together at which I thought the marriage was consummated'. Irvine's complaint was that Rossanna

---

[34] *The Assembly's Shorter Catechism Explained, By Way of Question and Answer* (2 parts, Belfast, 1764), p. 155.

[35] John McBride, *A Vindication of Marriage: As Solemnized by Presbyterians, in the North of Ireland* (n.p., 1702), p. 22.

[36] Ibid., p. 15.

[37] Andrew Holmes, *The Shaping of Ulster Presbyterianism and Practice 1770–1840* (Oxford, 2006), pp. 1–51.

did not maintain the promise that they had made to each other and had married another.[38] Other couples also referred to the fact that they had said the words of the Confession of Faith privately to one another prior to their first sexual intercourse or spoke of making a verbal promise of marriage that was followed by sexual intercourse.[39]

The leadership of the Seceder congregation of Cahans seemed uncertain how to deal with Thomas Irvine's claim that he had privately married Rosanna Lister. The minister and elders referred the matter to the Presbytery. The latter upheld Irvine's contention that he was married to Lister but Lister's then husband, David Harshaw, appealed to the Burgher Synod. The latter disagreed with the Presbytery's conclusion and declared Lister's marriage to Harshaw as the valid one.[40]

The ambiguity in Cahans concerning private marriages continued into the early decades of the nineteenth century. As late as December 1833, William Jackson justified the birth of his first child, two and a half months after the formal celebration of his marriage in August 1833, on the grounds that in January 'he and his wife became pledged to each other according to the form in the Directory for Marriage'. The elders were again unclear how to treat Jackson's claim that his child was 'lawfully begotten' and agreed to ask the Presbytery 'if a man and woman bind themselves privately to each other by that form acknowledged to be right when used before witnesses are they guilty of fornication if they cohabit together as man and wife?' The Presbytery responded, however, that Jackson and his wife had committed pre-marital fornication, presumably on the grounds that the marriage had not been solemnised in public, a direction that the authorities in all the Presbyterian congregations were trying to enforce by that time.[41]

The awareness of the theological difference between a private promise of marriage and a public solemnisation among members of the Cahans congregation may also indicate a Scottish influence on attitudes to the marriage service in some Ulster Presbyterian communities in the eighteenth century. There was a long tradition in Scotland of marriages based on verbal consent, which the civil courts continued to recognise as valid

---

[38] Cahans Session Book, 1751–1802, entry dated 1777 (PHSIB).
[39] See examples in ibid.
[40] Holmes, *The Shaping of Ulster Presbyterian Belief and Practice*, pp. 222–3.
[41] Cahans Session Book, 1824–1911, 29 Dec. 1833 (PHSIB); John Monteith Barkley, 'A history of the ruling eldership in Irish Presbyterianism' (2 vols., unpublished MA thesis, Queen's University Belfast, 1952), i, p. 238. See also Leanne Calvert, '"He came to her bed pretending courtship": Sex, courtship and the making of marriage in Ulster, 1750–1844', *Irish Historical* Studies, 42, 162 (2018), 258–62.

even though they were deemed 'irregular' by the Church of Scotland.[42] It is likely that this tradition of private marriage was brought to Ireland by Scottish settlers. This custom may also help to explain the prevalence of pre-marital sex that can be documented in Presbyterian communities in the eighteenth century.[43] The public solemnisation of the marriage might follow the private vows and consummation.

In the sixteenth century, the Protestant Reformation abolished the sacramental status of marriage arguing that the union of a man and a woman did not require divine intervention.[44] In 1563, the Council of Trent, however, reaffirmed the seven sacraments (which included marriage) of the medieval church. It also endeavoured to strengthen Catholic church regulations including those on marriage. The *Tametsi* decree of the Council directed that marital unions were to be celebrated in the presence of a parish priest before two witnesses. The marriage was to take place in the parish of one of the partners. It was the responsibility of the priest to ensure that the couple had the consent of their respective parents but lack of consent did not invalidate the marriage.[45] The Council reinforced the canon law on consanguinity and affinity that stipulated that two people who were related within the fourth degree (i.e. going back four generations) could not legally marry. The Anglican Reformation had by that time reduced the number to two.[46] The marriage of any couple discovered to be within the prohibited degrees was to be declared null and void and the man and woman involved were to be denied any possibility of being granted a dispensation.[47] In addition, *Tametsi* stipulated that the marriage of a Catholic to a non-Catholic had to take place in the presence of a Catholic priest and that marriages that did not follow this rule would be considered void.

In an Irish context it is important to note that the *Tametsi* decree could only be enforced after it had been published or promulgated in a parish. The promulgation of the decree in Ireland was uneven and took place over a long period of time. Throughout the seventeenth and eighteenth

---

[42] T. C. Smout, 'Scottish marriage, regular and irregular 1500–1940' in R. B. Outhwaite (ed.), *Marriage and Society: Studies in the Social History of Marriage* (London, 1981), pp. 206, 211.

[43] See Chapter 4.

[44] The Reformation reduced the number of sacraments to two: baptism and communion.

[45] Charlotte Christensen-Nugues, 'Parental authority and freedom of choice: The debate on clandestinity and parental consent at the Council of Trent (1545–63)', *Sixteenth Century Journal*, 45, 1 (2014), 51–72.

[46] Maebh Harding, 'The curious incident of the Marriage Act (No 2) 1537 and the Irish statute book', *Legal Studies*, 32, 1 (2012), 78–108.

[47] Entry for 'Tametsi' in *Catholic Encyclopedia*, consulted online: www.newadvent.org/cathen/14441b.htm. Accessed 28 January 2019.

centuries, successive synods of the Irish Catholic hierarchy deferred proclaiming the full text of the *Tametsi* decree, particularly those sections that required that marriages take place in the presence of a parish priest of one of the partners. Most clergy were also prepared to overlook Trent's insistence that banns be proclaimed and did not prohibit mixed marriages as *Tametsi* directed. The argument of the seventeenth-century hierarchy was that there were not enough parochial clergy in the country to facilitate this requirement and that the publication of banns of Catholic marriages was impractical considering the particular circumstances of the Irish church.[48]

Tametsi was proclaimed in many dioceses in Ulster and Connacht in the late seventeenth century but it was not strictly observed before the nineteenth century.[49] In 1714, the bishop of Clogher, Hugh MacMahon, wrote that although *Tametsi* was recognised as church law by the clergy in Ulster, there were problems in enforcing it. MacMahon explained that some of the priests made use of the concept of 'Epikeia', the canon law equivalent of equity, in order to permit some relaxation of the strict observance of the Trent decree. As the bishop noted, the priests issued dispensations from the strict enforcement of canon law 'in cases where they think the Holy See would dispense if presented with the facts'.[50] MacMahon, aware that the priests did not have permission from Rome to exercise such a flexible attitude to church law, expressed his disapproval but he also pointed out that the challenging circumstances of the Catholic church in Ireland, in general, and in Ulster, in particular, made it difficult to proclaim banns or to perform the marriage service in public. Although by the later eighteenth century more efforts were made to enforce the *Tametsi* decree in the province, in 1788, the bishop of Raphoe was only able to reassure Rome that the Tridentine directions on the marriages of Catholics to non-Catholics were observed in his diocese.[51]

In the ecclesiastical province of Tuam, there were attempts from the 1740s to regulate marriages more comprehensively. A synod of 1746 ordered that the Tridentine decree on marriage, which had been 'previously promulgated ... be strictly observed', and reminded the clergy as well as the laity of the penalties to be imposed for participating in or even

---

[48] Forrestal, *Catholic Synods in Ireland*, pp. 80, 105, 112, 115.
[49] Laurence F. Renehan, *Collections on Irish Church History*. Edited by Daniel McCarthy (Dublin, 1861), pp. 116–7, 139–41, 149–61, 289–90, 345–7.
[50] Patrick J. Flanagan, 'The diocese of Clogher in 1714', *Clogher Record*, i, 3 (1955), 125–6.
[51] Cathaldus Giblin (ed.), *The Diocese of Raphoe 1773–1805* (1980), p. 25.

attending clandestine marriages.[52] The situation in the west of Ireland was, however, compounded by the existence of the separate ecclesiastical jurisdiction of the wardenship of Galway, which did not proclaim the Tridentine decree until the 1820s. Consequently, it was possible for individuals to evade the strict enforcement of church law in the province by seeking permission to marry within the jurisdiction of the wardenship.[53]

In the archdiocese of Cashel, the records of provincial synods suggest that, as in Tuam, from the 1740s the provincial hierarchy were endeavouring to tighten the regulation of marriage and bring practices in their jurisdiction into line with the Tridentine guidelines. The full implementation of *Tametsi* in the archdiocese, however, took some time and was not completed until 1785.[54]

The recognition of the Tridentine decree took even longer in the province of Dublin. John Troy, who became archbishop of Dublin in 1786, maintained his opposition to the decree until his death in 1823. Troy's stance on *Tametsi* was supported by a majority of the priests in Dublin. In 1788, when the archbishop consulted the clergy in the archdiocese for their views on the promulgation of *Tametsi,* most argued against the introduction of the Tridentine decree. The priests contended that it would not only render existing mixed marriages invalid but it would also introduce a serious division between the civil law and that of the Catholic church. The state would continue to recognise marriages that the church would deem null and void.[55]

It was with some reluctance, following pressure from Rome, that Troy's successor Daniel Murray promulgated the *Tametsi* decree in the province in 1827, and the warden of Galway followed suit in the same year.[56] Prior to this date, the older version of canon law remained in place in both jurisdictions, and marriages without banns and not conducted in the presence of a Catholic priest were still officially sanctioned

---

[52] James Gerard McGarry, 'The statutes of Tuam from the Council of Trent to the nineteenth century' (unpublished MA thesis, University College Galway, 1932), p. 92.
[53] For the wardenship of Galway see documents in Galway Diocesan Archives catalogued in Edward MacLysaght and H. F. Berry, 'Report on documents relating to the wardenship of Galway', *Analecta Hibernica*, 14 (Dec. 1944); Martin Coen, *The Wardenship of Galway* (Galway, 1984).
[54] Sr M. Imelda, 'Calendar of Papers of James Butler Archbishop of Cashel and Emly 1712–1791' (NLI, Manuscript Room, Special List No 170B, pp. 140–49).
[55] DDA, Troy Papers, Green File 29/1/40.
[56] Correspondence of Irish Bishops to Archbishop Daniel Murray, 1824–1827 (DDA, Murray Papers, 30/8); Patrick J. Corish, 'Catholic marriage under the penal code' in Art Cosgrove (ed.), *Marriage in Ireland* (Dublin, 1985), p. 74.

by the church.[57] In 1825, James Doyle, the Catholic Bishop of Kildare and Leighlin told a Select Committee of the House of Lords that in the ecclesiastical province of Dublin, all mixed marriages conducted by either a Church of Ireland or a Presbyterian minister were deemed valid by the Catholic authorities.[58] Theoretically, according to Catholic canon law, prior to 1827, a private promise to marry could also still have been considered valid in these districts as the presence of a Catholic priest was not mandatory. Although such private marriages can be documented for early seventeenth-century Ireland, by the eighteenth century the vast majority of Catholics believed that marriage entailed an officiating clergyman of some kind. As the bishop of Kerry, Nicholas Madgett noted, 'by a happy and praise-worthy error', most couples did not realise that a clerical witness to their marriage was not strictly necessary.[59]

Of all the main Christian denominations, it was the Society of Friends that rejected most explicitly the theological necessity for a public ceremony. Yet, paradoxically, of all the churches, it was also the Society of Friends that exercised the tightest public control over the marriages of its members. Marriage in the Society was a carefully orchestrated event with all proposed marriages between members being discussed at Society meetings and solemnised in public. Members of the Women's Meetings undertook to visit the home of the woman to ensure that she had the consent of her parents and that she was in the right frame of mind to marry.[60] A written record of the marriage and the witnesses was also kept. Thus, when Jacob Hancock and Mary Grigg announced their intention to marry in 1792, they attended 'several meetings' of the Quaker community in Coleraine and the document

---

[57] Patrick J. Corish, *The Irish Catholic Experience: A Historical Survey* (Dublin, 1985), pp. 106–7; S. J. Connolly, *Priests and People in Pre-famine Ireland, 1780–1845* (Dublin, 1982), pp. 198–203.

[58] *Minutes of Evidence Taken before the Select Committee of the House of Lords, Appointed to Inquire into the State of Ireland, More Particularly with Reference to the Circumstances Which May Have Led to Disturbances in That Part of the United Kingdom 24 March–22 June 1825* (London, 1825), p. 314.

[59] Michael Manning, 'Dr Nicholas Madgett's Constitutio Ecclesiastica', *Journal of Kerry Archaeological and Historical Society*, 9 (1976), 86. See also the comment by Sir Thomas Staples in *Regina v Carroll*: 'The Roman Catholics in this country ... do always insist on having a Priest present at their marriages'. Edward Spencer Dix, *Report of the Cases of Regina v Millis, et Regina v Carroll, in the Queen's Bench in Ireland, in Easter and Trinity Terms, 1842* (Dublin, 1842), p. 115.

[60] Richard L. Greaves, *God's Other Children: Protestant Nonconformists and the Emergence of Denominational Churches in Ireland, 1660–1700* (Stanford, 1997), pp. 343–48; Minutes of the Lurgan Women's Meetings, 1794–1900 (PRONI, MIC16/29A).

recording their marriage vows was signed by four men, four women and twelve of their relatives.[61]

The Quakers were, however, unusual, in enforcing such a public witnessing of marriages. In other denominations, it is clear that until the 1840s, at least, the preference for most couples and their families was for a service performed in private. It was normal practice before the 1844 Marriages (Ireland) Act for marriage services in Ireland to be held in a private house rather than in a church.[62] The house was not necessarily the home of one of the partners to be married but could be that of the presiding priest or minister (see Illustration 1.1). In a court case in England, where church weddings were mandatory after the 1753 Marriage Act, a judge explained that in Ireland, 'persons of respectability were usually married in their own houses'.[63] The 1844 legislation stipulated that Church of Ireland and Presbyterian marriages should take place in a registered place of worship. Members of the Quaker and Jewish communities were exempted from this requirement but they were obliged to notify the newly established office of registrar of their intention to marry. The Act specifically, however, excluded marriages conducted by a Catholic priest, who was not obliged to give notice of any marriage, nor was it necessary to register Catholic chapels with the registrar's office.[64]

There was, therefore, never any parliamentary legislation passed that prevented Catholic marriages from being held in a private house. In 1850, however, the Synod of Thurles issued a decree directing that the administering of all sacraments, including marriage, should take place in a church and not in a private house. The synod was the first national Catholic synod held in Ireland since the Reformation and formed part of the reform programme initiated by Paul Cullen (Archbishop of Armagh from 1849 and appointed Archbishop of Dublin in 1852). Cullen directed a major overhaul in clerical discipline as well as a building programme of parish churches, which made it easier for members of the laity to attend church services.[65] Gradually, therefore, in the later

---

[61] Minutes of Coleraine Women's Meeting, May 1794–1798, Nov. 1800 (PRONI, MIC16/29, pp. 40–1).

[62] For Catholic marriages solemnised in private houses see, for example, the marriage and baptism register for the parish of St Michan's, Dublin, 1726–1730. Consulted on microfilm in NLI.

[63] Edward Ryan and William Moody, *Reports of Cases Determined at Nisi Prius, in the Courts of King's Bench and Common Pleas, and on the Oxford and Western Circuits from the Sittings after Michaelmas Term, 4 George IV, 1823 …* (London, 1827), p. 80.

[64] Marriages (Ireland) Act. 7 & 8 Vict. c.81. 1844.

[65] P. C. Barry, 'The legislation of the Synod of Thurles, 1850', *Irish Theological Quarterly*, (1 June 1969), 131–66; Emmet Larkin, 'The devotional revolution in Ireland, 1850-1875', *American Historical Review*, 77, 3 (June 1972), 625–52.

Illustration 1.1 This is the only known contemporary image of a marriage solemnised in a private house. The print of J. P. Haverty's painting of Daniel O'Connell in the background suggests a date in the 1840s or later.

37

decades of the nineteenth century, the celebration of Catholic marriages in a church became the norm. Priests were still, however, free to attend the subsequent celebrations in a private house at which a collection might be made or, alternatively, agree a sum which might be expected through a collection with the parties to be married. The change in venue is evident in the diaries of two priests, James and Thomas O'Carroll (who were also brothers). In Thomas O'Carroll's diary for 1846 he recorded that all the marriages that he conducted were in private houses but all of the marriages that his brother, James, celebrated in 1862–1864 were held in a parish church. The latter argued in his diary that the new practice of a church marriage increased the cost of the event for the family because more people accepted the invitation to the marriage festivities knowing that the couple had agreed a fee for the priest in lieu of a collection.[66]

Banns

The preference for a private service before 1850 also explains why there was strong resistance within Catholic and Protestant communities to the publishing of banns. In the seventeenth and early eighteenth centuries, the issuing of dispensations from reading the banns was justified by Catholic priests on pragmatic grounds that it was not safe to do so. By the middle decades of the eighteenth century, however, the opposition to banns had evolved into a matter of social pride and status. Publication of banns was perceived in local communities as a sign of poverty and an indication that the couple or their respective families could not afford the licence fee to dispense with the procedure.[67]

The dislike of banns was shared by the Anglican and Presbyterian communities. In the Church of Ireland, it was possible, as in the Catholic church, to purchase a dispensation from the publishing of banns. The surviving lists of licences issued suggests that this was a very common

---

[66] Diary of Reverend James O'Carroll, 1862 (The O'Carroll Diaries (unpublished typescript by Rev. James Feehan), pp. v–vi, 45–6) (Tipperary Studies, The Source, Thurles, Co Tipperary). Daniel Grace documents the move towards church weddings in his study of four parish registers in the diocese of Killaloe, 1831–1840. Most marriages still took place in the home of the bride but in the town of Kilrush, 61 per cent of marriages were solemnised in the chapel; 21 per cent took place in a private house and 7 per cent in the priest's house. See Daniel Grace, 'The income of Catholic priests in pre-Famine Ireland: Some evidence from the diocese of Killaloe', *Tipperary Historical Journal*, 30 (2017), 82–3.

[67] Corish, *The Irish Catholic Experience*, p. 179; Connolly, *Priests and People in Pre-famine Ireland*, p. 199.

and popular option which couples availed of, if they could.[68] Similarly, the Presbyterian church leadership struggled to enforce the regulations on publishing banns in advance of the marriage.[69] Throughout the eighteenth century, successive synods of the General Synod of Ulster persisted in directing ministers to follow the *Directory's* regulations on the promulgation of banns and frequently rebuked those who did not do so.[70] Despite the church instructions, however, the Presbyterian lay community continued to opt for private services. In 1803, the General Synod conceded defeat on the issue and agreed that ministers could choose to solemnise marriage after one public proclamation and in the following year, the ministers attending the Synod agreed that the proclamation could be optional.[71] The 1844 Marriage (Ireland) Act included provisions for the publication of banns in Presbyterian meeting houses on three successive Sundays before the marriage was solemnised. The first clause of the Act, however, permitted a week's notice to be given to the registrar about the intended marriage instead of public banns.[72] The Matrimonial Causes and Marriage Law (Ireland) Amendment Acts (1870, 1871) incorporated the Anglican guidelines on the publication of banns for marriages performed in Church of Ireland churches. The legislation also provided for the registration of marriages performed by Catholic priests but it did not specify the procedures to be followed by the latter in relation to marriage, an omission that subsequently led to legal debate on what constituted a legally valid Catholic marriage.[73]

---

[68] See, for example, Hilary D. Walsh, 'Ossory marriage license bonds', *Irish Genealogist*, 4 (1971), 331–41; Raymond Refaussé, 'Marriage licences from the diocese of Ossory 1739–1804', *Irish Genealogist*, 8 (1990), 122–44; (1991), 239–67; (1992), 393–428. See also manuscript licences in PRONI, CR1/26/E; D950/1/87; DIO/4/30/2.

[69] On payments for proclaiming banns in seventeenth-century Presbyterian congregations see William T. Latimer, 'The old session-book of Templepatrick Presbyterian Church, County Antrim', *Journal of Royal Society of Antiquaries of Ireland*, 5, 2 (1895), 130–134; 31, 2 (1901), 162–75; 31, 3 (1901), 259–72; Dundonald Session and Committee Book, 1678 (PHSIB).

[70] *Records of the General Synod of Ulster, from 1691 to 1820* (3 vols., 1691–1820, Belfast, 1890, 1897), i, pp. 53, 61, 72, 87, 204, 276; ii, pp. 280, 394, 446; iii, pp. 74, 81, 98, 252. See also W. T. Latimer's foreword to Richard Linn (ed.), 'Marriage register of the Presbyterian congregation of Banbridge, County Down, 1756–1794', *Journal of the Royal Society of Antiquaries of Ireland*, 39 (1909), 75–7.

[71] *Records of the General Synod of Ulster, from 1691 to 1820*, iii, pp. 268, 278; Holmes, *The Shaping of Ulster Presbyterian Belief and Pactice*, pp. 214–5.

[72] Marriage (Ireland) Act. 7 & 8 Vict. c.81. 1844.

[73] Matrimonial Causes and Marriage Law (Ireland) Amendment Act. 33 & 34 Vict. c.10. 1870; Matrimonial Causes and Marriage Law (Ireland) Amendment Act. 34 & 35 Vict. c.49. 1871. On the legal debate on the validity of a marriage solemnised according to Catholic canon law see pp. 54–7.

The civil law did not, therefore, require banns to be published for Catholic marriages, but following the proclamation of the *Tametsi* decree throughout the island, the Catholic authorities did. It is not clear when the popularity of securing a licence to dispense with marriage banns declined but, like the church service, the publication of banns had become the norm for Catholic marriages by the end of the nineteenth century.

Mixed Marriages

The term 'mixed marriages' usually refers in Ireland to marriages of Catholics to non-Catholics. As indicated already, the Council of Trent (1545–1563) specified that the marriage of a Catholic to a non-Catholic should be solemnised by a Catholic priest before witnesses. This created problems for the Catholic church in Ireland, because the state had imposed restrictions on marriages of Protestants to Catholics. In the early eighteenth century, the Irish parliament passed laws prohibiting 'mixed' marriages that were performed by a Catholic priest. The legislation of 1745 imposed severe penalties on Catholic priests who presided over the marriage of a Protestant and a Catholic.[74] Under a Catholic relief act of 1793, Catholic priests were permitted to marry a Catholic and a Protestant but only if the couple had first been married in a Church of Ireland service. Failure to do so would incur a fine of £500.[75] The passing of this act, combined with the lifting of the restrictions on Presbyterian ministers in 1782, appears to have led to a tolerance of clergymen from both groups performing mixed marriages. In 1825, for example, the Church of Ireland Archbishop of Dublin, William Magee, told a House of Lords Select Committee that Catholic priests presiding over mixed marriages:

[a]s far as I have been given to understand ... has become of late years frequent in Ireland, and so much so that now any attempt made by individuals to support the law in that particular is become exceedingly unpopular.[76]

---

[74] An Act for Annulling All Marriages to Be Celebrated by Any Popish Priest between Protestant and Protestant, or between Protestant and Papist. 19 Geo. II c.13. 1745.

[75] An Act for the Relief of His Majesty's Popish, or Roman Catholic Subjects of Ireland. 33 Geo. III c.21. 1793. See also the addendum to the minutes of a provincial synod in the diocese of Kerry in the 1820s, which made it mandatory for the Catholic partner to remarry in the Catholic church on pain of being excluded from the sacraments (Kerry Diocesan Archives, Killarney).

[76] *Minutes of Evidence Taken before the Select Committee of the House of Lords, Appointed to Inquire into the State of Ireland, More Particularly with Reference to the Circumstances Which May Have Led to Disturbances in That Part of the United Kingdom 24 March–22 June 1825,*

Thomas Costello, a Catholic priest from Limerick, agreed with the archbishop that such marriages were 'very frequent'.[77] It was not, however, until the passing of the Matrimonial Causes and Marriage Law (Ireland) Amendment Act (1871) that a mixed marriage solemnised by a Catholic priest was deemed officially valid in Irish civil law.

The view of the Catholic church on marriages of Catholics to non-Catholics was theologically and legally complicated. Medieval theologians unanimously agreed that marriages contracted between two baptised partners were valid provided there was no other reason why the couple could not marry. The Protestant reformation introduced some hesitancy into the theological debate but the majority of canonists in the sixteenth and seventeenth centuries maintained that the marriage of a Catholic to a Protestant constituted a valid if illicit marriage because both partners were baptised Christians. The discussion between the theologians focused on two issues: should the non-Catholic be expected to abjure his or her own faith, and should there also be an undertaking that the children would be brought up as Catholics. Throughout the early modern period, there was no agreement on the answers to these questions.[78] Successive popes adopted a pragmatic attitude in countries where, as in Ireland, the civil law imposed restrictions on Catholic marriages. As the German theologian, Bernard Häiring noted, in the seventeenth and early eighteenth centuries:

Mixed marriages entered upon without any papal or episcopal dispensations and without any guarantee of Catholic baptism or education of the children were blessed by the Church.[79]

There continued, however, to be confusion over the status of mixed marriages solemnised in a non-Catholic service in countries or regions where the Tridentine decrees had been promulgated. In 1741, Pope Benedict XIV issued an exemption from the *Tametsi* regulations for all mixed marriages conducted in the Netherlands, where the canon law was deemed to be in conflict with the civil law. A similar concession was granted to the Catholic church in Poland in 1748. In the late 1770s, the Irish hierarchy wrote to Rome indicating their uncertainty concerning

---

p. 422. See also Raymond M. Lee, 'Intermarriage, conflict and social control in Ireland: The decree "Ne Temere"', *Economic and Social Review*, 17, 2 (1985), 13.

[77] Cited in ibid.

[78] Alfred J. Connick, 'Canonical doctrine concerning mixed marriages - before Trent and during the seventeenth and early eighteenth centuries', *Jurist*, 20 (1960), 295–326; 398–418.

[79] Bernard Häiring, *Marriage in the Modern World* (Cork, 1965), p. 206 as cited in Eoin de Bháldraithe, 'Mixed marriages in the new code: Can we now implement the Anglican-Roman Catholic recommendations?', *Jurist*, 46 (1986), 430.

the validity of mixed marriages after the promulgation of *Tametsi* in a parish or diocese and requested that the Dutch exemption be extended to Ireland. Initially, the papal advisors prevaricated but in 1785, Pope Pius VII issued a statement declaring that marriages celebrated between Catholics and non-Catholics in Ireland that did not follow the guidelines in the Tridentine decree were valid. Although the papal declaration referred only to parishes where *Tametsi* had been proclaimed, the statement was interpreted as referring to all mixed marriages performed in Ireland. In 1887, the archbishop of Dublin, Paul Cullen, received confirmation from Rome that this was an acceptable interpretation.[80]

From the time of his return to Ireland, Cullen expressed a strong dislike of mixed marriages. He was concerned, in particular, at the ease with which Catholics could marry non-Catholics in Ireland and at the harm such unions were doing to the Catholic community. Despite the Vatican guidelines concerning the raising of children of mixed marriages in the Catholic faith, Cullen believed that these guidelines were not observed in many Irish families.[81] Cullen attempted to curb the number of mixed marriages by insisting that all such unions required a special papal dispensation. While this regulation was not universally adopted, Cullen succeeded in 1853 in making it a requirement in his new archdiocese of Dublin (see Illustration 1.2).[82]

The Marriage (Ireland) Act of 1844 had introduced civil registration of marriage for the first time. This enabled Catholics who ignored ecclesiastical advice and opted to marry a non-Catholic, to have a civil marriage in a registry office and then marry again in a Catholic service. Marriage registers for the towns of Athy and Wexford suggest that this was a common practice for mixed marriages in the late 1840s and 1850s.[83] Paul Cullen insisted, however, that mixed marriages celebrated by a Catholic priest should not follow the same ceremony as that of two Catholics. The marriage decree of the Synod of Thurles in 1850 included a clause copied from an

---

[80] Sr M. Imelda, 'Calendar of Papers of James Butler Archbishops of Cashel and Emly 1712–1791'; T. P. Cunningham, 'Mixed marriages in Ireland before the *Ne Temere* decree', *Irish Ecclesiastical Review*, 101 (1964), 53–6; Eoin de Bháldraithe, 'Mixed marriages and Irish politics: The effect of "Ne Temere"', *Studies: An Irish Quarterly Review*, 77, 307 (Autumn 1988), 284–99; Patrick Corish, *The Irish Catholic Experience*, p. 220.

[81] Barry, 'The legislation of the Synod of Thurles', 145–7.

[82] Ibid., 147–8; Corish, *The Irish Catholic Experience*, p. 221. The ecclesiastical province of Tuam followed the example set by Dublin.

[83] Catholic Marriage Register for Wexford, County Wexford, 1823–1867. Consulted on microfilm in NLI, Microfilm Positive 4254; Catholic Marriage Register for Athy, County Kildare, 1753–1853. Consulted by Dr John Bergin by permission of Monsignor John Wilson, parish priest of Athy.

NOTIFICATION.

MIXED AND CLANDESTINE MARRIAGES.

It is much to be deplored that, notwithstanding the admonitions of the Church, and the sad experience of the evils of Mixed Marriages, Catholics are still seen to rush into those fatal connexions.

It is, therefore, deemed necessary to call the attention of all whom it may concern to the following notification :—

1. Catholics who, without the requisite dispensations, contract Mixed Marriages, are guilty of a grievous offence against the laws of the Church, and in this Diocese incur, by the very fact, the penalty of Excommunication.

2. In the case where two Catholics, in this country, in despite of ecclesiastical authority, present themselves before a Protestant minister, a civil registrar, or any other unauthorized person, and attempt to contract marriage, such marriage is NULL and VOID in the eyes of the Church ; and the persons so attempting to contract are, by the very fact, Excommunicated.

3. All Catholics who are witnesses to Marriages, referred to in the preceding paragraphs, also incur the penalty of Excommunication.

4. As much scandal is given by these Marriages, parties so offending against the laws of the Church will not be admitted to Sacraments until, having first made reparation for their scandal, and having offered satisfaction for the offence thus given, they are absolved from the Excommunication incurred, by the authority of the Archbishop.

5. Should persons thus guilty present themselves for Communion in the Church before they have received Absolution from the Excommunication which they have incurred, and in the manner above provided for, they expose themselves to be treated as public sinners, and to be refused the Holy Sacrament.

✠ PAUL CARD. CULLEN,

Archbishop, etc. etc.

J. M. O'TOOLE & SON, Printers, 7 Great Brunswick-street, Dublin.

Illustration 1.2 The document is not dated, but Paul Cullen was created a cardinal in 1866 and died in 1878. The guidelines did not introduce any new rules but reinforced Cullen's attempts to discourage mixed marriages in the archdiocese of Dublin.

American Catholic Council decree that a mixed marriage should be solemnised without the use of any sacred rituals or vestments. In 1858, a papal direction, probably secured by Cullen, elaborated on what this meant: the marriage service was to be performed in the sacristy of the church and the officiating priest was not to celebrate mass or give a nuptial blessing.[84]

The papal address to the Polish clergy in 1748 referred to the children of mixed marriages being raised as Catholic and subsequent addresses contained similar statements. The decrees of nineteenth-century Irish synods, including the national synod of Thurles, also endorsed the view that in a mixed marriage the children should be raised as Catholic.[85] It is, however, difficult to determine the extent to which this instruction was followed in practice. As noted already, Cullen believed that it was not observed in the archdiocese of Dublin. There was allegedly a tradition in Ireland of the boys in the family of a mixed marriage being raised in the faith of their father while the girls followed the beliefs of their mother. The strength of this tradition is, however, also difficult to determine.[86] From the 1860s, disputes over the proselytising of children in orphanages and other institutions frequently centred on the offspring of parents who were or had been from different denominations. The right of a mother or father to determine the religious education of daughters or sons was not noted in the public discussion that these disputes provoked.[87] When disagreements over the rearing of children reached the civil courts, the judges usually, as David Jameson has documented, supported the father's choice of religious upbringing for his daughters as well as for his sons over the preference of their mother.[88] The analysis by Cormac Ó Grada et al. of the 1911 census, however, revealed that Irish mixed marriages consisted predominantly of a Catholic woman marrying a Protestant man and by that time, 70 per cent of the children of such marriages were raised Catholic.[89]

---

[84] *Decreta Synodi Plenariae Episcoporum Hiberniae Apud Thurles Habitae, Anno MDCCCL* (Dublin, 1851), p. 28.

[85] Barry, 'The legislation of the Synod of Thurles', 147.

[86] See, for example, Lee, 'Intermarriage, conflict and social control in Ireland', 14–15.

[87] See, for example, *Freeman's Journal*, 19 Feb. 1876; 20 Nov. 1894; 13 Dec. 1897; 31 Jan. 1913; 13 Jan. 1920. On proselytism see *Irish Times*, 29 Dec. 1860; 5 Aug. 1869. See also Maria Luddy, *Women and Philanthropy in Nineteenth-Century Ireland* (Cambridge, 1995), chapter 3.

[88] David Jameson, 'The religious upbringing of children in "mixed marriages": The evolution of Irish law', *New Hibernia Review*, 18, 2 (Summer 2014), 65–72.

[89] Alan Fernihough, Cormac Ó Gráda and Brendan M. Walsh, 'Mixed marriages in Ireland a century ago' (University College Dublin Centre for Economic Research Working Paper Series; WP14/07, pp. 9–11, 18). http://hdl.handle.net/10197/5480. Accessed 25 January 2019.

The religious education of the children of a mixed marriage became a politically sensitive topic in Ireland following the publication of the *Ne Temere* decree by the pope in 1908. The background to the issuing of the decree was the variation in practice throughout the Catholic world of the regulations concerning mixed marriages. The papal exemptions granted to non-Catholic countries, combined with the fact that the Tridentine decrees had not been promulgated in a number of countries with large Catholic populations, including the United States, had led to a proliferation of local regulations that did not conform to the guidelines outlined in *Tametsi*. In addition, the insistence that the marriage service be performed by the parish priest of one of the partners to the marriage, preferably the woman, was difficult to implement in cities with large migrant or emigrant populations. The *Ne Temere* decree reiterated the Tridentine guidelines on the requirements for a valid marriage and made some practical reforms to the parish residency requirement. The authors envisaged that the law would apply throughout the Catholic world and would, therefore, standardise the regulations regarding marriage. It was also aimed at eliminating the exemptions for mixed marriages that had been issued in 1785 for Ireland and at different times in the eighteenth and nineteenth centuries for other countries. As was often the case with papal decrees on marriage, however, a provision was included in the *Ne Temere* document for exemptions to be granted for some countries. The new regulations were to be applied 'unless it had been decided otherwise for some places'. The only exception that was made at the time of the issuing of the decree was in relation to marriages in Germany. This meant, in effect, that in Ireland all marriages of Catholics to non-Catholics had to be solemnised by a Catholic priest.[90]

There was no reference in *Ne Temere* to the necessity to raise the children of a mixed marriage as Catholic, but this was the central issue in the public controversy that was provoked when a Belfast priest tried to implement the decree. Late in 1910, a Presbyterian minister in Belfast, William Corkey, wrote to the local press to alert the public to the treatment of a member of his congregation, Agnes McCann, who had been married in a Presbyterian meeting house to Alexander McCann, a Catholic, some years before the *Ne Temere* decree had been published. The minister alleged that the McCanns had been visited by a parish priest who informed the couple that their marriage was not a valid Catholic marriage and that they should be remarried in a service solemnised by a Catholic priest. The fallout from this visit had dire personal

---

[90] De Bháldraithe, 'Mixed marriages and Irish politics', 290.

consequence for the McCann marriage. Agnes McCann refused to comply with the priest's instructions and, as a result, her husband took their children from her care. She was subsequently unable to locate their whereabouts.[91] The issue was raised in parliament and became the focus of Protestant anger against the Catholic church, at a time when there was a high degree of insecurity within the Protestant community at the prospect of the implementation of Home Rule. The *Ne Temere* decree seemed to prove to the Protestant community that 'Home Rule' would indeed mean 'Rome Rule' and that homes would be broken up on the direction of Catholic priests. As Jim MacPherson has noted, the McCann case gave 'concrete form to popular Protestant beliefs about the impact of Home Rule on their community'.[92] The Presbyterian minister, William Corkey, who had initiated the controversy, presented the papal document as a challenge to civil law in Britain:

This decree challenges the supremacy of British law. I hold in my hand a marriage certificate bearing the seal of the British Empire, and recording the marriage of Alexander McCann and Agnes Jane Barclay. This certificate declares that, according to the law of Britain, these two are husband and wife. This Papal decree says their marriage is 'no marriage at all.' Which law is going to be supreme in Great Britain?[93]

For their part, the Catholic clergy were divided on the issue. Some looked to Rome to calm the public hysteria through the provision of an Irish exemption from the decree while others applauded Alexander McCann for abandoning his wife and taking his children with him. The Jesuit theologian, Peter Finlay, for example, claimed that the Catholic husband 'was conscientiously bound to separate from the Presbyterian woman unless she consented to a revalidation of the marriage'.[94]

The controversy that followed the publication of the *Ne Temere* decree in Ireland undoubtedly contributed to a reduction in the number of mixed marriages. There were at the time exaggerated stories about priests recommending the break-up of families. In 1910, John Crozier, the Church of Ireland Bishop of Down and Connor, noted the 'terrible evils already resulting here from the Roman decree *Ne Temere*'. He claimed that 'case after case of desertion by the Roman husband has

---

[91] D. A. J. MacPherson, '"Exploited with fury on a thousand platforms": Women, unionism and the *Ne Temere* decree in Ireland, 1908–1913' in J. Allen and R. Allen (eds.), *Faith of Our Fathers: Six Centuries of Popular Belief in England, Ireland and Wales* (Newcastle, 2009), pp. 157–75.

[92] Ibid., p. 178.

[93] Cited in Lee, 'Intermarriage, conflict and social control in Ireland', 19.

[94] Cited in De Bháldraithe, 'Mixed marriages and Irish politics', 290.

come before us'.[95] It was also alleged, less convincingly, that many Protestant girls were being 'seduced' and abandoned by Catholic men.[96] The 1908 decree had clearly led to concern among Catholics who, like Alexander McCann, had married a non-Catholic in a Protestant service. The Irish hierarchy eventually succeeded in their efforts to secure a faculty from Rome to validate such marriages. The priest was only obliged to 'remind the Catholic of the obligation, which always binds, to provide as far as possible (*pro viribus*) for baptism and education of the children in the Catholic religion'.[97] As Eoin de Bháldraithe pointed out, the mild tone of this special dispensation, when compared with the harsher rhetoric of priests such as Peter Finlay, may have been designed to reduce the public embarrassment to the church caused by the original decree.[98] The dispensation only, however, applied to existing marriages. As noted already, the commitment to raise the children of a mixed marriage in the Catholic faith had a long history. Although it was not noted specifically in the *Ne Temere* decree, De Bháldraithe and Raymond M. Lee argue convincingly that it became an obligatory promise in Ireland because, after 1908, no priest would authorise a mixed marriage without it.[99]

Subsequent to the controversy aroused by the *Ne Temere* decree, members of the Irish Catholic community were alert to the problems associated with a mixed marriage.[100] For Protestants, too, the public debate had served as a 'cautionary tale' for anyone contemplating a marriage of this kind.[101] John Gregg, who was later to become the Church of Ireland Archbishop of Armagh, noted that 'a certain strong feeling has been growing up amongst our people as the result of this recent agitation which makes a mixed marriage rather an unpopular thing'.[102]

It is difficult to estimate the number of mixed marriages at any time in the period covered by this volume. They may have been more common

---

[95] John Crozier, Bishop of Down and Connor to John Victor Macmillan, 17 Dec. 1910 (Lambeth Palace Archives, Davidson Papers, vol. 420). See also Lee, 'Intermarriage, conflict and social control in Ireland', 20–21.

[96] *Irish Times*, 9 Feb. 1911.

[97] De Bháldraithe, 'Mixed marriages and Irish politics', 293.   [98] Ibid.

[99] Lee, 'Intermarriage, conflict and social control in Ireland', 15–16. Lee cites an unpublished paper by De Bháldraithe entitled 'The children of an inter-church marriage'.

[100] See, for example, DDA, Archbishop Walsh Papers, 1916–1917.

[101] Lee, 'Intermarriage, conflict and social control in Ireland', 25.

[102] J. A. F Gregg to John Crozier, Archbishop of Armagh, 29 Sept. 1911 (Lambeth Palace Archives, Davidson Papers, vol. 420, ff 247–50). See also De Bháldraithe, 'Mixed marriages and Irish politics', 291–2; Lee, 'Intermarriage, conflict and social control in Ireland', 25.

in the larger cities where there was a sizeable Protestant community in the eighteenth and nineteenth centuries and, of course, in the northern part of the island. John Crawford estimated that in inner city parishes in Dublin in the 1850s and the 1870s, there were couples in mixed marriages in 10 or 11 per cent of the Church of Ireland households. Crawford and other scholars have also indicated that, as the Church of Ireland population declined in Dublin in the early twentieth century, the number of mixed marriages increased. According to the 1901 census, 18 per cent of the 94 Church of Ireland households in St Luke's parish in Dublin, included married couples from different religious backgrounds.[103] Ó Grada et al. agreed that the number of mixed marriages was higher in the cities and may have increased in the late nineteenth century. In Dublin they suggest that between 1871 and 1911, 12 per cent of marriages were between couples from different religious denominations. They also concur, however, that mixed marriages became less common in the aftermath of the *Ne Temere* controversy. They estimate that in 1911 less than 1 per cent of co-resident married couples consisted of spouses from different religious denominations, which amounted to 33,834 marriages out of a total of 472,834.[104] Marianne Elliott agrees that while mixed marriages were reasonably common in the province of Ulster in the eighteenth century, hostility to such marriages increased in the post-Famine decades. One consequence of sectarian rioting was that 'mixed religious couples ... were hounded out of Protestant areas'.[105]

The 1844 Marriage (Ireland) Act

The 1782 Act for the Relief of Protestant Dissenters specified:

That all matrimonial contracts or marriages heretofore entered into, or hereafter to be entered into, between protestant dissenters, and solemnised or celebrated by protestant dissenting ministers or teachers, shall be, and shall be held and taken to be good and valid to all intents and purposes whatsoever ... and that all parties to such marriages, ... shall ... be ... intitled [sic] to all rights and benefits ... as all his Majesty's subjects of the established church ...[106]

The intent of the Act was to place marriages between two dissenters, by dissenting ministers, on an equal legal status as marriages performed by

---

[103] John Crawford, *The Church of Ireland in Victorian Dublin* (Dublin, 2005), pp. 66–7.

[104] Fernihough, Ó Gráda and Walsh, 'Mixed marriages in Ireland a century ago', pp. 5–6.

[105] Marianne Elliott, *The Catholics of Ulster: A History* (London, 2000), pp. 340–1. See also A. C. Hepburn, *A Past Apart: Studies in the History of Catholic Belfast, 1850–1950* (Belfast, 1996), pp. 241–2.

[106] An Act for the Relief of Protestant Dissenters, in Certain Matters Therein Contained, Geo. III c.21. 1782.

Anglican ministers. The Act was short and, as noted already, did not specifically prohibit a Presbyterian minister from legally marrying a member of the Church of Ireland and a Presbyterian. Nor did it define what was meant by a dissenting minister. A petition signed by twenty-two members of the Irish House of Lords (including thirteen bishops) protested that the Act would lead to an increase in the number of clandestine marriages, as it legalised marriages solemnised by ministers from the 'numberless sects of Protestant dissenter' without distinguishing between them. It also enabled couples who 'may have gone once or twice to a Meeting-House, or to hear a Field-Preacher' to describe themselves as dissenters and be married accordingly.[107] Although the petitioners were not successful in preventing the passing of the legislation, they were correct in their assessment of it. The Act seems to have opened the way to a considerable increase in the number of clergymen, unattached to a congregation or parish, who performed marriage services for money.[108]

Ten years after the Presbyterian relief act, the Irish parliament agreed to the removal of further restrictions on Presbyterian and Catholic marriages. It repealed the legislation of the early eighteenth century that prevented dissenting ministers from solemnising marriages between Catholics and Protestants. The new law permitted dissenting ministers to marry Roman Catholics and dissenters, but continued the prohibition on their marrying members of the Church of Ireland or two members of the Catholic faith.[109]

The absence in the 1782 Act of an explicit prohibition on dissenting ministers from solemnising marriages between dissenters and members of the Church of Ireland appears to have been interpreted by lawyers as well as by lay men and women as legitimising such unions. By 1841, it was noted in the Irish courts that there were thousands of couples who had been married in this way. The Presbyterian authorities were also keen to assert that their ministers could legally marry members of the Church of Ireland.[110]

Two legal developments in England also contributed to the relaxing of restrictions against marriages by Presbyterian ministers. The first was the decision in the case of *Dalrymple v Dalrymple*, which was heard in the London consistory court in 1811. The presiding ecclesiastical judge, Sir William Scott, deemed that under Scottish law a marriage contracted

---

[107] Petition signed 3 May 1782, *Journals of the Irish House of Lords* (1782), pp. 320–1.
[108] See Chapter 2.
[109] An Act for the Relief of His Majesty's Popish, or Roman Catholic Subjects of Ireland. 33 Geo. III c.21. 1793.
[110] See comments in *Regina v Smith* in Crawford and Dix, *Reports of Cases Argued and Ruled on the Circuits of Ireland*, ii, pp. 318–46.

privately without a religious service was valid. Scott also suggested that this was the law in England prior to the 1753 Marriage Act. This statement was interpreted by some legal authorities in Ireland to mean that a religious service was not essential for a marriage contract in Ireland where the 1753 Act had not been implemented. Contemporaries queried the accuracy of Scott's survey of the history of English marriage law but, nonetheless, Scott's judgment in *Dalrymple v Dalrymple* undoubtedly facilitated the widening of the judicial acceptance of marriages performed by Presbyterian ministers in Ireland.[111] The influence of the verdict in the Dalrymple case can be seen in the trial of William Marshall for bigamy in 1828. Marshall was a member of the Church of Ireland and, at the age of seventeen, he had run away from home to marry Ann Morris who was a Presbyterian. The marriage had been performed by an unplaced Presbyterian minister. The couple had a child together but within two years they had parted and Marshall had married again in a Church of Ireland service. Witnesses at Marshall's trial for bigamy alleged that the Church of Ireland minister had ignored claims that he was a married man, presumably on the grounds that the minister did not consider the marriage to Morris as legally valid. The assize judge, however, dismissed the attempts by Marshall's defence lawyer to use the statute law to argue that the first marriage was void because Marshall was a member of the Church of Ireland. Clearly influenced by the Dalrymple verdict, the judge expressed his 'great doubt' that 'according to the law of Ireland, any religious ceremony was required' for a valid marriage. Marshall was convicted of bigamy on the grounds that his first marriage was valid as the couple had promised privately to marry one another.[112] In other bigamy cases, also heard on the northern circuit, the marriages conducted by Presbyterian ministers in which one of the parties was Anglican were also recognised as valid.[113]

The second legal development in England that had an impact on interpretations of the marriage law in Ireland was the debate on marriage reform that led to the passing of the Act for Marriages in England in 1836 (6 & 7 Wm IV, c.85), which provided for civil marriages to be conducted

---

[111] For a modern critique of the historical validity of the judgement in *Dalrymple v Dalrymple* case see Rebecca Probert, *Marriage Law and Practice in the Long Eighteenth Century: A Reassessment* (Cambridge, 2009), pp. 60–7.

[112] *Belfast Newsletter* and *Freeman's Journal*, 25 March 1828. See also Crawford and Dix, *Reports of Cases Argued and Ruled on the Circuits of Ireland*, ii, pp. 330–1. Brian McClintock, 'The 1844 Marriage Act: Politico-religious agitation and its consequence for Ulster genealogy', *Familia: Ulster Genealogical Review*, 1, 2 (1986), 33–58.

[113] *Freeman's Journal*, 11 Aug. 1842. See also p. 303.

in the newly created General Registry Office and administered by the registrar rather than a clergyman. This Act did not apply in Ireland, although the creation of an Irish General Registry Office was, as noted already, later incorporated into the Marriage (Ireland) Act 1844. The public debate on the legislation in England in the 1830s increased support for transferring legal control of marriages from the ecclesiastical courts and church regulation into the civil domain. Consequently, there was a growing tolerance of the judge's view in the Marshall case that a religious service might not be necessary to validate a marriage in Ireland.

By the late 1830s, however, members of both the civil and ecclesiastical judiciary were beginning to express concern at the legal confusion that had arisen in relation to the status of marriages performed by Presbyterian ministers.[114] George Miller, the judge in the Armagh consistorial court, was one of the first to publish a critique of the historical assumptions incorporated in the judgment of *Dalrymple v Dalrymple* and its relevance for Ireland. Miller's analysis was part of a judgment in which he deemed a marriage performed by an unplaced Presbyterian minister invalid because neither of the parties whom he married were Presbyterian.[115] In 1840 a dispute over the succession to an estate came before the consistorial court in Armagh in *Lemon v Lemon*. Two women claimed to be the lawful widow of Thomas Lemon, a member of the established Church. Lemon had married twice. His first marriage was to a Roman Catholic and was witnessed by an unattached Presbyterian minister, while Jane McQuatty, who was possibly a Presbyterian, claimed that she had also married Lemon. Evidence provided in court that the marriage to Jane McQuatty had taken place was not conclusive. In his will Lemon had left a legacy to Jane as the mother of his sons, but he had not claimed her as a wife. Judge Miller ruled that the first marriage was null and void because neither party to it was Presbyterian. He also ruled that the second marriage was invalid because the documentation produced in court had not convinced him that it had taken place. Miller dismissed the argument that it had existed by repute or that the legacy that Lemon had left McQuatty and her two children was evidence that they were married.[116]

---

[114] See, for example, the comments of Justice Pennefeather in a trial for bigamy heard on January 1840. *Freeman's Journal*, 16 Jan. 1840.

[115] George Miller, *Judgment in the Consistorial Court of Armagh Involving the Question of the Law of Marriage in Ireland* (Armagh, 1840).

[116] Ibid.; Crawford and Dix, *Reports of Cases Argued and Ruled on the Circuits of Ireland*, i, pp. 516–22.

Miller's judgement on Lemon's first marriage, which was contrary to the trend of the civil courts to accept the validity of such marriages, argued that the presence of a 'clergyman episcopally ordained' was always assumed in Irish statute law on marriage.[117] Miller denounced the laxity in the law that had developed in the aftermath of the 1782 Act, as well as Scott's assumption that marriage in English and Irish common law was no more than a civil contract. Miller concluded by asserting bluntly that members of the established church who had been married by Presbyterian ministers were 'by law, in a state of concubinage, not of matrimony'.[118]

Not surprisingly, Miller's judgment provoked unease in northern assize courts where, in 1839 and 1840, a number of trials for bigamy were referred by the assize judges for the consideration of all twelve judges serving on the Queen's Bench. The main issue in dispute in each case was the validity of a first marriage performed by a Presbyterian minister in which one or both of the parties were members of the established church. The arguments of both the defence and the prosecution focused mainly on whether or not the verdict of Sir William Scott in the Dalrymple case applied to Irish marriage law. In all these cases, the counsel for the crown argued in favour of the notion that a civil contract of marriage was valid without a religious service.[119] In the trial of Samuel Smith, for example, the solicitor general suggested that it was possible to have a contract marriage that would be recognised in civil law even if the ecclesiastical court considered it invalid. The solicitor general also pointed out that Presbyterian ministers in Ulster regularly married members of the established church and dissenters and that 'a large portion of the population of Ulster' would be illegitimalised if such marriages were deemed invalid. Eight judges, however, decided that Smith's first marriage by a Presbyterian minister was invalid according to Irish law.[120] A year later, two more cases on the northern circuit raised the same issues and judgment in both cases was again referred to the judges on the Queen's Bench.[121]

---

[117] Ibid., p. 13.   [118] Ibid., p. 18.

[119] *Regina v Charleton* before the Monaghan Spring Assizes, 1839, in Robert Jebb, *Cases Chiefly Relating to the Criminal and Presentment Law, Reserved for Consideration, and Decided by the Twelve Judges of Ireland, from May 1822, to Nov. 1840* (Dublin, 1841), pp. 267–98; Crawford and Dix, *Reports of Cases Argued and Ruled on the Circuits of Ireland*, i, pp. 315–20.' See also *Rex v M'Laughlin* in ibid., p. 170.

[120] Ibid.

[121] Edward Dix, *Report on the Cases of Regina v. Millis et Regina v. Carroll in the Queen's Bench in Ireland in Easter and Trinity Terms, 1842* (Dublin, 1842).

By that time too, there was considerable public interest in the legal debate and the arguments on both sides were reported extensively in the Irish newspapers.[122] The case that aroused the most legal and public attention was the trial of George Millis, a soldier, for bigamy in 1842. In 1828 Millis, a member of the Church of Ireland, had married Esther Graham in the house of a Presbyterian minister in Tullyish, County Down. The couple had two children but in 1830 Millis had left his Irish family and gone to live in England. In 1836 he married for a second time in a Church of England service. The Irish judges in *Regina v Millis* were divided in their judgment on whether or not Millis was guilty of bigamy. The case was referred to the six law lords in the House of Lords. They too could not agree and, consequently, Millis was acquitted.[123] The case, however, underlined the ambiguous legal status of marriages conducted by Presbyterian ministers and led to rushed legislation through Westminster validating all such unions.[124]

Although the public controversy about the bigamy trials focussed on the legal doubt surrounding the validity of a marriage solemnised by a Presbyterian minister, much of the legal argument of the defence and the state concentrated on whether or not, under Irish statute law, the presence of an ecclesiastical minister was actually necessary to validate a marriage. Counsel for the prosecution meticulously examined Irish statute law on marriage and argued that in the absence of an Irish equivalent of the 1753 English Marriage Act, a private promise between two individuals to marry constituted a legal contract that should be recognised by the courts. The case of Elizabeth Leeson and William Fitzmaurice was cited in support of this argument. The defence, however, pointed to the central problem of Irish marriage law: the civil court might recognise a private contract as legally binding, but the ecclesiastical courts would not recognise it as a valid marriage and would, therefore, not accord it any of the legal benefits of a marriage. Consequently, the children of such a partnership would be deemed illegitimate by the ecclesiastical court and would, therefore, have no inheritance rights to the property of their parents. Nor would the ecclesiastical

---

[122] For an account of the public debate on the validity of Presbyterian marriages see McClintock, 'The 1844 Marriage Act: Politico-religious agitation and its consequence for Ulster genealogy', 33–58.

[123] For an analysis of the debate in the House of Lords see Rebecca Probert, 'R v Millis reconsidered: Binding contracts and bigamous marriages', *Legal Studies*, 28, 3 (Sept. 2008), 337–55.

[124] An Act for Confirmation of Certain Marriages in Ireland. 5 & 6 Vict. c.113. 1842; Faloon, *The Marriage Law of Ireland*, pp. 17–18.

court agree to separation or divorce proceedings for a private contract, which it did not recognise as a marriage.

In addition to the establishment of the office of the General Registrar, the 1844 Marriage (Ireland) Act provided for the appointment of local registrar officers. A couple intending to marry in a Church of Ireland, Presbyterian, Quaker or Jewish marriage service were obliged to give advance notice of their intended nuptials to the local registrar, who would issue a certificate of marriage that was to be presented to the officiating minister. The church or other place of worship where such marriages were solemnised also had to be registered with the registrar. As noted already, the Act also provided for civil marriages to be performed in the local registrar's office without any reference to a religious minister or church official.[125]

For the first time, therefore, the 1844 Marriage Act established the legal equality of all marriages conducted by Presbyterian ministers with those solemnised by Church of Ireland ministers. The new legislation also tightened up the administrative process for Protestant, Dissenter and Jewish marriages and insisted on the keeping of accurate and consistent records of marriages for the first time. The Act, however, explicitly excluded marriages performed by Roman Catholic priests:

> nothing in this Act contained shall affect any Marriages by any Roman Catholic Priest which may now be lawfully celebrated, nor extend to the Registration of any Roman Catholic Chapel, but such Marriages may continue to be celebrated in the same Manner and subject to the same Limitations and Restrictions as if this Act had not been passed.[126]

It was not until 1864 that marriages conducted by Catholic priests began to be registered in the General Registrar's Office.

Civil Law versus Catholic Canon Law

Apart from the requirement to register marriages with the civil authorities, therefore, the Catholic church was free to regulate marriage according to its own guidelines. While this independence from state control may have been viewed as a positive achievement by the Irish Catholic hierarchy in the nineteenth century, it also had the potential to lead to different interpretations by the church and the state as to what constituted a legally valid marriage. In the early decades of the nineteenth

---

[125] Marriage (Ireland) Act. 7 & 8 Vict. c.81. 1844. McClintock, 'The 1844 Marriage Act: Politico-religious agitation and its consequence for Ulster genealogy', 53–7.
[126] Marriage (Ireland) Act. 7 & 8 Vict. c.81. 1844.

century, a number of cases came before the Irish courts that pointed to the discrepancies between the civil law on marriage and Catholic canon law. It is likely that this issue was investigated with greater intensity because of the concurrent public debate on the validity of marriages conducted by Presbyterian ministers. The main issue of contention was the different regulations of church and state on consanguinity and the degrees within which a couple could marry.

In 1839, John Burke married a woman named Margaret Fitzgerald. Both were Roman Catholic and had obtained a dispensation to marry from the Catholic vicar general of the diocese because they claimed to be fourth cousins, i.e. within the prohibited degrees according to Catholic canon law. The couple were in fact second cousins, and one of the issues in dispute was that the vicar general was not competent to grant a dispensation for second degree consanguinity. Shortly after the marriage, Margaret went to live in America. Her husband remained in Ireland and married again in 1840 before a Catholic clergyman. A prosecution for bigamy ensued in 1843. In the trial the jury was unable to come to a verdict and the matter was sent to the Queen's Bench.[127] William Crotty, Bishop of Down and Connor, in a letter on the case published in a number of newspapers, noted that if the jury found Burke guilty of bigamy it would be a matter of grave consequence for the Catholic church. His argument was that, in the view of the church, the first marriage was invalid. Dr Crotty was speaking before the 1844 Marriage Act and was fearful of the implications of the pending Act for state interference in Catholic marriages. This Act, he wrote, 'will put our marriages on the Gretna Green establishment, by doing away with all those salutary restrictions by which the Catholic Church has endeavoured to restrain the too frequent intermarriage of persons related to each other, within certain degrees of kindred'.[128] The civil judges, however, all agreed that the first marriage was valid, arguing that the marriage of second cousins was permitted in Irish civil law even if it was prohibited under Catholic canon law.[129] The real issue was whether the law of the Catholic church or the law of the state would take precedence. As the barrister for the Crown commented, the civil courts should not invalidate a marriage 'in consequence of some hidden or unknown rule, and because a particular person did not give a particular dispensation'.[130]

---

[127] *Freeman's Journal*, 4, 6 April 1843.   [128] *Freeman's Journal*, 4 April 1843.

[129] *The Queen v John Burke* in *Irish Law Reports, Particularly of Points of Practice, Argued and Determined in the Courts of Queen's Bench, Common Pleas, and Exchequer of Pleas during the Years 1842 and 1843* (5 vols., Dublin, 1843), v, pp. 549–58. For further details of the case see *Freeman's Journal*, 3, 10 June 1843.

[130] *Freeman's Journal*, 14 June 1843.

Burke was found guilty of bigamy and sentenced to twelve months' imprisonment.

Clashes between the civil courts and the Catholic church continued into the early twentieth century. In a case reminiscent of the *Fitzmaurice v Fitzmaurice* case of the 1720s, William Arland Ussher questioned the validity of his marriage to Mary Caulfield in April 1910. The marriage had taken place very late at night in Ussher's house in County Galway. The service was performed by the local parish priest, Joseph Fahy. There was only one other person present at the marriage: Agnes Campbell, who was Ussher's cook. Caulfield was Catholic and had been a housemaid in the house. Ussher was brought up as a member of the Church of Ireland but he arranged to convert to Catholicism before the marriage took place. He was received secretly by Fahy into the Catholic church in an unused bedroom of his house shortly before the marriage, which took place in another bedroom. Ussher claimed that the secrecy was necessary because he was heir to a large estate, and if his sisters had discovered that he had converted to Catholicism, he might be disinherited.[131]

Following the marriage, the couple lived together and a daughter was born in January 1911. Ussher kept in contact with Fahy and urged the priest not to make public the documentation on the marriage. The union was not, however, a success and in December 1911, Ussher took a case in the Dublin courts to invalidate the marriage. His legal representatives argued that as there was no statutory requirement for the process involved in a Catholic marriage, they were obliged to follow the requirements of the Catholic church. The *Tametsi* and *Ne Temere* decrees had specified that at least two witnesses should be present at the marriage and, as there had only been one in this case, the marriage was not a valid Catholic marriage. Caulfield's defence did not dispute that the marriage did not conform to the process outlined in the papal decrees, but argued that it was, nonetheless, a valid marriage in Irish common law. Her barrister returned to the early nineteenth-century definition of a valid Irish marriage: a promise made by a man and a woman in the presence of an ordained clergyman. There was no statute law, he argued, that required the marriage to be witnessed. Ussher appealed the initial decision that the marriage was a valid one, but in 1912 the judges in the King's Bench rejected his appeal. J. Kenny's definition of a valid Catholic marriage in Irish common law closely echoed that of John Radcliff, the judge in the Dublin consistory court in 1832:

---

[131] Jameson, 'The religious upbringing of children in "mixed marriages": The evolution of Irish law', 65–8; *Ussher v Ussher, Irish Reports, King's Bench Division*, 1912, 2, pp. 445–528.

the only requirements to a valid and binding marriage between Roman Catholics capable of contracting are the consensus of the man and woman there and then to become husband and wife – openly expressed in the presence of a priest of holy orders.[132]

In effect, the Irish courts confirmed that the papal decrees of *Tametsi* and *Ne Temere* had no standing in Irish civil law.

Conclusion

Lawrence Stone described 'marriage law as it operated in practice' in England from the fourteenth to the nineteenth centuries as 'a mess'.[133] Stone wrote of a society in which people were joined together by customary unions or verbal contracts, participated in clandestine marriages that were difficult to prove or were married in a regular service but were later discovered to have married within the prohibited degrees of the established church.[134] Yet, by comparison with Ireland, the law on marriage in English society before and after the Marriage Act of 1753 looks fairly straightforward. In England, most people, including Roman Catholics and dissenters, married in an Anglican service and English statute law did not make special provisions for either group to conduct their own services. The vast majority of couples also appeared to have accepted the necessity for a church wedding even if, as in Ireland, the proclamation of banns was unpopular. As Rebecca Probert has noted:

Long before the Clandestine Marriages Act of 1753 made certain formalities essential to the creation of a valid marriage in England and Wales, the practice of celebrating a marriage in a church, or at least before an Anglican clergyman, had become virtually universal.[135]

Stone attributed the confusion concerning the marriage law in England to the absence of an agreed consensus as to what constituted a legally valid marriage. Yet, Probert's work would suggest that there was far more agreement in English society than there was in Ireland, where there were not only differing views between the state and individual churches but also within religious denominations. Until 1827, the Catholic church was divided into areas where the Council of Trent's definition of a valid marriage was implemented, and others where it was not. Within Presbyterianism, there were groups who placed more emphasis

---

[132] Ibid., 2, p. 456.
[133] Lawrence Stone, *Uncertain Unions: Marriage in England, 1660–1753* (Oxford, 1992), p. 31.
[134] Ibid., p. 16.
[135] Probert, *Marriage Law and Practice in the Long Eighteenth Century*, pp. 1–2.

on the scriptural definition of marriage, as essentially the private vows between a man and a woman, than the church leadership approved.

Outside of the churches' views, there was, also, a small substratum of people who did not participate in any religiously sanctioned marriage. Catholic diocesan records include reports by parish priests of cohabiting couples who ignored requests that they marry or separate.[136] Andrew Holmes has suggested that in the period 1770–1830, there was a 'sizeable group, possibly comprising at least one-fifth of the Presbyterian population who had no formal link with the church'.[137] This assertion also raises the intriguing possibility of the existence of a small group of Presbyterians who married privately and never solemnised their marriages in the presence of a minister. Some of those who appeared before Presbyterian sessions to confess sins of fornication prior to marriage or their participation in an 'irregular marriage', admitted that the offences had occurred many years before. It was only when membership of their local Presbyterian community became important for the baptism of their children, perhaps, that they felt the need to confess and participate in the Communion service.[138]

Prior to the second half of the nineteenth century, it is possible to document the laity frequently defying clerical censure in order to marry in a manner that conformed more to social than to religious requirements. Throughout the eighteenth century, all of the main churches struggled to implement their regulations in relation to marriage. Men and women planning to marry in Ireland in the period from 1660 through to 1844 could choose from a complex array of formal and informal services. Many chose to marry according to the guidelines of their respective churches, but for those who encountered financial or other impediments in doing so, there were other options. In 1714, Hugh McMahon, Bishop of Clogher, defended a relaxed attitude to implementing Catholic canon law on issues such as consanguinity and affinity, on the grounds that it would lead to defections from Catholicism to the Protestant church, because:

Excluded from the Sacraments and plied with censures, there is the danger they might pervert. This would mean the loss of the children who, otherwise, would be brought up as Catholics. Prelates here are frequently faced with difficulties of this kind: viz., if they insist on the law, they fear the parties will pervert; if they overlook the matter, they are shirking their duty.[139]

---

[136] See Chapter 8.
[137] Holmes, *The Shaping of Ulster Presbyterian Belief and Practice*, p. 306.
[138] See, for example, the case of Jain Stuart, who confessed to the Glascar session in 1808 that she had been married in an irregular marriage ten years before (Glascar Session Book, 27 Oct. 1808 (PHSIB)).
[139] Flanagan, 'The diocese of Clogher in 1714', 125.

Bishops in other dioceses expressed similar concerns and described how individuals who had been denied permission to marry by the Catholic authorities turned to the established church to legalise their union. In the 1830s, for example, Bishop William Crotty wrote angrily to a parish priest in his diocese of Down and Connor about a couple who were related within the degrees prohibited by Catholic canon law who were married in a Protestant church:

> Do these wretched individuals know that the Catholic church considers their union incestuous and invalid, that no Catholic can respect them as truly married in the sight of heaven, and that living as they do we are all obliged to class them as heathens and sinners of the worst and most infamous description?[140]

The authorities in the other churches also struggled to deal with the promiscuous attitude of the laity to their choice of marriage service. One of the most common offences condemned at Presbyterian kirk sessions was participation in an 'irregular marriage'. This included marriages by couple beggars but also those solemnised by more orthodox Church of Ireland ministers and Roman Catholic priests. The ambiguous legal status of Presbyterian marriages, particularly before 1782, undoubtedly encouraged many couples or their parents to insist that their marriage be solemnised in the established church before seeking forgiveness from their minister and elders in the session. In most kirk sessions there was also a small but regular trickle of offenders who had solemnised their marriage in the presence of a Catholic priest. In Aghadowey, for example, in the first decades of the eighteenth century, there was roughly one such marriage a year.[141] The reasons why a Presbyterian would choose to be married by a Catholic priest, even though it was illegal before the legislation of 1871, were undoubtedly varied. The rules of the Catholic church on mixed marriages, particularly in late eighteenth-century Ulster where the Tridentine decrees were partially in force, might have compelled some to have their marriage first solemnised by a Catholic priest before confessing their offence to their local session. This may have been a pragmatic solution to the problem presented by a mixed marriage, as both partners to the marriage were able to satisfy the rules of their respective churches.

In the Society of Friends, marrying someone from 'a different persuasion' resulted in expulsion or the removal of membership rights of the Society. Yet, despite this harsh punishment, 'marrying out' was not

---

[140] Draft letter of Michael Blake to Arthur McArdle, parish priest of Ahaderg, no date [c.1833] (PRONI, DIORC/3/1).

[141] Aghadowey Session Book, 1702-61 (PHSIB).

uncommon. Between 1755 and 1784, in the small Quaker community of Grange near Coleraine, on average two to three members a year were recorded as having married in a service solemnised by a Church of Ireland minister, a Catholic priest or, less commonly, a 'Presbyterian preacher'.[142] Most were, undoubtedly, young men and women, impatient at the confining rules of the community and their limited choice of marriage partners. The disownment record frequently notes that the transgressors were guilty not just of marrying outside the Quaker community but also of disobeying their parents.[143]

By the last decades of the eighteenth century, there are indications that all the church authorities were beginning to supervise the implementation of their respective regulations concerning marriage more stringently. In the Presbyterian church, for example, some sessions insisted that a couple who married in an irregular fashion should remarry.[144] In 1784, in Annahilt, the session declared that if any members of the congregation 'married irregularly' then they would not only be obliged to remarry but also to pay a fine of five shillings to be divided between the poor of the parish and the church.[145] In the late 1780s, members of the Carnmoney congregation suspected of participating in an 'irregular' marriage were summoned by the session to 'prove' their marriage with a witness.[146] The constitutions of the Presbyterian church, which were published by the General Synod of Ulster in 1825, also specified that all marriages had to be solemnised in the church in the presence of a minister.[147]

Almost all the laws relating to marriage passed by the Irish parliament were politically motivated, and concerned with the marriages of couples from mixed religious backgrounds and with the marriage of minors – particularly Protestant heiresses – without the permission of their parents. The fact that there was usually a property qualification before either category of legislation was applied, is also an indicator that the state's primary interest was in the protection of the landed estates held by

---

[142] Minutes of Coleraine Women's Meeting, May 1794–1798, Nov. 1800 (PRONI, MIC16/29).

[143] See, for example, the case of Mary Trean, 17 April 1795. Minutes of Coleraine Women's Meeting, May 1794–1798, Nov. 1800 (PRONI, MIC16/29).

[144] *Records of the General Synod of Ulster, from 1691 to 1820*, i, pp. 276–7; ii, pp. 359, 253.

[145] Barkley, 'A history of the ruling eldership in Irish Presbyterianism', i, p. 64.

[146] Leanne Calvert (ed.), 'Carnmoney Kirk Session Minute Chapter Book, January 1786–March 1804' (unpublished transcript of original in PHSIB).

[147] *The Constitution and Discipline of the Presbyterian Church; with a Directory for the Celebration of Ordinances, and the Performance of Ministerial Duties* (Belfast, 1841).

Protestant landlords rather than the regulation of marriage.[148] The latter was only the means to the former.

The majority of people of all denominations, however, married in some sort of ceremony in the presence of a clergyman although many, as the next chapter makes clear, sought out the services of a couple beggar rather than pay for the relatively high cost of a more orthodox ceremony.

---

[148] *The Statutes at Large Passed in the Parliaments Held in Ireland* (20 vols., Dublin, 1786–1801). For the legislation, 1692–1800, see Irish Legislation Database: www.qub.ac.uk/ild/?func=help&section=sources. Accessed 28 January 2019.

2   Couple Beggars

The reverend Joseph Wood died in July 1829. His obituary in the *Clonmel Herald* told the story of the 'strange vicissitudes' that he had experienced in his life. Born in the 1760s, he had graduated from Trinity College Dublin in 1795. He was ordained as a minister of the Church of Ireland in 1798 and served for some years as a curate in Ballinasloe, County Galway. According to his obituary, Wood left his ministry when he was cited as the defendant in a criminal conversation case.[1] Unable to pay the damages awarded against him, Wood was sentenced to imprisonment in Dublin. He escaped and fled to the Isle of Man, where he was re-arrested and returned to Newgate Prison. Here he began to make use of his clerical qualifications to marry 'such persons as were anxious to avail themselves of his services'. When his prison sentence was complete, Wood, unable to find another clerical appointment, began to work as a couple beggar in Dublin. He married Jane King in 1826 although, at the time of his death, another woman also claimed to be his wife. Jane King's father, Stuart was also a couple beggar. Wood was initially employed by Stuart King and took over the business of his father-in-law when he died. In the 1820s, Wood established a reputation as one of the best known couple beggars in Dublin. He usually performed the marriages in the King–Wood household in Smithfield, near the city centre.[2]

Wood lived for much of his life in a semi-legal world in which the state laws on marriage were interpreted in a flexible manner. He was an adulterer and a bigamist and, according to some accounts, frequently

---

[1] That is he was cited as an adulterer. For more information on criminal conversation cases see pp. 398–403.

[2] *Clonmel Herald,* 5 August 1829; *Evening Packet,* 31 March 1846; Herbert Wood, 'Report by Mr Herbert Wood on certain registers of irregular marriage', *The Thirty-Fourth Report of the Deputy Keeper of the Public Records and Keeper of the State Papers Ireland* (Dublin, 1902), p. 28. The registers were destroyed in the burning of the Public Record Office of Ireland in 1922.

drunk when solemnising marriages.[3] He also undoubtedly married couples that a more orthodox Church of Ireland minister would have refused to do. The most significant aspect of Wood's life, however, is not his messy private life and lack of interrogation of couples availing of his services, but the fact that he was ordained a minister by the archbishop of Tuam and bishop of Ardagh in 1799.[4] Wood's ordination qualified him to perform legally valid marriages. He was, as the judge in the consistorial court, John Radcliff, confirmed a 'priest in orders'.[5]

Who Were the Couple Beggars?

Wood was one of many unattached clergymen who performed marriages for payment in eighteenth and early nineteenth-century Ireland. The term 'couple beggar' was used to refer to a diverse range of men. It included Catholic priests, as well as Church of Ireland and Presbyterian ministers. Even before the 1782 legislation widening the legal recognition of marriages performed by Presbyterian ministers, local kirk-sessions acknowledged the problem of ministers conducting 'irregular' or 'clandestine' marriages. In 1776, William Randles was deposed as a Presbyterian minister for marrying couples irregularly in Newry. As the Presbytery of Moira and Lisburn recorded, Randles' business was extensive and 'universally known in ye country'. Despite his suspension as a minister, Randles continued to marry couples at least into the 1790s.[6] Another 'debarred' minister, John Caldwell, who married members of the Presbyterian congregation in Glascar in 1808 and 1809 subsequently moved to Dublin where he worked for some time with Joseph Wood.[7]

---

[3] C. R. Milward, *Reports of Cases Argued and Determined in the Court of Prerogative in Ireland, and in the Consistory Court of Dublin. During the Time of the Right Honourable John Radcliff LL. D* (Dublin, 1847), pp. 292–3.
[4] Wood, 'Report by Mr Herbert Wood on certain registers of irregular marriages', p. 28.
[5] See p. 27.
[6] Moira and Lisburn Presbytery Minute Book, 1670–1830 (PHSIB). See entries dated 11 Jan., 7 March, 18 April, 4 July, 4 Aug., 10 Oct. 1775; 9 Jan., 9 April, 1776; 11 Aug. 1778. See also entries in Glascar Session Book, 1760–1818 (PHSIB) dated 31 March, 26 May 1782; 26, 28 Oct. 1785; 15, 22 April 1787; 2 Dec. 1787; 31 May 1788; 18 June 1789; 28 March, [?] Sept. 1790; 2 Oct. 1791; 20 May 1792; 17 April 1793; 10 Oct. 1802; 27 May 1808.
[7] See entries dated 23 April, 10 Oct. 1809; 8 April, 15 April, 30 Sept., 9 Oct. 1810 in Glascar Session Book, 1760–1818 (PHSIB). For Caldwell's employment by Joseph Wood, see Wood, 'Report by Mr Herbert Wood on certain registers of irregular marriages', p. 27. See also references to John Abernethy, who was deposed by the Templeptrick Presbytery in 1801 for conducting marriages in a public house and in his own private house (Minutes of the Templepatrick Presbytery, 1795–1915 (PRONI, MIC1P/85/1)).

Most couple beggars, like Caldwell, Randles and Joseph Wood, had fallen out with their respective churches for a variety of offences, usually involving women or alcohol. Some couple beggars continued to hold official clerical positions but were not averse to marrying couples privately for cash payments. This group included Catholic priests such as Eugene Sheridan, a curate in Templemore, County Cavan, who was prosecuted for marrying a Catholic and Protestant in 1838.[8] Other priests, often members of regular orders and not attached to a parish, earned a living by conducting marriage services much to the annoyance of the resident parochial clergy. In 1739, for example, the Catholic warden of Galway conducted an enquiry into a marriage performed in a private house by Matthew Concannon, an unattached priest. The marriage was valid because Concannon was an ordained priest but instructions were issued to the clergy to warn 'ye flock yt they are not to entertain him'. The wardenship continued to struggle against the activities of unattached priests throughout the eighteenth century.[9]

Another minister who held an official position was the German Lutheran minister, Johann Georg Frederick Schulz. He had initially intended to undertake missionary work in Africa but his journey had been interrupted by a ship wreck off the Irish coast. Landing in Wexford, Schulz travelled to Dublin where he was offered and accepted the position of pastor of the Lutheran congregation in the city. Schulz was recognised by the Church of Ireland as a legitimate minister and received an annual stipend from the state for serving the small German community in Dublin as well as providing services in the German language for visiting seamen and others to the city. Schulz's official duties were conducted in the Lutheran Church in Poolbeg Street but his main source of income came from the marriages he conducted at his family home in Cullenswood on the edge of the city in Ranelagh.[10] Schulz was described in 1838 as a 'tall, thin, gaunt old man' with 'white whiskers all round his face'. According to one witness

---

[8] *Dublin Weekly Register*, 21 April 1838. See also below p. 87.

[9] Edward MacLysaght and H. F. Berry, 'Report on documents relating to the wardenship of Galway', *Analecta Hibernica*, 14 (Dec. 1944), 42, 87–88, 107–8. There were three couple beggars identified by Bishop William Coppinger in his list of ninety-three deceased Catholic clergy in the diocese of Cloyne and Ross, 1770–1799. See Eric A. Derr and Matt MacKenna (eds.), 'Episcopal visitations of the diocese of Cloyne and Ross, 1785–1828 [with index]', *Archivium Hibernicum*, 66 (2013), 326–28.

[10] John Warburton, James Whitelaw and Robert Walsh, *History of the City of Dublin, from the Earliest Accounts to the Present Time* (3 vols., Dublin, 1818), ii, p. 844.

Illustration 2.1 The stereotypical image of the couple beggar was of a dishevelled, drunken former minister. The minister in this image holds a prayer book in one hand and money in the other. There are glasses and an open bottle on the table beside him. The key in the groom's hand was used as a ring for the bride. It may also symbolise the sexual availability of the woman following the service.

at a later trial, Schulz 'read the ceremony the same as any other clergy-man would read it'. The service was in English and he spoke 'plain and distinct'.[11]

There was also a smaller number of men who operated as couple beggars who had never been ordained or were not members of a dissenting sect. The best known example is Samuel D'Assigny who was the son of Anglican vicar and author, Marius D'Assigny. Samuel graduated from Trinity College, Oxford in 1691 and published two pamphlets on religious issues. He was never, however, formally ordained. He appears to have fraudulently practised as a clergyman in the Church of England before he came to Dublin and worked as a couple beggar in the city. Given his education and family background, D'Assigny may have had the demeanour of a clergyman. He dressed as a minister when he performed marriage services, wearing a 'band and gown'. By the time of his death in 1737, D'Assigny was reported to have 'joined many thousand pairs in matrimony'.[12]

It is impossible to determine how many couple beggars operated in eighteenth- or nineteenth-century Ireland. The numbers, undoubtedly, increased in the 1780s and 1790s when the restrictions on Presbyterian ministers and Catholic priests were relaxed. Most couple beggars worked discreetly in town fairs or in rural areas and tried to avoid detection by church authorities.[13] They only appear in the historical record when they were prosecuted or if the validity of a marriage they witnessed was questioned. Richard Sandes, a Church of Ireland minister, for example, worked from what was described as a 'miserable hovel' on the road between Portlaoise and Mountrath in County Offaly. Sandes had been a curate in a church in Portlaoise but was degraded in 1828 for presiding over a clandestine marriage and for being drunk in the pulpit.[14] Undeterred by his degradation, Sandes continued to marry couples for which he was imprisoned in 1831 and again in 1841.[15] He was, according to one newspaper report:

---

[11] *Freeman's Journal*, 19 Dec. 1853. Another witness said that he was not sure if the service was in English.

[12] Herbert Wood, 'Report by Mr Herbert Wood on certain registers of irregular marriages', p. 23. See also *ODNB* for Marius D'Assigny (father of Samuel).

[13] Anaple Kissok told the Connor Presbyterian kirk-session in 1704 that she was married on the fair day in Shane's Castle 'at the back of a hedge with a priest' (John M. Barkley, 'The eldership in Irish Presbyterianism' (2 vols., unpublished MA thesis, Queen's University Belfast, 1952), i, p. 101). See also Jonah Barrington, *Personal Sketches of His Own Times* (3rd ed., 2 vols., London, 1869), ii, p. 326.

[14] *Nenagh Guardian*, 9 March 1842.   [15] Ibid.

at all times accessible to those happy pairs who sought him with a bottle of whisky in one hand and a half-crown in the other. He has united several hundred persons in unpermitted wedlock in his time, and was an object of terror to all parents within ten miles of his dwelling.[16]

Another couple beggar who has left a minimal record behind him is the Catholic priest, referred to in newspaper reports as Father Golding (or Goldging) who married couples in his home in Lisnaskea, County Fermanagh, which was known locally as 'a second Gretna Green ... where all "the runaways" in this and adjoining counties had recourse to have the hyemenal knot tied'.[17]

We know most about couple beggars who operated in Dublin and solemnised marriages for thousands of couples in the eighteenth and early nineteenth centuries. In addition to Joseph Wood and Johann Georg Schulz, one of the best documented couple beggars was Patrick Fay. Fay was born in County Meath and had been educated on the continent as a Catholic priest. He served for a number of years as a curate on a French man of war. Like other couple beggars, Fay moved easily between the Catholic church and the Church of Ireland. Following his return to Ireland, he converted to Protestantism in 1772 and shortly afterwards married Elizabeth Finlay, the widow of a Dublin shoemaker.[18] Fay's conversion may also have been related to his appointment as curate at the Royal Hospital Kilmainham in 1777. He was subsequently dismissed from this position for 'misconduct' and began work as a couple beggar.[19] Unlike others of his profession, Fay welcomed publicity. He issued printed certificates of marriages that he had solemnised according to the 'canonical rights of the Church of Ireland'. Fay did not seem to object when these were subsequently printed in newspaper notices by wives whose husbands had denied that they were married.[20]

Fay was clearly an enterprising business man. He received some property with his marriage and bought other houses in Dublin with his earnings from his marriage services. He also advertised his services in England. In 1782, he placed a notice in a Cumberland newspaper to deny rumours that he had been excommunicated. He reassured the readers that he:

---

[16] *The Drogheda Journal; or, Meath and Louth Advertiser*, 12 April 1831.

[17] *Northern Standard*, 2 June 1849.

[18] John Brady, *Catholics and Catholicism in the Eighteenth Century Press* (Maynooth, 1965), p. 150. See also *Rev. Mr. M.-'s Answer to Mr Fay's Reasons for Reforming From the Church of Rome* (Dublin, 1772).

[19] Brady, *Catholics and Catholicism*, pp. 262–3; *Northampton Mercury*, 13 Sept. 1788.

[20] See, for example, *Saunders's News-Letter*, 26 Sept., 11 Nov. 1784. See also *Saunders's News-Letter*, 18 Nov. 1780 and Chapter 11.

continues every office of his function, with the utmost secrecy, care, and dispatch, on terms much more reasonable than any other person in the same business ... Witnesses provided, if required; also, accommodations for consummation, with the necessary refreshments, etc. on paying a reasonable advance.[21]

Fay may have recognised the attraction of the flexibility of Irish marriage law for English couples and reports of his activities appeared regularly in English newspapers. Fay also, however, had plans to expand his business into an upmarket brothel. He informed his English readers that he had purchased land adjoining to his house in Essex Street in Dublin, which he intended to lay out in 'the most elegant taste with baths, recesses, etc. in the Turkish style' with a temple 'exactly on the same plan as the famous temple of Venus at Paphos, in the isle of Cyprus', which would be decorated with 'voluptuous paintings'; and a library stocked with books by 'amorous authors'.[22] Fay's ambitious plans were, however, squashed when he was finally degraded by the archbishop of Dublin. Fay publicly announced his resignation as a couple beggar in 1787.[23] Although prior to his degradation Fay could solemnise legally binding marriages, he, like Joseph Wood and other couple beggars, spent time in gaol, often for offences unrelated to his work as a couple beggar. In late 1787, Fay was found guilty of assaulting a woman and in 1788 he was indicted for forging the signature of the sheriff of County Meath. For the latter crime he was sentenced to death but this was later commuted to transportation to North America for life. In 1795, Fay reappeared again in a Dublin court, having returned to Ireland in defiance of his transportation sentence.[24]

Couple Beggars and the Law

Legal prosecution of couple beggars was mainly under the terms of the 1725 'Act to Prevent Marriages by Degraded Clergymen and Popish Priests ...'. The law made it a felony punishable by death for Catholic priests as well as 'degraded clergyman, or any layman, pretending to be a clergyman of the church of Ireland as by law established' to marry 'two protestants, or reputed protestants, or ... a protestant or reputed

---

[21] *Cumberland Pacquet and Ware's Whitehaven Advertiser*, 22 Jan. 1782.   [22] Ibid.
[23] *Saunders's News-Letter*, 26 Feb. 1787.
[24] *Saunders's News-Letter*, 30 Oct. 1787, 14 Feb., 5 June 1795; *Northampton Mercury*, 13 Sept. 1788; *Kentish Gazette*, 12 Sept. 1788, 3 July 1795; *Hereford Journal*, 11 Nov. 1789. See also Brady, *Catholics and Catholicism*, pp. 150, 232, 247, 260, 262–3, 266, 268, 294, 296.

protestant and a papist'.[25] We do not know how many degraded clergymen and Catholic priests were prosecuted for breaking this law. Newspaper reports in the 1730s occasionally refer to prosecutions and executions of clergymen. In the 1730s two priests were convicted at the Armagh and Trim assizes respectively for marrying Protestants. At the latter court, the priest was given a death sentence for the crime.[26] In 1740, Edward Sewell, a degraded Church of Ireland minister, was tried and executed for a similar offence. In his printed gallows speech, however, Sewell indicated that his mistake had been to marry, unknowingly, Richard Walker, the son of a prominent Dublin merchant: 'Had I surmised he had been the Son of the Man he was, or any other Person of Credit's Son, I would not for any Consideration have perform'd the Ceremoney'. Walker, Sewell claimed, had presented himself as a tradesman of 'no Fortune or Birth'. The implication of Sewell's last speech was that he would not have been prosecuted if he had married a poorer man.[27]

By the 1750s, the punishment for prosecution under the 1725 Act had been commuted to seven years' transportation. When, for example, Edward Ambrose Coghlan was found guilty in 1753 of marrying 'several soldiers and apprentices to Roman Catholics', he was transported to North America.[28] In 1829, when Belfast priest, James M. Vincent M'Carey was found guilty of marrying two Protestants (who had claimed to be Catholic), he was sentenced to a £500 fine and retained in prison until the fine was paid.[29] Prosecution of couple beggars under the terms of the 1725 Act was by that time increasingly rare.[30] At the sentencing of Richard Sandes under the act in 1841, the judge observed that although the law remained on the statute book, 'it was forgotten'. The judge was clearly not familiar with the commuting of earlier sentences to seven years' transportation or the fine allocated to M'Carey. He sentenced Sandes to what he described as the 'disproportionate' sentence of death specified in the legislation. He expressed his confidence, however, that it would be remitted. Sandes eventually served one year in prison. In the

---

[25] Act to Prevent Marriages by Degraded Clergymen and Popish Priests, and for Preventing Marriages Consummated from Being Avoided by Precontracts, and for the More Effectual Punishing of Bigamy. 12 Geo. I c.3. 1725.

[26] Brady, *Catholics and Catholicism*, pp. 52, 57.

[27] James Kelly, *Gallows Speeches from Eighteenth-Century Ireland* (Dublin, 2001), pp. 268–70.

[28] Brady, *Catholics and Catholicism*, pp. 81–2.

[29] *Clonmel Herald*, 4 April 1829. M'Carey was fined a second time for the same offence in the following year. See *The Drogheda Journal; or, Meath and Louth Advertiser*, 3 April 1830.

[30] Brady, *Catholics and Catholicism*, pp. 81–2.

course of the trial, it was pointed out that the 1725 law did not apply to Catholic priests marrying two Catholics. It may have been for this reason that Sandes converted to Catholicism in 1842 in an attempt to continue his couple beggar career as a Catholic priest. He was, however, subsequently expelled from the Catholic church for drunkenness.[31]

The 1725 legislation only provided for the prosecution of degraded ministers or Catholic priests who presided over mixed marriages. It could not, however, be used to prosecute the majority of Church of Ireland couple beggars who had not been degraded. The often complex legal process involved in degrading a minister deterred the authorities in the established church from initiating the process. It could take a long time and involve a series of civil and ecclesiastical court cases. In 1746, Jemmett Browne, the new bishop of Cork, Cloyne and Ross, attempted to enforce the Church of Ireland's canon law on the proclamation of banns and the requirement to marry in church. The bishop became embroiled in a long legal dispute with Marmaduke Dallas. The latter was an unattached minister who had married a couple in a private house without reading banns. Dallas vehemently disputed the bishop's claim that this constituted a 'clandestine' marriage. He argued that the manner in which he conducted the marriage service was the 'universal practice of all the clergymen in the kingdom'.[32] Dallas appealed his degradation in the civil and ecclesiastical courts and printed a number of pamphlets defending his actions.[33] He also asserted that he had the support of other clergymen who had attended the visitation in Cork at which he was denounced. One minister noted that when the archbishop of Dublin tried to enforce the same canon law in Dublin the clergy 'did not mind what he said'.[34] In the 1780s, when the archbishop of Dublin secured the degradation of Patrick Fay, it was also 'after a long process and very

---

[31] *Londonderry Standard*, 9 March 1842.

[32] Marmaduke Dallas, *A Short and True State of the Affair Betwixt the Rt. Revd. J–m–t, lord bishop of C-rk and R–ss and the Revd, M–rm–duke Dallas, A.M.* (Dublin, 1750), p. 6.

[33] *A Letter From a Clergyman in Dublin, to a Clergyman in Cork. In Answer to a Letter Published in Dublin, Dec. 8th, 1749. Vindicating the Conduct of the Bishop of Cork, in the Degradation of Mr. Dallas* (Dublin, 1749); *A Second Letter from the Reverend Marmaduke Dallas, A.M. To the Right Reverend Jemmet Lord Bishop of Cork and Ross: In Answer to His Lordship's Letter, Dated Nov. 20, 1740* (Dublin, 1750); *A Fourth Letter from the Reverend Marmaduke Dallas, A.M. to the Right Reverend Jemmet, Lord Bishop of Cork and Ross. To be Continued, 'Till the Bishop of Cork's Whole Letter Is Examined* (Dublin, 1750); *Philadelphicus's Second Letter in Answer to the Vindication of the Conduct of the B–p of C–k in a Letter Dated November 20, 1749* (Cork, 1749(?)).

[34] Jemmett Browne, *A Letter from a Clergyman [sic] of the Diocese of Cork, to His Friend in Dublin, Relating the Conduct of the Bishop of Cork, in the Degradation of Mr. Dallas* (Cork, 1749), p. 37. See also Marmaduke Dallas, *A Letter from the Reverend Marmaduke Dallas, A.M. to the Right Reverend Jemmet, Lord Bishop of Cork and Ross*, p. 8.

considerable expense'.[35] Similarly, efforts to degrade Joseph Wood only succeeded in 1824, a few years before his death and after he had been operating as a couple beggar for a considerable length of time.[36] As implementation of the 1725 law was infrequent in the later decades of the eighteenth century, degradation was not as serious a threat to a couple beggar as it had been in the 1730s and 1740s. Patrick Fay and Joseph Wood continued to work as couple beggars after they had been degraded. Fay, according to a newspaper report, no longer, however, issued written certificates that he had performed the marriage.[37]

Making a Living as a Couple Beggar

Couple beggars usually justified their occupation as a way of making a living when they were abandoned by church authorities. Before his degradation, Edward Sewell had been a Church of Ireland curate in Carlingford and in Dublin. He alleged that he had been seduced by a 'vile Woman' who claimed that he had married himself to her. Accused of bigamy, the church authorities succeeded in degrading Sewell. Unable to find employment as a teacher, he took up the 'Trade as it's so called of marrying' in order to support himself and his family.[38]

Working as a couple beggar could be a very lucrative business and yield far more than was necessary to maintain a family. When Samuel D'Assigny died in 1737, he was reported to have left a legacy of £1,000. Newspaper reports about Patrick Fay's activities noted the wealth that he had accumulated, with one commentator observing that the 'business he got in his line' was 'really astonishing'.[39] Patrick Fay himself boasted that he had made £600 a year through his marriage business. Other Dublin-based couple beggars may have had more modest incomes but still earned what would have been considered a relatively high income in late eighteenth- or early nineteenth-century Ireland. In 1900, the Public Record Office of Ireland acquired the registers of eleven couple beggars who operated in Dublin between 1799 and 1845. In his brief survey of the registers, the Deputy Keeper, Herbert Wood, calculated that their annual incomes ranged from £50 to £500.[40]

---

[35] *Finn's Leinster Journal*, 10 Sept. 1788.
[36] Wood, 'Report by Mr Herbert Wood on certain registers of irregular marriages', p. 28.
[37] *Finn's Leinster Journal*, 10 Sept. 1788.   [38] Kelly, *Gallows Speeches*, pp. 268–70.
[39] *Northampton Mercury*, 13 Sept. 1788.
[40] Wood, 'Report by Mr Herbert Wood on certain registers of irregular marriages', p. 24.

Joseph Wood's wealth can be discerned from the fact that two women claimed the right to his property as his widow. A couple of years earlier, in separation proceedings, one of the women had been granted an annual allowance of £26 from Wood's earnings.[41] The determination of maintenance costs in the consistory court was based on the husband's status and ability to pay. An annual payment of £26 to his wife suggests that Wood's overall income was not inconsiderable.

The extended King and Wood family operated a profitable business at what was referred to in court proceedings as the 'marriage house' in Haymarket near Smithfield in Dublin. The business was probably begun by Stuart King who graduated from Trinity College Dublin in 1787 and whose register of the marriages that he conducted in Haymarket began in 1799.[42] This would suggest that at some point between these dates, King was either dismissed by the Church of Ireland authorities or failed to secure a permanent clerical post and decided to pursue a career as a couple beggar. King, who died in about 1818, employed Joseph Wood and possibly other men as couple beggars. When Wood succeeded King in the business in Haymarket, he also employed other ministers. As noted already, John Caldwell, a Presbyterian minister from Ballybay, County Monaghan, for example, worked for Wood in 1821–1822.[43] Wood's brother-in-law, John King, served as clerk to Wood and issued certificates of the marriage solemnised by the couple beggar for fees ranging from one shilling and six pence to two shillings and six pence. If the couple came alone to the house, Wood's wife, Jane, or a servant acted as witnesses. Like many couple beggars, Wood kept a register of the marriages that he performed in which he or his clerk entered the name of the couple, their address, the witnesses to the marriage and the fee paid. Wood also claimed that he conducted the marriage service with great care. He was 'very exact and read further than is read in churches, as I am frequently called upon to witness the same, it makes me more particular'.[44]

Following Wood's death in 1829, his widow Jane took over the business and employed three or four couple beggars to conduct marriages in the 'marriage house'. John King continued also to work as a clerk and he and Jane Wood issued and signed marriage certificates.

---

[41] *Drogheda Journal, or Meath & Louth Advertiser*, 11 Jan. 1834; *Freeman's Journal*, 30 March 1846.
[42] Wood, 'Report by Mr Herbert Wood on certain registers of irregular marriages', p. 27.
[43] Ibid.
[44] Quoted in Milward, *Reports of Cases Argued and Determined in the Court of Prerogative in Ireland, and in the Consistory Court of Dublin*, p. 300; *Evening Packet*, 31 March 1846.

They also amended their register records on request and, presumably, on payment of a fee. Their registers included entries such as 'names changed by mutual consent' or 'names erased by mutual consent'. Although John King denied that his establishment arranged for the annulment of marriages, the deletion of the record of a union was most likely for this purpose.[45]

The registers of the couple beggars were the only official proof that the marriage had taken place. Consequently, they were a valuable piece of evidence in a bigamy trial. Among the services that Jane Wood provided was a search of the registers for a fee of 2s 6d. If an individual required a written certificate confirming that the marriage had occurred, there was an additional fee of 2s 6d.[46] Occasionally, the full register might also be lent to the court. The courts varied in their attitude to the registers of couple beggars, with some judges rejecting them as reliable evidence that a marriage had taken place. Others, however, acknowledged the clerical qualifications of men like Wood and Fay and determined that the marriages that they solemnised were valid. It was for this reason that the registers were purchased from private ownership in 1900.[47]

In the 1830s, Jane Wood left the house in Haymarket and lived for a while with a couple beggar called Stenson. When they quarrelled and separated, Wood employed another clergyman to conduct marriages in a house in Brunswick Street. In 1843, although described as an 'elderly woman', Jane Wood was still managing a couple beggar business.[48] Her brother, John King, seems to have inherited the Haymarket house which he subsequently rented to Isham Baggs, a former Church of Ireland curate assistant who performed marriages there. King worked for Baggs as a clerk for some time but also noted in a bigamy trial that he lived off the earnings of the house.[49] The continuation of the King and Wood enterprise, albeit in two separate establishments, into the 1840s, is evidence of the profitability of the business on the eve of the passing of the Marriage (Ireland) Act 1844.

---

[45] *Dublin Evening Mail*, 15 April 1846.
[46] Ibid. On the courts' perception of the marriages of couple beggars see also Wood, 'Report by Mr Herbert Wood on certain registers of irregular marriages', pp. 26–7.
[47] Ibid., pp. 22, 27. The registers had been collected by the Dublin Registrar Officers, John Haslar Samuels and his son, Arthur Samuels. For the attitude of judges to the registers see *Drogheda Journal, or Meath and Louth Advertiser*, 11 Jan. 1834; *Evening Packet*, 31 March 1846.
[48] *Freeman's Journal*, 30 Jan. 1843.   [49] Ibid. See also *Kerry Evening Post*, 6 Nov. 1833.

Schulz Register

The marriage registers kept by couple beggars and placed in the Public Record Office were destroyed in the bombing of the Four Courts in 1922. Fortunately, two volumes of a register maintained by Johann Georg Frederick Schulz were kept in the General Register Office and, thus, survived the fire. The volumes cover the years, 1806–1837 and list about 6,000 marriage entries. The registers are entitled 'Church Book for Marriages in the German Church'.[50] In some of the initial entries, Schulz noted that the marriage had been solemnised in the Lutheran church in Poolbeg Street where he was the pastor, but for most of the later entries he does not specify the location of the service. In court proceedings that queried the legality of some of the marriages Schulz conducted, the location of the ceremony was always given as Cullenswood in Ranelagh. In 1853, Schulz's daughter, Caroline confirmed that she only saw her father perform marriage services in the family home in Cullenswood.[51] In 1818, James Whitelaw noted in his history of Dublin that there were only twelve people in the German Lutheran congregation in the city.[52] It would seem, therefore, that Schulz, while officially the pastor of the small Lutheran congregation, built up a more lucrative business providing marriage services for couples who came to his house in Cullenswood.

Although most of the entries in the registers consist only of the names of the couple and the date of their marriage, Schulz occasionally included addresses and a reference to the man's occupation, particularly if he was a soldier. The registers provide, therefore, some statistical evidence of the work of one Dublin-based couple beggar in the early nineteenth century.

As noted above, Schulz conducted over 6,000 marriages in the fifteen year period from 1823 to 1837.[53] Figure 2.1 indicates that the figures rose steadily after 1829, which was the year of Joseph Wood's death. In 1835–1836, Schulz solemnised almost 900 marriages per year.

A newspaper report in 1788 suggested that Patrick Fay had frequently married five or six couples a day, which would suggest that he could have married up to 2,000 couples annually.[54] This figure may be an

---

[50] The original registers are in the General Registrar's Office, Roscommon, County Roscommon. See also Henry McDowell (ed.), *Irregular Marriages in Dublin Before 1837* (Dundalk, 2015).

[51] *Saunders's News-Letter*, 18 July 1853.

[52] Warburton, Whitelaw and Walsh, *History of the City of Dublin*, ii, p. 844; *Freeman's Journal*, 14 Feb. 1838; 19 Dec. 1853.

[53] The figures are compiled from the original registers in the General Registrar's Office, Roscommon.

[54] *Finn's Leinster Journal*, 10 Sept. 1788.

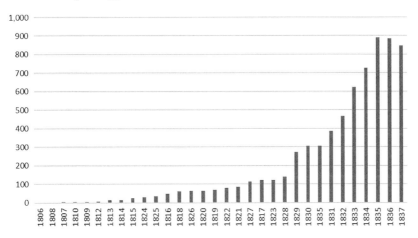

Figure 2.1 Number of marriages solemnised by Johann Georg Schulz,
1805–1837.
Source: Schulz Register, General Register Office, Ireland

exaggeration but it might also reflect the success of Fay's efforts in
publicising his trade. In 1843, John King, the son of Stuart King, told a
Dublin court that he had witnessed thousands of marriages in his family
home in Haymarket.[55] He estimated that there were usually at least three
marriages a day. This would suggest a total of over 1,000 marriages a
year, which compares favourably with the figures indicated by Schulz's
registers.[56] More modest figures were reported for less well-known
couple beggars. In 1840, for example, the Reverend James Maguire
was recorded as celebrating 500 marriages in two years.[57]

Table 2.1 lists the number of marriages registered in the city of Dublin,
in the ten-year period, 1830–1840 according to the 1841 Census. The
annual average is 1,968.45. It is not clear how this figure was calculated
but it clearly does not include marriages performed by couple beggars.[58]
According to the registers acquired by the Public Record Office of
Ireland, there were seven couple beggars working in Dublin during those
years. Three of these men were working for the Wood/King household

[55] *Freeman's Journal*, 30 Jan. 1843.
[56] Wood's obituary suggested a lower figure of 5,000 marriages over a sixteen-year period
which would indicate an annual average of just over 300. See *Clonmel Herald*, 5
Aug. 1829.
[57] *Dublin Monitor*, 30 April 1840.
[58] *Report of the Commissioners Appointed to Take the Census of Ireland for the Year 1841*
(Dublin, 1843), p. 100.

Table 2.1 *Total number of marriages in the city of Dublin according to the 1841 census*

Year	Total No. of Marriages
1830	1,949
1831	1,799
1832	1,840
1833	1,796
1834	2,022
1835	2,110
1836	2,022
1837	1,936
1838	1,985
1839	2,206
1840	1,988
Annual average	**1,968.45**

but others such as Schulz operated independently.[59] Even if one uses the lower annual estimate of 500 marriages per couple beggar, the total number of 3,500 is still far higher than the number of registered marriages. These figures are, therefore, strong evidence of the prevalence of marriages conducted by couple beggars in Ireland in the early decades of the nineteenth century and, probably, also in the second half of the eighteenth century.

In a relatively small number of marriages, Schulz recorded in his registers the place of origin of the couple. The places listed suggest that most came either from Dublin or the bordering counties of Kildare and Wicklow. Other couples travelled from Counties Carlow and Kilkenny. Schulz also married couples from outside of Ireland. These included men from Prussia and Hanover who were married by Schulz as part of his responsibilities as the Lutheran minister in Dublin, but there was also a small group of men and women noted as originating in Liverpool, Bristol and other parts of England. Some may have been sailors, stopping temporarily in Dublin port or soldiers stationed for a short time in the city, but it is also possible that some may have travelled to Dublin to be married. Given the absence of statute law on marriage, it was considerably easier to marry in Ireland than it was in England.

---

[59] Wood, 'Report by Mr Herbert Wood on certain registers of irregular marriages', pp. 27–8.

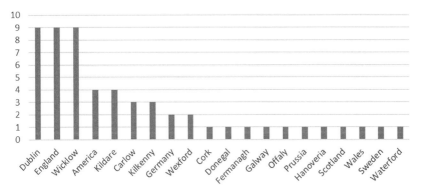

Figure 2.2 Addresses of couples married by Johann Georg Schulz.
Source: Schulz Register, General Register Office, Ireland

Why Use a Couple Beggar?

In 1788, when Archbishop John Troy asked the Catholic clergy in the archdiocese of Dublin for their views on clandestine marriages, many of the priests responded by explaining why members of their congregation preferred to be married by a couple beggar rather than a priest.[60] Most of the priests agreed that it was mainly the poorer sections of society who were married by couple beggars in Dublin and they nearly all identified the cost of a Catholic marriage as a strong motivating factor. Fees for Catholic marriages were a controversial topic in the middle decades of the eighteenth century and were clearly a source of considerable resentment. Father Callaghan of St Nicholas's parish expressed the view that there was a perception among the laity that the parish clergy would ask for fees that most couples could not afford. Callaghan, who advocated that the poor should be married for free, wrote that he had 'known some to be hurried to a couple beggar, by the harshness of a curate and his bargaining for dues'.[61] In Dublin in the 1780s, the lowest fee requested by a priest for a marriage service was estimated at half a guinea or 10s 6d. In other dioceses, a fee of a guinea or more is cited in eighteenth-century diocesan records.[62] In his response to Troy, Father Henry Nowlan noted the additional fees charged by the church for dispensations to marry within the prohibited degrees or without the

---

[60] For the wider context of this enquiry, see Chapter 1.
[61] Reply of Father Callaghan, 28 Oct. 1788 (DDA, Troy Papers, Green File 29/1/32).
[62] See, for example, 'Answers by Andrew Kenny, parish priest of Clare Galway, 1800' (Galway Diocesan Archives, Box 15).

proclamation of banns, which he claimed were 'particularly hard on the poor so that they are driven to those who will, with less expense, join them in marriage'.[63]

Couple beggars were more flexible in their charges and demanded what they thought the customer could afford. According to Herbert Wood's analysis of the registers of the Dublin couple beggars, the majority of fees recorded were under ten shillings and many were 'as low as 3s 3d'.[64] Wood also noted that in a small number of cases the words 'charity' or 'nothing' were recorded in the registers, entries that soften, perhaps, the image of the money-grabbing couple beggar.[65] In reports of trials in which couple beggars gave evidence, reference was made to fees of 5s and 7s.6d.[66]

The high fees demanded by Catholic priests for performing marriage services were among the grievances listed by the Rightboys, the agrarian secret society that was active in north and west Munster in the 1780s. In their printed demands, the Rightboys recommended that priests should accept a fee of five shillings for a marriage service and some supporters of the group believed that it should be half that amount.[67] In response, in June 1786, the Munster hierarchy issued a statement instructing that no more than five shillings should be exacted for issuing a licence to dispense with banns and that a priest's fee should be set at seven shillings and six pence.[68] This amounted to a total payment of twelve shillings and six pence, which was still a considerable sum of money, particularly for the labourers and cottiers whom the Rightboys claimed to represent. In an echo of Callaghan's description of priests in Dublin, the Munster bishops exhorted priests 'never to bargain mercenarily for their dues; nor *ever* to withhold … the sacraments, on pretence of their dues not being paid'.[69] The southern-based hierarchy also recommended that the fee for the marriage service should not be charged if the couple could not afford it. Despite the episcopal directive, two accounts of marriage in Cork in the first decade of the nineteenth century noted that although the nominal

---

[63] Response of Henry Nowlan, 21 July 1788 (DDA, Troy Papers, Green File 29/17).

[64] Wood, 'Report by Mr Herbert Wood on certain registers of irregular marriages', p. 28.

[65] Ibid., pp. 23–24. The charge for the certificate seems to have varied from one shilling and six pence to a guinea.

[66] *Dublin Morning Register*, 16 July 1829; *Freeman's Journal*, 19 Dec. 1853.

[67] James S. Donnelly, Jr., 'The Rightboy Movement, 1785–88', *Studia Hibernica*, 17/18 (1977/78), 165–73.

[68] Ibid., 172–3; Record of Synod, 1786 (Kerry Diocesan Archive); See also Brady, *Catholics and Catholicism*, pp. 235–9; 242–4; 244–7.

[69] James Butler, *A Justification of the Tenets of the Roman Catholic Religion and a Refutation of the Charges Brought against Its Clergy* (Dublin, 1787), appendix 1, pp. 3–7.

fee for the priest was 10s 6d, the sum normally paid was a guinea. This was in addition to the cost of the licence (from five shillings to a guinea) and a collection made among the guests who attended subsequent celebrations.[70] The sum collected could obviously vary depending on the circumstances of the couple and their respective families. In the diocese of Killaloe before the 1840s, sums as high as £10 18s 6d were collected.[71]

In the 1790s, Catholic bishops in the archdiocese of Armagh earned a considerable portion of their annual revenue through the granting of licences.[72] The relative importance of marriage fees in the overall income of the priest who conducted the service is difficult to estimate but local studies suggest that it could vary between regions and between parishes. Daniel Grace analysed the registers of three Catholic parishes in the diocese of Killaloe between 1820 and 1844 and estimated that marriage fees made up 41 per cent of clerical income in the parish of Dunkerrin, 38.5 per cent in Bourne and Corbally, and just 24 per cent in the parish of Rath and Kilnaboy, where the Christmas day collection at 41 per cent of income was more substantial.[73] In a similar analysis of marriage fees in six parishes in the same diocese between the 1830s and 1840s, Grace noted that the majority of couples paid between £1 and £3 in fees. On average only one in twenty of the couples paid no fee.[74]

Additional fees might also be paid by Catholic couples to the local Church of Ireland clergy. The practice of paying a fee to the local Church of Ireland minister for a licence to marry without banns had developed in the early seventeenth century. It enabled a Catholic couple to be married in a private house by a Catholic priest.[75] This custom survived in some areas into the eighteenth century but seems to have disappeared in others. In the wardenship of Galway, for example, the procedure was that the priest, having assured himself that there were no impediments to the couple marrying, secured leave or license to marry the couple from the Protestant warden of Galway or the Protestant Archbishop of Tuam. This licence normally cost 5s 5d from the warden and was technically for

---

[70] Horatio Townsend, *A Statistical Survey of the County of Cork* (Dublin, 1810), p. 84; Edward Wakefield, *An Account of Ireland, Statistical and Political* (2 vols., London, 1812), ii, p. 562. See also Daniel Grace, 'The income of Catholic priests in pre-Famine Ireland: Some evidence from the diocese of Killaloe', *Tipperary Historical Journal*, 30 (2017), 79.

[71] Ibid., p. 83.

[72] See 'Abstract of the returns of the several Roman Catholic Bishops of Ireland, relative to the state of their Church, January 1801' in Charles Vane (ed.), *Memoirs and Correspondence of Viscount Castlereagh, Second Marquess of Londonderry* (9 vols., London, 1848–1853), iv, pp. 97, 100, 102, 113, 114.

[73] Grace, 'The income of Catholic priests in pre-Famine Ireland', 77–9.   [74] Ibid., 84.

[75] Patrick Corish, *The Irish Catholic Experience. A Historical Survey* (Dublin, 1985), p. 106.

permission to conduct a marriage service in a place other than the Church of Ireland parish church or without the publication of the banns.[76] A higher fee of a guinea or twenty-seven shillings was paid to the archbishop in order to secure dispensations for marrying someone who was within the degrees of consanguinity or affinity prohibited by the Church of Ireland, although these were, as noted in Chapter 1, limited to the first and second degrees. The Catholic priests' fees would, presumably, have been in addition to these payments.

John O'Sullivan, Dean of Kenmare, acknowledged that when he first came to the area in 1839, marriage fees were the 'most fruitful source of dissension' between a priest and his parishioners. By the time O'Sullivan penned his 'Praxis Parochi' in 1850, the public protest at costly marriage fees had begun to dissipate, mainly because there were fewer weddings, as the average age of marrying couples rose and many people spent their marriage money on a ticket to America. O'Sullivan was critical of priests who had charged very high fees in the past: 'Was it not an ordinary thing to demand, 10, 15, aye 20 pounds for the marriage of a farmer's daughter, aye and abuse the people lustily into the bargain should there be any demur to it?'[77] O'Sullivan condemned the damage done to the Church by such financial demands. He was, however, in favour of the priest accepting the collection made at the meal that followed the marriage service in a private house as this money was 'offered freely' and did not provoke the same hostility as the request for fees. Priests, O'Sullivan believed, should therefore, display 'some semblance of gratitude' for the collection and not 'scamper away' as soon as it was received. O'Sullivan also regretted the move towards having a service in the chapel or the priest's house and to charge the equivalent of what might be offered at the 'public wedding' in the home.[78]

The high cost of a marriage performed by a Catholic priest accounts for many of the poor Catholic men and women who opted for the services of a couple beggar but it does not explain why Protestants, members of dissenting communities and Catholics who could afford a more orthodox service also did so. The fees charged for marriage services performed by Church of Ireland ministers did not give rise to the same level of hostility as those of the Catholic clergy, while Presbyterian ministers did not, according to the General Synod in 1804, take 'any

---

[76] See for example, 'Answers by Andrew Kenny, parish priest of Clare Galway, 1800' (Galway Diocesan Archives, Box 15). The payment may also have included a fee for reading the banns in the Church of Ireland.

[77] John O'Sullivan, 'Praxis Parochi', p. 706 (Kerry Diocesan Archives, Killarney).

[78] Ibid., pp. 707–14.

pecuniary Charge whatsoever' for solemnising marriages.[79] The term 'couple beggar' can, however, be misleading because there were reasons other than money why a couple might prefer not to marry according to the rite of their particular church.

In his identification of the reasons why clandestine marriages were so popular, the Augustinian provincial head, Father Francis Hickey, suggested that of every one hundred such marriages, 40 per cent were mixed marriages of Catholics marrying Protestants while 30 per cent were for other reasons such as a desire for secrecy; the absence of parental consent; parents, anxious 'to secure an advantageous match for their children'; or women seduced by men, including sailors or soldiers serving in the city for a short time who, according to Hickey, 'glory in their iniquity and seduce everywhere, as many as they can'. Alcohol was also in his view, and that of other clergymen, responsible for a 'considerable number' of the marriages. Hickey estimated that 10 per cent of the marriages performed by couple beggars were the result of a drunken spur of the moment decision.[80]

The legal difficulties facing couples of mixed religion who wanted to marry clearly led many to resort to a couple beggar to perform a marriage service for them. As indicated in Chapter 1, from 1793, under the Catholic relief legislation, Roman Catholic priests were permitted to preside over such marriages provided that the couple had been previously married by a Protestant minister.[81] Subsequent to the passing of this legislation, Catholic records note the remarrying of couples who had already been legally married by a Church of Ireland minister who, in some cases, was a couple beggar.[82] One priest pointed out to Troy that Catholics involved in a mixed marriage preferred to attend a couple beggar rather than be married in a Protestant church.[83]

Secrecy might also have been a strong motivating factor for approaching a couple beggar to preside over a marriage. As Edward Sewell found to his cost, young couples who did not have their parents' consent to marry could easily avail of the services of a couple beggar. When Albert

---

[79] *Records of the General Synod of Ulster: From 1691 to 1820. Published by the Authority of the General Assembly of the Presbyterian Church in Ireland, With the Sanction of the General Synod* (3 vols, Belfast, 1898), iii, p. 279.

[80] Reply of Francis Hickey OSA Provincial, Jan. 1789 (DDA, Troy Papers, Green File 29/1/40).

[81] See Chapter 1.

[82] See, for example, 'Catholic Marriage Register for Athy, County Kildare, 1753–1853'. Consulted by Dr John Bergin by permission of Monsignor John Wilson, parish priest of Athy.

[83] Reply of Francis Hickey OSA Provincial, Jan. 1789 (DDA, Troy Papers, Green File 29/1/40).

Maxwell decided in 1826 to marry Cornelia Bryan, a young woman he had met while a law student in London, he engaged the services of Joseph Wood. The pair met the couple beggar in Portobello, on the outskirts of Dublin city and then walked with him to a house in Mount Pleasant in Ranelagh, where Wood performed a marriage ceremony, according to the rite of the Book of Common Prayer. The house was empty at the time and there were no witnesses to the marriage. Following the service, the couple left the house separately and Cornelia continued to live in lodgings while Albert lived with his father and sister. They were not aware of Cornelia's existence and only heard about the marriage when Cornelia gave birth to a son the following year. Despite the secret nature of the marriage and Albert's subsequent attempts to query its validity, the Dublin courts confirmed that it was a legal marriage under Irish common law.[84]

Albert Maxwell's father said in court that his son had 'made a fool of himself'. It was not, however, only young men who preferred to marry in secret. Older men marrying women socially beneath them or considerably younger than them often also preferred a quiet service. In 1827, when former soldier Robert Poole proposed to marry Mary O'Brien, then employed as his children's maid, he approached a Catholic priest, Father Stafford, and asked him to conduct the service. Mary was a Catholic and one of Stafford's parishioners and seemed to be anxious for a Catholic service even though Poole was a member of the Church of Ireland. Stafford refused to marry the couple on the grounds that he could be prosecuted for presiding at a mixed marriage. He did, however, suggest that if the couple were first married by a Protestant minister that he could then remarry them in a Catholic service. Poole could have asked the local Church of Ireland minister to perform the service, but this would have entailed a more public ceremony than he desired. He clearly wished to keep his marriage to a domestic servant as discrete as possible. Following Stafford's refusal, Poole was advised by a neighbour to approach Joseph Wood, whom the neighbour and others assured him was a clergyman who could celebrate legally valid marriages. The couple accordingly went to Wood's house in Haymarket and were married by him. Wood issued the couple with a certificate, which they subsequently showed to friends to confirm that they had gone through a legal service.[85]

The fact that Wood performed his ceremonies in a manner that conformed to the Anglican service may also have been reassuring to a young woman like Mary O'Brien, who clearly wanted to celebrate her marriage

---

[84] Milward, *Reports of Cases Argued and Determined in the Court of Prerogative in Ireland, and in the Consistory Court of Dublin*, pp. 290–306.

[85] Ibid., pp. 329–30.

in a formal service. The only witness to the marriage (Poole's servant, James Hatch) recalled how Wood 'looked like a parson' with a 'band tied around his neck' and a piece of light-coloured pink silk around his shoulders. He was also described as reading from a book, although, like many who attended such weddings, Hatch was illiterate and could not say if it was the Book of Common Prayer.[86]

Mary kept the certificate that Wood had given to her and her new husband and produced it following Robert Poole's death, when his children by a previous marriage questioned Mary's right to administer her husband's estate. The judge upheld the validity of the marriage, mainly on the grounds that a number of witnesses, including his brother, said that Robert had acknowledged Mary as his wife and her children as his.[87]

The judge commented that Poole may have only gone through the motions of a marriage service 'to satisfy the scruples of the girl and not to make a public display by him' because he was marrying a servant.[88] When Christopher Smith, a fifty-year-old shopkeeper from Roscrea, also married a young maid servant, Joanna Leary, in April 1800, he cited his 'pride' as a reason for not having a public marriage ceremony. Instead, he opted for a clandestine marriage by a 'reformed priest' in the house of the woman's father, because he had four grown-up sons and was 'afraid of the opinion and censure of them and the world'. The witnesses to the marriage, which took place at night were under 'an injunction of silence'.[89]

About 5 per cent of the women married by Schulz were recorded as widows, perhaps older women who also preferred the discretion of a small private ceremony. In the initial years of keeping his register, Schulz frequently listed the names of witnesses to a marriage. Occasionally, too, he noted that among the witnesses were the parents of either the bride or groom. In other cases, where the witnesses had the same surname as one of the partners to the marriage, it might be assumed that the marriage had the approval of the wider family.

For some, the speed and ease with which a couple beggar could be hired as well as the simplicity, if not the crudity, of the service was essential. This was particularly the case with couples who had eloped or where a young woman had been abducted, willingly or by force. Matthew Harris, a Dublin-based couple beggar, described how in 1811 he was summoned by an anonymous letter to the Nassau Street home of jeweller, James Vignes. Harris spent 'no more than three minutes' in an

[86] Ibid., pp. 327–28.   [87] Ibid., pp. 325–45.   [88] Ibid., p. 330.
[89] Ibid., pp. 120–32. See also ibid., p. 216 for a similar case.

upstairs room in the house and during this time he 'performed the ceremony of marriage' for a couple whom he had never met before.[90] Despite the speed with which Harris completed the service, it was nonetheless deemed as valid because Harris had been ordained as a Catholic priest in Douay, France.[91]

Although Johann Georg Schulz did not usually record the occupation of the couples marrying, he does seem to have noted when the men were serving soldiers. In about 10 per cent of the marriages recorded by Schulz, he identified the husband as a soldier from a regiment stationed in Dublin. Serving soldiers should have secured the permission of their commanding officer to marry but it is unlikely that most of those who were married by Schulz had done so. Such marriages may have been perceived as a means of having sexual intercourse with a woman and were not taken seriously by the men, who did not expect to be garrisoned in Ireland for too long. Few women would have had the persistence of Jane M'Clanaghan, who married Ensign Sorell of the 31st Regiment in Newry in 1793. The couple were married by Mr Reynolds, an unattached Presbyterian minister, and the service took place in Reynolds' house with M'Clanaghan's sister and brother-in-law as witnesses. The marriage remained secret as Sorell did not have the army's permission to marry. Subsequently, Sorell was stationed in different parts of Ireland and then travelled to the West Indies with his regiment. Over the next six years, Sorell corresponded very intermittently with his wife. Hearing that his regiment had returned to England, M'Clanaghan and her sister travelled to London to meet him. Although M'Clanaghan produced a marriage certificate that had been authenticated by a local Presbyterian minister in Newry, Sorell denied that she was his wife and convinced his commanding officer that her marriage certificate was a forgery. The efforts of her friends to appeal to Lord Mulgrave, the colonel of the regiment, failed to persuade the army to recognise the marriage and M'Clanaghan returned to Ireland without her husband.[92]

Other marriages were, as Hickey noted, the result of a sudden decision determined in the course of an evening's socialising and consumption of

---

[90] *A Report of the Trial of Robert Robinson, for Bigamy: Tried in the Sessions House, Green-Street at the Commission of Oyer and Terminer* (Dublin, 1812), pp. 17–19.

[91] Ibid., pp. 23–4. For Harris, see also, *A Full and Correct Report of a Trial for Seduction, Wherein Nicholas Kavanagh, of Kilcullen in the County of Kildare, was Plaintiff and Edward Kelly, of New Abbey in Said County, Defendant …* (Dublin, 1827), pp. 7, 21; Wood, 'Report by Mr Herbert Wood on certain registers of irregular marriages', p. 27.

[92] *Memoirs of the Life of the Late Mrs Catharine Capp Written by Herself* (Boston, 1824), pp. 234–57.

alcohol. A female witness to the marriage of John Arnold and Mary Anne Howe in Dublin in 1836 said that she had been very surprised when she heard that the couple were to be married. She went with a group of people to the home of Johann Georg Schulz in Cullenswood and said that she was 'perfectly sober ... all the women were sober; the men were not quite drunk, at least when they made up the matter [i.e. when they decided on the marriage]; if the prisoner [i.e. Arnold] was drunk at the marriage it was on the road he got drunk.'[93] Arnold claimed that he was 'stone, dead, blind drunk ... and totally unconscious of what he had done'. The next day when he realised what had happened, he asked for a divorce to which Howe allegedly agreed, provided that he not marry again. The couple went back to Schulz, who pronounced a divorce by tearing up the marriage certificate.[94]

It was not, however, in Schulz's power to grant a divorce, and in court he denied that he had done so. When Arnold subsequently married another woman in a Catholic service, Howe accused him of bigamy.[95] Another couple, Patrick Byrne and Mary King, married by Schulz, also decided between themselves that their marriage was not a valid one and that there were 'no marital obligations'. 'They came to a mutual understanding that they should each be free to marry again as they did not well agree.' They also, however, ended up in court with Byrne accused of bigamy.[96]

Apart from the risk of later accusations of bigamy, such forgotten marriages might also be resurrected in cases involving disputed inheritance or property transfers. Charles William Wall was married by Schulz in 1839. He left his wife shortly after the marriage and married again. Although they were separated for thirty years, Mrs Wall was obliged in 1869 to ask for legal permission to sign a deed without her husband being present.[97]

The popularity of marriages by couple beggars may also have been due to the fact that, from an ecclesiastical point of view, there were usually no long-term consequences for the couples involved. Officially, in the Catholic church, from the middle decades of the eighteenth century, the penalty for marrying in this fashion was excommunication. This did not, however, mean a lifetime exclusion from Catholic services. In Munster, the clergy appear to have regularly ratified clandestine marriages and

---

[93] *Freeman's Journal*, 14 Feb. 1838.   [94] Ibid.   [95] Ibid.

[96] *Freeman's Journal*, 12 Aug. 1842; *Cork Examiner*, 15 Aug. 1842.

[97] *Dublin Evening Mail*, 23 Dec. 1869. See also bigamy case cited in *Kentish Independent*, 26 July 1862.

forgiven the offenders.[98] Similarly, in Dublin, priests were criticised for lifting 'easily and privately' the excommunication penalty on payment of the marriage fee to the appropriate parochial cleric.[99] In the Church of Ireland, it was possible for those married by couple beggars to confess their offence and be forgiven. Similarly, eighteenth-century session books of Presbyterian congregations regularly recorded the appearance of individuals who acknowledged their offence in marrying irregularly and were rebuked and forgiven by the minister and the elders. As noted in the last chapter, however, couples who married irregularly i.e. by a degraded or suspended Presbyterian minister were obliged to remarry.[100]

Finally, it might be noted that it was also possible for Irish people to marry in Scotland. The surviving register for the parish church in Portpatrick, 1720–1846, includes 235 entries for couples with Irish addresses. The reasons why men and women chose to marry in a Scottish Presbyterian church varied but were probably similar to those who had their marriages solemnised by a couple beggar. The absence of parental consent, different religious backgrounds and a belief that the presiding minister would not ask too many probing questions are likely to have predominated, although the emphasis in Scottish Presbyterianism on marriage as a private contract may also have appealed to couples from a dissenting background.[101]

The End of the Couple Beggar

The Marriage (Ireland) Act of 1844 and its amendment put Church of Ireland and Presbyterian couple beggars out of business because it specified that marriages presided over by a Church of Ireland or Presbyterian minister must take place in a church or meeting house registered with the newly appointed Registrar. The law, as noted already, did not apply to Roman Catholic priests but they continued to be prohibited from solemnising mixed marriages. In the years after the 1844 legislation was

---

[98] For example, see the 1785 visitation of Bishop Matthew McKenna in which he regularly listed clandestine marriages that had yet to be validated by the parish priest. Eric A. Derr and Matt MacKenna (eds.), 'Episcopal visitations of the diocese of Cloyne and Ross, 1785–1828 [with index]', *Archivium Hibernicum*, 66 (2013), 285, 286, 289, 300, 302.

[99] DDA, Troy Papers, Green File 29/1/40.

[100] *The Constitution and Discipline of the Presbyterian Church with a Directory for the Celebration of Ordinances* (Belfast, 1825), pp. 42–3.

[101] Most of the marriages date from 1770. Northern addresses predominate but there are also entries for men and women from other parts of the island. See Arthur Brack, *Irregular Marriages at Portpatrick, Wigtownshire 1759–1826* (Dumfries, 1997). See also PRONI, T1005 for a transcript of the Irish entries.

passed, a small number of Catholic priests were prosecuted for marrying couples of mixed religious background. In 1848, Thomas Butler, a soldier, wanted to marry Anne Murray, before his regiment left the country. The couple went to Father Eugene Sheridan, a curate in Templemore, County Cavan 'who married them in a private house, and to whom he [Thomas Butler] gave money to perform the ceremony'. Sheridan, it was noted, 'spoke in an unknown tongue' and a key was used in place of a ring. Sheridan's profile recalled the earlier perception of Catholic couple beggars. He was a degraded Catholic priest who had already been tried for drunken disputes with his neighbours.[102] Although degraded by the Catholic church, it is worth noting that Sheridan and other priests convicted of presiding over mixed marriages were tried under the terms of the 1844 Act and not the 1725 Act nullifying marriages performed by degraded clergymen.[103] The newly appointed local registrar officers were called to court to confirm that the marriages had been solemnised in locations that were not registered by the General Register Office.

The reform programme outlined in the Catholic Synod of Thurles in 1850 included harsher disciplining of priests who ignored church regulations, particularly in relation to the financial demands that they imposed on their parishioners. The decrees of the Synod led to the final end of the Catholic couple beggar. Initially, the Synod focussed, as other Synods had done, on limiting the sums of money that the clergy could collect for a marriage service. At Paul Cullen's insistence, however, the final decrees of the Synod also included, as noted in Chapter 1, a prohibition on marriage services celebrated in private houses and not in a Catholic church. This was designed to bring practice in Ireland into conformity with that elsewhere in the Catholic world and, in particular, in Italy.[104] The decrees of the Synod of Thurles also brought Catholic practice into line with the civil law as outlined in the 1844 Marriage Act. It, thus, sounded the death knell for the couple beggar, although it did not, as indicated in Chapter 1, totally eradicate the practice of marriages celebrated in a private house, as the civil law continued to recognise such marriages.

---

[102] *Dublin Weekly Register*, 21 April 1838; *Belfast Newsletter*, 25 July 1848. See also p. 64 and NAI, CRF 1848 S33 for Sheridan's petition for an early release from prison.

[103] Act to Prevent Marriages by Degraded Clergymen and Popish Priests, and for Preventing Marriages Consummated from Being Avoided by Precontracts, and for the More Effectual Punishing of Bigamy. 12 Geo. I c.3. 1725.

[104] P. C. Barry, 'The legislation of the Synod of Thurles, 1850', *Irish Theological Quarterly*, (1 June 1969), 143.

Conclusion

The popularity of couple beggars in Ireland before 1850 was a natural corollary to the absence of statute law defining how, where and by whom a marriage should be celebrated. Many couple beggars developed a flourishing business, particularly in the late eighteenth and early nineteenth century when there was considerable ambiguity around what constituted a legally valid marriage. As the civil law falteringly moved towards a recognition of all marriages conducted by Catholic, Protestant and Dissenting ministers, the couple beggar took advantage of the legal uncertainty to preside over services that were accepted by local communities as valid, even if they did not quite conform to the laws of either the state or the respective churches.

Couples chose to marry with a couple beggar for a myriad of reasons. The speed at which a marriage could be arranged and the unwillingness of most couple beggars to ask probing questions about parental consent or the precise marital status of either partner made them an attractive option. More devout Catholics participating in a mixed marriage may also have preferred to have their civil marriage solemnised by a couple beggar than go through a more formal service in a Protestant church. Undoubtedly, however, a primary motive for opting for a couple beggar to celebrate a marriage was the expense of a Catholic marriage. Stories abounded in ecclesiastical correspondence of clergymen who refused to marry impoverished couples until a fee had been paid. Before 1850, most priests also expected to perform a marriage service in a private house, which would be followed by a celebratory meal at which a collection would be made for the clergyman.

A marriage by a couple beggar may not have appealed to the middling ranks of Irish society but it was clearly an option for those at the lower end of the social hierarchy. The priests in the diocese of Dublin in 1788 acknowledged that it was mainly the poor who used the services of the couple beggar. This also suggests, as Chapter 1 indicates, a disregard for adhering to church regulations on marriage among some sections of Irish society before 1850. In post-Famine Ireland, the civil law and the regulations of all the churches aligned to eradicate the phenomenon of the couple beggar.

Part II

Ways to Marriage

3 Meeting and Matching with a Partner

I doe understande that your constanty hath been great ... Especialy showne in Refusinge Such matches as hath ofured, the meenest of which, I Doubt not, might and could produse, better reasons both from their parts and Estats; that they wear the persons whoe best Deserved to Injoy you; beinge ablest to maintaine youe...[1]

Thus, John Black wooed his future wife, Jean Eccles, in 1674. Eccles, the daughter of a Belfast merchant, clearly had other offers of marriage. Black had completed an apprenticeship in Belfast and was in the process of developing his own ship owning and trading business. He did not as yet have the wealth or the connections that some of his rival suitors could offer.[2] Yet, Eccles defied the expectations of her family and friends and assured Black of her love for him, resolving, according to Black, that she would 'raither Shune Ritches then Contentment'.[3]

The story of the Black–Eccles courtship, glimpsed tantalisingly in the letters that they both valued enough to preserve, raises questions about how and why marriage partners were chosen. The previous chapters outlined the legal options available to couples wishing to marry. The next two chapters focus on the choice of partner and the process involved in courtship. They ask: at what age did people marry, and where did they look for a partner? What role did family and friends have in the selection of a spouse, and how was the courting couple expected to behave? How important were financial considerations and how were dowries agreed? As with most issues relating to marriage, the answers to these questions are filtered by class, by locality and by changes in customs and practices over time.

---

[1] John Black to Jean Eccles, 21 Aug. 1674 (PRONI, Black Papers, D4457/4).
[2] Black became a freeman of city of Belfast in 1675. Jean Agnew, *Belfast Merchant Families in the Seventeenth Century* (Dublin, 1996), pp. 211–2, 224–5.
[3] John Black to Jean Eccles, 17 Sept. 1674; 21 Aug. 1674 (PRONI, Black Papers, D4457/4, 6).

Age at Marriage

The age at which people married in pre-Famine Ireland has provoked considerable debate among historians struggling to explain the exceptional rise in the size of the Irish population in the decades prior to the Great Famine (1845–1850). In the 1950s, Kenneth Connell argued that an important factor in the rise of the population was the early age at which young women married. Connell's work was subsequently criticised by scholars for its failure to identify class and regional variations.[4] Michael Drake, who was the first to query Connell's conclusions, also pointed to his reliance on the qualitative evidence provided by the report 'Inquiring into the Condition of the Poorer Classes in Ireland', which was commissioned by the House of Commons in 1833, rather than making use of contemporary statistical evidence.[5] It is, however, the scarcity of numerical data that makes analysis of the pre-Famine age at marriage so problematic.[6] As noted already, parish records were maintained and preserved erratically until the second half of the nineteenth century while the original returns for national censuses were nearly all destroyed in the fire in the Public Record Office in 1922. A small number of scholars have, in recent decades, tried to piece together what has survived. Their studies emphasise the regional and class variation in the ages at which people married.

In his study of late seventeenth-century County Wicklow, Brian Gurrin linked Protestant baptism and marriages records for 441 couples who married between 1681 and 1700. His analysis indicated that early marriage was common for women at that time in Wicklow: the median age at marriage was twenty and 38 per cent had married before they reached the age of twenty-one. Brides above the age of thirty were rare.[7] The marriage of girls who were between sixteen and nineteen was not uncommon. Gurrin noted, however, that the age of marriage for women increased in the course of the eighteenth century. It rose from an average

[4] K. H. Connell, *The Population of Ireland, 1750–1845* (Oxford, 1950); 'Peasant marriage in Ireland: Its structure and development since the Famine', *Economic History Review*, new series, 14, 3 (1962), 502–23.

[5] *Reports of the Commissioners for Inquiring into the Condition of the Poorer Classes in Ireland*: First Report, HC 1835 (369), xxxii, pts 1 & 2; Second Report, HC 1837 (68), xxxi; Third Report, HC 1836 (43), xxx (hereafter Poor Inquiry).

[6] Michael Drake, 'Marriage and population growth in Ireland, 1750–1845', *Economic History Review*, 16, 2 (1963), 201–313. See also Joseph Lee, 'Marriage and population in pre-Famine Ireland', *Economic History Review*, 21, 2 (1968), 283–95.

[7] Brian Francis Gurrin, 'Land and people in Wicklow, 1660–1840' (2 vols., unpublished PhD thesis, NUI Maynooth, 2006), ii, pp. 5–7.

of 21.8 years of age in the early part of the century (1720–1740) to 23.25 at the end (1781 and 1800).[8]

Analysing a Church of Ireland parish register for Blaris, Lisburn, County Down, dating to the late seventeenth and early eighteenth centuries, Valerie Morgan also noted a relatively low marriage age for women (in the late teens and early twenties). In Coleraine parish in the 1820s, the average age at marriage for men was 21.7 and for women, 21. This had risen by 1840 to 24–26 for men and 22–25 for women.[9] Emphasising the regional variation in age of marriage, William Macafee concluded that in another Ulster parish, there was no 'significant' change in the age of marriage for men over the seventy-five year period from 1770–1845. The mean stayed at 25–26. There was, however, an increase in the age of women as the mean rose from 21.8 in 1771 to 23.6 by 1845.[10] In more general terms, Liam Kennedy, Kerby Miller and Brian Gurrin concluded that in Ulster by 1841 'the age at marriage for women had risen to 26 years in most counties' and in Monaghan it was as high as 27. Among men, the highest age was also in Monaghan at 29.8 years, while the youngest age was in Belfast (26.6).[11]

Leslie Clarkson's study of the town of Carrick-on-Suir, County Tipperary, also identified relatively high marital ages for women in the late eighteenth century. Carrick was a prosperous wool town, and had a population of 88 males for every 100 females. In the 'fertility age range' (15–44) there were 77 males per 100 females. Clarkson notes that this left many women with partners who were in excess of 15 years their senior. The average age of marriage in the town was 25.9 years for women and 27.8 for men. Of those women who married, less than 3 per cent were aged between 15 and 19.[12] In contrast, Cormac Ó Grada's analysis of the registers of the Rotunda Lying-In Hospital in the inner city of Dublin revealed that the average age of

---

[8] Ibid., p. 9.
[9] Valerie Morgan, 'A case study of population change over two centuries: Blaris, Lisburn 1661–1848', *Irish Economic and Social History Journal*, 3 (1976), 5–16.
[10] William Macafee, 'The demographic history of Ulster, 1750–1841' in H. Tyler Blethen and Curtis W. Wood, Jr. (eds.), *Ulster and North America: Transatlantic Perspectives on the Scotch-Irish* (Chapel Hill, 1991), p. 51–4.
[11] Liam Kennedy, Kerby A. Miller and Brian Gurrin, 'People and population change, 1600–1914' in Liam Kennedy and Philip Ollerenshaw (eds.), *Ulster since 1600: Politics, Economy, and Society* (Oxford, 2013), pp. 65–6.
[12] L. A. Clarkson, 'Love, labour and life: Women in Carrick-on-Suir in the late eighteenth century', *Irish Economic and Social History*, 20 (1993), 18–34; 'The demography of Carrick-on-Suir, 1799', *Proceedings of the Royal Irish Academy*, Section C, 87 (1987), 13–36.

marriage for working-class women was about 21 in the 1810s, rising to 23 in the 1840s.[13]

A key criticism of Connell's work was that it did not recognise the importance of the social hierarchy in rural Ireland. Instead, he referred in general terms to the 'peasant' and overlooked the distinction between labourers and those with land tenure, as well as the subtle social divisions within the latter group. Kevin O'Neill's analysis of marriage in Killeshandra, County Cavan, as recorded in the national census of 1841, found a clear distinction in age at marriage within the different social levels. Farmers with large tenancies married late, at a mean age of 28.4, while labouring men without land married younger at 24.5 years. This was not, however, as O'Neill points out, 'considerably younger' than farmers with small- or medium-sized tenancies, with a mean age at marriage of 27.7 and 25.6 respectively. Women in all social classes married younger than men. O'Neill also documented a sharp decline of 5.1 years in the mean age at marriage for labouring women, from the late-eighteenth century through to the 1820s (Table 3.1).[14]

It is difficult to draw coherent conclusions from the different figures that emerge from these regional studies. There is, however, agreement on a number of key issues. First, it is clear that distinctions in social class should be considered when examining ages at marriage. Within medium- and large-tenant farming families, marriage was always later than in families further down the economic hierarchy. The reasons for this are partly related to the desire to maintain the unity of the family property and, perhaps too, a more general sense of social conservatism among

Table 3.1 *Age at first marriage in Killeshandra according to the 1841 census*

Size of farm	Men	Women
Small (1–12 acres)	27.7	23.8
Middling (13–25 acres)	25.6	21.55
Large (101 acres)	28.42	23.7
Labourers without land tenure	24.5	22.26

Source: Kevin O'Neill, *Family and Farm in Pre-famine Ireland: The Parish of Killashandra* (Madison, 1984), p. 178

[13] Cormac Ó Grada, *Ireland: A New Economic History 1780–1939* (Oxford, 1994), p. 7.
[14] Kevin O'Neill, *Family and Farm in Pre-famine Ireland: The Parish of Killashandra* (Madison, 1984), pp. 177–85.

middle-income farmers concerned to choose a partner who would bring an economic advantage to the family.

The studies on age at marriage that have been completed since Connell wrote his analysis confirm that age at marriage varied in different localities and was probably linked to the local economy and the availability of work. Historians also concur that the average age at which people first married rose in the 1820s and 1830s across all social classes. This rise coincided with a serious downturn in the Irish economy and an increase in the number of labourers without land tenure. In the census of 1841, 55 per cent of the Irish rural population was classified in this category.[15] As work opportunities declined, labouring men may have begun to delay marriage until they could provide for their families, while women had a wider choice of marriage partners and could afford, therefore, to wait for the most financially attractive suitor.[16] Kennedy *et al.* also linked the higher rates of marriage in Monaghan to a declining economy.[17] Labouring men continued, however, to marry at a lower age than other social groups. The regional variations in age at marriage of the 'labouring class' reported in the first report of the Commission for Inquiring into the Condition of the Poorer Classes in Ireland may (Table 3.2), therefore, merit more attention than the critiques of K. H. Connell's work acknowledged. Niall Ó Ciosáin has described the Reports of the Poor Inquiry as an 'unusual even unique' source for nineteenth-century Ireland. The printed reports included what appear to be 'verbatim transcripts' of conversations with men and women from all social classes, including the labouring poor. There is no other source for nineteenth-century Ireland that provides such direct testimony.[18]

The Report of the Poor Inquiry and other contemporary writing in the 1830s testify to the concern of the political and ecclesiastical establishment with the problems associated with early marriage and its perception as one of the causes of the chronic poverty of Ireland. This is particularly evident in the Ordnance Survey memoirs for parishes in the north of Ireland, in which the memoir writers praised the prudence of the Presbyterian community in delaying marriage until they had the means to maintain a separate household, while implicitly criticising

---

[15] Lee, 'Marriage and population in pre-Famine Ireland', 285; L. M. Cullen, 'Irish history without the potato', *Past and Present*, 40 (1968), 80–1.

[16] O'Neill, *Family and Farm in Pre-famine Ireland*, p. 185.

[17] Kennedy *et al.*, 'People and population change, 1600–1914', p. 66.

[18] Niall Ó Ciosáin, *Ireland in Official Print Culture, 1800–1850: A New Reading of the Poor Inquiry* (Oxford, 2014), p. 51.

Table 3.2 *Age at marriage of the 'labouring class' (Poor Inquiry (Ireland), 1836)*

County	Average Age of Marriage
Galway	18–21
Leitrim	16–22
Mayo and Sligo	under 20
Dublin	26
Kilkenny	20–25
King's County	17–20
Louth	25–30
Limerick	18–25
Clare	17–25
Kerry	18–21
Wicklow	23–28
Queen's County	26
Meath	20–25
Cork	20
Tipperary	18–22
Waterford	24–30
Armagh	19–30
Down	20–25
Fermanagh	18–25

Source: *Poor Inquiry (Ireland). Appendix (H), Part ii. Remarks on Evidence Contained in Appendixes (D) (E) (F) By One of the Commissioners* (HC 1836 XXXIV), pp. 669–72

Catholic couples for marrying early and without sufficient economic resources. In Kilroot parish in County Antrim, for example, the recording officer noted:

... that there have not been in memory any cases of extremely early marriage among the inhabitants of the parish. On the contrary, as is the case in most Scottish districts, where the people are civilised and educated, their marriages take place at a later period of life than in those districts where the inhabitants are less enlightened and in less comfortable circumstances. There seems to be a prudence and caution in their disposition which prevents the men from encumbering themselves before they have been assured of the probability of a provision, and they therefore seldom marry before the age of 28 or 30. The usual age at which females marry is from 20 to 25.[19]

---

[19] Angelique Day and Patrick McWilliams (eds.), *Ordnance Survey Memoirs of Ireland: Parishes of County Antrim, 1830–1, 1833–5, 1839–40. East Antrim: Glynn, Inver, Kilroot and Templecorran* (Belfast, 1990), p. 67.

The note taker for the parish of Ballyscullion in County Tyrone was more explicit when he recorded that Catholics married very early, while Protestants 'not so much'.[20]

In his critique of Connell's work, Michael Drake also cautioned against assuming that most people knew their precise age in the early nineteenth century. Even parents may have provided guesstimates of their children's ages.[21] Age was often determined by appearance and physical ability rather than by chronological years. Contemporary commentators may also have guessed the ages at which young couples were marrying with concepts of 'early' varying from teen marriage to under twenty-five.

Kevin O'Neill suggested that in looking at a couple's decision to marry early, it is useful to consider society's perception of marriage. In pre-Famine Ireland, the expectation was that the majority of the population would marry. If, in the dire economic circumstances of the 1830s, poor men 'had lost all hope' of acquiring employment, then they may also have believed that there was little point in delaying the marriage, which they were likely to undertake at some stage in their lives.[22] It is people in this frame of mind who were described, a little disdainfully, by local clergymen to the Poor Inquiry Commissioners.

The parish priest in Leighlin, County Carlow, reported that in the poorest sections of the town, people who married, 'had not a pair of blankets, a potato-pot, or beyond one meal in reserve for the next day'.[23] Another parish priest commented that 'the most destitute are the most reckless in contracting marriage, under a belief that nothing can render their situaton worse'.[24] Other witnesses who testified to the Poor Inquiry Commissioners reported that a poor labourer's decision to marry might also have been viewed as a means of alleviating his or her economic position. As in other rural societies, children were perceived as a material asset or, as one witness phrased it: 'their children are their wealth'. Children could help with farm work and also, most importantly, were expected to provide for their elderly parents.[25] In County Sligo, Dr Kenny reported how labourers explained to him why they married at an early age:

[20] Angelique Day and Patrick McWilliams (eds.), *Ordnance Survey Memoirs of Ireland: Parishes of County Londonderry I, 1830, 1834, 1836: Arboe, Artrea, Ballinderry, Ballyscullion, Magherafelt, Termoneeny* (Belfast, 1990), p. 55.

[21] Drake, 'Marriage and population growth in Ireland', 201–313.

[22] O'Neill, *Family and Farm in Pre-Famine Ireland*, pp. 185–6.

[23] *Poor Inquiry (Ireland). Appendix (H), Part ii*, p. 670.   [24] Ibid.

[25] Ibid., p. 671; L. A. Clarkson, 'Marriage and fertility in nineteenth-century Ireland' in R. B. Outhwaite, *Marriage and Society: Studies in the Social History of Marriage* (New York, 1982), p. 240.

If God give us a family, and we marry young, our children will support us when we are beyond work; but if we do not marry soon, we should be broken down before our children should be grown enough to support us.[26]

The Presbyterian minister, Mr Gibson, reported a similar belief in County Westmeath: 'The poor consider that when they have brought up a family they have made a provision for their old age'.[27] As will be discussed later in the volume, some of those who provided information for the Poor Enquiry also suggested that fear of an unmarried daughter being abducted also encouraged marriage at an early age among tenant-farmer families.[28]

The poor people who spoke with the Commissioners provided, therefore, a nuanced and informed view of the reasons for early marriage. A poor man's wife might not bring a dowry to a marriage but she could offer another valuable asset: her physical labour and, if necessity required, her ability to beg, particularly when her husband took seasonal employment away from home. A labourer called Waldron explained to the Poor Inquiry Commissioners how the decision to marry early could suit the financial circumstances of the three families involved. A young man living 'in misery' with his parents and large number of siblings might conclude that he would be better off married to 'some girl, and … a house of my own, and we will live for ourselves'. Similarly, a father might decide that it would ease the situation of his large family if he could find someone else 'to do' for one of his daughters. The daughter, according to Waldron, was often 'as anxious as her father' to leave the family home. The young couple married, therefore, 'without any fear of being worse off than before; for when he has no work, if he is ashamed to beg himself, the wife and children will beg and support him'.[29]

It is important, therefore, to consider the poverty in which many families in pre-Famine Ireland lived and the speed with which a new house and home could be established.[30] The ease with which it was possible to marry in pre-Famine Ireland may also have encouraged those with no dowry or match to be negotiated to marry quickly and at a young age. According to one witness, many early marriages were 'contracted at fairs in the heat of the moment', presumably in a quick service witnessed by a couple beggar.[31]

As is well documented, the Famine of the 1840s had a disproportionate impact on the lowest social groups in rural society. In particular, the proportion of labourers declined dramatically from 55 per cent of the

---

[26] *Poor Inquiry*. Appendix (H), Part ii, p. 671.   [27] Ibid.   [28] See p. 194.
[29] *Poor Inquiry*. Appendix (H), Part ii, p. 670.   [30] See p. 10.
[31] *Poor Inquiry*. Appendix (H), Part ii, p. 671.

population in 1841 to 25 per cent by 1881.[32] Historians have linked the rise in age of marriage in post-Famine Ireland with the devastating impact that the Famine had on the lower social groups in rural society. As Joe Lee noted, the 'age at marriage within classes possibly changed less dramatically than the sizes of the classes themselves'.[33]

There were also regional and class variations in the rise in marriage age in the decades after the Famine. In the west of Ireland, according to the 1911 census, women from small farms were still likely to marry young, as were those living in working-class communities in towns and cities.[34] Caitriona Clear attributes the latter to the opportunities that young men and women had of working together and getting to know one another over a period of time before they married.[35] Many urban workers were also migrants from rural areas and were, therefore, less likely to be influenced in their choice of partner by parental priorities. The paintings of William Conor vividly capture the relative freedom of the young men and women who worked in the textile mills and factories in early twentieth-century Belfast.[36] Overall, however, despite these local variations the general trend in post-Famine Ireland was towards a later marital age: rising gradually from the mid-twenties to twenty-eight in the early twentieth century. By 1911, the average age at marriage, nationally, for women was twenty-nine while that of men was thirty-three years.[37]

Society's expectation that most people would marry also changed. Coinciding with a rise in age at marriage was a remarkable increase in the number of people who never married. The proportion of men not married in 1841 was 10 per cent but this had risen to 24 per cent by 1901. The comparable figures for women were 12 per cent unmarried in 1841 and 20 per cent in 1901.[38] In 1871, 43 per cent of all women aged 15–45 were married. In 1911 only 36 per cent of women in this age range were married.[39] The highest percentage of women who were not married in

---

[32] Lee, 'Marriage and population in pre-Famine Ireland', 285.   [33] Ibid.

[34] Caitriona Clear, *Social Change and Everyday Life in Ireland, 1850–1922* (Manchester, 2007), pp. 75–6, 168–74.

[35] Ibid., p. 76.

[36] Judith C. Wilson, *Conor. 1881–1968: The Life and Work of an Ulster Artist* (Belfast, 1981).

[37] John Fitzgerald, 'Irish demography since 1740' in Eugenio F. Biagini and Mary E. Daly (eds.), *The Cambridge Social History of Modern Ireland* (Cambridge, 2017), p. 19; Lindsay Earner-Byrne and Diane Urquhart, 'Gender roles in Ireland since 1740' in Biagini and Daly (eds.), *Cambridge Social History*, pp. 319–20.

[38] Clarkson, 'Marriage and fertility in nineteenth-century Ireland', pp. 244–5.

[39] Marriage rates were at their lowest in Ireland in the 1930s. There were 22,045 marriages registered in Ireland in 2014. In 1932, 13,029 marriages were recorded in the Irish state; in 1974 the number was 22,833, and the numbers fell to under 16,000 in 1995. In 2014 there were 6,167 civil marriage ceremonies – that is non-religious ceremonies – and 392 civil partnerships. In 1964 the average age of the groom was 29.8 years; it was 26.2 in

their thirties or early forties was to be found in the east and north of the country. In 1881 and in 1911, however, the largest percentage of single women in this age group lived in the suburban middle-class areas of County Dublin. The number of people who did not marry was, however, also high in rural farming families. Thirty-eight per cent of middle-aged women were single in County Donegal in 1911.[40]

Caitriona Clear has pointed out that delayed marriage was not unique to Ireland and was increasingly common in middle-class families throughout the western world in the nineteenth century. The stark rise in the number of Irish people who remained single all their lives was, however, unusual.[41] Historians have asked why this was the case and, particularly, why Irish farmers were so reluctant to marry. Clear and Cormac Ó Grada query the traditional explanation that sons, and particularly the eldest son, waited for the father or widowed mother to die before deciding to marry and bring another woman into the family home. They have also questioned the validity of Timothy Guinnane's intriguing suggestion that celibacy was a choice made by farming men who, in the improved economy of the post-Famine era, no longer saw the financial need to undergo the personal difficulties involved in an arranged marriage. They had sufficient funds to finance their old age through the use of hired help or selling off part or all of their holding. Unmarried men also found 'substitute families' through living with siblings and other kin.[42]

Ó Grada and Clear have commented that most of the writing on marriage and celibacy in post-Famine Ireland focuses on the options available to single men with the assumption, as Ó Grada noted, that there was a 'limitless supply of women willing to marry the men if required'.[43] The emigration of single women from rural Ireland meant that this was evidently not the case. Both historians also point to the new opportunities open to men and women in the period. Clear, in particular, notes the increased access for farmers' daughters to education. Contemporary debate voiced concern that a convent education gave girls expectations of a more comfortable life than was available on the

---

1977. For brides the average age in 1964 was 26.3 and 24 in 1977. See the Central Statistics Office website: www.cso.ie. Accessed 9 March 2020. See also Rita M. Rhodes, *Women and the Family in Post-Famine Ireland. Status and Opportunity in a Patriarchal Society* (New York, 1992), pp. 109–16 for provincial breakdown of age at marriage, 1871–1911.

[40] Clear, *Social Change and Everyday Life in Ireland*, pp. 76, 172–3.   [41] Ibid., p. 77.

[42] Ó Grada, *Ireland: A New Economic History*, pp. 214–18; Clear, *Social Change and Everyday Life in Ireland*, pp. 77–80; Timothy Guinnane, *The Vanishing Irish: Households, Migration, and the Rural Economy in Ireland, 1850–1914* (Princeton, 1997).

[43] Ó Grada, *Ireland: A New Economic History*, p. 218.

average farm. It was, therefore, frequently the women who postponed marriage as they sought other options in life.[44]

It might also be added that most historians who have commented on the relatively high number of people who remained unmarried in early twentieth-century Ireland describe them as 'celibate'. Yet, as we shall see in Chapter 8, the high rates of venereal disease in the same period of time might suggest that this is not an accurate description.

Geographic Considerations – Marrying Someone Near

Most people, particularly in rural Ireland, looked to their own immediate locality for a marriage partner. An analysis of the marriage licences issued in the diocese of Ossory, 1739–1804, indicates that over 60 per cent of people married someone who lived in the same county as themselves. The addresses provided in the licence documentation also suggests that over 50 per cent of people chose a partner from within their own parish and some from within their own townland. The Ossory licences were mainly issued to members of the Church of Ireland.[45] An analysis of late nineteenth-century parish records indicates, however, that the custom of

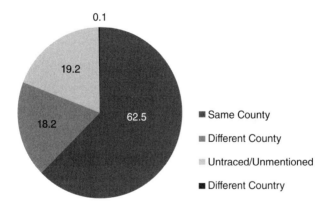

Figure 3.1 Place of origin of marriage partners in marriage licences in the diocese of Ossory, 1739–1804.
Source: Raymond Refaussé, 'Marriage licences from the diocese of Ossory 1739–1804', *Irish Genealogist*, 8 (1990), 122–44; (1991), 239–67; (1992), 393–428

---

[44] Ibid.; Clear, *Social Change and Everyday Life in Ireland,* pp. 79–80. On the perceived impact of convent education on Irish girls, see Angela Bourke *et al.* (eds.), *Field Day Anthology of Irish Writing, vol. 5: Irishwomen's Writing and Traditions* (Cork/New York, 2002), pp. 658–9.

[45] See Figure 3.2 and Tables 3.1 and 3.2.

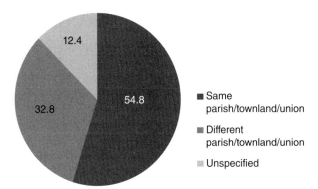

Figure 3.2 Place of origin of marriage partners from the same county in marriage licences in the diocese of Ossory, 1739–1804.
Source: Raymond Refaussé, 'Marriage licences from the diocese of Ossory 1739–1804', *Irish Genealogist*, 8 (1990), 122–44; (1991), 239–67; (1992), 393–428

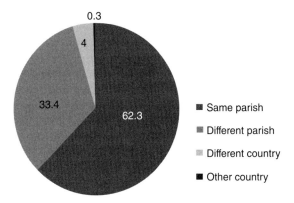

Figure 3.3 Place of origin of Roman Catholic marriage partners in County Kerry, 1856–1905.
Source: Database supplied by www.irishgenealogy.ie

choosing a partner from within the immediate locality was also common to Catholic couples. In County Kerry (1856–1905) for example, over 60 percent of couples married someone from within their own parish while over 50 per cent of Protestants did, a difference that reflects the small number of Protestants living in the county and the difficulty of finding a spouse of the same religious background living in close proximity.[46]

The continuous stream of requests for dispensations by Catholic couples to marry second or third cousins also testifies to the fact that

---

[46] See Figures 3.2 and 3.3.

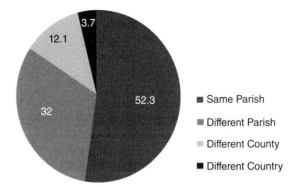

Figure 3.4 Place of origin of Church of Ireland marriage partners in County Kerry, 1856–1905.
Source: Database supplied by www.irishgenealogy.ie

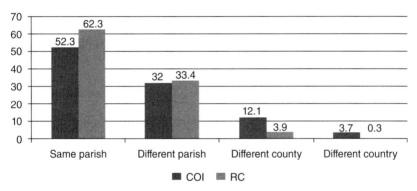

Figure 3.5 Place of origin of Church of Ireland and Roman Catholic marriage partners in County Kerry, 1856–1905.
Source: Database supplied by www.irishgenealogy.ie

many people not only knew their future spouse, but that there was a strong possibility they were also related. Caitriona Clear suggests, however, that this practice declined as the Catholic church imposed stronger adherence to church regulation in the late nineteenth century.[47] More constant was the expectation that marriage partners would come from the same social class and religious denomination. As indicated in Chapter 1, mixed inter-faith marriages were not encouraged by church authorities. The sons and daughters of farmers with middling- and

[47] Clear, *Social Change and Everyday Life in Ireland,* pp. 80–1.

large-sized holdings were under particular pressure to marry their social and economic equal. In one of William Carleton's stories, for example, a man who has the temerity to demonstrate an interest in a girl of higher social status than his own is told by his mother to go look for a girl he might 'have a right to expect', and not one that 'could lay down guineas where you could hardly find shillings.'[48] The diarist, Amhlaoibh Ó Suilleabháin had a sexual relationship with a maid servant in his home, with whom he had two children. He did not, however, think of marrying her, even after his wife died. She was of the wrong class. Instead, as we shall see, he made an effort to marry the sister of a priest, which would have been considered a far more respectable choice.[49] Samuel Clark, in an analysis of marriage patterns in County Roscommon between 1864 and 1880, noted that farm families were least likely to form marriage alliances with those classes arranged above and below them on the social scale.[50] A contemporary observed the same class limits in 1892:

A 'poor man' must not look for the hand of a rich peasant's daughter, nor must a man of the working-class or a farm servant dare to cast his eyes on a farmer's daughter. Young men and women sometimes marry out of their rank in life, but it is looked on as something 'dreadful'. I remember once telling a young man that he ought to pay his addresses to the daughter of a neighbouring farmer. The youth's reply was that the dog would be set on him if he went near the house.[51]

In towns and cities partners were normally also chosen within a local catchment area. Mary Daly, for example, noted that in late nineteenth-century Dublin there was a tendency among the working classes to choose marriage partners from the same residential area. In 1871, 21.3 per cent of couples marrying gave the same address while 7.9 per cent of the married couples that Daly examined lived in the same street and just over 39 per cent lived within a mile of each other.[52] Roy Foster pointed to a similar trend among urban middle-class families when he outlined the inter-connections between many of those involved in revolutionary politics in the early twentieth century.[53]

---

[48] William Carleton, 'Shane Fadh's wedding', *Traits and Stories of the Irish Peasantry* (London, 1890).

[49] Pierce Grace, *The Middle Class of Callan, County Kilkenny, 1825–45* (Dublin, 2015).

[50] Samuel Clark, *Social Origins of the Irish Land War* (Princeton, 1979), p. 118.

[51] A Guardian of the Poor, *The Irish Peasant: A Sociological Study* (London, 1892), pp. 133–4. The young man's father farmed about twenty acres and the woman's father farmed about sixty acres.

[52] Mary E. Daly, *Dublin: The Deposed Capital: A Social and Economic History, 1860–1914* (Cork, 1985), p.145.

[53] R. F. Foster, *Vivid Faces: The Revolutionary Generation in Ireland 1890–1923* (London, 2014).

As the nineteenth century ended, there is evidence of people venturing a little further for marriage partners. Rosaleen Fallon has explored marriage in the rural townland of Clonown in County Roscommon in the 1890s and later. She noted that in the nineteenth century marriages of residents to those with non-farming backgrounds was a rare occurrence. By the early twentieth century, however, men and women living in the townland were marrying into the local town populations and displaying a greater level of mobility in their selection of marriage partners.[54]

Michael Ahern identified a similar gradual widening of the pool from which marriage partners were chosen in the relatively closed world of the Quaker community in County Tipperary. The spatial limits of Quaker marriage within the county were narrow through the eighteenth century. Of the 361 marriages (between 1757 and 1856) contracted by Tipperary Quakers where both partners can be identified, 59 per cent found marriage partners from within the compass of the local monthly meeting, or within a Waterford–Cork–Limerick axis that formed the administrative area of the Munster quarterly meeting. Social contact through the Society's religious meetings was an important factor in promoting marriage between members. In the later nineteenth century there was a significant spreading out of the geographical marital links formed by Tipperary Quakers as expanding economic conditions saw business interests for Quakers extend and an influx of Quakers from other parts of the country to Tipperary.[55]

More generally, changing social conditions in late nineteenth-century Ireland such as an improved road and railway network, greater employment of women away from home areas and a declining rural population due to emigration motivated young men and women to look more widely for a marriage partner. By the end of the nineteenth century the bicycle had also made an impact on how far young people might travel, for instance, to a dance. Family connections and suitable financial arrangements remained, however, important requirements for a successful courtship.

How Did You Meet Your Partner?

Although we can document the geographical range within which most people looked for marriage partners, it is impossible to generalise about

---

[54] Rosaleen Fallon, A *County Roscommon Wedding, 1892: The Marriage of John Hughes and Mary Gavin* (Dublin, 2004), pp. 22–4.
[55] Michael Ahern, *The Quakers of County Tipperary, 1655–1924* (Clonmel, 2009), pp. 208–11.

the particular social occasions or spaces in which young and old encountered one another. Marriages were formed through the connections of family and friends as well as through a myriad of formal and informal social gatherings. As already indicated, many couples would have known one another from childhood while others, as we shall see, had scarcely met before they were matched by family members.

The expansion of urban Ireland in the eighteenth century created new social spaces for middle- and upper-class people to meet. Promenades, assembly rooms and concert halls opened up safe public spaces for women. Dorothea Herbert described in her 'Retrospections' the social world of the young members of the Protestant community in and around Carrick-on-Suir in the 1780s: 'we had always dancing in the Evening on the green Turf and regular Assemblies once a Week in Carrick'.[56] In a similar fashion, Amhlaoibh Ó Suilleabháin noted on a number of occasions in his diary that the '*mná óga uaisle an bhaile, agus no h-óganaigh uaisle*' [the young ladies of the town, and the young gentlemen] were promenading in the middle of the town green in Callan in County Kilkenny in the 1820s.[57] Ó Súilleabháin is careful, however, to distinguish between the 'ladies' and 'gentlewomen' who promenaded in Callan and the thousands of young '*ógmhná agus óganaigh*' [maidens and youths] who danced to music on a small hill in the local bog. The social distinctions may not have been so clear in late eighteenth-century Coleraine, where John Tennent recorded how he and other young apprentices amused themselves in the evening on the bowling green. He described it as 'a place where persons of every description goes at the time of Easter to divert themselves'.[58]

The authors of the memorials for the Ordnance Survey in the 1830s described the most popular amusements in the parish. These almost always included dancing. As the author of the Carnmoney memorial wrote: 'scarce a month passes without there being a dance in some farmer's house'.[59] Leanne Calvert also described the importance of dancing in the social lives of young Presbyterians in late eighteenth and early nineteenth-century Ulster. Usually organised in private houses,

---

[56] Dorothea Herbert, *Retrospections of Dorothea Herbert, 1770–1806* (Dublin, 1988), p. 81.
[57] Michael McGrath (ed.), *Cinnlae Amhlaoibh Uí Shúileabháin: The Diary of Humphrey O'Sullivan* (4 vols., Dublin, 1936–1937), i, pp. 80-1.
[58] Leanne Calvert (ed.), 'The journal of John Tennent, 1786–90', *Analecta Hibernica*, 43 (2012), 91, 117.
[59] Angelique Day and Patrick McWilliams (eds.), *Ordnance Survey Memoirs of Ireland 1830–1840*, vol. 2: *Parishes of County Antrim I, 1838–9: Ballymartin, Ballyrobert, Ballywalter, Carnmoney, Mallusk* (Belfast, 1990), p. 52. See also pp. 112–3. For images of dancing in rural Ireland from the eighteenth through to the early twentieth centuries, see B. Rooney (ed.), *A Time and a Place: Two Centuries of Irish Social Life* (Dublin, 2006), pp. 25–46.

evening dances provided an ideal opportunity for young people to meet with minimum supervision by parents or guardians. Local kirk sessions, not surprisingly, perhaps, were concerned at what took place not only at the dance but also in the fields afterwards.[60]

Another popular form of amusement recorded by the Ordnance Survey memorialists was attendance at local fairs. Some social commentators tutted with disapproval at the young farm servants who excitedly spent their earnings at the fair rather than saving for a marriage trousseau.[61] Yet, for most young women, the fair was, apart from the church, the one public gathering that they were permitted to attend. The 'riot and dissipation' at the annual Donnybrook Fair was notorious in eighteenth and early nine-teenth century Dublin. Games included young women running in their underwear and 'Kiss in the ring' in which a group of girls danced around a man who selected one of them for a kiss.[62] Jonah Barrington described the 'long dance' at the fair in which large groups of people participated: 'I have seen a row of a hundred couple[s] labouring at their jig-steps till they fell off actually breathless …'[63] It was not, however, until the evening that 'sweethearts made up their matches'. Barrington quoted a Dublin priest who noted the increase in the number of marriages that were celebrated in the week after Donnybrook fair.[64] Not surprisingly, couple beggars also found plenty of business at the fair.[65]

By the 1860s, the excesses of Donnybrook Fair had been curbed but the fairs in rural towns continued to be opportunities for couples to meet and for marriage bargains to be agreed.[66] In Ballinasloe, in the 1920s, a newspaper report noted that on Saturdays all the young people dressed up and came with their parents to the fair to partake in amuse-ments: 'A good deal of "matchmaking" takes place and the young people court and the old people discuss their fortunes. Many betrothed people meet for the first time at the fair and the marriages which follow are usually happy.'[67]

---

[60] Leanne Calvert, '"He came to her bed pretending courtship": Sex, courtship and the making of marriage in Ulster, 1750–1844', *Irish Historical Studies*, 42, 162 (2018), 251–3.

[61] See, for example, Mary Leadbeater, *Cottage Dialogues among the Irish Peasantry* (London, 1811), pp. 13–19.

[62] Séamas Ó Maitiú, *The Humours of Donnybrook: Dublin's Famous Fair and Its Suppression* (Dublin, 1995), p. 20.

[63] Jonah Barrington, *Personal Sketches of His Own Times* (3rd ed., 2 vols., London, 1869), ii, p. 331.

[64] Ibid., p. 332.   [65] See Chapter 2.

[66] Ó Maitiú, *The Humours of Donnybrook*; Report of the Commissioners of the Metropolitan Police for the Information of His Excellency, the Lord Lieutenant (NAI, CSORP, 1838/2642).

[67] *Irish Times*, 10 Oct. 1924.

Other opportunities for young people to meet informally were the celebrations around saints' days and other religious feast days. In the 1740s, farmer and land agent Nicholas Peacock provided his servants with drinking money to go to the public house or dances on feast days such as St Patrick's Day and Christmas.[68] He also gave 'ye boys and ye mades' money to drink at Patterns, the ostensibly religious festival at a holy site where music was played, young people danced and a great deal of alcohol was consumed.[69] The eve of St John's Day on 24 June was another occasion for all night vigils and dancing around the bonfire.[70] In Ulster, the popular appeal of some Presbyterian sects was also the cause of alarm. Thomas Ledlie Birch, the Presbyterian minister denounced the setting up of stalls and drinking tents in front of Presbyterian churches on Sundays and the drunken sociability of men and women who attended services.[71]

The ritual of church attendance, which developed as a more regular practice in the nineteenth century, created new possibilities of social interaction in a respectable manner as men and women walked to and from the local chapel as well as watching one another during the service. In his autobiography, William Carleton nostalgically recalled how as a teenager he had silently admired a young woman, Anne Duffy, whom he met at mass: 'She knelt ... on the left hand side of the priest, next [to] the altar; while I ... placed myself in the same position on the other side, so that we were right opposite to each other. ... I said no prayers that day. My eyes were never off her – they were riveted on her.'[72] Carleton also regularly followed Duffy home from the church. A more formal relationship between Carleton and Duffy never developed, primarily because Carleton had not the means to keep a wife of Duffy's social standing. Other couples also described how walking to and from church formed an important part of their courtship.[73] When Samuel Kingston attempted to court Lucy Lawrenson he chose to meet her on Sunday evenings at her

---

[68] Marie-Louise Legg (ed.), *The Diary of Nicholas Peacock, 1740–51: The Worlds of a County Limerick Farmer and Agent* (Dublin, 2005), pp. 65, 148, 152, 165, 171.

[69] Ibid., p. 65. See also p. 145.

[70] See, for example, McGrath, *Cinnlae Amhlaoibh Uí Shúileabhan*, pp. 76–7.

[71] Thomas Leslie Birch, *Physicians Languishing under Disease. An Address to the Seceding, or Associate Synod of Ireland, Upon Certain Tenets and Practices, Alleged to be In Enmity with All Religious Reformation* (Belfast, 1796), p. 38.

[72] *The Life of William Carleton: Being His Autobiography and Letters; and an Account of His Life and Writings, From the Point at Which the Autobiography Breaks Off, By David J. O'Donoghue* (2 vols., London, 1896), i, p. 52.

[73] See, for example, *Irish Times*, 24 Oct. 1865; *Belfast Newsletter*, 24 Oct. 1865; *Freeman's Journal*, 11, 18 March, 24 Oct. 1865.

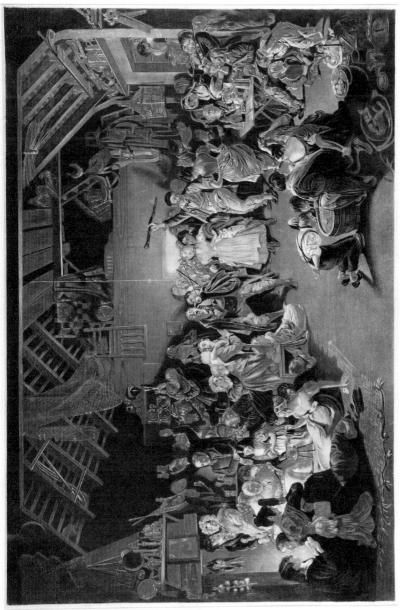

Illustration 3.1 Religious feast days were an occasion for dances and communal celebrations. Daniel Maclise's painting captures the opportunities such events provided for young men and women to socialise and physically touch without adult disapproval. The older woman in the left-hand corner is telling the marital fortunes of the younger women who sit around her.

local church so that he could walk her home. Although Samuel was a lodger in Lawrenson's mother's house, the walk from the church provided their only opportunity for privacy.[74]

Servants and other young people working away from home had the most freedom to socialise without being supervised by parents or other members of the family. In the Carnmoney Presbyterian session book, one woman described in 1804 how she and her husband permitted young men to visit their female servant at night and she acknowledged that she did not know when or if they had left to go home.[75] In court cases concerned with the breakdown of courtship in the mid- to late-nineteenth century, female plaintiffs often noted that they had first met their intended marriage partner while working as a servant.[76] Sadly, too, it was young single domestic servants who were most likely to be accused of infanticide or concealing the birth of infants born outside of marriage.[77]

Employers could, however, also act *in loco parentis* and supervise the activities of their employees. In the 1790s, the Coleraine merchant, Samuel Girvin, dismissed one of his apprentices when he discovered that the young man had 'slept out of his masters house [at] different times'.[78] Almost a hundred years later, when Sis Whelan was employed as a shop assistant in Bunclody, County Wexford, in 1899, she wrote of how her employer did not permit his female employees to have boyfriends: 'If Mr Lewis found out that any of them were talking to young men, he would not keep them'. Although Sis continued to meet with her boyfriend, Tom Eades, they were clearly careful not to be seen together in the hotel where Tom stayed when he came to see Sis.[79]

By the end of the nineteenth century, new leisure activities widened the number of social venues where men and women could meet without being censured by employers or parents. Cultural and historical clubs and societies began, for example, to accept women as well as men as members. The early photos of local archaeological field clubs

---

[74] Daisy Lawrenson Swanson, *Emerging from the Shadow: The Lives of Sarah Anne Lawrenson and Lucy Olive Kingston* (Dublin, 1994), p. 61.

[75] Leanne Calvert (ed.), 'Carnmoney Kirk Session Minute Chapter Book, January 1786–March 1804' (unpublished transcript of original in PHSIB). See also Calvert, '"He came to her bed pretending courtship"', 253, 255–7.

[76] See Chapters 4 and 6.

[77] Elaine Farrell, *'A Most Diabolical Deed': Infanticide and Irish Society, 1850–1900* (Manchester, 2013).

[78] Calvert, 'The Journal of John Tennent, 1786–90', 93.

[79] Rosemary Raughter (ed.), '"Your own for ever, Sis": Letters to Parsonstown, 1898–1903', *Bulletin of the Methodist Historical Society of Ireland*, 22, 1 (2017), 58, 74. See also p. 45.

suggest the sociability that they facilitated.[80] James and Margaret Cousins, who married in 1903, met at the annual conference of the Wesleyan Methodist Church in Ireland in 1899. They spent their courtship in Dublin indulging their mutual interests, visiting galleries, going to concerts, 'lectures and the like'.[81] When Margaret first met James she noted he did not have the physical attributes that she expected of a future husband; she did not like the fact that he was a vegetarian and she was disappointed in his marriage proposal. She believed, however, that this might be her one chance of marriage. Their shared cultural visits during their courtship enabled Margaret to develop her affection for her future husband: 'I was learning to appreciate his depth and purity of thought, his genius in expression, his understanding of the need for every human being to have freedom to grow in their own way'.[82]

Senia Pašeta has documented how political as well as cultural-nationalist developments in early twentieth-century Ireland opened up new public and social spaces for women. Pašeta conveys the sense of excitement of women who relished the new opportunities for engagement with cultural and political organisations.[83] As Marie Perolz exclaimed, 'I took part in everything'. She moved from 'one organisation to another regularly, often on a daily basis'.[84] The Gaelic League was very popular among young women who wanted not just to learn Irish but probably also to meet like-minded young men. The courtship of Éamon de Valera and his Gaelic League teacher, Sinéad Flanagan, is well-known, but others too encountered their future spouses through engagement in similar cultural clubs and societies.[85] Éamonn Ceannt, one of the signatories to the 1916 Proclamation, and Áine Ní Bhraonáin, met through the Gaelic League and they both spent much of their courtship at the Pipers' Club, of which Ceannt was a co-founder.[86] Travelling to summer schools in the Gaeltacht also opened up the possibilities of close engagement with the opposite sex.[87] More particularly, Lucy McDiarmid

---

[80] See, for example, Myrtle Hill and Vivienne Pollock (eds.), *Image and Experience: Photographs of Irish Women, c.1880–1920* (Belfast, 1993), p. 126.

[81] James H. and Margaret E. Cousins, *We Two Together* (Madras, 1950), p. 86. James Cousins was a poet. The couple went to live in India where Margaret was involved in the women's movement.

[82] Ibid., p. 87.

[83] Senia Pašeta, *Irish Nationalist Women 1900–1918* (Cambridge, 2013), pp. 17–32.

[84] Ibid., p. 26.   [85] *DIB*.

[86] *DIB*; Sinéad McCoole, *Easter Widows. Seven Irish Women Who Lived in the Shadow of the Easter Rising* (London, 2014), pp. 110–33.

[87] Foster, *Vivid Faces*, p. 123. See also Chapter 4.

described the 'kind of romantic intimacy' that developed between the young men and women involved in the preparations for the Easter Rising.[88] The attraction of a man in uniform was also testified by some of the witness statements given to the Bureau of Military History. Bridget Thornton described her feelings when she met two men who were involved in the rebellion. Edward Daly and Seamus Sullivan reminded her of 'British officers in appearance and inspired us girls with feelings of enthusiasm and caused us many heart throbs'. Another republican man brought to mind the 'attractive heroes in Irish history'.[89]

The early decades of the twentieth century were also, however, a time when many young Irish men spent much of their daily life in male company, either in the British Army during the First World War or in the Irish Volunteers and later in the armed forces on either side of the civil war. Some also served time in prison. In his memoirs, C. S. Andrews did not recall the Gaelic League as an opportunity to develop close relationships with girls. Instead, he claimed that he had 'never met any girls except in "convoys" at the Sinn Féin Club or at Gaelic League functions …' In old age, Andrews recalled the absence of social interaction with the opposite sex in his youth:

I did not realise it at the time but, in fact, I had not had a normal adolescence. Among my multitudinous friends I had never known a girl who was more than a passing acquaintance. My boyhood and early manhood, spent as they were at all male schools, football clubs and the IRA, had left me emotionally immature in the matter of inter-sex relations … which was at that time the not uncommon experience of a man of nearly twenty three years of age, as I was when I came home from the Civil War.[90]

Andrews subsequently socialised with women within republican circles, meeting them in flats in Dublin, and as he got to 'know women as friends and companions, a new world was opened to me'. It was also through this new network that he met his first wife, Mary Coyle, who was a member of Cumann na mBan.[91] The courting couple took advantage of the social activities available in the city to get to know one another: 'We went to the theatre once a week, often had tea together in the Grafton picture-house café followed by a film in one or other of the many city cinemas, attended whist drives … or occasional "hops"'.[92]

[88] Lucy McDiarmid, *At Home in the Revolution: What Women Said and Did in 1916* (Dublin, 2015), p. 80.
[89] Statement of Bridget Thornton (WS259, Bureau of Military History, Dublin).
[90] C. S. Andrews, *Man of No Property* (Dublin, 1982), pp. 19, 167.
[91] Ibid., pp. 27–31, 44–45.   [92] Ibid., p. 61.

Personal Advertisements

Not everyone was able to avail themselves of the social opportunities offered in the larger cities. In post-Famine Ireland, particularly in rural areas, the increased emigration of young men and women meant that the pool of possible spouses declined. Some, anxious to marry in Ireland, attempted to widen their choice of partner through personal advertisements that appeared sporadically in Irish newspapers in the early nineteenth century and became more frequent at the end of the century. The earliest known advert for a spouse appeared in the *Ennis Chronicle and Clare Advertiser* in 1801. A 'young man in the middle class of the community' specified that he was looking for a wife who had an 'animated countenance, be genteel in her person, possessing many mental accomplishments, and a small fortune.'[93] The author of the notice also noted his awareness that such advertisements were becoming more popular elsewhere in the United Kingdom.[94] The practice was slow to develop in Ireland but by the 1870s, matrimonial notices began to be printed in Irish newspapers. In the 1880s and 1890s, there were on average four to five personal advertisements in each weekly issue of the *Freeman's Journal.* Similar advertisements appeared in *The Irish Times* and the *Belfast Newsletter*. Initially, the notices were inserted by men but in the 1890s about a third were placed by women. The advertisements normally indicated the author's age, religion and occupation or annual income. The men were usually looking for a 'young lady', 'good-looking' and with 'means' or a business. Others wanted a wife who could assist her husband in business. In 1892, for example, a young Catholic draper who claimed to have £3,000 invested in his business sought a 'young lady having thorough knowledge of the general Drapery and a taste for business'. He indicated that 'money was no object' if a woman was 'found suitable'. She must, however, be 'tall, handsome and respectable'.[95] In addition to financial assets, some men also asked that the woman be educated or 'accomplished'.[96] There was clearly an element of wishful thinking in the listing of these desirable attributes but they do give us some indication of what a middle-class man looked for in an ideal spouse. Most of the women who inserted notices also looked for financial security but they tended not to emphasise physical attributes. Some already had their own businesses and, like the men, were looking for a partner to work with them. In January 1898, a woman who described

---

[93] *Ennis Chronicle and Clare Advertiser*, 5 Oct. 1801.   [94] Ibid.
[95] *Freeman's Journal*, 25 June 1892.
[96] See, for example, *Freeman's Journal*, 18 Oct. 1876; 9 July 1877, 9 Jan. 1891.

herself as young with a 'draper's shop in the best town in the south' indicated that she wanted a young man, 'Draper preferred', having £200 or £300 'or more'.[97] Other women wanted a man with a steady income and occupation. There appears to have been a marked preference for a member of the Royal Irish Constabulary, probably because it was a permanent and pensionable position.[98] Policemen who inserted notices were also keen to highlight their occupation. In January 1891, a head constable, aged thirty six and 'considered good looking' detailed the attractions of his employment: an annual salary of £104 and £700 in the bank.[99]

The majority of those who inserted notices in the *Irish Times* and *Belfast Newsletter* identified themselves as Protestant while almost all who advertised in the *Freeman's Journal* were Catholic. A small number of the latter also offered to provide clerical references as to their character and presumably their faith.[100] Unsurprisingly, all who specified their religious denomination wanted a partner of the same religion. It may have been for similar reasons that Irish emigrants placed matrimonial ads in the *Freeman's Journal* and the *Irish Times*.[101] Others may have preferred a spouse from home or wished to return to Ireland in later life. There was a poignancy about the notice inserted in the *Irish Times* in 1901 by a widow, aged forty, who described herself as an 'Irish gentle-woman' with a 'good appearance' and 'nice figure'. She was 'living alone' in a house in London but she had 'no means'. She wanted to correspond with a 'gentleman with means'.[102]

The number of matrimonial advertisements was never large and it decreased in the 1920s. The decline may have coincided with the rise in importance of the professional match-maker.[103] The personal ads along with the emergence of the latter reflect the social consequences of emigration as men and women began to find it difficult to meet with suitable spouses locally. The advertisements also gave individuals greater control over their choice of a marriage partner. Although a small number of farmers advertised for wives, most of the notices were inserted by men

---

[97] *Freeman's Journal*, 8 Jan. 1898.
[98] See, for example, *Freeman's Journal*, 13 Feb. 1886; 24 May 1892; 4 June 1902.
[99] *Freeman's Journal*, 9 Jan. 1891.
[100] See, for example, *Freeman's Journal*, 19 Nov. 1874; 9 Jan. 1891; 4 June 1902.
[101] See, for example, *Freeman's Journal*, 8 Jan. 1898; 26 Aug. 1905; 31 May 1906.
[102] *Irish Times*, 9 March 1901.
[103] The first Irish newspaper reference to a marriage agency was on 24 August 1912 when a 'respectable working man', aged thirty-eight, advertised in the *Belfast Newsletter* for a 'suitable young lady' aged about twenty-seven and asked that replies be sent to Gilbert's Matrimonial Bureau in Skipper Street, Belfast. This might have been inserted as a joke or, alternatively, an unsuccessful attempt to establish a marriage agency in Belfast.

and women living in towns and cities. The women who had established businesses of their own may also have felt sufficiently independent of their families to identify a suitable spouse for themselves. The personal ads were, therefore, an indication that by the late nineteenth century more young people felt free to choose their own marriage partner.[104]

Role of the Family and Friends in the Choice of Spouse

Most men and women still, however, relied on friends and family to help them find a partner. As already indicated, despite the popular lore attached to the professional match-maker, such individuals were rare before the twentieth century.[105] In the period covered by this volume, most 'matches' were negotiated by a parent, male relative, family friend or, sometimes, by a cleric. The task of the negotiator was to ascertain whether both parties were interested in considering a marriage match and, if so, whether the terms would be agreeable to both families.

When Protestant farmer and land agent, Nicholas Peacock, began to look for a wife early in 1746, he asked his friend, Arthur Bastable, to act on his behalf with the family of Catherine Chapman. Nicholas had met Catherine during a visit to her family home in County Cork at the beginning of January 1746 but by the end of the month, Bastable had written to him with the news that Catherine's father 'could not give his daughter half ye fortune I expected'.[106] It took more than a year for the discussion to resume. On 4 April 1747, another friend of Nicholas's sent him a letter 'about Miss Chapman'. Nicholas was clearly pleased by what he read because he answered the letter the same day and eight days later, he travelled to Cork to discuss the marriage with Catherine's father. According to his account of the meeting, Nicholas was a tough negotiator. He was about to return home without an agreement when Mr Chapman yielded and conceded to his terms.[107] The next day, Nicholas travelled back to Limerick and promptly purchased a wedding ring (for 7s 7d) and a locket ring (for 4s 4d). He sent a letter to Catherine on 21 April and by 6 May he had gone back to Cork to be married. Nicholas's plan to marry immediately was hindered by the necessity of acquiring a licence to dispense with the reading of the banns. Having paid 18s 11d to the local clergyman, Catherine and Nicholas were

---

[104] For the wider history of personal ads see H .G. Cocks, *Classified: The Secret History of the Personal Column* (London, 2009).

[105] Even in the twentieth century, most matches were organised by a family friend rather than a professional match-maker. See National Folklore Collection, Volume 2028, Marriage Customs Questionnaire.

[106] Legg, *The Diary of Nicholas Peacock, 1740–1751*, p. 52.   [107] Ibid., pp. 172–3.

married on 9 May.[108] The final negotiations, agreement and marriage ceremony took less than six weeks and, if Nicholas's diary record is accurate, the couple had met on two occasions prior to their marriage.

From the perspective of the twenty-first century, Nicholas Peacock's courtship and marriage may seem crude, over-concerned with financial matters and lacking in emotional connection. Yet, the courtship conducted by Nicholas was not unusual. Over eighty years after Nicholas Peacock's courtship, when the Kilkenny-based widower, Amhlaoibh Ó Súilleabháin, began to look for a wife in the 1820s, he went through a similar process. A local priest and friend, Father Síomóin Breatnach acted as the intermediary for Ó Súilleabháin to court his unmarried sister, Máire. Like Nicholas Peacock, Amhlaoibh travelled to the Breatnach home by invitation from Máire's brother and he spent two days '*ag suirighe le Máire*' [courting Máire]. The rest of her family stayed discreetly out of the way, as he noted in his journal. Ó Suilleabháin thought that he had managed to persuade Máire Bhreatnach 'as she gave me to understand that she would come home with me'.[109] The dowry was also agreed. Despite his optimism, Amhlaoibh did not marry Máire Bhreatnach, although he continued to regret the absence of a wife to look after his four children and to help him with his drapery business. As he agonised on the first anniversary of his wife's death: 'What will my four poor orphans do, if I marry again, and what should I do myself, or they either, or my business unless I marry.'[110]

Although Ó Súilleabháin's plan to remarry did not materialise, both he and Nicholas Peacock followed the same ritual. An intermediary, usually a relative or friend ascertained whether the woman's family was interested in discussing a marriage. This was followed by a visit to discover whether the girl was willing to consider the idea and then the financial arrangements were negotiated, normally by the parents of the couple. Both Peacock and Ó Suilleabháin were relatively old as grooms and were, therefore, in a position to conduct their own negotiations. If agreement was reached, then the marriage ceremony could follow very quickly. The ease with which it was possible to marry in Ireland, as outlined in Chapter 1, meant that most couples expected to marry very soon after the financial settlement had been agreed. As one group of priests explained in 1788, families were eager to have the ceremony completed as soon as agreement had been reached on the financial terms.[111]

---

[108] Ibid., pp. 174–5.   [109] McGrath, *Cinnlae Amhlaoibh Uí Shúileabháin*, ii, pp. 219–20.
[110] Ibid., p. 295.
[111] Reply of Dean Sherlock and five priests of St Catherine's parish, Dublin to Archbishop Troy, 23 Oct. 1788 (DDA, Troy Papers, Green File 29/36).

The Belfast-born medic and accoucheur, William Drennan, like Nicholas Peacock, took a long time to commit to marriage. He was in his mid-forties when he married Englishwoman Sarah Swanwick in 1800. Prior to that date, Drennan had experienced a number of aborted attempts at courtship that were partly due to his failure to engage an intermediary or to consult sufficiently with his family. He initially considered Belfast-based Margaret Jones as a possible spouse but encountered difficulties without an interlocutor to determine if she was interested in him as a husband. Drennan presented a pessimistic view of Margaret's body language and demeanour:

I met her eyes but seldom and when I did I thought I looked more readily than she... [The family's] invitation with Margaret's accompanying manner – translated – seems to be – we like you well enough as a calling acquaintance and as your silence for some time past seems to show that you have dropped all thoughts of a greater intimacy, we may venture safely now to give you all we can give you – friendship of a common acquaintance.

Drennan's sister, Martha, speculated that Margaret's 'very, very proper' behaviour might be because she had heard that Drennan was engaged to another woman or it might, indeed, have been an indication of 'real indifference'.[112] Eventually, Drennan summoned up the courage to write to Margaret but was quickly rebuffed. Margaret expressed surprise that anything in her behaviour had encouraged Drennan.[113] When Drennan met Sarah Swanwick, the woman whom he was eventually to marry, he again neglected to follow the accepted procedure for courtship. He did not make use of an intermediary but met Sarah through the social and business circle that he had developed in Dublin. The importance of keeping members of his family informed about his courtship of Sarah became clear when his sister expressed her anger at his failure to confide in her.[114]

More significantly for the successful progress of the courtship, Drennan's widowed mother refused to discuss any marriage settlement that she might agree for her son because the family knew so little about the woman that he claimed to love. Mrs Drennan might also have been influenced by an awareness that William had neither a large fortune nor significant family connections. It might have been considered reckless to select for a wife a woman who would bring him neither. Not surprisingly, therefore, the plans for the Drennan–Swanwick marriage stalled due to money matters. Sarah was clearly upset that William gave the

---

[112] Jean Agnew (ed.), *The Drennan–McTier Letters, 1776–1819* (3 vols., Dublin, 1998–2001), i, p. 195. Emphasis in the original.
[113] Ibid., i, p. 235.   [114] Ibid., i, pp. 563, 566, 567, 570; ii, pp. 40, 276–7.

impression that he withdrew his interest in her because she did not have a sufficient fortune.[115]

As was the case in the marriage between Nicholas Peacock and Catherine Chapman, the plans for the betrothal of William Drennan and Sarah Swanwick were renewed a number of years after the first approach failed. This time, however, family members made the initial approach. By that stage, William's family were eager to see him married even if it was to a woman without a large dowry. William's sister, Martha, and Sarah's cousin and her sister's sister-in-law, who lived in Dublin, discussed with their respective families how the couple could be brought together.[116] Once it was clear that both sides were agreed, the Irish family expected that the marriage ceremony would happen relatively quickly. William visited Sarah in England in October 1799 and was disappointed that he could not return immediately with her as his bride.[117] Sarah, adhering to the customs and norms of English society, insisted on a longer time gap between the agreement to marry and the ceremony. She travelled to Dublin in January 1800.[118] Within days of her arrival, Sarah and William were married in a private house in the presence of a Presbyterian minister and a small family group consisting of Sarah's relatives who were based in Dublin. Sarah's parents did not travel from England for the ceremony and none of Drennan's family was present.[119]

The experiences of individuals from the middling ranks of society such as Nicholas and Catherine Peacock, Amhlaoibh Ó Suilleabháin and William and Sarah Drennan, all demonstrate the important contribution of family and friends to a successful courtship. Above all, it was the view of the parents or guardians that mattered most. Although neither Peacock nor Ó Suilleabháin had to secure approval from their own parents, they both had to ensure the consent of their prospective bride's parents to the match. This was an essential part of the formal courtship ritual to be performed by a man. For her part, the woman was expected to inform her parents of any interest expressed by a young man. Sarah Swanwick, for example, passed William Drennan's first letter of interest in her to her parents.[120] Similarly, when Dorothea Herbert, the daughter of a Church of Ireland minister who lived in Carrick-on-Suir, County Tipperary, received a letter in 1785 from the Reverend Gwynn outlining his intentions, she handed it to her mother 'not daring to act uncouncel'd

---

[115] Agnew, *The Drennan–McTier Letters,* ii, pp. 417, 500.   [116] Ibid., pp. 499–508.
[117] Ibid., pp. 519–20. See also William Drennan's correspondence with Sarah Swanwick (PRONI, T581).
[118] Agnew, *The Drennan–McTier Letters* , ii, pp. 570–3.   [119] Ibid., p. 573.
[120] Ibid., p. 563.

Young and inexperienced as I was'.[121] Mrs Herbert sent the letter back by Dorothea's sister with a message that had Dorothea known what was in the letter she would not have opened it. This was a rebuke to Gwynn that he should have first consulted Dorothea's parents.[122] In 1828, when Myles John O'Reilly wrote his first courtship letter to Elizabeth Anne de la Poer Beresford, she passed the letter to her brother as her father, a clergyman, was away from home. In his response, Elizabeth's brother explained to O'Reilly that it was not appropriate for his sister to answer his letter as they had known each other for too short a time.[123] The necessity for securing the permission of parents or guardians for proposals of marriage was also emphasised in the testimonies presented in breach of promise cases, as we shall see in Chapter 5.

Children were conscious of the need to secure their parents' approval for a proposed marriage; the emotional rift caused by not having such support was unacceptable to many offspring. Strictly speaking, no clergyman could marry a couple without ensuring that both parties freely consented to the marriage and, if they were under age, had their parents' approval. The insistence of parents and other family members could, however, impose considerable pressure on the couple. Dorothea Herbert wrote of how her cousin, Fanny Blennerhasset, had refused her suitor seven times before finally agreeing to marry him. When the guests arrived for the wedding, however, 'the Bride Elect so piteously demanded a Respite that it was granted though all acknowledge she deserved none after her sevenfold refusal'.[124] As noted in Chapter 1, the Quaker community insisted that parents approved their children's choice of marriage partner and held the parent responsible if their son or daughter married someone unsuitable.[125] Mary Leadbeater noted the influence of parental choice in a letter to her cousin about the forthcoming marriage of an acquaintance:

I wish I could view her approaching nuptials (or to use an expression more adequate to my feelings on the occasion of her approaching sacrifice) with so much complacency as thou seems to do, I would willingly hope with thee that Abby would not give her hand unaccompanied by her heart to any man, but my dear cousin thou knows not what parental persuasion might be able to effect, I am sure had she been left to her own choice she would never have married William H.[126]

---

[121] Herbert, *Retrospections*, p. 138.   [122] Ibid., p. 139.
[123] John Beresford to Myles John O'Reilly ('History of the courtship and marriage of Myles John O'Reilly to Elizabeth Anne de la Poer Beresford', 1828–1829 (NLI, O'Reilly Manuscripts, no. 14).
[124] Herbert, *Retrospections*, pp. 125–6.   [125] See pp. 35–6.
[126] Cited in Kevin O'Neill, '"Pale and dejected, exhausted by the waste of sorrow": Courtship and the expression of emotion, Mary Shackleton, 1783–1791' in Willemijn Ruberg and Kristine Steenbergh (eds.), *Sexed Sentiments: Interdisciplinary Perspectives on Gender and Emotion* (Amsterdam, 2011), pp. 51–2.

When Leadbeater's own daughter, Deborah, contravened Quaker regulations to marry secretly her first cousin, Abraham, in a Church of Ireland service, Mary and her husband were reprimanded by the local Quaker community in Ballitore, County Kildare, for not exerting sufficient parental authority on their daughter's marriage choice.[127] As noted in Chapter 2, however, a young couple, such as Deborah and Abraham Shackleton, who were determined to marry, could nearly always find a clergyman or a couple beggar who would perform the ceremony without asking too many questions.

In 1749, Edward Synge, Bishop of Elphin, warned his teenage daughter, Alicia, of the dangers of a girl 'marrying her self', by which he meant a girl choosing her own marriage partner without consulting her family and friends. He told Alicia the story of a young woman who had married a man who was socially below her in economic status and had, thereby, forfeited a wealthy legacy from her uncle.[128]

Imagine then the Condition of such a young Woman ... educated with great care ... probably condemn'd to pass her days ... in a Caban ... her husband, as I am told, behaves himself very well to her. But it is not in his power to raise her or himself higher, or to provide better for her than his narrow fortune will allow. I can't help pitying her, tho' she has been her own Executioner...[129]

Synge may have been contemptuous of life in a 'Caban' but in rural farming families it was also the norm for parents or a guardian to identify a potential bride or groom for their sons and daughters and to appoint a relative or friend to make enquiries concerning the feasibility of a match. We have the most information on such arrangements for the nineteenth century although it is likely that family involvement was important throughout the period covered by this volume. In the families of large-tenant farmers, as Sean Connolly noted, the emphasis was on the benefit to the family of the marriage rather than the individual. Many of these matches were unromantic bargains. Peig Sayers complained about the undue influence of a dowry in relation to her brother in the late nineteenth century:

---

[127] Mary O'Dowd, 'Mary Leadbeater: Modern woman and Irish Quaker' in David Hayton and Andrew Holmes (eds.), *Ourselves Alone? Religion, Society and Politics in Eighteenth- and Nineteenth-Century Ireland: Essays Presented to S. J. Connolly* (Dublin, 2016), pp. 137–53.

[128] Marie-Louise Legg (ed.), *The Synge Letters. Bishop Edward Synge to His Daughter Alicia, Roscommon to Dublin, 1746–1752* (Dublin, 1996), pp. 155–6.

[129] Ibid.

Sean could have got many a fine girl to marry him but that wouldn't do his people at all for it wasn't a fine woman they wanted but money. Often Brighde would say with a snort of disgust that beauty didn't boil the pot. The old people cared for nothing but their own satisfaction even if that meant having the son troubled in his mind and tied to a good-for-nothing slattern for the rest of his days.[130]

A father or a widow whose son's marriage prospects depended on his inheriting all or part of the family holding, and whose daughter was similarly dependent on the provision of a suitable dowry, could clearly claim a substantial voice both in the timing of his children's marriages and in the choice of partner. Whether this power was exercised or not of course depended on the personalities of the parents and their expectations of what their children should and should not do. One woman, who was the daughter of a prosperous farmer, and married in 1880, articulated the significance of material wealth to the relationship: 'Father came in and gave me his blessing. He cared a great deal for my happiness and thought Richard and I were well suited to one another; besides which Richard's land and prospects were on a par with the dowry he would give with me'.[131] The Commissioners Inquiring into the Condition of the Poorer Classes in Ireland were told that if there was no land involved, in 1830s County Limerick, 'marriages are settled between the parties, often at fairs, but for those who have land, they are arranged by the parents'.[132]

A significant aspect of the courtship process was, of course, the negotiations and arrangement for the dowry, fortune or marriage portion that the woman brought to her new home. Even at the poorest economic level, some household goods might be exchanged on marriage, or there could be an agreement over the care of elderly parents if the father provided some land upon his son's marriage. Furthermore, as noted earlier, a poor woman's ability and willingness to beg could be attractive to an equally poor man who, traditionally, would not have been willing to beg himself. At all levels of society, therefore, marriage and material concerns were interlinked. It was also assumed that a courting couple was aware of the economic contribution that each would bring to the marriage. In 1860, a judge admonished a defendant for not inquiring about a woman's fortune, and other 'particulars' before he proposed to her and had discussions with her father. It was too late, he stated, to do so after the event and then discover that such matters were 'unsatisfactory'.[133]

---

[130] *Peig: The Autobiography of Peig Sayers* (Dublin, 1971), pp. 90–1.
[131] Mary Carbery, *The Farm by Lough Gur* (Cork, 1973), p. 261.
[132] Poor Enquiry, Appendix A, HC 1835, xxxii.   [133] *Belfast Newsletter*, 6 Dec. 1860.

Marriage Settlements

From the late seventeenth century, among wealthy landed and merchant families, negotiations for marriage normally included the drawing up of a formal, legally binding marriage settlement. The document provided for the exchange of money and property between the families of both partners to the marriage. The marriage settlement would note the dowry that the bride's father or guardian would pay the groom's father or guardian. In return the latter would agree the annuity to be given to the bride if she survived her husband. The amount of the annuity was calculated in relation to the size of the dowry. This was normally about 10 per cent. In other words, a dowry of £3,000 would yield an annuity of £300. The marriage settlement might also indicate the financial and property allocation for any children born to the couple. The normal practice was for the eldest son to inherit the bulk of the estate of his father, but younger sons were given cash sums or property that guaranteed them some financial security. The marriage settlement might also identify the marriage portion or dowry to be given to any daughters of the marriage.[134]

Although initially utilised only by families with considerable economic assets to control and distribute, by the early decades of the nineteenth century marriage settlements began to be employed by middle-class rural and urban families. Written agreements were also used by some families further down the social scale, particularly to make arrangements for elderly parents following the marriages of their children. The increased use of settlements across social classes formed part of the growing popularity of ensuring that inheritance issues were confirmed by legal documentation, which included, as we will discuss later, last wills and testaments.

A marriage settlement drawn up in Dublin in 1841 was typical of the kind of arrangement made in relatively wealthy farming families. The settlement for the proposed marriage of William Kain and Mary Kenny was agreed by their respective fathers. Mary had a dowry of £1,000 from her father while William was to take possession of farmland given to him by his father. The details of the land concerned was specified in the settlement. If Mary survived William, instead of an annuity, she was to have a life-time interest in the property. If there were children of the

---

[134] Deborah Wilson, *Women Marriage and Property in Wealthy Landed Families in Ireland, 1750–1850* (Manchester, 2009); Mary O'Dowd, *A History of Women in Ireland, 1500– 1800* (Harlow, 2005), pp. 83–6; Anthony Malcomson, *Pursuit of the Heiress: Aristocratic Marriage in Ireland, 1740–1840* (2nd ed., Belfast, 2006).

marriage then provision was made for them also. If there were no children, and if both partners died, then the property was to revert to the groom's two sisters. More immediately, William had to provide a £200 fortune for an unmarried sister, which was probably to come from the fortune brought by Mary. The settlement, like others of its kind, tried to cover all eventualities. The point was to safeguard the maintenance and support of the bride to be and any children of the marriage.[135]

Another settlement made in County Kerry in the early twentieth century noted what was to come to the couple from the groom's family on the payment of a dowry. The property consisted of 'the grass of six cows, five cows, horse cart tracking, household furniture, dairy utensils, farming implements and all other goods, cattle and chattels which may be on said lands and said dwelling house'. Further, it was stipulated in this settlement that while the groom's mother, Bridget Sullivan, a widow, lived, she was in charge of the household and that 'Michael Sullivan [groom] shall always preside in the dwelling house together with his said intended wife and shall be supported, maintained, kept and suitably clothed by the said Bridget Sullivan during her lifetime'. At the same time the settlement made it clear that both Michael Sullivan and his intended wife, Johanna, 'would work the farm jointly with the said Bridget Sullivan in the usual course of husbandry'.[136] Reflecting the possibly difficult position of a widow when a young wife joined the household, this settlement made clear that Bridget's position was protected and her situation agreed before the marriage took place. There was no ambiguity about her status. In other farmhouses, as we shall see, the widow's status was often less clear.[137]

By the early decades of the nineteenth century, the marriages of the offspring of tenant farmers with holdings of no more than six or eight acres might also involve a written agreement outlining the transfer of money and property. Petitions to the landlord or his agent from tenants on the Shirley estate in County Monaghan frequently refer to such agreements.[138] The size of the farms on the estate ranged from two to fifteen acres. The terms of the 'marriage articles' were negotiated between the fathers of the couple or, if either was dead, with another male relative.[139] The negotiators agreed on the amount of money or, in

---

[135] Settlement for marriage between Patrick Kain and Mary Kenny, 1841 (NAI, MS 999/22/2). For other examples see NAI, MS 999/30/3; 999/132/1; 999/138/4; 999/149/3.
[136] Cited from a private collection in Rhodes, *Women and the Family in Post-Famine Ireland*, p. 105.
[137] See Chapter 7 on marital relations.   [138] PRONI, Shirley Papers (D/3531/P).
[139] Occasionally a widow might negotiate on behalf of her daughter. See marriage settlement of Michael Marran and Mary Marran, 6 Sept. 1827 (PRONI, Shirley Papers, D/3531/P).

some cases, property, to be given by the bride's family to that of the groom and how many acres of land the newly married couple would have at their disposal and when they would secure the tenancy of the farm. The agreement would sometimes specify that the transfer of the farm would take place on the death of the father or that the father would give a portion of the farm to his son on marriage and bequeath the full tenancy to him in his will.[140]

In other cases, the father agreed that his son could take over the farm on marriage but that two or three acres would be reserved for himself and his wife. In 1842, for example, James Callan agreed to give a dowry or 'marriage portion' of £50 to Bryan Holland when Callan's daughter, Alice, married Holland's son, Thomas. Bryan Holland also agreed to give his son seven of the nine acres that made up the family farm, along with a mare, a foal and a cart. The agreement stipulated that Bryan would reserve the two remaining acres and a room and the kitchen in the farmhouse for himself and his wife.[141] The agreement thus ensured financial security for the newly married couple but also provided for aging parents, a concern that was also, as we have seen, important for labourers' families.

The landlord on the Shirley estate appears to have permitted such arrangements, but not all landlords were so benign, and they may have become less common in the decades after the Great Famine when landlords and large-tenant farmers aimed to consolidate rather than subdivide their landholdings. James Donnelly has noted the significance of securing land leases before making any marriage arrangements in post-Famine Ireland. He cited the observation of a tenant on the Jones' estate in County Cork, who took out a lease in the 1860s: 'I was unmarried then, and some people were match-making with me; they would not finish the match unless I had a lease, for they did not like the character of the landlord'.[142] Land agents could also use the opportunity of a tenant intending to marry to increase the rent. In 1887, the tenants on

---

[140] See, for example, the marriage settlement of Bridget Kieran and Owen Farnun, 4 Dec. 1845; petition of John Lannan, 15 March 1844; letter of Margaret Kearney, March 1845 (PRONI, Shirley Papers, D/3531/P).

[141] Marriage settlement of Thomas Holland and Alice Callan, 14 Oct. 1842 (PRONI, Shirley Papers, D/3531/P, Box 1). For other similar examples see Petitions of Michael Marrin, 28 April 1843; Anne Daly, 13 Feb. 1844; George Kernan, 22 Jan. 1845; William Power, 1 March 1845 (PRONI, Shirley Papers, D/3531/P, Box 1). The Life Association of Scotland (with Irish office in Upper-Sackville street), advertised that you could insure yourself and be protected from 'provisions under marriage settlements etc.' (*Irish Times*, 17 Nov. 1859).

[142] James S. Donnelly, Jr., *The Land and the People of Nineteenth-Century Cork: The Rural Economy and the Land Question* (London, 1975), p. 225.

the Devonshire estate complained that 'no parent was allowed the exercise of his right ... to get his son or daughter married without the consent and sanction of the agent, which was invariably withheld unless the new tenant consented to a considerable increase of the rent ...'.[143] Such approval appears to have been necessary on a number of estates, a consideration that had to be kept in mind when dowries were arranged.

Dowries

Despite the increase in the use of written marriage settlements, most families did not agree a settlement penned by a lawyer. Instead, the dowry was agreed through handshakes and verbal approval. Central to the agreement was, of course, the amount of the dowry to be given to the groom's family by the bride's. As we have seen, details of dowries surface in estate papers. They are also referenced in wills and reports of legal cases involving disputes about inheritance, the use of land and petitions for separation. While we know that dowries were very much part of the marriage system in pre- and post-Famine Ireland, we still do not have a comprehensive understanding of how dowries were used, or the value of dowries over time in different parts of Ireland and in relation to different classes. What is clear from looking at the available archival and printed sources is that a dowry, or fortune, was expected in marriages: lack of a dowry, or what was believed to be an insufficient dowry, was considered grounds for ending a courtship; and whatever its value the dowry was often a source of marital strife and violence in the home.

Dowry Amounts

In rural families in the late seventeenth century, dowries could still consist of farm animals and household goods rather than a cash sum. In 1682, for example, Ownye Ny Teig from County Clare agreed to provide her future husband, Laughline O'Hykie, with eight in-calf cows 'and all such cattle as she shall be able to get among her friends'. The gathering of some household goods and stock remained a common way of collecting a suitable dowry in rural Ireland into the eighteenth century.[144]

The evidence of wills can enable us to identify what fathers, and some mothers, left their unmarried daughters as marriage portions. Until the

---

[143] Tenants' memorial to the Duke of Devonshire, 4 Dec. 1885 (*Cork Constitution*, 18 Dec. 1885). Cited in Donnelly, *The Land and the People*, p. 225.

[144] O'Dowd, *History of Women*, pp. 86–7.

middle decades of the nineteenth century, making a will was, however, an occupation of the wealthy. Men and women who composed their last will and testament in the eighteenth century usually had considerable assets to be distributed after their deaths. Legacies to children included property, goods and cash sums that could form the basis for a dowry. In 1718, Ralph Evans, a bricklayer in Dublin distributed his sizeable property portfolio among his children, leaving his daughters, as well as his sons, houses in the city centre.[145] In 1725, Benjamin McDowell, a linen merchant from Rathmore, County Antrim, bequeathed to his two unmarried daughters the money left after his debts had been paid as well as 'all my cows, horses, cattle and other effects whatsoever' and a lease of property and the profits of a mill, to be equally divided between them.[146] It is impossible to chart the exact size of eighteenth-century dowries from the evidence of wills, not just because of the combination of cash with other goods and property but also because the will may represent only part of the documentation that outlined the distribution of the testator's property. Many testators would also have been bound by marriage settlements arranged with children or with their wife's family before they married. Cash provisions for unmarried daughters in eighteenth-century wills varied enormously from small bequests of £5 to large sums of £1,000 and more. In 1723, for example, Richard Kearney, a farmer in County Tipperary, left to his daughter, Anstis, £55 'to maintain her and find her in cloise until she will marry and to give it to her when she wants it'. When she married, Anstis was to have an additional £5 provided she married with the consent of her mother and her brother.[147]

By the 1850s, more middle-class farmers and merchants began to make wills, and the provisions that parents made for unmarried daughters enable us to get a firmer idea of the range of dowry payments at that time. A survey of wills from County Down from the 1830s through to the 1850s indicates that marriage portions for daughters ranged from £20 to £60, with an average sum of £40.[148] These figures match the sums noted in the petitions from the early nineteenth-century Shirley estate in the decades before the Famine. The amounts of the forty-four dowries cited ranged from £10 to £600, but thirty-three (75 per cent) were under £50 and the average sum was £40. Only three dowries were over £70 at £100, £212 and £600 respectively.[149] Twenty to thirty years later in

[145] Will of Ralph Evans, Senior, 10 Dec. 1717 (Registry of Deeds, Dublin, 23/213/13152).
[146] Will of Benjamin McDowell, 2 Dec. 1725 (NAI, MFGS 41/04/2).
[147] Will of Richard Kearney, 4 March 1723 (NAI, MFGS 41/04/2).
[148] Based on analysis of wills in NAI, MFGS 41/8.
[149] PRONI, Shirley Papers, D/3531/P.

the western counties of Galway, Leitrim and Mayo, bequests by fathers to unmarried daughters ranged from £120 to £500 with an average of £211.[150] In County Wexford at the same date, the range was from £50 to £500 with an average of £216.[151] Information from the wills we have investigated suggests, therefore, that the cash sum expected for a successful marriage was gradually rising in the nineteenth century, particularly among the middling sections of rural and urban society. In addition, fathers continued to give daughters cash as well as stock and household goods to assist with the setting up of a new home. In 1836, for example, Robert Gourley, a farmer in Comber, County Down, left his daughter, Mary, £20 in cash as well as a 'bed and bedding', a press and her spinning wheel.[152] The cash sum provided in a dowry should, of course, be related to the acreage of the father's farm and other assets that he might possess. Cormac Ó Grada calculated the value of dowries in relation to the total value of an estate when probate was complete. In contrast to our findings, he estimated that the relative value of dowries decreased over the nineteenth century and he suggested that the decrease in the amount paid by a family for a daughter's dowry was a by-product of the emigration of large numbers of single women from rural Ireland. Farmers could offer less for the marriage of a daughter who remained at home, knowing that they were unlikely to be outbid by a rival offer. Ó Grada argues that this paradoxically may indicate a positive development for Irish women, as fewer were forced into arranged marriages.[153] On the other hand, a married woman's status in the home was closely linked to the dowry that she brought on marriage, and there had to be some financial equivalency between the value of the bride's dowry and the farm where she was to reside.

Fathers also used wills to ensure that their children (daughters, in particular) married according to their wishes or those of their wives or executors. Some left very specific instructions. In 1715, for example, Abraham Watkins from Cork bequeathed £100 to his daughter as a marriage portion along with an annuity of £8 after her mother's death. Watkins stipulated, however, that if she married 'Derby Cartie, the fiddler' she was not to get 'one penny portion'.[154] Most men left the approval of their daughters' marriages to their widow and their eldest son

---

[150] Based on an analysis of wills in NAI, MFGS 41/38B; NAI, MFGS 41/47; NAI, MFGS 41/15.

[151] Based on an analysis of wills in NAI, MFGS 41/42.

[152] Will of Robert Gourley, 20 March 1836 (NAI, MFGS 41/8).

[153] Cormac Ó Grada, *Ireland before and after the Famine: Explorations in Economic History, 1800–1925* (Manchester, 1988), pp. 165–9.

[154] Will of Abraham Watkins, 12 July 1715 (Registry of Deeds, Dublin, 24/92/13174).

or to the executors of the estate. In 1850, John Duncan, a grocer from Comber in County Down, bequeathed £50 to each of his six daughters, to be given to them on their marriage provided that their chosen partner was approved by his widow and executors. If any of the daughters married without their mother's approval, their portion was to be redistributed as their mother and executors deemed appropriate.[155] Similarly, in 1864, George Taylor of County Sligo directed that his son was to pay his two sisters £100 each when they married with their brother's consent. Without his consent they were to receive no dowry.[156]

As a dowry of some kind, however small, was considered essential for a satisfactory match, it is not surprising that charities provided assistance for poor families. Most, however, catered for very small numbers of women and successful applicants had to meet specific criteria. In his will of 1792, for example, Thomas Charleton bequeathed property to fund marriage portions of £6.16s 6d to be given to 'the son of any day labourer of Counties Meath and Longford, being at the time of marriage between the ages of 15 and 30, and marrying the daughter of any day labourer of Counties Meath and Longford, being at the time of marriage between the ages of 15 and 40'. The fund was only open to members of the Church of Ireland and, given the size of the dowries distributed, was aimed at the very poorest group in society.[157] It was for this reason that philanthropists such as Mary Leadbeater urged young men and women to save for their marriages.[158]

Fortunes, Dowries and Negotiations

The legal testimonies given in breach of promise cases provide contextual detail on the negotiations involved in agreeing a dowry, which could involve members of both families and 'friends' who were usually members of the extended family. Juries were sympathetic to the expectations that men had of the fortune or dowry that women might bring to a marriage. In an unusual case of a man initiating a breach of promise to marry case, Patrick Quail sued John Murray and his wife Elizabeth in 1852. Quail was twenty-eight years old, and had a small farm of twenty-five acres in County Meath, while Bridget Murray's father held a farm about the same size in County Cavan. The latter had three daughters and

---

155 NAI, MFGS 41/8.
156 NAI, MFGS 41/47 Will Books Various Districts 1865–1883.
157 https://moxhamireland.wordpress.com/2016/07/21/charltons-endowment-charitable-trust-fund-marriage-certificates/
158 See, for example, Leadbeater, *Cottage Dialogues among the Irish Peasantry*, pp. 74–5, 81–87.

it was claimed that he intended to marry Bridget off 'advantageously ... with the least possible expense to himself in the item of her fortune'. Patrick and Bridget met in 1848 at the house of Quail's uncle, whose wife was a cousin of Bridget's, and he told the court:

there was some match-making gone on with; but the matter was deferred to a subsequent meeting, which took place in a public house, in the town of Kingscourt ... When the fortune was spoken of the old man offered £50, £25 in hand, and the rest in future payments.[159]

The couple got on well together, met numerous times and a wedding date was set for 18 August 1851. On the morning arranged for the wedding, Quail was informed by his proposed bride's father that the wedding was cancelled and that his daughter now intended to marry John Murray. It was claimed by the lucky groom's brother that the father had persuaded his daughter to marry Murray as he was 'richer' than Quail. Quail gave the father a bill for £7. 8s. 2d. for the costs he had incurred in preparing for the wedding. The jury recognised the justice of Quail's case and awarded him £25 damages.[160] The families were evidently in similar financial circumstances and all matters had been agreed before the marriage was to take place. In awarding him £25 the jury were also providing him with half the marriage portion. What is not clear is what the bride-to-be thought of the situation, or whether she had any say in either of these proposed marriages.

In 1906, Julia Brannigan, a farmer's daughter from Brittas in County Louth, sued Patrick Howell for £500. The case revealed the haggling that could take place in the negotiations for the dowry. Howell claimed in court that any promise of marriage was conditional on his receiving £250 as a marriage portion, which, in this case had not been fulfilled. Brannigan had offered a fortune of £200, and Howell alleged that he had initially demanded a dowry of £300 but had subsequently reduced it to £250. Her brother then offered £225, which Brannigan claimed Howell had accepted. But the defendant was adamant that he would take no less than £250 as he required that amount to pay off his debts. The jury awarded the plaintiff £30, a relatively small amount given the claim made. This award recognised that Brannigan had a case but also suggested that it was acceptable for Howell to demand a substantial dowry relative to the wealth of the intended bride.[161]

Women without access to a dowry were in a precarious position when it came to identifying a marriage partner. In the early 1870s, James Farrelly told Anne Carroll, very soon after meeting her, that he was in

---

[159] *Belfast Newsletter*, 6 Feb. 1852.   [160] Ibid.   [161] *Irish Times*, 28 April 1906.

love with her. The pair lived in Bray, County Wicklow, and there was correspondence between them amounting to eighteen letters. In one letter he inquired after her fortune and she responded that she did not have one and had not the means to acquire one. He wrote to ask whether her 'friends' would provide a fortune and then he asked her to come to Dublin and apologised for talking about money. The correspondence ended and he married someone else who had an acceptable dowry of £50. In court, Farrelly denied that a promise to marry had been made and said it was conditional on Carroll getting a fortune. He admitted to the jury that 'I was looking for money and that was the reason why I corresponded with the girl'. His father did not know of his courtship, which, as noted already, in normal circumstances would have been frowned on. We do not know what Carroll's background was, but the fact that she had no fortune to bring to a marriage suggests a lower-class status. Farrelly said that he would have married her for £100 or even for £50, which he had received from his new bride. He admitted to telling Carroll that he loved her on first meeting her, but 'there was no talk of money then'. He lost the case and Carroll was awarded £40, which may very well have afforded her a dowry.[162]

The haggling and negotiations for a dowry that was acceptable to both families could be lengthy and might end in failure if a compromise could not be agreed. In 1860, John McGarry was courting Marianne Delany and determined to marry her. McGarry asked a cousin formally to approach her father for permission. An interview was arranged with the latter and money was discussed. McGarry had £5,000 (£2,000 in the business and the rest in Scottish securities) and asked for £1,000. Delany, who was a pawnbroker with shops in Dublin, demurred and thinking of his large family of four daughters and one son, offered £700 to McGarry, £300 on the wedding day, £200 two years later and £200 on death. This kind of staggered payment was relatively common in marriage negotiations. The birth of a child, for instance, was sometimes a milestone for the payment of a second instalment. In this case McGarry pressed for £1,000. Delany observed, 'you are like a man who was bargaining for a sheep or a cow; is it my daughter you want or is it money?' McGarry still insisted on £1,000 with Delany refusing to offer this amount, and after some negotiations with the defendant's solicitor the proposed marriage was cancelled. The defendant, when sued for breach of promise to marry, did not offer any defence in court but had his barrister ask the plaintiff's father to allow him still to marry his daughter. The father, responding

---

[162] *Irish Times*, 4 Dec. 1874.

through his barrister, stated he 'would rather die first'. The jury upheld Marianne Delany's case and awarded £500 damages.[163]

The all male juries in breach of promise cases understood the financial and economic necessity of women to marry, and even where economic motives were blatantly obvious they still awarded substantial damages. In 1897 Catherine Darcy, 'a young lady of prepossessing appearance' in her early twenties sued Terence Dunne, a man of 'mature age'. Darcy had only spoken to Dunne once, before she, her father and uncle went to Portumna and met the defendant, his sister and uncle. They all went into a private room in a public house. Darcy was asked whether she was satisfied with Dunne and she said she was although she had only met him once before. At the meeting Dunne produced a cheque for £450 and asked the plaintiff's father what he would offer as her fortune. Her father suggested £50. Dunne wanted £60, but then accepted the £50. The wedding date was set; the plaintiff spent £15 on her wedding trousseau. The couple were to go 'half in half with the marriage money'; her side were to have twenty guests while the defendant was to have twenty-four. Subsequently, Darcy received a letter from Dunne calling off the wedding. In court she admitted Dunne was an old man but that she was willing to marry him. When asked whether she was anxious to marry him she replied 'I was'. When asked why, she replied that he 'was well off'. The barrister then asked whether it was the £450 or Dunne that she was marrying and she responded she was 'marrying both'. Dunne claimed he broke off the engagement because the marriage money had not been paid. However, it appeared that the fortune was to be paid on the morning of the wedding. Dunne's defence was, therefore, not accepted by the jury.[164]

The position of siblings within the household could also shape the dowry discussions. In a breach of promise to marry case in 1892, it was reported that the male defendant, from County Cork, and some friends proceeded to the plaintiff's house in Farranfore, County Kerry, where a match was proposed 'as was the custom of the country'. It was agreed that the defendant should get the plaintiff's father's farm on condition of paying over a sum of money. It was noted that the match-making 'went on for some hours', and when the terms were finally agreed upon, the woman's brother said if he did not get £80 for himself no one should come near the farm. On hearing this the defendant broke off the negotiations. The plaintiff claimed that further negotiations began later that year but with all the marriage arrangements made the

---

[163] *Irish Times*, 4 Dec. 1860; *Freeman's Journal*, 5 Dec. 1860.
[164] The jury awarded Darcy £100. *Freeman's Journal*, 8 April 1897.

defendant did not turn up on the wedding day.[165] In other cases, the father of the prospective bride had to balance the amount of the dowry demanded by her suitor against the cash sums to be set aside for other daughters.[166]

Dowry Problems

The centrality of the dowry for both families as well as for the married couple's financial security meant that it was important that both sides upheld the commitments agreed in the negotiations. Unpaid or partially paid dowries could lead to considerable tension and arguments within and between families. Court proceedings tell stories of angry husbands taking goods from the homes of their fathers-in-law when the full dowry was not paid.[167] Refusing to pay a dowry in full would surely have been the cause of much domestic strife. It is difficult to know how common it was for dowries not to be paid, or at least not to be paid in full, or what the consequences were of non-payment. Anecdotal evidence suggests that a wife might be sent back to her family when a dowry was not paid.[168] It is also clear that unpaid dowries could result in violent conflict within and between families.

In 1892, Michael Conroy of Ferbane, County Offaly sued P. W. Corrigan for £44, the amount of eleven monthly instalments due under a marriage agreement made in July 1891. The plaintiff married the daughter of a man called Michael Fox, but only on the condition that he got a £50 fortune. Fox could not pay at once, so Corrigan went as surety for the payments. No payments were made. Fox said he had given a watch worth £6 and a cart worth £30 to his son-in-law and he wanted that deducted from the £50. The plaintiff said the cart and the watch were no use to him and he did not accept them as a set-off against the money. Corrigan said he would pay the money, but thought credit should be given for the watch and cart. The recorder ordered that the

---

[165] *Freeman's Journal*, 22 April 1892. The plaintiffs are almost always women. In this instance no names were provided and the case was postponed until June 1892. The outcome of the case is unknown, and there appears to be no further report of the case which suggests that it may have been settled outside of court.

[166] See, for example, the breach of promise case reported in *Irish Times*, 4 Feb. 1873; *Belfast Newsletter*, 4 Feb. 1873; *Freeman's Journal*, 4 Feb. 1873.

[167] See, for example, the case of Thomas Coughlan who was sentenced to twelve months' imprisonment for removing some cows from his father-in-law's land (NAI, CRF 1843 C31).

[168] David Fitzpatrick, 'Divorce and separation in modern Irish history', *Past and Present*, 114 (1987), 172–96.

watch and cart be returned and he would then issue a certificate ordering the full amount be paid at £5 a month.[169]

Some parents regretted handing over property to their children's spouses. As noted already, in marriage agreements and wills a father or husband might try to secure the position of a widow or new bride by noting in writing the expectation they had of the status of that individual in the household of the newly married couple. Whether such settlements shaped people's subsequent behaviour is unclear, but what is evident is the belief that certain conditions, such as the loss of status of a widow or widower, could have a material impact on that individual in a household. The older generation might find it impossible to give up their power to a son or son-in-law when a new bride entered the family home. The result could be not just a private family dispute but a violent disagreement which ended in fatalities. In 1904 in County Mayo, Edward Hopkins, a farmer aged thirty-two, was shot dead by his father James. Edward had married two years previously and had been promised half the farm from his father, but afterwards the father refused to give it up. Edward sued him and won £10 for the losses sustained. The father then tried to have Edward evicted from the house but the county court judge determined that he should give over half the house. In April, some cattle were seized to pay the decree, but James Junior, a younger brother, claimed that they were his and they were returned. More cattle were seized a few days before, and this brought matters to a crisis. The gun used to kill Edward belonged to James Junior, and was kept in a shop some distance from the farm. It was believed that it was taken by the father with his son's connivance. They were both arrested and committed for trial.[170]

Conclusion

One of the most significant changes that gradually took place in the eighteenth and nineteenth centuries in terms of individuals meeting a potential spouse was the expansion in the spatial range in which the search took place. The move into towns and cities broadened the spaces for courtship. Urbanisation and modernisation changed the expectations of what men and women wanted from marriage. The independent working woman or man was confident enough to advertise his or her requirements while, in the early twentieth century, compatibility rather than parental choice predominated. More generally, the increased

[169] *Irish Times*, 23 July 1892.   [170] *Irish Times*, 19 March 1904.

access of girls to education raised their expectations of what they wanted from life and many opted not to spend it in the farming community of their parents.

From the seventeenth through to the early twentieth century, financial and material considerations formed a central part of the negotiations for probably the majority of marriages. Marriage was used by families as a means to accumulate additional economic resources or to retain land within a particular family. The size of a dowry could vary, depending on class, family income and the numbers of daughters requiring a marriage portion. The perception that the dowry and arranged marriages became more pervasive in post-Famine Ireland is, however, not supported by the evidence that we have examined. From the seventeenth through to the early decades of the twentieth century, fathers and guardians from the middling ranks of society were aware of the need to provide a dowry or marriage portion for their daughters. Further down the social scale a woman might offer household goods or even her own labour. Dowries, whatever shape they took, made marriages an explicit business deal. Assets, and the rights brought with them, provided the expectation of a wife's control of her own household, the support of a husband and the safety of a family unit in which all might prosper.

Marriages, of course, did not always work out like this in reality, but dowry payments acknowledged the reality of the financial basis of marriage. Exploring the history of dowries demonstrates, therefore, that money or its equivalent was, for most of the period, arguably the most important feature in arranging a marriage but, as we will see in the following chapters, it was not the only consideration.

4   Courtship Behaviour

In 1869, the marriage of Daniel Coghlan and Ellen McCarthy was negotiated around the kitchen table in Coghlan's family home, situated in the hinterland of Skibbereen, County Cork. Present were members of both families who shared dinner and, probably, also whiskey. The two fathers negotiated a suitable marriage settlement. Also at the meal was Thomas O'Brien, a friend of both families, who had acted as the intermediary. The marriage negotiations fell through and Daniel sued Ellen for breach of promise. During the court case, the questioning between O'Brien and Mr Clarke, the barrister for Ellen McCarthy, revealed the short courtship of the couple who had only met the evening of the aforementioned dinner:

MR CLARKE: They had at that time ample opportunity of becoming acquainted with one another?
WITNESS: Yes. They first sat at one side of the table and they were removed to the other side of the table and remained together again. At least I found them so removed, after I had absented myself for a while.
MR CLARKE: Did they remain up all night?
WITNESS: I left them at one side of the table and when I came back again they were at the other side of the table.
MR CLARKE: Still together, like love birds?
WITNESS: Still together.[1]

As noted in the previous chapter, the courtships of couples in nineteenth-century rural Ireland were sometimes brief and lacking in romance, if not physical closeness. Yet, other evidence presented in breach of promise suits indicates that many courtships, particularly in middle-class families, were of a longer duration and followed agreed forms of behaviour that signalled to the couple's families and the wider local community that a formal courtship was in process. Courtships were indicated by suitors being known and acknowledged by the family, mainly through visits by

[1] *Irish Times*, 30 July 1869. See also Katie Barclay, 'Place and power in Irish farms at the end of the nineteenth century', *Women's History Review*, 21, 4 (Sept. 2012), 581–2.

Illustration 4.1 The illustration depicts a courting couple. The man is visiting the woman's home. Her mother, clearly pleased with the match, has set the table for tea. There may be some implied sexuality in the exaggerated size of the man, the settle bed behind the couple and the apple that the younger sister is eating.

136

the man to his intended bride's home; by the community's recognition that the couple's behaviour in public demonstrated that they were courting; and by the exchange of gifts, tokens and letters.

In 1819, Elizabeth Berwick sued a Mr Cryne for breach of promise. She owned a school in Dun Laoghaire and the defendant was a butcher who lived nearby. The newspaper report of the subsequent court proceedings suggested that Cryne perceived that a match with Berwick would help 'promote his domestic happiness' as well as his business. Neighbours commented on how Cryne 'continually sought [Berwick's] company … and in fact the whole village had long laid down that the marriage would soon take place, as they were inseparable'. They also noted that the couple went together to chapel every Sunday in the same vehicle, and knelt together side by side. One witness testified that when on one occasion he passed Berwick's house, he saw the defendant mending the bolt on a window shutter.[2] Although we have no intimate details of this courtship, for the local population the ways in which this couple presented themselves in public – attending chapel together, and the act of house maintenance – all signalled an inevitable marriage.

James Cassidy, who ran a public house in Dublin, gave precise details about his unusually long courtship to the court. He testified that he had known the plaintiff, Mary Josephine Brennan, for ten years when he had worked as a vintner's assistant. He courted her for four years until 1892. He saw her twice on Sundays, 12:30–1:30 p.m. and 8:30–11 p.m., and then a couple of times during the week. In the day, he saw her in his father's shop and at night he would meet her there and go for a walk, weather permitting; if not, they retired to the house and played cards or some other amusement. Over the duration of the courtship, she gave him presents, including a rosary beads, but he did not return these when the relationship ended. He also received a plait of her hair 'to wear next to your heart'. Despite having courted Brennan for four years, when Cassidy's employer died, he married his widow, whom he had courted for three to four months.[3]

The witnessing of physical touch, whether it was kissing, which appears to have been the most intimate act to perform in public, or sitting on someone's knee, was used by barristers in breach of promise cases as clear evidence that a relationship existed between a couple. In 1894, when Thomas Boyd was sued by Susan McCormick, he acknowledged that she had often sat on his knee.[4] Catherine Murphy and James Walsh had known each other since they were children. When they were

---

[2] *Ennis Chronicle*, 27 July1819.   [3] *Irish Times*, 14–15 Feb. 1894.
[4] *Irish Times*, 27 July 1892; *Freeman's Journal*, 27 July 1892.

both teenagers, James, fulfilling the wishes of his dead father, proposed to Catherine and she accepted. He 'shook her by the hand and kissed her, and said she was as much his wife as if they had stood before a priest'. She told the court that following the proposal he had 'come in once and sent in for me and wanted to kiss me. I said the priest would kill me if I allowed him, and he said was I not his own, and I said I could not let him.'[5] Catherine's reticence may have been due to her youth and also to the increasingly strong policing of sexual morality by the Catholic clergy in post-Famine Ireland.[6] In 1883, when Margaret O'Halloran was asked by her barrister whether John Ryan, whom she was suing for reneging on his proposal of marriage, had kissed her, she hesitated before answering yes and the barrister immediately made it clear, in case any slight was given to her character, that since the couple were engaged this was a perfectly respectable thing to have done.[7]

As literacy became more widespread, letter writing was another common – albeit more private – ritual of courtship. As indicated in Chapter 3, John Black and Jane Eccles preserved their courtship correspondence. When Robert Emmet was arrested for rebellion in 1803, the prison authorities found love letters from Sarah Curran on his person. They were not signed but a letter that Emmet wrote from prison in which he referred to 'Sarah' was intercepted and, as a consequence, the Curran house in Rathfarnham, Dublin, was raided by the army. More letters from Emmet were found despite the attempt by Sarah's sister, Amelia, to burn a bundle of love letters kept by Sarah.[8]

Another well-known political leader, Daniel O'Connell, also courted his future wife, Mary, through a regular correspondence. As Daniel's letters to Mary testify, the rhetoric of courting letters became increasingly romantic in the early nineteenth century:

I have received many letters from you and you certainly cannot conceive what pleasure they afford me, my sweet, my delightful darling. You are my comfort, and the soother of my cares … in absence you are present in my imagination, and your image like a fairy vision visits my dreams and makes my sleep blessed. My love, you are dearer to my heart than ever was woman to man.[9]

In breach of promise court cases, the letters of plaintiffs and defendants were read out in court, much to the amusement of the public and the embarrassment of their authors. Many of the letters were emotional and

---

[5] *Irish Times*, 15 July 1873; *Belfast Newsletter*, 16 July 1873.
[6] *Belfast Newsletter*, 18 Dec. 1879.   [7] *Freeman's Journal*, 26 July 1883.
[8] Patrick Geoghegan, *Robert Emmet: A Life* (Dublin, 2002), pp. 28–9.
[9] Daniel O'Connell to Mary O'Connell, 24 Jan. 1801 in Maurice O'Connell (ed.), *The Correspondence of Daniel O'Connell* (8 vols., Dublin, 1971–1980), i, 1792–1814, p. 41.

intimate in style. Susan Harris made her feelings plain to Thomas Boyd when she wrote: 'I wish I could put myself in the envelope, for I never thought so much in my life. Although you are absent you dwell in my heart. I think of you most when the moon shines brightly. I close with fond love. – Yours to death Susan Harris'.[10]

There were eighty to ninety letters presented as evidence in the case of Anna Sutton and William Nolan. They were both from business families in Cork and Limerick and it was noted in court that it was through a 'distant connection' that Anna and William had met. At the end of one of William's letters there were thirty or forty crosses 'which counsel was informed meant kisses', a comment that brought mirth to the court. In another letter William wrote:

need I tell you how I love you – how every day strengthens that love? No: it is needless, for it has become part of my being to cherish you in my heart of hearts, and to love you with a love that death can only efface. I remain dearest and loved Anna ever your own faithful and loving, Willie.

William also quoted the poet, Thomas Moore, in his letters to Anna, another reflection of the increased use of romantic language of the late nineteenth century.[11]

A collection of 104 letters survive of the courting correspondence of Sarah (Sis) Whelan to her future husband, Thomas (Tom) Eades over a three-year period between 1898 and 1901. Sis initially worked as a shop assistant in a drapery shop in Birr, County Offaly, but in 1899 moved to a shop in Bunclody, County Wexford. Tom was employed in a hardware store in Birr.[12] Although Sis's employer disapproved of his female employees having friendships with young men, he did not, according to Sis, 'mind about the letters'.[13] The letters were usually short and focused on arrangements for meetings or Sis's enjoyment of time spent with Tom. They wrote every few days to one another and through the letters it is possible to trace the progress of their courtship and their growing affection for one another. The couple appear to have met at a Methodist meeting, and going to church activities together remained an important part of their courtship. In 1900, Tom cycled the seventy-three miles from Birr to Bunclody to spend the day with Sis and attend a watchnight service in the Methodist chapel.[14]

---

[10] *Irish Times*, 27 July 1892; *Freeman's Journal*, 27 July 1892.
[11] *Irish Times*, 22 March 1879; *Freeman's Journal*, 22 March 1879, 10 June 1890.
[12] Rosemary Raughter (ed.), '"Your own for ever, Sis": Letters to Parsonstown, 1898–1903', *Bulletin of the Methodist Historical Society of Ireland*, 22, 1 (2017), 36–116.
[13] Ibid., 59.   [14] Ibid., 67–8.

If the letters of Sis Whelan and Tom Eades document their intimacy and affection for one another, other courtship letters reveal the lack of romance in the relationship. In a breach of promise case in 1905, the plaintiff, Ellie Gorry, addressed the defendant as 'Dear Mr. Maguire', with the barrister commenting there was 'not much love in it'. The account of the courtship at the trial described how the Gorrys and Maguires were neighbours and that Ellie's sister was married to Laurence Maguire's brother. The marriage between them was agreed by both families. Ellie admitted that she had not verbally given her agreement to the marriage but that her sister had said: 'Silence gives consent'. When Ellie was questioned about Laurence only visiting on Sundays, and then not when it rained, she said rather forlornly that she thought he was marrying her for herself and not the money.[15]

Gift giving was another important element in the ritual of courtship. Gifts included rings, which were taken to mean a marriage had been proposed, and other pieces of jewellery as well as a variety of other items. By the end of the nineteenth century photographs were often swapped between couples.[16] Tom Eades, for example, sent Sis Whelan at different times several bunches of flowers, boxes of apples and a bracelet. Sis sent him a photo of herself.[17] Newspaper advertisements for Valentine cards began in the 1850s, revealing the new consumerism around the material culture of courtship and 'romantic' relations. In 1862, the Dublin stationery and bookshop, J. Wiseheart and Sons announced that they would stay open late on 14 February due to the increased demand for Valentine cards. Among the items that they advertised were 'Marriage Certificates, Love Summonses and Bank of Love Notes'.[18] Gifts of rings prior to marriage were also increasingly considered public manifestations of the couple's commitment. Gemstone engagement rings began to make an appearance in the 1880s and by the early twentieth century, diamond engagement rings were becoming the norm among those who could afford them.[19] Rings and other gifts were expected to be returned if the relationship broke down. Robert Tennent, however, retained the locks of hair that he collected from thirteen different women in the years from 1818 to 1827. Two were from Hannah McGee who sent Tennent one half of a broken ring when she broke off their relationship under parental

---

[15] *Irish Times*, 13 Feb. 1905.   [16] See for instance, *Freeman's Journal*, 9 Nov. 1893.
[17] Raughter, '"Your own for ever, Sis"', 47, 53, 57, 60, 63, 74, 103.
[18] *Freeman's Journal*, 13 Feb. 1862. See also ibid., 13 Feb. 1851; 14 Feb. 1859; *Cork Examiner*, 8 Feb. 1864, 6 Feb. 1866; *Waterford News and Star*, 17 Feb. 1865.
[19] Linda Ballard, *Forgetting Frolic: Marriage Traditions in Ireland* (Belfast, 1998), p. 44.

pressure. She expressed a vague hope that they, like the ring, might be joined together at some stage in the future.[20]

The number and quality of the gifts exchanged between couples were taken as evidence of the seriousness of the relationship. James Cassidy attempted to downplay the significance of his friendship with Mary Josephine Brennan by suggesting that the gifts he had received from her were 'very small'.[21] By contrast, Mary O'Connell complained that Daniel's gifts to her were too extravagant. They included, in addition to his portrait and a lock of his hair, jewellery and items of expensive clothing. Mary's correspondence communicates her sense of anxiety that O'Connell was not only sending her courtship gifts but attempting to dress her in a manner that he found acceptable.[22]

Secret Courtships

The public displays of courtship enabled the parents of the couple to supervise their conduct. Not all courtships, however, proceeded in public or with the approval of the couples' parents. Parental disapproval did not always end a budding relationship. Instead, a courtship might proceed in secret with friends and family called on to provide places where the couple could meet without the knowledge of parents or guardians. When William Drennan thought to meet with Margaret Jones in private to ascertain her feelings, he asked his sister, Martha, to find out when she would be travelling to Dublin; he preferred not to meet with her in Belfast because he suspected that her father might not approve of him as a potential son-in-law. Some years later, when William initiated his plan to court Sarah Swanwick, he urged, Martha to encourage Sarah's sister to invite her to Dublin as he considered his going to England to visit her in her parents' house, 'imprudent'.[23] Similarly, when law student James Emmerson began to court Letitia Tennent in the early nineteenth century, it was also without her father's knowledge. The couple met in the Belfast homes of friends and family, including her

---

[20] PRONI, D1748/G/802/1–17; D1748/G/407/6. The authors are grateful to Dr Leanne Calvert for these references. On Tennent's female friendships before marriage, see Jonathan Jeffrey Wright, 'Robert Hyndman's toe: Romanticism, schoolboy politics and the affective revolution in late Georgian Belfast' in Catherine Cox and Susannah Riordan (eds.), *Adolescence in Modern Irish History* (Basingstoke, 2015), pp. 15–41.

[21] *Irish Times*, 15 Feb. 1894.

[22] See, for example, Daniel O'Connell to Mary O'Connell, 24 Jan. 1801 in *The Correspondence of Daniel O'Connell*, i, pp. 50–56.

[23] Jean Agnew (ed.), *The Drennan–McTier Letters, 1776–1819* (3 vols., Dublin, 1998–2001), i, pp. 158–60, 563–4.

aunt's house, much to the annoyance of her brother and Letitia's father, William.[24] Letitia was William Tennent's only legitimate child and was heiress to most of the vast wealth that he had accumulated through his sugar and other businesses. William was protective of Letitia and clearly wanted her to marry a husband who would help enhance his family's social and economic standing. When William learned of the connection between his daughter and the fortuneless James Emmerson, he was furious. His daughter, however, noted that her father's anger was mainly because she had not told him of Emmerson's approaches to her, which had been initiated two years before he learned of them. Letitia was also well aware that she was dashing her father's ambitious plans for her marriage. As she wrote to Tennent, 'was I married to a peer tomorrow, it might gratify your ambition but it would break my heart'.[25]

While Letitia asserted that her feelings for Emmerson 'can never change but with death', she, nonetheless, refused to marry him without her father's formal approval. Letitia maintained her opposition to her father's wishes for over a year and claimed repeatedly that Emmerson would marry her regardless of any fortune that she might bring to him: 'neither of us are ambitious and provided we had but a competince [sic] we wish for no more'.[26] William Tennent eventually relented and agreed to the marriage. In his will, he left the bulk of his estate to Letitia and James but requested that James change his name to Emmerson Tennent.[27]

Two other well-known courtships that continued without parental approval were those of Sarah Curran and Robert Emmet and Mary and Daniel O'Connell. Curran's father, the lawyer, Richard, only found out about his daughter's connection to Emmet when, as noted already, police raided his house following Emmet's arrest and discovered the letters from him to Sarah.[28] Daniel O'Connell courted his future wife, Mary, in defiance of his patron and benefactor, his uncle Maurice. Like James Emmerson and Letitia Tennent, Daniel met Mary in the neutral space of the city rather than incur the wrath of his uncle through meeting her in Kerry. In Dublin, he explained to Mary: 'I would have many more opportunities of seeing and conversing with you than in that prying, curious, busy town of Tralee'.[29] Mary did, however, conform to the

---

[24] Letitia Tennent to William Tennent, 1 Feb. 1830 (PRONI, D1748/B/1/318/17); same to same, 21 Jan. 1831 (PRONI, D1748/B/1/318/18).
[25] Letitia Tennent to William Tennent, 21 Feb. 1831 (PRONI, D1748/B/1/318/19).
[26] Letitia Tennent to William Tennent, 21 Jan. 1831 (PRONI, D1748/B/1/318/18).
[27] Letitia Tennent to William Tennent, 27 May 1831 (PRONI, D1748/B/1/318/20); ODNB.
[28] DIB; Geoghegan, Robert Emmet, pp. 119, 200, 203, 218–25, 256–7.
[29] The Correspondence of Daniel O'Connell, i, p. 34. Emphasis in original.

practice of informing her mother about her relationship with her cousin, Daniel, despite the latter's command not to 'show my letters to any of your family'.[30] Other members of the extended O'Connell family were recruited to assist with the secret courtship. Mary's sister and brother-in-law conveyed letters between the couple. Another male relative to whom Mary addressed letters which were to be secretly passed on to Daniel was reprimanded by her brother, Richard, for the inappropriateness of corresponding with his sister, a single woman.[31]

Going against a parent's wishes could have serious financial as well as social consequences for the defiant couple. As we have seen, fathers often left very specific instructions in their wills that their daughters were to seek the approval and consent of their mothers and older brother before they married. Defying the advice of parents could at worst lead to disinheritance and alienation from the family. Following his discovery of Robert Emmet's courtship of his daughter, Richard Curran banished his daughter from the family home and when she died in 1808, he rejected her last request to be buried alongside her sister in the family's graveyard.[32] Maurice O'Connell also punished his nephew for his secret courtship and marriage by dividing his inheritance, initially intended for Daniel, between him and his brother with dire consequences for the financial status of Daniel's growing family.[33]

Love or Money?

While the financial arrangements for a marriage were of utmost importance, love and physical attraction also played a part in marriage arrangements. Mary and Daniel O'Connell clearly married for love. In their letters to one another, both are explicit in their expressions of emotional and physical attraction.[34] Although, in the long term, the O'Connells sacrificed money and material wealth for love, they both, as Erin Bishop points out, agreed that material wealth was as important as emotional support for a successful marriage.[35] William Drennan agonised over whether or not he was being over particular in his search for a wife, declaring that he was willing to settle for 'some little round girl with a taste for the harpsichord and some little fortune'.[36] Drennan's mother, increasingly impatient with her son's failure to marry, urged him to find a 'lively,

---

[30] Ibid., i, pp. 57–8.   [31] Ibid., i, p. 57.   [32] Geoghegan, *Robert Emmet*, pp. 30, 36.
[33] ODNB.
[34] See, for example, *The Correspondence of Daniel O'Connell*, i, pp. 41, 54, 64.
[35] Eirin I. Bishop, *The World of Mary O'Connell, 1778–1836* (Dublin, 1999), p. 33.
[36] Agnew, *The Drennan–McTier Letters*, ii, p. 271.

sensible, agreeable girl that will be able to put some life into him'.[37] In the end, however, Drennan chose for his wife the only woman that he had declared to his sister that he actually loved and who had 'not a 6d'. He had to persuade his mother that Sarah Swanwick had a 'kind of fortune' in that she was 'liberal in her mind', well-educated and, for good measure, she was a dissenter.[38] Letitia Tennent was also fulsome in her proclamations of her love for James Emmerson, much to her father's chagrin. Love was, therefore, clearly important to individuals in courtship, even if in the formal process of arranging the marriage it was not given a high priority.

An emphasis on love and physical attraction in courtship could also result in personal tragedy and, in extreme cases, mental illness. In the annual report of the district, criminal and private lunatic asylums in Ireland to March 1857, twenty-five men and seventy women were defined with a mental disease caused by 'love and jealousy'.[39] In 1862, thirty-eight men and eighty women were defined with mental disease having been caused by 'love, jealousy and seduction'.[40] In 1869, 69 men and 103 women were so defined.[41] Such diagnoses were no longer in use by the late 1870s.

The practical aspects of marriage, including fortunes, settlements and living arrangements were well recognised, but by the end of the nineteenth century romantic gestures of affection were also expected in courtship. Barristers, in breach of promise cases, frequently noted mockingly when they were absent. In the Dublin case of Abigail Bowers *v* William Morris, the plaintiff was the daughter of a respectable gentleman, and the defendant held property near her father's residence. An intimacy sprung up between them and he proposed marriage. The marriage settlement was agreed and shortly afterwards Morris stopped answering letters. It was then discovered that he had married someone else. The plaintiff's barrister, trying to persuade the jury that there had been no courtship here, asked 'where were all the romantic walks, the moonlight rambles, light and music and all that sort of thing'.[42]

As noted in the last chapter, growing levels of education including, by the turn of the twentieth century, university education for women also meant that more men and women were determined to marry the person

---

[37] Ibid., i, pp. 261–2.   [38] Ibid., ii, pp. 516–7.
[39] *The Eighth Report on the District, Criminal, and Private Lunatic Asylums in Ireland with Appendices* (Dublin, 1857), p. 44.
[40] *The Twelfth Report on the District, Criminal, and Private Lunatic Asylums in Ireland with Appendices* (Dublin, 1870), p. 69.
[41] *The Nineteenth Report on the District, Criminal, and Private Lunatic Asylums in Ireland with Appendices* (Dublin, 1863), p. 86.
[42] *Irish Times*, 29 Nov. 1862; *Belfast Newsletter*, 28, 29 Nov. 1862; *Freeman's Journal*, 1 Dec. 1862.

of their choice rather than be compelled to marry someone chosen by their family. It is noticeable that in the stories of the courtships of Éamon de Valera and Sinéad Flanagan and of Éamonn Ceannt and Áine Ní Bhraonáin, the approval of parents is rarely noted and may, by that time, have been a formality in middle-class and, particularly, Dublin-based families. Even in rural towns such as Birr, by the end of the late nineteenth century parental consent does not appear to have been a priority for courting couples. Cis Whelan befriended the mother of her fiancé and future husband, Tom, but her courtship correspondence makes very few references to her own parents.[43]

C. S. Andrews downplayed the presence of mothers who attended meetings of the Gaelic League along with their daughters: 'Any of [the] girls I liked particularly always seemed to have their mothers around. Mothers were not deliberately installed as chaperons; it happened that way.'[44] Kathleen Daly's family expressed concern that she planned to marry Tom Clarke, a man who was twenty years older than her. Clarke spent fifteen years in prison in England and when he was released in 1898, he went to stay with the Daly family in Limerick. Kathleen's uncle, John, was a close friend of Clarke, having spent time in prison with him. Clarke's attraction to Daly took him by surprise as he later explained to her:

You wonder how it came that I took to you – Oh I'll tell you that – I couldn't help it – do you recollect the morning in the dining room I astonished you by tossing your hair – that was done on the impulse and my own astonishment was far greater than your own – even yet when I think of it I can't understand how it came about – I couldn't help it.[45]

Daly's widowed mother and her uncle were strongly opposed to a marriage between Kathleen and Tom. By the time the couple met, however, Kathleen had established her own successful clothing business in Limerick, also in defiance of her family. Her family insisted that she wait for at least a year 'to take time to make sure her heart and her head were in unison on the matter'. They also wanted Tom to be in paid work before he married. Despite strong family opposition, however, Kathleen eventually persuaded her uncle and mother to permit her to travel to New York, where Tom had gone both to find work and to promote the Irish republican cause. The couple were married in 1901 in the Bronx.[46]

---

[43] Raughter, '"Your own for ever, Sis"'.
[44] C. S. Andrews, *Man of No Property* (Dublin, 1982), p. 167.
[45] Cited in Sinéad McCoole, *Easter Widows: Seven Irish Women Who Lived in the Shadow of the Easter Rising* (London, 2014), p. 16.
[46] Ibid., pp. 15–22.

Pre-marital Sex

As noted already, kissing and a woman sitting on a man's knee were acceptable as public displays of affection for courting couples. As a young teenager in the 1770s, Mary Shackleton Leadbeater watched with fascination the courtship of her sister, Margaret, by Samuel Grubb. It involved a great deal of physical touching, with Margaret sitting on Samuel's knee and being pulled by him into the second parlour in the house where the young couple spent a 'long time' in the evenings alone together. There is, however, no evidence to suggest that either Margaret or her sister Mary, who did not marry until she was in her thirties, had sexual intercourse before marriage.[47]

In her study of the sexual activity of Ulster Presbyterians, Leanne Calvert concluded that 'couples participated in a range of sexual behaviours that stopped just short of intercourse'. This included 'grabbing, groping, touching' and bundling. The latter involved couples lying and sometimes, sleeping in bed fully clothed. Calvert suggests that a great deal of the flirtatious behaviour of young Presbyterians took place in and around a bed and, like Margaret Shackleton and Samuel Grubb, their activities were not always closely supervised by adults.[48]

Clearly some couples went beyond the limits of physical touching implicitly, if not explicitly, tolerated in the Quaker and Presbyterian communities. Not surprisingly, it is difficult for historians to analyse the level of sexual activity of courting couples. Since the late 1970s, however, historians have queried the image of Ireland as a sexually chaste society in which pre-marital sexual intercourse was rare. In a pioneering study based on a small selection of parochial records pre-1864, Sean Connolly suggested that the number of illegitimate births in nineteenth-century Ireland was low by comparison with other European societies.[49] Illegitimacy rates averaged between 4 and 5 per cent in the pre-Famine period and about 3 per cent after that. Connolly noted, however, that up to 10 per cent of

---

[47] Mary O'Dowd, 'Adolescence girlhood in eighteenth-century Ireland' in Mary O'Dowd and June Purvis (eds.), *A History of the Girl: Formation, Education and Identity* (London, 2018), pp. 58–9. See also Kevin O'Neill, 'Almost a gentlewoman: Gender and adolescence in the diary of Mary Shackleton' in Mary O'Dowd and Sabine Wichert (eds.), *Chattel, Servant or Citizen: Women's Status in Church and State* (Belfast, 1995), pp. 91–102.

[48] Leanne Calvert, '"He came to her bed pretending courtship": Sex, courtship and the making of marriage in Ulster, 1750–1844', *Irish Historical Studies*, 42, 162 (2018), 253, 255–7.

[49] S. J. Connolly, 'Illegitimacy and pre-nuptial pregnancy in Ireland before 1864: The evidence of some Catholic parish registers', *Irish Economic and Social History*, 6 (1979), 5–23.

women in his sample were probably pregnant at the time of their marriage.[50] He also highlighted regional variations in patterns of illegitimacy and the difficulties regarding the reliability of Catholic registers for an analysis of births outside marriage.[51] The north east, in Connolly's study, appeared to be an exception where levels of pre-marital pregnancy were higher than in other parts of Ireland. Paul Gray and Donald Akenson expanded Connolly's analysis to explore in particular the illegitimacy rates in the north east. They have both argued that there was a high number of pregnant brides in the region but a low rate of births to mothers who never married.[52] In other words, pre-marital sex was usually followed by marriage.

This conclusion conforms to the evidence provided through the Presbyterian session minute books, which indicate that pre-marital sex was tolerated, if not approved, so long as the couple married subsequently. In Carnmoney between 1767 and 1819, the sessions considered thirty-eight cases of fornication and seventy-nine of pre-marital fornication (i.e. where the couple had married subsequently). By contrast there were only twenty cases concerned with the paternity and maintenance of twenty children born outside marriage.[53] In Cahans, 1786–1821, the session considered 106 cases of fornication and 92 cases of pre-marital fornication and in Glascar, between 1760 and 1817, 44 cases of fornication and pre-marital fornication.[54]

As Paul Gray noted in his study of illegitimacy, Ulster Presbyterian society has been portrayed as paradoxically both sexually promiscuous and as a society in which sexual behaviour was strictly controlled by the session and presbytery. The toleration of sex before the formal service of marriage is not, however, necessarily an indicator of a sexually liberal society. The presiding elders and ministers in many sessions exercised a sliding scale of breaches of the sexual moral code. Fornication that was not followed by a marriage ceremony was not acceptable, particularly if it could be proven that one of the partners subsequently reneged on a promise of marriage. Some sessions, in the later part of the eighteenth century, however, only took a serious interest in fornication if it resulted

---

[50] Ibid., and S. J. Connolly, *Priests and People in Pre-famine Ireland, 1780–1845* (Dublin, 1982).

[51] Connolly, 'Illegitimacy and pre-nuptial pregnancy in Ireland before 1864', 5–23.

[52] Paul W. P. Gray, 'A social history of illegitimacy in Ireland from the late eighteenth to the early twentieth century' (unpublished PhD thesis, Queen's University Belfast, 2000), p. 123; Donald H. Akenson, *Small Differences: Irish Catholics and Irish Protestants, 1815–1922: An International Perspective* (Montreal, 1991), pp. 28–38.

[53] Leanne Calvert (ed.), 'Carnmoney Kirk Session Chapter Minute Book, January 1786– March 1804' (unpublished transcript of original in PHSIB).

[54] Cahans Session Book, 1786–1821 (PHSIB); Glascar Session Book, 1760–1818 (PHSIB).

in a pregnancy. The session enquiry was as much about the need to secure financial support for the child through the identification of the father as it was about reprimanding the couple.[55]

While Ulster Presbyterian society has been singled out by historians for its tolerance of sex before marriage, it is more difficult to assess the extent to which such practices were prevalent in Catholic or Church of Ireland communities. In his detailed study of marriage and baptismal registers for the parish of Wicklow, Brian Gurrin noted that in the mid-eighteenth century '5.5 per cent of all marriages ... presented a child for baptism before their marriage was eight months old (thirty-three weeks) and an additional 1.9 per cent presented during the ninth month (thirty-eight weeks) of the union. The equivalent Catholic (Wicklow parish) statistics were 10.1 and 1.3 per cent.'[56] These figures are similar to those estimated by Donald Akenson and Paul Gray for the Presbyterian community and also coincide with Connolly's estimate of pregnant brides.[57]

Between 1696 and 1711, there were thirty-eight petitions relating to accusations of fornication or pre-marital sex presented to the vicar general of the Killaloe diocesan court.[58] As in the session minute books, fornication represented the most common form of sexual offence documented in the surviving court records. The theoretical punishment of public censure was also very similar to that of the Presbyterian session, although the petitioners to the vicar general in Killaloe were concerned to have their punishment commuted to a cash fine.[59] All the petitions were presented by men and a number refer to the shame of being compelled to admit their guilt in public. Florence McNamara, for example, confessed to an act of fornication with Hanna McNamara. He explained to the vicar general that he was a young gentleman as yet without an inheritance and, as a result of his actions, 'very much under his father's frown' and 'commanded ... out of his house'. McNamara successfully petitioned the court to have his sentence commuted to a ten-shilling fine.[60] Similarly, Amos Carr, in 1711, told the vicar general in his petition that a 'public penance would tend to his utter ruin and destruction'. He was

---

[55] See also John J. Marshall (ed.), *Vestry Book of the Parish of Aghalow, Caledon, County Tyrone, With an Account of the Family of Caledon, 1691–1807* (Dungannon, 1935) for a similar concern in the Church of Ireland with financial support for infants born outside marriage.

[56] Brian Francis Gurrin, 'Land and people in Wicklow, 1660–1840' (2 vols., unpublished PhD thesis, NUI Maynooth, 2006), ii, p. 23.

[57] Gray, 'A social history of illegitimacy in Ireland from the late eighteenth to the early twentieth century'; Akenson, *Small Differences*, p. 34.

[58] BL, Add MS 31881–2.

[59] See Papers of the Consistory Court of Killaloe, 1671–1824 (BL, Add MS 31881–2).

[60] BL, Add MS 31881, fo.75.

'entirely depending on the pleasure of his father who will not give maintenance if he publicly performs penance'. He too was permitted to commute his punishment to a 40s fine.[61]

While the ecclesiastical court appeared to be sympathetic to young men found guilty of occasional acts of pre-marital sex, it was less understanding if the woman became pregnant and the man either refused to recognise the child as his or refused to marry the woman. There are nine petitions in the Killaloe collection relating to breach of promise suits. All were initiated by women, six of whom had become pregnant by the men who had seduced them with promises of marriage.[62] In the Catholic diocese of Ossory in the early 1750s, priests also reported accusations of fornication and breaches of promises to marry.[63]

The surviving records of all the main denominations, therefore, suggest that in the seventeenth and eighteenth centuries, pre-marital sex was not uncommon and that a figure of 10 per cent of brides who were pregnant seems to be a conservative estimate. Brian Gurrin notes, however, that Irish rates of pregnant brides contrast strongly with the English situation, where '20 to 25 per cent of brides were pregnant when they entered the church in the early modern period, but in some parishes the figure was as high as 30 or even 50 per cent'.[64]

One factor that may have influenced the lower illegitimacy rates in Ireland is the ease with which it was possible to marry by contrast with England. A qualified clergyman could be summoned within hours of the decision to marry. Sexual intercourse could very quickly be followed by marriage, or an agreement to participate in a quick marriage ceremony could be used as a bribe to have sexual intercourse. The Ordnance Survey memoir of the Presbyterian community in Carnmoney suggested that pre-marital intercourse was also used as a means of securing and increasing a dowry from the girl's father.[65]

In the middle decades of the eighteenth century, the Catholic warden of Galway publicly denounced couples who rushed into marriage: 'hurried away by unbridled passion, they run hastily to the priest, they tell him a thousand lies, they leave nothing untried to compass their end of

---

[61] Ibid., fo. 117.
[62] Mary O'Dowd, 'Men, women, children and the family, 1550–1730' in Jane Ohlmeyer (ed.), *Cambridge History of Ireland* (Cambridge, 2018), ii, pp. 337–63. See also Chapters 3 and 9.
[63] Christopher O'Dwyer (ed.), 'Archbishop Butler's visitation book', *Archivium Hibernicum*, 33 (1975), 1–90; 34 (1975), 1–49.
[64] Gurrin, 'Land and people in Wicklow, 1660–1840', ii, p. 23.
[65] A. Day and P. McWilliams, *Ordnance Survey Memoirs of Ireland Parishes of County Antrim 1, 1838–9* (Belfast, 1990), ii, p. 59.

prevailing on him to give his sanction by his presence to their unchristian measures.' The warden's solution was to announce that henceforth he would require three days' notice of a couple's intention to marry, a warning that in itself indicates the speed with which couples could marry in Ireland, even when apparent restrictions were introduced.[66]

A pregnant bride was not, therefore, as socially shameful as giving birth to a child outside marriage. In the 1830s, the Poor Enquiry gave considerable space to 'bastardy', noting the levels of illegitimacy in various parishes around the country, taking evidence on the support of illegitimate children and attitudes towards the mothers, and indeed fathers, of these children. In County Kildare evidence was provided that signified the status of both mother and child:

A young man of the lowest class would feel degraded by marrying a woman who had an illegitimate child by another ... girls who have had bastards seldom can get anyone to marry them except those men by whom they were seduced; they are looked on as degraded persons, and scarcely associated with ... bastards are looked on in the same view; a small farmer would refuse a match with a bastard.[67]

The witnesses also told the familiar story of fathers rarely admitting paternity, and in some places women used the petty sessions courts to not only name, and shame, the father publicly but also to sue for 'wages for nursing the child'.[68]

As has been well researched elsewhere, unmarried mothers became the subject of reform, and a level of institutionalisation by the end of the nineteenth and into the twentieth centuries.[69] Despite the public discourse, however, the illegitimate birth rate in Ireland had decreased by that time by comparison with the figures available for the eighteenth century and continued to be 'less than that recorded for most other European countries'. For the years 1921–1923, births outside marriage amounted to 2.6 per cent of all registered births in Ireland. Between 1926 and 1929 there was a small but gradual annual increase in the figures that caused a degree of panic amongst the guardians of Irish morality, particularly in the Catholic church.[70] The rise was attributed to a loss of parental control and responsibility during the period of the war of independence and civil war. That parental control, it was argued,

---

[66] Galway Diocesan Archives, Box 9, file 1.
[67] Cadamstown parish, County Kildare, *Poor Enquiry, Appendix (A) and Supplement, Being Answers to Questions Circulated by the Commissioners*, p. 62.
[68] Ibid., p. 66.
[69] Maria Luddy, 'Unmarried mothers in Ireland', *Women's History Review*, 21, 1 (Feb. 2011), 109–26.
[70] For numbers of illegitimate births between 1864 and 1945 see E.W. McCabe, 'The need for a law of adoption', article in Adoption of Children: General File (NAI, Department of the Taoiseach, S10815A).

had never been restored. Moral laxity was seen to be a result of the prevalence of 'commercialised dancehalls, picture houses … and the opportunities afforded by the misuse of motor cars for luring girls'.[71] For the Church, the state and many welfare workers, the way forward was to introduce legislation that would raise the age of consent, introduce harsher punishments for solicitation and regulate the dancehalls in a stricter fashion. Much of this type of legislation found its way onto the statute books by the early 1930s.[72] There was little relief or support, however, for unmarried mothers before the 1970s.

Infanticide

Another indicator of pre- and extra-marital sexual activity is the level of infanticide cases prosecuted in Irish courts. James Kelly has analysed reports of 235 infanticide cases in Ireland between 1721 and 1800.[73] Elaine Farrell uncovered 4,645 cases of suspected infant murder in the fifty year period from 1850 to 1900.[74] Cliona Rattigan, who analysed the following fifty years, found 280 murders of infants under the age of one year between 1900 and 1919; 141 between 1900 and 1919; and 141 between 1927 and 1950.[75] The majority of the infants were born to single, usually poor women. Many were employed as domestic servants and living away from home. The figures represent suspected cases of infanticide that were identified by the police. It is likely that there were far more incidents of concealment of birth and deaths of infants that were never recorded. The women, and it was mostly women who committed infanticide, often acted alone and for a variety of reasons were unable to marry the father of their child, some of whom were already married. The shame of having a child outside marriage was undoubtedly a strong factor in their decision to kill their newly born infant.

Seduction: The Legal Option

The social shame attached to a single woman giving birth to a child was often perceived as dishonouring not only her but her whole family. Court

---

[71] NAI, Department of Justice File, H 171/1.

[72] Maria Luddy, 'Sex and the single girl in 1920s and 1930s Ireland', *The Irish Review*, 35 (Summer 2007), 79–91.

[73] James Kelly, 'Infanticide in eighteenth-century Ireland', *Irish Economic and Social History*, 19 (1992), 5–26.

[74] Elaine Farrell, *'A Most Diabolical Deed': Infanticide and Irish Society, 1850–1900* (Manchester, 2013).

[75] Cliona Rattigan, *'What Else Could I Do?' Single Mothers and Infanticide, Ireland 1900–1950* (Dublin, 2012), pp. 6–7.

records reveal how the woman's male relatives often sought to impose their own form of punishment on the man involved. In 1836, for example, a group of men broke into the house of Pierce Hearn in Carrick-on-Suir, County Tipperary. They forced him before a clergyman 'to compel him to marry' a girl named Ellen Gibbs, with whom he had had a child. The priest refused to marry the couple. Hearn complained later to the local magistrate who sought advice from the Lord Lieutenant on what law was applicable when a man was abducted and forced into marriage.[76]

There was also a legal alternative to private and violent revenge. The man could be sued for seduction by the woman's parent or guardian. In the middle ages, a master could sue another man who sexually seduced his servant for the loss of the services of the servant, particularly if she became pregnant following the seduction. In the course of the eighteenth century the tort of seduction, as it was called, was expanded to enable a parent or guardian to sue the male seducer of an unmarried daughter for the loss of her services and/or comfort. Although such cases have been documented in England from the middle decades of the seventeenth century, in Ireland, the use of the tort of seduction in legal actions seems to date from the late eighteenth century. Between 1793 and 1925 at least 297 cases of seduction came before the Irish courts. In addition, seduction cases (at least thirty-seven) were heard by the Dáil courts, 1919–1922, with awards being made by the republican judicature to the plaintiffs and directions given for maintenance support for the children born of the liaisons.[77]

When accusations of seduction came to court a woman's experience of courtship, pre-marital pregnancy and abandonment became stories of heartless seduction. A case from 1832 reveals the courtroom rhetoric that also indicated the shame attached to sexual seduction. Mrs Sarah Boyd sued Samuel McCord for the seduction of her only daughter, Jane Boyd. McCord 'had addressed [Jane] as an honourable suitor and proposed marriage, which had been accepted'. It was noted in court that 'in country life a proposal of marriage when followed by an assent, is usually a passport to a general welcome and a friendly reception; and the unsuspecting girl had, relying on the honour of her lover, in a moment of weakness, fallen a prey to her seducer.'

A baby boy was born of the relationship, but no marriage ensued. While it was argued by a barrister that 'no damages ... would be

---

[76] Tipperary (NAI, OP/1836/27/5). For a similar case from County Longford see Longford (NAI, OP/1836/21).

[77] See for instance, cases listed in Dáil Éireann Court Register Book (NAI, DE1/1 2B102).

commensurate with the evil sustained', the jury could take into account 'the dishonour, ignominy and degradation, brought on her [the mother's] family by [the] defendant, independent of the serious injury a woman of her age must in reality suffer in the loss of her daughter's services, and in whose society and virtue she can now no longer feel consolation; such damages being the only means by which she could punish the destroyer of her peace and happiness'. That the jury took the case very seriously can be seen by the award of £100 in damages plus costs to the plaintiff.[78] The majority of women noted that the only reason they had yielded to the sexual advances of a seducer was that he had promised marriage. This, of course, elides any sexual desire that might have been felt by the woman herself. It puts all the blame for the illicit intercourse onto the seducer.

In 1852, a Mrs Dunne sued John Largan for the seduction of her daughter, Theresa. The plaintiff was a widow with a small property in Carlow town. The defendant was a neighbour of the Dunnes as well as being Mrs Dunne's landlord and a school teacher. He was about fifty when he volunteered to teach her seventeen-year-old daughter, and then seduced her under a promise of marriage. The family sent her away to hide the subsequent pregnancy but Largan, much to the family's shame, publicly vilified her character instead of keeping her condition secret. It was also implied that Largan was the victim of a conspiracy on the part of Dunne that was designed to compel him to marry her. The judge, in his summing up, was sceptical of this claim and stressed the young age of the girl who had been seduced by a much older man. The jury agreed and granted Mrs Dunne damages of £200.[79]

Despite efforts on the part of the defence to question the character of the unmarried mother, in the vast majority of seduction suits the sympathy of the judge and jury was with the woman and her family. Plaintiffs were successful in about 95 per cent of the cases. The financial reward may not, however, have compensated for the shame of the details about the woman's life that emerged in open court. Most of the parents or guardians who sued for damages for the seduction of a daughter or ward were from a lower social or economic class than the defendants. The aim of the suit was as much about securing maintenance for the unmarried mother and her child as it was about her sexual seduction. Often too, the case involved a broken promise of marriage with breach of promise proceedings occurring concurrently with those of seduction.

[78] *Connaught Journal*, 3 Sept. 1832.   [79] *Freeman's Journal*, 30 Nov. 1852.

Changing Attitudes to Pre-marital Sex?

Roy Foster has pointed to the liberal attitudes to pre-marital sex among the group that he describes as the 'revolutionary generation'. Republican Pearse Beaslaí, for example, recorded in his diary how Bride Fitzgerald, the sister of the local priest, slipped into his room every night when he was staying in the Irish college in Ballingeary, County Cork. Cumann na mBan member, Mabel Fitzgerald, was pregnant when she married fellow republican, Desmond, secretly in France, while Grace Gifford's marriage to Joseph Plunkett on the eve of his execution was undoubtedly due to her pregnancy.[80] The divorce proceedings of Maud Gonne and John MacBride revealed that she had had two children with her French lover before she married.[81]

Rosamund Jacob confided in her diary about her physical attraction to men. In 1915, she wrote of her sexual attraction to a young male friend, Tony Farrington:

I certainly am in some ways a man in disguise – a man turned inside out. My love for Tony is more masculine than feminine; I love him, not spiritually and patiently and unselfishly as a woman is supposed to love a man, but physically and impatiently and selfishly, as a man loves a woman. The idea of him being happy apart from me has no charms for me at all. I'd rather have him unhappy near me than happy far away. Its more a craving and a passion for him than proper love. And the very fact of picking someone younger than myself to love is like a man.[82]

Jacob had a number of lovers, the most well-known of whom was republican activist, Frank Ryan. Jacob and Ryan met at the Gaelic League in Dublin in 1925. It was she rather than Ryan who initiated sexual intimacy three years later in July 1928:

... when he started to go I asked him to stay the night with me. He was perfect – didn't shirk it – shut the door – refused with obvious reasons, looking painfully miserable – admitted he'd like to – any man would like to accept such an invitation – I cdn't argue it, he was so unhappy over it – then he did take me and kiss me, and when I made to stop, he pulled me down on the sofa and lay there, holding me tight, partly on top of me, his face against mine, all hot and panting and deliciously excited, showing most plainly *how* tempted he was, for more than half an hour.[83]

---

[80] R. F. Foster, *Vivid Faces: The Revolutionary Generation in Ireland 1890–1923* (London, 2014), pp. 123–4; Grace Plunkett, *All in the Blood* (Dublin, 2012), pp. 233–4, 247.

[81] Anthony J. Jordan, *The Yeats Gonne MacBride Triangle* (Westport, 2000).

[82] Cited in Leeann Lane, *Rosamund Jacob: Third Person Singular* (Dublin, 2010), p. 197.

[83] Ibid., pp. 183–4. See also pp. 173–9; Fearghal McGarry, *Frank Ryan* (Dundalk, 2002).

Throughout their relationship Ryan was more reserved about it than Jacob. While he visited her at night for sexual intercourse, he also wanted to keep their liaison secret 'as he thought it was a sin'.[84] Ryan's attitude may have been more typical among republican men than it was for the more open-minded Jacob. There is considerable evidence that many in the revolution generation were not comfortable with their sexuality or sexual expression. Terence MacSwiney went to the extreme of circumventing the temptation of 'beastly sexual passion' by avoiding the company of young women.[85] Éamonn Ceannt expressed his sexual desire, but also his reticence, in his letters to his fiancée:

Somehow I have a great faith in this love making of ours. ... You may remember agreeing that a certain sweet pleasure is only an outward sign and is not the real thing. That was the night I tried to explain away your scruples as to kissing. You remember, don't you, sweetheart? We shall have quite a number of little epochs in this eventful time, and up to this we have had none that it causes pain or fear or shame to look back upon. So much the better.[86]

A couple of weeks later, he wrote:

Tabhair dom póg [Give me a kiss] Aye, I feel your arms circling round my neck, my head is gently bent down till your sweet lips meet mine in a kiss. Now, as you say yourself, you needn't be afraid. All the same I won't ask you to be too prodigal of those little expressions of your great love I have often said that to you, and it only seems to make you gentler, more tender. If that were possible.[87]

In his memoir, C. S. Andrews recalled that he had received no sex education at school. Most of his knowledge had come from army friends returning from the front during the First World War. They produced condoms and 'filthee [sic] pictures'. Andrews admitted that as an adolescent boy he did not understand the purpose of the condom and was ashamed to have 'glanced' at the pictures. He noted, however, that 'like all these boyish experiences, they were remembered'.[88] By the time he was twenty-three and had begun to court his future wife, Mary Coyle, Andrews acknowledged that he was better informed and 'knew all the slang words used to describe the variations of the love-making process and the acrobatics of the marriage bed'. He and Mary had little

---

[84] Lane, *Rosamund Jacob,* p. 174. See also pp. 176–80. It might also be noted that Jacob was from a Quaker background while Ryan was a Catholic.

[85] Ibid., p. 17.

[86] 10 Dec. 1903 (NLI, 'Ceannt and O'Brennan Papers, 1851–1953,' MS 13069/2/12). See also McCoole, *Easter Widows,* pp. 110–33.

[87] 24 Dec. 1903 (NLI, 'Ceannt and O'Brennan Papers, 1851–1953,' MS 13069/3/7). Underlining in the original manuscript.

[88] C. S. Andrews, *Dublin Made Me* (Dublin, 1979), p. 79.

opportunity, however, to test his knowledge in a practical sense. As an older man, he recalled his frustration that the public rituals of courtship did not permit many opportunities for more private intimacy:

for a man and a woman in the situation Mary and I found ourselves in, picture-houses, theatres, cabarets, or the Hill of Howth or Powerscourt Demesne or Glenasmole did not fulfil all our needs. We wanted to be alone but there was nowhere we could be alone. At that time attaining privacy was a common problem for courting couples; hence the popularity of the cinema.[89]

Conclusion

It is clear that courtship behaviour varied not just across social class but also depended on individual inclination and disposition. There were agreed patterns of behaviour, particularly in middle-class society, that signalled to family, friends and the wider community that a couple were courting and the expectation was that the courtship would end in marriage. Nor should women be perceived as entirely passive actors in the courtship game. Women like Letitia Tennent who defied their fathers to marry the men of their choice were actively shaping their own futures. Jonathan Wright has documented the courtship of Eliza McCracken with Letitia's cousin, Robert James Tennent, and traced the way in which she exercised considerable agency both in her relationship with Tennent and with her father, who strongly opposed the match.[90]

Not everyone, therefore, observed or followed the rules of courtship. This is particularly evident in relation to pre-marital sex. While impossible to quantify, one of the facts to emerge from a study of breach of promise and seduction cases is the prevalence of sex as part of courtship. Jurors did not appear to punish women when evidence of pre-marital sexual activity, often signified by the birth of an illegitimate child, came to light. The reporting of such cases in the newspapers throughout the period also suggests that rather than being hidden, the problems that arose from pre-marital sex and the manner in which men and women conducted their love lives, found very public expression through these accounts.

While the Presbyterian church authorities were tolerant if not approving of couples who consummated their relationship before marriage, the statistical evidence in scattered sources also indicates a significant

---

[89] C. S. Andrews, *A Man of No Property* (Dublin, 1982), p. 82.

[90] Jonathan Jeffrey Wright, 'Love, loss and learning in late Georgian Belfast' in D. W. Hayton and Andrew R. Holmes (eds.), *Ourselves Alone? Religion, Society and Politics in Eighteenth- and Nineteenth-Century Ireland* (Dublin, 2016), pp. 169–91.

number of pregnant Catholic brides. The single mother may have been shunned by society but there was less shame attached to the birth of children within seven or eight months of marriage.

There is evidence in middle-class urban society of changing attitudes to courtship in the early decades of the twentieth century, with more men and women anxious to make their own choice of spouse. Paradoxically, at the same time, despite the liberated attitude of individuals such as Rosamund Jacob, the perception of pre-marital sex as a 'sin' became more prevalent in the late nineteenth century. In other words, while young couples had more freedom to choose a partner by the 1900s, they had less freedom to spend intimate time with each other.

5   Breach of Promise

In 1871, Mary Mays, a young woman in her twenties, living with her widowed mother who farmed seven acres, sued Miller McIntyre who was forty-three years old and a farmer of fifty-six acres, which he held for an annual rent of £93. The couple, both Methodists, had met at a prayer meeting and continued to see each other until he proposed in August 1870. Mays accepted his offer and her 'mother readily consented on account of the reputation the defendant had acquired as a well-conducted, religious man'. The marriage licence was secured, and McIntyre bought a wedding dress and ring for Mays and a suit for himself. The wedding was set for 11 October, but on the 5th of that month McIntyre sent a workman on his farm to break off the engagement, saying he had heard stories disparaging her character, although he himself did not believe them. Mays sought damages of £800. McIntyre offered no defence but asked for a mitigation of damages. She was awarded £200 and 6d costs.[1] This was one of hundreds of cases taken by women against men who had reneged on their promise to marry. This was a relatively clear-cut case: the marriage had been agreed, the necessary preparations had been made and McIntyre had shown himself to be unreliable and dishonourable. The damages awarded by the jury recognised that Mays had been unjustly treated. The court case and the award of damages publicly vindicated her reputation. In this chapter, we explore the law on reneging on a promise of marriage and the court proceedings that might follow. We look at what these law suits tell us about perceptions of femininity and masculinity and about ideal behaviour, particularly of women.

The Law

A breach of promise to marry is a fundamental break of a promise, by either a man or woman, to carry through a marriage. The legal action had

[1] *Irish Times*, 2 March 1871.

its origins in the canon law definition of marriage as a promise between a man and a woman. Ecclesiastical courts had an obligation to ensure that when a promise of marriage was made, both parties recognised that they had entered into a clandestine but valid marriage. Medieval ecclesiastical courts regularly heard cases related to allegations of broken promises often made in private with few or no witnesses.[2] Breach of promise cases, brought usually by single mothers, were heard, for example, by the medieval diocesan court in Armagh.[3] As indicated in the previous chapter, a small number of breach of promise cases are also recorded in the surviving documentation of the Killaloe diocesan records for the early eighteenth century. They were all initiated by single mothers who claimed that they had agreed to sexual intercourse because a promise of marriage had been made. The best documented case was that brought by Anne Stammers of Nenagh against Thomas Dalton. Witnesses testified that they had been present in a private house in 1721 when Stammers and Dolan had

entered into a contract of marriage by taking then an oath to each other upon the Holy Evangelist ... and by kissing each other confirmed it by repeating these words 'I Thomas Dalton take the Anne Stamers to be my lawfull and wedded wife' and 'I Ann Stamers take thee Thomas Dalton to be my lawfull and wedded husband'.[4]

The witnesses also said that Dalton had promised to bring a priest to marry the couple but this does not seem to have happened. Anne, however, subsequently gave birth to a daughter whom the witnesses alleged Dalton claimed as his. Although we do not know the outcome of the case, John Hawkins, the vicar general who presided over the Killaloe court, prevented Dalton from marrying another until the case was resolved.[5]

As in other disciplinary issues relating to marriage, the Catholic and Presbyterian authorities followed similar guidelines to the ecclesiastical courts in relation to allegations of breaches of promises to marry. All the Christian denominations agreed that a promise to marriage was binding and should be upheld by church authorities.[6] Surviving documentation

---

[2] See Chapter 1.
[3] See, for example, Angela Bourke *et al.* (eds.), *Field Day Anthology of Irish Writing: Volumes 4 and 5: Irish Women's Writing and Traditions* (Cork, 2002), v, pp. 478–9.
[4] Killaloe Consistory Court Book (BL, Add MS 31881), p. 189.
[5] Ibid., pp. 180, 189. See also Philip Dwyer, *The Diocese of Killaloe from the Reformation to the Close of the Eighteenth Century* (Dublin, 1878), pp. 353, 363; Mary O'Dowd, 'Men, women, children and the family, 1550–1730' in Jane Ohlmeyer (ed.), *Cambridge History of Ireland* (4 vols., Cambridge, 2018), ii, pp. 298–320.
[6] See Chapter 1.

is scattered but we can identify occasional references to Catholic authorities disciplining members of their congregation who reneged on promises to marry. Between 1734 and 1752 when Nicholas Madgett was parish priest in Tralee and O'Dorney, 'more than a thousand' complaints about breaches of promise to marry were referred to him. Most of the complainants were women who, in Madgett's view, had made the mistake of too 'easily admitting intercourse with her partner'.[7] The Church could use the threat of excommunication to compel espoused couples to marry but, as the many cases of infanticide dealt with by the common law courts testify, it was difficult to find sufficient evidence to prosecute men who defaulted on their promises.[8]

The Presbyterian sessions took allegations of broken promises of marriage very seriously. The elders made enquiries in the community as to their validity and summoned witnesses to the alleged promise to appear before them. In 1714, Andrew Sprule appeared before the Connor session to complain that he was 'wronged by Jonat Scott ... who is now under proclamation of marriage with Robert Carnohan and that notwithstanding of promises often made by the same Jonat Scott to him Andrew Sprule that she would marry him and appointed to meet him at Ballymonah and he went according to her appointment but she came not as yet'. The session ordered the clerk to delay proceeding with the marriage arrangements until further enquiries could be made, with a request to discover whether the parents had given their consent.[9] In 1773, the enquiry of the Cahans session into the promises made by William Harkness and Elizabeth Gray included a written petition signed by Harkness, in which he cited a letter from Gray, as well as the detailed questioning of witnesses. Harkness claimed that despite the failure of Gray's mother and other relatives to agree a match with his father and 'others', Gray had given him her hand and 'promise[d] to be true to him & no other & your Petitioner said the same that he would be true to her & no other'. Gray, however, was subsequently promised in marriage to another, a match that was presumably arranged by her mother following the breakdown of negotiations with Harkness's father. Harkness alleged that he and Gray

[7] Michael Manning, 'Dr Nicholas Madgett's Constitutio Ecclesiastica', *Journal of Kerry Archaeological and Historical Society*, 9 (1976), 87. See also Eric A. Derr, 'Episcopal visitations in the dioceses of Cloyne and Ross, 1785–1828 [with index]', *Archivium Hibernicum*, 66 (2013), 289.

[8] Elaine Farrell, *A Most Diabolical Deed: Infanticide and Irish Society, 1850–1900* (Manchester, 2013) and *Infanticide in the Irish Crown Files at Assizes, 1883–1900* (Dublin, 2012).

[9] Connor Session Book, 1708–1720, 12 Oct. 1714. Cited in John M. Barkley, 'History of the ruling eldership in Irish Presbyterianism' (2 vols., unpublished MA thesis, Queen's University of Belfast, 1952), i, pp. 104–5.

had then met secretly and confirmed their vows to one another. The elders were asked to consider whether the obligations to Harkness 'were so strong as she could not be married to another man'. A majority determined that although Harkness and Gray had acted 'sinfully', she was free to marry another man. The Moderator disagreed with the decision, as did members of Harkness's family. Five months later, Harkness acknowledged his offence in pursuing Gray even though she had been promised to another, and in disobeying his parents following the collapse of the match-making negotiations.[10] The elders decided that as he had not been successful in his courtship of Gray, that they would rebuke him in private rather than subject him to a public punishment in the meeting house.[11]

As is clear from the Harkness/Gray case, the church authorities had little effective power in breach of promise allegations. When a man or a woman brought a breach of promise allegation to their respective church authorities, they could expect at best that the offending party would be ordered to fulfil their promise on pain of being evicted from the church. Furthermore, as William Harkness discovered, even with the support of the Moderator, this punishment was not guaranteed. If the promise had been followed by sexual intercourse and the woman became pregnant, she might also plead with the church authorities for assistance in securing maintenance from the offending father. There was, however, no assurance that this would be successful. As indicated already, young men cited for a breach of promise in the Killaloe court frequently petitioned for a cash fine to be substituted *in lieu* of a public penance. None offered to maintain the child nor were they required to do so by the court.[12]

In England, by the late seventeenth century, actions for breach of contract to marry were beginning to move into the secular courts where the successful plaintiff would be awarded a financial sum of damages from the defendant.[13] In Ireland, civil suits for breach of promise seem to have begun in the middle years of the eighteenth century.

Secular Law

The civil action was based on the perception of a promise to marry as a legally binding contract. Failure to uphold the contract entitled the other party to sue for damages. The action evolved throughout the

[10] Cahans Session Book, 24, 30 Jan. 1773 (PHSIB). See also Andrew R. Holmes, *The Shaping of Ulster Presbyterian Belief and Practice 1770–1840* (Oxford, 2006), p. 222.

[11] Ibid.

[12] See BL, Add MS 31881; O'Dowd, 'Men, women, children and the family', pp. 337–8.

[13] Saskia Lettmaier, *Broken Engagements: The Action for Breach of Promise of Marriage and the Feminine Ideal, 1800–1940* (Oxford, 2010), pp. 21–6.

nineteenth century, but it remained a legal process that was very support-ive of a plaintiff's case. However, breach of promise cases were not always straightforward. The law recognised that such promises were often per-sonal in nature and difficulties might arise to prevent or make the proposed marriage untenable. Such promises were like a contract and, like other contracts, some sort of evidence was required if a prosecution was to be successful and damages awarded. Michael Sinnott, in one of the few studies of Irish breach of promise to marry cases, provides a clear analysis of such cases in terms of the legal and evidential elements of the action in nineteenth-century Ireland.[14] Our study adds to that analysis by extending the period under review and looking closely at the meanings ascribed to the actions of couples before the relationship broke down. In Ireland, almost all the breach of promise cases, from the late eighteenth to the early twentieth centuries, were brought by women.[15] Essentially, the woman who brought the case was seeking money, 'damages', for a broken promise of marriage. In taking a case she was implying that her reputation had suffered, that her ability to find a suitable husband to support her was perhaps irreparably impaired and that her future was bleak and she was condemned to spinsterhood.

Breach of promise to marry cases provided lawyers with lucrative incomes and newspapers with titillating stories for their reading audience. The actual court cases themselves were a form of public entertainment and the court room the arena of performance for wit-nesses, barristers, judges and, after 1869, defendants and plaintiffs. Exploring the history of breach of promise cases in Ireland provides, as we have seen in Chapter 4, an insight into courtship rituals, reveals the significance of monetary considerations in marriage negotiations and the value that was placed on women's and men's reputations. Such cases also throw light on the appropriateness of cross-class relation-ships, particularly where they related to an employer and a servant, and the significance of social status among plaintiffs and defendants. The prominence of breach of promise cases in the newspapers throughout the period also reinforces our view that rather than being hidden, issues

---

[14] Michael Sinnott, 'The action for breach of promise of marriage in nineteenth-century Ireland' in Niamh Howlin and Kevin Costello (eds.), *Law and the Family in Ireland, 1800–1950* (London, 2017), pp. 44–65; Alan Shatter, *Family Law in the Republic of Ireland* (2nd ed., Dublin 1981), pp. 25–30. For a recent study of breach of promise to marry cases in Ireland see Maria Luddy, *Matters of Deceit: Breach of Promise to Marry Cases in Nineteenth-Century Limerick* (Dublin, 2011).

[15] That women took the majority of cases in England in this period is attested by Ginger S. Frost, *Promises Broken: Courtship, Class, and Gender in Victorian England* (Charlottesville, 1995), and Lettmaier, *Broken Engagements*.

relating to sexuality and how people conducted their love lives found very public expression through these reports, and suggests that the press, both local and national, was a significant medium of sexual gossip for the reading public.

Numbers

It is difficult to gather accurate figures about the numbers of breach of promise cases that were pursued through the Irish civil courts before 1865. For the period from 1760 to 1919, we have some information on 524 cases. From 1865 to 1919, when statistics of cases were reported annually in the Judicial and Criminal Statistics for Ireland, 401 cases went to court.[16] Between 1764 and 1864, 123 cases were recorded. This figure is very likely to be an underestimate, as before 1865 no official figures were kept. Of the 123 cases tried between 1764 and 1864, only 7 of the plaintiffs were men. After 1865 there were at least ten male plaintiffs.[17] In Victorian England it was believed that breach of promise to marry cases had become 'epidemic' by the 1860s. Ginger Frost notes that in the decades between the 1860s and 1890s the numbers of such trials nearly doubled, with an average of thirty-four cases a year in the 1860s, a figure which rose to an average of sixty-seven cases a year by the 1890s.[18] In Ireland in the decade of the 1860s about sixty-nine cases went to trial, and this had decreased only slightly in the 1890s when a total of sixty-two cases were brought to court. The level of breach of promise cases in Ireland rose in the first decade of the twentieth century, when eighty-seven cases came to court between 1900 and 1909. Why was this the case? The lower rates of marriage and the difficulty in securing a husband in post-Famine Ireland made a breach of promise to marry an even more serious transgression than in the earlier period. The break-down of a courtship in post-Famine Ireland may have been seen as a greater social failure for a woman whose options for marriage were already considerably more limited than in the pre-Famine period. This might explain why women were more willing to take such cases to court in the later nineteenth and early twentieth centuries.

The general success of women in winning breach of promise cases also suggests that jurors saw a breach of promise as a sombre matter, affecting

---

[16] For the period after 1865 figures have been collated from the judicial and criminal statistics for Ireland, 1866–1920.

[17] The figures indicate that breach of promise suits were taken overwhelmingly by women and, unless specifically noted, in this text 'plaintiffs' refer to women and 'defendants' refer to men.

[18] Frost, *Promises Broken*, Chapter 1.

the woman's ability to marry in the future. There was, however, a steady flow of such cases appearing in the Irish courts throughout the period, and it remained a popular form of litigation. The majority of breach of promise to marry cases were between individuals of the same class, and over the period it was an action most often taken by women at the lower end of the middle class. There was a financial cost to taking such cases and women without much means needed to be sure that if they took a case the damages won would also allow for the payment of costs.

Common Law Courts

Given the public nature of breach of promise cases, it is unlikely that every case came to court, and indeed matters may have been settled out of court to prevent embarrassment to either party. Frost has noted in her work on breach of promise cases in England between 1859 and 1921, that at least a fifth of the cases were withdrawn before they got to the actual courtroom.[19] In Ireland, from the 1860s, at least 110 cases entered for court proceedings were either withdrawn or settled out of court. In 1857, for instance, the case between Devereux and Henry, settled for £300, was cancelled just as it came to court.[20] In 1847, the case of Richard William Croker and Catherine Stoddard was settled out of court with the newspaper report noting that this was 'a great disappointment to a large auditory which attended to learn the facts and the fun it was supposed they would produce'.[21]

The public maintained an overwhelming curiosity in these cases throughout the period. The accounts of breach of promise cases were a regular feature of the national and local press, and papers such as the *Belfast Newsletter*, the *Freeman's Journal* and the *Irish Times* also reported on cases that came before the English courts. Indeed, about a quarter of the reports appearing in the Irish press on breach of promise cases were cases from the English courts, which occasionally involved an Irish woman.[22] Many of the papers alerted the public to forthcoming cases. For instance, the *Cork Constitution* noted in 1851 an upcoming case which,

---

[19] Ibid., Chapter 2.   [20] *Belfast Newsletter*, 29 June 1857.
[21] *Belfast Newsletter*, 17 Dec. 1847.
[22] For instance, the *Nation* newspaper reported in 1869 that a 'Miss Morony, a young Irish lady of great personal attraction and of good position in the county Clare', obtained £2,000 damages in an action against an officer of the army in Croydon assizes. Similarly, in 1873, the *Belfast Newsletter* drew readers' attention to a case in the London Court of Common Pleas in which Miss Kate Humphrey, the daughter of a Dublin solicitor, sued Nicholas Vincent Wise, a medical student and a gentleman farmer near Cork. *Belfast Newsletter*, 13 Dec. 1873.

according to the gossip of the courts, is likely to present more than the usual amount of interest excited in such cases. The fair plaintiff is said to be one of the most engaging of our city belles and the defendant, a wealthy captain in a marching regiment ... damages are laid at £3,000. The letters of the defendant, who moved among society of the highest families in the counties of Cork and Limerick will, it is said, afford no small amount of fun.[23]

All kinds of difficulties could, and did, present themselves to intending marriage partners. Defendants often lost interest in plaintiffs and married someone else, even when a courtship had gone on for a long time. Less often the plaintiff lost interest in the defendant and married someone else. Some men used the promise of marriage as a means of persuading women into a sexual relationship, and then abandoned them months or even years later. Sometimes families interfered and parental permission for the marriage was not granted or relatives, siblings or children disapproved of the marriage because of a fear they might lose out in some way in relation to an inheritance or, perhaps, in emotional affection. The amount to be paid as a dowry was often disputed and could lead to the breakdown of a relationship. All of the stories presented by the barristers in court were expected to show their client in the most positive light. Defendants had to provide valid reasons for not proceeding with the marriage and their stories had to be believed by the jury.

There is a similarity about all breach of promise cases in terms of their narrative and exposition in the courts. The stories told in court were fairly standard and perhaps expected by the jury: the injured and wronged woman facing the dishonourable man, not for financial gain but to reinforce her respectability in a public setting.

The language of the courts and the ways in which breach of promise cases were reported changed subtly by the end of the nineteenth century. Whatever rhetorical devices barristers had used over the decades had either diminished considerably or were not reported in the papers. The 'sensational' aspects of the cases were no longer highlighted. The reporting became mundane and matter of fact. Women were, however, still expected to be virtuous and respectable when appearing in court, and men were expected to be considerate and manly in their defence. These cases were essentially about people who had changed their minds, realised they had made mistakes or felt compelled by circumstances to agree to marriages they did not necessarily desire. Breach of promise cases also continued to reveal society's expectation that women should marry, a belief echoed perhaps in the success women had as plaintiffs in these cases.

---

[23] *Cork Constitution*, 25 Nov. 1851.

Breach of promise trials were, therefore, of huge interest to the public. The case of *Blake v Wilkins* in 1817 was so eagerly anticipated that every lodging house in Galway, 'even the humblest in the town was filled to overflowing'. 'Lodging house keepers', reported the *Freeman's Journal*, 'are making now a rich harvest. Beds a pound a night but then it is not so expensive when you get others to join you. Three of us slept in one bed last night in a double-bedded room, and four in the other bed. It was like the black hole of Calcutta'. Blake, in his thirties, was retired on health grounds from the Royal Navy and had sued the widow Wilkins for breach of promise. She was described as a 'vain old lady of 65, possessed of a fee-simple estate of £800 a year'. The court case was the source of much merriment when the defendant's barrister, the well-known advocate Charles Phillips, ridiculed his own client and in the process also won her the case. She was not appreciative, and when Phillips left the court Wilkins attempted to attack him with a horsewhip.[24] In the 1841 Cork case of *Campion v Drew*, where damages were claimed at £5,000, the 'most intense interest and anxiety were evinced by all parties to hear it'. The case was to begin at 9 a.m. but 'long before that hour the grand jury gallery presented a brilliant array of female beauty and fashion'. There were no seats available by 10 a.m., and many women were left standing.[25] In 1863, at a case that came before the Galway assizes the 'court was densely crowded. Several ladies occupied the bar seats, and his lordship accommodated two with seats on the bench'. The case involved a clergyman and the daughter of a 'gentleman'.[26] Throughout the period these cases would have been the talk of the neighbourhood where the plaintiffs and defendants resided.

Much recent historical work has looked upon the court as a theatrical space where witnesses, barristers and judges perform. Before 1869 neither defendant nor plaintiff could appear on their own behalf and the evidence was thus taken from friends, servants and family members. Juries, as previously noted, were overwhelmingly sympathetic to female plaintiffs. In the period between 1865 and 1919, of the 401 cases that came to trial, 331, or over 82 per cent, were decided in favour of the plaintiff, and 46, just over 11 per cent, for the defendant. People's stories were shaped by the legal system. If a suit involved a plea for damages, plaintiffs would emphasise their reduced value in the marriage place, how the breach had made them ill, and so on. It is not clear whether juries worried about women making up these stories, even if this was a defence sometimes used in court. There was some public discussion of the

[24] *Freeman's Journal*, 19 April 1817.   [25] *Freeman's Journal*, 14 Aug. 1841.
[26] *Belfast Newsletter*, 16 March 1863.

possible abuse of breach of promise cases, but this made little impact on the numbers of such cases appearing before the Irish courts. A commentator in the *Irish Times* observed in 1879:

Except the desire to be married, there is nothing the heart of a woman so yearns after as the opportunity of announcing that she is engaged. Nothing can exceed the attachment of a woman to an eligible suitor when he has a large fortune. There is no limit to the rage of a woman 'scorned', as every breach of promise action shows. Starting with these axioms, we find in them, all the materials for the construction of ... the most sensational, legal drama which the episodes of courtship contribute for the enjoyment of a gaping crowd in a law-court. The solution of it all is that the next best thing to a wealthy suitor is the possession of the wealthy suitor's money.[27]

In *O'Dwyer v Maguire,* the defence argued that the plaintiff was a 'clever woman of the world, who knew the game she had to play, and who had entered into a design to entrap the defendant into an agreement to marry her.' She had knowledge, it was declared, of legal technicalities as she had been involved in settling her father's legal suits for debt.[28] This argument made little impression on the jury. Whether women were making up stories or not, the juries decided their verdicts on the range of evidence provided, and the likelihood that the events described actually happened.

Knowing the significance of marriage to women's status in society, juries may have accepted the plaintiff's case more readily because marriage was such an important aspect of women's lives and a case of breach of promise was likely to damage her prospects of finding a suitable spouse. Even when sexual transgression had taken place the jurors remained sympathetic. Although, for example, Eliza McLoughlin was seen on another man's knee kissing him, the jury still awarded her £100 in damages.[29] Mary Ellen Fitzpatrick had been seduced by William Vint, both of County Antrim, and she gave birth in December 1872. He then refused to marry her, claiming that the child was not his. The defence tried to prove the looseness of her character but 'nothing tending to evidence of this was proved except that she allowed herself to be kissed by different young men who had seen her home from dancing parties. It was however deposed that this was one of the Ulster customs among the class to which the parties belonged'. She was awarded £150.[30]

---

[27] *Irish Times,* 28 Jan.1879.
[28] *Irish Times,* 18 Dec. 1879; *Belfast Newsletter,* 18 Dec. 1879; *Freeman's Journal,* 19 Dec. 1879.
[29] *Irish Times,* 7 March 1877.
[30] *Irish Times,* 26 March 1873; *Belfast Newsletter,* 26 March 1873.

The common narrative in the stories told in the court was that a promise had been made, and that it had been broken. The woman, as plaintiff, suffered loss in some way, to her emotions, her reputation, her livelihood or her ability to marry. The cases were presented as tragedies where women required compensation and the restoration of their good name. Romance, love, presents, tokens and sometimes letters all formed part of the story. Friends and family were called as witnesses to the courtship, the promise and the breach, while plaintiffs were expected to have suffered physically and emotionally from the breach; it was anticipated that this suffering would be apparent in their countenance or in their dealings with friends and family. Under the direction of the judge, the jury made the important decisions as to who would win the case and how much in damages and costs were to be paid. Given the numbers of cases that came before the courts it appears that women saw this as an opportunity to rectify a perceived wrong and, perhaps, given the success of plaintiffs in securing damages, as a way of acquiring some monetary reward for being jilted.

Just as women were expected to be feminine and demure in court, men whether as witnesses, defendants or plaintiffs, were expected to be masculine and vigorous. The rhetoric of the court was that it was unmanly to abandon a woman with whom a promise of marriage had been agreed. Such men were open to contempt. In *Brennan v Cassidy* the barrister for the plaintiff noted that when the defendant suddenly married someone else he had left the 'unfortunate girl he had courted for years to be a laughing stock among her friends and neighbours'. It was, he said, a 'shameless, unmanly, and disgraceful thing for a man to do'.[31] Men left themselves open to ridicule when they took breach of promise cases, as did Thomas Butler when he sued Mrs Kealy. She claimed that the plaintiff 'had no property in the world but six children, of which he was anxious she could become the parent'.[32] James Murray had also, according to the defence, committed a 'cruel and unmanly wrong' when he jilted Emma Bickley in 1869.[33] It was widely believed that men were much less affected by breach of promise cases than women. Men, it was argued, deserved no sympathy from the court for their actions.

Women had to present themselves in particular ways in court. Their looks and dress were noted. In evidence, their status, education, family backgrounds, occupations, morality and character were also discussed. In Cork in 1838, in *Rubie v Fitzgerald*, the defendant's barrister noted that Anne Rubie was not in court. He claimed she was older than she

---

[31] *Freeman's Journal*, 14 Feb. 1894.   [32] *Belfast Newsletter*, 10 May 1854.
[33] *Irish Times*, 6 July 1869.

stated and that if she had been pretty then her family 'would have dressed her up and paraded her and sat her in the back row with a sad face' to elicit sympathy from the jury.[34] Miss Delany, on the other hand was at the 'interesting age of 19 and in addition to the greatest of all charms – youth – she was a lady of considerable accomplishments and of superior education'.[35] Women's age was often an issue: where defendants might describe a woman as old if she was beyond thirty while a plaintiff's barristers would argue that she was young. The latter described women who had not reached the age of twenty-one as infants and women in their twenties as young girls, or as very young. It was common for barristers to claim that their clients had not wanted to bring a claim to court and had only been persuaded of this action by family and friends. Women were expected to display modesty, gentleness, passivity and reticence, although in actually taking a case, they were making a statement about their own social value as women in a society that prized marriage.

Barristers performed in the court. They were witty and entertaining. They would try to elicit as much sympathy from the jury as possible. They shaped the coming narrative in their opening statements, often appealing to the jurors' sense of justice. In the 1804 *Fitzgerald v Hawkesworth* suit, the plaintiff's barrister asserted that the case was 'calculated to interest manly sensibility and engage the serious attention and sympathy of every man wishing to maintain the moral and social obligations'. The jury would

find the case before them one in which the duplicity and art of the defendant was commensurate with his professions of affection and that the moment he pretended love, he determined to deceive. They would find hypocrisy and love in the same man; enthusiasm and dissimulation, cunning and candour in the same letters; and in those letters, and under his own hand, they would be able to trace the arts and wiles of the deceitful lover. On the other hand they would see in the plaintiff long constancy, continued affection, and undeviating virtue, up to the present moment. They would behold an affecting picture of patience and long suffering, the lady slow to promise, but having promised, most faithful to the last.[36]

Some barristers impressed the seriousness of the jilted woman's situation on the jury. In an 1893 case, the plaintiff's barrister observed that 'frequently in actions of breach of promise people look for allusions to the sentimental and tried-to-be humorous speeches of counsel. But in this case there was nothing of that kind ... it was a case of a most melancholy and painful character ...' and he proceeded to relate the story of a young woman ruined by a man who had promised her marriage.[37]

---

[34] *Freeman's Journal*, 3 Aug. 1838; *Belfast Newsletter*, 7 Aug. 1838.
[35] *Freeman's Journal*, 4 Dec. 1860.   [36] *Ennis Chronicle*, 24 May 1804.
[37] *Freeman's Journal*, 29 March 1893.

Barristers also won over juries by their wit. When a defendant's barrister asked what damages were sought he was told £3,000. Pretending to be shocked, he stated his belief that there was a 'clerical error' and damages were to be £30, whereupon the plaintiff's barrister replied, 'And I at first supposed it was £30,000'.[38] In *Meagher v Cross*, the plaintiff's barrister played considerably to the jury and the court with grave humour when speaking of the defendant, who was an undertaker in Limerick. The defendant's barrister, following his lead, mocked the range of 'widows and spinsters' in the case, noting that 'a widow scented a husband as the camel was said to scent water afar in the desert'.[39] It was the humour and gentle, if not sometimes blatant, mockery of either the plaintiff, defendant or the witnesses that kept the crowds coming to these courts. Barristers quoted Shakespeare, Dickens and other novelists. They referred to classical literature. In doing so, they revealed not only their erudition but also the literary culture that shaped their perceptions of courtship and marriage.

Barristers also made it clear in court that women suffered differently from men in breach of promise cases. In *Little v Lynch* the plaintiff's barrister asserted,

we all know that woman is made to be won by affection ... If a man be affected, he can go abroad and mix in the pleasures of the world, he can go to plays, balls and public assemblies and forget his grief in the amusements afforded by society; but wound a woman's heart once; take her happy home from her, and you send her an outcast upon the world. Win her heart and betray it, and you send her a bankrupt on society, without a hope except that death may relieve her from the canker, which consumes her heart. She is left to the contempt of her own sex, and rendered an incubus on the happiness of her friends and relatives.[40]

In 1877, Daniel Egan from Roscrea, County Tipperary, sued Jean O'Reilly for breach of promise. When he was asked by the defendant's barrister whether he had come to court 'to recover damages for blighted affections' he stated 'Not exactly'. He claimed his prospects in life were injured, and that although he was only thirty, 'it was not since this courtship commenced I began to look older.' When asked if he had been in love with the girl, he replied 'yes', and he believed that she loved him. He stated that he was 'very much grieved and disappointed when she did not marry [him]'.[41] This was exactly the narrative that women followed in court, and it worked for Egan as the jury awarded him £250 in

---

[38] *Belfast Newsletter*, 12 Nov. 1830.   [39] *Irish Times*, 13 May 1904.
[40] *Belfast Newsletter*, 31 Oct. 1831.
[41] *Irish Times*, 13 Dec. 1877; *Freeman's Journal*, 14 Dec. 1877.

damages. Other male plaintiffs were not so fortunate. While the suits of some were successful in that hundreds of pounds in damages were awarded, the pleas of others were dismissed or mocked by the court. This was exemplified in the case of Samuel Mullens who sued Mary Johnson in 1891 and was awarded £1 in damages.[42]

Dáil Courts

The establishment of the provisional courts by the first Dáil in 1920 were intended to maintain law and order in the early years of the new state. Consequently, the judges in the court dealt with a range of social issues including breach of promise cases, maintenance for deserted wives and children and seduction.[43] The Dáil courts adhered to the law as it existed when the courts were first established. Further research is required on the extensive records of the courts to discover how many cases of breach of promise were processed by the republican judges. There is, however, evidence of the court making awards to women who presented complaints of breach of promise. In 1923, for example, Thomas Mulcahy successfully appealed an award of £200 made for breach of promise to marry Kate Gallagher, and in another case, in 1925, a woman was awarded £100 plus costs although the defendant did not attend the proceedings.[44] The case taken by Kate Roche against Thomas Hartnett provided the court with a detailed account of her courtship by Thomas Hartnett. She sued him for breach of promise to marry her, while her mother and brother took a case against Hartnett for seduction. Roche had first met the defendant when she was a schoolgirl, although aged nineteen at the time. Hartnett had inherited a farm of a hundred acres. They met regularly on Sundays. Her mother did not like Hartnett and

---

[42] *Nation*, 16 May 1891.

[43] The new system of Dáil Courts, known also as republican courts, was established in 1920. A key reason for their establishment was to undermine British rule in Ireland. During the War of Independence the Royal Irish Constabulary, the magistracy and the Dublin executive in the country was collapsing. The Dáil Courts offered a legal infrastructure that ran in parallel to the petty sessions courts. They dealt with a whole range of issues, including land disputes, trespass, assault, etc. The courts were closed in the summer of 1922 and legislation passed by the Irish Free State government in 1923 allowed the business of these courts, about 5,000 cases, to be concluded by 1925. For further information see, Henry Hanna and Denis A. Pringle, *The Statute Law of the Irish Free State, 1922–1928* (Dublin, 1929); Mary Kotsonouris, *Retreat from Revolution: The Dáil Courts, 1920–24* (Dublin, 1993); *The Winding Up of the Dáil Courts, 1922–1925* (Dublin, 2004); Heather Laird, *Subversive Law in Ireland, 1879–1920: From 'Unwritten Law to the Dáil Courts'* (Dublin, 2005).

[44] Dáil Éireann Court Register Book (NAI, DE1/1 2B102, fo. 3, 59; DE1/2 2B102, fo. 85, 12).

believed that he was not a suitable match for her daughter. The couple continued, however, to meet in secret and to write to each other. He gave her small gifts of sweets, apples and chocolate. Hartnett told Roche that as soon as he had his own house they would marry. The couple had been seeing each other for about fifteen years. Roche noted that when they met together 'we behaved as lovers during our meetings. If I asked him was he speaking to any other girl, he'd say that he loved no-one but me. He always kissed me, loved me, and promised me marriage'. Finally, he told her that they would be married in June 1920. 'If anything occurred he said it would be of great assistance in helping on the marriage with my people'. No doubt Hartnett was suggesting that they have sex and that she would become pregnant. She refused. However, in October 1920 the couple were sitting up against a ditch when Hartnett argued that her mother 'couldn't say anything against the marriage, if I was in that condition'. She finally gave in and 'allowed him to do what he liked to me then'. The 'seduction', as she called it, took place down a lane. The couple, according to Roche's evidence, had sex on one more occasion and then Kate discovered that she was pregnant. Kate also admitted that her mother had made two other matches for her but she had rejected both because she wished to marry Hartnett. When the case finally came to an end in 1921, the Dáil court dismissed the breach of promise action, stating that there was no corroboration for the promise being made. Kate's mother and brother were allowed £100 and costs, for the seduction claim. Originally Roche had sought £3,000 for the breach of promise case, while her mother and brother looked for the same amount for seduction. Hartnett appealed on the grounds that the damages were excessive and then withdrew his appeal. Roche sought a retrial, which was finally listed for hearing in July 1924, by which time the courts had been wound up.[45]

Damages

Numerous factors appear to have influenced juries in deciding the level of damages to be paid. In a substantial number of cases the defendant admitted that a promise of marriage had been given, but that circumstances whether personal, familial or financial had made the marriage impossible. Jurors took account of how long the couple had been courting, whether a reasonable time had elapsed for the proposed marriage to occur, how the defendant behaved throughout the courtship, the

---

[45] *Kate Roche and Others v Thomas Hartnett* (NAI, Dáil Éireann Court Register Book, H 15/16).

couple's social compatibility and whether there were witnesses to any promise of marriage. They also took note of the ways in which the couple interacted in company. The jury's role was, very often, essentially to decide how serious the breach was by examining the contextual details provided by the lawyers and witnesses, and then assessing the level of damages to be awarded. Factors such as the proximity of the wedding date, and whether the plaintiff had purchased wedding clothes or arranged a wedding feast, also helped to determine the level of damages awarded. The jurors were often themselves parents and no doubt were thinking of their own daughters when cases came before them. Lawyers often spoke to jurors in terms of parental care and this may also have influenced how juries decided and assessed damages. Juries expected to hear tales of the physical deterioration of the jilted woman, and her physical decline in the event of being abandoned by her expected husband. Barristers knew what stories to construct to elicit the greatest sympathy from the jury for their clients.

Money was a significant feature of breach of promise cases. Whoever lost had to pay not only damages but often the legal costs of the winning party, and these were determined by the jury. In Limerick, for example, damages ranged from £3,000 to less than £20, which was similar to other Irish courts. Of the eighty-one cases for which damages were documented in the period from 1764 to 1864, the average award for a breach of promise was £209. Individual awards varied between a very precise £3,596 in the 1816 case of *McCarthy v Grace* to £5 in an 1833 case. In the eleven cases decided in the 1830s, the average award was £399, an average distorted by the award of £3,000 in the 1837 case of *Head v Purdon*. Between 1865 and 1919 the average award in a case was £183. According to the judicial statistics, the highest possible award was £5,000, which appears never to have been made, and the lowest awards were around £3. The majority of awards were between £5 and £200, with over 209, about 44 per cent of the damages, being within this range. In a few cases, the damages awarded were so small that the plaintiff had essentially lost the case. In 1883, for instance, Thomas Halliday Kingsley, a London-based medical assistant approaching, as the report noted, 'middle age' sued Miss Eliza Annie Peile of Dublin for alleged breach of promise and was looking for damages of £2,000.[46] The jury acknowledged that there had been a marriage contract between the couple and that the contract had not been rescinded by mutual agreement, but the plaintiff was allowed only a farthing in damages. Technically, Kingsley

---

[46] *Irish Times*, 13 Jan. 1883.

was in the right but the jury clearly sided with the defendant. At the same time Peile had sued the plaintiff for misrepresenting his situation to her, and the jury awarded her the £100 damages she sought, plus costs. Kingsley was thus considerably out of pocket in this case and the jury's verdict and the award of what was described as 'derisory damages' publicly declared that he had been morally wrong to take the case.[47]

One of the largest awards made in the period was the £3,500 damages and £96 in costs awarded to Mary-Anne McCarthy in a suit against William Grace in 1816. Unusually the case had come before the courts previously and damages had been awarded, but second case was taken in order to increase the award. Mary-Anne McCarthy, who lived in Killarney, was a cousin of Daniel O'Connell and he appears to have acted as her guardian as well as representing her in court. At the time of the trial McCarthy was about eighteen years old, 'of a most respectable family and connections, of great personal beauty, educated with the greatest care, and distinguished for the delicacy of her manners and purity of her conduct'.[48] The defendant, William Grace, was a 'gentleman of high birth ... of honorable [sic] profession, of unimpeached character, with great advantages of personal appearance, a good fortune in possession, and a still better one in expectancy'.[49] Letters were produced in court to show that there had been a promise of marriage. O'Connell testified that Grace had acknowledged the promise, but that he had since inherited a substantial sum of money (£18,000) and he had, therefore, asked to break off the match. O'Connell then suggested that the defendant had lied to him about these circumstances. The judge advised the jury that 'if ever there was a promise of marriage solemnly, deliberately, and repeatedly made, this, in my judgment is that'.[50]

Issues of class, as evident in this case, played a significant role in the level of damages awarded. The higher the social class the greater the award. This rule is also evident in cases in which the defendant and plaintiff were from different classes. In 1812, in Cork, a young man of wealth was accused of seducing a maid in his father's house under promise of marriage. She had a baby and the jury awarded her 100 guineas in damages, a large sum for a servant at the time.[51] These cross-class alliances between an employer and servant were more often cases of seduction, though many appeared in court as breach of promise

---

[47] *Irish Times*, 20 Jan. 1883.
[48] *Trial of William Grace, Esq., Captain in the Queen's County Regt. of Militia for a Breach of Promise of Marriage to Miss Mary-Anne McCarthy of Killarney Before Mr. Justice Mayne and a Special Jury at Tralee Assizes March 27, 1816* (Cork, 1816), p. 4.
[49] Ibid.   [50] Ibid., p. 28.   [51] *Freeman's Journal*, 2 April 1812.

cases. Often illegitimate children had been born of the relationship, with the father refusing to recognise the infant as his own. Juries awarding damages in these cases were ensuring men took some responsibility for their actions.[52]

It was also the jury's work to assess damages. In the *McCarthy v Grace* case the jury took note of the financial circumstances of the defendant and the social damage caused to the plaintiff. The defendant, Grace, could clearly afford the damages. O'Connell had testified that McCarthy's health had gone into serious decline since the breach and her 'spirits had suffered a considerable depression by reason of the defendant's conduct towards her'; he noted that he feared she would become consumptive.[53] The breakdown of health, depression, a 'changed person', the 'injury to reputation', were the consequences noted by barristers in jilted women. Sympathetic juries took such physical and mental deterioration seriously and awarded damages accordingly.

In cases where couples were from a lower social class, juries generally awarded damages within the context of the financial circumstances of the defendant. In 1877, for example, Mary Gorman, a dressmaker aged twenty-seven, sued John Phillips, a builder, about forty-seven years old, for breach of promise and damages of £760. The jury awarded her £30.[54] Susan Harris, a dairymaid, sued Thomas Boyd, a coachman, both employed in the same house, for breach of promise in 1892. She sought damages of £500. The court was informed that 'impropriety' took place between them on several occasions and eventually she left her employment. By the time the matter came to court the defendant had acquired two houses and a farm. The substantial award of £55 damages reflected his newly acquired wealth.[55]

To put these damages into some context it is useful to note typical wage and income levels in Ireland over the period. These are general figures and it should be kept in mind that there were regional variations in income levels. Maura Cronin, in her study of labour in Cork city, has shown that in 1839 a general labourer could earn between 10d and 1s per day; by 1900 they could earn between 2s 6d and 2s and 8d per day.[56] In 1885, agricultural labourers were earning in the region of 9s to 12s per week. An unskilled labourer working in Dublin in 1885 might have earned in the region of 15 to 20 shillings per week. Skilled workers were

---

[52] See Chapter 11 on desertion for more on the responsibility of husbands towards their wives and families.

[53] *Trial of William Grace*, pp. 19–20.   [54] *Irish Times*, 24 Nov. 1877.

[55] *Irish Times*, 27 July 1892; *Freeman's Journal*, 27 July 1892.

[56] Maura Cronin, *Country, Class or Craft? The Politicization of the Skilled Artisan in Nineteenth-Century Cork* (Cork, 1994), pp. 28–9.

getting 33 shillings weekly. Domestic servants who 'lived in' earned £10–£12 a year in Dublin in 1901.[57] In 1904, Charles Cameron surveyed the earnings and expenses of the poor in Dublin and noted that a tailor could earn only 10 shillings per week and from that paid rent of 2s 6d, which left 7s 6s to cover food, fuel, clothing, and so on.[58] In the 1880s the average annual salary for a police constable was £75, while a school teacher had £49 and the perk of a house to live in. Mona Hearn notes that, in the 1880s, a young middle-class man hoping to marry on £300 a year and expecting to start a family would have to budget very carefully. Food would have taken up at least 30 per cent of that income and about 8 per cent would have gone towards the payment of servants.[59] By the early 1900s, a dispensary doctor would earn about £200 from dispensary work alone. A shop assistant could earn between £1 10s to £2 per week. Leading barristers could earn up to £5,000 a year, but the average earnings were closer to £800–£1,000.[60] These figures indicate that an award to a plaintiff of even the relatively small sum of £30 could make a significant difference to the financial status of a skilled worker or domestic servant.

The case of *Rubie v Foley* caused considerable excitement in Cork as both parties were of the 'strong farmer' class. She was a Protestant and he a Catholic. The couple had become acquainted in November 1835, and Rubie claimed that though they had not spoken of marriage, 'he was always coming after her, quite undisguised'. He used to come and see her twice or three times a day, and Foley had visited her relatives and been accepted as her suitor. Foley married another. In court it was noted that Foley's father had a 'large' farm but Rubie's father had told Foley he could only give his daughter a £200 fortune. There was some evidence that Foley had given Rubie a gold ring. The defence claimed that Rubie 'was on the wrong side of 30 and cut her wise teeth long ago'. Her family, it was claimed, fixed their 'eye on a young clown – a man who knows nothing but his spade and shovel, and his cart and horse, and how to dig potatoes – a man who never went home sober and because she is a little too far gone for market, they say "we'll get him for a husband for her, or if not, a little lob of his money"'. Declaring Foley to be a 'mere peasant living in a thatched cabin, that nobody would marry' seems to have

---

[57] H. D. Gribbon, 'Economic and social history, 1850–1921' in W. E. Vaughan (ed.), *A New History of Ireland: Ireland under the Union II: 1870–1921* (Oxford, 1996), pp. 320–4.
[58] Sir Charles A. Cameron, *How the Poor Live* (Dublin, 1904), pp. 6–7.
[59] M. Hearn, 'How Victorian families lived' in M. Daly, M. Hearn and H. Pearson, *Dublin's Victorian Houses* (Dublin, 1998), pp. 66–70.
[60] R. Barry O'Brien, *Dublin Castle and the Irish People* (London, 1909), p. 387.

worked for the defence. The verdict for the plaintiff was low at £20 damages. Issues of age, class and religion, and the fact that a proposal of marriage appears not to have been made, were probably factors that made the case a relatively fruitless one for the plaintiff.[61]

By contrast, an award of £4,000 was made to Miss Kate Graves in her claim against Jonas Morris in Cork in 1875. Both individuals were from 'distinguished families' and Morris had £15,000, which he controlled when he came of age, and was set to inherit a property worth a further £8,000 a year from his grandfather. Graves had previously been engaged to John Arnott, the founder of Arnott's department store, but that engagement had been broken off. There was no dispute that a promise of marriage had been made and the judge, in his summing up, declared that 'there could not be a shadow of a doubt that this contract had been violated and broken in the most plain and decisive terms by this gentleman'.[62] He guided the jury to consider 'compensation that should be given to set the young lady in as advantageous a position as possible before the eyes of those who had been feasting themselves with the scandal and gossip which they had been hearing'. The jury made the substantial award of £4,000, which had the intention of securing the reputation of the woman involved and being a large enough award to punish the defendant.

Unsurprisingly, not all defendants could afford to pay the damages awarded against them, or they chose to defy the court order and refused to pay them. Eliza Hanlon, for instance won £50 plus £34 8s 10d. costs in her suit against James Kelly, but he did not pay her the money. He allegedly sent her a letter with two farthings in it, saying that is all she would get. Kelly later offered £20 in full satisfaction of the debt but the court decided that the full amount was to be paid in instalments.[63] Sometimes damages were irrecoverable. John Johnson was taken to court by Hamilton Perry in 1838 to enforce the payment of damages. Johnson had been declared insolvent and admitted that the jury in the case had awarded £70 against him, though they also announced him a 'pauper'. Perry was willing to let this judgment go if Johnson would marry his daughter, but Johnson stated he would prefer to go to prison. It was claimed that Johnson's father was a 'farmer in comfortable circumstances'. However, in reality, it seems that Johnson and Perry were of the 'humble sort'. Perry was advised to withdraw his petition otherwise

---

[61] *Freeman's Journal*, 3 Aug. 1838.
[62] *Freeman's Journal*, 28 July 1875. See also *Freeman's Journal*, 27 July 1875.
[63] *Irish Times*, 7 Feb. 1877.

Johnson would go to prison for a 'very long period'. The petition was thus withdrawn.[64]

Younger women courting older men was a common enough occurrence in these court cases, but one always noted by lawyers as laughable and somehow unnatural. Juries recognised that older men often had considerable wealth, and such relationships were understood and accepted as a pragmatic economic transaction. Mary Ann Kavanagh, aged twenty-six, sued John Magarry, a man 'almost sixty', in Dublin in 1830. She was the daughter of a respectable publican, and damages were laid at the considerable sum of £1,000. The promise was fully proved, though the defence sought to lessen the impact of whatever damages might be allowed by noting that Mary Ann was a barmaid. She was 'the Hebe of the tap-room, who administered to the consolation of certain good fellows, who met every evening in Patrick Street, at her father's house, against a sexagenarian, who belonged to that class of worthy persons, who in the spirit of thrifty benevolence, write "money to be lent" over their doors.' The defence implied she got him drunk and convinced him that she was in love in order to induce him to propose. But he then realised that he was 'engaged in a perilous adventure'. He broke it off but the defence noted it was best for both of them as 'He has escaped from her and she from him ... What injury has she suffered? Surely not one of you will think that she was in love? She might have protested it to the old pawnbroker, but it required a credulous senility to believe her... She is better off now than if she were married to him and his £14,00 a year and his £14,000 in bank stock'. The jury, however, clearly accepted that the old man had committed himself and awarded £700. Those in court considered the damages excessive.[65]

In the case of *Williams v Good*, heard at Cork County Crown Court in 1876, the requested damages were £3,000. Sophia Williams was twenty-three years old, while the defendant, William Baker Good, was seventy. Williams, who came from Macroom, lived with her brother and his wife, who was a relation of the defendant. Good had lived in India where he had a business and made a large fortune. He was a widower, without children, who returned to Ireland in 1875. Good proposed three times and was finally accepted. In her testimony, Sophia stated that she

---

[64] *Freeman's Journal*, 7 May 1838. For other cases see, *Belfast Newsletter*, 29 June 1857; *Sunday Independent*, 19 Jan. 1913.

[65] *Freeman's Journal*, 9 Nov. 1830; *Connaught Journal*, 18 Nov. 1830. For cases see, *Irish Times*, 9 May 1879; *Freeman's Journal*, 9 May 1879.

referred the third proposal to her brother and that 'It was ultimately arranged that I should accept him'. When asked by his lawyer whether she liked him at first, she stated, 'I never told him that', which gave rise to laughter in the court. The defence lawyer asked, 'If your brothers had not agreed the match you would not have consented? No.' In this case, with the defendant agreeing to a verdict for damages and using the age gap as mitigation, the jury awarded the substantial sum of £2,000 and costs.[66] The jurors accepted that this was a financial transaction and understood that a man of this age had little physical attraction to a young woman. His attraction was in his social status and his money, perhaps enough to make up for physical deficiencies.

Juries had little sympathy for men who married someone else immediately after breaking an engagement, or without telling the woman that they were courting someone else. In 1894, Bridget Moynihan, who worked as a cook in Dublin, took a case against Thomas Meehan, a farmer in County Tipperary. He asked Bridget for £20, which she gave him as part of her fortune. He then met with her in Dublin and told her he had to break the engagement as his father had left him in financial difficulties and he gave her back her £20. He told her he was going to America. She then heard that he had not gone to America but had married another woman, from whom he got £80. In a feat of true justice, the jury awarded the plaintiff £80 in damages.[67]

Juries also took account of the length of courtship when assessing damages. At the Limerick assizes in 1880, Maryanne Griott of Ballymorris, County Clare, sued Robert Ryan, of the same place, to recover £1,000 damages. The couple had courted for seventeen years and the plaintiff's lawyer described the case as 'the most heartless breach of faith that was ever submitted to a jury'. At the time the case was taken, the plaintiff was thirty-four years old, and the defendant thirty-nine. The defendant, who married someone else, continued to visit Maryanne up to the week before his marriage. The priest testified that he knew of the engagement and refused to marry the defendant to a new wife, but Ryan got a letter from the bishop, which made him do so. The priest's testimony secured the case for the plaintiff; the defendant offered no defence other than denying there had been any promise of marriage. The jury awarded Girott the full £1,000 originally sought, a rare occurrence, and it was reported that there 'was great applause in court, the galleries being filled with ladies.'[68]

---

[66] *Freeman's Journal*, 7 Aug. 1876.   [67] *Freeman's Journal*, 31 May 1894.
[68] *Irish Times*, 8 March 1880; *Freeman's Journal*, 8 March 1880.

Conclusion

The testimony given in court was by necessity biased. Where both plaintiff and defendant presented their cases, as they were able to do after 1869, there is a possibility of understanding how the relationship had evolved and how it had broken down. The narratives of these cases were shaped by the plaintiffs and defendants, by the barristers and the judges, and in turn were filtered to the general public through the newspaper reports. It is likely, though impossible to prove, that these reports, including the verbatim quoting of letters, shaped how Irish men and women conducted their own romances.

Women certainly felt themselves wronged when promises to marry were broken. Taking their cases to court was very rarely about enforcing the promise; indeed, many of the men had married other women by the time the case got to court. In only a few instances did the jury, or the barristers, suggest that a marriage might still occur between the couple. Expected gender roles were evident in the stories told in these cases. However, it is also worth noting that 'typical' gendered expectations of the roles of men and women in society expressed in the courts were rhetorical and legal strategies used by barristers to win a case. What juries were doing, to some extent, was reinforcing the expectation that men be honourable and keep their promises, impressing upon the defendants, and the public, that the performance of masculinity implied an adherence to the duties of men. Men's failures were being punished. It was understood that sexual inter-course outside marriage could be a dangerous threat to respectability, but within the context of a promise of marriage women were shielded from a loss of character. Given their success in prosecuting such cases, this was a legal process where women started with an advantage even though they were presenting their experiences in court, possibly the most public forum for airing personal tales. Women of the lower-middle classes, in particular, felt able to take such cases in greater numbers as the nineteenth century progressed. Indeed, the court offered them a degree of financial protection, and perhaps vindication, by making awards for damages. Juries, in awarding damages, were also making pronouncements on acceptable male and female behaviour. Whereas in general society only women were held responsible for the serious consequences of pre-marital sexual intercourse, these breach of promise cases went some way to place responsibility on men for their actions and to make them publicly accountable for their behaviour, particularly in post-Famine Ireland, where social and economic constraints made marriage less likely for all men and women.

6   Abductions

On the night of 4 March 1822 in the townland of Aughrim, near Liscarroll in County Cork, twelve well-armed men entered the house of Richard Goold, the son of a prosperous farmer. The abductors were searching for the eldest daughter of the family. In one of the bedrooms they found sixteen-year old Honora Goold and asked her whether she were the eldest daughter. She said she was not but the men did not believe her. They ordered her to dress and forcibly took her from the house. Placing Honora onto a horse ridden by James Brown the party sped off. At one stage the group stopped at a public house where six other men joined them. In that group was a blacksmith, Walter Fitzmaurice, a noted leader of the Rockite agrarian movement, and a man accused of murder and other crimes. The abduction party then headed off into the hills of West Limerick and eventually, riding through the night, came to the house of David Leahy, a comfortable farmer, who lived with his wife and two sons. A maid and a niece of Leahy's wife, Mary Cahill, who was a little older than Honora, were also in the house that morning. James Brown soon realised that they had abducted the wrong daughter, but he still proposed marriage to Honora, who refused him. Over the next few weeks Brown repeatedly raped Honora in an attempt to force her to marry him. Honora was moved from cabin to cabin during her incarceration and, eventually, David Leahy suggested to Honora that she would be released if she signed a document saying she was in his house of her own free will. She agreed, and when she was finally rescued she was found alone in a cabin 'in a most pitiable condition'. The abduction, deemed a 'barbaric and preeminently atrocious case',[1] was widely reported in the British and Irish press. The youth of the woman, the intense search for her and the involvement of a noted Rockite, at a time when the authorities sought to

An earlier version of this chapter was published as Maria Luddy, 'Abductions in nineteenth-century Ireland', *New Hibernia Review/Iris Eireannach*, 17, 2 (Summer 2013), 17–44.
[1] *Freeman's Journal*, 27 Aug. 1822.

impose law and order against agrarian disturbances in the countryside, made it a case of great interest.[2] Once recovered, Honora gave information to the police about her abductors, most of whom were eventually captured, with Fitzmaurice giving himself up to the authorities. James Brown escaped and it was thought that he had left the country for America. When the case came to court Honora, attired in 'mourning dress', signifying that she was grieving for a loss, gave her testimony 'correct and distinct, interrupted only by those bursts of acute sensibility which the narration of the unparalleled outrage committed upon her caused in the recital of it before the font of justice'.[3] The Leahys claimed that they had been terrorised into supporting the abduction, but they were convicted and sentenced to seven years' transportation. Fitzmaurice, at his trial in August 1822, pleaded guilty to the charge of abduction. Having probably made an agreement with the authorities he was pardoned. A man named Costello was executed for his involvement in the crime, and in all eleven other individuals were imprisoned or transported for their participation in the abduction.

Essentially, abduction can be described as the practice of carrying off a woman with the purpose of compelling her to marry a particular man who would then have access to the available dowry of money, land or other property, linked to the woman. In Irish folklore terms for abduction included 'snatching', *sugan*, *fuadach chun posta*, and 'left-handed marriage'.[4] The fact that abduction stories can be found in the folklore of the country indicates that such tales were part of rural culture.[5] The history of abductions in Ireland has received some attention from historians, with most of the research focusing on the eighteenth century and on the higher levels of society.[6] James Kelly and Thomas Power agree that

---

[2] For details of the case see *Freeman's Journal*, 9, 22 Aug. 12 Sept. 1822; *Limerick News*, 1, 5, 26 Aug., 9 Sept. 1822. British newspapers that covered the case include, *Caledonian Mercury*, 28 March 1822; *Trewman's Exeter Flying Post*, 4 April, 29 Aug. 1822; *Morning Chronicle* 24 April, 17, 30 Aug., 7 Sept. 1822; *Jackson's Oxford Journal*, 10 Aug. 1822; *Glasgow Herald*, 12 Aug. 1822; *The Examiner*, 11 Aug. 1822. The Goold case was also published in various editions of *The Newgate Calendar, or, the Chronicles of Crime* (Philadelphia, 1840 ed.), pp. 65–7.

[3] *Freeman's Journal*, 27 Aug. 1822.

[4] Sean Ó Suilleabháin, *Handbook of Irish Folklore* (Detroit, 1970), p. 200.

[5] See various stories in *Béaloideas: Journal of the Folklore Society of Ireland*.

[6] James Kelly has pioneered the study of abductions in Ireland. See his 'The abduction of women of fortune in eighteenth-century Ireland', *Eighteenth-Century Ireland/Iris an Dá Chultúr*, 9 (1994), 7–43. For other accounts see Toby Barnard, *The Abduction of a Limerick Heiress* (Dublin, 1998); Michael Durey, 'Abduction and rape in Ireland in the era of the 1798 rebellion', *Eighteenth-Century Ireland/Iris an Dá Chultúr*, 21 (2006), 27–47; Thomas P. Power, *Forcibly without Her Consent: Abductions in Ireland, 1700–1850* (New York, 2010), which, despite its title, focuses mostly on the eighteenth century. Kiera Lindsey, '"The absolute distress of females": Irish abduction and British newspapers,

abduction was about money and status; Power also suggests that abduction was a display of communally sanctioned violence against women. Kelly argues that those involved in abductions in the eighteenth century came from a 'narrow band of society'.[7] For the first half of the nineteenth century this 'narrow band' was considerably wider than might be expected, with servants abducting servants, and landless labourers abducting women of little fortune. Likewise, there was often considerable community and local opposition to abductions. Abduction was a noted phenomenon of the eighteenth and nineteenth centuries and, within the context of the history of marriage in Ireland, reflects the desire, and in some cases the ability, of couples to overcome parental decisions on their marriage partners, but perhaps, primarily, the desire among individuals and families for the property and status that was achievable through marriage. Abduction was most often a crime of considerable terror and violence and it is worth exploring for what it says about marriage strategy; attitudes to marriage and consent; parental authority and property; women's agency in choosing a marriage partner and the value of women in Irish society. Exploring the phenomenon of abduction in Ireland between the seventeenth and twentieth centuries allows us to reveal the extent of the phenomenon, to look at the motives behind and assess reactions to abductions, including the role of the family and wider community in this often very violent enterprise. Finally, this chapter will analyse how abductors were punished and evaluate the significance of rape in abduction trials.[8]

The wider literature on abduction tends to be written by anthropologists, is geographically specific and focuses heavily on social norms, the impact of the law and the relationship of abduction to marriage and raising social status. These are elements that can be found in the case of Irish abductions.[9] Kathryn Sloan's work on 'runaway daughters' in late nineteenth-century Oaxaca, Mexico, reveals the complex

---

1800–1850', *The Journal of Imperial and Commonwealth History*, 42, 2 (2014), 625–44. Abductions are also mentioned in A. P. W. Malcolmson, *The Pursuit of the Heiress: Aristocratic Marriage in Ireland 1740–1840* (2nd ed., Belfast, 2006). There is a broader literature on medieval abductions in France and England. See for example, Garthine Walker, '"Strange kind of stealing": Abduction in early modern Wales' in M. Roberts and S. Clarke (eds.), *Women and Gender in Early Modern Wales* (Cardiff, 2000), pp. 50–74; Gwen Seabourne, *Imprisoning Medieval Women: The Non-judicial Confinement and Abduction of Women in England, c. 1170–1509* (Farnham, 2011); Caroline S. Dunn, *Damsels in Distress: The Abduction of Women in Medieval England* (Cambridge, 2012).

[7] Kelly, 'The abduction of women of fortune', 40.

[8] Power, *Forcibly without Her Consent*, has valuable comments to make on nineteenth-century abductions in Ireland.

[9] See *Anthropological Quarterly*, 47, 3 (July 1974). Special issue.

interrelationships between parents and children over marriage choice, and the ways in which courts were used to mediate these relationships. Parental approval for a marriage was often circumvented by means of *rapo*, the abduction of a woman by physical force or violence in order to satisfy the sexual desires of men. However, Sloan reveals that such cases were most often collusive, used as a means to force parents to accept their daughter's partner of choice. Bound up with all of this were issues of sexual honour, the symbolic culture around *rapo* and the changing relationships between the state, the rise of liberalism and individual freedoms.[10] In Ireland it is evident that a small number of abductions were perpetrated to force a marriage against parental consent, though Irish courts were rarely involved in resolving these collusive abductions.

Abduction and the Law

As Power has noted, the laws relating to abduction in Ireland followed closely those operating in England.[11] The first relevant act was that of 1634, which was a specifically Irish statute. This act 'for the punishment of such as shall take away maidens that be inheritors' followed the stipulations of an earlier English act of 1557–1558.[12] In 1707, a new act was passed in the Irish parliament, which focused especially on the property implications of an abduction.[13] A separate section of this act related to a particular Irish abduction. In April 1707, the thirteen-year old heiress Margaret MacNamara had been taken from her home by John O'Bryan and others. O'Bryan is said to have forced MacNamara to marry him, before a couple beggar, under threat of rape. O'Bryan was a Catholic and MacNamara a Protestant. MacNamara's mother applied to the House of Commons for relief, and the act of 1707 addressed some of the circumstances of the O'Bryan/MacNamara abduction. The 1707 act stipulated that anyone over the age of fourteen who abducted and married, with the woman's consent (but not that of her parents), an heiress, or woman of substance under the age of eighteen, could be sent to prison for three years on conviction, as could his abducting companions. Importantly, the abductor would have no access, at any stage, to the profits from his

---

[10] Kathryn A. Sloan, *Runaway Daughters: Seduction, Elopement, and Honor in Nineteenth-Century Mexico* (Albuquerque, 2008).
[11] Power, *Forcibly without Her Consent*, pp. 54–8.
[12] An Act for the Punishment of Such as Shall Take Away Maidens That Be Inheritors. 10 Charles 1, c.17. 1634.
[13] Power, *Forcibly without Her Consent*, p. 56.

abductee's estate, which was to be vested in trustees.[14] If a woman was abducted without her consent then all of the abductors were liable to a death sentence on conviction. Any Anglican clergyman who performed such marriages was to be deprived of his living. As Kelly notes, the real fear here was the abduction of a Protestant by a Catholic and the law makers were determined that an abductor should not benefit materially from the crime.[15] The penalties under this act were severe, but it proved ineffective since few abductees were willing to prosecute or give evidence in court.

A section of the 1735 Act 'for the more effectual preventing [of] clandestine marriages' stipulated that where the parties were under the age of twenty-one and married without the written consent of a father or guardian then the marriage was void.[16] In 1829, the 1828 Offences against the Person Act which covered England and Wales, was applied to Ireland.[17] Under this act, the punishment for the abduction of a woman or girl, against her consent, for the purposes of a forced marriage or rape was clearly specified: 'every such offender, and every accessory before the fact of such offence, shall be guilty of a felony', and 'being convicted thereof, shall suffer death as a felon'. Every 'accessory after the fact to such offence' could be transported for life or 'for any term not less than seven years or, to be imprisoned with or without hard labour' for no longer than three years.[18] In addition, if a girl under 16 was abducted, the perpetrator would be guilty of a misdemeanour and could be fined and/or imprisoned.[19] Like all of the legislation on abductions the real point was to reinforce parental authority and to protect property.

Further legislation, the Offences against the Person Act of 1861, retained punishment for the forcible and violent abduction of women.[20] After the passing of the 1885 Criminal Law Amendment Act any person who took a girl, under eighteen, from her parents' or guardian's custody with intent to have her 'unlawfully and carnally known by any man' was guilty of a misdeamour, and on conviction was liable to up to two years' imprisonment with or without hard labour.[21] In practice, as we will see later, the majority of those committed in cases of abduction were released; the full severity of the law, that is the death sentence, was rarely imposed for this crime.

---

[14] An Act for the More Effectual Preventing the Taking Away and Marrying Children against the Wills of Their Parents or Guardians. 6 Ann c.16. 1707.

[15] Kelly, 'The abduction of women of fortune', 11–12.

[16] An Act for the More Effectual Preventing Clandestine Marriages. 9 Geo. II c.11. 1735.

[17] A Bill for Consolidating and Amending the Statutes in Ireland relating to the Offences against the Person. 10 Geo. IV c.34. 1829.

[18] Ibid.   [19] Ibid.

[20] An Act to Consolidate and Amend the Statute Law of England and Ireland Relating to Offences against the Person. 24 & 25 Vict. c.100. 1861. The concern with property remained a feature of the 1861 Act.

[21] An Act to Make Further Provision for Women and Girls, the Suppression of Brothels, and Other Purposes. 48 & 49 Vict. c.69. 1885.

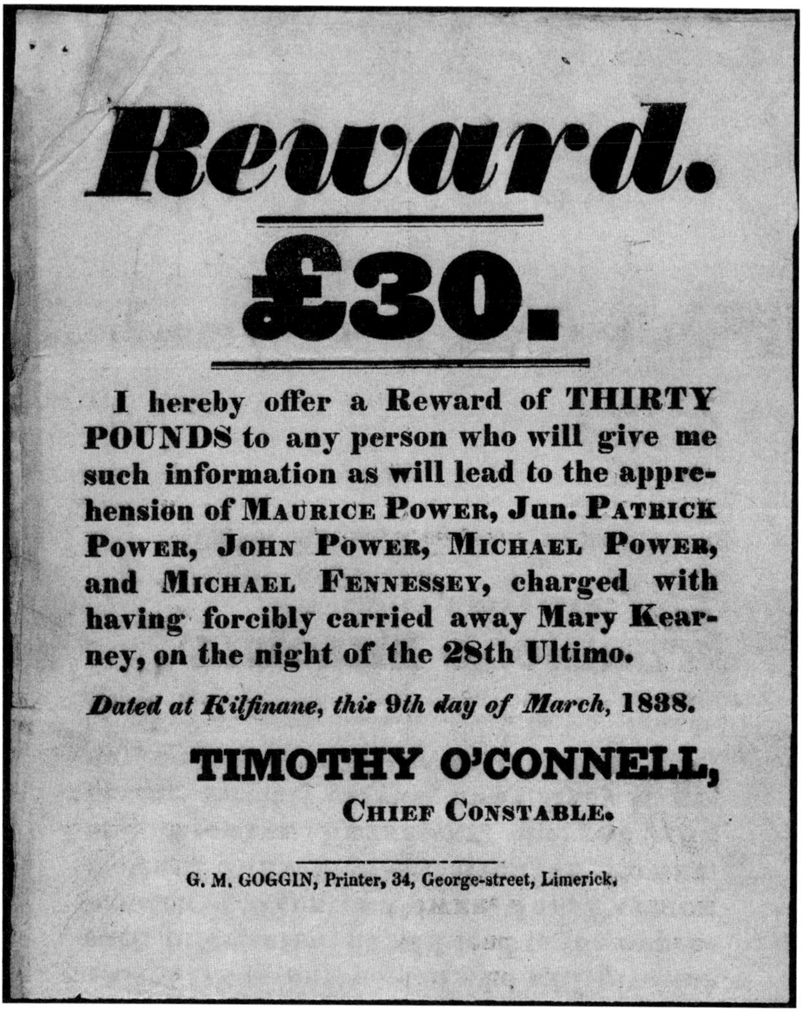

Reward.

£30.

I hereby offer a Reward of THIRTY POUNDS to any person who will give me such information as will lead to the apprehension of MAURICE POWER, Jun. PATRICK POWER, JOHN POWER, MICHAEL POWER, and MICHAEL FENNESSEY, charged with having forcibly carried away Mary Kearney, on the night of the 28th Ultimo.

Dated at Kilfinane, this 9th day of March, 1838.

TIMOTHY O'CONNELL,
CHIEF CONSTABLE.

G. M. GOGGIN, Printer, 34, George-street, Limerick.

Illustration 6.1 Rewards were commonly offered for information on abductions, particularly in the eighteenth century where wealthy women had been abducted. Such rewards were less common by the 1830s.

The Extent of Abductions

Before examining abductions in more detail it is useful to look at the extent of the practice, though reliable information on the numbers of abductions is only available from the eighteenth to the twentieth centuries. All of the official statistics associated with abduction need to be treated with caution, and it seems likely that abductions were under-recorded in official records. For instance, the parish priest of Moyarta, County Clare, Malachi Duggan, noted in 1824 that in a period of about forty years there had been in the region of forty abductions in his parish.[22] However, newspaper reports and official statistics account for forty-one abductions in the whole of County Clare from 1700 to 1814.[23] There are a number of reasons why abductions are under-recorded in official returns. Generally, over the period, 'successful' abductions might not necessarily be publicly acknowledged. For instance, in an inquest on a murder victim that took place in Tullamore in 1835, it was revealed that the victim's son-in-law, Jeremiah Mara, had probably committed the murder. Mara had had a relationship with the victim's daughter but she had refused his offer of marriage. He explained to the coroner that he was then 'driven to the necessity of taking her away by force'.[24] The couple did marry and lived with her father. The property of the murder victim was put at risk when a second daughter was about to marry, and Mara believed that if that marriage occurred he would have lost out on an inheritance from his father-in-law's farm. Essentially what we see here is that Mara had, through abduction, secured his marriage to a relatively well-off farmer's daughter. It was in essence a successful abduction. However, that there was an abduction at all only comes to light because of the inquest report.[25] Another difficulty with abductions is that they were not always recorded as such. In some cases, the police mistook abduction for rape or an incident of rape as

---

[22] *State of Ireland, Minutes of Evidence Taken before the Select Committee Appointed to Inquire into the Disturbances in Ireland, in the Last Session of Parliament, 13th May–18th June 1824,* HC 1825 (20), vii, pp. 209–10.

[23] There is a discrepancy in the overall figures for abduction. Kelly notes 180 abductions between 1701 and 1800; Power provides a figure of 136 to 138 for abductions between 1700 and 1802. Our research suggests the number of abductions between 1700 and 1802 was at least 215. The figures suggest that the phenomenon was more widespread in the eighteenth century than has been previously noted. Assessing the number of abductions also allows for a more thorough investigation of, among other issues, the social levels of both abductors and abductees. See Power, *Forcibly without Her Consent,* p. 102; Kelly, 'The abduction of women of fortune', p. 41.

[24] *Freeman's Journal,* 8 Aug. 1838.

[25] Ibid. In a murder case brought to court in County Mayo in 1844 it was revealed that the victim was killed during an unsuccessful, and unrecorded, abduction. See, *Mayo Constitution,* 30 July 1844. Another abduction came to light in a trial relating to the posting of threatening notices in Limerick in 1844. See *Nenagh Guardian,* 31 July 1844.

an abduction. In 1827, for instance, a rape case was pursued as an abduction.[26] Bridget Jordan's case was reported in 1839 as 'an assault with intent to violate' whereas in fact she had been abducted and taken to a house and kept there against her will.[27] In 1841 Mary Gibbons was raped in Galway but the police classified her attack as an abduction.[28] While rape cases were not necessarily cases of abduction, there was sometimes, at least, a belief that such a violation would force a marriage between the perpetrator and victim.[29]

For the eighteenth century there are few official statistics for abductions, and numbers are calculated from newspapers, prison registers, prisoners' petitions and cases, proclamations and the calendar of presentments. The current estimate for abductions in Ireland between 1700 and 1799 is 213.[30] In general, the number of abductions relating to the aristocracy was small, constituting about seven incidents in total.[31]

Table 6.1 *Abductions in Ireland 1700–1799*

Year	1700–1710	1718–1730	1731–1740	1741–1750	1751–1760
Abductions	7	15	7	16	24
Year	1761–1770	1771–1780	1781–1790	1791–1799	No decade known
Abductions	40	41	39	15	9

Source: Authors' database

There is a considerable increase in the numbers of abductions from the 1760s, which may reflect the emergence of the agrarian protests of the Whiteboys and Rightboys. The fact that the crime was economically motivated may explain why there appears to be a considerable reduction in abductions after 1790, when war brought prosperity to the country. The largest number of abductions in the eighteenth century was in County Tipperary, with forty-six cases up to 1799; Kilkenny witnessed twenty-six cases; there were twenty-six recorded cases in Cork; and

[26] *Finn's Leinster Journal*, 21 July 1827.
[27] Chief Secretary Office, Registered Papers, Outrage Reports (NAI, 9656/21/1839). [Hereafter NAI, CSORP/OR].
[28] NAI, CSO/RP/OR 1767/1841/11.
[29] See for instance, *Finn's Leinster Journal*, 31 Aug. 1822.
[30] The upheaval caused by the 1798 rebellion has made it difficult to assess levels of abduction for the last decade of the eighteenth century. Durey has identified sixteen cases of abduction between 1797 and 1799, though these have not been included in the totals given above. See Durey, 'Abduction and rape', 27–47. See also Power, *Forcibly without Her Consent*, pp. 54–8. Figures calculated from authors' database.
[31] Malcomson, *Pursuit of an Heiress*, pp. 62–7.

eleven in Limerick.[32] The regional pattern of abductions was to change quite dramatically in the nineteenth century. From 1800–1850 the estimated number of abductions in the country was in the region of 1,479. During this period the five counties with the greatest number of abductions (roughly 630) were Limerick, Clare, Roscommon, Tipperary, and Mayo. Substantial numbers of abductions also occurred in Galway and Kerry. From 1700–1850 there were fewer abductions in Ulster (about sixty-four) than in any of the other provinces. Given the figures that we have it is evident that recorded abductions were at their height in the 1830s and 1840s, and that the first half of the nineteenth century is a much more significant period for abductions than the entire eighteenth century. Why might this be so? Population growth was unprecedented at the time. As we have noted elsewhere in this volume, the period is also regarded as one of industrial decline and chronic poverty.[33] Landless peasants, labourers and men with small acreages, those from the lower reaches of society, were more strongly affected by economic downturns and some sought to improve their economic position by property acquisition through abductions.

From the 1860s the numbers of abductions declined considerably, with a recorded 120 cases from 1860 to 1918. Also in this period the nature of abductions changed and there were many more collusive abductions and elopements. Trials for abductions in the late nineteenth and early twentieth centuries were more often about exerting parental authority than prosecuting a vicious case of abduction.

There were of course abductions before the eighteenth century, though they are not well documented. One of the most well-known occurred in 1668 when fifteen-year-old Mary Ware was abducted in Dublin. Ware knew her abductor, James Shirley, and, like many abductees, she had rejected his offer of marriage. Ware was kept captive by Shirley and his accomplices for several days and nights and, according to Ware's account, she was raped and then forced to participate in a marriage. Mary managed eventually to escape from her captors and she took legal proceedings against Shirley, initially to annul the marriage on

---

[32] These figures have been gathered from a search of local and national newspapers, and official records such as 'Committals, Trials, Convictions, &c Ireland. Return of the Number of Persons, Male and Female Committed to the Several Gaols in Ireland for Trial, at the Different Assizes, Commissions of the Peace, and at the General Sessions… 1813–14 (264) (Ireland)'. Similar returns cover the period to 1851. Various prison reports for Ireland cover the period 1821–1850 and judicial statistics provide data on the years between 1812 and 1851.

[33] Cormac Ó Grada, 'Poverty, population and agriculture, 1801–1845' in W. E. Vaughan (ed.), *A New History of Ireland V, Ireland under the Union 1, 1801–70* (Oxford, 1989), pp. 108–57.

the grounds that she had not agreed to it and secondly to charge Shirley with rape. The case was a celebrated one as Ware's grandfather was the well-known antiquarian and writer, James Ware, and her father was Auditor General in the Irish administration. Mary Ware won the case in the Dublin consistory court on the annulment of her forced marriage but the indictment for rape took much longer to process.[34] Shirley was eventually acquitted in 1672, four years after the abduction and sexual assault had taken place. The long and unsuccessful attempt to have Shirley prosecuted for his actions demonstrated how difficult it was in the early modern period to secure a guilty verdict for rape, for which the punishment was death. Shirley clearly received sympathy and support within influential political circles in both England and Ireland.[35]

In the militarised masculinity of late seventeenth-century Ireland, abductions of women were not, therefore, always taken as serious offences by the men who participated in them. In her statement describing her rape and abduction, Mary Ware related how Shirley's accomplices laughed at her cries for help. Another man admitted leaving the cabin where she was kept even though he could hear her screaming.[36] The Irish Jacobite, Patrick Sarsfield was involved in two abductions when he was a young soldier and based in London. In 1682, he was among a group of men who assisted in the abduction of a wealthy widow. Most of the group were sentenced to prison time or fines but Sarsfield managed to escape punishment. Within months, however, he had seized Lady Elizabeth Herbert, another widow to whom he had already proposed. She had refused him and his abduction of her did not change her mind. Francis Gwynn, the clerk of the privy council, reported that the abduction was viewed with amusement by 'the town' in London. People were laying bets on whether or not the couple would marry. They did not, and Lady Herbert's attempt to prosecute Sarsfield was hindered by the note she had signed during her captivity agreeing not to prosecute her abductors.[37]

---

[34] Dudley Loftus, who defended Mary Ware in the Dublin consistory court, published his legal arguments in *The Case of Ware and Sherley as It Was Set Forth in Matter of Fact and Argued in Several Points of Law in the Consistory Court of Dublin, in Michael Term 1668* (Dublin, 1669).

[35] Mary O'Dowd, 'Ware versus Shirley' in Marian Lyons (ed.), *Mystery Stories from Early Modern Ireland* (forthcoming).

[36] *Calendar of State Papers Ireland, 1666–1669.* Ed. Robert Pentland Mahaffy (London, 1908), pp. 566–71.

[37] Piers Wauchope, *Patrick Sarsfield and the Williamite War* (Dublin, 1992), pp. 22–7; *Calendar of State Papers Domestic: Charles II, 1683 January–June.* Ed. F H Blackburne Daniell (London, 1933), pp. 136–7, 223; Kelly, 'The abduction of women of fortune', 10.

It is clear from the evidence that for many men from the late seventeenth century through to the early nineteenth century abductions were a significant means through which to secure a marriage and hence the 'fortune' that went with the abducted woman. In those decades when abductions were most frequent, the 1760s to 1770s, and the 1830s, it is important to note the presence and geographic extent of agrarian disturbance. The Whiteboys, Rightboys, Rockites and Ribbonmen were, among other groups, particularly active in these decades in Munster, and there are certainly cases where abductions formed the purpose of an attack on a household. For instance, a group of Tipperary Whiteboys abducted the daughter of Philip Dwyer in 1775 in 'order to bestow her on one of their needy companions'.[38] While abductions were not a common activity in any agrarian movement, the disruption caused to the implementation of law and order more generally may well have facilitated the practice at a time when there was a stronger likelihood that the authorities were too busy to pursue the perpetrators.[39]

Arthur Young, writing of his visit to Ireland in the late eighteenth century, commented 'it is scarcely credible how many young women have been of late years carried off and ravished, in order (as they generally have fortunes) to gain to appearance a voluntary marriage.'[40] Abductors in the eighteenth century have been characterised as members of the gentry in reduced circumstances attempting to improve their status through abduction. In 1718, Rebecca White was taken from her uncle's house in Cappagh, County Tipperary, by a group of armed men. She was an heiress and a local family, named Fitzgerald, was behind the abduction. The victim was intended for Thomas Fitzgerald. A marriage, officiated by a couple beggar, duly took place a few days after the abduction.[41] A member of the local gentry, a man named Thomas Johnston, made an unsuccessful attempt to abduct Charlotte Newcomen in Longford in 1772. She was a

---

[38] *Hibernian Journal*, 21 April 1775. For similar cases see *Hibernian Journal*, 24 April 1775, 1, 3 Jan. 1776; *Ennis Chronicle*, 16 Feb. 1792. For other cases where there was some involvement by agrarian groups in abductions see *Freeman's Journal*, 16 March, 24 April, 1822; *Mayo Constitution*, 11 March 1830; *Galway Weekly Advertiser*, 30 Oct. 1830; *Roscommon and Leitrim Gazette*, 11 May 1833, 21 Feb. 1835.

[39] Agrarian societies were primarily concerned with regulating landholding and the payment of church fees and tithes. For their opposition to marriage fees charged by Catholic priests see pp. 77–81. For further information on these groups see M. R. Beames, *Peasants and Power: The Whiteboy Movements and Their Control in Pre-famine Ireland* (Sussex, 1983); James S. Donnelly, Jr., *Captain Rock: The Irish Agrarian Rebellion of 1821–1824* (Madison, Wisconsin, 2009); Michael Huggins, *Social Conflict in Pre-famine Ireland: The Case of County Roscommon* (Dublin, 2007).

[40] Arthur Young, *A Tour in Ireland* (2 vols., 2nd ed., London, 1780), ii, p. 240.

[41] Denis G. Marnane, *Land and Violence: A History of West Tipperary from 1660* (Tipperary, 1985), p. 21.

very wealthy heiress and resisted her abduction with considerable courage. Johnston was described as a 'young man of great parts, but [of] consummate vanity, one who was capable of the most daring acts of violence ... and at the same time capable of the basest fraud to cover it up'.[42] Johnston was fatally wounded in the abduction attempt; Newcomen went on to marry William Gleadowe, a prominent Dublin banker. Another infamous case from the eighteenth century was that which led to the death of Mary Anne Knox of Derry, shot by John MacNaghten of County Antrim, in an attempted abduction in 1761. Knox had a fortune of £6,000 and MacNaghten, having inherited an estate from an uncle, had lost most of it in gambling debts.[43] Sir Henry Hayes was convicted of abducting Mary Pike in Cork in July 1797. Pike was a Quaker with a fortune of £20,000. Hayes, had been knighted in 1790, and in the same year was appointed sheriff of Cork city. At the time of the abduction he was a widower with four children, and aged thirty-five. Pike had just turned twenty-one. After the abduction, a marriage ceremony took place with Pike resisting the entire time. Hayes was unable to consummate the marriage and, finally acknowledging that Pike was distressed and resistant, he left her, and the country. Pike was rescued and Hayes eventually brought to court where he was sentenced to death, then reprieved and sentenced to transportation for life to Botany Bay. He succeeded in securing a pardon after ten years and returned to Ireland in 1812, where he died in 1832. Mary Pike never married and suffered from serious mental illness for much of her adult life. She also died in 1832.[44]

Reporting on an abduction case in 1787 the *Dublin Evening Post* described the phenomenon as a

breach of social ties so horrid in its nature, and so injurious in its consequences that even the nations which continue in barbarism, which were never enlightened by the sun of civilisation, have not been disgraced with it, has of late been too common in this country – I mean the running away with girls of fortune. The Cherokee or Esquimaux [Eskimo] will look with esteem on the daughter of his fellow creature, and would shudder at the idea of forcing her by violence from the breast of an aged and fond parent; but our Irish *gentlemen*, who take the title from

---

[42] Quoted in Power, *Forcibly without Her Consent*, p. 12. See also Letter from Sarah Colvill to Robert Colvill, 1772 (PRONI, Dunraven Papers, 1772, D3196/L/5/1).

[43] Darinagh Boyle, *Half-Hanged MacNaghten* (Derry, 1993).

[44] *The Trial of Sir Henry Browne Hayes, Knt. For Forcibly and Feloniously Taking Away Miss Mary Pike on the 22nd Day of July, 1797* (Cork, 1797); Máire Mhic Giobúin, 'Sir Henry Browne Hayes, abductor' in Liam Clare and Máire Ní Chearbhaill (eds.), *Trouble with the Law: Crimes and Trials from Ireland's Past* (Dublin, 2007), pp. 37–54; Kelly, 'The abduction of women of fortune', 20–1, 35–6.

an estate of 30 or 40 pounds a year, scorns such savage honesty, and thinks nothing of such a deed.[45]

As Power has shown, most of the abductions perpetrated by the landed or gentry classes occurred in the period before 1770, and after this time there was a move towards abductions being perpetrated by men from lower economic classes.[46]

According to Kelly, between 1701 and 1800, about eighty abductions were instigated by individuals who held five or more acres, were yeomen farmers or members of the gentry, with thirty-nine abductions being carried out by those who held less than five acres and were labourers, small farmers, artisans or small businessmen.[47] In these cases the targets were women who were to inherit substantial amounts of money or land, and whose financial value had the means to enhance the status of the abductor, pay his debts or secure further property.[48] A butcher abducted Sarah Cannon of Kilworth, County Cork, 'a young lady entitled to a considerable fortune' in 1785.[49] She was quickly rescued by a local Justice of Peace who brought her to his own house only to find that early the following morning a 'riotous and outrageous mob, to the number of two hundred men, armed with guns, blunderbailes, pistols, swords, and sledges', headed by her abductor, surrounded his house requesting that Sarah be handed over. She was hurried away to the home of a great uncle where that night she was again abducted. It was reported that Sarah was detained in an unknown place until 17 June, when she was brought to the house of a Bartholomew Symmons and 'is so closely guarded no assistance can be rendered'.[50] The authorities knew where Sarah was held, but she was not rescued. It is unclear how this case developed, but given that Sarah had already been absent for some time from her home, and any rescue party appeared to have given up, she may very well have accepted her fate at her abductor's hand.

In 1812, Malachi Duggan noted on his arrival as parish priest in Moyarta, County Clare, that abductions were a major problem. He

---

[45] *Dublin Evening Post*, 16 Jan. 1787.   [46] Power, *Forcibly without Her Consent*, p. 13.

[47] Kelly, 'The abduction of women of fortune', 42.

[48] Other such cases include that of the abduction of Mary Max in 1777, by her cousin Samuel Phillips. She had a fortune of between £30,000 and £40,000. Susanna Grove of County Tipperary, was abducted by Hugh Grady in 1756 and forced into marriage. Her fortune, which consisted of property, allowed Grady to pay off debts relating to his own property. See Power, *Forcibly without Her Consent*, p. 19. See also, *Pue's Occurrences*, 31 March, 18 Aug. 1753, 30 March 1754, 8 June, 9 Nov. 1756; *Corke Journal*, 14 June 1756.

[49] *Volunteer Evening Post*, 22 Oct. 1785. See also *Freeman's Journal*, 7 July 1785; NAI, The Catalogue of Proclamations.

[50] Ibid.

informed a parliamentary committee in 1824 that in the first decade of the century abductions had been quite common as young men of no means wanted to marry girls from a better-off class who had a dowry. For the most part, he observed, little action was taken against the abductors. However, the execution of a young man for a killing that occurred during an abduction in 1814 had acted as a check and there were no further abductions until 1824. At the time Duggan was giving his evidence there were seven young men from Moyarta in jail for attempted abductions. Duggan also suggested that the fear of abduction was a factor in early marriages:

The facility with which the crime of abduction and an attempt at it escaped punishment, created apprehension in the body of the people, for their daughters, and induced them to dispose of them in marriage before they were hardly arrived at the age of puberty; the practice of marrying young became general, and a subject of imitation, and settled into a fashion, so much so, that it was a reproach on a young girl to exceed twenty before she was married.[51]

Cornewall Lewis, who had been involved in the poor inquiry in Ireland in the 1830s, claimed that abductions were so common in pre-Famine Ireland that they 'affect[ed] the marrying habits of the population'.[52] In the 1830s, a priest in County Clare noted that 'many plans were laid to get possession of a girl who had a fortune, through fear of this, a farmer was anxious to get his daughter married out of harm's way'.[53] Another commentator observed that it was 'considered most desirable by farmers that their daughters should be settled when young, that they may be withdrawn from the dangers and schemes to which their fortunes expose them'.[54]

In 1833 a newspaper comment observed that the practice of abduction had declined dramatically, and where it did survive it was noted as

a remnant of manners long gone by in this country. It was a matter of history that the ordinary mode of courtship in former times in Ireland was one similar to the present occurrence which substituted the violence of a ruffian for the consent of a woman, as a necessary ingredient in the marriage contract. In proportion as

---

[51] *State of Ireland: Minutes of Evidence Taken before the Select Committee Appointed to Inquire into the Disturbances in Ireland, in the Last Session of Parliament, 13th May-18th June 1824.* HC 1825 (20), vii, pp. 209–10.
[52] George Cornewall Lewis, *Local Disturbances in Ireland* (London, 1836; reprinted Cork, 1977), pp. 239–40.
[53] *First Report of Commissioners of Enquiry into the Condition of the Poorer Classes in Ireland* [hereafter Poor Inquiry, 1835], Appendix A, HC 1835 xxxii, p. 420.
[54] Ibid., pp. 416, 420, on age at marriage see also pp. 92–100.

nations become more civilized, they have paid respect to the characters and feelings of a female.[55]

However, in 1836, a Mayo magistrate described the practice as a 'barbarous and brutal custom … [which] would render it dangerous for any woman of character to dwell in this country' and as 'one of the most lawless and pagan habits of the Irish peasantry'.[56] In fact, abductions were to continue in numbers large enough to be of public concern until the 1850s.

Who Was Abducted?

There was, therefore, clearly an intent to benefit financially from these abductions and women with relatively small marriage fortunes also found themselves endangered. The primary motive for abductions continued to be economic throughout the period. Access to land was a vital form of survival for poorer individuals and their families in the eighteenth and early nineteenth centuries. The value of the property associated with an unmarried woman was an enticement for men and that value was assessed by the status of the father, or rumours of a fortune. Bridget Grealish was abducted in Galway in 1839, the police noting she 'had a good fortune'.[57] Catherine McNamara's father was described as a 'comfortable farmer', holding twenty-two acres. Pat Creighton, the father of her abductor, held five acres.[58] Whether Creighton, the abductor, was to inherit from his father is unknown and his taking of Catherine McNamara may have been an attempt to obtain property or money that might secure his own future. In 1840, Margaret Walsh, the daughter of a farmer, was abducted by a group of four brothers, the McCarthys, all described as labourers. Margaret was reputed to have a fortune of £200.[59] Whether this rumour of a large fortune reflected reality is unknown, and it is unlikely that fathers provided the full 'reputed' fortune to an abductor. Likewise, John McNamara held 5 acres, and the family of the woman whom he abducted, Anne Scally, held about 16 acres. The abduction of Honora O'Donnell so that she would marry Michael Connors, a man she had previously refused to marry, took place

---

[55] *Ballina Impartial*, 29 July 1833.
[56] *Mayo Constitution*, 12, 24 Feb. 1836. There were in the region of 176 abductions in the 1830s and 122 in the 1840s.
[57] NAI, CSO/RP/OR, 675/1839/11.
[58] *Mayo Constitution*, 2 March 1835; *Belfast Newsletter*, 6 March 1835; NAI, Convict Reference Files 1840 C83.
[59] *Freeman's Journal*, 26 Aug. 1840; *Belfast Newsletter*, 1 Sept. 1840; *Connaught Journal*, 3 Sept. 1840; NAI, CRF 1841 Mc16.

on the night before her wedding to another man. She had a house of her own and a £15 fortune.[60] These abductors were, therefore, improving their financial position. However, labourers' daughters were not immune to abduction. For instance, the daughter of Michael Healy was the victim of an attempted abduction in October 1830.[61] While the daughters of farmers appeared to have been targeted most often, the daughters of shopkeepers and publicans were also abducted. In the eighteenth century, Kelly suggests, most of the victims of abduction were mainly 'young Protestant women of fortune' and the abductors were 'Catholic men of the lower gentry'.[62] In the nineteenth century, abductions were primarily within the Catholic community and were carried out by men from the farming and labouring classes.

An acute awareness of class was evident in the case of Mary Kenny, abducted in County Mayo in 1838. She was raped and kept by her abductors for three days and nights until she was rescued. She prosecuted her abductor, a servant, noting 'I have thirty pounds fortune, he has nothing: I could not think of marrying such a barbarian'.[63] A curious case from 1842 also signifies a recognition of class differences as an impediment to marriage, whether forced or not. Brothers John and James Roper held Catherine Haggan against her will overnight in an attempt to force a marriage. Catherine told John 'that even if she was willing to marry him he hadn't the marriage money'.[64] The marriage money probably refers to the money needed to secure a licence, a ring and wedding clothes, and the ability to cover the fees involved. Catherine is clearly suggesting that her abductor could not afford a legal marriage ceremony. The brothers set her free the following morning and paid compensation to her father.[65] Police and newspaper reports in the nineteenth century rarely noted the social class of abductors unless there was a major class discrepancy, suggesting that many abductions were within particular class boundaries. Patrick Foy abducted Bridget Smyth in 1840 and it was noted they were on 'an equal footing in life within the view of their respective friends'.[66] The same was true of John McGrath and Mary Commins.[67] In 1805, the attempted abduction of a woman named Brien, a servant maid to Michael Kelly, a farmer, near Donoughmore, County Tipperary, by a man whose surname was Murphy and who was also a servant in the house, was met with considerable resistance by the woman.

---

[60] *Freeman's Journal*, 5 July 1850.   [61] NAI, CSO/RP/OR/44/1830.
[62] Kelly, 'The abduction of women of fortune', 37.
[63] *Galway Weekly Advertiser*, 4 Aug. 1838.   [64] *Mayo Constitution*, 2 Aug. 1842.
[65] *Mayo Constitution*, 2 Aug. 1842.   [66] NAI, CRF 1840 F38.
[67] NAI, CRF 1845 McG6.

As a result she was violently assaulted and died within hours of the attack.[68] Honora Bruder was abducted in 1836 by five men in County Limerick. Honora, who was repeatedly raped during her ordeal, had been a servant in a farmer's house along with her abductor, Jeremiah Kelly. Kelly had wanted to marry her and she had refused him.[69] Although there would seem to be little financial incentive to abducting a servant, in some cases it was an act of revenge for refusing a marriage proposal. It should also be noted that women servants could and did have small savings that they intended to use as their dowry on marriage. Male servants also had aspirations beyond their class. Servants would have some idea of the 'value' of a daughter of the household in which a woman lived. Seven men abducted Honora McMahon from her bed in 1834. Honora, it was noted, was to have a fortune 'but not a large one'.[70] They took her without her clothes and put two handkerchiefs on her mouth. The principal abductor was a servant in her mother's household, John O'Dea, a cousin of hers. When they got her to a house they tried to persuade her to marry O'Dea, but she refused. The abductors took her to different houses over the space of a couple of nights and the occupant of the last house finally took her home. On rare occasions, two women might be abducted at the same time. Whether this was an attempt by the abductors to ensure they had kidnapped the appropriate woman to secure a dowry, or whether both women had dowries and were thus worth abducting is unclear. In 1816, the two stepdaughters of Dennis Finn were abducted in County Wicklow. Immediately, a party was organised to rescue them but it was hours before the girls were reached. In the meantime the principal abductor, Terry Flackey, escaped into the mountains where he was not followed as 'the pursuers were ignorant of the passes'.[71] Mary and Anne Gardener of Castlegal in Sligo were abducted in 1848 when returning home from a friend's house. The two women were brought to different locations. Anne escaped and then she and her mother went to rescue Mary. The girls' mother, also Anne, was a widow and held approximately twenty acres of land. Mary Gardener's abductor, Michael Higgins, held land of about three acres.[72]

The determination of abductors to secure a 'fortune' is evident in their behaviour, as we have seen in the case of Honora Goold, who although the wrong abductee was still 'worth' taking. If a dowry or fortune was not forthcoming in a mistaken abduction, the abductor often returned to the

---

68 *Ennis Chronicle*, 16 May 1805.   69 NAI, CSO/RP/OR/233/1836/12.
70 *Ballina Impartial*, 21 July 1834.
71 *Ennis Chronicle*, 26 Oct. 1816; *The Morning Post*, 26 Oct. 1816.
72 *Sligo Journal*, 10 March 1848.

scene of the crime to abduct the woman of value. In 1830, a young woman named Haran, 'of considerable fortune',[73] was on the eve of her marriage when a group of abductors surrounded the house with the aim of carrying her off – but accidentally took her married sister, who was clearly of no value to them. Once they discovered their error they returned her to the family home and seized the unmarried sister.[74] On the night of 22 April 1838, five armed men broke into the house of James McNamara and forcibly took away his daughter Margaret. She too, was taken away by mistake as it was McNamara's eldest daughter Mary who was to inherit the five acres held by her father. To prevent another attack McNamara had his daughter Mary married to a man named Sheahan the following day.[75] Mary Anne McShea, described as a 'little girl', was abducted in Mayo in 1833.[76] During the court case it was claimed that Mary Anne was taken as her sister, the intended victim, had been sent to Newport to hide.[77] It is clear that at stake in these cases was the 'fortune' and that only a particular woman in the household was of value to the abductors. This also suggests that the younger daughters in poor families may have had little in the way of property as a dowry and were not, therefore, a target for abduction.

In the same way, widows were targets most often because of the property they held after the death of a husband. In 1827, Ellen Cowhig, aged about twenty, a widow with one child, whose husband had died the previous year leaving her in the possession of property, was abducted from her father's house in County Limerick.[78] The attempt to retain property within the wider family also appears as a motive in the abduction of widows. Michael Cannon abducted Catherine Tiernan in 1841 following the death of her husband, a cousin of Cannon's.[79] Other abductors were related to their victims, suggesting again an attempt to retain property or assets within the realm of the wider family group.

Abductions were frequently ruthless and violent events. An abduction party could consist of up to fifty people, armed and perhaps unruly; they must have offered a terrifying sight to the women who

---

[73] *Belfast Newsletter*, 26 Feb. 1830.   [74] Ibid.   [75] NAI, CSO/RP/OR/233/1838/12.

[76] The ages of the victims of abductions are unclear in a number of cases. Newspaper reports often use the term 'young girl' or 'young woman' and in reported court cases journalists seem to guess the age of the victims from their appearance. Claiming them to be young would have aroused the sympathy of the reader.

[77] *Ballina Impartial*, 29 July 1833.

[78] *Belfast Newsletter*, 8 April 1828; *Ennis Chronicle and Clare Advertiser*, 12 Dec. 1827, 9 April 1828; *Connaught Journal*, 25 Oct. 1827.

[79] NAI, CSO/RP/OR, 5335/1841/16; CSO/RP/ OR, 5835/1841/16.

were being abducted. A group of men attacked the house of Johanna Shea, 'a poor widow with eight children'[80] in County Clare. Johanna's husband had died a few days before the abduction. On the night of the attack the men had dragged Shea 'and her daughter Mary Shea' out of bed naked and one of the abductors 'did present a loaded pistol' aimed at Johanna swearing he would shoot her if she made any noise. The party then tied a handkerchief around the mouth of Mary Shea and 'by force and violence took her about ten miles distance when she was rescued by her friends'. In a petition to prevent leniency in sentencing the abductors, Johanna noted that her daughter was 'only seventeen and her peace of mind [is] ruined for ever'.[81] What made the abductions even more frightening was that family members who tried to protect a young woman were assaulted and sometimes seriously injured. In 1770 a father was killed and his wife seriously injured when they attempted to prevent the abduction of their daughter.[82] It was terrifying also for the abductee, often carried away over unfamiliar countryside, disorientated and fearing violence and rape at the hands of her abductors.

Family and Abduction

Kinship ties were evident in the often large groups that participated in abductions. Brothers Denis and Martin Creighton abducted Catherine McNamara in 1835.[83] When Mary Hargidan was abducted in Sligo in 1834, her abductors were Pat Kildea, his father and three of his female relatives.[84] In 1848, a woman was arrested shortly after her own wedding for assisting her brother in a recent abduction.[85] Such instances of family collusion suggest abduction was a viable and acceptable means of securing an individual's financial security. In a highly unusual case three soldiers, one named O'Connor, were arrested for abducting Jane Matthews, with the intention that O'Connor would marry her. It was reported that the force used was considerable and that she had put up a strong resistance. The journalist noted that 'the character and conduct of the young person were extremely good; and what aggravated the violence was that she disliked O'Connor and was attached to another'.[86] What was unusual

---

[80] NAI, Prisoners' Petitions and Cases 1778–1836.   [81] Ibid.
[82] *Belfast Newsletter*, 20 Feb. 1770. For other cases of extreme violence see *Mayo Constitution*, 24 Feb. 1830; 10, 17 Feb. 1834.
[83] NAI, CRF 1840 C83.   [84] *Sligo Journal*, 14 March 1834.
[85] *Tuam Herald*, 1 April 1848.   [86] *Connaught Journal*, 28 July 1825

about the case was that her parents had urged O'Connor to abduct their daughter and they appeared as witnesses against their daughter in his defence. The jury, and judge, were horrified at the parents' conduct. O'Connor was found guilty but recommended for mercy as he had not raped the girl.[87] In this instance the family was determined to secure their daughter's marriage to a particular individual, and went to extraordinary lengths to effect it.[88]

Women did offer resistance to their abductors. In 1805, a servant woman named Brien died after resisting an attempt, by a fellow servant, to abduct her.[89] Honora Ryan, who was abducted three times in 1823, managed to escape from her abductors on each occasion, but not without injury.[90] In one instance an abductor tried, unsuccessfully, to force his victim to drink some laudanum. The morning after the abduction he sent for a clergyman who tried to persuade the woman to marry her abductor, but she vehemently refused to do so.[91] Others resisted being raped, and consistently refused to be married to their abductor. Some of the abductors had a priest ready to celebrate the marriage. Many of these clerics were most likely to have been working as couple beggars, who did not baulk at the forced nature of the event. In 1771 a couple beggar, Mathew O'Brien, was charged with marrying Anne Browne to Richard Meagher after her abduction.[92] As we explained in Chapter 1, a woman who was compelled to marry against her will could apply to have the marriage voided by either or both church and state. There is, however, little surviving evidence that abducted women availed themselves of this option.

Abductions were reported in the press and this served a number of functions. It was a way of warning those parents who read the papers to be fearful of their daughters' care. The reports also alerted families to the extent of abductions in the country. In the nineteenth century the press provided more detail on abductions and in some instances, at least, this was a form of entertainment for the reading public. Some of the stories could be read as adventure stories, dramas, tales of resistance and rescue,

---

[87] Ibid.; *Ennis Chronicle and Clare Advertiser*, 30 July 1825.

[88] In 1841, O'Connor was appointed by the Irish Poor Law Commissioners as a returning officer for the Union of Athlone. Given his previous history, questions were asked in the House of Lords about this appointment. See *Belfast Newsletter*, 11 June 1841.

[89] *Ennis Chronicle*, 16 May 1805.

[90] *Freeman's Journal*, 1 April 1823. See also, *The Morning Chronicle*, 2 April 1823; *The Morning Post*, 3 April 1823.

[91] *Belfast Newsletter*, 18 May 1824.

[92] *Finn's Leinster Journal*, 5, 9 Jan. 1771. See also, *Dublin Gazette*, 26 Feb. 1757.

and female virtue. The reporter, for instance, who wrote the *Belfast Newsletter's* account of the abduction of Catherine McNamara in 1835, did so with style and verve. He saw the origins of the abduction in 'John Creighton, a hamlet rake and village debauchee, living in the neighbourhood, [who] took it into his head, by one bold stroke, to secure himself in a pretty wife and handsome fortune'.[93] Abduction stories were also warnings and suggested loss. The loss to the family was economic: the dowry or fortune that came with the woman was 'lost', as was the value of her chastity. It is interesting to speculate at what point an abducted woman had most value. Was she valuable because it was known she had a dowry? Was the value of the woman only realised when marriage followed an abduction and the dowry, or property, was handed over? Or, for the abductor, was the woman's value made more real and probable when a loss of virginity was assumed because she had been missing from her family, or when sexual violence was perpetrated, both events making it difficult for a woman to marry respectably? For abductors, sexual intercourse or rape appears to have been an important point of ownership. For instance, widows were unlikely to be virgins, but even widows who were abducted were raped.[94]

The story of Honora Goold, as it appeared in the *Newgate Calendar*, made clear the loss that could be experienced by a family in cases of abduction. The author in this particular publication made clear that the motive of her abductor, James Brown, even in abducting the wrong woman, could be fulfilled. Brown, it was noted, was intent on improving his economic position and 'knowing the opulence of her family could make him independent, provided he could insure the consent of the astonished girl he had forcibly carried off'.[95] What perhaps made the tale more exciting for readers was the hint that rape had occurred, but the author frames it coyly. Having noted that Brown shared a bed with Goold he wrote 'the reader need not be told the rest – the purity of female innocence was grossly violated in the person of this young and lovely creature; and her destroyer arose from his bed of lust ...'.[96] Goold's abduction was considered sensational at the time; the trial of her abductors was also widely covered, and the way in which she presented herself in court and gave her evidence proved her worthy of protection.

[93] *Belfast Newsletter*, 6 March 1835.
[94] See, for instance, the case of Ellen Cowhig, *Belfast Newsletter*, 8 April 1828.
[95] *The Newgate Calendar*, p. 66.   [96] Ibid., p. 67.

Collusive Abductions

If any agency can be ascribed to women in abductions it is in the realm of collusive abductions, whereby women ensured that they exercised their choice in a marriage partner despite what might have been decided by their parents. A Mr Furlong from Limerick claimed in his evidence to the Poor Inquiry in the 1830s that 'half of them run away with and carry off the girl with her own consent'.[97] It is difficult to assess the accuracy of this statement. We certainly have evidence from enough cases to show that a considerable number of women were taken against their will. It is equally clear, however, that some abductions were collusive. Catherine Roche was abducted in 1810 and kept away for one night. She later stated that she had gone willingly with her abductor.[98] Declan Barron's abduction of Mary Hogan in 1828 may have been a collusive abduction. In court she said she was willing to marry him, if her father approved. When the prisoner was asked whether he would marry her, he agreed and was discharged.[99] Mary Flanagan of Adare was abducted in December 1839, by a gang headed by John Moloney, 'who had', according to the police, 'been courting the girl for some years'.[100] In 1839, Catherine Cohalan, from Aughrim in County Galway, was abducted from her home by a man named James Cohalan. Her seizure had been agreed by the couple because Catherine did not wish to marry Michael Campbell, a man whom her father had arranged for her to marry the following week. Catherine stated in evidence that she had 'sent a note to James Cohalan to come to me and I would go away with him as I did not like the man my father wanted me to marry'. She avoided marrying Campbell but also in the process lost her dowry.[101] A girl named Spillane, the only child of a woman who had realised £60 by begging, had agreed to marry a young labourer. He, on hearing that her mother was in treaty with someone else for a son-in-law, organised an abduction party, broke into her cabin and carried her off. This couple also married.[102] In 1843, Thomas Kennedy, who was indicted at Castlebar assizes for the abduction of Bridget Mea, was found guilty of assault only, as it was not clear to the jury whether or not Mea had gone willingly with the defendant. Jurors clearly expected some form of resistance from the abducted women and it was not evident in this case.[103]

---

[97] *Poor Enquiry*, Appendix A, p. 692.   [98] *Waterford Mail*, 20 Aug. 1810.
[99] *Belfast Newsletter*, 28 March 1828.
[100] NAI, CSO/RP/OR 254/1839/11; *Freeman's Journal*, 15 Dec. 1839.
[101] NAI, CSO/RP/OR 276/1839/11.   [102] *Belfast Newsletter*, 27 Feb. 1838.
[103] *Freeman's Journal*, 8 March 1843.

Abductions could, then, be collusive and strategic attempts to force parental permission for a marriage and to compel them to improve the dowry on offer. During the trial of Brien O'Neill for the abduction of Bridget McParlan it came to light that the couple had known each other and that she had been keen to marry him. However, O'Neill was not happy with the dowry McParlan's father offered, and the abduction was a way to force the father to provide more money. During the trial Bridget stated that she would 'marry him now if he pleased'. The trial was stopped, the couple left the courthouse and after a while the Catholic chaplain announced that a marriage had been solemnised between the parties and so the judge directed an acquittal.[104] Edward Branbury was described as the son 'of a considerably wealthy man', but he would not give his son, Edward any funds, which he apparently needed to marry Agnes Turner. Consequently, he abducted her and this forced the parents to compromise.[105] Many women did end up marrying their abductors but it is impossible to provide any accurate figures relating to such marriages. A man named Burke abducted Bridget Burns of Easky, County Sligo, in 1838. This was possibly a collusive abduction since her parents had rejected him as a husband for their daughter, but after the abduction her mother explained that: 'She never would have consented to give her daughter to said Burke, but now since this has happened and that no Christian will ever marry her daughter after being carried away she would give her consent'.[106] The prosecution of Michael Ryan at the Nenagh assizes in 1848 for the abduction of Mary Dunn in 1834 did not go ahead when it was revealed that the couple had married.[107] In these cases couples were revealing their strong opposition to their parents' disapproval of their chosen marriage partners. A collusive abduction was probably the most effective means by which an individual could secure the marriage partner of their choice.

What were community views on abductions? People rarely intervened when a woman was abducted in public. When Edward McEvoy's daughter was abducted in broad daylight on a market day in Swinford, County Mayo, there were about forty men in the abduction party. It was noted that 'no one would or dared interfere'.[108] This may have been due to the large force that often made up an abduction party, many of whom were

---

[104] *Belfast Newsletter*, 5 Aug. 1828; *Ennis Chronicle and Clare Advertiser*, 9 Aug. 1828; *Carlow Morning Post*, 7 Aug. 1828; *Finn's Leinster Journal*, 9 Aug. 1828.
[105] *Mayo Constitution*, 2 March 1835.   [106] NAI, CSO/RP/OR 26/1838/32.
[107] NAI, CSO/RP/OR 15/1848/37.
[108] Sir Francis Lynch-Blosse to Henry Waldron, 19 January 1833, private index (NAI, 1833/47).

well armed, and does not necessarily mean that the community more widely condoned the abduction. However, there were some interventions. For example, in 1834 when Elizabeth Carden was abducted in Mayo, the villagers followed the abduction party and succeeded in rescuing the girl.[109] Mary Feenigan was similarly rescued by neighbours from an attempted abduction in Sligo in 1838.[110] Sometimes, however, as we shall see, there was community support for an abductor.

Abductions in Post-Famine Ireland

If we examine abduction as essentially a crime of economics then the impact of the Great Famine can be traced in the reduction in the number of abduction cases after the 1850s. As already noted in Chapter 3, during the Famine, the number of landless labourers and tenants with an acre or so of land – those most commonly involved in abductions – was considerably reduced. Changing moral values around family, sexuality and land ownership also contributed to the reduction in the number of abductions. They became an unacceptable way to secure a wife. Around 120 cases of abductions were noted from the 1850s. Like many other law suits we have uncovered for this study, the law was applied inconsistently in post-Famine abductions. For instance, in 1860 John Molloy, a labourer, was indicted for the abduction of Mary Conway, a girl under the age of fifteen. On cross examination it was elicited that there had been a 'little courtship' between the two. The jury acquitted the prisoner.[111] William Fortune was not so lucky when he abducted Anne Smith, who was under sixteen, from Carrick-on-Suir in 1864. This was clearly a collusive abduction and the couple had been meeting secretly against the wishes of Anne's mother. Anne's stepfather had apparently encouraged the relationship. The couple ran away and were found four days later living as man and wife in Clonmel. Fortune was convicted.[112]

There were clearly many more collusive abductions in this period. A man named Smyth ran away with Miss Courtney in 1878 and was apprehended in Glasgow, just after the couple had been married. He was tried in Antrim and declared to the court that he did not realise that he had committed any offence. He denied that any 'familiarity had taken place between them before the marriage', and his entire concern was to have her as his wife.[113] His wife was the daughter of a magistrate in

---

[109] *Mayo Constitution*, 10 Feb. 1834.
[110] NAI, CSO/RP/OR 38/1838/26. For a similar case see *Ballina Impartial*, 2 Feb. 1835.
[111] *Freeman's Journal*, 27 July 1860.   [112] *Freeman's Journal*, 11 March 1864.
[113] *Freeman's Journal*, 26 July, 7 Sept. 1878.

County Derry, who disapproved of their relationship. This fact may have influenced Smyth's relatively harsh sentence of four months' imprisonment with hard labour.[114] In those abductions that occurred after the Famine there seems to have been very little, if any, violence used and none of the victims appear to have been raped. This suggests that collusive abductions were a way of defying parental opposition to a relationship. In a small number of cases, abductors were evidently trying to improve their economic and social circumstances. In 1891, John Doyle found himself before the Wicklow assizes on a charge of abduction for removing Sarah Jane Haughton from her mother's charge. Doyle was a labourer, while Haughton's widowed mother ran a sixty-three-acre farm. Doyle worked on the farm for eighteen months. Sarah Jane went missing for two days before she was returned home by the local sergeant and another man. Doyle was found not guilty, although the judge made it clear that 'there was nothing against the character of the young girl'.[115]

Justice

Bringing abductors to trial, and convicting them, was not always a straightforward process. Juries and witnesses could be intimidated. Rewards were offered for information leading to the capture and prosecution of abductors. In some cases the principals were sought but any members of the abduction party willing to give evidence against them were promised pardons. Kelly has observed that most abductors, until the late eighteenth century, escaped trial and punishment because abductees were reluctant to pursue a prosecution to trial.[116] Many of those prosecuted tended to be fined or imprisoned for short periods of time. However, from the 1770s prosecutions were pursued more forcefully and the attention of the authorities focused primarily on the abduction of women of substantial fortune. The abduction of the Kennedy sisters in County Kilkenny in 1779, for instance, resulted in the execution of three men.[117] Between the years 1800 and 1850 there were in the region of 2,000 individuals committed for their involvement in abductions.[118]

---

[114] Ibid.   [115] *Freeman's Journal*, 23 July 1891.
[116] Kelly, 'The abduction of women of fortune', 31.
[117] See Margery Weiner, *Matters of Felony: A Reconstruction* (London, 1967); *Hibernian Journal*, 20, 30 Oct., 1,6, 8 Dec. 1780; *Finn's Leinster Journal*, 21 April 1779. Between August 1779 and March 1781 eight men found guilty of the crime of abduction were executed. See Kelly, 'The abduction of women of fortune', 33.
[118] These figures are calculated from Outrage Reports, *Reports of Commissioners into the General State of Prisons in Ireland* (1803–1850), and Criminal Statistics and select committees on the state of Ireland.

Table 6.2 *Abduction trials and outcomes, 1826–1838*

Year	Committals	Acquittals	Convicted	Executed	Jail	Transportation
1826	43	7	12	2	0	0
1827	59	10	15	0	0	0
1828	60	15	11	2	0	0
1829	61	17	8	1	0	0
1830	64	10	9	2	0	0
1831	38	13	1	0	0	0
1832	58	32	3	1	0	0
1833	54	13	9	5	0	0
1834	93	26	20	2	0	10
1835	71	22	15	3	0	0
1836	34	23	10	0	0	1
1837	34	8	5	1	0	0
1838	29	12	12	0	8	1

Source: *Report from the Select Committee of the House of Lords Appointed to Enquire into the State of Ireland … 1839*, XI, XII, p. 1.

Of this number around 350 were convicted with sentences ranging from execution, to transportation, to a few months in jail. Over 160 men were sentenced to death for the crime, with at least 16 actually being executed between 1815 and 1842, when the law changed.[119] Over the period 1800–1850 just over forty men were transported for seven years or more. The available evidence suggests that the majority of individuals who made up the abduction parties were acquitted or not tried. For instance, in the five-year period from 1815 to 1820, 275 individuals were committed for being involved in an abduction, of that number 17 were sentenced to death, 7 to jail terms and 11 to transportation; just under 87 per cent were released. What appear to be reliably accurate statistics on the outcome of trials for abductions are available for the years between 1826 and 1838.

Very few prisoners spent time in jail, and a number of those sentenced to death had those sentences either commuted or discharged. For instance, Patrick Barker, who was being held in Tipperary town gaol having been convicted of abduction in March 1835, after being sentenced to death, found himself given a free pardon and was out of gaol by August of the same year.[120] At the same time James Dillon was in

[119] The laws in England and Ireland regarding the death penalty were assimilated in 1842. The death penalty for the crimes of rape and abduction was abolished.
[120] *Report from the Select Committee of the House of Lords Appointed to Enquire into the State of Ireland in Respect of Crime* HL 1839, p. 1412.

Limerick city gaol facing a death sentence for his part in an abduction. His sentence was subsequently commuted to transportation for seven years.

From 1845 to 1850, 179 committals saw 43 convictions, with 38 sentenced to jail, and 6 to transportation; thus 74 per cent of those committed were released. Most of those sentenced to death were reprieved. It is clear that while abductors were vigorously pursued by the police and relatives, convictions did not always follow. This may be due to the unwillingness of abductees, or others, to give evidence in court, and where the social class of abductors and abductees was fairly similar, sentences were not generally heavy. The judicial and criminal statistics from 1866 reveal that eighty-five people were arrested for being involved in abductions, with forty-two being convicted, and thirty-one of those were imprisoned for short periods.[121]

Intimidation and threats of violence were common reasons for not prosecuting an abduction. In one case in Roscommon a local Justice of the Peace observed that the abductors 'are of a very respectable family and no doubt but their relatives will exert themselves to prevent prosecution'.[122] George Goold petitioned the Lord Lieutenant in 1823 for government assistance, emphasising his family's hardship after the abduction of his sister, Honora. Having prosecuted the abductors he noted that the family were forced to leave the area and sell their cattle 'at a very low price'.[123] In 1823, John Casey was found not guilty of assisting in the abduction of Mary McGarry as no witnesses appeared to testify against him. The principal abductor in the case had gone to America.[124] In 1828 Michael Fenton sought legal advice from the Chief Secretary's Office on compelling a witness to testify in an attempted abduction case. He had already gathered witnesses in the case but the woman involved, Mary McDonnell, refused to identify her abductors. Shortly after the attempted abduction she had married another man to 'prevent a reoccurrence'.[125] A Mayo policeman noted in 1838 that in one particular abduction the abductors 'are so connected in this part of the country by marriage and otherwise, that it will be very difficult to arrest them'.[126] In Roscommon, when the police arrived at the house of a girl who had been abducted they were refused admittance; once they got

---

[121] Figures from 1879–1890 do not appear to exist.
[122] Cited in Huggins, *Social Conflict*, p. 122.   [123] NAI, CSO/RP/1823/982.
[124] *Ballina Impartial*, 5 May 1823. For another similar case, see *The Morning Post*, 22 July 1850.
[125] Letter from Michael Fenton, Castletown, Dromore West [County Sligo], 9 Feb. 1828 (NAI, CSO/RP/OP/1828/176).
[126] NAI, CSO/RP/OR 53/1838/21.

into the house the girl stated that she did not want to prosecute, as some of the abduction party were 'friends of hers'.[127] In 1839, Catherine Guinan, the daughter of a cattle dealer, had a dowry of £300 and was abducted by Michael Mullery. Mullery was a member of a large faction group. Catherine was rescued and Mullery and his accomplices were prosecuted. Mullery, it was noted in the magistrate's report, 'by threats and violence afterwards to the injured party ... will so intimidate them that they can laugh to scorn the magistrates of the law'. It was unsurprising when the police were informed that 'the parents of the girl now wish to decline to prosecute'.[128]

Likewise, witnesses sometimes had to be protected. The Crown Solicitor for Munster, Matthew Barrington, noted in 1829 that 'We had a very serious case of abduction last year against a man named Halihy, in the County of Cork; he was hanged, and we were obliged to remove the woman out of that county to Limerick, and bring her and keep her there till the assizes, though her father was a very respectable farmer'.[129] In 1839, John Kilfeather, alias Gilfillan, was indicted for carrying away Catherine Hoey, a girl of fourteen. She gave evidence against him in court and it was noted that there 'seemed to be a bad feeling pervading the country people assembled as those whom she had prosecuted were from county Donegal and were much liked by the people in general'. She had police protection when passing through Lifford and Strabane going to the Derry assizes where it was feared she might be assaulted by the crowd.[130] Even after a successful prosecution, witnesses could be in danger. Dennis Daly was executed in Cork in 1829 for his part in the abduction of Ann Gallagher. There was some local sympathy for Daly, who had handed himself in to the authorities. More than a thousand people were estimated to have attended his funeral in Glanworth, County Cork, and the crowd intended the funeral procession to pass the abductee's home. The local magistrate remonstrated with the crowd but he and the policemen with him came under attack and fired at the crowd killing one of them and wounding at least six others. The police were quickly reinforced by a military party. An English newspaper observed that in Ireland 'abduction [was not] viewed, amongst the poorer classes, in the light of a crime'.[131]

---

[127] NAI, CSO/RP/OR 19/1838/25.   [128] NAI, CSO/RP/OR 509/1839/11.
[129] *The Morning Chronicle*, 31 July 1829. See also, evidence of Mathew Barrington, *Report from the Select Committee on the Irish Miscellaneous Estimates with Minutes of Evidence and Appendix*, H.C. 342, 1829, p. 77.
[130] *Freeman's Journal*, 1 Aug. 1839; NAI, CRF 1839 R35.
[131] *Connaught Journal*, 3 Sept. 1829; *Belfast Newsletter*, 15 Sept. 1829; *Carlow Morning Post*, 31 Aug. 1829. See also, *The Hull Packet and Humber Mercury*, 15 Sept. 1829.

Parents might insist on a prosecution even when the abducted daughter was unwilling to pursue one. In 1828, Catherine Trainer was abducted from her home and the intention of the abductors was to bring her to a man named Thomas King who wished 'to defile her'. Trainer told the court that she was now married and did not wish King to be 'injured on her account'. She admitted to being abducted but 'not so much against her will, as against the will of her parents'. She liked the prisoner 'very well' and would have married him if her family had agreed to the marriage. She then refused to provide any account of the rape and the prisoners were acquitted.[132] Catherine Farrelly, who had been abducted in County Cavan in 1835, was rescued and returned to her family. She quickly married another man but her parents insisted that she prosecute her abductor, a report on the case noting that she 'goes by their directions'.[133] Catherine Tiernan, abducted by Michael Cannon in 1841, was intent on prosecuting her abductor. However, at the trial, she was told that it was the family's wish that she should marry Cannon and that her mother had given her blessing for Catherine to do so. Catherine's version of events then changed and she told the police that the abduction was pre-arranged.[134] Fear of a reprisal from the abductor's family or his friends and relatives may have persuaded some victims to intervene on the abductor's behalf. This may have been the reasoning behind a petition sent to support Patrick Connolly, sentenced to death, which was later reprieved to transportation for life, for the abduction of Anne Finnigan in County Monaghan in 1836. Finnigan and her father wrote a petition to the Lord Lieutenant asking that the sentence be reduced further. Anne noted that the event of the abduction was a moment of 'unguarded folly and youthful levity', and stated that she had now forgiven Connolly from her 'heart and soul'.[135] Margaret Brien, who had been abducted by John Gleeson, refused to be sworn at his trial, stating that 'she had forgiven the prisoner'.[136] The trial of the abductors of Bridget Fetherston was postponed when Catherine Wheeler, a material witness, had 'absconded to avoid giving evidence'.[137] Clearly there were problems with prosecuting these abductors and the low rate of convictions, whether due to lack of witnesses, intimidation or other causes, suggests that abduction was a less risky enterprise than might have been suggested by the law.

---

[132] *Belfast Newsletter*, 5 Aug. 1828. [133] *Galway Weekly Advertiser*, 11 March 1837.
[134] NAI, CSO/RP/OR 5335/1841/16. [135] NAI, CRF 1836 C1.
[136] *Nenagh Guardian*, 22 March 1845. [137] *Anglo-Celt*, 31 July 1846.

Rape and Reputation

The common belief was that an abducted woman, especially if she were gone for any length of time, had lost her honour. Her virtue and chastity were compromised and it was assumed that it would be impossible for her to marry respectably. While abductors were seeking to raise their status or secure money or land, they realised that the abductee's absence from her home for any length of time would very probably secure a marriage on these grounds. The more ruthless abductors simply raped their abductees. In 1823, one young man from County Laois carried off the daughter of a 'respectable' person named Haughy. This may have been one of those cases where an intention to rape, rather than to enforce a marriage, was the principle aim. The father collected a party and pursued the offender, who when caught refused to marry the girl. The woman's reputation having been ruined, the abductor was beaten by the girl's father in such a manner as 'to endanger his life'.[138] Similarly, at a trial for assault, the prisoner's father pleaded in court that the dispute that led to the assault occurred when the prisoner's sister was

followed to a fair ... and from thence taken away by one of the prosecutors and after detaining her for eight days he refused to marry her and sent her home after destroying her reputation and still not being contented with the destruction of an unfortunate female, when the prosecutors at a publick [sic] meeting met the prisoners they boasted of their amour with their dishonourable sister and threatened destruction to any person who dare oppose them.[139]

It was noted in court that the father's grief at his daughter's loss of chastity had 'ruined his constitution'.

As the incidents of abduction already cited indicate, it was possible for an abducted woman to marry another man following their abduction, although whether such men had to be persuaded with an enhanced dowry, or if they came from a lower section of society, is unclear. Bridget Smith, abducted in Mayo in 1840, did not marry her abductor but 'another person' as her parents wished.[140] In Roscommon in 1841, Anne Burke, who had been abducted by James Beatty, married a man named McLoughlin. They were married within a short time after the abduction and the reason given for the haste was 'so little had any stain attache[d] to her character'.[141] In Sligo in 1838, Mary Feenigan was abducted by a group of men, but within three days she was married to a man named

---

[138] *Connaught Journal*, 10 Feb. 1823.
[139] Prisoners' Petitions and Cases, 11 May 1825 (NAI, VI 24 1 2596).
[140] NAI, CRF 1840 F38.   [141] NAI, CRF 1841 B15; CSO/RP/OR, 38/1838/26.

Kilroy who had nothing to do with the abduction.[142] So it clearly was possible to marry after being abducted. It is possible too that some of these marriages were already in negotiation prior to the abduction. What we have seen in abductions from the eighteenth through to the twentieth century is that it was generally a crime of violence and intimidation. Victims were generally mistreated and sometimes raped. There was a better chance of conviction if the woman could show, most often through physical injuries that had been witnessed, that she had resisted the abduction in some way. Women who had endured this often horrendous ordeal then had to give evidence in court if her abductor was to be prosecuted. Such prosecutions, as we have seen, were not always successful.

In actual court cases it was more likely that an abductor would be sentenced to death if the abduction also involved rape. Jeremiah Herlehy and Timothy Cremen were both executed in May 1828 for separate abductions. What distinguished these particular abductions was the fact that both men repeatedly raped their victims, whom they managed to conceal for up to ten days.[143] Abduction trials were serious, and had more serious outcomes, when rape and/or serious physical assault were involved. Defendants also used the fact that they had not raped their victims as a mitigating factor in their prosecution. A character reference from a Catholic priest for Patrick Foy, who had been involved in an abduction in 1840, noted his 'one redeeming feature, I think credible to the unfortunate man, [was] that he committed no violence to the prosecutrix'.[144] Foy, who had been sentenced to death, had his sentence reduced to transportation for life, and that sentence was further reduced to eighteen months' imprisonment with hard labour when mitigating circumstances were taken into account. The fact that some abductors married their abductees also ensured that prosecutions were not continued. Some abductors attempted to have their sentences mitigated by declaring that the abduction had not harmed the victim's chances of marriage. For instance, a petition from one abductor, whose sentence had already been commuted to two years' imprisonment, observed 'that the said prosecutrix was married shortly after the occurrence aforesaid to a man whom her parents selected for her and with whom she is ever since living she not having suffered in the least degree either in person or character'. Consequently, the petition continued, the abductor should be released.[145]

---

[142] *Mayo Constitution*, 4 March 1830; NAI, CSO/RP/OR, 38/26/1838.
[143] *Belfast Newsletter*, 8 April, 2 May 1838.   [144] NAI, CRF 1840 F38.
[145] NAI, CRF 1845 T5.

Many abduction cases, when they came to court and were not resolved by a marriage, were more about the crimes of rape and assault than about the abduction *per se*. In a number of cases the crime of abduction was reduced to a case of assault. There is no doubt that a loss of chastity was recognised, by the family and the community, as a severe assault on a woman, and a stain against her family. Successful convictions for rape in the eighteenth and nineteenth centuries could lead to sentences of execution or transportation; the severest sentences passed on those convicted of abduction suggest that the crime of rape was also being severely punished.

Rape as a crime complicates our understanding of abduction, especially where it led to marriage. Matthew Barrington, Crown Solicitor for the Munster Circuit, claimed in 1829 that 'it is a mode that girls have of swearing a rape against a man, to try to get married to him'. He believed that out of fifteen recent rape trials only two had been genuine cases.[146] The tendency of Irish magistrates to allow couples to marry where there was an accusation of rape came in for severe criticism in the 1830s, a decade in which there was a substantial number of abductions. H. D. Inglis, in his travels in Ireland in 1834, noted that at Ennis assizes nearly forty cases of rape were entered for trial. He observed, however, that in nine out of ten cases 'the crime is sworn to, merely for the purpose of getting a husband; and the plan generally succeeds'.[147] By 1837, Irish magistrates were informed that they should no longer allow the charge of rape to be compromised by marriage. Allowing such a compromise, it was believed, encouraged women to make false accusations in the hope of compelling men to marry them. It also allowed men to believe that the worst that could happen to them if convicted of rape was to be compelled to marry the 'victim of his lust'.[148] Given the leeway that magistrates allowed in the area of rape, it was understandable that abductors believed that when prosecuted, a marriage would, even when rape had occurred, secure their freedom.[149]

---

[146] Evidence of Mathew Barrington, *Report from the Select Committee to Inquire into Irish Miscellaneous Estimates*, p. 77.

[147] H.D. Inglis, *A Journey throughout Ireland* (London, 1838), pp. 163–4.

[148] Anon., *Instructions for the Guidance of Resident Magistrates* (Dublin, 1837), pp. 6–8. While arrests for the crime of rape occurred, convictions were less forthcoming. For instance, there were 4 convictions from the 149 arrests for rape in 1816. The letter to the magistrates was published in the press. See, for instance, *Tralee Mercury*, 13 Sept. 1837.

[149] Five prisoners accused of rape had their cases dismissed before the Cavan assizes as they had all married their accusers. See *The Enniskillen Chronicle and Erne Packet*, 30 July 1835.

It is also worth considering more generally whether women used rape as a strategy for marriage. For poor single women, marriage could be a good survival strategy. Witnesses who appeared before the Poor Law Enquiry Commissioners in the 1830s commented that 'men sometimes marry to get rid of charges of rape' and 'it frequently happens that women threaten to swear a rape against a man, to force him to marry her; it mostly ends in marriage; they are often married in the dock during trial'.[150] It was widely believed that many rape charges were attempts to secure marriage and it is mostly male authority figures, such as magistrates, judges and priests who expressed these views. The parish priest in Kilmore Erris, County Mayo, in his evidence to the commission noted that as a result of the number of rape cases 'got up merely for the purpose of forcing marriage... a regulation has been imposed upon the catholic clergy of this diocese, not to marry such parties while a prosecution is pending'.[151] In 1836, Catherine Slevin admitted that she had had a sexual relationship with Michael Higgins before she had him charged with rape. She stated that she had 'instigated the said prosecution with a view of compelling [Higgins] to marry me'.[152] Higgins was sentenced to death and a flurry of petitions was sent to the Lord Lieutenant to have his sentence reduced. The judge in the case bemoaned the number of rape cases that saw perjury being committed by women, convictions being made and then petitions being presented that argued for a mitigation of sentence allowing the couple to marry.[153] In 1836 Mary Leary signed a petition for the 'free pardon, conditionally on his [prisoner] marrying memorialist either before or after his release'.[154] At the Kerry summer assizes in 1838, Baron Richardson revealed his abhorrence of the crime of rape and noted that the last time he had been at the Kerry assizes 'between twenty and thirty odious and disgusting crimes of that kind' came before him. He remarked that 'in the whole of the cases sent down to me for trial, there was nothing like the character of rape'. Richardson argued that the greatest scrutiny was required of these 'trumpery cases'.[155] While the practice seems to have declined in the late 1830s, some further cases surfaced in the 1840s and later.[156]

---

[150] Poor Law Enquiry, appendix A, pp. 56, 83.   [151] Ibid., p. 53.

[152] NAI, CRF 1836 H1.

[153] NAI, CRF 1836 H1. It is not known what became of Higgins.

[154] NAI, CRF 1836 H5.

[155] *Tralee Mercury*, 18 July 1838. Reports of two such cases tried by Richards in 1837 can be found in *Tralee Mercury*, 15 March 1837.

[156] In 1892, when Bridget Ruane refused Michael Knight's proposal of marriage, he raped her. She then agreed to marry him, noting 'I said I'd have anything before my character would be scattered on account of him'. Knight later reneged on the proposal and Ruane prosecuted him; the charges were dropped when he renewed his proposal (NAI, Mayo Assize Files, 1892).

James Wallace, according to the magistrate, was convicted 'on clear evidence'[157] of a rape on Catherine Reynolds in 1843. Wallace was sentenced to transportation for life. The victim's father petitioned for the release of Wallace stating that his daughter wished to marry the man. The petition was unsuccessful and the magistrate who tried the case, and whose advice was sought, opposed the idea that such a strategy could be used to secure the prisoner's release.[158] That the law was unevenly enforced is clear from a similar case in the same year. In that case Pierce Gorman had been convicted at Nenagh assizes of raping Catherine Maher and was sentenced to transportation for life. The magistrate who tried the case supported a petition declaring that the couple wished to be married, and the prisoner was released.[159] In 1847, William Dillane was convicted of rape and also sentenced to transportation for life. The judge who presided over the trial believed that the woman involved had made a deliberate effort to 'capture' the prisoner as her family had nothing and the prisoner was the son of a farmer. The only verdict he could give at the time was transportation as the jury had found the prisoner guilty. In the petition papers for a mitigation of sentence the same judge argued for a reduction of the sentence to eighteen months' hard labour as the prisoner was now willing to marry the woman, who consented to the proposal on the understanding that the marriage would take place before the prisoner was released from prison. This condition made the judge certain that she had planned the encounter with the prisoner that led to the rape.[160] John Hayden raped a servant with whom he worked in Kilkenny. He was convicted and sentenced to transportation for life. The victim, Mary Grany, and her parents signed (with their mark) a petition to have the prisoner released as he said that he wanted to marry Mary. However, Mary then visited the local priest and told him that her parents had forced her to sign the petition and she had no wish to marry Hayden, who had promised to support her family.[161] The cleric informed the Lord Lieutenant's office and Hayden was duly transported.[162] There are numerous examples of such cases in Ireland, particularly from the 1820s to the 1840s. The practical implications of a successful rape charge gave some women an opportunity to secure a marriage and hence, particularly in pre-Famine Ireland, a possible means of subsistence.

Returning to abductions, it is clear that sometimes prosecutions were followed through by the families to achieve justice or secure revenge

---

[157] NAI, CRF 1843 G9.
[158] NAI, CRF 1843 W19. Wallace was transported in August 1843.
[159] NAI, CRF 1843 G9.   [160] NAI, CRF 1847 D43.   [161] NAI, CRF 1843 H20.
[162] Hayden was transported on the 8 May 1843. See Irish Prison Registers.

against the abductor. In some cases it was a way to force a marriage between the abductor and abductee. This was more evident in those cases where rape had occurred during the abduction. The concern with the abductee's reputation however, was compromised by a court case. In court the full details of the case were revealed and the violence and rape were made known to the public, who crowded into the courts to view these trials. The victim was the one who had to provide the necessary evidence for a successful prosecution. If chastity was so important, why did families, and the women themselves, then go to court? It appears that women were perceived as victims if they suffered severe violence or sexual assault, which they were expected to strongly resist. Were the women mere chattels to be exchanged, or was a prosecution an expression of a woman's or a family's outrage at the pain suffered by them in an abduction? The court cases in themselves were not about dowries or property or fortune, and it is interesting to consider that when an abduction was successful the dowry or fortune was still handed over by the family. A refusal to pay a dowry might, of course, have endangered the life of the woman. By the time the cases came to court the damage to a woman's reputation was done; it was too late to undo that damage, so what, if anything, was being restored to the family through these court cases? Seeing justice done to a perpetrator may have been what was really required by the family but, as we have seen, many abductors never endured the full force of the law.

Conclusion

The centrality of rape to many of these abductions appears significant. Rape has, as a number of historians have shown, historically specific constructions and meanings.[163] It suggests the relationship between social and sexual power. Rape was an expression of power over the abducted woman and its meanings for her were evident. She would lose her virtue; she would find it difficult to marry someone else, and so the abductor was shaping her future. She had to show she resisted in order to establish coercion, so she needed to fight her attacker and retain the marks of injury. Within the context of abduction, rape was an assumed part of the process. It is not clear whether a woman's reputation could be secured or repaired by proving that a rape had not occurred; it certainly assisted in reducing the sentence of the abductor, but it is not obvious if

---

[163] See for instance, Sharon Block, *Rape and Sexual Power in Early America* (Chapel Hill, 2006).

evidence to this effect secured, or rescued, the reputation of the woman involved.

Consensual abductions revealed the willingness of some couples to defy parental authority. Like many marriages in eighteenth- and nineteenth-century Ireland, abduction was itself an economic transaction, a transaction that could be carried through with considerable violence. We know little, if anything, about what abductors lost when they engaged in this violent activity. It is not at all clear how their actions shaped understandings of masculinity in the period, or whether abductors lost any status in their own communities as a result of their actions. We need further to explore the values or moral economy that informed gender relations in pre-Famine Ireland, before we can fully understand the import of abduction. What we now know, however, is that abduction was an extensive practice in the first half of the nineteenth century. It was, in the majority of cases, an act of violence. There is usually a strong class element to these abductions. The primary function of an abduction was to compel a marriage that would improve the fortunes of the abductor. For much of the eighteenth century relatively wealthy women were targeted by the minor gentry. By the early nineteenth century, abductions were more common in the lower classes, with lower-class women, and the daughters of shopkeepers and publicans, being targeted by men also of the lower classes. Over the period, the numbers of abductions increased incrementally until the 1830s and 1840s, and then faded away by the early twentieth century. Although abductors and abduction parties were prosecuted, at least 70 to 80 per cent of those involved in abductions were not convicted of an offence, and many had capital and other sentences significantly reduced. Given the status of virginity, and the impact of the loss of virginity outside marriage upon a woman's reputation and ability to marry, a successful abduction offered almost a guarantee of marriage and the dowry that went with it. Intimacy and violence, consent and resistance, reputation and loss, were the central components of abduction and reveal much about gender relations, relations between parents and their children, and the law and the community in Ireland.

Part III

Happy Ever After?

7   Marital Relations

I must first vent myself. I wonder how thou could be so stupid as to imagine I would send money to Dublin to answer a bill of mine and not tell thee where it was to be applied ... I am quite put out by thy neglect ...

Don't be displeased at my writing as I did in the beginning of this. It is all out now and I have no more to say. Thou art always my entirely beloved and dear, dear wife say my heart flowing with affection.[1]

The letter from William Leadbeater to his wife, Mary, whom he had asked to conduct some financial business while she was in Dublin, neatly encapsulates an affectionate relationship between husband and wife. William communicated his annoyance with his wife as she had clearly misunderstood his request but by the end of the letter, he acknowledged his need to vent his frustration and was concerned to reassure his wife of his love and devotion. The Leadbeater marriage is unusually well documented. In addition to the couple's correspondence, Mary Shackleton Leadbeater kept a journal from the age of eleven to shortly before her death in her sixty-eighth year in 1826. Through the pages of the journal, it is possible to trace the chronology of her marriage to William Leadbeater from their first meeting, their courtship, marriage and parenthood through to old age. Despite the frustration expressed in the letter cited above, the Leadbeater marriage was a very happy and affectionate one. Mary regularly recorded in her diary how much she missed her 'dear William' when he was away from home. In 1801, after ten years of marriage, she wrote of 'how lonely I feel in his absence and what tender anxiety invades me while he is so far away ... I would not change these sensations for the tranquillity of a maiden life'.[2] Mary also noted how William took an active role in caring for their six children and how they relied on one another for emotional support when their four-year-old

---

[1] William Leadbeater to Mary Leadbeater, 28 April 1802 (NLI, MS 8003).
[2] Journal of Mary Leadbeater, April 1801 (NLI, MS 9324, p. 45).

daughter, Jane, was accidently burnt to death in the family home in 1798.[3] The couple also shared work tasks: managing an inn, a small farm and a household of children as well as caring for Mary's mother, who lived with them and suffered from dementia towards the end of her life. William was also clearly proud of his wife's fame as a writer and brought guests staying at the inn to visit the family home.[4] Through the pages of his wife's journal, William emerges as the ideal husband, caring for his children as well as his wife. In the two years before she died, Mary was ill and frequently bed-ridden. She recorded how William looked after her: acting as a 'nurse-tender', taking her out for short rides in a horse and cart and buying her a 'bed chair' on one of his business trips to Dublin, which enabled her to sit more comfortably.[5]

In previous chapters we looked at the process of courtship and the negotiations that went into making a marriage. In this chapter we explore what happens after the marriage was agreed. We look first at the planning of the wedding festivities: the buying of a dress and the preparation of the wedding meal. In the second section of the chapter, we explore relationships between husbands and wives and the different ways in which patriarchy was expressed. To what extent did husbands exercise their authority under the laws of church and state to control their wife's behaviour? What evidence is there that husbands were aware of their status as heads of household and anxious to enforce it? We examine these questions with the caveat in mind that it is impossible, even in a well-documented marriage like that of the Leadbeaters, to catch more than a glimpse of the intimate human relationship between a husband and a wife.

Wedding Festivities

As Chapters 3 and 4 indicate, a marriage service could quickly follow an agreement on a marriage settlement or dowry. In such circumstances, the wedding celebrations were often brief and might consist of no more than a meal attended by a small family group. Other courtships, as we have seen, took longer, followed an agreed pattern of behaviour, and the couple and their families had more time to prepare for the wedding service and the subsequent festivities.

---

[3] Journal of Mary Leadbeater, 11 March, Dec. 1798 (NLI, MS 9320, pp. 225–9).
[4] Mary O'Dowd, 'Mary Leadbeater: Modern woman and Irish Quaker' in David Hayton and Andrew Holmes (eds.), *Ourselves Alone? Religion, Society and Politics in Eighteenth- and Nineteenth-Century Ireland: Essays Presented to S. J. Connolly* (Dublin, 2016), pp. 137–53.
[5] Journal of Mary Leadbeater, February, May 1826 (NLI, MS 93446, pp. 6, 18, 31, 38).

The most popular time of the year for marriages were the days before Lent, and particularly Shrove Tuesday, as all Christian denominations prohibited weddings during Lent.[6] Folklore accounts describe the rituals that took place on the day of the wedding, with mummers arriving to accompany the bride to the wedding venue.[7] This is a custom, however, that only became popular in the second half of the nineteenth century when the marriage service moved from the bride's home to the church.[8] Prior to that time, the procession to the church was a rare occurrence and largely confined to wealthy family weddings. As a special honour, however, the diarist Mary Delany followed this custom when she organised the wedding of her maidservant, Sarah Hipwell in her house at Delville near Dublin in 1751. The wedding party, which consisted mainly of the domestic servants in the household who were bedecked with white ribbons provided by Delany, walked from Delville to the nearby church at Glasnevin where Delany's husband, Patrick, performed the service. A larger party subsequently attended the dinner that Delany arranged, which had 'as much beef, mutton, and pudding as they could devour'.[9] Mary Shackleton Leadbeater also described participating in a procession for a Quaker wedding that she attended in Carlow in 1777. Wearing the long black hood and cloak that her mother had insisted she wear, the eighteen-year old Shackleton was embarrassed at joining the other girls in the procession who were all dressed in their finery of light-coloured dresses.[10]

The main post-marriage celebration, as in the Delville household, was normally the meal attended by members of the two extended families, friends and the minister who performed the service. The hospitality offered by the bride's family was considered an important demonstration of the family's social standing and material wealth. Most

[6] Brian Francis Gurrin, 'Land and people in Wicklow, 1660–1840' (2 vols., unpublished PhD thesis, NUI Maynooth, 2006), ii, pp. 428–9; Daniel Grace, 'The income of Catholic priests in pre-Famine Ireland: Some evidence from the diocese of Killaloe', *Tipperary Historical Journal*, 30 (2017), 81.
[7] Linda Ballard, *Forgetting Frolic: Marriage Traditions in Ireland* (Belfast, 1998); Caoimhín Ó Danachair, 'Some marriage customs and their regional distribution', *Béaloideas*, 42/44 (1974–1976), 136–75.
[8] See 36–7, 87 above on the move towards marriages in church. See also Hugh Dorian, *The Outer Edge of Ulster. A Memoir of Social Life in Nineteenth-Century Donegal*. Edited by Breandán MacSuibhne and David Dickson (Dublin, 2000), pp. 304–6.
[9] Cited in Ballard, *Forgetting Frolic*, p. 106.
[10] Mary O'Dowd, 'Adolescent girlhood in eighteenth century Ireland' in Mary O'Dowd and June Purvis (eds.), *A History of the Girl: Formation, Identity and Education* (London, 2018), p. 63.

descriptions of wedding meals in the eighteenth and nineteenth centuries emphasise the extent and the variety of food offered. Mary Delany provided an impressive array of dishes when her goddaughter, Sally Chapone, married in 1764. There were twenty separate offerings of fish, fowl, meat and vegetables as well as nine desserts.[11] At perhaps a lower level of *haute cusine*, in 1847, Mrs Ann Leo told Nenagh petty sessions how she had cooked and supervised the preparation of a dinner for the wedding of Biddy Kennedy, the daughter of a comfortable farmer, Jerry Kennedy. The father had promised her a payment of five shillings for her labour. He told Leo that he wanted everything perfect, 'for I wouldn't give it to say to her people-in-law and the company that the bridegroom will bring wud [sic] him that every half port was not clean and dacent [sic]'. The court was informed that Leo had overseen the preparation of an extensive menu for the wedding. It consisted of 'a goose ... a piece of pork, a foot in height ... a bit of mutton, praties and cabbage'. Following this came 'a mutton pie, a black pudding and a taste of pastry'.[12] John Gamble, the travel writer, who attended a wedding in County Antrim in 1812, also described an 'abundant' meal and 'the moment dinner was over, the table was removed, and the company began dancing. The music was a fiddle and a dulcimer. The dances were reels of three and of four...'.[13]

In the years before the national Synod of Thurles directed that all Catholic marriage services should be conducted in the local parish church, priests regularly attended not just the service but the subsequent celebrations at which a collection was made on their behalf.[14] The service was usually held in the evening. Father Thomas O'Carroll recorded in his diary of 1846, the times at which he attended a wedding (7:00 to 8:00 p.m.) and when he got home in the evening (usually 11:00–11:30 p.m.). O'Carroll also described the difficulties of travelling to and from remote parts of rural Tipperary in the dark. On most occasions, he appears to have stayed for as short a time as possible and gave the impression in his journal that he was relieved to get home.[15]

---

[11] Cited in Ballard, *Forgetting Frolic*, p. 106.

[12] *Nenagh Guardian*, 4 April 1849. Cited in Grace, 'The income of Catholic priests in pre-Famine Ireland', 82. See also Ballard, *Forgetting Frolic*, pp. 106–7 for descriptions of other wedding meals.

[13] John Gamble, *A View of Society and Manners in the North of Ireland: In the Summer and Autumn of 1812* (London, 1813), pp. 94–5.

[14] For the Synod of Thurles' directions on marriage see pp. 36, 42–4, 87.

[15] Diary of Thomas O'Carroll, 1846 (The O'Carroll Diaries (unpublished typescript by Rev. James Feehan), pp. 3–4). (Tipperary Studies, The Source, Thurles, Co. Tipperary).

The Kenmare-based Catholic Dean John O'Sullivan also noted what he considered the tediousness of attendance at rural wedding festivities:

It requires much patience and resignation to come to a country house in the evening with a roaring fire roasting, boiling, baking, cooking in a variety of ways various and sundry joints of fowl, beef, mutton, bacon superintended by a dirty slattern melting from the action of the heat and the steam, and the smoke with so many streams of perspiration oozing from every pore of her body ... The priest ... must preside and officiate at the carving for the company. He must make a semblance of eating something; for if he have common sense he will have eaten his dinner at home as usual, and be he ever so hungry, if he have got a glimpse at the cook and her *modus operandi*, I defy him to make much use of the dinner ...[16]

O'Sullivan admitted, however, that what he found most difficult about the long evening was keeping up the conversation:

The subjects most interesting to them were the ones I knew nothing about, what would be interesting to me was high Dutch to them, then the unintentional offences offered by some of them through ignorance or through tipsiness, the coarseness of their language to each other ... made the whole scene a most repulsive and disagreeable one.[17]

Nevertheless, O'Sullivan, as noted in Chapter 1, urged priests to continue to attend 'public weddings' because it was a way to get to know their parishioners and to earn their respect: 'the people let out freely and unguardedly what they thought about the whole world ... It is not in human nature not to feel attached to the man that sits at the same table, that sleeps under the same roof, that makes himself part and parcel of the company that assembles upon such occasions.'[18] Other descriptions of the wedding meal confirm the central role of the priest in the proceedings. Some, however, may have enjoyed the wedding festivities more than Dean O'Sullivan. In his account of the wedding in County Antrim in 1812, John Gamble wrote of how the priest was 'grand carver, grand talker too, and grand laugher'. The good humour of the priest was no doubt helped by the drinking of whiskey before the meal began.'[19]

Not all wedding celebrations were such raucous affairs. Dorothea Herbert attended a wedding in 1785, which she related was 'in a Private Stile and we had Nothing but Cards and a Supper with a few Jokes about the first kiss from Mr Rankin.'[20] Marriages in the Society of Friends were

---

[16] John O'Sullivan, 'Praxi Parochis' (Kerry Diocesan Archives, Killarney), pp. 709–10.
[17] Ibid., p. 711.   [18] Ibid., p. 712.
[19] Gamble, *A View of Society and Manners in the North of Ireland*, p. 94. See also Ballard, *Forgetting Frolics*, p. 108.
[20] Dorothea Herbert, *Retrospections of Dorothea Herbert, 1770–1806* (Dublin, 1988), p. 119.

an opportunity to bring the community together but in a more sober manner than the celebrations described by Dean John O'Sullivan. The witnessing of the marriage was often followed by a round of social visits and small gatherings. In 1819, Henry Palmer, who lived near Clonmel, County Tipperary, described his surprise when he visited a Quaker friend and was invited upstairs to a room which was 'filled all round with friends, sitting so stiff and so smiling, so clean and so fine at a table covered with plumb cake, and glasses of wine to congratulate a bride and bridegroom married the day before.'[21]

As we discussed in Chapter 1, by the end of the nineteenth century the majority of marriage services were conducted in a church or meeting house. Services were also increasingly held in the morning as canon law decreed. A wedding meal remained a normal part of the celebrations but by that time it may have been hosted in a local hotel rather than in the bride's home. Hotels begin to advertise the provision of wedding breakfasts from the 1880s. The improvement in transport increased the popularity of honeymoons, which in turn determined the scheduling and length of the wedding festivities as the newly married couple frequently had to catch a train after the meal. In 1861, for example, the breakfast for Emily Ward's wedding in County Down took place between 1:00 and 2:30 p.m. but the bride and groom had to leave at 2:15 to catch the train to Belfast and then to Dublin.[22] Other accounts of weddings in the early twentieth century describe similar short celebrations, which were followed by the bride and groom departing for their honeymoon.

The size of the wedding party, as in more recent times, depended on the preferences of the families and the bride and groom, but large crowded affairs were rare. Most descriptions from the eighteenth through to the early twentieth century are of relatively small affairs attended by members of the extended family and a small selection of friends. When Mary Coyle and Tod Andrews married in Haddington Road Church in Dublin in 1928, they invited no guests to the church but had a wedding breakfast in Mary's family home. It was attended by members of the couple's immediate families and although there was a bottle of champagne in the house, it remained unopened.[23]

As the stories told by jilted women in breach of promise suits revealed, an important part of the last stages of the courtship was the purchase of a

---

[21] Henry Palmer to Mrs Kitty Cope, 8 March 1819 (NAI, Private Accessions, 999/782/1). In her diary Mary Leadbeater also describes the visits she and her husband William received following their marriage (Journal of Mary Leadbeater, 1791 (NLI, MS 9316)).
[22] Ballard, *Forgetting Frolic*, p. 96.
[23] C. S. Andrews, *Dublin Made Me* (Dublin, 1979), p. 86.

dress by the bride. The garments worn by men on their wedding day attracted less notice. Mary Shackleton Leadbeater wrote enviously of the wedding outfit of light-coloured poplin with mob cap and calamine shoes worn by her friend, Jenny Lecky, whose wedding she attended in Carlow. A few years later, another teenage girl, Dorothea Herbert, described the wedding dress of a young relative who was a wealthy heiress: 'the bride was dress'd in a White Sarsnet and a White silk bonnet with a very long Veil to it – Her Dress was very rich with fine Lace and costly Trinkets'. Herbert was one of two bridesmaids, both of whom were also dressed in white. The beauty of the garments was undermined a little by the anxiety of the bride, whom Herbert described as 'quite disfigured by continual fretting and Anxiety'.[24]

While wealthy brides such as Herbert's relative might choose to be married in white, the ritual of the white wedding dress did not become popular in Ireland before the 1930s. Before that time, as Linda Ballard explains, the wedding gown tended to follow contemporary fashion and was often designed with subsequent 'wearability' in mind. In the nineteenth century, a wedding dress was often a two-piece outfit that could be worn with different skirts or blouses at a later stage. Few people had the resources to have a dress that could be worn only once. Fashion trends dictated the shape, colour and length of the dress. In the 1860s, Maria Sweeney had a fashionable blue dress with lace trim made for her wedding in Ballymote, County Sligo. She wore it the following week to Mass but the priest allegedly 'disapproved of the figure-revealing style' and Sweeney never wore it again.[25] By the 1920s, short dresses or 'elegantly fashionable day or street dresses' were popular with brides, if not all the clergy.[26] Most dresses were bespoke, made by the many dressmakers employed in Irish towns and cities, but by the 1890s department stores such as Brown Thomas in Dublin were advertising readymade wedding garments.

Forms of Patriarchy

After the wedding celebrations, the bride and groom settled down to married life. Over the past forty years, historians of marriage in England have attempted to analyse and categorise the changing nature of marital relationships over time. In the 1970s, Lawrence Stone suggested that it

---

[24] Herbert, *Retrospections*, pp. 121–2.
[25] See explanatory notice and dress on display in 'The Way We Wore' exhibition in the National Museum of Ireland, Collins Barracks, Dublin.
[26] Ballard, *Forgetting Frolic*, pp. 77–81.

Illustration 7.1 James Herron and Sarah Harris were married in St Peter's Church, Drogheda, Co. Louth, 23 July 1874. Heron was a sub-constable in the Royal Irish Constabulary and the son of a farmer. Harris was the daughter of a vintner. Her brown silk dress is deposited in the Ulster Folk and Transport Museum along with the family bible that the couple had received as a wedding present (Ballard, *Forgetting Frolic*, p. 79).

was possible to detect a significant shift in attitudes to marriage in the early modern period. Marriage in the sixteenth century was characterised by emotionally cold and pragmatic connections motivated by consider-ations of financial and social gain, but by the eighteenth century, affec-tionate and companionate marriages were more common. Paradoxically, Stone also argued that the patriarchal status of the husband was reinforced in seventeenth-century England, partly as a consequence of the Protestant Reformation.[27] The Stone model has proved controversial and has been criticised by many scholars for presenting too polarised a view of the history of marriage. Historians such as Barbara Hanawalt and Keith Wrightson have pointed to the existence of affectionate and com-panionate marriages throughout the medieval and the early modern period as well as the continuity of loveless matches.[28] Case studies of individual marriages have also raised questions about patriarchy and the prevalence of husbands who dominated and controlled the lives of their wives.[29] Patriarchy was usually diluted by the circumstances as well as the personalities of individual husbands and wives. Medieval historian, Barbara Hanawalt, referred to marriage as a partnership.[30] More recently, Joanne Bailey, in her study of marriage in England, 1660–1800, described the prevailing marital relationship of the period as one of co-dependency. Both spouses worked to maintain the household and the wife's manage-ment of the home and children bestowed on her a considerable amount of informal power.[31] Linda Pollock has also critiqued the Stone model, suggesting that it is too simplistic to categorise marital relations as affec-tionate or oppressive. Relationships between husbands and wives did not remain static and changed over the duration of the marriage depending on circumstances and the personalities of those involved.[32]

Historians of marriage in the nineteenth and early twentieth century also emphasise the theme of partnership and co-dependency, but have contextualised it and suggest that there was an increased gender divide in marital responsibilities. Hall and Davidoff's classic study of middle-class

---

[27] Lawrence Stone, *The Family, Sex and Marriage in England 1500–1800* (New York, 1977).
[28] Barbara Hanawalt, *The Ties That Bound: Peasant Families in Medieval England* (Oxford, 1986), pp. 205–23; Keith Wrightson, *English Society 1680–1680* (London, 1982), pp. 92–104. See also Joanne Bailey, *Unquiet Lives: Marriage and Marriage Breakdown in England, 1660–1800* (Cambridge, 2003), pp. 1–11; Helen Berry and Elizabeth Foyster (eds.), *The Family in Early Modern England* (Cambridge, 2007), pp. 1–17; Linda Pollock, 'Rethinking patriarchy and the family in seventeenth-century England', *Journal of Family History*, 23 (1998), 3–27.
[29] See, for example, Amanda Vickery, *The Gentleman's Daughter: Women's Lives in Georgian England* (Yale, 2003).
[30] Hanawalt, *The Ties That Bound*, pp. 205–23.   [31] Bailey, *Unquiet Lives*, pp. 85–109.
[32] Ibid., p. 10.

English Victorian families drew attention to the impact on marital relations of urban expansion and the physical separation of the suburban home and the city-based workplace. A wife's responsibilities increasingly focussed on creating a comfortable home for her husband who travelled away from the house to work.[33] Paradoxically, as middle-class women put their energies into the private world of the home, the English parliament passed a series of acts aimed at establishing married women's economic independence from their husbands. The Married Women's Property Acts (1865, 1870, 1882) enabled married women to maintain income that they earned either through their own labour or inheritance, and to own and dispose of property independently of their husbands. The emergence of the first women's movement and the campaign for female suffrage also initiated a public discourse on women's role in marriage and in wider society. Despite recognition of the 'New Woman', however, historians are hesitant to identify major changes in attitudes to marital relations before the Second World War. Society continued to perceive the husband as head of the household, and constraints on a wife's ability to function both legally and financially independently of her husband remained in place.

There has been very little research undertaken on marital relations in Ireland for any period of time. Erin Bishop's analysis of the O'Connell marriage, completed in 1999, is the most detailed historical analysis of an Irish marriage.[34] Anthony Malcomson and Sean Connolly have explored marital relations in wealthy Irish aristocratic families but Rosemary Raughter's edition of the diary of Methodist convert, Elizabeth Bennis, was the first text to provide an insight into a middle-class, urban-based marriage in the eighteenth century.[35] More recently, Leanne Calvert's work on Presbyterian families has opened up discussion in an Irish context of the nature of patriarchy in marital relations.[36] Based on a selection of primary sources and drawing on the work of these scholars,

---

[33] Leonore Davidoff and Catherine Hall, *Family Fortunes: Men and Women of the English Middle Class 1780–1850* (London, 1987).

[34] Erin I. Bishop, *The World of Mary O'Connell, 1778–1836* (Dublin, 1999).

[35] See Rosemary Raughter (ed.), *The Journal of Elizabeth Bennis 1749–1779* (Dublin, 2003); Rosemary Raughter, 'A time of trial being near at hand: Pregnancy, childbirth and parenting in the spiritual journal of Elizabeth Bennis (1749–79)' in Elaine Farrell (ed.), *'She Said She Was in the Family Way': Pregnancy and Infancy in Modern Ireland* (London, 2012), pp. 75–90. On Irish aristocratic marriage see A. P. W. Malcomson, *The Pursuit of the Heiress: Aristocratic Marriage in Ireland 1740–1840* (2nd ed., Belfast, 2006).

[36] Leanne Calvert, '"Do not forget your bit wife": Love, marriage and the negotiation of patriarchy in Irish Presbyterian marriages, c. 1780–1850', *Women's History Review*, 26, 3 (2017), 433–54; '"A more careful tender nurse cannot be than my dear husband": Reassessing the role of men in pregnancy and childbirth in Ulster, 1780–1838', *Journal of Family History*, 42, 1 (Jan. 2017), 22–36.

this chapter aims to assess the extent to which the conclusions of historians on marriage in England have a relevance for a study of marital relations in Ireland. It explores the different levels of control, affection, intimacy and power in selected Irish marriages.

When Dean John O'Sullivan asked young men in his parish of Kenmare in the early decades of the nineteenth century why they were eager to marry at what O'Sullivan considered a young age, they invariably replied that they needed someone to wash their shirts.[37] This may have been a glib response to an interfering priest, but the young men's comments echo those of Nicholas Peacock and Amhlaoibh Ó Suilleabháin, who agreed that the main purpose in securing a wife was to have someone to look after the house and children and, in Ó Suilleabháin's case, to help with his drapery shop. In nineteenth-century breach of promise cases, the utility of marriage was also stressed. Similarly, men who placed personal advertisements seeking a wife identified the need for a working partner, particularly if they ran a family business.

Yet, just as it would be incorrect to assume that love and physical attraction were missing from courtships that focussed on monetary arrangements, it would also be misleading to conclude that a short courtship led inevitably to an unhappy marriage. There is a significant change in tone in Nicholas Peacock's diary after he married. The morose references when he was single to his being 'at home alone' or having spent the day 'museing and reading' and the evening drinking with his male companions 'till drunk' or falling over were replaced by entries that described a more active social life.[38] Shortly after his marriage, he wrote proudly that he had spent the day 'reading and walking with my wife'.[39] Catherine (whom he affectionately refers to as 'Catty') and he dined out with other couples as well as hosting dinner parties in their home, something that Peacock never recorded doing before his marriage. There are also frequent references to 'Catty and I' visiting Catherine's family in Cork as well as regularly staying overnight with Peacock's relatives in their large house at Court near Adare in County Limerick.[40] In addition, Peacock refurbished his domestic space for his new wife. Within months of his marriage, he enlarged his bedroom, put in a new window and had a bed made.[41] In 1748, Peacock celebrated the christening of his first

---

[37] O'Sullivan, 'Praxis Parochi', p. 709.
[38] Marie-Louise Legg (ed.), *The Diary of Nicholas Peacock, 1740–51: The Worlds of a County Limerick Farmer and Agent* (Dublin, 2005), pp. 62, 116–7, 151, 167.
[39] Ibid., p. 176.
[40] Ibid., pp. 183, 185, 186–7. Peacock also worked as a land agent for the owners of Court, the Hartstonges.
[41] Ibid., pp. 27, 179.   [42] Ibid., pp. 30, 187.

Illustration 7.2 This illustration depicts an idyllic scene of married life in a rural cottage. The father plays with his children while his wife does some needle work. An older woman (possibly the husband's mother) sits by the fire while another woman (possibly the husband's unmarried sister) rocks an infant in a cradle. See also the upturned chair used as a pen for the child.

child with a lavish feast.[42] For some years after they were married, he continued to pay the female servants in the house but gradually he transferred this responsibility to Catherine and recorded in his diary money given to his wife and Catherine's payments to servants.[43]

In summary, therefore, Nicholas Peacock got what he desired on marriage: someone to 'take care of my house'. He also, however, got much more. He now had a companion with whom he read, took walks and socialised. It is difficult to discern from his brief diary entries whether Nicholas Peacock established a strong controlling power in his extended household. Indirect evidence would suggest that he did not. Before the children were born, Catherine regularly spent nights away from her husband and the marital home, either with her family in County Cork or with Nicholas's relatives at Court. There are many diary entries indicating that Nicholas travelled to collect his wife from both houses.[44] Following the birth of her first child, Catherine tended to travel and return to Court on the same day but still spent time away from her husband either there or in her family home.[45] A wife who frequently stayed outside the family home does not seem compatible with a husband who maintained a strict regime in his household hierarchy. As Catherine began to share the household tasks with her husband and as their family expanded, the diary entries suggest that they were developing a companionship as well as a partnership or a co-dependency in the management of their domestic affairs.

As noted already, William Leadbeater was very supportive of his wife's literary ambition. He looked after their children while she spent extended periods of time in Dublin negotiating with printers. Although William was obliged legally to travel to Dublin to sign the printer's contract on his wife's behalf, there is little evidence that he exercised a domineering control in the Leadbeater household.[46] The fact that Mary was thirty-five when she married and five years older than her husband may have strengthened her sense of being an equal partner. Nevertheless, when Mary first went to Dublin shortly after they married, William indirectly reminded her of his status in the household, writing that Mary's mother, Elizabeth, was anxious that she return home as soon as possible: '[she] desired me to say … that thou art now given to another and that thou must mind what thy husband says to thee'. William assured Mary that she could stay as long she liked even if he did 'suffer a little for want of thy company'.[47] Later, in 1807 when Mary spent six weeks in Dublin,

---

[43] See, for example, ibid., pp. 181, 204, 205, 206, 213, 216, 219, 228.
[44] See ibid., pp. 178–81.   [45] See ibid., pp. 206, 228.
[46] O'Dowd, 'Mary Leadbeater: Modern woman and Irish Quaker'.
[47] William Leadbeater to Mary Leadbeater, 31 Jan. 1791 (NLI, MS 8003).

William again cared for their five children although his letters also convey a sense of his impatience at Mary's long absence from the home. By 1812, however, William was more relaxed about Mary's visits to Dublin, reassuring her that although he missed her, he 'would not choose to hurry' her. In Mary's absence, William noted that their eldest daughter Elizabeth was 'very helpful and diligent and manages the family'.[48]

The founder of the United Irishmen, William Drennan, had a more idealistic vision of the perfect marriage. When, as an 'oldish unmarried man' Drennan wondered if he had been too demanding in his search for a wife, he described an idyllic picture of a happy family:

Often, said the American farmer, when I plough my low grounds, I place my child on a seat which I have screwed to the beam of the plough. The motion pleases him and he looks up to me, with a smile of delight on a cheek glowing with health, as I lean over the handle, various are the thoughts which crowd into my mind. My wife sometimes sits knitting in the field, and praises the docility of my horses, and the straitness of my furrows. Here is a subject for a picture to contrast with an authorling burning his shins at a solitary fireside.[49]

It was a vision of a patriarchal family with the father and son bonding through physical labour while the wife sat passively by and applauded. Drennan's life after marriage to Sarah Swanwick may not have fulfilled this vision, but he was more inclined to control the relationship than William Leadbeater appeared to be. In the early years of his marriage, Drennan, like Nicholas Peacock, seems to have relished the company and expanded social life that his marriage initiated. Shortly after his marriage, William Drennan described how he and his wife, Sarah 'had been a good deal abroad, but not incessantly'.[50] They had attended the theatre and Sarah was 'under my tuition' in chess.[51] In addition, the couple hosted supper and breakfast parties, all organised by Sarah.[52] William also made some adjustments to his house in preparation for Sarah's arrival, although he romantically wrote to Sarah that his house was waiting for her to 'supply it with life and to animate its furniture'. Like Peacock, Drennan did not refurbish the bedroom until after the wedding, partly, he claimed to Sarah, slightly tongue in cheek, out of modesty: 'I dare not venture to ask you the colour of your night ribband, nor whether you ever slept out of a four post bed, nor whether you prefer a worse room street ward to a better and more convenient room'.[53]

---

[48] William Leadbeater to Mary Leadbeater, 3 May 1812 (NLI, MS 8003).
[49] Jean Agnew (ed.), *The Drennan–McTier Letters, 1794–1801* (3 vols., Dublin, 1999), ii, p. 213.
[50] Ibid., ii, p. 581.   [51] Ibid., ii, p. 585.   [52] Ibid., ii, p. 587; iii, pp. 543, 544–5.
[53] William Drennan to Sarah Swanwick (25 Nov. 1799) (PRONI, T2884/20).

As a bachelor, William had noted how he 'doted' on children and he was clearly delighted with the large family that he and Sarah accumulated within a relatively short period of time. After nine years of marriage, Sarah had given birth to eight children.[54] William's letters to his sister, Martha, give an impression that he and Sarah discussed in a companionate fashion their children's welfare and upbringing. Nevertheless, as an obstetrician, William took a stronger interest than most men of his time in the health and education of his children. His correspondence is full of advice and instructions both to his wife Sarah and to Martha when his sons stayed with her, on how to feed the children, how to care for their illnesses, what books they should read and who their play companions should be[55]

Before he was married, William supervised the employment and work of his household servants and was a demanding employer who regularly dismissed or complained about the quality of his employees' work.[56] Following his marriage, he continued to take considerable interest in servants employed in his Dublin home and regularly commented in his letters on the problems that they had with particular maids or male employees.[57] The surviving letters from William to Sarah after they were married also suggest that he often directed her in managing the household.[58] In his letters to his sister, William rarely criticised Sarah but in 1807, after seven years of marriage, his correspondence hinted at a certain tension in the marriage. The family was experiencing financial difficulties as William's medical practice in Dublin had not expanded in the way that he had hoped. When his long awaited legacy finally arrived in 1807 with the death of his cousin, William decided to move the family to Belfast. When explaining his decision to his sister, William noted in patriarchal terms the influence of Sarah's sister, Mary Hutton, on his wife in their Dublin household. He described Mrs Hutton as a 'most self-sufficient woman, humbled at home, yet would be a school-mistress abroad'. Drennan claimed that his sister-in-law 'would direct [Sarah] in everything, even in what relates to my house'.[59] Moving his wife to Belfast would prevent Mrs Hutton from exercising any influence over

[54] See family tree in Agnew, *The Drennan–McTier Letters*, ii, p. 744. For 'doted' quote see ibid., ii, p. 271.

[55] See, for example, ibid., iii, pp. 59, 82, 85, 150, 179, 202–3, 218, 220, 225, 231–2, 265–6, 279, 282, 495–6, 590–1; William Drennan to Sarah Drennan, 1809 (PRONI, T2884/74).

[56] See Drennan's correspondence in Agnew, *The Drennan–McTier Letters*, ii, in which he refers regularly to his servants.

[57] See, for example, ibid., iii, pp. 179, 202, 220–1, 227–8, 288–9, 291–2, 300–1.

[58] See for example, William Drennan to Sarah Swanwick, 1 Sept. 1805 (PRONI, T2884/43).

[59] Agnew, *The Drennan–McTier Letters,* iii, pp. 609–10.

her. Drennan also noted among his reasons for leaving Dublin the cost of household expenses and hinted that Sarah could have managed domestic affairs 'at somewhat less cost'.[60] His plan was that his family would live for a time with his sister so that she could 'initiate Sarah a little into the mode of Belfast housekeeping'.[61] Elsewhere, William laughingly referred to himself as the 'king of the house', which indicates that he was, at least, conscious of a hierarchy in the household.[62] Joanne Bailey has suggested that wives in early modern England derived a considerable amount of indirect power and influence through their control of the household and the overseeing of the financial arrangements for the house, servants and children.[63] William Drennan, however, took an active role in the management of his household and must, therefore, have limited the indirect power and influence of his wife. Drennan depended on his wife to share the care for his large family and household but his correspondence suggests that their relationship was more accurately described as a co-dependency than as a partnership.

The Drennan marriage was complicated by William's relationship with his sister, Martha, and is a reminder that other members of a family could exert a strong influence on the relationship between husband and wife. In his courtship correspondence with Sarah, William described Martha as 'my oldest, my once dearest, my ever to be respected correspondent, my best adviser in every difficulty, in every real or supposed misfortune, my best consoler, and first friend'.[64] Following his marriage, William continued to write frequently to his sister. Sarah corresponded with her sister-in-law but their correspondence lacked warmth and real affection. Sarah may, in fact, have felt more uneasy about Martha's proprietorial hold over William than about her husband's interference in the management of the household. Martha's husband, Samuel McTier, wrote to his wife that he had been hurt by her 'showing too evident a partiality' for William.[65] Martha insisted that William confide in her and, as noted in Chapter 3, his first attempt to court Sarah failed partly because he had not told his sister about the new woman in his life. It was Martha who communicated the news about William's courtship to their mother and appears to have done little to alleviate her upset at her son's secretive behaviour.[66] Years later, Martha still resented William's silence and he continued to feel obliged to apologise to her for not having confided in her.[67]

---

[60] Ibid., p. 610.   [61] Ibid., pp. 616–7.   [62] Ibid., p. 315.   [63] Bailey, *Unquiet Lives.*
[64] William Drennan to Sarah Swanwick, 26 Sept. 1793 (PRONI, T2884/4).
[65] Agnew, *The Drennan–McTier Letters,* i, p. 113.
[66] Ibid., i, pp. 564–6, 573–4, 578. For Drennan's courtship, see pp. 117–18.
[67] Ibid., ii, pp. 276–7.

Martha's care for William's and Sarah's son, Tom was also a source of tension between the sisters-in-law. Tom was initially sent to his aunt's house in Belfast in 1802, shortly after Sarah had given birth to their second son, William. Martha, who was childless, relished the opportunity to play a maternal role and was dismissive of Sarah's requests for the return of her son. When Tom returned to Dublin after a two year stay in Belfast, William felt obliged to send his second son, William, as a substitute.[68]

Martha's childlessness was obviously an important factor in her relationship with her husband, Sam. She admitted that she could not always 'banish the thought that ... I am a lost woman.'[69] As noted already, the correspondence between Sam and Martha McTier suggests that their marriage was also complicated by Martha's relationship with her brother. Sam expressed in writing his affection for his wife. He wrote of missing her and the 'sometimes pleasing silence' as they sat together.[70] Martha's letters to Sam are more restrained although this may have been because they were read aloud to other members of the family. Sam warned Martha that her letters went through 'many readings'.[71] He urged her to include any 'soft whisper' that she had for him at the end of the letter so that when he read it aloud to her mother, she would not be aware of any interruptions. The surviving letters suggest, however, that Martha did not adopt this practice. She also ignored Sam's request to her that she not encourage William's courtship of Margaret Jones as he thought it would be the 'greatest folly' to do so while Margaret's father was still alive.[72] On this occasion, at least, Martha placed concern for her brother above that of the wishes of her husband. When Sam died without making a will, Martha was forthright in her criticism; 'He knew the law – nor can I ever think he designed this division but if it turns out so, blameably negligent indeed he was both to me and his memory'.[73] Martha's description of Sam on his gravestone as a 'safe companion' and a 'prudent adviser' summed up her attitude to him.[74]

Of all the marriages examined for this volume, that of Daniel and Mary O'Connell is the best documented. During long periods of time when Daniel was away from the family home in the early years of their marriage, he corresponded regularly with his wife and she with him. Daniel drew on the language of the new companionate marriage in the early nineteenth century. He referred to Mary as his 'friend and companion'

---

[68] Mary McNeill, *Little Tom Drennan: Portrait of a Georgian Childhood* (Dublin, 1962).
[69] Agnew, *The Drennan–McTier Letters*, i, p. 83.   [70] Ibid., p. 56.   [71] Ibid., p. 97.
[72] Ibid., pp. 115–16.   [73] Agnew, *The Drennan–McTier Letters*, ii, p. 158.
[74] Ibid., iii, p. 244.

and consulted her on public as well as private affairs.[75] The couple did, however, acknowledge Daniel's superior status in the marriage. Mary pledged 'to obey his will' although Daniel assured her that he would not insist on her wifely duty but hoped that she would do everything with gratitude for his loving attitude to her.[76]

O'Connell's frequent absences meant that Mary was left to deal with the management of financial as well as of household and family matters. Daniel did, however, maintain a supervisory role and took an interest in his children's education and, as they grew into adulthood, in the future careers of the boys and in the negotiation of marriage settlements for the girls.[77]

O'Connell's patriarchal control of his family was, therefore, limited by his frequent absences and the demands of his busy public life. He often instructed Mary to do as she thought fit, although she usually did as he advised.[78] Mary was, nonetheless, capable of resisting O'Connell's control, refusing, for example, to live in Kerry particularly while Daniel's uncle, Maurice, who had opposed their marriage was alive.[79] She also expressed her frustration and, at times, her anger, at her husband's financial extravagance.[80]

Erin Bishop suggests that Daniel O'Connell used his correspondence with Mary and his children to construct a comforting image of a happy and stable family life which belied the reality of his actions:

Despite the many letters he composed expressing his desire to be reunited with his wife and children ... O'Connell considered his duty to his profession or to his country more important than personal happiness derived from being with his wife and family. He was willing ... to keep his political appointments but ... often allowed business engagements to keep him away from his family, ... despite the deep disappointment and loneliness his choices caused his wife and children.[81]

Patriarchy and forms of resistance to it are also evident in the marriage of Elizabeth and Mitchell Bennis. The Bennis family lived in mid-eighteenth century Limerick where Mitchell ran a saddlery business. Following her conversion to Methodism in 1749, Elizabeth Bennis kept a spiritual diary in which she recorded not just her religious thoughts and exercises but also wrote about her husband and children. Elizabeth's

---

[75] Daniel O'Connell to Mary O'Connell, 23 Aug.1802 (NLI, O'Connell Papers).
[76] Bishop, *The World of Mary O'Connell*, p. 34.
[77] Ibid., pp. 58–87; Erin Bishop (ed.), *My Darling Danny: Letters from Mary O'Connell to Her Daniel, 1830–1832* (Cork, 1998).
[78] Ibid., p. 36.   [79] Ibid., pp. 36–7, 51–2, 143–5.   [80] Ibid., pp. 88–107.
[81] Ibid., pp. 56–7. See also Helen Mulvey, 'The correspondence of Daniel and Mary O'Connell' in M. R. O'Connell (ed.), *The Correspondence of Daniel O'Connell* (8 vols., Dublin and Shannon, 1972–80), i, xxiii.

conversion to Methodism was a source of tension between husband and wife because Mitchell refused to become a member. For her part, Elizabeth was torn between her husband's 'affections' and her adherence to Methodism: 'The loss of my husband's affections weighs me down to the dust, and if I would dare to choose I would say, let me lose all this world can give, but leave me happy in this. But ... O Lord, let me lay my hand on my mouth and say, thy will be done.'[82] Ultimately, however, it was Mitchell's tolerance and affection for his wife that prevented the 'discord' between them from becoming permanent. Mitchell's patience was, at times, sorely tested. Elizabeth often participated in family and social events reluctantly, disliking the 'company of worldly people' and the time taken away from prayer and her spiritual duties.[83] At a gathering for a dinner party on 29 December 1758, Elizabeth described how she 'found no relish for their enjoyment. I was amongst them as a fish upon dry land, labouring to keep my thoughts stayed upon God'. A few days later, on New Year's Day, she and Mitchell had an angry exchange with Mitchell 'railing at and abusing the truths and people of God.[84] In 1767, when the family moved house, Elizabeth arranged to have her own room 'retired from the rest of the apartments of the house, where I may have the opportunity of being alone at any time. The want of such a place has often grieved me ...'[85]

Despite Elizabeth's anti-social behaviour and their disagreements over religion, Elizabeth and Mitchell continued to maintain a strong bond and affection for one another. Elizabeth devoted a considerable amount of time to the organisation of the Methodist community in Limerick. Her commitments to Methodism meant that she frequently met with male preachers on her own. Men also visited her in her home on a regular basis. In 1763, Elizabeth noted in her diary that some of the family's acquaintances had suggested that she had been unfaithful to her husband. Mitchell, however, accepted Elizabeth's assurances that the rumours were untrue and permitted her to continue to meet with other Methodist members. Mitchell's trust in his wife had, according to Elizabeth, brought the couple closer together as her 'heart filled with the tenderest affection towards him, so that I could use no other language than the language of love, and ... the Lord had wrought also on him, so that peace was made in both breasts and our hearts more closely united together.'[86]

Elizabeth and Mitchell Bennis clearly reached a compromise concerning Elizabeth's religious activities. Elizabeth did, however, recognise her

---

[82] Rosemary Raughter (ed.), *The Journal of Elizabeth Bennis, 1749–1779* (Dublin, 2003), pp. 62–3.
[83] Ibid., p. 138.   [84] Ibid., p. 139.   [85] Ibid., p. 198.   [86] Ibid., p. 158.

husband's role as head of the household in other ways. In her journal, she makes occasional reference to her wifely duty to obey her husband. She notes, for example, that she participated in social or family events 'in obedience to my husband'. Elizabeth also appeared powerless to prevent her husband making what she considered to be bad business and financial decisions. On more than one occasion she endeavoured without success to persuade him to be more prudent and lamented in her journal the loss of substantial sums of money, which she attributed to her husband's 'obstinacy'.[87]

Later, in 1772, Elizabeth was confronted with another form of male control when her daughter, Eleanor, confided in her that her husband was physically abusing her. Elizabeth was at a loss as to what to do as she was reluctant to interfere in her daughter's marriage. She acknowledged that her only resource was prayer and was grateful to record a few weeks later that 'the tyrant has calmed his rage'.[88] The abuse was still continuing, however, four years later in 1776.[89] There appears to have been no question of Elizabeth encouraging her daughter to leave her husband. Elizabeth Bennis met and corresponded with Methodist founder, John Wesley (1703–1791) and would have adhered to his views on marital relations. Wesley supported the traditional hierarchy in marriage and believed that it was a husband's duty to rule his household but to do so in a 'mild, gentle and wise' fashion.[90] Divorce and remarriage were only possible if one of the partners committed adultery.[91]

In the 1840s, William and Lucy O'Brien, like the O'Connells, also maintained a relationship by correspondence. William's involvement in the Young Ireland rebellion in 1848 resulted in his transportation to Tasmania. The couple were separated for over three years during which time they maintained a regular correspondence. William issued instructions to Lucy on the management of the household and the rearing of their children. William, like Daniel O'Connell, may also have been consciously constructing an idyllic portrait of his marriage that was at odds with the reality. During his time in Tasmania, William kept a diary for Lucy's benefit. Richard Davis, William's biographer, suggested that this was a carefully edited version of his life in exile. A sociable man, William had many female as well as male friends in Tasmania, but few references to his women companions appear in his diary.[92]

---

[87] Ibid., pp. 225–7.   [88] Ibid., pp. 241, 244.   [89] Ibid., p. 269.
[90] Bufford W. Coe, *John Wesley and Marriage* (London, 1996), p. 103.
[91] Ibid., pp. 56–7.
[92] Richard Davis, *Revolutionary Imperialist William Smith O'Brien* (Dublin, 1998), pp. 300–1, 311–314.

Linda Pollock defined the patriarchal figure in a family as 'the person one apologized to; requesting his forgiveness validated his power without at the same time necessarily preventing a dependent's chosen course of action'.[93] It could also be added that a controlling patriarchal figure is not necessarily the husband or father in the nuclear family. Another member of the extended family might assume that role. In the families analysed here, the person who conforms best to Pollock's definition of a patriarchal figure is Maurice O'Connell, uncle of Daniel, referred to in the family as 'Hunting Cap'. When Daniel O'Connell decided to marry his cousin, Mary, without Hunting Cap's knowledge, he undoubtedly believed that he could subsequently apologise to his uncle and ask his forgiveness. He did not, however, expect Hunting Cap to prevent his 'chosen course of action' and confidently assured Mary that he would inherit a substantial sum of money on his uncle's death. O'Connell was shocked to discover that his uncle maintained his resistance to his marriage until the end of his life and, as a consequence, significantly reduced his intended inheritance for his nephew.[94] The fact that Daniel O'Connell's parents were more supportive of their son's choice of spouse was of little importance. It was Daniel's father's brother who held the most wealth in the extended family and, hence, was perceived as the patriarchal head of the family. Maurice O'Connell was also recognised as the head of the family by other members of the extended O'Connell family. He was appointed as executor to their wills, and when Abigail Gould was physically abused by her husband, James, she too turned to her uncle Maurice's assistance. Abigail was shocked and upset when her uncle insisted that she maintain the family unit with her husband 'with that patience, that resignation that becomes a good Christian and the calmness of a gentlewoman'.[95] Sugar-merchant, William Tennent, exercised a similar position in his family as his brothers and sisters looked to him rather than to their father for advice, instruction and financial help. William's father, the Reverend John Tennent also recognised that the financial success of his eldest son bestowed on him a status in the family and he too referred his other children to William for advice.[96]

Pollock has also suggested that 'the intervention of other people, both family members beyond the nuclear family as well as friends and

---

[93] Pollock, 'Rethinking patriarchy and the family', 5.
[94] Bishop, *The World of Mary O'Connell*, p. 53.
[95] Abigail Gould to Maurice O'Connell, 27 April 1791 (University College, Dublin (UCD), O'Connell Papers, P12/2A/31); will of Daniel O'Sullivan, 20 March 1792 (UCD, O'Connell Papers, P12/5/200).
[96] See correspondence of William Tennent (PRONI, D1748/B/1).

servants ... weakened the patriarch's ability to exercise full authority...'.[97] As we have seen, in the Drennan family, William's correspondence suggests that he perceived his sister-in-law as attempting to undermine his authority in his household. Mitchell Bennis's control over his wife was clearly threatened by her friends in the Methodist community, while Elizabeth's moral support for her daughter might have helped to limit, if not prevent, her son-in-law's behaviour. The actions of other members of the family could, however, support and strengthen the position of the patriarch. Within months of starting her journal in 1749, Elizabeth Bennis refers to her mother-in-law's opposition to her religious activities, which may have reinforced her son's dislike of Methodism.[98] As Leanne Calvert has documented, Belfast-based Isabella Campbell Allen also complained that her mother-in-law attempted to undermine her relationship with her husband by presenting her as extravagant and a poor manager of their shared household.[99] In a similar fashion, Martha McTier supported her brother's views of the upbringing of his children against the wishes of his wife.

There are, of course, great difficulties in examining correspondence and diaries for evidence of intimate relations. All to a certain extent created an image of a happier or more contented relationship than might have existed in reality. Like his brother-in-law, Sam McTier, William Drennan was conscious as he wrote to his sister that his letters might be read aloud to other members of the family. He quickly followed up the one letter in which he wrote critically about his wife and her sister with another cautioning his sister not to circulate the letter 'as it contained several things I should not wish open to every eye'.[100] The correspondence of Daniel O'Connell and his wife, Mary, documents the many expressions of love and affection that they exchanged throughout their married life. This was, in the main, a private correspondence not shared with other readers or listeners. It might, therefore, be considered as strong evidence of the mutual love and companionship that sustained the marriage. Erin Bishop's study of the O'Connell marriage notes, however, that Daniel destroyed letters in which Mary expressed her anger at him, particularly in relation to accusations that he had had an affair.[101] There are also, undoubtedly, gaps in the Bennis diary, the main purpose of which was to record its author's spiritual life, and the

---

[97] Pollock, 'Rethinking patriarchy and the family', 5.
[98] See, for example, Raughter, *The Journal of Elizabeth Bennis*, p. 125.
[99] Calvert, '"Do not forget your bit wife"', 442–5.
[100] Agnew, *The Drennan–McTier Letters*, iii, p. 613.
[101] Bishop, *The World of Mary O'Connell*, p. 42.

references to her family are incidental and may omit many family crises and concerns. Although a member of the Society of Friends, which encouraged the keeping of a spiritual journal, Mary Leadbeater's diary was more secular than religious in emphasis. During her married life, in particular, her diary recorded daily life in the village of Ballitore as well as within her own family. It was, however, circulated among members of the extended Leadbeater family and Mary was clearly cautious about what she should record. She did not, for example, describe any serious disagreements between herself and her husband, William. As the letter cited at the start of the chapter suggests, the couple's correspondence presents a more realistic picture of their marriage.[102]

The seemingly contradictory mixture of love and affection and a husband's right to be obeyed – is not that surprising. All the churches agreed that marriage should be about mutual love and respect. Few clergymen would have disagreed with the description in the Presbyterian catechism published in Belfast in 1764 of the duties of a husband and wife. There should be: 'the most tender and affectionate love, on both sides ...; the strictest fidelity to the marriage-bed and covenant ... and the promoting [of] the temporal and spiritual welfare of each other ...'[103] All would also have agreed with John Wesley that the husband held the superior position in the marriage. Wesley, as well as clergymen of other denominations, frequently used the analogy of the relationship between Christ and the Church to describe the connection between a husband and wife.[104] The Catholic warden of Galway drafted a number of sermons on marriage and exhorted a newly married couple 'to love each other tenderly'. He directed the husband to 'love your spouse as Christ loved the Church, that you should guide her as your companion, that you should always have for her an affection full of tenderness'. For her part, the wife was 'to have for your husband that friendship that complacence, that respect and submission which the Church always had for Christ her spouse. You are both of you to have but one head and one soul'.[105]

At a lower social level, it is very difficult to discern if husbands and wives acted towards one another in the loving way that church guide-lines dictated. Irish proverbs emphasised the control of the husband in the home:

---

[102] On the language of letter-writing, see Calvert, '"Do not forget your bit wife"', 433–54.
[103] *The Assembly's Shorter Catechism Explained. By Way of Question and Answer ...* (Belfast, 1764).
[104] Coe, *John Wesley and Marriage*, p. 103.
[105] Sermon on marriage, no date (Galway Diocesan Archives, Box 7).

'Smachtaigh do ben' [rule your wife]

'Na tabhuir cumachta dot mhnaoi os do chion oir da liege tu dhi saltradh are do chois anocht sailteoraid si ar do chionn amaireach' [do not give your wife authority over you, for if you let her stamp on your foot tonight, she will stamp on your head tomorrow].

'Smachtaigh do ben amail dodhenta do mac no do charad' [rule your wife as you would your son or your friend].[106]

Some English visitors to Ireland thought that Irish wives were treated badly by their husbands. In an oft-quoted passage, Edward Wakefield wrote that 'an Irishman assumes over the partner of his bed an authority which is seldom claimed or submitted to in England'.[107] Wakefield was shocked by the physical labour that Irish women undertook and described them as 'more like beasts of burden than rational beings'. The chronic poverty of late eighteenth and early nineteenth-century Irish rural society meant that all members of the family, husbands and wives, sons and daughters, had to engage in hard manual work for survival. The work of women and men in the fields, which Wakefield denounced, may, in fact, reflect the co-dependency and partnership of husbands and wives in labouring families where even very young children were expected to help with farm labour.

Before the late nineteenth century, it was rare for a married couple to have any private or intimate time together. The typical farmhouse or cabin was not designed to include private spaces. In the cabins and cottages of the poor, there was only one room and very little furniture. A bed was a luxury and in most poor households all members of the family slept, frequently naked, on rushes or straw laid out on the floor.[108] Sexual modesty was observed by the parents sleeping in the middle with the sons sleeping on the father's side and the daughters on the mother's side. In Aghadowey, in October 1704, a man was accused of adultery with a servant girl. The Presbyterian session examination revealed that he and his wife slept alongside the maid. The elders appear to have believed the man's defence that although he lay naked beside the two women, his wife lay between him and the maid.[109] In the

---

[106] Carl Marstrander, 'Bídh Crínna', *Ériu*, 5 (1911), 126–7, 136–7, 138–9.

[107] Edward Wakefield, *An Account of Ireland, Statistical and Political* (2 vols., London, 1812), i, p. 801.

[108] Anne O'Dowd, *Straw, Hay and Rushes in Irish Folk Tradition* (Dublin, 2015), pp. 158–74. Mary Leadbeater urged men not to bring their newly wed wives home to a bed on the floor but to wait before they married until they could afford a 'bedstead to raise one up from the floor'. See Mary Leadbeater, *Cottage Dialogues among the Irish Peasantry* (London, 1811), pp. 74–5.

[109] Entry dated 24 Oct. 1704 (Aghadowey Session Book, 1702–1761 (PHSIB)).

nineteenth century, Caesar Otway was one of many observers, who described similar sleeping arrangements:

what is called sleeping in *stradogue* and is *regulated* as follows ... the whole family ... lied down *decently*, and in order; the eldest daughter next the wall farthest from the door, then all the sisters, according to their ages; next the mother, father, and sons in succession, and then the strangers, whether the travelling pedlar, or tailor, or beggar; thus the strangers are kept aloof from the female part of the family, and if there be an apparent community there is great propriety of conduct.[110]

In the 1830s, a labouring man, Dominic Frehill, described how he, his wife and his five children lay in one bed, 'heads and points' with some lying one way and others in the opposite direction.[111] In other households, the married couple had some privacy as they slept in the bed while the children lay on straw on the floor.[112] Visitors and farm workers slept with members of the family of both sexes. In 1846, in a court case involving the murder of the farmer who owned the house, his daughter described the flexible sleeping arrangements in the household:

I slept in the same room with my mother and father; and my three sisters also. Hayes [a farm servant] and Jerry, my brother usually slept on the loft. Andy would sleep with my father and mother and Billy [farm servant], sometimes with them and sometimes on the loft.[113]

As noted in the introduction, standards in housing rose steadily after the Famine and by 1891 more than half of Irish rural families lived in dwellings with at least four rooms. These new houses facilitated the development of a greater level of private space within households and, consequently, the provision of separate bedrooms for parents and children.[114] In the larger cities of Belfast and Dublin, housing for poor families remained unhygienic and cramped with large families living in one or two rooms.[115]

---

[110] Caesar Otway, *Sketches in Erris and Tyrawly* (Dublin, 1841), p. 32; O'Dowd, *Straw, Hay and Rushes*, pp. 186–7. In 1678, Richard Head described a similar arrangement with the husband and wife lying in one direction and the children in another. See ibid., p. 161.
[111] O'Dowd, *Straw, Hay and Rushes*, p.161.   [112] Ibid., p. 166.
[113] *Saunders's News-Letter*, 3 Aug. 1846; *Anglo-Celt*, 7 Aug. 1846; *Leinster Express*, 8 Aug. 1846; *Downpatrick Recorder*, 29 Aug. 1846. Andy Hayes was accused of murdering his employer in collusion with the farmer's wife.
[114] T. W. Freeman, *Pre-Famine Ireland: A Study in Historical Geography* (Manchester, 1957), pp. 146–52; Barry O'Reilly, 'Hearth and home: The vernacular house in Ireland from c.1800', *Proceedings of the Royal Irish Academy*, Section C, 3 (2011), 193–21; Angela Bourke, *The Burning of Bridget Cleary. A True Story* (London, 1999), pp. 46–7.
[115] Frank Cullen, 'The provision of working- and lower-middle-class housing in late nineteenth-century urban Ireland', *Proceedings of the Royal Irish Academy*, Section C, 3 (2011), 217–51. Caitriona Crowe, *Dublin 1911* (Dublin, 2011); Jacinta Prunty, *Dublin Slums, 1800–1925: A Study in Urban Geography* (Dublin, 1998); Ellen Rowley, 'Housing

The arrival of a new wife, particularly into a farming household where an older couple were still living, could lead to tensions concerning the hierarchy of control and what sort of respect was due to the new arrival. A wife might expect that her dowry would buy her a degree of authority within the household. There is, however, ample evidence to demonstrate that there was a common belief in Irish rural society that farm land should belong to the family that traditionally owned it. By working on the farm, new wives might exercise ownership or rights to that land that discomforted other members of the family, including their husbands. Family disputes frequently revolved around such discomfort. A particular source of tension was the woman's control of the hens in the farmyard. As Angela Bourke has noted: 'Only one flock of hens could run in a farmyard'.[116] Thomas McQuelter and Mary Bane murdered McQuelter's father, referred to as Thomas Senior, in a dispute over his wife's rights to the yard for her hens. This relationship had the added complexity that Thomas Junior had married without his father's permission. Mary Bane's family had, however, agreed to the marriage and had provided a dowry of £20. In the lead up to the murder, the family had argued over hens and the father threatened to banish the hens; Thomas replied that 'he would have hens and eggs when the devil would be picking his bones'. While this was a dispute between men, hens and eggs were an exclusively female occupation. Thomas was defending his wife's rights to access farm resources and highlighting the legitimacy of her place. In doing so, he was emphasising that his wife had a recognised position on the farm.[117]

Selling eggs was also one of the principle ways in which a farmer's wife could earn an income independent of her husband. Margaret O'Brien's husband clearly resented the money his wife made from the selling of eggs. During the acrimonious proceedings for a divorce *a mensa et thoro* in 1911, Joseph O'Brien claimed that his wife had derived a 'substantial income' from her 300 hens and that she had made him pay for 'whatever eggs he ate!'[118] Angela Bourke has also pointed to the oral storytelling tradition that linked resentment at the independence that women acquired through keeping hens with the stereotypical belief that women talked too much. Hens and women made too much noise:

---

in Ireland, 1740–2016' in Eugenio Biagino and Mary E. Daly (eds.), *The Cambridge Social History of Ireland* (Cambridge, 2018), pp. 212–32.
[116] Bourke, *The Burning of Bridget Cleary*, p. 44.
[117] *Irish Times*, 31 July 1863. See also Katie Barclay, 'Farmwives, domesticity and work in late nineteenth-century Ireland', *Rural History*, 24, 2 (2013), 143–60.
[118] *Irish Times*, 10 March 1911.

'poultry-keeping, like talkativeness, was a sign that a woman was not under a man's control'.[119]

Marriage settlements that arranged for the older generation in the household to live in certain rooms or have access to specific resources could also be a source of tension between the newly arrived wife, her husband and her in-laws. In 1891, at the Carlow assizes, James Heany was indicted for the murder of his wife, Mary Anne Heany, aged thirty-two. They lived on a farm near Drumlish in County Longford with their three children and James' father. James pleaded not guilty. The *Irish Times* reported that the family had:

one of those family arrangements by which some of the land was to belong to the husband and some to the wife, and the house itself was divided between different members of the family, the prisoner and his young wife occupying one part, and the other being occupied by Heany, the prisoner's father ... Mary Anne Heany was anxious to assert her own rights, and the prisoner, listening to a great deal that the father told him, was determined to assume some mastery over the house and farm, and this led to frequent quarrels about the land.

On the day of the murder, Mary Anne was making hay on what she considered her land and her husband threatened her life. Later that day, she came to dig potatoes and her husband, who was cutting oats, dragged her into the corn field and killed her with a scythe.[120]

Childlessness could also lead to tension in a marriage. As indicated already, Martha McTier described herself as a 'lost' woman when she and her husband failed in their efforts to have children. In Chapter 3, we noted how the birth of children was perceived, particularly among poor families, as important for the future of the family: the provision of workers for the farm and the security of the parents in old age. A failure to produce children could lead not just to unhappiness between husband and wife but also in the wider extended family. In 1850, Dean John O'Sullivan recalled a woman who after two years of marriage had no children and resorted to having sex with her neighbour because she could no longer bear 'the taunts of her husband's relations'.[121] Bridget and Michael Cleary were also child-less after seven and a half years of marriage, a fact that might have contributed to Bridget's killing by Michael in 1895.[122] The failure to produce children could also lead to the withholding of part of a dowry payment.

A rare glimpse of a husband and father from a farming background exercising a form of patriarchal control is documented in the correspondence of the Prendergast family. Four of the children of James and

---

[119] Bourke, *The Burning of Bridget Cleary*, pp. 44–5.   [120] *Irish Times*, 17 Dec. 1891.
[121] John O'Sullivan, 'Praxis Parochi' (Kerry Diocesan Archives, Killarney).
[122] Bourke, *The Burning of Bridget Cleary*, p. 45.

Elizabeth Prendergast from Milltown, County Kerry, emigrated to Boston in the early 1840s. James wrote regularly to his children, passing on news from home and acknowledging the remittances that they sent to him. James wrote not only on behalf of himself and his wife but he also took responsibility for advising other young people from the locality on caring for their family back home. As he wrote to his son Thomas in 1843:

> ... please to inform Mrs McKenna that the money sent home by Judy Sullivan Quart to her Father that the mother got none of it therefore she expects you will speak to Mrs Gnaw to advise the little girl in the next remittance not to forget herself as she was surprised at the daughter that she did not send her something according to promises.[123]

James also looked after his son Michael's wife, Ellen, and their children when Michael emigrated in 1847.[124] James controlled the correspondence between the family in Ireland and in Boston. To his son Michael's annoyance, his father opened letters addressed to Michael from his brother, James.[125] For his part, the father complained that Michael wrote to James without consulting him, blaming the scribe who wrote the letter for his son's deception: 'Patt Mahony placed a great trick in advising my son to trouble you contrary to my knowledge when he had no need'.[126] When Michael followed his siblings to North America, James continued to control his correspondence, advising him to send the letters for his wife, Ellen, to him.[127] James's wife never wrote to her children while her husband was alive, and wrote what she acknowledged as the 'first letter I ever addressed ye' when James died in 1848.[128]

If the correspondence of James Prendergast indicates the control that he chose to exercise over his family, it should also be acknowledged that his letters communicate his affection for his children and his wife. In 1847, for example, when Elizabeth was ill for a number of months, James reassured his children that she was recovered 'thank God. I would be poorly if she did not. I would not deny it in any account'.[129]

'All I Have in the World to My Dear Wife': Patriarchy and Last Wills and Testaments

It is difficult, therefore, to generalise about patriarchy and the way in which it manifested itself in a marriage. Last wills and testaments enable

---

[123] Shelley Barber (ed.), *The Prendergast Letters. Correspondence from Famine-Era Ireland, 1840–1850* (Amherst and Boston, 2006), p. 58.
[124] Ibid., pp. 115–19, 147, 154.   [125] Ibid., pp. 64–5.   [126] Ibid., p. 65.
[127] Ibid., p. 116.   [128] Ibid., p. 146.   [129] Ibid., p. 108.

the historian to gauge some measure of the esteem in which a man held his wife and also to trace the way in which the legal obligations of a husband for his widow changed during the two hundred and sixty-five years surveyed in this volume. In the medieval period, under English common law, the legal entitlement of widows was fairly straightforward. A widow could claim a third of her husband's real estate for the duration of her life. If the widow remarried, she brought the dower from her first husband with her, which would then legally be controlled by her second husband. By 1660, the development of marriage settlements among propertied families led to the replacement of dower with jointure, by which land or a cash annuity was held in trust to be granted to the wife if she survived her husband. As indicated in Chapter 3, the amount of the annuity was usually related to the size of the marriage portion or dowry that the wife brought to the marriage. The popularity of jointures among wealthy families led gradually in the course of the eighteenth century to the disuse of dower. And, as already noted, in the nineteenth century, marriage settlements began to be used by middle- and lower-class rural and urban men and women with some wealth to pass on to the next generation.

Until 1890, common law distinguished between bequests of real estate and personal property. The former related to the landed property of the testator while the latter referred to the movable property in his or her possession at the time of death. This included cash or money invested in shares and banks, household furniture, jewellery and animal stock as well as many of the items that a wife brought to the marriage. Before 1695, it was the 'custom' in many parts of Ireland for a man's personal property to be divided into three parts: one for his widow, one for his children and the testator was free to dispose of the final third as he wished. If there were no children of the marriage, a widow would receive all the goods after the debts of the deceased had been paid. Under the terms of the 1695 Statute of Distribution, this three-fold division was abolished and a man was free to choose how he divided all his personal property. If he did not leave a will then the widow was entitled to a third with the remainder going to his children. If there were no children, the widow received half the goods and other close relatives the rest.[130]

A combination of the replacement of dower with jointures and the 1695 Act eroded the direct legal entitlement of the widow to a share in her husband's real and personal property. If there were no marriage settlement agreed prior to the marriage, a husband was free to determine

---

[130] Paul Ward, *Family and Succession Law* (Dordrecht, 2006), p. 23; J. C. Wylie, *Irish Land Law* (5th ed., Haywards Heath, West Sussex, 2013), pp. 852–3.

the personal estate that he would leave his wife in his last will and testament. In 1890, the Intestate Estates Act partially amended the erosion of a widow's automatic right to a share in her husband's estate. The Act abolished the distinction between the real and personal estate of the deceased husband and specified that if a man died without making a will and held a total estate valued at £500 or less, then his widow was entitled to inherit his full estate. If the estate was valued at more than £500, then a sum of that value was to be charged on the real and personal property and given to the widow.[131]

As noted in Chapter 3, before the nineteenth century the practice of making a written will had been mainly confined to the wealthier sections of society: men, and some women, with property to distribute to the next generation. A will was also often only one of a series of documents involved in disposing of property on the death of a husband or wife. The marriage settlement would have specified how most of the property was to be divided with a will being used only to add additional benefits for a man's wife or children or to make small bequests to family and friends.[132] In the nineteenth century, however, it became increasingly common for men and women (single and widowed) from more varied economic backgrounds to make wills. The 1890 Act accelerated this trend because if a man did not make a will, his widow could inherit his whole estate if it was valued at less than £500 and leave his children with nothing. A significant number of the men (and women) who made wills in the late nineteenth century were illiterate and signed their name with a mark. This suggests a recognition of the importance of a will even if the testator could not write it him or herself.[133]

For middle-class families with wealth invested in land or a business, a will might, as with the wealthier propertied class, be only one in a series of legal documents involved in the transfer of property to the widow and the testator's heirs. As, however, the practice of making a will became more common among men and women of all economic backgrounds, so too the last will and testament became the most popular means by which a husband provided for his widow and children.

---

[131] Ibid.

[132] Kevin Costello, 'Married women's property in Ireland, 1800–1900' in Niamh Howlin and Kevin Costello (eds.), *Law and the Family in Ireland, 1800–1950* (London, 2017), pp. 66–86.

[133] The probating of wills was the responsibility of the ecclesiastical courts until they were abolished with the disestablishment of the Church of Ireland. From 1871, the Court for Marriage and Probate took responsibility for the probate of last wills and testaments. The original records for both jurisdictions were destroyed in 1922. This analysis is based on transcripts and copies in NAI, the Registry of Deeds and the records of the Genealogical Society in PRONI.

Most men accepted that they had an obligation to provide for their widow after their death, but the way in which they did so varied. For some, the provision for a widow was interpreted as leaving her sufficient for her maintenance but little more. In life, as in death, husbands appear to have been guided by the principle that they were obliged by society, if not strictly by common law, to maintain their wives with sufficient food and lodging, i.e. to give them their 'necessities'. This usually took the form of either an annual allowance or a cash sum to be paid by the main heir to the widow. The sums granted varied and it is difficult to generalise about the cash payments left to widows by farmers or by small business-men in towns. In most cases, it depended on the wealth of the testator. In wills examined for this volume dating from the 1840s through to the 1890s, widows received cash sums varying in amounts from £30 to £300 while the annuities ranged from £6 to £30.

In addition to a cash sum or annuity, almost all husbands whose wills have been analysed also provided for the lodging or living arrangements of their wives after their deaths. This usually involved giving the widow permission to reside in the family home for the rest of her life (unless she remarried). The instructions on the widow's living quarters could often be quite specific. The husband might identify a particular room or section of the house as his widow's living quarters, with a warning to his principal heir that the widow was to be maintained and treated in the same way as when the testator was alive. In 1836, Robert Gourley left his 'dearly beloved wife', Mary, their marital bed along with her 'wheel and reel' and permitted her to live in the family home and to be maintained by his son 'in any particular as she has heretofore received'. Like some other husbands, Robert also gave his wife the option of living separately from her son and if she chose to do this, then she should be allowed to have 'whatever sum she may think most reasonable for her support during her life to be paid off my farm by my son James'.[134] In 1864, George Taylor of Ballinafull, County Sligo, instructed that if his wife preferred to live on her own, that his son should build her a 'separate room ... fitted up for her' and that he was to provide his mother with a ton of 'good potatoes', a supply of turf 'brought home and stacked' every year along with a cash annuity of £6.[135] Other men might not have had the means to act so generously towards their wives, but even small tenant farmers directed their sons to provide for their widows. In his will of 1889, Pat McGowan, a farmer in Rossinver in County Leitrim, left his

---

[134] Will of Robert Gourley, 20 March 1836 (NAI, MFGS 41/8). For Gourley's legacy to his daughter, see p. 127 above.
[135] Will of George Taylor, 19 Jan. 1864 (NAI, MFGS 41/47).

farm to his two sons but bequeathed 'one cow's place with the lower room of the house' to his wife and daughter along with one of the two cows on the farm for their support.[136]

The combination of lodgings, maintenance in the form of food and other domestic comforts and, if financially feasible, an annual cash sum was, therefore, a common way in which farmers in rural post-Famine Ireland made provision for their wives following their deaths. It is clear, however, that provision for the widow was only one of the purposes of a will; provision for a man's children was equally important. It was not uncommon for a testator to direct that his real and personal property be divided equally between the widow and the surviving children, 'share and share alike'. Joseph Bealin, for example, a merchant in Boyle in 1888, bequeathed all his real and personal property to be shared between his wife, Rose Anne and his six children.[137] Such provisions were more likely to be made when the children were under age and the widow was left with the sole responsibility for their upbringing and providing for their education or apprenticeship.

About a quarter of the testators in the wills surveyed, however, bequeathed economic and household control to their wives by leaving them all their property with instructions that a son or heir inherit only after the death of their mother, the widow. Many men also passed on the role of head of the family to their wives and expressed in their wills their affection as well as their trust in their ability to manage the family and its financial affairs. Thomas Cooley, the postmaster in Castlebar, County Mayo, in the 1860s left all his property 'of every nature and kind whatsoever' for his wife, Mary's 'sole use and benefit'. He declared in his will that he had 'the fullest confidence that she will make the same distribution of my property among my children which I rightly would make'.[138] Such wills, therefore, reflect the esteem in which the testators held their wives and suggest that they perceive their marital relationship as one of partnership rather than one in which they were the controlling spouse. Furthermore, as noted in Chapter 3, bequests to unmarried daughters were sometimes also conditional on their marrying with the consent of their mothers.

This type of will was, however, more likely to be made by small business men in towns rather than farmers living in rural areas. Throughout the period examined for this volume, there was a strong tradition of shopkeepers, craftsmen and owners of businesses bequeathing businesses to their wives for their lifetimes. In 1727, for example, Edward

---

[136] Will of Pat. McGowan, 6 Nov. 1889 (NAI, MFGS 41/15).
[137] Will of Joseph Bealin, 19 Aug. 1888 (NAI, MFGS 41/38B).
[138] Will of Thomas Cooley, 12 Apr. 1866 (NAI, MFGS 41/47).

Painter, described as a dealer, left to his wife a house in Ann Street in Dublin and 'all his assets and affects, real and personal, ready money, plate, rights, books, debts, bonds, notes and leases, movable and immoveable'.[139] George Deniston, a Dublin merchant, devised all his 'worldly substance and estate as well real as personal' to his wife for life in his will dated to 1717. Their son only inherited the estate after his mother's death. Deniston also appointed his wife as the sole executor for his last will and testament.[140] In 1737, John McSweeny of Cork City, shoemaker, bequeathed all his goods to his wife and two children and a child yet to be born. He requested that they live in their house together and if his widow was incapable of maintaining them, then the property should be sold for her benefit.[141] Joseph White of Cork City, blacksmith, also left everything to his wife and son in 1740, with his wife as his executor.[142] Similarly, in 1777, Robert Lyon of Cork City, shopkeeper, left all his 'worldly substance' to his wife and nominated her as his sole executor.[143]

The custom of traders and artisans leaving their wives in charge of their businesses continued through the nineteenth century. Nor was it a tradition confined to large cities such as Dublin or Cork. Wills from Counties Mayo, Waterford and Wexford in the 1880s and 1890s suggest that shopkeepers and craftsmen living in small rural towns adopted a similar practice. In 1891, Michael Joyce, a shopkeeper in Ballinrobe, County Mayo, left all of his cash savings, his farm and his business to his wife and children to be divided among them all equally: 'share and share' alike. Joyce also directed that his wife continue the business after his death for the benefit of herself and the children.[144] James Doyle, a shopkeeper from Newtownbarry (now Bunclody) in County Wexford also asked his wife, Mary, to continue his business when he made his will in 1892. If, however, she chose not to do so, then James directed that she sell the business and provide cash sums for his two sons, one of whom was training to be a priest. If Mary opted to continue the business, James left it to his wife's discretion to determine if their eldest son, James, merited inheriting the business on her death. He could only do so if he was 'subject and obedient' to his mother in the conduct of the business. If James did not live in a 'quiet, orderly and peacable manner' with his

---

[139] Will of Edward Painter, 12 Aug. 1727 (Registry of Deeds, Dublin, Memorial No. 37975).
[140] Will of George Deniston, 20 March 1717 (Registry of Deeds, Dublin, 20/404/11044).
[141] Will of John McSweeny, 18 May 1737 (PRONI, T/581/5, p. 335).
[142] Will of Joseph White, 1740 (PRONI, T/581/5, p. 405).
[143] Will of Robert Lyon, 8 Dec. 1777 (PRONI, T/581/5, p. 49).
[144] Will of Michael Joyce, 6 July 1891 (NAI, MFGS 41/15).

mother, then his father instructed that he receive only a cash sum of £300, with the residue of his estate following his wife's death going to his second son.[145]

'For Her Sole and Separate Use': Married Women's Separate Estates

Apart from leaving their wives in charge, there were other ways in which men and women could overrule the patriarchal tendencies of the law. In the early eighteenth century, it was not uncommon for a father to leave land or money to his daughter and to stipulate in his will that the woman's husband was not to 'intermeddle' with the legacy which was for the 'separate use' of the daughter. John Hooper, a merchant in Lurgan, County Armagh, for example, left money to each of his three daughters to their 'sole and separate use' regardless of 'whether she be sole or married and not withstanding her coverture … not to be subject or liable to the control, intermeddling, debts or engagements of … any husband.[146] Hannah Villiers, a widow from Waterford left money to her daughter Mary in 1744. It is clear from the will that Mary's husband 'had failed in his fortune' and her mother was concerned to bequeath an annuity to her daughter that would be for her 'separate benefit' and her husband was not to 'intermeddle' in it.[147]

With the passing of the Married Women's Property Acts (1865, 1870, 1882) in the second half of the nineteenth century, the practice of fathers and, sometimes, mothers, leaving cash sums and property for their daughters' separate use became more prevalent. In 1882, for example, a Waterford upholster, James Scott, provided £1,000 for his widow and a marriage portion of £300 for his unmarried daughter and left the residue of his estate to his two daughters, one of whom was married, 'in equal shares absolutely for their sole and separate uses free from the control, debts and engagements of their husbands or of any husband with whom they are either of them may intermarry with'.[148]

Continuing Tradition of Patriarchy

If husbands could bypass the laws on patriarchy through their last will and testament, the law also enabled them to make use of the document to

---

[145] Will of James Doyle, 29 May 1882 (NAI, MFGS 41/42).
[146] Will of John Hooper, 1 Jan. 1709 (Registry of Deeds, Dublin, 100/33/69469).
[147] Will of Hannah Villiers, 3 Jan. 1745 (Registry of Deeds, Dublin, 116/397/81091).
[148] See also Costello, 'Married women's property in Ireland', pp. 72–5.

reinforce their power over their families, even from the grave. Widows were left bequests while they remained as widows, but if they remarried the bequest could be reduced or withdrawn altogether. John Duncan, a grocer from Cumber, County Down, who died in 1850, provided generously for his widow, Agnes, leaving her all his property in Cumber and the tenant right of a farm. Yet, if Agnes remarried, John instructed that she would be 'deprived of all benefit arising from this my last will and testament'. Other men made less harsh provisions in the event of their wife remarrying, usually limiting their benefits to an annual cash sum. As Susan Staves commented on wills in nineteenth-century England, men felt obliged to support their wives when they were on their own but disliked the idea of providing assistance that might also be enjoyed by another man.[149]

What Changed in Marital Relations, 1660–1925?

We can identify key legal changes that had an impact on marital relations, particularly from a financial perspective, although it is difficult to document precisely what difference this made at the level of an individual marriage. The evolution of the concept of a married woman's separate estate was the most significant change in giving wives legal and financial independence. Leanne Calvert has documented how Isabella Campbell Allen was able to use her separate control of an annuity of £500 'as a bargaining tool in marriage and employed it as a tactic on occasions when she felt her independence threatened'.[150] Kevin Costello's analysis of the impact of the married women's property acts on Irish women suggests, however, that few seized the opportunities to establish businesses independently of their husbands.[151] It is important to note that the motivation behind the second Married Women's Property Act (1870) was not the widening of provisions for middle- or upper-class women who, it was argued, had access to trusts and separate estates which were recognised in the chancery court. Instead, the parliamentary enquiry into the need for a change in the law in relation to married women's economic status focussed on working-class women in the new industrial towns of the north of England and, in the case of Ireland, Belfast. Isabella Tod appeared before the commission in 1868 and argued that married working women would benefit from a change in the law. Wives whose husbands did not

---

[149] Susan Staves, *Married Women's Separate Property in England, 1660–1833* (Cambridge, MA, 1990), p. 36.
[150] Calvert, '"Do not forget your bit wife"', 442.
[151] Costello, 'Married women's property in Ireland', pp. 66–86.

work, either through 'idleness' or problems with alcohol, should not risk losing all their earnings to their husbands. This was a particularly pressing problem in Belfast where women found it easier to find paid employment than men. Husbands could be left at home while their wives went to work.[152] Tod told of a Belfast woman whose husband sold the furniture in the family house while she was working, even though she had paid for it through her wages, and of another woman who was discouraged from opening a small school because all her income would be taken by her husband. Tod assured the commission that such women were aware of the legal restrictions on their income and that they would welcome a change in the law.[153] The 1870 Married Women's Property Act enabled wives to retain control of their wages as well as of any money left to them by will. This law provided working-class women in cities such as Belfast and Dublin with legal protection against husbands taking their income without their consent. The 1882 Act expanded married women's financial independence by asserting that they could own property and have access to credit in their own name without interference from their husbands.

There are also other signs of change in what was expected in marriage in the early twentieth century. Feminists Hanna Sheehy and Margaret Gillespie viewed their marriages differently than their mothers had done. Sheehy kept her own surname, adding that of her husband to it, and her husband similarly incorporated his wife's surname, referring to himself after he married as Frank Sheehy Skeffington, much to the annoyance of his father who thought he was betraying the family name.[154] The Sheehy Skeffingtons also opted to be married wearing their university graduation gowns as a gesture towards female admission to third-level education. Margaret Gillespie changed her surname to that of her husband, James Cousins, but she too viewed companionate friendship as central to marriage and the couple chose a collaborative structure for their jointly authored biography entitled *We Two Together*.[155]

Other couples linked to socially or politically radical groups in Dublin in the early twentieth century also placed shared intellectual and cultural interests at the centre of their relationship. León Ó Broin and his wife, Cait Ní Raghallaigh, spent their honeymoon at a summer school on international law and politics in Geneva.[156] Unlike the young men

---

[152] Jonathan P. Hamill, 'A study of female textile operatives in the Belfast linen industry: 1890–1910' (unpublished PhD thesis, Queen's University Belfast, 1999), pp. 213–16.

[153] *Report of the Royal Commission on the Laws of Marriage* (London, 1868).

[154] Leah Levenson and Jerry H. Natterstad, *Hanna Sheehy-Skeffington: Irish Feminist* (Syracuse, 1986), p. 15.

[155] James H. Cousins and Margaret E. Cousins, *We Two Together* (Madras, 1950).

[156] León Ó Broin, *Just Like Yesterday* (Dublin, 1986), pp. 62–3.

encountered by John O'Sullivan, the dean of Kenmare in the mid-nineteenth century, Ó Broin did not expect his wife to spend her day on domestic duties. At an early stage in their marriage, when he encountered Cait on her knees scrubbing the floor, he exclaimed that he had not married her to do that 'sort of thing' and 'ordered' her to employ help.[157] Mary Maguire and Pádraig Colum shared throughout their married life an interest in writing and literature. They married in 1912, although Mary was initially apprehensive at the idea of marriage as she had no 'taste for exchanging the independent and interesting life I was living for pottering around a kitchen, planning meals, hanging curtains and so on ...'.[158] Similarly, Margaret Ward cited Hanna Sheehy Skeffington's 'lifelong dislike of housework': 'Like the lilies I dust not, neither do I darn, and wash-up only in acute domestic crisis when I have worked through all the ware in the pantry and piled it perilously in the kitchen.'[159]

Hanna Sheehy Skeffington, Margaret Cousins and fellow suffragist, Anna Haslam, provided the first explicit accounts of sexual relations between husband and wife or, as in the Cousins marriage, the absence of it. Both Cousins and Haslam acknowledged in different ways their lack of knowledge about the physical side of marital relations. Cousins wrote in her section of the joint memoir that, prior to marriage, she 'knew nothing of the technique of sex' but that she had trusted in her husband's 'knowledge, his will and his integrity'. Nevertheless, the twenty-five year old university graduate was clearly shocked by the physicality of sex with her husband:

I remember that I grew white and thin during our first married year. People thought this was due to my being a vegetarian. But I knew it was due to the problems of adjustment to the revelation that marriage had brought me as to the physical basis of sex. Every child I looked at called to my mind the shocking circumstance that brought about its existence. My new knowledge, though I was lovingly safeguarded from it, made me ashamed of humanity and ashamed for it. I found myself looking on men and women as degraded by this demand of nature.[160]

As their biography revealed, the Cousins' marriage became a celibate one as Margaret decided to wait 'until the evolution of form has substituted some more artistic way of continuance of the race'.

Anna Haslam also had a celibate marriage. She confided to Marie Stopes:

[157] Ibid., pp. 79–80.   [158] Mary Colum, *Life and the Dream* (London, 1947).
[159] Cited in Margaret Ward, *Hanna Sheehy Skeffington: A Life* (Dublin, 1997), p. 29.
[160] Cousins and Cousins, *We Two Together*, p. 108.

... My husband & self ... preferred abstinence – after the first week we were married – never after that – we slept together for over 60 years – and were a most loving couple – everyone thought us an ideal pair. We had decided before we married that we were too poor [to have children] ...[161]

Lucy Lawrenson may have had similar expectations of a celibate marriage. When Samuel Kingston proposed to her in 1913, she seems to have suggested a 'modern' marriage of friendship rather than one based on sexual intimacy. In order to persuade Lawrenson that there was more to the relationship between a husband and wife than friendship, Kingston wrote an eight-page statement that he entitled 'A Psychological Proposal'. He explained that for him 'mutual sex attraction' was essential for a successful marriage. He tried to allay what he perceived as Lawrenson's 'fear that for the woman to give rein to her natural tenderness and romance is to give an opportunity to the man to put her in the subordinate position you so morbidly dread'. Marriage, he claimed involved a 'certain amount of <u>mutual</u> subordination'.[162] While Kingston did not accept a marriage without sex, he articulated his support for a different type of modern marriage. He described to Lawrenson the sort of women promoted by his mother as suitable marriage partners:

'Now,' she says, 'here is so-and-so, who would make you a most excellent wife ... she has a large dowry, she is an excellent cook, house-keeper and "manager"; she has nice, quiet, ladylike, domesticated tastes, she is musical and well-educated, agreeable and good-tempered, good-looking and respectable. You like her and she likes you. She would make you very happy and comfortable. What more can you want?'[163]

Kingston rejected the traditional role of a wife as described by his mother. He told Lawrenson of his dream of a marriage in which 'we would be real lovers as well as real friends and comrades, free and equal ... helping, supporting, encouraging each other in work and aspirations and ideals'.[164] With some prompting from her mother, Lucy eventually accepted Kingston's proposal. In another modern move, Lucy and Samuel tried to persuade the officiating clergyman at their wedding to omit the word 'obey' from their marriage vows, but it was to no avail.[165]

---

[161] Anna Haslam to Marie Stopes, 20 Aug. 1918 (Brynmor Jones Library, The University of Hull, Marie Stopes Papers, DX/66/2).

[162] Samuel Kingston, 'A psychological proposal' (21 June 1913) (NAI, PRIV1234/4/1/1(3). See also Daisy Lawrenson Swanson, *Emerging from the Shadow: The Lives of Sarah Anne Lawrenson and Lucy Olive Kingston* (Dublin, 1994), pp. 62–4; Caitriona Crowe on the *History Show*, 18 Nov. 2018. www.rte.ie/radio1/the-history-show/programmes/2018/1118/1011747-the-history-show-sunday-18-november-2018/. Accessed 12 December 2019.

[163] Kingston, 'A psychological proposal'.   [164] Ibid.

[165] Lawrenson Swanson, *Emerging from the Shadow*, pp. 68–9.

Lucy may have initially won the argument on a celibate marriage. The couple's daughter, Daisy Lawrenson Swanson, suggests in her biography of her mother and grandmother that her parents may have been practising some form of birth control in the early years of their marriage. She quotes from Samuel's diary for 1917:

On June 21 – the fourth anniversary of 'putting the question' – Lucy and I had a frank discussion on our domestic arrangements and decided to undertake the full duties – and privileges – of matrimony, a decision so important that it constitutes the event of the year for us.[166]

By August of that year, Lucy was pregnant with their daughter, Daisy.

The Sheehy Skeffingtons appear to have enjoyed a happy sexual relationship, although Leah Levenson and Jerry H. Nattersted noted that prior to her marriage Hanna was not that well-informed about sex. She recorded in her diary that 'no one had ever presented "worthy thoughts" on the subject, least of all ... those who taught me!'[167] Just over a year after they were married in 1903, the Sheehy Skeffingtons ordered two marriage manuals.[168] This may have been a search for advice on forms of contraception as their son, Owen, was not born until six years after the couple had married. Hanna Sheehy Skeffington also told her friend, author and diarist, Rosamund Jacob that she and her husband slept in separate bedrooms: 'she thinks that's the most civilized way, never liked sleeping with anyone. She is very ascetic.'[169]

Cormac Ó Grada and Niall Duffy's study of the correspondence received by Marie Stopes indicates that the Sheehy Skeffingtons were not the only Irish couple seeking advice on birth control and contraceptives. They estimated that there were 'several hundred' letters from Ireland in the Stopes archive for the period 1918–1940. Ó Grada's study of 100 letters revealed that most were from middle class men and women who were either married or about to be married. About half of the letters came from non-Catholics living in the north of Ireland. Other correspondents were resident in Dublin. More Irish men than women wrote to Stopes, but the women were more likely to ask for advice on birth control. The men focussed on sexual problems such as impotency or premature ejaculation. The analysis of the Irish letters to Stope compliments Ó Grada et al's exploration of the 1911 census, in which they found that a 'substantial minority' of married couples were practising birth control.[170] Mary E. Daly also noted the regional, religious and

---

[166] Ibid., p. 78.   [167] Levenson and Nattersted, *Hanna Sheehy-Skeffington*, p. 16.
[168] Ibid.   [169] Rosamund Jacob Diary, 10 Nov. 1919 (NLI, MS 32,582 (39)), p. 94.
[170] Cormac Ó Grada and Niall Duffy, 'The fertility transition in Ireland and Scotland, c. 1880–1930' in S. J. Connolly, R. A Houston and R. J. Morris (eds.), *Conflict, Identity*

occupational variations in the size of families in the 1911 census with Protestant professional couples having on average the smallest families: 3.76 children for those married between 20 and 29 years. This compared with 9.47 children for families of semi-skilled occupations and 7.64 children in the households of labourers. Daly's research on the 1926 census indicated that these trends continued into the 1930s, with Protestant couples and professional families continuing to have fewer children. Farmers in rural Ireland had the largest families, with an average of 5.6 children for couples married for 15 to 19 years.[171]

Conclusion

The census data of the early twentieth century confirms, therefore, that some couples were actively taking measures to limit the size of their families. As Daly notes, however, more generally, the Irish family size in the 1920s was 'significantly higher than elsewhere in Europe'.[172] Data from the eighteenth century also suggests a relatively high household size, ranging from a mean of 4.6 to 5.5.[173] This chapter has focussed on relationships between husband and wife and the various ways in which patriarchy was exercised. Although we do not explore the role of children in a marriage, the discussion on relations between husbands and wives must also be placed in the wider context of relatively large families and households. It is impossible to generalise about the implications for marital relations of large numbers of children but large, crowded households are, nonetheless, a constant throughout the period covered by this volume.

and Economic Development in Ireland and Scotland, 1600–1939 (Preston, 1995), pp. 89–102; Cormac Ó Gráda, Timothy Guinnane and Carolyn M. Moehling, 'Fertility in South Dublin a century ago: First look' (University College Dublin Centre for Economic Research Working Paper Series; WP01/26, 2001–11). http://hdl.handle.net/10197/503. Accessed 25 January 2019.

[171] Mary E. Daly, 'Marriage, fertility and women's lives in twentieth-century Ireland (c. 1900–c. 1970)', Women's History Review, 15, 4 (2006), 571–4. For the Irish medical view of contraception see Anne Daly, '"Veiled obscenity": Contraception and the Dublin Medical Press, 1850–1900' in Elaine Farrell (ed.), She Said She Was in the Family Way': Pregnancy and Infancy in Modern Ireland (London, 2012), pp. 15–33.

[172] Daly, 'Marriage, fertility and women's lives', 574.

[173] This figure incorporates all those living in a house including servants. Brian Gurrin, 'Population and emigration, 1730–1845' in James Kelly (ed.), Cambridge History of Ireland (Cambridge, 2018), iii, pp. 205–8; L. A. Clarkson, 'Irish population revisited, 1687–1821' in J. M. Goldstrom and L. A. Clarkson (eds.), Irish Population, Economy, and Society: Essays in Honour of the Late K. H. Connell (Oxford, 1981), pp. 13–35; Stuart Daultrey, David Dickson and Cormac Ó Gráda, 'Eighteenth-century Irish population: New perspectives from old sources', The Journal of Economic History, 41, 3 (Sept., 1981), 601–28.

It is challenging to come to any general conclusions about Irish definitions and experiences of patriarchy. Legally, a husband was recognised as head of the household and allocated a status superior to their wives throughout the period covered by this book. Married women were in theory expected to submit and to obey their husbands. The extent to which the narrow legal definition of patriarchy was implemented in practice depended on a range of variables including economic circumstances, the individual personalities of husbands and wives and the expectations of what the respective roles of husband and wife should be. There is considerable evidence of partnership and co-operation, although there is also evidence of men's awareness of their right to demand a wife's obedience and of women accepting without much protest that they should obey. And, as Chapter 10 documents, husbands were found guilty of domestic abuse throughout the period covered by this book.

We began this chapter with one man, William Leadbeater expressing both his frustration and his lifelong love for his wife. We finish with another man not known for his public displays of emotion but who privately wrote of his sexual longing for his wife. As a young husband, Éamon de Valera wrote love letters to his wife, Sinéad, which communicated his physical yearning for her. In 1911, as he spent time away learning Irish, de Valera wrote to Sinéad:

I need a kiss, urgently ... I want to press my wife to my heart, but we are 150 miles apart. Darling, do you think of me at all? – can you sleep without those long limbs wrapped around you? – those same limbs are longing to be wrapped around you again – two weeks – fourteen days – how can I endure it? You do not know how sorrowful I am ...[174]

There can be no generalising about intimate relationships between married couples. Emotions shaped such relationships as clearly as economics and status. Emotions might be expressed in words, in letters, but within an intimate life they find expression also in gesture, touch, in looks and in more practical realms of support and care. Many such intimacies are hidden from us as historians.

---

[174] *Irish Times*, 25 Nov. 2000; Diarmaid Ferriter, *Occasions of Sin: Sex and Society in Modern Ireland* (London, 2009), p. 90.

8   Adultery and Sex outside Marriage

Dr Philip Cross, a retired army surgeon, was convicted of poisoning his wife in 1887.[1] The Crosses and their five children 'lived in a comfortable position, receiving and visiting the surrounding gentry'. However, in 1886 Dr Cross began a liaison with a young governess at a neighbouring estate and Mrs Cross began to show the classic symptoms of arsenic poisoning by the spring of 1887. Her husband insisted she was suffering from heart disease. Mrs Cross died in early June 1887. Cross had her buried immediately, signed a death certificate saying she had died of typhoid fever, and married the young governess a few days later.[2] All of this haste aroused suspicion about his wife's death; the body was exhumed and it was found that she had been poisoned. The use of poison was taken as evidence of premeditation and intent to murder.[3] The judge in the case was clear that he had no sympathy for Cross. He directed the jury to consider 'If he [Cross] was not a loving husband he had no right to be there: foul adultery, heartless and callous indifference on the occasion of her death, that after the very scant funeral rites were performed he left to join that creature again, he hurried with wicked speed to replace the faithful wife then in her grave – all this had been proved without doubt'.[4] Cross was found guilty and hanged in January 1888.

As other chapters in this volume indicate, marital infidelity was not uncommon in the period under review. It is impossible, however, to know how extensive extra-marital sexual behaviour was in any period. Having previously examined pre-marital sex, here we explore the attitudes expressed towards adulterous behaviour and couples who cohabited without marrying; how such behaviour reflected upon marital relationships and what it says more generally about sexuality in Irish society.[5]

---

[1] RIC Return of Outrages for 1887 (NAI, CSO ICR 2).   [2] *Irish Times*, 15 Dec. 1887.
[3] RIC Return of Outrages for 1887 (NAI, CSO ICR 2); *Cork Examiner*, 10 Dec. 1887.
[4] *Irish Times*, 15 Dec. 1887.
[5] There are a number of histories on the topic of adultery. See, for instance, David M. Turner, *Fashioning Adultery: Gender, Sex and Civility in England, 1660–1740* (Cambridge, 2008); Susan Law, *Through the Keyhole: Sex, Scandal and the Secret Life of the Country*

Adultery and the Churches

Legally, adultery was a prosecutable crime in the ecclesiastical courts. The punishment was normally a public shaming with the offender or offenders being obliged to stand in front of the congregation in three different churches on successive Sundays.[6] In the collection of petitions presented to the Killaloe diocesan court dating to the years from 1700 to 1711, twenty-three related to accusations of adultery. Adultery was the second-highest offence recorded among the cases listed in the court records after fornication or pre-marital sex. Unlike the latter, however, most of the adultery cases listed provide no details of the particular circumstances. As in the prosecution of single fathers, the ecclesiastical courts had limited control over those who failed to turn up to face their accusers. The most severe sanction for absence from court was a publicly proclaimed excommunication.[7] Although administered by clergy who were members of the established church, the ecclesiastical court was open to all denominations. A sanction of excommunication might not, however, have been considered too seriously by Dissenters or members of the Catholic church. In 1804, a judge in a Dublin court noted that prosecutions for adultery in the ecclesiastical courts were by that time 'so unusual as to be nearly obsolete'.[8] It is likely, therefore, that, as in England, the number had declined significantly by the middle decades of the eighteenth century and were mainly those necessitated by the legal request for a parliamentary divorce.[9]

In the Presbyterian church, adultery was treated as a far more serious offence than fornication or pre-marital sex, partly because it was considered grounds for a divorce, according to the Westminster Confession of Faith. Within the session, regardless of sectional denomination, the hearing of a charge of adultery could continue for several months while the elders examined the man and woman accused, as well as neighbours and relatives concerning the behaviour of the couple and the veracity of

---

Houses (Gloucestershire, 2015). For an Irish case study see Éamonn Darcy, *The World of Thomas Ward: Sex and Scandal in Late Seventeenth Century County Antrim* (Dublin, 2016).

[6] See, for example, BL, Add MS 31881, p. 24.

[7] Ibid. The Killaloe collection of petitions only includes cases in which the accused queried a sentence of the court or had a request to make to the vicar general. The actual number of adultery cases dealt with by the court at this time is unknown.

[8] *A Report of the Trial on an Action for Damages Brought by the Reverend Charles Massy against the Most Noble the Marquis of Headfort for Criminal Conversation for Damages with Plaintiff's Wife* (Dublin, 1804), p. 87.

[9] See Chapter 12.

the accusation.[10] Another measure of the seriousness with which it was considered was that when the information was gathered, accusations of adultery were usually referred by the kirk-session to the presbytery. As Presbyterian communities regarded adultery as a heinous offence, it is not surprising that the number of cases considered in eighteenth-century sessions was small. In Carnmoney, for example, between 1786 and 1804, there were only three cases of adultery discussed by the session compared with seventy-nine incidences of pre-marital fornication and thirty-eight cases of fornication.[11] In Glascar, between 1760 and 1818, the session examined two incidences of adultery and one of these was only suspected rather than proven or admitted.[12] In the Burgher Secession community of Cahans, Andrew Holmes identified three cases of adultery and twenty-three cases of fornication between 1752 and 1758.[13] Not all repented their sin of adultery. In the 1720s, Mary Walsh confessed to adultery 'but did not repent fully', and the last heard of her was that she was leaving for England. Likewise, Mary Carmichael, on a confession of adultery, was advised to 'to get into some lodging with good people where she might have a religious conversion'. She too moved residence and the congregation lost touch with her.[14]

Until the last quarter of the nineteenth century, the Catholic church did not have the same administrative structures to supervise and prosecute its members who broke their marriage vows as the Presbyterian or established churches. Eighteenth-century visitation reports from Catholic bishops suggest, however, that local priests were aware that many of their parishioners were not following the church's teaching on monogamous marriage for life. In the early 1750s, the bishop of Ossory, Richard Butler established a regular system of meetings of the priests in his diocese in which they communicated to him instances of 'public sinners', which included adulterers, bigamists and couples who were cohabiting.[15] The clerical accounting of the state of parishes in the diocese was not systematic but the priests' reports reveal that in almost every parish there were at

---

[10] See, for example, the questioning of John Wales and Margaret Macrea at the Cahans session in 1756 (Cahans Session Book, 1751–1802, pp. 63–9 (PHSIB)).

[11] Leanne Calvert (ed.), 'Carnmoney Kirk Session Chapter Minute Book, January 1786– March 1804' (unpublished transcript of original in PHSIB).

[12] Glascar Session Book, 1760–1818 (PHSIB).

[13] Andrew R. Holmes, *The Shaping of Ulster Presbyterian Belief and Practice 1770–1840* (Oxford, 2006), p. 173.

[14] Plunkett/Usher's Quay Session Book, 1726–1766, 16 Jan. 1731; 31 Dec. 1736. Now in the custody of Clontarf and Scots Presbyterian Church. Examined by courtesy of Hilary Fairman.

[15] Christopher O'Dwyer (ed.), 'Archbishop Butler's visitation book', *Archivium Hibernicum*, 33 (1975), 1–90; 34 (1975), 1–49.

least one or two couples who were known to be flouting the church rules on marriage. The most common offenders were men who had 'eloped' from their wives and were living with other women. Other couples who claimed to be married were suspected of having 'pretended marriages'. As in the ecclesiastical court, the clergy were expected to publicly denounce the sinners. In 1758, for example, Father Tim Brien reported the following public sinners in the parish of Drum:

John G. & Margaret R., concubine to John G., whose wife is alive by name Honor K.; Thomas H. and Grace P. live together unmarried these several years past. Said two couples after three publick admonitions are to be publickly excommunicated if th[e]y do not reform.[16]

Just over thirty years later, Mathew McKenna, Bishop of Cloyne and Ross, presented a similar account in his visitation report. McKenna noted that in the majority of parishes that he visited, there were married couples who were not living together; cohabiting couples who were not married; married men living with women other than their wives and single women variously described as 'kept', 'concubine', 'mistress', 'idle' or 'ladies of pleasure'.[17] In the parishes of Clonmeen and Killcorny, County Cork, for example, McKenna recorded that:

ye flock very irregular. John Mac Aulife does not cohabit with his wife. <u>now does</u>. Denis Donevan & Peg Winaby in publick adultery. 3 years excommunicated … Dinahy of Cluainmine entertained a lady of pleasure & is suspected of adultery … Callaghan McCarty impregnated 2 sisters this year and is suspected to continue in the crime with one of them. Finely Keeffe guilty of adultery with his servant, whom he visits still.[18]

McKenna used his visitation report as a working document and noted when he had succeeded in reforming one of his parishioners. In the above extract, he, or the local parish priest, may have persuaded John Mac Aulife to live with his wife and hence, he subsequently entered the additional note of 'now does'. Such additions are, however, relatively rare, which would suggest that McKenna and his colleagues made little headway in changing the sexual habits of erring members of the diocese.

McKenna's immediate successors as bishops did not keep such detailed records and merely referred to 'public scandals' in particular parishes without providing details.[19] The behaviour of parishioners may not, therefore, have changed but was simply not reported in the same detail. In other dioceses in the early nineteenth century, members of the

---

[16] Ibid., 11. The surnames were withheld from the 1975 printed edition of the visitation.
[17] Eric A. Derr and Matt MacKenna (eds.), 'Episcopal visitations of the diocese of Cloyne and Ross, 1785–1828 (with index)', *Archivium Hibernicum*, 66 (2013), 271–314.
[18] Ibid., 290.   [19] Ibid., 365, 366, 368, 370, 372, 375.

Catholic hierarchy reported the number of cohabiting and adulterous couples in their parishes. In 1826, George Plunkett, Bishop of Elphin, claimed that when he first began as bishop in the western diocese in 1814, there were 'innumerable couples' who 'had lived as man and wife who had never been married and many others in flagrant and notorious adultery'.[20] In 1842, the bishop of Cork, John Murphy, wrote to Paul Cullen in Rome that he had 'a melancholy list of 64 couples who have for years lived in fornication, adultery, incest'.[21] Catholic clergymen regularly complained that their inability to administer the issuing of dispensations, particularly for couples marrying within the prohibited degrees, also encouraged cohabitation.[22]

By the 1840s, the Catholic clergy were beginning to enforce the church laws on marriage more effectively. In 1850, Dean John O'Sullivan urged priests to persist in denouncing cohabiting couples publicly. He admitted that it might take two to three years, to persuade a couple who had been together for a long time to separate but the priests should persevere. In particular, O'Sullivan advised that a parish priest should be 'untiring in his public denunciation' of couples who could not get a church dispensation to marry and chose instead to live together. As O'Sullivan noted, 'if they once get a family it will be very difficult to separate them'.[23]

The evidence is scattered and we have no consistent documentation as to how adulterers or cohabiting couples were viewed within local communities. In 1775, a group of Whiteboys, leading a crowd of over 100 people, went to an unmarried couple who were living in 'scandal' in County Kilkenny. The couple was forced to swear that they would separate and they were warned that if they did not keep to the separation the Whiteboys would return and strangle them both. This attack may, however, have been provoked by particular or personal circumstances rather than representing more widespread communal disapproval.[24] Ineffective recording of births, marriages and deaths also meant that it was not difficult for a cohabiting or adulterous couple to convince their neighbours that they had married before they moved to the locality. It was often only when difficulties developed in the partnership that the

---

[20] Emmet Larkin, 'Church and state in Ireland in the nineteenth century', *Church History*, 31, 3 (Sept. 1962), 300.

[21] Cited in Emmet Larkin, 'The devotional revolution in Ireland, 1850–1875', *American Historical Review*, 77, 3 (June 1972), 637. An incestuous relationship often referred to those living within the prohibited degrees.

[22] See, for example, Francis Garvey to Warden of Galway, 1783 (Galway Diocesan Archives, Box 7/D18/F1).

[23] John O'Sullivan, 'Praxis Parochi' (Kerry Diocesan Archives, Killarney), p. 710.

[24] Cited in J. S. Donnelly, 'Irish agrarian rebellion: The Whiteboys of 1769–1776', *Proceedings of the Royal Irish Academy*, lxxxiii, section C (1983), 309.

truth of the relationship might emerge. Some neighbours may also have had a fairly tolerant attitude to cohabiting couples. In 1851, a priest in Armagh wrote to Cardinal Paul Cullen about one of his parishioners, Edward Duffy:

[he] did not tell me the truth about sending his pretended wife away. He has her concealed in some of his neighbour's houses every day and they go together every night. When I can get them to live separately every night, I will inform your Grace of it. Duffy's now pretended wife and his first wife were first cousins. To avoid scandal it might be desirable to grant them a dispensation in the above impediment in the second degree of affinity, if they separate for some time.[25]

The public controversy triggered by the adultery of Katherine O'Shea with Charles Stewart Parnell reveals the changing atmosphere in late nineteenth-century Ireland. Yet, even at that late stage, there were many willing to overlook the political leader's sexual indiscretions – although criticism of Mrs O'Shea was less nuanced. In her own account of her relationship with Parnell, O'Shea described the subterfuge tactics of the adulterous couple. She would watch Parnell speaking in the chamber of the House of Commons from the Ladies' Gallery and he 'would signal by certain manipulations of his handkerchief' when he wanted to see her.[26] Parnell also wrote formal letters or notes to Mrs O'Shea and incorporated into the correspondence 'some word or sign that let me know a place or time of meeting in London or near my home'.[27] When Parnell was arrested for his political activities, he arranged with an unknown visitor to the prison to deliver letters to O'Shea addressed to 'Mrs Carpenter'. He also wrote to her in 'invisible ink'.[28] Myles Dungan suggests that it is likely that O'Shea was having sex with her husband and Parnell at the same time.[29]

Newspaper reports of criminal conversation cases revealed similar intimate details of adulterous couples' furtive activities. As will be explained in more detail in Chapter 12, domestic servants and hotel employees were summoned to court to testify about what they had seen and how they had concluded that a married woman and her gentleman friend were having sexual intercourse. They were asked about the woman's clothes and demeanour following her meeting in a closed (often locked) room with her putative lover. Dishevelled bedclothes might also

---

[25] Thomas Dunleer to Cardinal Cullen, 21 March 1851 (Dublin Diocesan Archives, Cullen Papers 39/2 File IV: Armagh Priests, 1851).
[26] Katharine O'Shea, *Charles Stewart Parnell: His Love Story and Political Life* (2 vols. New York, 1914), i, p. 165.
[27] Ibid., p. 176.   [28] Ibid., pp. 201–2.
[29] Myles Dungan, *The Captain and the King: William O'Shea, Parnell and Late Victorian Ireland* (Dublin, 2009), p. 63.

be assumed to provide key clues. In the trial of Anthony Patrick Mahon, an army surgeon, for adultery with the wife of Thomas Hodgens, a barrister, the servants were questioned about the 'tossed' state of Mrs Hodgens when she came out of Mahon's room and what they had heard as they stood outside the room:

BARRISTER FOR HODGENS: How was Mrs Hodgens dressed the morning you saw her coming out of Mahon's room?

THOMAS M'GEE (SERVANT): It was a white morning gown.

BARRISTER FOR HODGENS: What kind of noise did you hear?

THOMAS M'GEE (SERVANT): It was the noise of a bed shaking ...

ANNE WALSH (SERVANT): was often employed to make his bed, his bed had all the appearance of two persons having slept in it, cannot say if a man and woman slept in it but there were the marks of two in it.[30]

Printed reports and newspaper accounts of trials for criminal conversation were, therefore, an important medium through which the public became aware of adulterous affairs. As in the case of Philip Cross, prosecutions for murder could also include stories of adultery. From the late seventeenth century, under English criminal law, a husband who killed his wife's lover could offer a defence of provocation and might be prosecuted for manslaughter rather than murder.[31] As the eighteenth-century legal commentator, William Blackstone, wrote, 'if a man takes another in the act of adultery with his wife, and kills him directly upon the spot ... it is not absolutely ranked in the class of justifiable homicide, as in [the] case of a forcible rape, but it is manslaughter. It is however the lowest degree of it'.[32] It is not clear from the surviving records how frequently this defence was used in Ireland. It might have been difficult to prove that the husband had discovered his wife *in flagrante* with another man. In 1848 Dennis Long, a farmer, suspected his wife of having an adulterous affair with a man named Walsh, one of his farm labourers. In order to secure some evidence against his wife he told her he would be away overnight and would return late the next day. He however, returned early and caught his wife and Walsh together in his house. 'With the fury of a lion, and in a moment of temporary insanity'

---

[30] Printed Report of Criminal Conversation Trial (Anthony Patrick Mahon, defendant; Thomas Hodgens, plaintiff (Dublin, 1835), p. 13. Consulted online. Harvard University, Studies in Scarlet. https://curiosity.lib.harvard.edu/studies-in-scarlet/catalog/41-9900403 63840203941. Accessed 15 January 2020. See pp. 398–403 for more information on law suits involving criminal conversation.

[31] See Chapter 10.

[32] K. Kesselring, 'No greater provocation? Adultery and the mitigation of murder in English law', *Law and History Review*, 34, 1 (2016), 107–213; William Blackstone, *Commentaries on the Laws of England: In Four Books. Book the Fourth* (13th ed., London, 1800), pp. 190–1.

he grabbed a spade and killed Walsh. When tried in 1849, Long escaped serious punishment. The judge and jury agreed that he had been provoked by his wife's activities to such an extent that his actions were the result of 'temporary insanity'. The charge of murder was reduced to manslaughter and the addition of a verdict of insanity underlined the view that Long was not to blame for his actions. Long received a jail sentence of two months.[33]

The courts might uphold the manly honour of a husband who murdered a man whom he discovered with his wife but they were less sympathetic if he killed his wife for adultery.[34] One of the most infamous murder trials of the nineteenth century was that of the artist, William Burke Kirwan, who was indicted for the murder of his wife, Sarah Maria Louisa, in September 1852. The couple had paid a visit to Ireland's Eye, about a mile off the coast at Howth harbour. During the course of the visit Sarah, who was considered a strong swimmer, drowned. The coroner later confirmed the death as one caused by accidental drowning. The couple had been married in 1840 and having lived with Kirwan's father eventually moved to a house in Upper Merrion Street, Dublin. They had no children. After the coroner's verdict, and the burial, some rumours spread that Kirwan had murdered his wife, and the police began to investigate. What they uncovered brought the case to a shocked and fascinated public. For at least ten years, and while he was married, Kirwan had an ongoing relationship with a Miss Teresa Kenny, mother of his seven children. Kenny, when questioned by the police, claimed that Sarah had known of the relationship. While there was no proof that Kirwan had murdered his wife, the circumstances of his private life saw him arrested for her murder.[35] The evidence in the case was circumstantial, a fact that rarely led to a murder conviction. However, Kirwan was found guilty of murder and sentenced to death, later commuted to transportation for life. The case caused considerable debate in legal and medical circles and many believed that Kirwan had been convicted more for his double life than for murder.[36]

---

[33] *Tuam Herald*, 2 Dec. 1848; *The Limerick and Clare Examiner*, 17 March 1849.
[34] Kesselring, 'No greater provocation?', 214–21.
[35] NAI, CRF 1853 K. John Simpson Armstrong, *Report of the Trial of William Burke Kirwan, for the Murder of Maria Louisa Kirwan, His Wife, at the Island of Ireland's Eye, in the County of Dublin on the 6th September, 1852, before Mr Justice Crampton and the Rt. Hon. Baron Greene, at the Commission Court, Green Street, on the 8th and 9th December, 1852* (Dublin, 1853). Kirwan was finally released in 1879.
[36] R. S. Lambert, *When Justice Failed* (London, 1935). For a recent account of the case see Michael Sheridan, *Murder at Ireland's Eye* (Dublin, 2012).

While the adultery of Charles Stewart Parnell and Katharine O'Shea received a great deal of attention in late nineteenth-century Ireland, the Irish parliamentarian and journalist, Thomas Power O'Connor claimed in his memoir that Parnell was not the only sexual miscreant in the Irish Parliamentary Party.[37] He noted that Katharine O'Shea's husband had had a number of adulterous affairs before his wife met Parnell. O'Connor described his school friend, Michael Francis Ward, who represented the borough of Galway, 1874–1880, as 'the most immoral man – sexually – I have ever known'.[38] O'Connor alleged that 'the glimpse of a bar-maid with a V-shaped blouse would be sufficient to light … the fire of [Ward's] fiery sensuality and that same night, and for weeks after he would disappear – it will be easily understood where – and would be lost to everybody'.[39] The leader of the party before Parnell, Isaac Butt, was known to have fathered a number of children outside of his marriage, while Francis Biggar had a 'weakness for women, some of dubious character'.[40] O'Connor wrote cynically about Biggar who presented himself as an 'apostle of sexual purity' but, although a bachelor, had in reality fathered a number of children. Biggar was cited in a breach of promise case in a London court and, according to O'Connor, wanted to defend his reneging on the marriage by arguing that he was obliged to provide for a number of children.[41]

Although he wrote scurrilously of the lives of members of the Irish Parliamentary Party under Parnell, O'Connor was careful to distinguish their antics from those of the next generation of Irish parliamentarians. He wrote respectfully of the party led by John Redmond. Most were married men whose wives remained at home in Ireland and looked after the family business. O'Connor acknowledged that some may have got themselves into 'temporary scrapes' but the Irish MPs, for the most part 'led lives of rigid virtue'.[42] 'Eve', he noted, 'never, or very rarely, entered this bleak paradise'.[43]

The later generation of politicians were not, however, immune from sexual adventures outside marriage. Despite his puritanical public image, the Irish Free State minister, Kevin O'Higgins was 'beset' by his love for Lady Hazel Lavery. A married man with two young children, O'Higgins wrote passionately and recklessly to Lavery about his physical attraction to her:

---

[37] T. P. O'Connor, *Memoirs of an Old Parliamentarian* (2 vols., London, 1929), i, pp. 227–9. See also Dungan, *The Captain and the King*, pp. 82, 339.
[38] O'Connor, *Memoirs of an Old Parliamentarian*, i, p. 20.   [39] Ibid., p. 22.
[40] *DIB*; For Butt's children, see O'Connor, *Memoirs of an Old Parliamentarian*, i, p. 33;
[41] Ibid., pp. 132–4.   [42] Ibid., ii, p. 65.   [43] Ibid., p. 64.

I am lost and desolate without you – I want you – all the enchantment – sight and sounds and the *touch of* you. I want to hold you to me and hear you say again and again and again that you love me and are [mine] forever and that you treasure in your [heart] every golden moment we have spent together in the glory of our [love] [Dear] heart I love you utterly – you always – All yours.[44]

Prostitution

If we are looking for evidence of sexual opportunity outside of marriage then exploring the history of prostitution and the prevalence of venereal diseases can be enlightening. Clergymen from all denominations denounced prostitution, but despite clerical condemnation it was common in eighteenth- and nineteenth-century Irish towns and cities. Prostitution thrived, particularly in Irish garrison towns, and it would be naive to assume that only unmarried soldiers used prostitutes for sex. In her autobiography, Margaret Leeson delineated her experiences as both a sex worker and as a brothel owner in Dublin in the last quarter of the eighteenth century. Leeson described the different categories of women who received financial reward for sexual favours. These included women maintained in lodgings by wealthy men; women who worked in brothels managed by former kept women like Leeson and poverty-stricken street walkers or 'strollers'. Leeson wrote gleefully about the married men who held high political or ecclesiastical positions, who frequented her Dublin brothel. Her more regular clientele were, however, the business and tradesmen of Dublin and the soldiers stationed in the city's barracks. It is likely that many of these men were also married.[45] That married men also used prostitutes was noted in an official report in 1871. In his evidence to a Royal Commission on the contagious diseases acts, Rev. Maguire from Cork City confirmed that married as well as single men paid for sex in the city. He observed 'That half our married men and half our youths would be preserved from misfortune if they did not meet these unfortunate women [prostitutes] in the streets'.[46]

There were sixty-eight women categorised as prostitutes among the inmates of the Limerick House of Industry between 1774 and 1793.

---

[44] Cited in Sinéad McCoole, *A Life of Lady Lavery 1880–1935* (Dublin, 1996), p. 128. The dashes indicate the parts of the letter that Lavery subsequently scored out. She also took steps to ensure that her letters to O'Higgins were destroyed.

[45] Margaret Leeson, *The Memoirs of Mrs Leeson*. Edited and Introduced by Mary Lyons (Dublin: Lilliput Press, 1995).

[46] *Royal Commission on the Administration and Operation of the Contagious Diseases Acts, ii, Minutes of Evidence* (c. 408–1), H. C., 1871, p. 677.

They were 'variously described as 'whore', 'strumpet' or 'harlot'. Statistically, the women specifically described as prostitutes represented only a small minority of the inmates but it is likely that more were described under headings such as 'shulers', 'strollers', 'vagabonds' or by the more general description of 'bad woman' or 'bad girl'.[47] Prostitution was clearly considered a problem in Limerick in the early nineteenth century, and on a number of occasions, such women were arrested by the municipal authorities and had their heads shaved.[48]

Mathew McKenna's visitation of the diocese of Cloyne and Ross indicates that prostitution was not confined to cities and towns in the late eighteenth century. His account describes the parish of Union Hall in County Cork as being particularly noted for 'girls of pleasure' while the parish of Great Island and Carrigtwohill had two 'body' or bawdy houses, a common name for a brothel.[49] Court cases also incidentally reveal rural venues for alleged prostitution. In 1843, for instance, in a suit for restoration of conjugal rights, Christopher Conron admitted that in 1838–1839, he was 'living, sleeping and cohabiting' with two sisters, Anne and Mary Barry. He told the court that he had rented a house and small farm near Cork so that the three of them could live together. When he went to England on the death of his father, he claimed that the Barry sisters had made use of the house for the 'reception of men'.[50]

Diarmuid Ó Grada identified fifty-four brothels operating in Dublin in the eighteenth century, the majority of which were run by women.[51] In 1838 there were 402 brothels recorded in Dublin, and that figure had risen to 1,287 by 1842.[52] The Dublin Metropolitan Police suggested that there were 74 brothels, but a total of 72 other houses frequented by prostitutes in Dublin in 1894, and about 367 women associated with those dwellings in the city. For many women prostitution was a transient occupation, resorted to in times of utter distress. Married women, along with single and widowed women, found their way into prostitution.[53] The precarious nature of being married to a soldier can be evidenced in

---

[47] David Fleming and John Logan (eds.), *Pauper Limerick: The Register of the Limerick House of Industry, 1774–93* (Dublin, 2011), pp. xx, xxii.

[48] Ibid., p. xiv.

[49] Derr and MacKenna, 'Episcopal visitations of the diocese of Cloyne and Ross, 1785–1828', 310, 311, 314.

[50] Anne Barry claimed to have married Conran and sued him for restoration of conjugal rights. See *Freeman's Journal*, 3 July 1843; *Southern Reporter and Cork Commercial Courier*, 27 July 1843; *Cork Examiner*, 31 July 1843; 1, 6 Dec. 1843.

[51] Diarmuid Ó Grada, *Georgian Dublin: The Forces That Shaped the City* (Cork, 2015), pp. 293–6.

[52] *Criminal and Judicial Statistics*, 1914–1916, lxxii.

[53] Maria Luddy, *Prostitution and Irish Society, 1800–1940* (Cambridge, 2007), chapter 2.

the tale of Susanna Price, who took to prostitution and crime to support herself when her soldier husband was sent overseas. In 1840 she was sentenced to seven years' transportation for larceny.[54]

A rare account of activity within a brothel was provided in the prosecution of the owners in 1824. James and Margaret McNally managed a brothel in Athlone, County Westmeath. A woman who worked there, Mary Flynn, described how 'there used men [sic] come every evening; upstairs in the house the men and the women used to retire; there was a bed in the room – for the accommodation of a bed McNally charged one shilling'.[55] We get a brief glimpse of a more upmarket brothel from a court case conducted in Belfast in 1851. The *Belfast Newsletter* noted that a huge crowd turned out in the court to hear the tale of a 'fast' young gentleman of family and fortune, who had prosecuted 'a fashionable female' for robbing him of fifty sovereigns in a brothel. A number of the 'young ladies' of her establishment were also in court. The prosecutor had expected to summon several witnesses but was advised that 'as many of those parties moved in [a] highly respectable sphere, the course would give rise to much unpleasantness and disgrace in families'. The newspaper noted that much of the detailed evidence the gentleman gave to the court to support his case was 'of course, altogether unfit for publication'. It was noted that he had visited the place at least twenty to thirty times, and had been there several times within the last six months, sometimes in company with other gentlemen. Wine was sold on the premises; champagne was £1 a bottle and the defendant had on one night paid a bill of £7 for his wine consumption.[56]

Sexually Transmitted Diseases

Further evidence of the existence (and even perhaps the extent) of pre-marital and extra marital sex was the range of advertisements appearing in the *Freeman's Journal*, and other papers, offering all kinds of remedies for ailments relating to venereal diseases. Information and remedies took a number of forms. Books and pamphlets were advertised; visiting doctors offered to see afflicted patients in private and a range of pills and potions were offered for sale. Throughout the 1820s ads ran in the *Freeman's Journal* for 'The French Pills'. The pills, priced at two shillings and six pence per box, came with 'full and direct instructions'.[57] By 1837 new

---

[54] NAI, CRF 1840 P20.   [55] *Athlone Sentinel*, 24 May 1845.
[56] *Belfast Newsletter*, 6 Aug. 1851.
[57] *Freeman's Journal*, 18 Dec. 1821. This same advertisement was repeated in the *Freeman's Journal* almost weekly between 1821 and 1823.

'remedies' were appearing, such as 'Franke's Specific Solution of Copaiba' described as a 'certain and most speedy cure for all urethral discharges, gleets, spasmodic strictures, irritation of the kidneys, bladder, urethra, and prostate gland.' Appended to these advertisements were a number of testimonials from medical doctors.[58] Perry's Purifying Pills were available from 1838 and advertised in the centre of the front page of the *Freeman's Journal*. Many of these advertisements fed into the ignorance and fears individuals felt around these diseases. The desire for secrecy was acknowledged, and acquisition of these diseases was often, for men, viewed as a mishap, a disease 'frequently contracted in a moment of inebriety', an unfortunate and unlucky event for which the individual should not have to suffer.[59] As the decades passed the advertisements became more elaborate and included drawings. The 'Cordial Balm of Syracium' would 'restore to [the customer] enjoyment of all the comforts of life'.[60] An advertisement for a treatise on venereal disease and Perry's Purifying Specific Pills took up almost a complete column on the front page of the *Freeman's Journal* for months between 1839 and 1841. The fact that they ran for such a long time, throughout the nineteenth century, suggests that there was a ready market for these types of 'cures'.[61]

In the 1850s when Cork medic Dr Townsend treated a married woman, 'Mrs S., aged 23', for a miscarriage, he described his treatment as 'mecury [*sic*] with chalk, Dover's Powder and a stay in the country'. 'I never', he wrote, 'either to the lady or any member of her family hinted that, in my opinion, she suffered from syphilis'. He felt able, however, to discuss the matter with her husband, and discovered that two years before the husband had contracted syphilis, had treatment and was assured he was cured.[62] Between 1847 and 1854, 414 married women and 6,550 'other women' were treated for venereal diseases in the Westmoreland Lock Hospital.[63] One doctor, writing to the *Dublin Medical Press and Circular* in 1886, made an astonishing observation when he noted 'I see a good deal of syphilis amongst ... young married women. It is not uncommon for young women to get syphilis immediately on marriage; many women who have been married for years get it

---

[58] Ibid., 14 March, 1837.
[59] Ibid., 20 Aug. 1838. The advertisement for Perry's Purifying Specific Pills appeared in the *Freeman's Journal* at least fifty-one times in 1840 and 1841.
[60] Ibid., 4 Jan. 1840.
[61] *Belfast Evening Telegraph*, 12 Jan. 1907, cited in Michael Boyle, 'Women and crime in Belfast, 1900–1914' (unpublished PhD thesis, Queen's University, Belfast, 1997), p. 219.
[62] 'Transactions of the county and city of Cork Medical and Surgical Society', *Dublin Quarterly Journal of Medical Science*, 27, 55 (1859), 236–8.
[63] *Report from the Select Committee on Dublin Hospitals* (Dublin, 1854), 12, p. 4.

from their husbands'.[64] He believed that 'such husbands gave their wives disease through having gone astray once only'. It was commonly believed that only prostitutes spread venereal diseases, even though it was admitted in the medical literature, that it was mostly husbands who gave their wives a disease. The danger of sexuality outside marriage was a constant theme in publications on these diseases. Many doctors also believed that respectable women and middle-class wives should not be informed of the nature of a presenting illness if that illness was a venereal disease.[65]

The most significant intervention in relation to venereal disease came from the Royal Commission on Venereal Disease, which began its work on 19 November 1913, and produced its final report in February 1916.[66] Dr Brian O'Brien, Chief Medical Inspector to the Irish Local Government Board, reported to the Commission in 1914 that venereal disease was almost non-existent in rural Ireland, and uncommon in the smaller towns. When asked about the 'splendid result' of almost no syphilis being evident, O'Brien responded 'that there was very little immorality' in rural Ireland.[67] However, he admitted that incidents of gonorrhoea might not have declined.[68] He did note that syphilis had a special prevalence in Dublin, which he attributed to poverty, bad housing and 'girls who go wrong'.[69] He also reported on incidents of venereal disease in Belfast, and to a lesser extent in Cork.[70] One doctor in Belfast had sixty-six women gynaecological patients who attended the Ulster Hospital for Women and Children tested for syphilis. Of the sixty-six, twenty-seven tested positive, which suggests that the rates of sexually transmitted

---

[64] *Dublin Medical Press and Circular*, 92 (1886), 486.

[65] Alfred Fournier, *Syphilis and Marriage* (London, 1881) was translated and published for the Royal College of Surgeons in England. In his book, Fournier advised doctors dealing with wives who had contracted a venereal disease that 'it is your moral duty to deceive her in this matter by hiding from her the name and nature of her malady', p. 169.

[66] *Royal Commission on Venereal Diseases, Final Report* (Cd. 8189), 1916. For a good general discussion of venereal disease see Lesley A. Hall, 'Venereal diseases and society in Britain, from the Contagious Diseases Acts to the National Health Service' in Roger Davidson and Lesley A. Hall (eds.), *Sex, Sin and Suffering: Venereal Disease and European Society Since 1870* (London, 2001), pp. 120–36.

[67] Evidence of Dr Brian O'Brien, 27 Feb. 1914, Qs 8208, *Royal Commission on Venereal Diseases, Final Report*.

[68] Ibid., Qs 8017–8.   [69] Ibid., Qs 8022.

[70] In Belfast, O'Brien noted that the number of patients with venereal disease treated in the infirmaries associated with the workhouses were men: 207 in 1911, 184 in 1912, and 119 in 1913. For women: 83 in 1911, 102 in 1912 and 141 in 1913. For the South Dublin Union the figures were: men: 195 in 1911, 225 in 1912 and 173 in 1913. In the North Dublin Union there were 84 in 1911, 96 in 1912 and 96 in 1913. Women, he noted, were not treated in the Dublin workhouse infirmaries and were sent instead to the Westmoreland Lock Hospital (ibid., Qs 8117–8120).

disease might have been higher in Belfast than has been acknowledged.[71] In O'Brien's view the treatment of the disease in Ireland was inadequate. He recommended that the means for diagnosis and institutional treatment should be subsidised by the government and that outpatient departments in hospitals, where men might be treated, should stay open late in the evening. He doubted that women would be keen to seek treatment. Like many medical men he was opposed to the notification of the disease, believing that notification would put people off seeking treatment.[72] O'Brien also noted that many cases of syphilis were treated by chemists and that quack medicines were also available and advertised in the press. He believed that most of the quack medicines came from England and 'sold to a very considerable extent' in Ireland.[73] Similarly, he observed that the great majority of women with venereal diseases were not treated in institutions and some were not treated at all, particularly in the early stages of the disease.[74] It is possible then that many more individuals were infected with these diseases than appeared in the statistics.

In England, by the end of the nineteenth century, the problems of venereal diseases and marriage were intertwined particularly as it related to parenthood. Venereal diseases represented a threat to the health and, thus, the future of the nation. Such concerns were not as prominent in Ireland at this time but resurfaced in the 1920s.[75]

With the establishment of the Irish Free State, nationalist rhetoric that linked sexual immorality with British soldiers was no longer credible. There was, however, growing concern about sexual morality in the country. The Inter-Departmental Committee of Inquiry regarding Venereal Disease was established in 1924 to 'make inquiries as to the steps necessary, if any, which are desirable to secure that the extent of venereal disease may be diminished'. The committee's report revealed that 'venereal disease was widespread throughout the country, and that it was disseminated largely by a class of girl who could not be regarded as a prostitute'.[76] Soldiers who contracted a sexually transmitted disease were obliged to identify the place and source of infection and it was suggested that, rather than being confined to urban areas, the disease

---

[71] Ibid., Qs 8198–8206.
[72] Ibid., Qs 7992–8295. His evidence was also reprinted in *The British Journal of Nursing*, 21 (March 1914), 256.
[73] Evidence of Dr Brian O'Brien, 27 Feb. 1914, Qs 8216– S8221, *Royal Commission on VD*, 1914.
[74] Ibid., Qs 7828.
[75] Susannah Riordan, 'Venereal disease in the Irish Free State: The politics of public health', *Irish Historical Studies*, 35, 139 (2007), 345–64.
[76] Report of the Inter-Departmental Committee of Inquiry Regarding Venereal Disease, p. 3 (NAI, 'VD in the Irish Free State', Department of the Taoiseach File, S 4183).

was to be found 'in every parish in Ireland'. It was also noted that prostitutes constituted the source of infection in only 30 per cent of cases. The Catholic priest and commentator, R. S. Devane maintained the older view that the source of the disease was to be found in the British army; and, in particular, among the Black and Tans who had travelled around the country. He wrote: 'In the past few years we have had wave after wave of men passing over the country ... It will be found that, *in many cases*, the girls who acted as camp followers to Black and Tans, etc., were the same who pursued the Free State troops, conveying in not a few cases infection'.[77]

The Report of the Committee of Inquiry Regarding Venereal Disease together with a number of other reports assessing sexual crime and prostitution in the state was never published. While the government had considered publishing an edited version of the VD inquiry, the Archbishop of Dublin, Edward Byrne, who was shown a copy of the report, suggested that it be delayed until it became evident that the incidence of VD had actually declined.[78] The publication of the report, it was believed, would have drawn attention to the conclusion that sexual immorality was far more common than the rhetoric of the newly established Irish Free State acknowledged.

Sexual Partners and Mistresses

A common theme in European folklore relates to the *ius primae noctis* or *droit de seigneur* – the sexual claims that landlords made to young virgin brides on their estates. In his study of such stories in Irish folklore, Seamus MacPhilib noted how they usually portrayed the landlord in a very negative light and described the ways in which local people tried to avoid granting him his *ius primae noctis*. They hid the news of the wedding from him or put an old woman in the bed to wait for him rather than the young bride. MacPhilib also linked the Irish folklore traditions of the *ius primae noctis* with other popular stories that described the 'sexual oppression or lasciviousness' of landlords as they demanded sexual favours from the wives of their tenants in lieu of rent; kept mistresses in houses on the estate and fathered numerous children outside of marriage, usually with daughters or wives of tenants.[79] According to many of these

---

[77] Ibid., p. 29. Emphasis in the original.
[78] Dr McDonnell's report on his interview with the Archbishop and a memo, 13 May 1927 (NAI, Department of the Taoiseach file, S4183).
[79] Séamus Mac Philib, '*Ius primae noctis* and the sexual image of Irish landlords in folk tradition and in contemporary accounts', *Béaloideas*, 56 (1988), 97–140.

stories, local girls were afraid to pass by a landlord for fear of attack. In County Antrim, one landlord was 'described as being so lustful that any girls who were due to pass by his house were said to have worn a 'protection' or had their private parts smeared with jam by their mothers, to feign menstruation or venereal disease'.[80]

These stories were a mixture of fact and fiction. As in other European countries where similar folklore survives, there is no convincing evidence that *ius primae noctis* existed in reality. Men in wealthy families, however, maintained mistresses, frequently from a lower class to themselves, and fathered children with them. Discrete notes survive in family papers of payments made by solicitors to estate owners' mistresses and their children. According to MacPhilib, one member of the Knights of Glin family in County Limerick in the mid-eighteenth century had several children born outside of marriage by a local woman, while a descendant in the nineteenth century was known as '*Ridire na mBan*' (the Knight of the Women).[81] In the 1790s, Arthur, 1st Earl of Annesley, was attracted to Sophia Connor who was the wife of his gardener, Martin Connor. According to her later trial for bigamy, Lord Annesley 'took a liking' to Mrs Connor and 'his rank in life made an impression on her. His lordship carried her off in his carriage to Dublin, where they lived together'. Annesley contrived to reconcile Mr Connor to the loss of his wife and Sophia later claimed that her husband had come to terms with the situation and had 'brought no action of crim con against Annesley', and that 'he did not disturb their happiness, but kept himself in a state of seclusion'. At some stage Annesley claimed to believe that Connor had died, and in 1797 he married Sophia and had two children by her. He died in 1802, and in 1810 a charge of bigamy was brought against Sophia to disprove her claim to be the Countess of Annesley and her son's right to his father's estate. As no evidence could be produced for her second marriage, she was found not guilty. She went to live in Paris until her death in 1850.[82]

Other landlords and men in positions of power in a local community undoubtedly behaved in a predatory manner, believing that their place in society allowed them to act as they wished with women in the locality. In April 1869 it was reported to the Lord Lieutenant that Hugh Bradshaw of Philipstown, County Tipperary, a landowner and magistrate, had been found murdered. There were those who believed that this was a typical agrarian murder instigated by his unhappy tenants. However, as one

---

[80] Ibid., 125.   [81] Ibid., 123.
[82] *Saunders's News-Letter*, 1 Nov. 1810. See also A. P. W. Malcolmson, *The Pursuit of the Heiress: Aristocratic Marriage in Ireland, 1740–1840* (2nd ed., Belfast, 2006), p. 7.

newspaper report put it, 'Landlords are prone to vices other than those signified by their unjust and tyrannical dealings with their tenantry'.[83] One of the main suspects in the case was a man named Allis, whose family were tenants of Bradshaw and who may have feared eviction by him. However, the local magistrates discovered in their investigations that Allis's sister, 'a very young girl', had been seduced by Bradshaw, a married man, and that she had been recently sent to England, a fact that implied pregnancy. In his report the magistrate noted 'this is but one of the very many acts of this character of which Mr Bradshaw had been accused' and he wrote he had no reason to believe that these stories were untrue. It appeared that Bradshaw was also having a sexual relationship with his housekeeper. He had previously acknowledged that he was the father of two illegitimate children born in the workhouse.[84] In this case no evidence could be found against Allis, and the community gave nothing away. No one was ever convicted of the murder, suggesting local support for the murderer and no sympathy for Bradshaw.

Stories of predatory landlords and male employers can give the impression that the women concerned had no choice or agency of their own. The judges and juries in trials involving adulterous relationships were inclined also to represent the women in this way. Occasionally, however, the voice of the woman comes through in police investigations of the case. When Maggie O'Connor, a domestic servant, and Patrick Shanny, a married man and her employer, were tried and acquitted of infanticide and concealment of birth in 1893, she stated clearly to the police: 'I allowed him to take liberties with me four times ... I was so fond of him and he was so good to me. I thought that no harm would come of it, he was such an old man. I would allow no young man to take such liberties with me'.[85] O'Connor was clearly genuinely fond of Shanny, and their sexual relationship was seemingly consensual and mutually

[83] *The Tipperary Free Press and Clonmel General Advertiser*, 4 May 1869. The authors are grateful to Dr Des Marnane for bringing this case to their attention. For a similar case see Nancy Murphy, *Guilty or Innocent? The Cormack Brothers: Trial, Execution and Exhumation* (Nenagh, 1997). Murphy analyses the October 1852 murder of John Ellis, a tenant and land agent in North Tipperary. A local landowner wrote of Ellis's character: 'His habits were immoral, flagrantly and scandalous[ly] immoral. As steward to a highly respected gentleman, he possessed facilities, and the command of money and used them to effect the ruin of several females; and it is generally believed that some of their relatives (worked on perhaps by other motives also) avenged their ruin in his blood'. Quoted in ibid., p. 29.

[84] NAI, CSO/RP/11937/1869.

[85] Quoted in Elaine Farrell, *'A Most Diabolical Deed': Infanticide and Irish Society, 1850–1900* (Manchester, 2013), p. 163. For fuller details of the case see Elaine Farrell (ed.), *Infanticide in the Irish Crown Files at Assizes, 1883–1900* (Dublin, 2012), pp. 194–204.

desirable. O'Connor's sexual ignorance led her to believe she would not become pregnant if they pursued such a relationship. It is also evident from the case that Shanny's wife and O'Connor's mother were cognisant of the facts, and their local community in Limerick city were also aware that O'Connor was pregnant outside marriage. Parental knowledge, in this instance at least, did not reveal any level of parental control

In his 1785 visitation report of the diocese of Cloyne and Ross, Bishop Mathew McKenna referred frequently to 'kept' women, 'concubines' and, less frequently, to 'mistresses'. This may reflect clerical fastidiousness in referring to women living with married men but the references suggest that this was not an uncommon phenomenon at the time.[86] Margaret Leeson narrated in her memoirs her life as a young woman when she was maintained by a succession of men. Written for publication, Leeson's account may not be a wholly accurate account of her life. A more honest view of a 'kept' woman is documented in the letters of Anne Henry to her lover, William Tennent, the Belfast businessman. The latter had a number of mistresses by whom he had more than twelve children. Henry was the mother of at least five. She met Tennent sometime before 1798 when he was imprisoned for four years in Scotland because he was suspected of membership of the United Irishmen. In 1798, Tennent's father, a Presbyterian minister, wrote that he had heard a rumour that a Scottish woman had arrived in Belfast claiming to be married to William and that he was the father of a number of her children. This may have been Anne Henry. Tennent's father passed on a message from William's mother that 'she would grudge and grieve to hear of your marriage with any of those base whores'.[87] William clearly agreed with his mother's sentiments as he did not marry Henry nor any of the other mothers of his existing children. When he returned to Belfast from Scotland he set about developing his sugar and other business interests. During this time Anne lived with William in Belfast along with her mother and five or six children, not all of them Anne's. William also began to build a second house in Belfast where he planned that Anne would live when he married. William made it clear to Anne that he would marry another woman, and that when he did their relationship would come to an end.[88] In February 1805, he began to search for a wife who would enhance his social and financial standing. He chose Eleanor

---

[86] Derr and MacKenna (eds.), 'Episcopal visitations of the diocese of Cloyne and Ross', 280, 283, 292, 296, 299, 302, 306, 311.
[87] Rev. John Tennent to William Tennent, 22 Oct. 1798 (PRONI, D/1748/B/1/317/16).
[88] Anne Henry to William Tennent, 20 Feb. 1805 (PRONI, D1748/B/1/136/11); same to same, 22 Feb. 1805 (PRONI, D1748/B/1/136/12).

Jackson, the daughter of a fellow United Irishman, whom he married in February 1805. Anne's pain, when he wrote to her from Dublin that he was about to marry, is palpable in her response:

Mr Knox brought me your letter. It has me completely miserable. It is vain for me to describe my feelings. May you be as happy as I am distracted. My sincere wish – my happiness did not last long. I thought myself blessed to be in the home with you. To please you was at all times the height of my wishes. You know it was my sincere attachment to you that caused me to be in my present situation. I will love you as long as I have life. This is more than I can bear.[89]

Despite William's talk of marriage, Anne had clearly hoped that he would not marry and would continue living with her. She reminded William of the time 'that you told me I had it in my power to prevent you from ever marrying. I wish I could do that now'.[90] William's marriage also meant that Anne, who was again pregnant with William's daughter, Theresa, had to move out of his house into the one that he was building for her. Within days of receiving the news that William was to marry, Anne was distressed and angry at the change that William's marriage imposed on her and her children. William had until his announcement of his marriage given her an allowance of £30 per month but was now proposing to change it to a £300 annuity. Anne queried why this reduction was necessary, as it was but a 'small income' to support her and her children. She also reminded William that her new house was not ready:

I ought to have all my cloths taken out of your house. I ought to leave it as soon as you would let me. My house is not ready yet. The back parlour and back room smokes greatly … the walls are extremely wet. I must buy cots. … I still hope you will have some regards for me and a wish to know [how] I am doing. The children will have but little opportunity to speak about me nor do I wish them to do it. … Oh what will become of me … I could behave myself but this is too much …[91]

Henry's description of her life in Belfast indicates that it was secretive and hidden. Apart from William Tennent, she saw few people other than her immediate family circle of her mother and her children. When Tennent was building the new house in Belfast in 1804–1805, Anne wrote of how she went down to see it in the morning when there was no one around as she was always 'ashamed to go out either when I am with child or after I have one'.[92] In 1805, following the announcement of Tennent's marriage, Anne told him in a letter that she intended from

---

[89] Anne Henry to William Tennent, 20 Feb. 1805 (PRONI, D1748/B/1/136/11).
[90] Anne Henry to William Tennent, 17 Feb. 1805 (PRONI, D1748/B/136/9).
[91] Anne Henry to William Tennent, 22 Feb. 1805 (PRONI, D1748/B/1/136/12).
[92] Anne Henry to William Tennent, 17 Oct.1804 (PRONI, D/1748/B/1/136/2).

then on 'to keep myself from being seen as much as possible. I have no
business to see anybody but my children. My conduct will be well
watched I am sure and almost sure I will not speak but there will be
some remarks placed on it'.[93] Later, when she moved into the new house,
she wrote to Tennent that she had not been out since 'I came here ... my
mother buys anything that is wanted'.[94]

Henry was more fortunate than many 'kept' women, because William
Tennent provided for her and her children.[95] When his wife died after less
than two years of marriage, he resumed his relationship with Anne Henry
and never remarried. She remained, however, living in a separate establishment and although her children regularly stayed with their father in his
rural residence in Tempo, their mother did not. Henry's letters also
suggest that she and Tennent resumed their relationship against the wishes
of both their families. In an undated letter written after Tennent's wife had
died, Henry wrote of sneaking out of her house unbeknownst to her
mother or daughter Jane to see Tennent: 'I long for a wet evening but
you must let me know the night you intend to keep in town because I must
say to my mother that I am asked out to tea that evening as I never go out
she would think it strange if I would without letting her know of it'.[96]
Henry also avoided meeting members of Tennent's family. In 1817, for
example, she wrote from Belfast to Tennent in Tempo noting that she
'kept more out of the way than if you were at home nor do I go to the upper
Garden but when I am sure I will not meet with any of your family'.[97]

No correspondence from William Tennent to Anne Henry survives,
but he clearly had great affection if not love for her. He was with her for
many years before he married, and maintained a relationship with her
following the death of his wife. Nonetheless, he also had other lovers and
when he married, he wrote in very romantic terms of his sense of loss
when his wife died in 1807. In a draft letter, he recalled to his wife's
family friend, Eleanor Bond, the 'pleasant and delicious days that we
enjoyed together'. He described their daily routine: 'When I came home
she was at the door to receive me in her endearing embrace. If I stayed
longer than expected she was on the road and in the avenue to meet me
with that sweet smile of goodness which won my heart and fixed it to

---

[93] Anne Henry to WilliamTennent, 22 Feb. 1805 (PRONI, D1748/B/1/136/12); Anne
Henry to William Tennent, Feb. 1805 (PRONI, D/1748/B/1/136/12).
[94] Anne Henry to William Tennent, no date (PRONI, D1748/B/1/136/16).
[95] See *Freeman's Journal*, 10 Dec. 1842, for a law suit in which barristers for a soldier
claimed that he was not legally obliged to continue his annuity to his lover after he
married another woman.
[96] Anne Henry to William Tennent, no date (PRONI, D1748/B/1/1/36/7).
[97] Anne Henry to William Tennent, 17 Sept. 1817 (PRONI, D1748/B/1/136/15).

herself. But now, alas, I have no one to receive me …'.[98] Tennent's wife, Eleanor, appears to have been aware of his relationship with Henry and of his large family as the children spent time in Tennent's house in Belfast. His daughter, Isabella, for example, lived with Henry but went over every Saturday to her father's house.[99]

Tennent entrusted Anne Henry with the upbringing of his children. She advised him on their education and reported to him on their activities. One of Tennent's eldest children, William, whose mother was another of Tennent's mistresses complained that his father treated Henry far more generously than he did his mother.[100] Tennent also appeared to have ignored the surprise and shock of friends and neighbours and brought his only legitimate offspring, his daughter Letitia, to stay with Anne Henry in her Belfast house after her mother's death. Eleanor Bond wrote to him that she had heard

from everyone ever since I came here that she [Letitia] is at home, with many, several [of] your children – but not a wife's – let me go further – that their <u>mothers</u> are in the town. Reflect a moment, would you think it right for another so to do? Would you have taken her dear mother had she been so situated?[101]

Bond advised Tennent to send Letitia to a boarding school.[102] Tennent funded the education of all his children, although he took special care with Letitia's and took Eleanor Bond's advice to have her educated in Dublin. Letitia also spent a great deal of time in her grandmother's home in Monaghan. She did, however, also get to know her half sisters and brothers in Belfast. At a later stage, in the discussions concerning Letitia's own marriage, the 'experiment' of her upbringing was raised as an issue that might hinder her chances of making a good match.[103]

Letitia Tennent cannot have been unaware of the impact on her father of her comment in one of her letters that she and her new husband were enjoying married life and that she was sure that James enjoyed her company and 'seems to have no inclination to look for happiness beyond our own fireside; he has neither taste nor wish … for company … and I am certain that so long as I can make home comfortable and agreeable to him he will never look for employment elsewhere …'[104]

---

[98] Draft letter, William Tennent to Eleanor Bond, 5 March 1807 (PRONI, D/1748/B/1/26/5).
[99] Anne Henry to William Tennent, no date, c. 1805–1806 (PRONI, D1748/B/1/136/16).
[100] William Tennent Junior to Robert Tennent, 28 Feb. 1803 (PRONI, D/1748/B/218/1).
[101] Eleanor Bond to William Tennent, no date (PRONI, D1748/B/1/26/16).
[102] Eleanor Bond to William Tennent, 5 Oct. 1807 (PRONI, D1748/B/1/26/15).
[103] Letitia Emmerson to William Tennent (PRONI, D1748/B/1/318/XX). See pp. 141–2, 144 for Letitia Tennent's courtship.
[104] Letitia Emmerson to William Tennent, 13 Sept. 1831 (PRONI, D1748/B/1/318/22).

Conclusion

When tales of sexual immorality came to court, Irish people flocked to hear the details. Newspapers revelled in the descriptive accounts of sex supplied by lawyers in court, or those who witnessed intimate encounters, whether in murder trials or criminal conversation disputes. The reading public enjoyed these sexual narratives and no doubt sided with defendants or litigants as their emotions dictated. The curiosity of family and neighbours made a sexual life outside marriage a difficult undertaking for most couples. Despite such difficulty we can see in this chapter the level of non-conformity that existed in sexual matters amongst individuals and couples, over a long time period. It can be viewed, for instance, in cohabitation, adultery, the keeping of mistresses and the advantage taken of women servants in households. We note also women's consensual sexual behaviour. The idealisation of women as asexual beings did not always translate into actual behaviour, and the ways in which illicit sexuality was reported kept it firmly in the public domain. Both the Church and the law increasingly oversaw the implementation of sexual norms in society and perpetuated ideals for male and female sexual behaviour. Whatever those norms were, there were always those who sought to kick against them.

The contradictions between public rhetoric on sexual morality and the private lives of individuals is also evident, particularly in the latter part of the time period explored in this volume. As we have seen Kevin O'Higgins was a minister in the government of the Irish Free State, which promoted strong supervision of the sexual behaviour of Irish citizens. Yet, although a married man, he was by his own admission besotted by Lady Lavery, a married woman. Given the hidden nature of adulterous relations, it is difficult to be precise about changing attitudes to sex outside marriage. Newspaper reports detailing the stories of sexual misdemeanours that were told in courts in the nineteenth century fade away in the 1920s. Their disappearance from public inspection does not, however, mean that they no longer took place.

9   Bigamy

In February 1726, William Taylor appeared before the elders of the Presbyterian church in Plunkett Street/Usher's Quay in Dublin. He reported to the session

that the Woman which they say is his Wife lives in Cavin Street and if it be thot fit he wod bring her here. He was desired to bring her. She came and being askt if she was married to Wm Taylor, she sayd that she was about nine years agoe, and that she did not know any thing of his haveing another Wife when she married him. That about 3 months after wards she heard of it, and left him, & has never lived with him since. And she married anotr man, who has now left her and gone with another Woman. And William Taylor some time agoe proposed to take her again and designed to leave the Hospital[1] [where he resided] and they were to come together next Easter. She was told her great sin in marrying as she did, and that she cannot lawfully live with this man. She was desired to consider the matter, and if she did not believe what we sayd to speak to her own Minister about it, for she sayd she belongd to the Establist [sic] Church.

He [Taylor] was admonisht to considr his sin in marrying as He did, & liveing in adultrie, and the sin which he has been the cause of in others, & the Evil of goeing to live with this woman who has another Husband now liveing. He was advised to live single and told the Judgmt of the session: that he can neither live with this woman nor marry anothr without being guilty of adultry. He was desird to considr what was sayd to him and attend our next meeting.[2]

Taylor's situation – his involvement in bigamy and adultery – reveals his repudiation of conventional expectations of marriage and the duties of a husband. Taylor appeared before the session over a period of eight years but was not readmitted to church services. He was told by the session that 'his case is so involved by his sinful marriages, that we cannot tell how to make his way clear'. It was observed that 'he does not

---

[1] Royal Kilmainham Hospital was established in 1684 for retired and injured soldiers.
[2] Plunkett Street/Usher's Quay Session Book, 1726–1766, 14 Feb. 1727, 21 March 1727, 18 Feb. 1729 (now in the custody of Clontarf and Scots Presbyterian Church). The authors are grateful to Hilary Fairman for permission to consult it.

express any sense of his sin and guilt but endeavours to vindicate what he has done'.[3]

As will be discussed in more detail in Chapter 12, the Irish Presbyterian church sanctioned the granting of divorce and permission to remarry if an individual could convince a Presbytery that his or her spouse had deserted or had committed adultery. The Presbyteries heard petitions from men and women who had married again when, as they claimed, their first spouse had disappeared or married another. Others told the Presbytery that they, like Taylor's second wife, had only discovered after they had gone through the marriage service that their spouse was already married.[4] Most of the petitioners who admitted to a bigamous marriage were seeking readmission to church services, particularly baptism for their children. The Presbyteries' response to such requests varied but the elders were often surprisingly tolerant of men and women whom they deemed had genuinely believed that their first spouse was dead. In 1730, for example, when James Turner admitted to the Aghadowey session that his first wife was still alive when he married the second, the elders and minister were forgiving and noted that 'as the fact was committed so long ago as the wars and his being in the army took him away from where his first wife found it convenient to stay, it is agreed that he only shall stand once Sabbath day'.[5] A similar leniency seems to have been granted to John Glespy, who acknowledged to the Glascar session in 1818 that the husband of his late wife, to whom he had been married for twenty years, lived for five years after their marriage. The case was referred to the Presbytery of Down but the Presbytery sent it back to the local session 'to deal with him as they thought fit'. The session agreed to rebuke Glespy in public and restore him to the congregation.[6]

As the Taylor case suggests, it was easier to maintain a long term bigamous relationship in the anonymity of a large city like Dublin than in a rural area. There are more cases relating to bigamy recorded in the minute book of the Presbyterian session of Plunkett Street/Usher's Quay in Dublin than in any of the other session or Presbytery minute books looked at for this study. In the seven-year period, from 1726 to 1733, six individuals came before the Dublin session who had, like Taylor, either remarried while their first spouse was still alive or had married someone who had a living spouse. In one of the longest running cases, Mary

---

[3] Ibid.   [4] See Chapter 12.

[5] Evidence from the Aghadowey session minutes, 1702–1761 cited in John M. Barkley, 'A history of the ruling eldership in Irish Presbyterianism' (2 vols., unpublished MA thesis, Queen's University Belfast, 1952), i, p. 168.

[6] Evidence from the Glascar session minutes, 17 April 1818, cited in Barkley, 'A history of the ruling eldership', i, p. 266.

Lewsley was suspended from the community because she had married a man who had another wife 'some years' prior to her appearance before the session in November 1728. The session was sympathetic and accepted the view of a male and female member of the church that Lewsley had been deceived into marrying the man and that when she discovered that he was married she had left him. In May 1729, Lewsley was restored to the congregation and permitted to receive communion. Less than two years later, however, Mary Lewsley was summoned to reappear before the session because she had begun to live with the man again and had had a child by him. Lewsley claimed that she had been again deceived by the man who told her that his wife was dead. When she discovered that this was untrue she had left him once more. The session took over two years to consider Lewsley's 'scandalous sin', during which time she was urged to fast and pray for forgiveness. Eventually, however, Lewsley was once again admitted as a member of the congregation.[7]

Catholic canon law prohibited remarriage under any circumstances while a spouse was still alive. Unlike the elders in the Presbyterian church, the Catholic clergy required proof that a former spouse was dead. The difficulties that this law presented may have encouraged some to take their chances and remarry in the hope that their former marriage might not be discovered. In 1752, parish priests in the diocese of Ossory reported five cases of bigamy, which suggests that while it was not prevalent it was not an uncommon phenomenon.[8] There were also accusations that itinerant priests were willing to marry couples whose spouses were still alive. In late eighteenth-century Galway, a man applied to the local parish priest to marry him. He acknowledged that he had been married before and that his first wife was still alive but living with another man. When the priest refused to marry him, the man complained of the 'hardship' of church law and announced that 'he would marry and though he acknowledged the impropriety of his act he said he would do penance before he would die'. To the local priest's annoyance, the man was subsequently married by an itinerant priest.[9] In another incident that also reflected an impatience with Catholic regulation on remarriage, Father John O'Sullivan reported that he had spent four years denouncing a woman who had cohabited with a man whose wife had emigrated to America fourteen years before and 'was never heard of since'. O'Sullivan

---

[7] Plunkett Street/Usher's Quay Session Book, 1726–1766, pp. 45, 47, 53, 63, 111, 114, 115, 116, 122, 123.
[8] Christopher O'Dwyer (ed.), 'Archbishop Butler's visitation Book', *Archivium Hibernicum*, 33 (1975), 1–90; 34 (1975), 1–49.
[9] Galway Diocesan Archives, Box C/8.

noted that: 'It was very difficult to get them to separate for they with no small share of plausibility contended that the fair presumption was in favour of the wife being dead when she had not been heard of directly or indirectly for the space of fourteen years.'[10]

Even couples who wished to abide by canon found it impossible to locate proof that a husband or wife, who had disappeared many years before, was deceased. In 1873, James Carroll appealed to Paul Cullen, Archbishop of Dublin, for amelioration of his marital position. He and his wife were Catholic and had been married in a Catholic service. Carroll was aware that his wife had been married twenty years previously to a soldier who had deserted her. They had both agreed not to give the full facts to the priest who married them in case the marriage would be delayed. Subsequently, Carroll confessed to a priest who told him that he should not consider his marriage as valid until the death of his wife's first husband was confirmed. He had two children with his wife and said he had endeavoured to act in accordance with the rules provided by his confessor. He noted, however, that his position was unbearable and 'my life an [sic] hell on earth'. He had done all he could to look for the former husband, even placing advertisements, but to no effect.[11] Francis Byrne devised a more ingenious solution to his failure to find his separated wife, Mary Clarke. He secured a death certificate for a woman of the same name and presented it to the priest, who married him![12]

The ecclesiastical authorities in the Catholic and Presbyterian churches thus imposed penalties on members of their congregations who violated their respective institution's regulations on bigamy and remarriage. It is important to note, however, that bigamy was from 1635 a criminal offence that was prosecuted in the civil rather than the ecclesiastical courts. An individual who wished to invalidate a marriage in civil law on the grounds of bigamy was obliged to seek a solution in the civil courts. The destruction of court records means, however, that we have little information on rates of bigamy before the nineteenth century. In this chapter we will, therefore, make use of surviving nineteenth-century court records and newspaper reports of trials to explore the motives behind bigamous marriages and what they reveal about how

[10] John O'Sullivan, 'Praxis Parochi', p. 700 (Kerry Diocesan Archives, Killarney). The differing laws on consanguinity observed by Catholic canon law and the state could also result in a Catholic who remarried following the voiding of his or her marriage by the Catholic authorities being accused of the crime of bigamy in the civil courts. See Chapter 1.

[11] Laity, July–Dec. 1873 (DDA, Cullen Papers 335/7/42).

[12] Bernard Farrell to Cardinal Paul Cullen, Nov. 1876 (DDA, Cullen Papers, File 1, Secular Priests, 1876, 322/6/94).

some individuals understood marriage and commitment. How were these illegal marriages discovered? How did defendants justify their behaviour and what sentences were imposed on those found guilty?

The Law on Bigamy

The criminalisation of bigamy in England and Wales dates to an act of 1604, which decreed the death penalty for those convicted, the exception being where a first spouse, even if living, remained continually overseas for seven years, or a divorce or annulment had been secured.[13] Bigamy was committed when a married person, whose spouse was still alive, went through a ceremony of marriage with another person, whether the second marriage took place in Ireland or abroad.[14] Marriage itself was tied up with the legitimacy of children, rights to property and inheritance, and the use of family assets. Bigamy undermined the whole concept of marriage, and the legal security that a legitimate marriage offered to wives and families. If allowed, bigamy, it was believed, could disrupt the stability of society.

The English legislation of 1604 was not enacted in Ireland until 1635.[15] This was followed by additional legislation in 1725, which made bigamy an act punishable by death or transportation. If a first spouse was absent from the country for seven years or more there could be a presumption of death, but if he or she returned even after that period then the second marriage was deemed null and void.[16] It is unclear how many, if any, bigamists in Ireland were executed for this offence. In 1724 John Cavendish was capitally convicted for bigamy 'but he, throwing himself on the Clergy, was only sentenced to transportation for life, with a confiscation of his goods and chattles'.[17] In England six people were executed for bigamy between 1674 and 1800.[18] The consolidating

---

[13] Bernard Capp, 'Bigamous marriage in early modern England', *Historical Journal*, 52, 3 (2009), 539. The type of 'divorce' secured was not specified in the 1604 legislation and was the subject of subsequent legal debate.

[14] Offences against the Person Act. 24 & 25 Vict. c.100, section 57. 1861.

[15] An Act for the Restraining of All Persons from Marriage till Their Former Wives and Former Husbands Be Dead. 10 Charles 1, c21 Ir. 1635.

[16] An Act to Prevent Marriages by Degraded Clergymen and Popish Priests and for Preventing Marriage Consummated from Being Avoided by Pre-contracts and for the More Effectual Punishing of Bigamy. 12 Geo I c3 Ir. 1725.

[17] *Finn's Leinster Journal*, 20 April 1774. Anyone who could read, and thus was deemed capable of becoming a clergyman, could claim immunity from capital punishment for certain offences. See Neal Garnham, *The Courts, Crime and the Criminal Law in Ireland 1692–1760* (Dublin, 1996), p. 23.

[18] Maria Nicolaou, *Divorced, Beheaded, Sold: Ending English Marriage, 1500–1847* (Barnsley, 2014), p. 31.

Irish act of 1829 saw the maximum sentence reduced to 'being trans-ported beyond the seas for a term of seven years'.[19] Current figures for Ireland show that forty-three bigamists were transported to Australia and Van Diemen's Land between1805 and 1852, when transportation ended. No woman bigamist appears to have been transported. In 1861, under the Offences against the Person Act, the maximum sentence was reduced to penal servitude of not less than three years and not more than seven, or imprisonment, with or without hard labour, for not more than two years.[20]

In bigamy cases, it was not sufficient to prove a marriage by reputation; a witness to the marriage had to be called to court, or the original register produced. The first wife was not considered a competent witness, whereas the second wife was.[21] A prosecution was dependent on the first or second wife, or a member of their families, informing the authorities of a bigamous situation. The first wife could not prosecute as it was the second wife who was considered the victim in these cases. James Connell, tried in Dublin in 1808, was discharged when his second wife failed to 'appear to prosecute'.[22] When Mary Anne Clarke 'a plain-looking young woman, bearing an infant in her arms', went to court in 1840, to charge her husband with bigamy she claimed that he had remarried three months after he had become her husband. However, his second wife failed to appear to give evidence against him and the first wife was not allowed to summons her to court. The judge noted that the second wife must 'complain voluntarily' as it was she, in the eyes of the law, who was the 'injured party'. The husband was discharged.[23] Such cases suggest some level of collusion between a bigamist and his second wife, and reveal that there may have been an agreement between them concerning the charge of bigamy.

Extent of Bigamy

By the early nineteenth century, bigamy trials were a common feature at assizes throughout the country. In 1812 the prosecution, opening the case for bigamy against Robert Robinson, noted that it was a crime 'too often committed, and seldom prosecuted in this country; [it is] a crime

---

[19] An Act for Consolidating and Amending the Statutes in Ireland Relating to Offences against the Person. 10 Geo. IV c.34. 1829. s.26.

[20] 24 & 25 Vict. c.100, s.57.

[21] Leonard Shelford, *A Practical Treatise on the Law of Marriage and Divorce* (Philadelphia, 1841), pp. 185–90. On marriage by reputation see also Chapter 1.

[22] *Dublin Evening Post*, 22 Sept. 1808.

[23] *Freeman's Journal*, 18 Jan. 1840. For a case in which the magistrate refused to prosecute because a wife could not prosecute, see also *Connaught Journal*, 4 June 1829.

[which] stands pre-eminently high in the scale of offences; a crime at once preying on the best interests of society, and annihilating the happiness of the individual who happens to be its victim'.[24] Not much had changed by 1829 when a clergyman, who was present in the court, took the opportunity to direct the attention of the magistrates to the 'fearful growth of that crime and to the baneful effects on the morals of the people'.[25]

In Ireland, bigamy was primarily a lower-class phenomenon and bigamists rarely married outside of their own class. At a time when divorce, as we shall see later in the volume, was not a feasible option for most couples, desertion and self-made divorces became the means by which many husbands and wives separated. As discussed in Chapters 1 and 2, the ambiguity of Irish law on what constituted a valid marriage meant that some believed or claimed to believe that their first marriage by a couple beggar or a Presbyterian clergyman had not been a valid one. They did not expect to be prosecuted for marrying again. Others argued that they had secured a divorce from the couple beggar which was not, however, within the legal remit of the latter to issue.[26] An exploration of the penalties imposed allow us to gauge the risks that individuals took in undergoing a second, or even third, marriage while their first spouse was still alive. The figures we have relating to committals to prison, and judicial and criminal statistics, suggest that between 1805 and 1919 there were at least 1,030 individuals arrested and/or prosecuted for this offence, averaging about eight cases per year.[27] These figures are under-estimates as they do not include any cases for the years between 1815 and 1821, or for the single years 1897 and 1918.

At least 692 individuals (about 67 per cent) were convicted on bigamy charges between 1805 and 1919. The greatest number of arrests and the highest conviction rates are to be found in 1827, which saw twenty-seven arrests and twelve convictions; 1828 with thirty arrests and twenty-one convictions; 1842 with twenty-one arrests and thirteen convictions; and 1843 with sixteen arrests and nine convictions.[28] It is worth noting the increase in bigamy cases in the 1840s, a decade, as we have seen in Chapter 1, when there was considerable controversy concerning marriage law in Ireland and, in particular, marriages conducted by Presbyterian

---

[24] An Eminent Barrister, *A Report of the Trial of Robert Robinson, for Bigamy, Tried in the Sessions House, Green Street* (Dublin, 1812), p. 2.
[25] See Chapter 1.   [26] See Chapter 2.
[27] If we accept an average of eight cases per year then the years between 1815 and 1821 would have produced in excess of fifty-six cases of bigamy.
[28] The figures for 1815–1821 are not available. Figures from prison committals and judicial and criminal statistics from 1865 are probably more reliable than the earlier figures.

Table 9.1 *Bigamy cases, 1805–1919*

Date	Crimes committed	Acquitted	Not proven/No bills	Convicted
1805–1814	56	41	5	3
1815–1821		no figures available		
1822–1830	96	28	26	42
1831–1840	79	21	27	28
1841–1850	114	22	20	72
1851–1860	72	19	2	51
1861–1870	95	13	3	72
1871–1880	92	10	5	75
1881–1890	87	8	5	70
1891–1900*	90	3	0	67
1901–1910	116	10	3	91
1911–1919*	133	5	3	120

* No figures available for 1897 and 1918.
Source: *Prison Committals* (Dublin, 1805–1861) and *Criminal and Judicial Statistics, Ireland* (Dublin, 1865–1919)

ministers.[29] The widespread social disruption caused by the Great Famine in that decade may also have had an impact on bigamy figures.

In 1919 there were twenty-four cases of bigamy before the courts: all the accused were convicted, with fourteen individuals serving prison sentences. It is clear that by the early years of the twentieth century, bigamy was an unacceptable transgression and conviction rates were greater than ever before. The number of arrests for bigamy was higher in the first two decades of the twentieth century even though the population of the country had declined considerably since 1850. Between 1911 and 1919, as revealed in Table 9.1, there were 133 arrests for bigamy with 121 convictions. The social disruption caused by the First World War saw a number of soldiers being convicted of bigamy. The greater movement of individuals into large towns and cities in Ireland in this period also provided opportunities to marry again within a community where an individual and his or her family were not known.

Who Were the Bigamists?

An examination of 205 bigamy cases from 1818 to 1877 gives us some indication of the backgrounds of those convicted of bigamy.[30]

[29] See Chapter 1. See also Maebh Harding, 'The comeback of the medieval marriage *per verba de praesenti* in nineteenth-century bigamy cases' in Niamh Howlin and Kevin Costello (eds.), *Law and the Family in Ireland, 1800–1950* (London, 2017), pp. 24–43.
[30] The cases are derived from the authors' Irish Prison database.

Table 9.2 *Sample of 205 bigamists, 1818–1877*

	Numbers	Age					
		20s	30s	40s	50s	60s	70s
Men:	187	92	50	24	16	2	3
Women:	18	12	3	1	1	1	

Source: Authors' database

As Table 9.2 notes bigamy was a crime of the younger man and woman. When occupations were noted, the men were almost all from the lower classes and included labourers (thirty-four), servants (nine), sailors (six) and members of the artisan class: weavers (three), masons (four), shoe-makers (four), carpenters (four). At a middle-class level, there were two apothecaries and one barrister. Many of the occupations of these men offered them mobility and an ability to practise their trade in new loca-tions. Serving as a soldier was an advantage for men who wished to commit bigamy, as they were often able to hide their marital status and they were, of course, regularly on the move to another posting. Over the period 1805–1919, where we have information on occupations of those prosecuted for bigamy, at least 200 individuals were soldiers. Fourteen of the women had no occupation listed, while one was an artificial flower seller, another a labourer and two were servants.

Bigamy was, however, a crime committed overwhelmingly by men. In the cases noted in the available Irish prison registers, 95 per cent of those convicted were men. It is also evident that women received lesser sen-tences than men. Bigamy prosecutions were also generally successful, particularly after the resolution of the ambiguity over the status of Pres-byterian marriages. Between 1822 and 1840 the average conviction rate was 44 per cent. Between 1841 and 1850 it was 63 percent, and from 1851 the conviction rate never went below 72 per cent. Between 1911 and 1919 the conviction rate was about 90 per cent.[31]

About forty men were transported for bigamy, the last being in August 1853. The sentences became generally lighter as the nineteenth century progressed and, after the 1850s, there was less consistency in sentencing, with prisoners receiving years or months with or without hard labour.

---

[31] Ginger Frost has noted that in England and Wales there were an average of ninety-eight bigamy trials per year between 1857 and 1904. Ginger S. Frost, *Living in Sin: Cohabiting as Husband and Wife in Nineteenth-Century England* (Manchester, 2008), p. 72.

Table 9.3 *Sentences of sample of 205 bigamists, 1818–1877**

	7 years transportation	5 years penal servitude	4 years penal servitude	18 months	12 months	6 months	3 months +	Discharged
					Prison			
Men:	34	16	14	20	16	16		
Women:				1		4	1	12

* Seventy-one individuals unaccounted.
Source: Authors' database

The women fared much better than the men. The shortest sentence awarded to a woman was to be detained for twenty-four hours.[32]

Whatever numbers we have it is also useful to keep in mind that there were probably many other couples in bigamous relationships who were never prosecuted.[33] For instance, we have no idea of the extent to which Irish migrant workers might have established second families in Britain in the nineteenth and twentieth centuries. Similarly, we do not know how frequently Irish men and women were involved in bigamous marriages when they left for countries beyond Britain. References to such cases exist. The Reverend Collin, who kept a marriage register relating to the Lutheran temple in Philadelphia between 1794 and 1806, noted a number of Irish couples who came to him to marry. In January 1794 he wrote that Margaret Power came to see him to ask for a second marriage certificate as her husband, who had left her on the evening of the marriage, had taken the first one with him. She was a twenty-seven-year-old widow and he was twenty-six; both were natives of Ireland. In taking the certificate her husband took away proof of the marriage. A married woman was a more respectable woman and a marriage certificate was necessary to prove her marital status if she required a decent occupation, even that of servant.[34]

While the figures for bigamy are not large, an exploration of the crime offers another perspective from which we can view how marriage was understood in the period and how individuals endeavoured to rid

[32] This sentence was imposed on Bridget Tierney/Scannell in Limerick in 1874. Source: bigamy database.
[33] Frost maintains that perhaps one in five bigamy cases in England Wales made it to court. Frost, *Living in Sin*, pp. 72–3.
[34] E. Klepp and B. G. Smith, 'The records of Gloria Dei Church: Marriages and "remarkable occurrences," 1794–1806', *Pennsylvania History*, 53, 2 (April 1986), 129. Further Irish cases appear on pp. 132, 133, 134, 136, 137, 140, 145, 147.

themselves of an unwanted partner, and, more widely, how couples viewed separation and divorce. Readers of Irish newspapers would have been familiar with reports of bigamy trials and, as with other court proceedings relating to marriage, the salacious details in English bigamy cases were also copied by Irish newspaper editors.[35]

Mixed Marriages

As we have seen in Chapter 1, legislation to validate marriages performed by Presbyterian ministers was enacted in 1738 and 1782. The latter act unintentionally contributed to an increase in bigamous marriages as it was interpreted by many as permitting dissenting ministers to preside over marriages between Presbyterians and members of the established church. This was not an accurate reading of the legislation and, consequently, there was considerable confusion among the public as well as within the courts as to what constituted a valid marriage conducted by a Presbyterian minister. The result was emergency legislation to validate marriages by dissenting ministers, some of which were in fact bigamous under the existing law.[36]

The differing religious beliefs of partners to a marriage could also be used as a defence to undermine a charge of bigamy. As noted in Chapter 1, an act passed by the Irish parliament in 1745 voided any marriage of two Protestants or of a Protestant and a Catholic celebrated by a Catholic priest.[37] This prohibition was not lifted until 1871. Before that time, therefore, a 'mixed marriage' that had been witnessed by a Catholic priest could be used as a defence in a bigamy trial, with defendants pleading that one of the partners to the marriage had lied or had not revealed their religious background to the presiding minister.[38]

In 1842, Daniel Robinson married Anne Griffith, a Catholic, before a Catholic priest, John Madden. The cleric declared that 'he had heard he [Robinson] was a protestant, but he did not tell me he was'. The priest did not make further enquiries to ascertain Robinson's true religion. Griffith and Robinson had lived together before their marriage and had had children. Madden stated that 'it was to take them out of this course of sin' that he had married them, the necessity of respectability

---

[35] The most infamous case of the period was the 1776 trial of the Duchess of Kingston for bigamy. The trial was held in Westminster Hall at the House of Lords. Over four thousand spectators filled the hall, with tickets costing in the region of £20. See Matthew J. Kinservik (ed.), 'The Production of a Female Pen': Anna Larpent's Account of the Duchess of Kingston's Bigamy Trial of 1776 (Yale, 2004).

[36] See pp. 48–53.

[37] An Act for Annulling All Marriages to be Celebrated by Any Popish Priest between Protestant and Protestant, or between Protestant and Papist. 19 Geo. II c.13. 1745.

[38] See pp. 40–53, 55–6.

overcoming any religious qualms the cleric might have had. The judge, however, declared that Robinson's marriage to Griffith was null and void and Robinson was acquitted of a charge of bigamy.[39] The verdict, issued at a time when the validity of marriages by Presbyterian ministers was being questioned, provoked public controversy, with one southern newspaper commenting that it was 'additional proof of the insulting character and immoral tendency of the Established Church in this country. The sacred institution of marriage is considered by the law to be null, in the case of persons of different creeds being united by any minister but one of the establishment'.[40]

The validity of a 'mixed marriage' was also the key argument in one of the most infamous bigamy trials of the nineteenth century: that of Major William Yevelerton and Theresa Longworth. The couple had first met in 1852 but by 1858 Yelverton had developed a relationship with another woman, Emily Forbes, whom he later married. The real issue in dispute was whether there had been a valid marriage between Yelverton and Longworth. The case was tried five times, with two trials in Dublin and two in Edinburgh; the final decision was made in the House of Lords. In the first Irish case a Mr Thurwall had taken an action against Yelverton for payment of over £250 for board and lodgings provided by him to Theresa Longworth, whom he claimed was Yelverton's wife. Theresa was a Catholic and Yelverton a Protestant. The defence's case was that there had been no marriage and hence she was not Yelverton's wife. Longworth claimed the couple had been first married in Scotland and then in Ireland, but the marriage had remained a secret. Yelverton denied any marriage had taken place but noted that the couple had cohabited for many years. The Irish judgement awarded Thurwall the costs he had incurred in keeping Longworth, clearly implying the couple had married. At the same time, Longworth had instituted cases in England and Scotland for a restitution of conjugal rights. Yelverton appealed and eventually the House of Lords ruled that the first marriage, between a Catholic and Protestant, conducted by a Catholic priest was invalid, and thus Yelverton's marriage to Emily Forbes was lawful.[41]

By the 1860s, bigamy cases based on the religious disparity of the couple to be married were rare. In 1865, Thomas Fanning pleaded not

---

[39] *Cork Examiner*, 15 Aug. 1842.   [40] *The Southern Patriot*, 9 March 1844.

[41] Anon., *The Yelverton Marriage Case, Thelwall v Yelverton, Comprising an Authentic and Unabridged Account of the Most Extraordinary Trial of Modern Times* ... (London, n.d., c. 1861); Arvel B. Erickson and John R. McCarthy, 'The Yelverton case: Civil legislation and marriage', *Victorian Studies*, 14, 3 (March 1971), 275–291; Lauren Harmsen Kiehna, 'Sensation and the fourth estate: *The Times* and the Yelverton bigamy trials', *Victorian Periodicals Review*, 47, 1 (Spring 2014), 87–104.

guilty to a charge of bigamy. His first wife was a Protestant and they had married in a Protestant service. His second marriage to a Catholic was celebrated by a Catholic priest. Fanning's defence was that he was in fact a Protestant, but that he had lied to his second wife and told her and the presiding priest that he was a Catholic. The prosecution cited similar cases tried in English courts in which the defendants were found guilty because they had deceived their wife and the minister. The judge in the Irish court, however, reserved judgment and the case was referred to the judges on the Queen's Bench for a verdict.[42] A minority of the justices pronounced in favour of upholding the conviction and finding Fanning guilty of bigamy but the majority, citing the 1745 Act, determined that the second marriage was null and void. The case against Fanning was dismissed. Among the judges who argued that the second marriage was valid and that Fanning should be indicted for bigamy was Thomas O'Hagan, who became the first Catholic lord chancellor in 1868. In his judgment he described the 1745 Act as 'one of the last lingering remnants of the penal laws'. It may not, therefore, have been a coincidence that it was during O'Hagan's time as lord chancellor that legislation was passed that legitimised marriages of Protestants and Catholics celebrated by Catholic priests.[43]

Uncovering Bigamy

How were bigamous marriages uncovered? First wives were frequently alerted to their husband's second marriage by accident. For instance, in 1822 the *Ennis Chronicle* announced the marriage of a Miss McNamara to Lieutenant John Wilson Pollin of the 40th regiment. The notice was copied by a number of newspapers and the first Mrs Pollin, living in Naas, County Kildare, read the notice and informed the father of the new bride of her situation. Lieutenant Pollin was soon lodged in jail.[44] Anne Read had married Martin Kavanagh in 1821, and saw him prosecuted for bigamy in 1830. In 1839 her brother-in-law informed her that her husband had now taken a third wife. Anne was told the couple would 'take tea in a certain house in Boot Lane on a certain evening' and she turned up to confront Kavanagh. His new wife declared 'she had as much call to Martin Kavanagh as she [Anne] had'.[45] Esther Ferris, a servant, discovered that her husband, also a servant, was married when she went to meet him from his place of work and saw him with another woman who turned out to be his first wife. When Anne McCloskey was arrested for

---

[42] *Waterford Chronicle*, 24 Nov. 1865.   [43] *Freeman's Journal*, 4 May 1866; *DIB*.
[44] *Freeman's Journal*, 19 June 1822.   [45] *Clonmel Herald*, 25 Dec. 1839.

bigamy in Belfast in 1891 she asked the policeman whether it was her first husband who had told on her.[46] James Welles's bigamy was uncovered in 1895 when his second wife found a letter he had penned to his first wife, inquiring as to her situation and how things stood between them.[47]

Generally, it was either a first or second spouse who informed the authorities about a bigamous individual. Sometimes other members of the family became involved but bigamy seems rarely to have been condemned or notified to the police by neighbours. This suggests that bigamy was often tolerated by the local community and that people were reluctant to report it to the authorities. In 1875, for instance, the parish priest at Arklow noted that a Mr Byrne, alias Kinsella, who came from Arklow had been arrested on a bigamy charge. The priest was about to go to the justice of the peace 'to have him duly committed' but he had 'world and all of difficulty in poking out the facts in Arklow to convict him'.[48] Evidence presented in the prosecution of bigamists in late nineteenth-century Belfast also indicates that within working-class communities in the city, bigamy was not considered a serious crime. As one witness testified in a case in 1892, she was sure that the second wife knew that her husband was already married.[49] Men and women also admitted that they had known that their spouse was married and had used a false name when signing the marriage register. It was a common practice for women and some men to use their mother's surname as an alternative to their own.[50]

Excuses for Bigamy

The ease with which it was possible to marry in Ireland meant that bigamous marriages might occur after one of the partners had had a very short-lived courtship that had culminated in a brief ceremony witnessed by a couple beggar. Bigamists could, therefore, attempt to argue that they had never been validly married to the first spouse. Others claimed that they were too drunk to have known what was going on during the first ceremony. The couple beggar, Joseph Wood, married John Lovenden who subsequently married again and was tried for bigamy. Lovenden's

---

[46] PRONI, BELF/1/2/2/1/32.
[47] *Ulster Gazette*, 2 Feb. 1895. In 1912 in Belfast one bigamist was caught when the same witness was used in two marriages that took place five months apart. *Irish Independent*, 19 June 1912.
[48] DDA, Cullen Papers 322/1 File I: Secular Priests, 1875.
[49] PRONI, ANT/1/1B/1/3/22.
[50] See, for example, ibid.; PRONI ANT/1/1B/1/1/12; ANT/1/1B/1/4/28; ANT/1/1B/1/13/12.

defence was that he had no knowledge of his first marriage 'until the morning after, when he found himself, on awaking, stretched on the floor of a miserable apartment out of which he ran as soon as possible, and never since saw the woman to whom it was alleged he was married, until this prosecution was set on foot'. After conviction Lovenden provided a number of strong character references to the court. The judge in the case seemed to accept Lovenden's story to some extent, and in consideration 'of the excellent character which he had heretofore borne, and the peculiar circumstances connected with his first marriage', he reduced the punishment to six months' imprisonment with hard labour.[51] In a similar defence, Miles Flynn argued in 1842 that he had never been legally married as he had been drunk and went through some sort of ceremony that he could not remember.[52] In 1833, John Devenish, a 'plain, sober, staid looking person, aged 40 and upwards', was charged with bigamy.[53] His second wife, Agnes Moran, described as 'a lass in her teens, not more than 17', said she was standing outside her father's house in Plunkett Street, Dublin, when a man named James Taylor introduced her to the prisoner as an unmarried journeyman hatter who earned £3 a week. Taylor then 'popped the question' and she agreed to accompany the two men to a public house to drink porter, and once she was drunk they got her to consent to marriage.[54] They all then went to the Haymarket and Devenish and Moran were married by the 'reverend functionary Mr Allen'. The 'happy pair' then adjourned from the 'Irish Gretna Green' to lodgings in Thomas Street, where they stayed for two days 'in connubial bliss, when an obstruction arose in the shape of a former spouse accompanied by a fine pledge of bygone affection, a boy of two months'. A separation immediately ensued and the husband was subsequently committed to trial for bigamy.[55]

Other men appeared to be serial offenders. Although most bigamists were prosecuted for marrying twice, a small number were charged with more than two marriages. Bernard Murray, aged sixty, for example, was arraigned for bigamy and polygamy at the Carlow assizes in 1838. He had first married in 1811 while in the militia at Killarney but had left his wife behind when his regiment was transferred to England. He then married two more women, both of whom were widows and testified at his trial. His second wife, Harriet Seaton (referred in the newspaper

---

[51] *Dublin Morning Register*, 16 July 1829.
[52] NAI, CRF 1842 F8. See also the case of Henry Knott, sentenced to eighteen calendar months on his conviction in 1864, who claimed he was drunk and had been persuaded to contract the second marriage by Elizabeth Shannon, 'who gave him drink for this purpose' (NAI, CRF 1864 K8).
[53] *Ballina Impartial*, 10 June 1833.   [54] Ibid.   [55] Ibid.

report as the 'remains of an exceedingly handsome woman') accused Murray of stealing £40 and other valuables from her. She admitted, however, that she had continued to live with him for a year after he told her that he had another wife. His defence attempted to portray Seaton in a negative fashion, implying that she might have lived in a brothel and that after she had left Murray, she had married for money. Murray's third wife appears to have been treated more kindly by the court. Described as 'a respectable looking elderly woman, rather good-looking', the newspaper report commented that she seemed 'less inclined to be severe with the prisoner' than was his second wife. Murray was found guilty and was transported for life.[56] Frederick Woolfries (alias Woodward, alias Russell) also married three times. He was already married to two women in England when he stayed at Miss Annie Gamble's father's house in Ramelton in Donegal and over a period of six weeks the couple became engaged and married.[57] Bryan Dennis Molloy appears to have held the record for multiple marriages. In his polygamy trial in Dublin in 1884, he was accused of having four wives when he married a fifth in a registry office in Dublin. Molloy, who had spent some time in a number of lunatic asylums and was the son of a magistrate, conducted some of his own defence. At the end of the trial, the judge directed the jury to return a verdict of guilty but insane at the time he went through his various marriages.[58]

Other men who chose to marry a second time had either been separated for some time from their first wife or claimed that they thought that she had died. David McAnerny told the court that he had been 'cajoled to marry a woman double his age [he was seventeen] and who treated him in the most 'unconjugal manner ... absenting herself from home for months at a time' and he said that he believed that she had died during one of her absences. He then remarried.[59] In 1893, Charles Wildrige, in a statement to the police on arrest, noted that he had lived with his first wife for about six weeks in his mother-in-law's house. She then left him and he did not see her for some time. He went to Port Glasgow and she joined him there, but she left again and went back to Belfast. He noted that she left him a number of times and finally deserted him, apparently for good, in about 1880. He had seen her since but

---

[56] *Southern Reporter and Cork Commercial Courier*, 27 March 1838; *Belfast Newsletter*, 27 March 1838.
[57] *Anglo-Celt*, 11 June 1904; *Irish Times*, 4 March 1905.
[58] *Freeman's Journal*, 22, 29 May, 5, 7, 9 June 1884. The trial attracted considerable attention in England.
[59] NAI, CRF 1842 Mc14.

stated that 'I saw her last week when she came to my house asking for money. She has turned out unfortunate and has been bad for the past eighteen years. She is now living as a prostitute and has been several times in gaol'. That he was deliberate in his deception of his second wife is evidenced by the fact that he signed his name Charles Moore for his second marriage. She told the court that she thought he was a widower.[60]

A more poignant story was told by Nellie M'Keag who was arrested on bigamy charges in April 1899. In 1891 she had married and had a child when she and her husband lived in Liverpool. M'Keag's mother, however, brought her back to Belfast in 1894 because she was in such bad health. While she was in Belfast her husband fathered three children with two different women and insisted that his wife support and look after these children, along with cooking for the two women who lived in her house. Following her departure from her husband's household, he informed her that they were not legally married. In 1897, 'considering herself free', she married a man named Norton in Belfast, who at the time of the bigamy charge was serving a nine-month sentence for larceny. M'Keag herself had just come out of hospital when she was arrested for bigamy. Her barrister advised her to plead guilty to the offence and to appeal to the mercy of the court as she had already endured a 'considerable amount of punishment'.[61]

Charles Wildridge's defence that he married again because his first wife was 'bad' was echoed by other defendants and their supporters. The men and their families drew on the rhetoric of the ideal wife and mother to condemn their spouses, whom they frequently accused of adultery and neglect of their wifely duties. Most had no qualms about exposing their first wives to public scrutiny and censure. Robert Connor, convicted of bigamy at the Belfast assizes in 1879, stated, in his petition for a remittance of his sentence, that his first wife had been in America for two years, and returned six weeks before their marriage. He had been acquainted with her before her departure. At the time of the marriage he was not aware of her immoral conduct while away, and she gave birth four months after the marriage. Upon being informed of his wife's behaviour, Connor left her without consummating the marriage. Under these circumstances he had always considered the marriage null and void and not binding on him. He claimed that if he had lived with her after the discovery of her 'dishonour', he would have been an 'object of scorn' to his family and friends.[62] Hugh McClean told the police that he had lived with Agnes Curry, his first wife, for one month and she then put him out

[60] PRONI, ANT/1/18/1/4/46.   [61] *Belfast Newsletter*, 12 April 1899.
[62] NAI, CRF 1883 C7; CRF 1882 C60.

of the house. He also alleged that she was the mother of five children by different men.[63] According to the police report, Benjamin Thomas Collins said when he was arrested: 'I may have broken the laws of man but I have not broken the laws of God. My wife is a bad woman. She diseased me and I could not work for three years. Dr Wilson of the Sleare Road can prove this'.[64]

In 1849 John Fox's mother claimed, in a petition for a mitigation of her son's sentence of seven years' transportation, that his first wife 'engaged in bad behaviour with another man and never looked after her husband'.[65] James Gillespie was considered an 'honest, industrious tradesman'. A police report noted that his first wife's conduct 'before her marriage as well as after was bad and immoral' and that she was considered after her marriage to be little better than a common prostitute and this was given as the reason why her husband enlisted. Mary Anne Gill, his second wife, was considered 'a steady well conducted young woman'.[66] David Guthrie, aged twenty-nine, who was tried for bigamy in Downpatrick in March 1880, pleaded guilty. He admitted that he had married his first wife in June 1872 'and having had cause to be dissatisfied with her conduct he left her and sometimes afterwards he joined the army'.[67] He served through the African campaign and he was discharged on pension in 1879. He had not heard from his wife for the seven years while he was in the army. When he returned home he renewed an acquaintance with a young woman whom he said knew about his previous marriage. They had married. The court found Guthrie guilty of bigamy and he was sentenced to five years' penal servitude. After two years in prison he petitioned for release on the grounds that not only had he now spent a considerable amount of time in prison but also that he was 'willing to pardon his [first] wife the faults which were the cause of his reckless and criminal conduct and to live with her in the future'. The sentencing judge commenting on Guthrie's petition noted that there should be no mitigation of sentence as 'it was necessary to stop him going about deluding women'.[68]

The custom of wife-selling was cited in English bigamy trials and there are occasional references to its use as a defence in Irish trials. Unusually, Henry O'Neill was sold by his wife. He was astonished to be convicted of bigamy and sentenced to seven years' transportation in 1839. The charge of bigamy had been proven in court; however, O'Neill, asking questions

---

[63] PRONI, ANT/1/18/1/19/1.   [64] PRONI, ANT/1/2C/6/95.
[65] NAI, CRF 1849 F9. Fox, aged twenty-one, actually died in prison in August 1849. See Smithfield Prison General Register (NAI, 1844–1849, 1/14/1).
[66] NAI, CRF 1862 G15.   [67] NAI, CIF 1882 G 8.   [68] Ibid.

of his second wife, noted that the couple had lived together before marriage. He then asked her:

Did you not buy me?
Judge (in great astonishment) – Buy you! What did you mean?
Traverser [i.e. O'Neill] – I mean, did she purchase and pay for me?
  (To the witness) Answer me that question upon your oath.
  Witness – I did buy you from your first wife.

Traverser – What did you pay for me?
  Witness – She asked £2, but I gave her £3 thinking you very cheap at that.

Traverser – Was not the bargain entirely between you and her?
  Witness – It was; she said that her father gave you some pounds with her, and as she had bought you with his money, she had a right to sell you if she liked.

O'Neill believed this was enough to prove that the first marriage was now null. The judge, when passing sentence, observed, 'that the punishment had never been inflicted on a more deserving subject'.[69] In 1829, two men were summoned to appear at Ballina assizes on bigamy charges, one of them being accused of selling his wife for £20.[70] However, there is no evidence that wife selling was a widespread phenomenon in Ireland as it was in parts of rural England.[71]

Spousal Collusion

The details provided in the records of the Antrim assizes for the late nineteenth century indicate that the second spouse was often aware that their new partner was already married. In 1894, Mary Coleman admitted that she had 'kept company' with the prisoner for about a year and a half.

---

[69] *Freeman's Journal*, 21 March 1839.   [70] *Chutes Western Herald*, 3 June 1829.
[71] See Samuel Menefee, *Wives for Sale* (Oxford, 1981), which records two cases of wife selling in Ireland, one in Dublin in 1756 and another in Belfast in 1882. Brian Gurrin writes about a case of wife selling in County Wicklow in the eighteenth century in Gurrin, 'How much for the wife? A case of popular divorce in eighteenth-century Wicklow', *Ulster Folklife*, 54 (2011), 45–7. In Dublin in 1790 a joiner and a bricklayer made a bargain by which the former sold his wife to the latter for two guineas and ten pots of porter. The poor woman knew nothing of the agreement till the purchaser came to possess himself of his property, 'which so much alarmed her, that she shrieked out in the greatest consternation. Her screams collected a number of her own sex, who learning the nature of the bargain, and irritated at the innovation made upon their liberties, seized upon the two dealers in female flesh, hoisted them upon a pole, and colted them about the streets, hooting them as objects of ridicule and contempt' (*Dublin Chronicle*, 24 June 1790).

She ascertained that he was a married man before they married and knew that his wife was alive. She obviously did not mind too much and noted in her deposition that her husband was married under the name of Wilson and she knew before she married him that his real name was Pickering.[72] What appears remarkable in these cases is that second wives insisted on going through a marriage ceremony even though they were aware that it was invalid. Perhaps this was to secure respectability in the community, where gossip would quickly announce that a marriage had taken place. Another woman who did not look too closely into the past of the man she married was Mary Anne Charley. John Kane 'and his two little girls' had come to lodge with her in Belfast in about 1888. She claimed to know nothing about the children's mother. Kane lodged with Charley for about three years before he married her. She knew that his name was John Kane and could not provide any explanation as to why he signed the marriage register as John Mulligan. She noted that the 'prisoner was a good man to me'. She had heard that his wife was dead 'but was not sure'.[73]

Leniency in Court

Despite the harsh penalties for the crime of bigamy included in the legislation, there was considerable variation in the sentences meted out to offenders. Judges frequently made the punishment fit the crime and could be lenient in their sentencing. In 1789 a man was pilloried for bigamy and the newspaper report noted that he 'owes the preservation of his life to the lenity of his first wife he had wantonly quitted'. His second wife had brought the case against him. His first wife claimed not to have married him, though she declared that he was an 'unfortunate creature, by whom she had two children'. However, witnesses to the marriage testified that it had occurred. 'The court sensible of the prisoner's guilt thought the woman highly culpable for perjuring herself, [but] she was pitied for her tenderness to a person, once we may suppose, the object of her affection'.[74] In 1816 Robert de la Pere Robinson, confined for four years on a charge of bigamy, petitioned for release on the grounds that the young woman who was the cause of his imprisonment 'was married last Sunday to Edward Archer Langley of Stafford Reg of Militia from which circumstances, I buoy myself up with the pleasing idea of obtaining my liberty.' He was released within six days as if he had not committed a crime.[75] By the time

---

[72] PRONI, ANT/1/18/1/4/2B.   [73] PRONI, ANT/1/18/1/3/22.
[74] *Ennis Chronicle*, 20 Aug. 1789.
[75] NAI, Prisoners' Petitions and Cases, 12 April 1816, VI–19–1–1390.

William Marshall was convicted of bigamy in Fermanagh in 1828, he had children by both of his wives. In pronouncing sentence the judge, who gave the prisoner one year's imprisonment, advised him not to 'flatter himself that the punishment he was now about to award him was the only one that awaited him'. The prisoner was told that the law would compel him to support his first wife and children, and his second family and that 'this will be a burden and punishment to you all the days of your life'.[76] A second wife, who had a child, and declared that she did not wish to punish him, brought Thomas Bevan to court. When asked why she had him committed she stated that his first wife had come 'and kicked up a row'. Bevan was given only six months' imprisonment. The judge stated 'this was one of the cases where the court might depart from the rule laid down to transport in bigamy cases. There was no evidence that he ill-used his first wife, and he had treated Miss Wilson (his second wife) well, and there did not seem much money or much beauty gained by the second marriage'.[77] William Patrick Chambers, who pleaded not guilty to bigamy at the Belfast assizes in March 1896, received a sentence of one month's imprisonment, without hard labour. The judge had believed the prisoner, 'who gave a pitiful tale of the treatment to which he had been subjected by his wife' and 'in the circumstances of the case, he would inflict a comparatively light punishment'.[78]

Others were not so fortunate and received harsher penalties. Richardson McIntyre was sentenced to three years' penal servitude in 1892. The severe sentence resulted from him mistreating his second wife.[79] Mary Jane Dignam was convicted of bigamy in 1893 and was jailed for four months when her second husband refused to have her back. If he had allowed her to come home, she would not have been punished.[80] Patrick Wilton (also named as Wilson in the newspapers) pleaded guilty to a bigamy charge in Cork in 1896. Before sentencing the judge noted that he had abandoned his first wife and children and then 'there was the betrayal of a young and virtuous girl'. However, it was noted that the second wife already had an illegitimate child and therefore the 'injury was not so great as if he had undergone marriage with a virtuous girl'. He was sentenced to eighteen months with hard labour.[81]

Sentences became harsher in the Irish Free State. In 1925, Patrick Keane was convicted of bigamy and received two sentences of five years' penal servitude, to run concurrently. The sentence was appealed as being too severe and it was pointed out to the court that the average sentence in

[76] *Belfast Newsletter*, 28 March 1828. See also p. 50 above.
[77] *Cork Examiner*, 11 Feb. 1850.   [78] *Belfast Newsletter*, 18 March 1896.
[79] *Belfast Newsletter*, 21 March 1892.   [80] *Belfast Newsletter*, 11 May 1893.
[81] *Cork Examiner*, 18 July 1896.

such cases was between eighteen months and two years. The appeal was allowed and the ruling was reduced to two sentences of eighteen months' hard labour to run concurrently. The judge was clearly making a point that both women had been wronged by the bigamist.[82]

Defeating a Bigamy Charge

Being unable to prove that a first marriage had occurred was one way of defeating a bigamy charge. In January 1824, Lettitia Robinson, in an attempt to ensure the appearance of witnesses in the case she was pursuing against her bigamous husband, placed a notice in the *Belfast Newsletter* offering a reward of five pounds for the apprehension of two individuals, William Bailie and John Magee, who could provide evidence in her case against Peter M'Conaghty of Portaferry. Both had failed to appear at the first hearing and in consequence M'Conaghty was bailed until the next assizes.[83] Similarly, Patrick Murray, arraigned upon a charge of bigamy in 1830, was discharged when no witnesses appeared to prove the case.[84]

The differences between Catholic canon law and that of the state, as noted in Chapter 1, could also be used as a defence in bigamy trials. In October 1818, William M'Clenaghan married his cousin, Sarha M'Geehan in the Church of Ireland Cathedral in Derry. Both were Roman Catholic. While the marriage was valid in common law, it was not recognised in Catholic canon law because the *Tametsi* decree had been proclaimed in the diocese of Derry and Raphoe and, therefore, the service should have taken place in a Catholic church. The couple lived with M'Geehan's parents for a year. However, according to the newspaper report, due to the 'unrelenting bigotry' of the Catholic church the local Catholic priest denounced the couple from the altar and 'deprived [them] of the rites of their Church'. Mc'Geehan's father fell ill and the priest said he could not attend him while the couple resided in his house. They left their home, and their appeals to the local Catholic bishop to resolve the situation received no reply. M'Clenaghan then left the area for a number of years, returned, courted and married another woman who lived in the same neighbourhood. The Catholic priest who carried out the second ceremony later declared that, being new to the area, he did not know that M'Clenaghan had been previously married. The case attracted the attention of the press because of the Catholic church's view

---

[82] *Kerryman*, 14 Feb. 1925.   [83] *Belfast Newsletter*, 28 Jan. 1824.
[84] *Freeman's Journal*, 15 Feb. 1830.

that M'Clenaghan's first marriage was null and void. Although an arrest warrant was issued for M'Clenaghan, he absconded before his trial.[85]

Women Bigamists

As noted already, women were rarely tried for bigamy, but when they were their cases often attracted a lot of public attention. Mrs Georgiana Lear, 'a lady' and the daughter of an attorney in Cork was aged about thirty-four when she was charged with bigamy. She appeared on the first day in court with her mother and was 'attired in a puce coloured pelisse, fashionable velvet bonnet, surmounted by a veil'.[86] She had married her first husband John Lear in 1812, when she was about eighteen years old. The couple had five children but 'before the birth of her last child, some levities were discovered on her part', and in consequence the couple separated in 1822. The eldest of the five children lived with the father and the youngest with the mother. The middle three children were at boarding school. Following the couple's separation, John Lear went to live in England. It was alleged in court that between the end of the first marriage and her marriage to William Alexander, Mrs Lear had 'associated herself with several persons in this town'. In January 1829, Georgiana married William Alexander, a sixty-year-old wealthy widower who lived in Dublin. She clearly knew of him but first met him on a Dublin street, after which she wrote to him telling him she was a widow with a little girl, in need of pecuniary assistance and asked for a meeting. They subsequently married and he was then informed that she was already married and he made her leave his house. Her defence, like that of many other bigamists, was that she believed her first husband had died and she produced an announcement from a newspaper dated 1813 to prove this fact. Her counsel also noted that John Lear had been absent from the country for more than seven years. The fact that a number of witnesses also believed that John Lear had died led the jury to return within ten minutes of retiring with a 'not guilty' verdict.[87]

As noted already, women who were prosecuted for bigamy generally received far more lenient sentences than male bigamists. They could be discharged without serving a prison sentence, or they might just spend a very short period of time in custody. Elizabeth Campbell was charged

---

[85] *Belfast Newsletter*, 1 Aug. 1826. The report is repeated verbatim in the *Westmeath Journal*, 3 Aug. 1826.
[86] *Southern Reporter and Cork Commercial Courier*, 30 April 1829.
[87] *Belfast Newsletter*, 30 April, 1 May 1829; *Freeman's Journal*, 30 Jan. 1829, 28 April 1829. *Southern Reporter and Cork Commercial Courier*, 30 April 1829.

with bigamy in 1824 but the bill had been ignored by the Grand Jury. Her counsel asked the court that she be freed but the prosecutor was not willing, stating that Campbell had threatened to 'have the life of the prosecutor'. She appeared in court 'dressed in a fashionable green shawl, Leghorn bonnet, and black lace veil'. She was believed to be about forty years old. The defendant was discharged after the judge cautioned her 'not to be too liberal in the use of her tongue' in future.[88] In 1846 a Mrs Scott was acquitted at her second trial for bigamy as the prosecutor wanted to delay the case until he had further information on the first marriage. The court was not willing to postpone the case any longer.[89] In 1887 Laura Smith received a sentence of one day's imprisonment for her bigamy. The prosecutor was the father of her second husband. The judge noted that no injustice had been done to the second husband as he was fully aware of Smith's circumstances. Her first husband had been sentenced to five years' penal servitude and, when he was released, it was believed that he had gone to America. The judge noted that he could see no harm could be done to a husband in a bigamy case, whereas a woman was a victim if her husband left her and married another. A man, he declared, could not be so victimised and did not have 'much to complain of'.[90] Jury members and judges who never imposed the full rigour of the law on women bigamists may also have shared this sentiment

The Case of Soldiers

Soldiers feature prominently among those prosecuted for bigamy and it is no coincidence that they also represented about 10 per cent of the men who were married by the couple beggar Johann Georg Frederick Schulz. As soldiers were frequently moved from one barracks to another in England and Ireland, it was relatively easy for them to hide a second marriage. A Sergeant Dunton was arrested in Cobh in 1896 for having married a woman from the town while also having a wife and three children living in Plymouth.[91] In 1901, Ellen Brookes admitted having married a soldier who had deserted her after a few months. She later received a letter from him stating that their marriage was not legal as he already had a wife. She claimed she had never any intention of committing bigamy and believed she was free to marry. She was acquitted.[92] Arthur Owens, who, in 1917, was released early from a nine month

---

[88] *Westmeath Journal*, 23 Sept. 1824.   [89] *Cork Examiner*, 24 April 1846.
[90] *Wicklow Newsletter*, 17 Dec. 1887.   [91] *Belfast Newsletter*, 2 March 1896.
[92] *Irish Times*, 12 Feb. 1901. For another case regarding soldiers see *Irish Times*, 23 Dec. 1903.

prison sentence to rejoin his regiment noted that he had met his second wife before he married his first wife and the pair had had a child. According to the report, he married his second wife in order 'to make her ... an honest woman and to get her an allowance'.[93] Another soldier, Isaac Crowe, had one wife in England and another living on the Curragh camp in Kildare.[94] The chances of being caught, if the soldiers resided in the same country as their first wives, were more likely in the early twentieth century when soldiers' dependants began to be paid a separation allowance. Being able to claim an allowance may also, of course, have made a soldier more attractive as a partner even if a woman was already married or knew that her husband had a living wife.[95]

Conclusion

The voices of bigamists come through the various depositions and evidence they gave to the police or to the courts during their trials. Much of the information provided is of course self-serving. John Woods, alias Cummings, made a statement to the police when he was arrested in 1892. It is one of the few direct comments made by a bigamist about why he committed bigamy:

I am now going to give an account of my reasons for committing bigamy. I was married to my first wife about 10 years ago. I was reared up with my grandmother and her husband's name was Woods. I married under that name. My own name being Cummings. My first wife knew this from the first month that we were married. We led a most miserable life. She was always casting up my friends and telling me I did not know who my father was and my mother. She said she was a whore. I left her but went back again thinking I could settle and make a home but she always asked me for Christ's sake to leave her and give her a chance to get a good tradesman who could keep her and that she would never acknowledge me as a husband until I gave her my own name Cummings. What had I to do? She did not want me and would not make a home. I met Sarah Savage. I told her my circumstances and I married her. She has proved a most virtuous and good wife. I will not say a word about Agnes Woods's character but Sergt Nesbitt of the RIC seen a sample of it in the street. I think it was better for me to do what I did than live with a woman who did not want me and live in sin and misery and perhaps something worse come of it. Hoping you will consider my case and be as lenient as you can. I plead guilty ... If I could of paid for a divorce I would have had my liberty. Instead I had to live a wretched and miserable life with a woman who did not want me or [was not] willing to make a home with me.[96]

[93] NAI, CRF 1917 O18.   [94] *Dublin Daily Express*, 24 Sept. 1915.
[95] See, for example, cases reported in *Dublin Daily Express*, 29 July, 9 Sept., 6 Dec. 1916.
[96] PRONI, ANT/1/2C/40.

Woods at once provides an excuse and a reason for his bigamy. He, like most unhappily married people, could not afford a divorce. He is also, like many bigamists, searching for some kind of marital contentment, which he seems to have achieved with his second wife.

Bigamy cases generally involved desertion and abandonment, states with practical and emotional consequences that must have been difficult for those who were deserted and for second spouses who must, in some cases at least, have also felt betrayed. The men and women who committed bigamy were on the whole servants, porters, labourers, soldiers and sailors. The majority were not improving their economic state, but perhaps endeavoring instead to find some happiness in their lives. Most only married twice. Bigamy pretended a marriage and thus respectability existed, which may have been preferable for many to open cohabitation.

There was little change in the numbers of bigamists tried between 1850 and 1919. One change that becomes evident from the 1860s is that more bigamists were marrying in the registrar's office.[97] A comment in the *Irish Independent* in 1911 noted that couples opted for civil marriage as they did not like the publicity of a religious ceremony and that 90 per cent of bigamy cases came from civil ceremonies.[98] We cannot generalise about the experience of marriage through these bigamy cases, but it is worth noting that many bigamous relationships involved emotional and financial commitments. In essence, they reveal evidence of men and women willing to interpret the law on marriage flexibly to suit their own ends and ensure themselves some level of happiness.

---

[97] See for example, the case of Mary Jane Dignam, *Belfast Newsletter*, 28 April 1893.
[98] *Irish Independent*, 21 Dec. 1911.

Part IV

The Unmaking of Marriage

10 Marital Violence

William Kelly, a falconer, was committed to Kilmainham gaol in 1763. He was described as 'a very desperate fellow', and was charged with assaulting a woman 'very desperately, who interposed to prevent his beating his wife in the cruellest manner: for kicking and knocking [her] down before Mr Morgan's house several times, and driving by force from thence his wife, who came for redress of his barbarity to her'.[1] Unfortunately, as with many early domestic abuse cases, we do not know what became of any of these individuals, or whether Kelly was punished for beating his wife. We do know that not all marital abuse went unpunished in the eighteenth century. In Dublin in 1766, for instance, Mathew May was charged with beating his wife and, in July 1770, James Helpany was sent to jail for kicking his wife in the stomach.[2] Marital disharmony was expressed in different ways through desertion, separation, divorce, bigamy and husbands refusing credit to their eloping wives. Marital dissatisfaction was also revealed through violence – primarily non-lethal – but also through murder.

The history of marital violence has been seriously studied by historians since the 1970s. The emergence of second-wave feminism was one spur to this investigation into spousal violence, as was the development of the new social history. Recent work on domestic conflict has extended our knowledge of the role of class in marital violence, the ways in which such violence was both apparent to the wider community and how the court system dealt with this issue.[3] Studies by Foyster and Bailey extend into the lower social classes, and raise questions about the pace and timing of

---

[1] *Freeman's Journal*, 25 Oct. 1763.
[2] Representative Church Body Library, St John's Watch Record, P328.3.1–7. www.ireland.anglican.org/about/rcb-library/archive-of-the-month?&page=7. Accessed April 2012.
[3] See Elizabeth Foyster, *Marital Violence: An English Family History, 1660–1857* (Cambridge, 2005); Lisa Surridge, *Bleak Houses: Marital Violence in Victorian* Fiction (Athens, Ohio, 2005); Lawrence Stone, *Uncertain Unions: Marriage in England, 1660–1753* (Oxford, 1992); *Broken Lives: Separation and Divorce in England, 1660–1857* (Oxford, 1993); Joanne Bailey, *Unquiet Lives: Marriage and Marriage Breakdown in England, 1660–1800* (Cambridge, 2003); Carolyn A. Conley, *Certain Other Countries: Homicide, Gender and National Identity*

changes in attitudes to marital violence, and how the economic interdependence of couples shaped the nature of power in marital relationships. Foyster argues that for centuries marital violence was not necessarily viewed as deviant behaviour, and she shows convincingly that marital violence remained very much in the public realm until well into the nineteenth century. Much of the recent Irish work on the subject places such violence within the framework of the family, where the violent behaviour can also focus on parents, siblings, other adults and children.[4] Indeed, intimate violence is a critical dimension of family history. Lindsey Earner-Byrne, following the work of Linda Gordon, argues for the significance of studying violence in the family within its social, economic and cultural contexts as a means of understanding how Irish society identifies and deals with these crimes today.[5] Many of the individuals we will discuss lived in households, sometimes very cramped, where children, in-laws, other relatives and even lodgers might reside.[6] Often, spousal violence spilled over to affect these individuals as well. While much of this violence occurred within the family context, the focus in this chapter will be specifically on violence between spouses.

Shani D' Cruze has observed that 'Whilst the basic physical realities of violence may be disturbingly repetitive, the socio-cultural context and

in *Late Nineteenth-Century England, Ireland, Scotland and Wales* (Ohio, 2007) takes a comparative approach and has some references to marital violence. Likewise, Conley's, *Melancholy Accidents: The Meaning of Violence in Post-Famine Ireland* (Kentucky, 1999), covers familial and spousal violence in Ireland. Pauline M. Prior, *Madness and Murder: Gender, Crime and Mental Disorder in Nineteenth-Century Ireland* (Dublin, 2008), has sections on spousal murder, as does Richard McMahon, *Homicide in Pre-famine and Famine Ireland* (Liverpool, 2013). Liz Steiner-Scott, '"To bounce a boot off her now and then...": Domestic violence in post-famine Ireland' in Maryann Gialanella Valiulis and Mary O'Dowd (eds.), *Women and Irish History* (Dublin, 1997), pp. 124–43, is the best historical account we have to date on the subject in Irish history. See also the important work of Diane Urquhart, 'Irish divorce and domestic violence, 1857–1922', *Women's History Review*, 22, 5 (2013), 820–37. Cara Diver, *Marital Violence in Post-Independence Ireland, 1922–1996* (Manchester, 2019) was published too late for the authors to note its arguments.

[4] Lindsey Earner-Byrne, '"Behind closed doors": Society, law and familial violence in Ireland, 1922–1990' in Howlin and Costello (eds.), *Law and the Family in Ireland, 1800–1950* (London, 2017), pp. 142–59; 'The family in Ireland, 1880–2015' in Thomas Bartlett (ed.), *The Cambridge History of Modern Ireland, 4, 1880 to the Present* (Cambridge, 2018), pp. 641–72; Lindsey Earner-Byrne and Diane Urquhart, 'Gender roles in Ireland since 1740' in Mary E. Daly and Eugenio Biagini (eds.), *The Cambridge Social History of Modern Ireland* (Cambridge, 2017), pp. 312–26.

[5] Linda Gordon argues that an historical understanding of the contexts of marital violence is essential to understanding contemporary attitudes to the subject. Linda Gordon, *Heroes of Their Own Lives: The Politics and History of Family Violence, Boston, 1880–1960* (Chicago, 2002).

[6] For the impact of violence in the family in relation to committals to lunatic asylums see Catherine Cox, *Negotiating Insanity in the Southeast of Ireland, 1820–1900* (Manchester, 2012), pp. 105–17.

meanings, as well as the techniques and technologies of violence, have their historical specificities.[7] Over the many decades covered by this current study there were times when violence between spouses seemed of little concern to the authorities; and there were other times when the authorities took a keen interest in such abuse. Interpersonal violence between spouses became more publicly visible through newspaper reporting from the early nineteenth century. The aim here is to explore the contexts of this violence, to consider the evolution of the legal discourses and judicial practices around this issue and to examine what this violence tells us about power, control and intimacy within marriages.

Extent of Violence

In the period covered by this book there were thousands of assaults perpetrated upon individuals for various reasons. The return of the Inspectors of Prisons ending in 1828 revealed that in the seven-year period between 1821 and 1828, 112,838 individuals were committed for trial for all kinds of offences, with 65,512 convicted. As many as 1,896 were given the death penalty and 332 were executed; of that number 155 were executed for murder. It is not possible to divide these figures into assaults on spouses, or even spousal murder. Spousal violence is, therefore, more likely to go unrecorded than recorded in historical sources.[8] Securing figures for spousal murder required a year-by-year analysis of newspaper sources from the late eighteenth to the twentieth century. We believe we have uncovered a substantial number of these murder and manslaughter cases: 713, for the period between 1772 and 1925, plus an additional eighty-five attempted murders in the same period. Again, there are difficulties with these figures, due to a lack of court records, and different names being provided for perpetrators in different newspaper accounts of the same murder. There are also problems with linking details recorded for individuals in prison registers with newspaper reports of trials. Frustratingly, too, it is frequently impossible to discover the final outcome of a trial which was not reported in a newspaper.

It was widely believed in the late nineteenth century that spousal assault was rare in Ireland, while it was thought to be a common practice

---

[7] Shani D'Cruze, 'Introduction: Unguarded passions: Violence, history and the everyday,' in *Everyday Violence in Britain, 1850–1950* (Harlow, 2000), p. 1.

[8] *Returns of the Inspectors of Prisons* (Dublin, 1822–1829). *Criminal and Judicial Statistics for Ireland*, 1866–1919. For instance, the annual number of common and aggravated assaults in 1876 was 1,526.

in England. In the evolution of Irish national identity in post-Famine Ireland, it was argued that such beliefs distinguished the Irish from the English. Irish men were held to be morally superior to English men. As one Irish judge was reported as saying in 1885, 'a husband is charged with assaulting his wife. It is an unusual case in this country and it was all their pride that very few such cases of the kind happened in Ireland no matter what might occur in other countries'.[9] But this judge was mistaken and there were hundreds, and more likely thousands, of spousal assaults in Ireland every year. Women and men who came before the courts charged with spousal assault or murder put their private lives on public display. Exploring marital violence allows us to examine spousal relationships in some detail and provides us with a sense of the commonalities that characterised unhappy marital unions.

The Law

In the period under discussion the governance of the domestic space was based on an understanding of authority and deference, which saw male heads of households as responsible for the social and moral order of the household. To maintain such order men could use moderate physical correction in their households. This included the physical chastisement of the wife. William Blackstone, whose works formed the foundation of legal interpretation noted:

The husband also (by the old law) might give his wife moderate correction. For, as he is to answer for her misbehaviour, the law thought it reasonable to entrust him with this power of restraining her, by domestic chastisement, in the same moderation that a man is allowed to correct his servants or children.[10]

What 'moderate' meant in reality or, indeed, how justified husbands were in chastising their wives, was an ongoing debate over the period. Historians have shown that the definition of marital cruelty changed over the centuries.[11] The development of what constituted spousal cruelty came from the Irish ecclesiastical courts and filtered down to petty session courts. In 1827, the judge in the Dublin consistory court, Dr John Radcliff, provided a definition of cruelty which he used as a guideline for granting a judicial separation or a divorce *a mensa et thoro*:

---

[9] *Kilkenny Journal*, 13 June 1885.
[10] W. Blackstone, *Commentaries on the Laws of England* (13th ed., 4 vols., London, 1800), i, p. 444. Doggett demonstrates that the commonly-held view that a husband could beat his wife with a rod no thicker than his thumb is a myth. See Maeve E. Doggett, *Marriage, Wife-Beating and the Law in Victorian England* (Columbia, 1993), p. 7.
[11] See Footnote 3, above.

'There must be something which renders the cohabitation unsafe, or is likely to be attended by injury to the person or health of the party'; in other words there needed to be a threat to life.[12] Magistrates and judges in the lower courts allowed for separations in cases of marital violence. They also made comments about acceptable and unacceptable levels of spousal violence in their individual courts, but their sentencing patterns were always uneven and inconsistent. Magistrates appear to have been particularly idiosyncratic in their judgements and were either unaware of the law or in many instances adapted it to accord with their own views on what a suitable punishment might be.

While courts were generally sympathetic to the plight of abused wives, what constituted a common assault, or an aggravated assault, in cases of domestic abuse was not always clear and it remained an ill-defined offence throughout the period. According to one widely used nineteenth-century legal authority a 'common assault means an assault not accompanied by circumstances giving it the character of an offence something more than an assault'.[13] Striking at another person with a cane, stick or other object and any action indicating the intention to use violence against the person was considered an assault. If a death followed the attack, then it became manslaughter or murder.

Domestic abuse cases were brought by wives against husbands as well as by husbands against wives. Plaintiffs appeared before a justice of the peace or magistrate to swear out a deposition that they were in fear of their lives or bodily harm from someone who had threatened or attempted to do them an injury. The court could then order the person complained of to find articles (sureties) of the peace and, in default, commit them to prison.[14] According to Doggett, these articles of the peace were freely available to women in England from the eighteenth century. This may have also been the case in Ireland. Irish women were certainly using justices and, from the late eighteenth century, magistrates, to bind over accused offenders to keep the peace and protect

---

[12] C. R. Milward, *Reports of Cases Argued and Determined in the Court of Prerogative in Ireland, and in the Consistory Court of Dublin, During the Time of the Right Honourable John Radcliff, LL. D* (Dublin, 1847), p. 159; William Duncan, 'Desertion and cruelty in Irish matrimonial law', *The Irish Jurist*, 2 (1972), 213. See Chapter 12 for definitions of marital cruelty as grounds for a judicial separation. See also, Urquhart, 'Irish divorce and domestic violence, 1857–1922', 820–37.

[13] E. P. Levinge, *The Justice of the Peace for Ireland* (3rd ed. updated by L. S. Montgomery) (Dublin, 1872), pp. 688–90.

[14] Doggett, *Marriage, Wife-Beating*, chapter 1. For policing more generally in eighteenth-century Ireland see Timothy D. Watt, *Popular Protest and Policing in Ascendancy Ireland, 1691–1761* (Woodbridge, Suffolk, 2018).

themselves from abusive husbands.[15] Articles of the peace did not, however, allow a woman to live separately from her husband, and many wives must have been fearful when a husband's sentence ended.[16]

Neal Garnham has explored the extent to which individuals took out indictments in the period between 1736 and 1795. Looking at forty-eight sample assizes in that period he discovered that women initiated fewer than one prosecution in five. From a total number of 4,620 indictments for assault in the period, women initiated 801 (i.e. *c.* 17 per cent).[17] While Garnham provides social and financial reasons as to why these figures are low, the numbers also reveal that some women were aware of the value of the court system to them and used it to their advantage. It has been argued that in England courts became tougher in their sentencing of assault cases from the late eighteenth century. By then interpersonal violence had become a serious matter for the courts, which began to prosecute this category of violence on a greater scale than previously.

In 1828, a substantial change was made to the prosecution of domestic assault cases. In that year the Offences against the Person Act, which applied to Ireland from 1829, made assault both a more serious crime and an easier one to prosecute. The Act was considered a chief point of departure in the prosecution of assault cases. It laid out a threshold for degrees of interpersonal violence while allowing courts leeway in sentencing.[18] Magistrates could now convict summarily for minor offences. They could also, in serious cases such as murder, attempted murder and assault causing grievous bodily harm, send an individual for trial before a judge and jury to the assizes. The Act itself was a consolidating one that also rationalised a whole range of legislation relating to offences against the person. The Act also equated punishments for attempted murder by poisoning, drowning, strangling, or wounding a victim, with those for attempted murder by shooting, stabbing or cutting. The level of harm that might be inflicted on an individual, rather than the method used to inflict that harm, now determined the sentence. Magistrates had powers to summarily convict in assault cases, and women could

---

[15] Ibid., pp. 11–15. See also S. Mendleson and P. Crawford, *Women in Early Modern England, 1550–1720* (Oxford, 1998), pp. 141–5.

[16] Doggett, *Marriage, Wife-Beating*, pp. 14–15.

[17] Neal Garnham, *The Courts, Crime and the Criminal Law in Ireland, 1692–1760* (Dublin, 1996), pp. 57–60. The figures do not identify perpetrators and it is not possible, therefore, to calculate how many represent marital violence.

[18] Gregory Thomas Smith, 'The state and the culture of violence in London, 1760–1840' (unpublished PhD thesis, University of Toronto, 1999).

henceforth access local petty sessions courts to deter their abusive husbands. Historians have argued that this Act brought widespread knowledge of marital abuse into the public domain, because the press reported on proceedings in petty sessions.[19] Under this Act, the maximum sentence was a fine of £5 or two months in prison. Sentences varied widely. While it is difficult to gauge the actual numbers of wives who brought their husbands before the sessions, it is clear from the evidence currently available that women did make use of this new legislation to control their husbands. For example, in 1835, fifty-six-year-old John Dowling was ordered to find two sureties of £5 each to keep the peace with his wife Eliza after she prosecuted him for beating her.[20]

In 1847, Anne Lynan charged her husband Michael with an assault. She was clearly injured when she appeared in court, although he claimed that he did not hit her, that she was a drunkard and had ruined him, selling his furniture and pledging his clothes. The court did not believe him and he got one month in jail.[21] It is worth noting that women's bodies and their presentation in court also went some way to securing convictions. Women who appeared before magistrates visibly cut and bruised were usually successful in their prosecutions.

Domestic Violence Cases

Domestic violence was not, therefore, a hidden crime in Ireland; it was widely reported in the local and national press. However, it was not until the 1960s and 1970s that spousal abuse was regarded seriously by campaign groups as an issue that demanded substantial changes in the law to protect, primarily, women and children.[22] Spouses fought over many issues: money, relationships with in-laws, the dereliction of domestic duties, alleged misbehaviour, infidelity, the uses of family resources, child-rearing and jealousy. Oftentimes such disputes were exacerbated by alcohol, and arguments that started out with verbal abuse soon escalated to physical violence. Domestic abuse could be severe, and continue over many years.

Women who brought information against their husbands were expected to pursue the case. Jane Murray ended up in Carlow gaol in 1824 when

---

[19] See Doggett, *Marriage, Wife-Beating*; Surridge, *Bleak Houses*; Martin Wiener, *Men of Blood: Violence, Manliness, and Criminal Justice in Victorian Britain* (Cambridge, 2006).
[20] Authors' assault database; NAI, Maryborough Prison, General Register 1821–1839. 1/55/25.
[21] *Freeman's Journal*, 12 May 1847.
[22] Diver, *Marital Violence in Post-Independence Ireland*.

she gave information that her husband 'cruelly beat her'. However, when she did not proceed to a prosecution (in other words she abandoned the case, 'in order not to hurt her four small children'), she was herself imprisoned, with her children. In a petition to the authorities for release she informed them that her husband had since enlisted in the army, effectively abandoning her.[23]

Men's use of violence against their wives was often a means to enforce spousal obedience. Not all women who were assaulted by their husbands took them to court but those who did were demonstrating that their husband's control over them was limited and that violence was unacceptable within the marital relationship. It is likely that consistent abuse eventually forced some women to bring their husbands to court. They clearly wanted their husbands to stop beating them. Perhaps they also wanted to shame their husbands in public in an effort to improve their behaviour. What they believed might result from a court case is a moot point. Did they think the violence would stop? Did they believe that an authority greater than that of the husband was vested in a justice or magistrate, and that their views would control the husband's behaviour? We do not know whether the violence abated after a court appearance, a period in jail or the imposition of a fine. Given what we now know about the psychology of spousal/partner violence it is unlikely that such punishments had much effect.

Wives' public testimony made intimate violence visible to the wider community and brought it to the attention of campaigners and legislators, who sought to control male behaviour by enacting new laws. For all the changes made in the law, the levels of violence in spousal relationships could never be accurately measured. Murder was unacceptable, but what really constituted acceptable and unacceptable violence against wives remained an ever-changing construct of magistrates, judges and juries. In 1888, when the neighbours of Patrick Butler of Galway tried to stop him beating his wife, he told them 'he married her, she was his wife and he could do what he liked with her'.[24] As Foyster argues 'marital violence was not always seen as deviant behaviour, and could be viewed instead as a feature of a "normal" functioning relationship'.[25] What concerned judges and others was a man going 'too far' and causing serious injury to his wife; or the man who neglected his husbandly duties, for instance in not supporting his wife and family, and who also engaged in violence against them.

---

[23] 17 May 1824 (NAI, Prisoners' Petitions and Cases, VI 23 2, 2440).
[24] NAI, Crown Files at Assizes, Galway, 1888.   [25] Foyster, *Marital Violence*, p. 57.

Provocation

The issue of provocation, however it might be claimed in court, was taken seriously by magistrates, judges and jurymen over the entire period of this study. The concept of provocation provided a framework for blame, and allowed men and women to argue that the behaviour of the offending spouse could no longer be tolerated. Husbands accused of violence towards their wives often resorted to arguing that she was somehow a bad wife. One individual claimed his wife had provoked him by not having his supper ready for him and he was released on recognisance. An old man who had beaten his wife so badly that she ended up in hospital was also released on recognisance as it had been 'shown that the prisoner got some provocation'.[26]

A case from the late eighteenth century provides some indication of the parameters that limited wives' access to justice. In this particular case obedience to the husband was paramount. Mary Amyott prosecuted her husband Francis Amyott, a professor of the French Language at Trinity College, Dublin, in 1792, just two months after their wedding. She claimed that she had been beaten about the head and body and left out in the cold for two hours with nothing to cover her, when she refused to have sexual relations with him. Her lawyer noted the moral obligations of society to protect wives from abusive husbands, and especially one who was a foreigner (Amyott was French), as Irishmen were 'celebrated throughout Europe for their manly attachment to the rights of the fair sex'. The defendant's lawyer tried initially to have the case dismissed, noting that women who brought charges against their husbands were guilty of 'perjury'. While this point was dismissed, the recorder of the court noted that 'it was the general rule of law that a wife cannot be evidence against her husband'. The recorder of Dublin City, in his summing up, noted that 'domestic broils between husband and wife are more frequently the offspring of caprice and mutual obstinacy than of any just foundation or sufficient'. The jury found the defendant not guilty. They very well may have held the same views as the recorder that 'in the present instance ... the wife had deviated from the injunctions of her husband ... had slighted his authority, and resisted his lawful commands'.[27] In other words she had provoked his abusive actions by refusing

---

[26] *Limerick Reporter*, 13 Oct. 1882; *Cavan Weekly News*, 20 Aug. 1878; *Munster News*, 29 Nov. 1876.

[27] Vincent Dowling, *Trials at Large* (Dublin, 1792), part 1 and 2, p. 632. See also Brian Henry, *Dublin Hanged: Crime, Law Enforcement and Punishment in Late Eighteenth-Century Dublin* (Dublin, 1994), pp. 55–6.

to have sexual relations with him. Marital rape was not a legal concept until the twentieth century; it was criminalised in Ireland in 1991.

Sometimes it was unacceptable for a husband to use provocation as a defence. In 1829 James Kelly, a jaunting car-keeper in Dublin, was indicted for assaulting his wife, Catherine. She appeared in court with an infant in her arms and deposed that one morning when her husband came in from work, she was holding her sick child whom she had just bathed. He asked her 'was there no sign of breakfast' and she replied 'if you earned anything, give it to me and I'll get your breakfast', implying that he was not a good provider. He took up a loaded whip and beat her with it. Her sister came in and saw her covered in blood. The court was told that he was constantly in the habit of abusing his wife and that he was twice previously bound to keep the peace. The couple had been married for eight years and had three living children. Catherine told the court that her husband frequently threatened to kill her and often put her out of bed after midnight and she was obliged to shelter herself and children in the watch house; he had bitten one of her fingers so she no longer had the use of it. In this instance the husband, because of his violent history towards his wife, could not get away with the provocation of his wife not having his breakfast ready. He was found guilty and got six months' imprisonment.[28]

Cases in the eighteenth and early nineteenth centuries show courts' concerns with how wives conformed to their husband's commands. However, courts could also be supportive in cases where the violence appeared extreme. The following case shows how marital violence was not always casual violence, and sometimes its intensity was extraordinary. In 1803 James Murphy was 'indicted for unlawfully, wickedly, cruelly and unnaturally contriving, and intending the destruction of Ann Murphy', his wife. The judge noted that Murphy had beaten his wife, ill-treated her, and kept her confined for six months without 'sustenance and necessaries'. The judge described Murphy's crime as worse than murder. He sentenced him to two years in jail for starving and attempting to murder his wife, and gave him a 100 pound fine. It was reported that Murphy was willing to make his wife 'ample recompence [*sic*] for all that is past, by taking a house for them both, and going into business without having any more to do with any of his family, who (says he) brought all this miserable business on him'. His counsel told the court that Murphy had agreed to make a settlement on his wife, if part of his fine was remitted, and that there was a mitigation of part of his

---

[28] *Ballina Impartial*, 28 Sept. 1829.

punishment. The court was willing to consider remission once a 'settlement was properly secured'.[29] We do not know whether Murphy served any jail time, or indeed whether he and his wife lived together again. Murphy tried to excuse his behaviour towards his wife by blaming the influence of his family on the marriage. His willingness to literally pay for his crimes held sway in court and may have succeeded in keeping him from prison. It is likely that his wife depended on him for financial support. A much more pragmatic response to violence came from another victim of abuse. Between 1835 and 1841, Mary McTigue summoned her husband for assault on numerous occasions before the Castlebar petty sessions. Clearly, the court appearances and fines had done nothing to control her husband's behaviour. In June 1841, she declared to the court that she was 'determined never to go back to him'.[30]

What real protection the law offered to abused wives is questionable, as many men sentenced for relatively brief periods in gaol offered only a short respite to their wives and children. John Mayne was found guilty of assaulting his wife Sarah Mayne in 1803, and 'was in conformity to her earnest desire, merely held over to bail of £100 to be of the peace to her for seven years'. She had deposed that from repeated threats and assaults from him she was in dread and fear of her life.[31] In 1808, 'a brutal fellow named Curran' was tried in Dublin for assaulting his wife, by splitting her lip, and beating her with a hammer. He was sentenced to three months imprisonment and ordered to give security for his good behaviour for what looked like a murderous assault.[32] Women who prosecuted their husbands for assault were not always safe. In 1855, Thomas Kearney was charged with attacking his wife, stabbing her in the cheek and arm with a knife. He had been brought before the court for assault the day before the attack but she pleaded to have him released. The following day he attacked her with a knife and left her seriously injured.[33]

Perpetrators

Throughout the period there appears to have been little discussion within the Irish press about the extent or meaning of domestic assault. An examination of a sample of 150 men arrested for assaulting their wives between 1825 and 1857, reveals that the majority of men were from the labouring classes, and included labourers, bricklayers, porters and dealers, while others were artisans with trades, such as carpenters,

---

[29] *Freeman's Journal*, 3 March 1803.   [30] *Mayo Constitution*, 29 June 1841.
[31] *Ennis Chronicle*, 20 Jan. 1803.   [32] *Ennis Chronicle*, 13 July 1808.
[33] *Freeman's Journal*, 9 Feb. 1855.

coopers, shoemakers, etc. Offenders ranged in age from nineteen years to over sixty. All of the cases were for assaulting a wife, and the sentences varied greatly, ranging from a husband at the Macroom sessions in 1825 being imprisoned for three months or liable for a fine of £5 to be paid to the prosecution, to a labourer named Thomas Monks who in 1843 faced a fine of 1s 6d or to be confined for three days. Other cases also reveal the variety of sentences. In 1846, a dealer named Burrowes Jordan was imprisoned for one week and was to remain in prison until he gave security to keep the peace with his wife. He was to guarantee £20 and also to secure two sureties of £10 each for fourteen years. The court was informed that he was in the habit 'for a considerable time past' of ill-treating and beating his wife. In the most recent incident he had stabbed her.[34] His more severe sentence reflects the attempt made on the life of his wife.

Men of the middle, upper-middle, gentry and landowning classes rarely ended up in court on spousal assault charges. Given the family status, reputation and the nature of wives' dependency at these levels of society, women were unlikely to take a brutal husband before the petty sessions. Most often, domestic violence at these social levels came to light in the divorce courts. These perpetrators were not being charged with assault but their violent and cruel actions were grounds for divorce.[35] Such discrepancies in dealing with marital violence suggests that the legal system offered different solutions for different classes.

Changing the Law

There was a concern among some MPs that the 1828 Act was too lenient on abusive husbands.[36] A Bill for the Better Prosecution and Punishment of Aggravated Assaults on Women and Children was introduced into the House of Commons in March 1853. Henry Fitzroy, who introduced the bill, argued that he 'was only asking [MPs] to extend the same protection to defenceless women as they already extended to poodle dogs and donkeys'. If found guilty under the cruelty to animals' Act, a person could be subjected to three months' imprisonment, with or without hard labour.[37] Fitzroy's bill was designed to extend the penalties that could be imposed for brutal assaults. A fine

---

[34] *Freeman's Journal,* 4 Dec. 1846.
[35] For cruelty as a grounds for divorce see Chapter 12.
[36] The 1828 Act was extended to Ireland in 1829 as An Act for Consolidating and Amending the Statutes in Ireland Relating to Offences against the Person. 10 Geo. IV c.34. 1829; Offences against the Person Act. 24 & 25 Vict. c.100. 1861.
[37] *HC Parliamentary Debates,* 1853, col. 1418.

of up to £20 or a term of imprisonment, with or without hard labour, not exceeding six months was now possible. Another important point in the bill was that the complaint did not have to be made by 'the party aggrieved'; it could be brought by a third party who had witnessed the assault. The bill received the Royal Assent in June 1853.[38] In 1854 the government sought information from various police forces within the United Kingdom on the numbers of assaults made on women and children in the year to July 1855. The return from the Dublin Metropolitan Police revealed that 15 individuals were sent for trial for assaults on women and children, 344 were summarily convicted and 863 individuals were discharged. This means that a total of 1,222 individuals were arrested by the DMP on the charge of assaulting women and children.[39] Further legislation in this area saw the introduction of the 1861 Offences against the Persons Act (also applicable to Ireland) which retained the 1853 Act without alteration.[40]

Examining a sample of 150 men arrested for assaulting women between 1858 and 1864, we see again that the majority of men were from the labouring and skilled artisan classes. The sentences handed out reflected the impact of the new legislation and suggest a greater intolerance towards spousal violence. A number of individuals were both fined and imprisoned for assaulting their wives. For instance, in May 1860, fifty-three-year-old Francis Adderly, a labourer, was convicted of severely assaulting his wife, Mary. He was fined five pounds and sentenced to two months in jail.[41] What becomes more common after the 1853 Act is that husbands were bound to keep the peace with their wives after conviction and a term in prison or a fine. This may have afforded some protection to abused wives, but it is difficult to tell how thoroughly such sentences were policed.

Extent of Assault

From 1865 there was an annual return noted in the judicial statistics for the number of assaults perpetrated on women and children.[42] The figures are available for both the Dublin Metropolitan District and the

---

[38] Doggett, *Marriage, Wife-Beating*, pp. 106–9.
[39] *Assaults on Women and Children (Dublin). Return of the Number of Men Charged at or Summoned to the Different Police Offices in Dublin, During the Past Year, for Assaults on Women and Children; Stating How Many Have Been Sent for Trial, and How Many Have Been Summarily Convicted.* HC 1854–55 (221).
[40] Doggett, *Marriage, Wife-Beating*, p. 109.
[41] NAI, Prison Register, Cork Male Prison.
[42] *Criminal and Judicial Statistics for Ireland* (Dublin, 1865–1895).

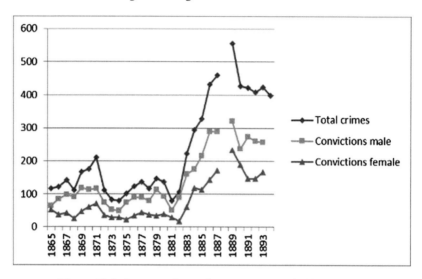

Figure 10.1 Aggravated assaults on women and children, Dublin Metropolitan District, 1864–1894.
Source: Dublin Metropolitan Police Statistics, 1866–1894

country as a whole (which do not include the Dublin figures). The figures are not as revealing as one might expect. They cover assaults on women and boys under the age of fourteen, and distinguish perpetrators on the grounds of sex, but the victims are not categorised. Women also committed aggravated assaults on other women, men and children, and are included in the available figures.[43] Keeping this in mind, the available figures tell us only of the extent of aggravated assaults, their increase and decrease over the decades.

In the DMP district in the years between 1865 and 1875 a total of 1,421 aggravated assaults against women and children were recorded, which amounted to an average of 129 assaults per annum (Figure 10.1). Over the same period 943 men were convicted of this offence, and 404 women. What is very noticeable is that the likelihood of conviction, if an individual was arrested for this crime, was very high: over 95 per cent. The judicial returns for 1869 provided a comparison of

---

[43] For women assaulting women, a common enough occurrence, see, for example, *Leinster Leader*, 30 July 1887, where it was reported that Kate McDonnell summonsed Mary More for assault for pulling her hair. For other cases see *Leinster Leader*, 24 Oct. 1891; *Freeman's Journal*, 23 April, 1878; NAI, CIF 1846 B9.

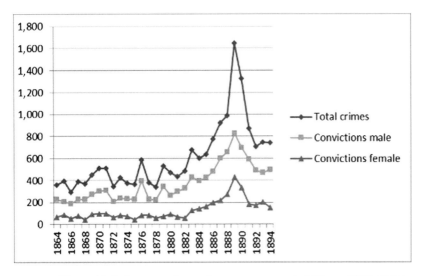

Figure 10.2 Aggravated assaults on women and children, 1865–1894, Ireland (excluding DMP).
Source: *Criminal and Judicial Statistics for Ireland* (Dublin, 1866–1895)

aggravated assaults against women and children in Ireland, England and Wales. The total for Ireland was 450, for England and Wales 2,690. The report notes that, per head of population, there were fewer crimes indicating 'a lower moral tone', such as aggravated assaults on women and children, evident in Ireland than in England and Wales.[44]

The DMP stopped reporting on this crime from 1894 but between 1885 and 1894, 3,853 aggravated assaults on women and children were recorded, an average of 385 per annum, a considerable increase in the numbers reported between 1865 and 1875. We can surmise that either more assaults were being committed or, more likely, more perpetrators were being brought to justice in this period. Between 1885 and 1893 (no figures are available for 1888; nor are convictions noted for 1894), 2,144 men were convicted of these assaults, as were 1,311 women.[45]

The difference between the DMP statistics and those for the rest of the country is that the latter provide us with the form of punishment received

[44] *Return of Judicial Statistics for Ireland, 1869*, p. 17.
[45] Dublin Metropolitan Police Statistics, annual reports, 1865–1894.

Table 10.1 *Sentences of those convicted of aggravated assaults on women and children, Ireland, 1864–1894*

		Sentences																						
	Total no. convicted		Over 6 months		3 to 6 months		2 to 3 months		1 to 2 months		15 days to 1 month		14 days and under		Reformatory school		Industrial school	Fined only		Whipped	To find sureties		Other punishments	
Year	M	F	M	F	M	F	M	F	M	F	M	F	M	F	M	F	M	M	F	M	M	F	M	F
1864	230	70	3	–	22	–	13	–	30	–	53	–	12	–	–	–	–	106	–	–	28	–	33	–
1865	210	87	1	–	8	–	16	–	25	–	39	–	21	–	–	–	–	142	–	–	29	–	16	–
1866	187	52	4	–	21	–	16	–	23	–	28	–	14	–	–	–	–	75	–	–	33	–	25	–
1867	228	76	–	–	19	–	24	–	30	–	44	–	20	–	–	–	–	97	–	–	38	–	32	–
1868	229	44	3	–	24	–	17	–	28	–	41	–	13	–	1	–	–	92	–	–	34	–	20	–
1869	274	92	6	–	23	–	22	–	28	–	44	–	29	–	2	–	–	149	–	–	46	–	17	–
1870	302	100	9	–	31	–	37	–	48	–	36	–	17	–	–	–	–	140	–	–	57	–	18	–
1871	307	100	2	–	25	–	21	–	47	–	49	–	29	–	4	–	–	168	–	–	51	–	11	–
1872	210	61	2	–	22	2	16	1	28	4	23	6	18	2	5	–	–	62	35	–	27	7	7	4
1873	238	82	3	–	41	–	14	–	17	10	30	15	8	6	6	–	–	80	36	–	33	13	6	2
1874	232	71	11	–	49	4	19	3	22	14	36	14	13	4	–	–	–	55	19	–	26	10	1	3
1875	230	44	3	–	53	2	33	3	25	5	29	4	8	5	3	–	–	51	21	–	23	2	2	2
1876	396	83	13	–	62	3	57	5	37	7	39	5	49	6	2	–	1	115	32	–	18	9	3	16

Year																							
1877	228	83	4	–	49	8	39	8	19	8	23	6	10	4	2	2	–	50	26	–	21	11	11	10
1878	222	60	3	–	41	2	39	5	35	12	26	6	6	5	1	–	–	53	16	–	14	10	4	4
1879	345	74	16	–	48	3	54	3	50	5	35	9	10	6	–	1	–	80	31	–	46	13	6	4
1880	265	91	8	–	53	2	38	6	22	9	23	10	12	3	–	–	–	82	39	–	23	20	4	1
1881	299	66	4	–	53	2	59	5	46	3	34	13	11	4	–	1	–	52	22	–	37	14	3	3
1882	329	60	20	1	55	2	48	3	31	5	36	9	12	3	3	–	–	76	22	–	49	14	2	1
1883	430	127	20	–	88	8	73	7	49	9	45	26	23	23	–	1	–	92	38	–	34	13	3	2
1884	394	145	3	–	67	2	78	11	60	26	60	48	39	17	1	–	–	58	31	–	23	5	6	1
1885	423	161	4	–	51	1	67	9	60	23	90	53	44	14	–	1	–	61	44	–	41	13	4	3
1886	478	201	3	–	68	7	60	11	63	23	76	54	79	31	1	–	–	62	44	–	55	30	3	1
1887	601	220	9	4	63	9	61	7	91	44	105	55	66	47	–	–	–	113	36	–	91	18	2	–
1888	654	273	11	2	71	10	89	7	91	44	133	84	59	38	1	–	–	91	63	–	102	24	6	1
1889	826	432	9	1	47	8	53	10	100	36	177	98	71	54	1	–	–	217	183	–	138	37	13	5
1890	699	335	7	–	54	17	69	15	84	41	152	67	59	33	–	–	–	170	125	–	98	34	6	3
1891	592	182	2	2	27	4	63	3	72	19	127	73	54	25	2	1	1	130	30	1	111	23	3	4
1892	491	174	2	–	40	1	53	5	74	20	116	55	32	21	–	–	–	74	35	–	93	33	7	4
1893	470	203	1	–	40	5	48	10	63	21	108	69	41	16	1	–	–	77	26	–	86	50	5	6
1894	496	153	–	–	57	5	90	5	60	22	90	48	33	20	–	–	–	64	24	2	89	25	11	4

by those convicted of this offence.[46] What is noticeable in these figures is the rise in the number of individuals tried on this charge, and the greater number of convictions. By the 1890s, magistrates appear to be more inclined to convict than before. Sentences were also harsher, with 195 individuals being sentenced to more than a month in jail, and 171 receiving a sentence between fourteen days and a month. Fewer were fined: seventy-four men and thirty-five women. What may have been happening in terms of the increase in numbers was that assaults upon women and children were becoming more unacceptable. The rise in prosecutions may also reflect the establishment in 1889 of the Society for the Prevention of Cruelty to Children which had an impact on the number of domestic abuse and child neglect cases which were heard by Irish courts.

How effective the police were in combating domestic violence is open to question. The police manuals of the period directed them not to interfere in domestic matters. Figures may also reveal the areas where police were more active. Aggravated assaults against women and children were higher in Dublin than in any other Irish city, including Belfast. This may have more to do with the diligence of the police or reflect a more heavily policed city than the unacceptability of the crime. It should also be recognised that, from the 1880s, legislation relating to the welfare of children was introduced. The period from the 1880s is widely recognised as an era when the 'rights' of children within the family become a focus of attention and concern for philanthropists, welfare activists and, in turn, legislators. In 1889 the Prevention of Cruelty to Children Act, which also applied in Ireland, was passed. A further Act relating to child cruelty was enacted in 1894 and a consolidating act reached the statute books in 1908.[47] The implementation of this legislation made the 1853 Aggravated Assaults against Women and Children Act, at least where it related to children, redundant.

Whatever the legal situation, sentencing in cases of domestic violence remained inconsistent. In 1906, Alexander Kelly was charged with having seriously assaulted his wife who, it was noted, 'still bore the marks of her husband's brutality'. She told the court that her husband had knocked her down, kicked her several times on her side, and kept beating her head against the floor until she became unconscious. Although he had been twice previously convicted and imprisoned for assaulting his

---

[46] *Criminal and Judicial Statistics for Ireland 1864* (3418), lvii 653. Figures for wife beating are noted in Urquhart, 'Irish divorce and domestic violence', 825–6. However, some of these figures need to be treated with caution and those noted for murder considerably underestimate the numbers of such cases between 1853 and 1920.

[47] See, Maria Luddy, 'The early years of the NSPCC in Ireland', *Eire/Ireland*, 44, 1&2 (Spring/Summer 2009), 67.

wife, his sentence for the third crime was four months' hard labour (the maximum could be six months). He was warned that if he came before the magistrates again he would receive the maximum penalty.[48] In 1908 Andrew Murphy, aged fifty-seven, appeared before the Dublin Police Courts charged with a serious assault on his wife. His sentence was six weeks' hard labour and bail or fourteen days. He also had two previous convictions for the same offence.[49]

Wives Assaulting Husbands

Women also assaulted their husbands, but such assaults were prosecuted much less frequently in the courts. In 1906, a woman named Codd was charged by her husband with assaulting him, although he had earlier been bound to 'keep the peace to his wife' having previously assaulted her. She was ordered to find bail for her future good conduct.[50] A pregnant Mary Anne Doyle violently assaulted her husband when she found him in a brothel in Purdon Street in Dublin. She had caught him in bed with the brothel keeper, whom she also assaulted by throwing bottles and glasses at her. All three were brought to court, where it was noted that they all had serious cuts and wounds. The husband was sent off to the prison hospital for treatment; the brothel keeper to Jervis Street hospital; while Mary Anne Doyle was considered too near her confinement to be punished and was allowed out on her own bail.[51] In May 1891, Ellen Watson was summoned by her husband for assaulting him. He claimed she had struck him in the face when she was drunk. She had also thrown boiling tea at him. In 1890 she had been imprisoned for three months for assaulting him and he now wanted a separation and he said that he would look after their six children himself. Ellen claimed her husband had joined the Salvation Army and would not give her money for food. If freed, she agreed that she would no longer live with her husband. The judge sentenced her to two months with hard labour.[52] When Mary Flanagan stabbed her husband of four years in the neck in a dispute over clothes, she noted to the police, 'If I kick and beat my husband, what is that to any other person?'[53] Winifrid Dwyer walked free from the court having, on the advice of the magistrate, pleaded guilty to assaulting her husband. She had inflicted serious wounds to his head. The fact that she was nine months pregnant at the time of the assault may have swayed the magistrate, but perhaps more decisive and influential was the fact that she had brought a large fortune to

[48] *Donegal Independent*, 29 June 1906.   [49] NAI, CIF M70 1909.
[50] *Freeman's Journal*, 1 Jan. 1878.   [51] *Freeman's Journal*, 19 March 1878.
[52] *Irish Times*, 2 June 1891.   [53] *Galway Express*, 19 July 1890.

the marriage which her husband had drunk away during their three-year union. He had also previously been convicted of assaulting her.[54]

Magistrates were reluctant, in some cases at least, to interfere in domestic conflict, but again there was little consistency in the ways magistrates acted in this period. In 1801 the prosecution of Elizabeth Quinn against Robert Quinn, her husband, for assault and battery received considerable press attention. Elizabeth was 'strenuously recommended ... to settle amicably with her husband' and return to live with him. In order to persuade her to follow such a course her husband's counsel offered to settle on her £300, in case she should survive her husband, and enter into security for £1,000, 'never more to molest her on returning to the loving and penitent affection of her tender husband'. Elizabeth informed the court that she felt her life would be endangered by returning to her husband and another proposal was put forward that allowed her a separate maintenance on condition that she drop the prosecution. She was much more amenable to this solution, and it was accepted by the court.[55]

Domestic violence trials could, therefore, end in a judgement sanctioning a judicial separation similar to those agreed in the ecclesiastical courts. In 1833, a blacksmith named Doran was indicted for assaulting his wife, Catherine. In the Recorder's Court she testified that her husband assaulted her violently and she was obliged to leave him. The couple had two children. The prisoner claimed it was jealousy that made her leave him and she was very often tipsy. She denied this and said she would not proceed with the prosecution if he promised not to assault her in future. The prisoner was asked by the court how much money he would allow her weekly for support and he suggested 5s and the case was dismissed on those terms.[56] Common law courts did not have the power to grant legal separations until 1871, when the powers of the ecclesiastical court were transferred to the Matrimonial Causes Court as part of the process of the disestablishment of the Church of Ireland. However, and perhaps following John Radcliff's 1827 definition of cruelty,[57] it appears that some justices and magistrates took ecclesiastical court rulings as a precedent for suggesting that couples separate and that maintenance be paid by the husband.[58] In 1838 a 'very respectable-looking woman', named Anne Lube, accompanied by three of her children, appeared to complain against her husband Patrick Lube, a painter, for a violent and brutal assault. She noted to the court 'I do not ... want to punish him; my only reason for applying here is to see if your worship

[54] Ibid.   [55] *Ennis Chronicle*, 29 Jan. 1801.   [56] *Connaught Journal*, 5 Sept. 1833.
[57] See p. 314–15.   [58] See Chapter 12.

could induce him to allow me something weekly for the support of myself and children as I am afraid while he continues in his present course to live with him'.[59] She was informed by the clerk that 'we cannot do anything for you in that way, unless he consents. All that lies in our power is to punish him for the assault'. The husband was then sent for and when he arrived he was intoxicated, which clearly influenced the magistrates in their judgement. The magistrates requested to know what he would allow his wife weekly as his salary was a guinea a week and his employment permanent. He suggested six shillings a week, and that he would take care of their son. He was asked by the court, 'Would it not be a great deal better if you consented to live peaceably and quietly with your wife, who appears to be a very sensible and well-conducted woman?' It was suggested that he had taken up with another woman. He eventually agreed to pay his wife seven shillings a week, but the court insisted that the couple remain living together in the same house as it was 'not our wish that you should separate more particularly as he may yet reform and drop his evil habits'. His wife agreed, noting 'but I must take care, while he continues drinking to keep out of his way as much as possible'.[60] How they managed to live together afterwards is unknown.

After the introduction of the 1871 legislation, courts did suggest couples separate. Further legislation, for example the 1878 Matrimonial Causes Act and the 1895 Summary Jurisdiction (Married Women) Act, which did not apply to Ireland, allowed magistrates to grant judicial separations, maintenance orders and the custody of young children to wives whose husbands were convicted of aggravated assaults. The 1895 Act allowed women to seek maintenance and separation orders on a much broader scale than before.[61] It is likely that Irish magistrates framed their own responses in court within the context of this legislation, even though it did not apply to Ireland. However, a solution to an abusive relationship was not always left to the courts. Clergymen were sometimes requested to bring couples to a resolution. In 1911 at the Mullingar quarter sessions, Julia Flood informed the court that her husband drank too much and beat her. She had been forced to find shelter with her sister. On other occasions she had been obliged to flee to a neighbour's house. The neighbour, who gave evidence in court, noted that 'it was with reluctance he gave evidence where husband and wife were concerned'. The husband wanted her to return to the family home but she

---

[59] *Freeman's Journal*, 6 March 1838.   [60] Ibid.
[61] Doggett, *Marriage, Wife-Beating*; Mary Lyndon Shanley, *Feminism, Marriage, and the Law in Victorian England, 1850-1895* (Princeton, 1989). Alan Shatter, *Family Law in the Republic of Ireland* (Dublin, 1977), chapter 14.

refused. The judge made no decree but wanted to hear what the clergy-man of the parish had to say. The latter attended the court and the judge decided to leave the matter to him to settle.[62] This was not the only occasion on which a magistrate or judge sought a couple's reconciliation through a priest or minister, and further examples of such action will be seen later.[63]

Even after a couple had separated, abuse could still take place. In Carlow in 1891, a man was charged with stabbing his wife after she successfully sued him for the price of two pigs. After leaving court he went to her house and took the two pigs away. He also assaulted her and stabbed her with a knife. He told the court, 'My wife and I got into grips and I did not use the knife till I got the blows'. Although he had previously been bound to keep the peace after another assault, the jury acquitted him because it was believed that she had provoked him, and there was 'no corroborative witness'.[64] Other women who were abused took the option of returning to their families in order to escape a husband's violence.[65]

Family Involvement

Family members and neighbours could play an active role in assisting the wives of abusive husbands. Ellen Sutcliffe summoned her son-in-law, Daniel Walsh, at the Abbeyleix petty sessions in 1875, for assault. She claimed that she tried to stop him beating his wife and he then 'turned on her', knocked her down and kicked her while she was on the ground. She had given up her farm to him on his marrying her daughter and there was an understanding that she would live in the house with the couple, and be supported by him. Walsh was sent to jail for a month, with hard labour. At the end of his imprisonment he was to give £10 and a further two securities of £5 each to keep the peace for six months or be imprisoned for six months.[66] This was a fairly severe sentence, and while he was not prosecuted by his wife for assault, the sentence reflects the court's acknowledgement of his violence towards her.

On other occasions, family intervention took the form of violence against the abusive husband. For instance, in 1830, John Philban was beaten and stoned by his wife's brothers 'for beating his wife'.[67] John Flannelly, of Shrule, County Mayo, was in the process of beating his wife

---

[62] *Irish Times*, 18 April 1911.   [63] See pp. 384–5.
[64] *Carlow Sentinel*, 14, 18 July 1891.
[65] *Mayo Constitution*, 3 June, 5 Aug. 1830, 25 July 1837.
[66] *Leinster Express*, 16 Oct. 1875.   [67] *Mayo Constitution*, 25 Oct. 1830.

when her sisters and brothers caught him and beat him to death, exclaiming 'you are a long time deserving that'.[68] In 1873 a number of Limerick men were prosecuted for assaulting their brother-in-law, who had been abusing their sister. The prosecuting barrister addressed the jury asking 'Was this a way a man was to be treated in a free country and under a free form of government because he had beaten his wife?' suggesting that a man could do as he wished to his spouse.[69] Sometimes those who came to the aid of an abused wife put themselves in danger. In 1834, when attempting to prevent Pat Hefferan from assaulting his own wife, Pat Byrne was stabbed twice with a knife or chisel and died.[70] An unusual and uncommon communal response to a violent husband occurred in Callan, County Kilkenny, in 1775. A man named Walsh was taken by a crowd of about 150 people, led by the Whiteboys, to a turnpike gate in Callan, hung by the neck until he was unconscious and when revived was given the option to 'take with his wife or to divide half his worldly substance with her'.[71]

Neighbours and family members often provided refuge to abused wives, and some at least knew about the circumstances in which a husband was violent to his wife. The woman might carry, in black eyes, cuts and bruises, the physical signs of abuse. Word-of-mouth *via* siblings or other family members or neighbours could also make the matter known, and abused wives returning to their parental homes were clearly objecting to the violence they endured. Other than taking revenge through violence, as noted in the examples above, the way in which families dealt with abusive husbands depended on a number of factors. There might be financial complications arising from dowry payments, or for poorer families a problem with ensuring support for an abused wife and her children. Indeed, it may also be true that the presence of children made it more difficult for a poorer couple to separate. As we have noted elsewhere, the work of a husband as well as of his wife and children was often vital for the family's survival. The idea that marriages were for life did not carry much sway among many from a poor background, who resorted to desertion or bigamy when they felt their marriages were unsuccessful.

How and when to intervene in a violent marriage was not always an easy decision for neighbours or family members to make. Suing an abusive husband was one way in which families sought to bring abusers to account

---

[68] *Mayo Constitution*, 15 March 1842.   [69] *Limerick Reporter*, 25 Feb. 1873.
[70] *Ballina Impartial*, 7 July 1834.
[71] Cited in J. S. Donnelly, 'Irish agrarian rebellion: The Whiteboys of 1769-1776', *Proceedings of the Royal Irish Academy*, lxxxiii, section C (1983), 309.

for their actions, though these cases were not always successful. In 1831 a Mr Pescoe, 'a respectable-looking old gentleman', with several cuts and bruises claimed he had been assaulted by his son-in-law, Captain Hicks, a navy man.[72] Pescoe complained that his son-in-law knocked him down and struck him with the iron heel of his boot on his eye when he had attempted to save his daughter (married to Hicks) from his dreadful treatment. Mrs Hicks appeared in court with her thirteen-year-old daughter supporting her, and with cuts on her head and a black eye. While in court she burst into tears and then fainted. Her behaviour, it was reported, 'overpowered the feelings of magistrates and every person present'. When she recovered, she swore that she had been married sixteen years and had four children living; she had been obliged to separate from her husband on two occasions due to his violent and barbarous treatment but returned to the family home 'induced by his entreaties and promises of mild and kind behaviour'. The last occasion for a beating occurred when he came home drunk and asked for more alcohol and she 'in the most gentle and affectionate manner begged of him not to insist on more', whereupon he knocked her down with his clenched fist, jumped on her stomach then held her down with one leg and continued thumping her. She was rescued by a man passing by the house and she and her children left their home for the night. Hicks provided no defence, but said that his father-in-law was the cause of all the trouble. Hicks was ordered to find bail of £200 and two sureties of £100; Mrs Hicks and her father were bound to £50 each to prosecute; and Miss Hicks (the daughter?) to £10. Within three days Pescoe and Hicks, together with the latter's wife, were back in court noting that Hicks could not make bail and requesting the court that he be let out, and also that they, Pescoe and his daughter, be allowed to drop all the charges. Mr Hicks 'expressed great sorrow and regret' for his behaviour and informed the court that 'any proceeding against him would be productive of disorder among his family, and final ruin'. Both applications were granted. 'So much for matrimonial squabbles!' as the *Freeman's Journal* noted.[73] Hicks and Pescoe may have decided not to continue with the assault charges for financial reasons. Given Hicks' previous treatment of his wife, it is unlikely that he stopped beating her.

Petitioning for Release

Many of the petitions presented to the Lord Lieutenant to mitigate the sentences of men accused of domestic abuse were sent by wives.

---

[72] *Freeman's Journal*, 9 Aug. 1831.   [73] Ibid.

In 1873 one magistrate noted that 'wives are invariably in the habit of memorializing for the release of their husbands. The reason is obvious'.[74] There was some recognition on the part of magistrates as to how precarious the economic lives of women and children were without the financial contribution of a husband. In 1883 Patrick Delany committed a serious assault on his wife when he struck her with a large stone and then attempted to strangle her. Having decided to prosecute him Mrs Delany, when in court, denied anything had happened and claimed that she was drunk when she spoke to the police. The presiding magistrate noted that 'the system of prevarication is getting so prevalent the police will have to exercise great caution in taking charges from women against their husbands. They make a statement to the police and then they entirely withdraw from it. If they wish to get murdered I can't help it. From what I see in this court, I have a very poor opinion of the women in Dublin.'[75]

Exploring appeal files, Liz Steiner-Scott looked at 1,012 cases of spousal assaults and noted that for the period 1853–1920 the average length of sentence was three months, and 22 per cent of those petitioning had received a sentence of six months with hard labour. However, as Steiner-Scott recognises, these appeal cases were only a small proportion of all abuse cases, and few of those convicted of assault appealed their sentences.[76] Steiner-Scott also concluded, from the evidence of these petitions, that a man convicted of assaulting another man (often with considerable violence) on average received a sentence of four months with hard labour.[77] However, from the hundreds of cases of domestic assault viewed for this chapter many husbands received lesser sentences for assaulting their wives, and it is also evident that hundreds of such men were never prosecuted at all. Many were also prosecuted and convicted a number of times, although this did not seem to diminish their violent actions. John Wolff, for instance, was charged in 1893 with having assaulted his wife. He had thrown a loaf of bread at her and a glass of milk in her face. The magistrate stated that the assault was not serious, but it was his fourteenth conviction, so he received one month's imprisonment and was to find bail for his future good behaviour.[78]

There was, as noted already, little public outcry against domestic violence in Ireland, though in the early decades of the twentieth century, the suffragist paper, *The Irish Citizen*, did offer criticism of the court system and its dealings with abusive husbands. In an article on 'Wife

---

[74] NAI, CIF, M40, 1873.   [75] *Irish Times*, 13 Aug. 1883.
[76] Steiner-Scott, '"To bounce a boot off her"', p. 133.   [77] Ibid., p. 137.
[78] *Irish Times*, 12 Sept. 1893.

Beating', in September 1919, L. A. M. Priestly-McCracken, argued that abusive husbands got light sentences or a small fine because they were the main breadwinners in the family. She suggested that such men should be given longer sentences with hard labour, and if necessary their wives and children should be supported out of public funds. She also suggested that just as there was a society to protect children from cruelty there should also be a society to protect wives from abusive husbands.[79] The 'debate' did not go further than that. Indeed, many feminists of the period believed that violence in the home was a 'working-class' problem, and that, therefore, marital violence was a class problem rather than a reflection of a wider social issue.[80]

Murder and Manslaughter

In the worst cases of marital violence death was often the final outcome. Reports of spousal murders in the newspapers of the eighteenth century were short and provided few, if any, details of the actual crime. 390 homicides were reported in the *Hibernian Journal* between 1780 and 1795. Of this number it was recorded that twelve involved husbands murdering their wives.[81] The reports of the inspectors general of prisons provide us with information on the number of individuals who were convicted of assault with intent to murder, conspiracy to murder, murder and manslaughter between 1827 and 1833. During the period 1838–1864, there were 3,533 murders recorded, and drawing on information in newspaper and other sources, there were at least 150 (*c.* 4.25 per cent) cases of alleged spousal murder and manslaughter charges during those years.[82] Richard McMahon's research shows that between 1841 and 1850 there were 1,562 reported cases of alleged murder or manslaughter in Ireland.[83] Of that number twenty-three (1.47%) were alleged murders or manslaughter of spouses. Overall this appears a very small percentage of murders. However, our trawl through the newspapers, and other sources, of the same period suggests that there were fifty-eight (3.65%) alleged murders or manslaughter of spouses – more than double McMahon's estimate – revealing that spousal murder was more common than previously noted.

---

[79] L. A. M. Priestly-McCracken, 'Wife-beating', *The Irish Citizen*, Sept. 1919, p. 27.
[80] Jo Aitken, '"The horrors of matrimony among the masses": Feminist representations of wife beating in England and Australia, 1870–1914, *Journal of Women's History*, 19, 1 (2007), 107–31.
[81] Henry, *Dublin Hanged*, p. 47.
[82] From 1865 the figures for homicides are made up of murders and manslaughter.
[83] McMahon, *Homicide in Pre-famine and Famine Ireland*, p. 12.

Table 10.2 *Violent deaths in Ireland, 1876–1895*

Dates	Murder	Manslaughter	Attempted	Murder spousal murder/manslaughter
1876–1895	936	1,828	169	150+

Source: *Criminal and Judicial Statistics for Ireland*, 1877–1896

Between 1876 and 1895 there was a total of 2,933 murder, manslaughter and attempted murder cases recorded. During the same period there were at least 150 spousal murders or manslaughter cases, accounting for 5.46 per cent of the total. So the number of spousal murders or cases of manslaughter appears to have been rising in a period of declining population. Between 1895 and 1925 there were 150 reported cases of alleged murder or manslaughter of spouses in Ireland. Vaughan notes that murder rates fell in Ireland from the 1850s and, on average, after 1859 remained below 100 per annum.[84] Between 1772 and 1925 there were at least 713 spousal murders, and at least 103 wives were alleged to have murdered their husbands. Over the same period there were another eighty-five failed attempts at spousal murder tried in the courts. There is no doubt that our figures from 1772 to 1850 are an underestimate, as not all murder or manslaughter cases were reported in the papers, or accurately recorded in other sources.

The Context of Murder

What were the contexts, then, in which spousal murder occurred? In many cases there was a history of domestic violence that culminated in a murder or attempted murder. In some instances, class difference was an issue and the reality of married life with someone from a lower class became unbearable. Some husbands and wives had simply tired of their spouses. In a few cases murder or attempted murder was a revenge for infidelity and in others it arose from domestic or family disputes about the use of family resources. Jealousy was often deemed the motive for a murder or a manslaughter, a motive ascribed when police, coroners and juries could provide no other explanation for the crime. It did not necessarily mean that a spouse was involved in an adulterous relationship, but jealousy was a word that offered a motive when no other was discernible. Caroline Conley's work on homicide in post-Famine Ireland

[84] W. E. Vaughan, *Murder Trials in Ireland, 1836–1914* (Dublin, 2009), p. 22.

identifies many of the causes of violence more generally in Irish society. She also identifies disputes over land, family resources and other matters as the bases for spousal murders. Likewise, Karen Brennan, writing of murder in the Irish family between 1930 and 1945 sees similar reasons for such violence, revealing the continuity in disputes over dowries, land and resources between couples and in families over the centuries.[85]

Spousal Murder

That spousal abuse was an element in the relationship is evidenced in a large number of cases. James Hickey murdered his wife after a year of marriage. On the fateful evening he had arrived home drunk, and demanded that his wife get out of bed and provide him with his supper. His brother also resided in the house and told her to stay where she was. But she got up, fearful of her husband, who was known not to treat her well. He then told her that he had lost his coat, and asked her to go with him to find it. He then shot her, and absconded. She was six months pregnant at the time.[86] Mary McGuinness, strangled to death by her husband in 1830, had 'always complained of her husband being wicked to her ... often went to the priest and complained of the treatment she received'.[87] William Copeland was accused of murdering his wife, Catherine, in 1840. At the inquest into the death of his wife, the jury concluded that she had died from injuries inflicted by Copeland. Various relatives of Catherine deposed that she applied to them for food at various times and when given food she ate voraciously; Catherine had come into the house of Humphrey James, her brother-in-law, about three weeks before the murder, and appeared quite weak and said Copeland had nearly murdered her. It appeared that about two years previously, he was bound over to keep the peace to his wife; immediately after he turned her out of the dwelling house, and put her in an outhouse, and cohabited with a beggar-woman, named Mary Dunn, until a few weeks before the murder. A local clergyman deposed that he had recently seen Copeland drag the deceased out of his house, strike her on the shoulder, take her by the neck, push her out on the road, and tear her clothes. This clergyman did not interfere with Copeland's actions at the time. The coroner, Dr O'Rourke, determined that she died from starvation and there were no marks of violence on the body. The coroner's jury verdict: 'We find that

---

[85] Conley, *Melancholy Accidents*; Karen Brennan, 'Murder in the Irish family, 1930–45' in Howlin and Costello (eds.), *Law and the Family*, chapter 10.

[86] *Saunders's News-Letter*, 6 March 1809.

[87] *Ballina Impartial*, 9 Aug. 1830; *Mayo Constitution*, 3 June, 5 Aug. 1830.

Catherine Copeland's death was caused by the common necessaries of life having been withheld from her by her husband William Copeland, and also by the bad treatment received from him at sundry times.' Following the verdict, Copeland absconded and evaded justice.[88]

The idiosyncrasy of the law is evident in the case of Murtagh Gately, who in September 1791 struck his wife Jane over the head with an iron hammer. Jane languished for two weeks before dying of the assault. In the meantime a doctor had prescribed something to ease her pain but her husband did not fill the prescription. Gately had previously been tried, and acquitted, of assaulting his wife. At the trial for murder, an uncle of Gately's wife graphically described the attack that killed her. It was also noted at the trial that Gately 'had been in the habit of beating her about the body'. The jury found him guilty of murder, having deliberated for more than an hour, but the judge would not accept the verdict and told the jury to reconsider and to reduce the sentence to manslaughter. The judge may have believed that the assault, while indirectly the cause of the wife's demise, was not its direct cause. Within two minutes of further consultation the jury agreed with the judge. Gately was sentenced to be burnt in the hand, imprisoned for twelve months and ordered to keep the peace for seven years.[89]

Class

As we have seen in earlier chapters, there was a general consensus in Irish society that cross-class alliances should not be entertained and such alliances went against the natural order of society. In 1731 William Ormsby, 'the son of a gentleman of position and fortune in the County of Sligo', was tried for the murder of Catherine Conaghan. She was a 'peasant' and had initially refused his advances but eventually the couple were married privately by a Catholic priest, although Ormsby was a Protestant. In 1726 a child was born. Ormsby 'scorned to acknowledge the daughter of a peasant as his wife' and he enjoyed a social life within the higher levels of society alone and unaccompanied by his wife. While rumours had circulated in Sligo and Dublin that Ormsby had married, he never admitted the fact and decided to end the marriage. Given that he was a Protestant and she a Catholic and they had been married by a Catholic cleric, the marriage was invalid. Before a resolution could be agreed Catherine was found dead, and a coroner's jury brought in a verdict of murder against Ormsby. He absconded, which was suggestive

---

[88] *Wexford Independent*, 14 Aug. 1840.   [89] *Hibernian Journal*, 12 Dec. 1791.

of his guilt, and he managed to evade the law for three years. Eventually he was arrested and brought to trial in 1731. The trial began at nine o'clock and ended at four but the jury took until 9 a.m. on the following morning to reach a verdict. The length of the jury's deliberations suggests that the members had some difficulty agreeing a verdict. Ormsby was, however, found not guilty.[90]

Class was also the factor that shaped the fate of Ellen Hanley, aged fifteen and murdered in 1819. Hanley was an orphan in the care of an uncle who was a rope maker. John Scanlan, a retired lieutenant of the marines, and a member of the Catholic gentry, fell in love with Ellen and in June 1819 the couple eloped, Ellen taking her uncle's savings with her. It is likely, given the secrecy involved, that the pair were married by a couple-beggar. Consequently, Scanlan later argued that their marriage was not binding. On 6 September, a body washed up on the shore of the Shannon river. It had been in the water for a considerable length of time and was badly decomposed, with no hair or flesh on the skull, and with a broken arm and leg. It was noted that Mrs Scanlan had a curious pair of double eye teeth, but the teeth had been knocked out of the corpse discovered in the water, making identification more difficult. Clothing belonging to Mrs Scanlan was identified and eventually the body was reported to be hers. Stephen Sullivan, John Scanlan's servant, who had assisted in the crime, fled, and Scanlan was arrested for murder.

Daniel O'Connell defended Scanlan at his trial where the evidence was overwhelming that the accused was involved in Ellen's murder, although he blamed Sullivan for all that had happened, and insisted that it had occurred without his knowledge. He was not believed and was sentenced to death. O'Connell, writing to his wife, observed 'It is very unusual with me to be so satisfied but he is a horrid villain'.[91] Sullivan was caught and tried for the murder some months later. He had no barrister to represent him and defended himself. The jury convicted him within fifteen minutes. At his execution Sullivan admitted that Scanlan had wanted to get rid of Hanley because she 'always called him her husband'.[92] At the time this was not a widely reported case, but it later found international fame in the play by Dion Boucicault *The Colleen Bawn*.[93]

---

[90] Oliver J. Burke, *Anecdotes of the Connaught Circuit* (Dublin, 1885), pp. 82–3.

[91] Maurice R. O'Connell (ed.), *The Correspondence of Daniel O'Connell* (8 vols., Dublin, 1972), ii, p. 243.

[92] For accounts of the trial see *Belfast Newsletter*, 24 Sept. 1820; *Saunders's News-Letter*, 1 Aug. 1820. See also, NAI, CSO/RP/1820/1054; CSO/RP/1820/1133; CSO/RP/1820/1413.

[93] The play was an enormous hit for Boucicault. The story of Hanley's murder was fictionalised by Gerald Griffin in *The Collegians* (London, 1829).

Getting Away with Murder

Throughout the period, barristers and sometimes judges suggested to juries that a husband had been provoked to murder a wife and this often led to a diminished charge if the perpetrator was found guilty. In 1871, for instance, sixty-year-old labourer John Swiney, spent two months in jail awaiting trial for strangling his wife. He was convicted of manslaughter and then discharged. The mitigating factor was probably that his wife, Mary, had been addicted to drink.[94] John Reilly was charged with attempting to murder his wife in 1901. The court believed that he had been given ample provocation. The prosecution put forward a charge of malicious wounding rather than attempted murder, which he pleaded guilty to, and it was noted there was 'a great deal of provocation'. He stated that 'she left me and went away with other men'. The couple had married in September 1901, and afterwards he took her to a 'nice comfortable house. He gave her £12 and gave her charge of the house'. Three months later, she brought a young man in as a lodger to the house and the husband considered that she paid too much attention to him. Reilly claimed that she said that he was an old man and that she was sorry she married him, and that the 'marriage was a matter of form'. He declared that she did not keep the house clean and when the lodger came she stayed in his room. He also asserted that she left him having stolen £8 7s 6d from his box. He was, he stated, provoked to commit what was originally considered to be a murderous assault.[95]

In 1913, Peter Gubbins had an indictment for murdering his wife reduced to a manslaughter charge. He had beaten her, and left her with broken ribs and a lacerated liver, from which she died. He was found guilty of manslaughter, under 'great provocation', and sentenced to seven years' penal servitude. The court was told that his wife was of weak mind, and had been in the lunatic ward of the workhouse, and drank a considerable amount. All were considered forms of provocation.[96]

Women who were caught in adulterous affairs received little sympathy in the courts where murder was tried. Such affairs were classed as a provocation to the husband who often received a light sentence for murdering adulterous wives. John Woods murdered his wife Anne in April 1792. It appeared that his wife was having an affair with a regimental musician. The trial revolved very much around this issue, placing the blame on the wife. The judge observed in his summing up that the wife's

---

[94] NAI, Printed Outrage Reports 1871; *Irish Times*, 2 March 1871.
[95] *Irish Times*, 15 Oct. 1902.
[96] *Dublin Daily Express*, 30 Dec. 1913; 6 Jan., 7 Feb. 1914.

behaviour had driven the offender 'to the most frantic pitch of rage and indignation', and that in consequence he had committed the crime 'in a state of temporary madness'. The jury returned a verdict of manslaughter and Woods was sentenced to be burned in the hand and to be jailed for six months.[97] Samuel Smith murdered his wife in Armagh in 1843. A neighbour informed the police that Smith had come to his house on the night of the murder and said 'that he had caught James Devlin, the pensioner, in the act with his wife'. It was also claimed that Smith, on the morning of the murder, had called his wife 'a whore'.[98] Smith received an eighteen month sentence on the grounds that he had been provoked.

Land and Dowries

Just as dowries and land issues played a role in domestic abuse, so too did such disputes lead to murder. Andrew Robinson was found guilty of murdering his wife in 1829. It was a 'love match' and the couple had married against the wishes of their parents before a Presbyterian minister. They lived with Robinson's father for six or seven months after the marriage. There appears to have been no dowry forthcoming from her family, which Robinson's father had expected. It was understood that she had been killed because the fortune was not received.[99]

In 1887 Margaret Brosnan had her indictment for the murder of her husband reduced to a charge of manslaughter. She had hit him with a hatchet and it was reported that although they had only been married for six months she had a 'dread' that her husband was going to sell his interest in the farm that he had received on his marriage (he also paid off a debt on the farm to the value of £140). This would have left her with no means of subsistence as a widow. She got twenty years' penal servitude.[100]

Catherine Grier was acquitted of the attempted murder of her husband in 1908. Grier was aged about fifty and her husband about twenty-five. It transpired that they had met on a public road when she gave him whiskey with a strange taste. He went home and subsequently vomited and his vomit had strychnine in it. The couple had married in 1906 and they lived on Catherine's 'good farm', with her two unmarried sisters. Given the composition of the household it is not surprising that 'some unpleasantness arose' and the young husband went back to live with his own people.

---

[97] Dowling, *Trials at Large*, i, pp. 37–49. See also pp. 266–7 on the law of provocation.
[98] NAI, Outrage papers, Armagh, 1843/16211.
[99] *Ballina Impartial*, 17 Aug. 1829; *Westmeath Journal*, 13 Aug. 1829; *Kerry Evening Post*, 8 Aug. 1829.
[100] Printed return relating to agrarian outrages 1879–1880; *Kerry Evening Post*, 23 Aug. 1879.

Mrs Grier worried that he would succeed to the land on her death as the couple had no children and, hence, she attempted to kill him.[101]

Not surprisingly, therefore, family dynamics caused considerable distress in some families and often led to extreme violence. In 1918 Richard Purser was found guilty of murdering his wife, with the assistance of his mother. His wife, Annie Ashmore, in her mid-twenties, had a dowry of £100, but she did not get on with her mother-in-law or her family. The local clergy intervened, and arrangements were being made for a separation, which would have involved giving back the dowry. It was also claimed that the husband had dealt irregularly with the dowry money. It was agreed that the dowry should be held in the joint names of husband and wife, but Purser withdrew the cash from the joint bank account and deposited it in his own name.[102]

Family Involvement in Murder

As we have seen above, there were also spousal murders that involved other family members, and these cases could be dealt with severely by the courts.[103] One of the most infamous and widely reported spousal murders that involved family and neighbours was that of Bridget Cleary. In 1895, Michael Cleary and a number of relatives were tried for the murder of Bridget Cleary, his wife. According to the police report in the days before she disappeared:

it was generally believed in the locality that she [Bridget] had been bewitched and her identity changed, and on the nights of 14th and 15th March, her husband, her father, and several others, in carrying out the prescription of a 'witch doctor' named Denis Gainey, subjected her to the most brutal ill treatment.

It was understood by Cleary and others that his wife was a 'changeling'. When she became ill and did not quickly recover her husband had

---

[101] NAI, Printed Outrage Reports, 1908.

[102] *Nationalist and Leinster Times,* 12 Oct. 1918; 9 Nov. 1918; *Freeman's Journal,* 16, 23 Oct. 1918. The mother and son were tried separately. The defence strategy was to claim that the son was insane, or had insane tendencies. See *Irish Independent,* 10–13 Dec. 1918; *Evening Herald,* 10 Dec. 1918; *Freeman's Journal,* 11 Dec. 1918. The mother was also found guilty but recommended to mercy. See *Cork Examiner,* 13 Dec. 1918. She was sentenced to be hanged on 7 Jan. 1919, but the sentence was reprieved.

[103] For instance, Bridget Brennan, assisted by her two sons, killed her husband, Jeremiah, in County Kerry in 1830. They were all sentenced to be hanged. *Kerry Evening Post,* 12 May 1830; 11 Aug. 1830. Mary McCann and her son were found not guilty of the murder of her husband Thomas, at Ballingarry, County Limerick in 1914. The judge noted that there was not enough evidence to allow the jury to reach a verdict. *Dublin Daily Express,* 14 May 1914; *Weekly Freeman's Journal,* 17 July 1915.

recourse to a local herbalist, Denis Gainey, who suggested she be given a herbal concoction. Again, the police report describes what happened next. 'The deceased ... was forcibly held by four men of the party, compelled to swallow a herb concoction and drenched with urine on the face, mouth and person. She was then placed on the kitchen fire and burned to some extent, while questions were put to her as to her identity'. She was to receive the same treatment on the following night, *'the motive being to drive out the witch which was supposed to possess her'*. Paraffin oil was poured over her to increase the flames, and the lower part of the trunk, abdomen, hips and thighs burned until the bones and internal organs protruded.' Afterwards Cleary, with some of his accomplices, buried the body and suggested to neighbours that Bridget had gone away. Given the circumstances of the murder this appeared an extraordinary act of rationality, signifying Cleary knew what he was doing. He, and others, were sentenced to various prison terms for their actions.[104]

Neighbours

The place of neighbours in matters relating to assault or murder is immensely revealing about interpersonal relationships and how people lived together. In the cities and towns of Ireland, especially where families were living together in tenements, neighbours shared stairways, privies, water pumps, and were very knowledgeable about what went on in each others households. They heard violence through the walls, or witnessed it in neighbouring rooms when assistance was sought, particularly by children, or on the streets. That neighbours could also become inured to the sounds of violence can be seen in the case of Samuel Harrington, who was found guilty of manslaughter and received a sentence of five years' penal servitude. The couple had been married for twenty-six years and he had continually mistreated her. In September 1882, he had quarrelled with her, stripped her naked and stuffed her with her head foremost down a narrow well with about seven inches of water. Neighbours heard her screams but thought it was only the usual beatings and did nothing to help.[105] Generally, in murder trials neighbours provided substantial information to the courts about the events leading up to, and including the murder, and its aftermath, even if they had not witnessed the actual murder itself.

---

[104] RIC Return of Outrages for 1895. Italics in the original. See Angela Bourke, *The Burning of Bridget Cleary* (London, 1999), for a full investigation of the case.
[105] *Kerry Evening Post*, 20 Dec. 1882.

Sentences

Over the entire period 1782–1925, at least forty individuals were executed for killing their spouses. Up to 1836, individuals condemned to death were usually hanged 'on the day next but one after that on which the sentence should be passed'. After 1836 the interval could be longer.[106] Mary Ann McConkey was executed in 1841 for poisoning her husband, an act that showed premeditation. While it could not be proved that she had purchased any poison, her case was lost when it was revealed in court that she had begun a relationship with a younger man, James Smith, a year before her husband's death. She had lived with Smith 'in a state of criminal intercourse for three months'; she had also recently given birth and the child's parentage was uncertain. This was a set of circumstances that found no sympathy with a jury.[107]

Vaughan has calculated that ninety-one individuals were executed in the period between 1862 and 1919. Our calculations suggest that nine of these executions, about 10 per cent, were for spousal murders.[108] Other than death the most severe sentence that could be passed was transportation for life. At least twelve individuals had their death sentences commuted to transportation for life, while two were sentenced to seven years and fourteen years respectively. In 1857, transportation was replaced by penal servitude. That women could often be treated more leniently than men is shown in the fact that Una Berhagra had her murder conviction commuted to transportation for life in 1846, while William Walsh, her accomplice, was hanged for the offence.[109]

Women who had the assistance of lovers in securing the demise of their husbands were dealt with harshly. In this period nine women were either hanged, along with their accomplices, or transported for life for colluding in spousal murder. In 1830 Ellen Connell, a 'comfortable farmer's wife', and Denis McCarthy, a forty-six year old day labourer, were hanged for the murder of Ellen's husband. She was thirty-six and had been married for twenty years. There were seven children from the marriage and the eldest child, being sixteen years old, was present at the executions.[110] In 1838 Catherine Galvin and Barry Colgan were both

---

[106] Vaughan, *Murder Trials*, p. 330.   [107] NAI, CRF 1841 McC17.

[108] Richard Bourke was executed in 1862; Edward Walsh in 1871; ? Flanagan in 1888; Dr P. H. E. Cross in 1888; James Heaney in 1891; John Boyle in 1893; Philip King in 1898; Mary Daly in 1903; James Campion in 1904. Another woman, Annie Walsh, was executed in 1925 for the murder of her husband in 1924.

[109] *Saunders's News-Letter*, 3 Aug. 1846: *Anglo-Celt*, 7 Aug. 1846; *Leinster Express*, 8 Aug. 1846; *Downpatrick Recorder*, 29 Aug. 1846.

[110] *Tralee Mercury*, 29 March 1830.

executed for the murder of Catherine's husband, James.[111] In 1841 Mary Hallinan, and her lover, a policeman, were both sentenced to death; he was executed in September 1841, while her hanging was delayed as she was found to be pregnant.[112] This couple had been having an affair for some time, and James Hughes the local parish priest had intervened and tried to have the policeman moved from the area. It was the possibility of the policeman's removal from the region that seems to have precipitated the murder.[113]

In 1815, Anthony Shevlane and Mary McKeal were convicted of murdering Shevlane's wife. The principal evidence was provided by Shevlane's daughter, aged eight. The child had been barely six years old when the murder was committed and had been thought too young to give evidence. When she did do so, she told the court that she had been lying in bed with her mother on the morning of the attack, when her father struck her mother with a spade and Mary McKeal stabbed her mother in various parts of the body with a knife, until she was dead. The child was frightened and pretended to be asleep. It appeared that McKeal was pregnant and the couple wanted to marry.[114] This was one of a number of murder/manslaughter cases in which children gave evidence against their parents, an ordeal that must have affected them greatly. In 1840, in a case in Downpatrick, the woman accused of murdering her husband 'shrieked in hysterical phrenzy' when her young daughter was brought out to testify against her.[115]

During the same period there were seventy individuals, all men, who were deemed insane or suffering temporary insanity whilst committing the crime. The usual sentence in these instances was to be detained in a lunatic asylum at the Lord Lieutenant's pleasure.[116] Only one woman appears to have been committed to an asylum for killing her husband. About twelve individuals committed a murder and then committed suicide, which also led to a belief that the individual had been insane. For instance, in Boyle in 1869, John Monson committed suicide after killing his wife, by striking his head with a stone. He was deemed insane.[117] A small number of husbands, about seven, murdered their wives and children and then committed suicide.

---

[111] *Ballina Impartial*, 18 March 1833; *Wexford Conservative*, 16 March 1833.
[112] *Ballina Advertiser*, 6 Aug. 1841; *Leinster Express*, 7 Aug. 1841.
[113] *Ballina Advertiser*, 30 July 1841.
[114] *Freeman's Journal*, 18 Aug. 1817; *Belfast Newsletter*, 15 Aug. 1817.
[115] *Ballina Advertiser*, 7 Aug. 1840.
[116] For further information on the insanity plea see Pauline Prior, *Madness and Murder: Gender, Crime and Mental Disorder in Nineteenth-Century Ireland* (Dublin, 2008), pp. 90–117.
[117] NAI, Printed Outrage Papers, 1870.

Some individuals literally got away with murder. About twenty-three individuals absconded after they had murdered their spouses, and few of these seem to have been caught. Over the period thirty-seven individuals were discharged, twenty-eight were found not guilty, and thirty-two were acquitted, most often on the grounds of lack of evidence. The defence of provocation, as we have seen, also let people get away with murder. John Hare was indicted for the wilful murder of Anne Hare, his wife, in 1831. He struck her with an umbrella, threw her on the ground, and inflicted 'divers wounds on her', from which she died. He was found not guilty of her murder and discharged from the court. On the night of the murder it was claimed his wife 'had taken too much ardent spirit, which she was in the habit of doing'. Her behaviour may have been seen as provocative and a mitigating factor.[118]

Manslaughter Charges

One conclusion that is evident from the available figures is that a considerable number of murder indictments were reduced to manslaughter charges, which of course did not carry the death penalty. From the total of manslaughter charges, in the region of 148 from 1772 to 1925, over seventy cases occurred after 1880. By the end of the nineteenth century spousal murder indictments were more likely to be treated in court as manslaughter cases, with sentences ranging from a few months in prison to decades. In 1833 Anne Salmon had a charge of murder reduced to manslaughter, for which she received a sentence of six months. The circumstances surrounding the death of her husband echoed that of many murder/manslaughter cases in which alcohol played an important role. In Salmon's case, a witness noted that he had seen the couple strike each other and that Salmon had taken a knife from her husband and stabbed him.[119] Shopkeeper James McMaster was charged with the manslaughter of his wife, Margaret, in 1868. It was observed at the trial that he was a widower with ten children when he married the deceased and that they had been married about five years. She was a widow without any children. It appeared she could not agree with her step children and as a result, they had all left their father's home. Margaret drank to some extent and had a violent temper, and she and the husband were continually quarrelling. She died from injuries inflicted when beaten by her drunken husband. The jury agreed that there were

---

[118] *Freeman's Journal*, 22 Feb. 1831.
[119] *Wexford Conservative*, 4 Sept. 1833; *Chute's Western Herald*, 2 Sept. 1833; *Northern Whig*, 2 Sept. 1833.

numerous mitigating factors in the case: she did not get on with his family; she drank and was bad tempered and quarrelsome. McMaster was convicted of her manslaughter and sentenced to twelve months' imprisonment.[120] In 1901, Edward Thomas French, a dispensary doctor, may have been saved from the gallows because of his drunkenness. He stabbed his wife several times in the heart, liver and wrist. Two servants came to her rescue and held him down, but his wife died within twenty minutes. He was drunk at the time and had been drinking heavily for the previous month, and when drunk, it was noted that he had a 'mania for attacking his wife', of whom he was jealous. He was charged with manslaughter and sentenced to penal servitude for life.[121]

Attempted murder cases were similar in context and violence to murder and manslaughter cases, the difference of course being that the intended victim survived the attack, and the sentences were less severe. These cases also reveal diverse contexts, whether it is in the makeup of the family, or the reasons given for the attempted murder. In 1899 Anthony Convey was convicted of attempting to murder his twenty-four-year-old wife, Mary. He went to the house of Michael Smith where his wife was lodging and deliberately fired three shots at her. She was not wounded. He believed her guilty of immorality; the couple had not lived together for nine months prior to the attack and their married life was noted to be unhappy. He was imprisoned for one year with hard labour.[122]

Conclusion

It is difficult to assess how Ireland's rates of spousal homicide relate to similar rates in other countries over a similar timespan, as the comparative material does not yet exist.[123] Clearly more husbands killed their wives, than wives killed husbands. Husbands used their wives' behaviour, their disobedience, intemperance, infidelity, lack of female virtue and inadequate fortunes, as excuses for causing their deaths. It is striking that in some of the murder cases noted above, husbands and wives were not living together. Where they were it was evident that there was

---

[120] Printed Outrage Reports 1868. NAI, CRF 1869 Mc7.
[121] NAI, Printed Outrage Reports 1902.
[122] NAI, Printed Outrage Reports, June 1899.
[123] Conley's work suggests the possibility of a comparative framework. However, the actual numbers of spousal murders are not entirely clear in her work. See, Conley, *Certain Other Countries*. Her *Melancholy Accidents* also presents some quantitative problems. For instance, on p. 68 she notes that in the period between 1866 and 1892 there were 140 spousal killings in Ireland. Our own research records at least 175 such murders in the same period.

considerable tension in the household for months if not years before a murder took place. Verbal and physical conflicts could, in the context of alcohol, spiral out of control. Money and property were also the causes of violence, as was the distribution of household resources. Some women feared the loss of their homes and other property and killed to protect their interests. Both men and women sought new partners, having tired, for whatever reason, of their spouse. Certain acts of violence were judged legitimate when particular contexts were taken into consideration. A drunken wife, a brutish and violent husband could, for example, result in murder charges being reduced to manslaughter charges. Episodes of violence, while confined to spouses, also drew in children, other family members, servants, neighbours and the authorities, in the form of police, coroners, magistrates, juries and judges. Violence was rarely a totally private affair.

11   Desertion

In 1698, Jenat Colbert was very clear about her reasons for leaving her husband. She declared to the Templepatrick Presbyterian session that she could not have a life with him as 'he will not labour to get them bread, but she is willing to dwell with him if he will make any provision for his family'. He in turn then deserted her. In December 1698,

the Minister as desired wrote to the Session of Templepatrick about Alexr Collbeart who appears as also Jenat Collbeart his wife they being examined severally and failings having been on both sides they were also confronted, the man did show a willingness to dwell with his wife and maintain her as he could but she did show herself unwilling to stay with her husband unless he oblige himself to dwell in this parish which the Session could not force him to do, she was reproved and told [the] hazard of a voluntary causeless deserting her husband, the man was advised to seek counsel whether he may not be legally divorced seeing she will not cohabit with him.[1]

Jenat Colbert appears to our modern eyes as an assertive woman, knowing what she wanted and unwilling to do the bidding of the authorities. She seems not to have cared much for her husband and, though it is not revealed in the above extract, she may have had some independent means of supporting herself and her children. As we have seen in other chapters, economic considerations were an important criterion when choosing a marriage partner. It allowed the possibility of subsistence for poorer women and their children; the status of being a wife, even one who was deserted, shaped women's access to welfare resources. Marriage was also a way to contain the poverty of women and children and sometimes men. While men might have been expected ideally to be the family breadwinners, earning enough to feed, clothe and house their wives and children, in reality poorer women were always obliged to assist in supplementing or securing the family income, as were children. As we have discussed in earlier chapters, men who engaged in unskilled labour

---

[1] Cited in John M. Barkley, 'History of the ruling eldership in Irish Presbyterianism' (2 vols., unpublished MA thesis, Queen's University Belfast, 1952), ii, pp. 77–9.

found it difficult to support their wives and children without the work of the entire family unit. For many women, the desertion of their husbands brought them and their children, to destitution and they, consequently, ended up in the workhouse. Desertion could occur at any point in a marriage, sometimes within a couple of days of the service or, alternatively, years later. Soldiers were a particularly difficult group to chase for maintenance. As noted already, they required the permission of their commander to marry and many soldiers never sought such permission and the army authorities then refused to recognise the dependency of the wife and any children of the relationship.[2] As will be clear from Chapter 12, throughout the period covered by this volume, securing a formal, civil divorce was an expensive and lengthy process. Most men and women who wished to leave an unhappy marriage did not, therefore, secure a divorce. Instead, they opted for desertion of their spouses and, also, frequently, any children that they might have had. In this chapter, we explore the evidence for desertion of marriages and the changing legal process which enabled the state to prosecute husbands who abandoned their wives and children.

Elopement Notices

The large number of newspaper notices placed by husbands cautioning the public that they would not pay any bills accumulated by their run-away wives testifies to the way in which men and women took matters into their own hands to abandon a difficult marriage, without consulting a lawyer or, in many cases, their spouses. From the early eighteenth century through to the early 1840s, elopement notices appeared in Irish newspapers. Between 1750 and 1800, about 900 husbands 'advertised their wives', as it was called, in the *Belfast Newsletter*.[3] There was a similar number of notices inserted by husbands and, occasionally, by wives, in the Dublin-based *Saunders's News-Letter* between 1773 and 1837. Although

---

[2] In 1858, the clerk of the Limerick Union communicated with Lieutenant Col. Dickson of the Royal Limerick Company Regiment, inquiring as to the marital status of Private John Griffin, whose wife was in the workhouse. In reply the guardians were informed that if Private Griffin were married, it was without the knowledge or permission of his commanding officer, thus they could not 'entertain' any charge for the wife's maintenance (Board of Guardian Minutes, Limerick, 10 April 1858. BG/110 A/30. 3 April 1858–29 Sept. 1858. https://www.limerick.ie/discover/explore/historical-resources/limerick-archives/archive-collections/limerick-union-board. Accessed January 2017. All following references to the Limerick Board of Guardians can be accessed at this address.

[3] For an analysis of the *Belfast Newsletter* notices see Mary O'Dowd, 'Marriage breakdown in Ireland, c. 1660–1857' in Niamh Howlin and Kevin Costello (eds.), *Law and the Family in Ireland 1800–1950* (London, 2015), pp. 14–20.

the notices appeared in city-based newspapers, the advertisers came from both urban and rural areas. Most of the notices that appeared in the *Belfast Newsletter*, for example, were placed by men who lived in the rural hinterland of Belfast. Similarly, the men who publicly proclaimed the elopement of their wives in the *Ennis Chronicle and Clare Advertiser* gave addresses from townlands outside the town of Ennis.

While not all men who 'advertised' their wives in this way noted their occupation, of those that did most came from the middling to lower ranks of rural and urban society. They were craftsmen, small farmers and shop keepers: men who had a small amount of cash or capital invested in a farm or family business in which the wife was often an active partner. The departure of a wife could, therefore, have had financial implications for the family income, particularly if the wife accumulated debts in her husband's name or took cash or goods from the household when she left. Some signed their notice with an 'x' indicating that they were illiterate. The wording of notices was often very similar, which suggests that they were written by a scribe or that the newspaper had a common formula available for those who could not compose their own notices.

The legal rational behind the elopement notices lay in a husband's responsibility to pay for the maintenance or the 'necessaries' of his wife, which was interpreted as 'food, lodging, clothing, medical attendance and medicine'.[4] If, however, a wife left the marriage voluntarily then the husband was no longer responsible for supporting her in this way.[5] The public notice to traders was, therefore, to warn them of the husband's repudiation of any debts that she might accumulate. If the wife was involved in the family business, the husband might also use the notice to indicate that she was no longer acting on his behalf. Most notices also stated that the wife had left the marital home without provocation from her husband. The insertion of this clause was also legally important because it asserted that the husband had done nothing that had led to his wife's departure. If, at a subsequent court proceeding, a wife could argue that she left the marital home because her husband had been physically abusing her or had committed adultery, then she would have been entitled to claim maintenance from him. An unprovoked elopement guaranteed her no such right.

---

[4] Joanne Bailey, *Unquiet Lives. Marriage and Marriage Breakdown in England, 1660–1800* (Cambridge, 2003), p. 57. See also Mary Beth Sievens, '"The wicked agency of others": Community, law, and marital conflict in Vermont, 1790–1830', *Journal of the Early Republic*, 21, 1 (Spring 2001), 20–1.

[5] Ibid.; Isaac Espinasse, *A Digest of the Law of Actions and Trials at Nisi Prius …* (2 vols., Dublin, 1790), i, pp. 119–25.

The public announcement might also form part of a formal or informal separation agreement between the couple.[6] In other instances, the couple may have agreed verbally to live apart and the notice placed in the newspaper in which the husband noted that he and his wife had 'mutually agreed' to separate might represent the only written document of their agreement.[7] Mary Beth Sievens, who analysed similar notices in the North American state of Vermont, argued that they are evidence of self-made divorces through which husbands and wives made their own arrangements for marital separation without consulting legal or ecclesiastical authorities.[8]

The concept of self-made divorces is particularly relevant when considering the concentration of notices in the *Belfast Newsletter* in the second half of the eighteenth century. Divorce and remarriage was permitted within the Presbyterian church if a husband or wife could credibly claim to have been deserted by their spouse and that they had done nothing to provoke their departure. Assertions in newspaper advertisements by husbands that wives had eloped without cause fitted neatly into the definition of 'wilful desertion', which the Westminster Confession of Faith asserted was necessary to justify a divorce and remarriage. In 1786, for example, Thomas Thompson appealed successfully to the Down Presbytery for permission to remarry even though his former wife was still alive. He explained that she had eloped from him and 'behaved very improperly', a phrase that occurs repeatedly in newspaper notices denouncing eloping wives.[9]

The majority of the notices that appeared in the *Belfast Newsletter* were from Counties Antrim and Down, incorporating the area included within the remit of the Seceder Presbytery of Down, which heard a number of requests for divorce in the late eighteenth century, all on the grounds of desertion. A comparison, however, of the small number of divorces processed in Presbyteries with the large number of elopement notices in the northern newspaper suggests that most of the husbands who inserted notices in the *Belfast Newsletter* did not seek a formal divorce

---

[6] See *Belfast Newsletter,* 20 May 1763, 20 Sept. 1782, 3 Sept. 1790, where separations are noted.

[7] See, for example, notices placed by John Ivory in *Dublin Mercury,* 7 March 1769, and by James Shiers in *Saunders's News-Letter,* 30 Aug. 1773; William Hackett in *Saunders's News-Letter,* 30 Nov. 1809. See also notice of Walter Blake in *Saunders's News-Letter,* 30 May 1787 in which he claimed that his wife, reneged on their 'mutual' agreement when her brother returned from overseas. Catherine and her brother may have realised that an agreement signed by Catherine had no legal validity.

[8] Sievens, '"The wicked agency of others"', 20–1.

[9] Minutes of the Presbytery of Down, 1785–1800 (PHSIB). See also *Saunders's News-Letter,* Hugh, May, 17 June 1783; Thomas Ellis, 20 May 1783; Edward Gunnell, 15 Nov. 1783.

from the church but proceeded to make their own arrangements to end their marriages. In 1814, for example, James Kirkwood told the Down Presbytery that he had been married by an irregular clergyman but that his wife had deserted him and could not be persuaded to live with him again. Accordingly, 'they then gave under their hands with mutual consent they were to have not further intercourse nor after claim'.[10]

For another group of men there was a common theme in their advertisements: anger at the wife's departure and the desire to shame her publicly. Men condemned their wives' abandonment of the family home and what they perceived as their unacceptable conduct, often in euphemistic terms. Luke Tute claimed that he had reasons to believe that his wife was 'not complying with the rules of a wife' while John Sheil from Lackan near Monasterevin claimed that his wife, Mary, had 'behaved in a manner not becoming a good wife'.[11] While William Dempsey expressed his dissatisfaction with his wife's conduct more discreetly, he nonetheless, succeeded in opening up her behaviour to public scrutiny. He noted in his advertisement in the *Saunders's News-Letter* that he would not mention Anne's faults out of respect for her father and friends.[12]

Other husbands sought revenge on the man with whom a wife had eloped. In 1773, Thomas Kennedy of Blessington, County Wicklow, provided a detailed description of John Nowlan, for whom his wife had left him ('5 Feet 7 Inches high, pale Face, crooked Nose, round Shoulder, fair Complexion, sandy Beard, and two or three Cuts in his Forehead'). Kennedy offered a two-guinea reward for any information on the location of Nowlan or his wife, whom he described as twenty-six years of age with 'brown Complexion, and full Eyes'.[13] Peter Wall also promised to prosecute his wife and her lover ('a snuff man from Birr') 'as far as the Law will permit'.[14]

A small number of women responded through public notices to refute the assertions of their husbands and give details of their marriages.[15] Most claimed that they had not left the marital home voluntarily but had fled in fear of their lives. Sara Kelly, for example, claimed in 1772 that she had lived 'under the iron paws (which I often felt)' of her husband for six years and that for the 'Preservation of Life itself, and the Safety of my Family', she had no choice but to go to her father's house.[16] In 1810,

---

[10] Minutes of the Presbytery of Down, 1837–1841 (PHSIB).
[11] *Saunders's News-Letter*, 5 March 1779, 8 Aug. 1793.
[12] *Saunders's News-Letter*, 2 Aug. 1793.   [13] *Saunders's News-Letter*, 4 May 1773.
[14] *Saunders's News-Letter*, 26 Oct. 1778.
[15] See, for example, the notice placed by Ellen Louisa Hill Forster in the *Freeman's Journal*, 26 Aug. 1820.
[16] Notice placed by Sara Kelly in *Saunders's News-Letter*, 9 April 1773.

Jane Robinson from Stoneybatter in Dublin claimed that her husband had used a pitch-fork, sword and firearms against her and that she was in the process of taking a suit against him in the ecclesiastical court.[17]

The allegations of domestic abuse, whether true or not, most often elicited a sympathetic reaction for wives, particularly those with children, who had deserted their husbands. However, the volume of elopement notices placed by husbands suggests also that many women left their husbands at their own volition and were intent on living separate lives. Some took their children with them and, to their husbands' annoyance, some also removed, from the family home, cash and goods that would enable them to set up a separate household. A small number of men denounced their wives for taking 'wearing apparel' but more focused on other goods and cash that the wife had taken with her.[18]

In their notices, the women frequently stated that they had returned to their parents' home, suggesting that their actions were supported by their family. Others asked neighbours to verify the violence of their husbands. The family and communal support offered to the fleeing wives also suggests that elopement was socially acceptable, particularly if domestic abuse was involved. While the rationale for the notices reflect the patriarchal ideology of the law: a wife who accumulated debt in her husband's name was also exploiting the law to her advantage.

Desertion and the Poor Law

Elopement notices disappear from Irish newspapers in the 1830s and this may be related to the introduction of the Poor Law in 1838. The new law led to the introduction of a nationwide system of poor relief with the establishment of workhouses where the destitute poor were to be relieved.[19] Legislation relating to desertion came into force with the introduction of the Poor Law. The Act for the More Effectual Relief of the Destitute Poor in Ireland provided for the punishment of persons deserting and leaving their wives or any children 'whom such persons may be liable to maintain, so that such wives or children should become destitute and be relieved in the workhouse of a union'. This Act was repealed in 1847 and

---

[17] *Saunders's News-Letter*, 26 Nov. 1810.

[18] For references to women taking 'wearing apparel' see notices placed by William McAnally in *Saunders's News-Letter*, 19 Dec. 1782; James Costello in *Saunders's News-Letter*, 28 Feb. 1797; John M'Ateer, *Belfast Newsletter*, 20 Nov. 1829; Thomas Hunter, *Belfast Newsletter*, 25 Dec. 1829.

[19] Virginia Crossman, *Poverty and the Poor Law in Ireland, 1850–1914* (Liverpool, 2013). See also, Virginia Crossman, 'Viewing women, family and sexuality through the prism of the Irish Poor Laws', *Women's History Review*, 15, 4 (2006), 541–50.

from that time men 'deserting or wilfully neglecting to maintain their wives or children 'so that they become a burden on the union in indoor or outdoor relief' were prosecuted under the Vagrancy Acts. They could be imprisoned for a period of up to three months with hard labour.[20] The law authorised the guardians of the Poor Law union workhouse in which the wife and/or children were maintained, to take a case against her husband. The legislation did not make provision for a maintenance payment to the wife, but rather allowed the board of guardians to sue the husband for the cost of maintaining his wife and any children on the poor rates. The purpose of the Act was to ensure that individuals did not become a burden on publicly-funded welfare. Unmarried mothers were obliged under the Poor Law Act of 1838 to maintain children born outside of marriage until the child reached fifteen years. The fathers of such children had no legal obligation for their maintenance and it was not until 1863 that Poor Law guardians in Ireland could pursue the men for support if their illegitimate children were living in the workhouse.[21]

For the various boards of guardians who oversaw the workhouse system in Ireland, the main concern was to keep the rates low. There was always a fear that the destitute and poor were abusing the Poor Law system. When husbands refused to join their families in the workhouse they were also liable to prosecution. In 1851 the Kerigan family was discharged from the Westport workhouse 'in consequence of the father having refused to enter with the family'. The minutes of the meeting at which this decision was made noted 'that it is preferable to proceed against the parties who do not enter the workhouse as the law recognises the necessity of relieving deserted families and provides for the punishment of those who are liable for their support'.[22] Guardians felt obligated to follow the rules of the Poor Law system, but that did not mean that they always acted harshly. As Virginia Crossman has shown, there were significant differences in the way in which the Poor Law system evolved and operated in different parts of Ireland.[23]

Under Poor Law legislation, offenders who failed to maintain their families were summarily tried before magistrates. We cannot assume that

[20] Thomas A. Mooney, *Compendium of the Irish Poor Law and General Manual for Poor Law Guardians and Their Officers* (Dublin, 1887), p. 901. From 1847 tried under the Vagrant Act. 10 & 11 Vict. c.84. 1847. Under the Army Act of 1881, the pay of soldiers could be sought to cover the cost of maintaining wife and children (ibid., pp. 522–4).

[21] Poor Relief (Ireland) Act. 25 & 26 Vict. c. 83. 1862.

[22] Board of Guardian Minutes, Westport, 19 Feb. 1851 (NLI, Westport Union, Minute Books of the Board of Guardians, Aug. 1850–March 1860, Mss 12,613–12,625). Powers given by Sec 58 of Act. 1 & 2 Vict. Cap 58 allowed a husband to be punished if he refused to come into the workhouse to be maintained with his wife and children.

[23] Crossman, *Poverty and the Poor Law*, passim.

all desertions were known to the authorities. However, between 1864 and 1919 there were 12,769 individuals proceeded against for neglecting to maintain their families.[24] From the records available between 1864 and 1880, where a gender breakdown is possible, 4,266 men and 1,021 women were proceeded against for deserting their families. Figures from various prison registers provide us with a little more detail as to who the deserters were. Almost all of these individuals were convicted and received sentences ranging from fourteen days to a month in prison. In a sample of 2,300 cases dating between 1838 and 1924, 1,930 men were brought before the petty sessions for deserting their wives, their families or, if widowed, their children. The number of women similarly charged was 370. The majority (about 58 per cent) of those tried were aged between thirty-one years and forty years, while about 25 per cent were aged between twenty-one and thirty years. The oldest deserter appears to have been James Doyle, who in 1852, at the age of seventy-six, abandoned his wife. He was imprisoned for fourteen days with hard labour for his crime.[25] Where occupations were provided, 414 individuals claimed they were labourers, and seventy-nine noted that they were servants. Other occupations included bakers, bricklayers, carpenters and dealers. The majority gave no indication of employment, which of course implied to the courts that they were unable to support wives and families. The majority of these desertions, 1,302, occurred between 1846 and 1851, marking the worst years of the Great Famine and its immediate aftermath, revealing another aspect of the social upheaval of that calamity.

The various government reports on the state of Ireland and its poor, conducted throughout the 1820s and 1830s, reveals the ease with which families could fall into destitution. Evidence to the Poor Inquiry of the 1830s noted, for instance, in Cork, that 'there are almost always labourers out of employment, and there are a great many whose work is very uncertain, having employment one week and not the next, and consequently they are often in the greatest distress … Such labourers often send their families to be supported in the house of industry for a season'.[26] On employment it was noted that in the parish of Killimore in the barony of Longford, Co. Galway that there was no paid work for labourers between September and March'.[27] In Wexford it was stated

---

[24] *Criminal and Judicial Statistics for Ireland*, 1864–1919. Note figures are missing for some years, including 1883.

[25] Authors' database.

[26] *Selection of Parochial Examinations Relative to the Destitute Classes in Ireland* (Dublin, 1835), pp. 236–8.

[27] Ibid., p. 197.

that when the labourers were not working, 'their wives and children are often obliged to beg'.[28]

As noted already, the principal legal and moral responsibility of husbands was to financially support a wife and children. Many husbands were unable or refused to support their wives and families. For poorer women there were periods of precarious dependency on men, such as when they were pregnant. And, as noted already, the family economy depended on the contribution of all members. The desertion of either spouse could throw a family into destitution. For example, a woman named O'Mara sought admission to the Waterford workhouse in 1870 for a few nights before she returned to Cork. She had four 'little children with her … all in a starving state'. Her husband had left her in Bandon to find work in Waterford. She had had one letter from him and nothing more. She went looking for him and discovered that he had found work but within four weeks of securing a job he had 'eloped' with another woman.[29]

In the 1840s, and later, some unions offered rewards, ranging between 10s to £1, for information leading to the apprehension of deserting husbands and parents.[30] Some boards of guardians were willing to go to considerable lengths to prosecute deserting husbands. In 1872 Michael Riordan was brought back from Liverpool to face charges of deserting his wife. He promised the magistrates that he would take his wife back to Liverpool with him and he was released from custody. He then absconded, leaving his wife an inmate of the workhouse.[31] Again in 1872, Edward Moore, who had deserted his family, had left the country and was discovered to be living in Manchester. The board of guardians of the North Dublin Union had some discussion about whether it was worth pursuing Moore. There had already been two warrants issued for his arrest and the last one had cost the board ten pounds. The guardians discussed whether it was necessary to pay a detective five pounds to travel to Manchester to bring the man back. It was finally agreed that this was a matter of principle and that the expenses should be paid and the man punished.[32] It is not known if in such instances, deserting husbands continued to pay for the maintenance of their wives/families. What is often evident in cases where husbands left for Scotland or England is that many had set up home with new partners and in some cases established

---

[28] Ibid., p. 232.   [29] *Tipperary Free Press and Clonmel General Advertiser*, 23 Sept. 1870.
[30] Board of Guardian Minutes, Ballymoney Union, 24 June 1848 (PRONI, BG/5/A/5).
[31] Board of Guardian Minutes, Limerick, 13 Sept. 1872. BG/110 A/54. 3 April 1872–25 Sept. 1872.
[32] *Freeman's Journal*, 30 May 1872. Russell was brought back to Ireland and sentenced to three months' imprisonment with hard labour. *Freeman's Journal*, 3 June 1872.

new families. It would have been financially difficult to support two families. Many of these deserting husbands had no intention of returning to their original family. In 1892 the Derry board of guardians prosecuted James Golding; he claimed he had just gone to Scotland to find work and had no intention of deserting, but it was revealed that this was the second time he had left his family.[33]

Given the high levels of emigration from nineteenth-century Ireland it is very likely that many deserting wives and husbands left the country. A witness to the Poor Enquiry of the 1830s noted the case of a woman who had given birth to a child, the father of whom was already married. He refused to support it, and shortly after its birth deserted his entire family and went to America.[34] In 1855, Thomas Roberts applied to the magistrates in Cork for a search warrant for a bed. He claimed it had been stolen from him by his wife who had deserted him to go to America with another man. The couple were found on the packet ship, together with the bed. All were taken ashore and the husband, being less concerned with the fate of his wife, sought only the immediate return of the bed.[35] When Julia Farrell left her husband William she took about £15 from him, together with a bed, some bedding, some china and some clothing. She was in her fifties and her new man was in his early twenties. There was nothing to prove that the wife's paramour had stolen any goods, and the case was dismissed. Originally the husband had planned to emigrate with his wife to America. It is not clear if he did that or left the country alone.[36] It is, however, through such incidental cases that we can uncover instances of desertion and the nature of marital relationships among some couples.

In instances of desertion the court was always keen to ascertain if the couple involved were married. A valid marriage certificate or other proof, such as witnesses to a ceremony, was acceptable to courts in proving a marriage had occurred. Such proof then made the husband liable for the maintenance of his wife and family. Some of these cases reveal instances of long-term co-habitation. The South Dublin Union prosecuted Archibald Robinson for leaving his wife, Mary Robinson, destitute. The latter swore that the couple had married in December 1827 in Monkstown church, according to Protestant rites. At the time the defendant was coachman to Sir William Betham and the only witness to the marriage was a fellow servant, James Lacey, who had since died. Mary claimed that

[33] *Derry Journal*, 12 Aug. 1892. Golding received a sentence of fourteen days in jail.
[34] *Reports of the Commissioners for Inquiring into the Condition of the Poorer Classes in Ireland: First Report, HC 1835* (369), xxxii, pts 1 & 2, Appendix A. Bastardy, p. 54.
[35] *Cork Examiner*, 28 March 1842.   [36] *Cork Examiner*, 4 April 1855.

they had lived happily for fourteen years, when he turned her out on the streets and took up with another, younger woman. They had had six children, only one of whom survived infanthood. The defendant claimed that Mary was not his lawful wife and that they had lived together for several years but never married. When the couple separated, he gave her £15 'in quittance of all demands real or imagined' and claimed that he 'behaved with much generosity towards a woman not his legal wife'. This 'self-made' divorce may have been an element in other desertions or separations, coming to light only incidentally in a court case. It was not the central point in this case, as there was no evidence that the couple had ever married. In this instance the magistrate dismissed the case without prejudice to allow proof of the marriage to be uncovered.[37]

In 1823, Daniel Barry was imprisoned on suspicion of killing his wife and child. However, Barry stated that the family had to leave Ennis, where he could not find any work. He and his wife separated, placing their child 'on the publick'. This left the wife free to engage in peddling and her husband to roam the country looking for work. It was their intention to meet up again when their circumstances improved.[38] This was a strategy used by the family to ensure its survival. It reveals that children and wives were not always 'truly' deserted. It also testifies to the family as an 'interdependent unit', particularly in pre-Famine Ireland. Many strategies were used to maintain that unit. The temporary 'desertion' of a family was one such strategy. The husband might look for work in England or Scotland, or another part of Ireland, while the wife and children would beg to secure their own subsistence.[39]

Collusive Desertions

That collusive desertions were a fairly regular occurrence is also testified to in the surviving sources. In 1846, in the Ballymoney Union, a number of women whose husbands had deserted them refused to 'swear informations against their husbands' and were discharged from the workhouse the following day.[40] In June of 1847 the Ballymoney guardians

---

[37] *Freeman's Journal*, 23 Feb. 1843.
[38] Prisoners' Petitions and Cases, 1778–1836, 18 Sept. 1823 (NAI, VI/21/1/1812).
[39] Mary Cullen, 'Breadwinners and providers: Women in the household economy of labouring families 1835–6' in Maria Luddy and Cliona Murphy (eds.), *Women Surviving: Studies in Irish Women's History in the 19th and 20th Centuries* (Dublin, 1990), pp. 85–116.
[40] Board of Guardian Minutes, Ballymoney Union, March 1846–Aug. 1847, 31 Oct. 1846 (PRONI, BG/2/A/4).

were informed by the master of the workhouse that 'there are many of the female paupers receiving letters in the workhouse supposed to be from their husbands who had deserted them'. The guardians asked the Poor Law Commission if the master could open such letters.[41] What is intriguing here, of course, is that letters are used as a form of communication, given that many inmates of workhouses in these early years were illiterate. What these letters consisted of is unknown; they may simply have provided an address where the husband might be located. In 1862 the Poor Law board in Tralee wrote to the Poor Law Commissioners asking their advice on how to deal with women 'who declined to grant informations against their husbands' on entering the workhouse. They were particularly keen to have a response as to whether the mere fact of a woman being admitted 'is in itself sufficient evidence of her having been deserted by her husband'.[42]

Where collusive desertions occurred the 'deserted' spouse had no intention of assisting in the prosecution of the 'deserter'. For instance, Mary Barry left the Limerick workhouse a day after entering when she was told that the clerk was about to write to the colonel of her husband's regiment.[43] Thomas Gibbon's wife also left when the clerk stated that he would make an application for her husband's pension.[44] By their actions these women were saving their husbands from prosecution. Michael Coghlan was discharged from the Limerick workhouse in 1845 when it was disclosed that 'his wife and children who are outside are in employment'.[45] The board saw no reason why his wife could not support her husband.

What is evident from the minutes of various workhouses is that women who were inmates of a union, and who appear or were noted to have been deserted, may have been only temporarily abandoned. Husbands sometimes sent for their 'deserted wives'. In 1858 Mary Crowley, an inmate of the Limerick workhouse, asked the board of guardians to provide her with £1 so that she could join her husband in America. She claimed that her husband had sent her an 'American order for £1' but that the failure of a bank had meant that she lost the money.

---

[41] Board of Guardians Minutes, Ballymoney Union, Feb. 1847–May 1848, 7 June 1847 (PRONI, BG/5/A/4).
[42] Board of Guardian Rough Minute Book, Tralee Union, 14 Dec. 1861–6 Dec. 1862 (Kerry County Library, Tralee, BG 1154 1 AA17).
[43] Board of Guardian Minutes, Limerick, 13 Sept. 1845. BG/110 A7. 11 June 1845–20 May 1846.
[44] Board of Guardian Minutes, Limerick, 19 July 1845. BG/110 A7. 11 June 1845–20 May 1846.
[45] Board of Guardian Minutes, Limerick, 6 Sept. 1845. BG/110 A7. 11 June 1845–20 May 1846.

The guardians provided her with a total of £5 to emigrate.[46] In 1883, the Poor Law Commission received a positive response to the query as to whether the husband of Mary Bourke, and the parents of James Donohoe, all in America, were willing and able to support their respective kin if they emigrated.[47]

Not only might desertions be collusive but it was also evident that many genuinely deserted wives knew exactly where their husbands resided or worked and were willing to use that information to their advantage. Eliza Wright provided evidence against her husband to the Dublin South Union board in 1856. She knew that he was working as a whip maker in London, earning good wages. She was keen for the members of the board to intervene on her behalf.[48] They turned the case over to the relieving officer to pursue further. John Browne was sentenced to three months in 1857 for deserting his wife, Sophia. She, in a petition to secure his release, informed the authorities that the couple had been separated for a number of years and that her husband allowed her 3s. 6d per week for support. When the husband discontinued the financial aid, she had to enter the workhouse. This was a very good way for her to secure her continued maintenance as all she needed to do was inform the relieving officer of her husband's whereabouts, which she did. The husband was then willing to continue to support her and she was anxious to have him released from prison. He was freed within a few days.[49]

Boards of guardians often refused entry to the workhouse if the members believed that a wife was not truly destitute, and this was acceptable under Poor Law regulations. They often did not believe the stories told to them by those seeking admittance, and comments made make it clear that they understood that a wife's place was by her husband. Stories needed to be consistent to be accepted by the guardians. Ellen Stokes, a woman with three children, gave different versions of her situation when she appeared before the Poor Law guardians in Galway in July 1842. She declared to the board that she had seen her husband a few days before 'but he was doing no good for her'. Before that she claimed she had not seen him for twenty months and that he had a second wife. The board rejected her application for admittance to the workhouse.[50] Wives whose husbands were willing to support them also

---

[46] Board of Guardian Minutes, Limerick, 10 April 1858. BG/110 A30. 3 April 1858–29 Sept. 1858.

[47] Board of Guardian Minutes, Limerick, 21 April 1883. BG/110 A76. 11 April 1883–26 Sept. 1883.

[48] Board of Guardian Minutes, South Dublin Union, 20 Aug. 1856 (NAI, Book A9–A11, July 1856–Dec. 1858).

[49] NAI, CIF 1857 B23.   [50] *Galway Vindicator*, 16 July 1842.

received little sympathy. An application by a woman for entry to the Enniskillen workhouse in 1875 was rejected when it was revealed that her husband, who was in America, had left money for her to follow him but she did not wish to emigrate. The guardians advised her to go to her husband.[51] In 1878 in Tralee, the relieving officer reported that Alice Callaghan was 'greatly to blame herself for the misunderstanding between herself and her husband'.[52] Consequently, she was not allowed into the workhouse. Johanna Daly was refused entry to the workhouse on a number of occasions. She claimed that her husband had deserted her but although he had been in court for desertion the case was dismissed, as he was 'perfectly ready to support his wife but that she had refused to live with him'.[53] Daly, in times of utter necessity, sought entrance to the workhouse; how she survived outside the workhouse system is, however, unknown.

However, guardians were not always insensitive to the needs of separated or deserted wives. In 1866, Charles Seabrooke, who used four different aliases, was arrested in London having deserted his wife and four children in Dublin in 1864, from which time they had been resident in the North Dublin Union. The guardians allowed his wife to leave the workhouse in order to support herself, but two of the children remained there. It was not unusual for guardians to allow such arrangements. In this particular case Seabrooke claimed that when he left the family three years previously he was in debt and had gone to England to find work and 'he lost sight of her [his wife] until quite recently'. His wife claimed he had another wife and child in England.[54] The Westport guardians had employed a married woman named Mary Dineen as a trained nurse in 1906. The Local Government Board objected, noting that 'it is stated that Mary Dineen is married and has one child… They accordingly desired to direct the attention of the guardians to their circular letter of the 4th July 1904 in which it was pointed out that the retention of married women on the nursing staff was objectionable and that it was desirable that female offices should resign their positions on marriage'. The Board requested another appointment be made. However, the guardians persisted in retaining Mrs Dineen and asked the Board to reconsider as 'through no fault of her own she has been separated from her husband (who resides in Dublin) for over twelve months and there is

---

51 Board of Guardian Minutes, Enniskillen, 6 July 1875 (PRONI, BG/14).
52 *Tralee Chronicle*, 22 March 1878.
53 *Tralee Chronicle*, 7 May 1881. See also Crossman, *Poverty and the Poor Law*, pp. 112–4.
54 *Freeman's Journal*, 26 Feb. 1866. He was imprisoned, with hard labour, for three months.

no likelihood whatever of their ever being re-united. She is a lady of the highest character'.[55] In 1915, a letter was read to the Westport Board of Guardians from George Sweeny in Achill, informing the guardians that his wife and five children became inmates of the workhouse without his consent, and if the guardians did not send them back to him he would take legal proceedings. The board ordered their solicitor to proceed against Mr Sweeny for the maintenance of his wife and family.[56] At a meeting of the same guardians in July 1915 all of the Sweenys appeared before the board. Sweeny's wife stated that she would not return to his house as he mistreated her and the children and that they were afraid of him. The family remained in the workhouse while the husband was prosecuted for the cost of their maintenance.[57] This last case reveals that boards of guardians did have some understanding of the perils involved in living with a violent husband. It was unusual to keep a wife and children in the workhouse once the husband had requested their return to the family home. But these cases are not typical of guardians' responses to deserted wives. Both of these women and their circumstances would have been well-known to the relevant boards of guardians. They were respected individuals who were deemed 'good' wives and in need of the guardians' support. Most other deserted women who came before the boards would have had more chequered histories, and made intermittent or fairly constant use of the workhouse. They were looked on with much less sympathy.

Reasons for Desertion

The reasons given by men and women for deserting their spouses were similar to those of husbands and wives who assaulted and abused each other, who separated and divorced and who committed bigamy: the women did not act as 'proper wives', the husbands were poor earners, violent and drunkards. Sometimes the opportunity just presented itself. This was likely the case with the husband of Anne Sullivan who, in 1826, deserted his wife and family after receiving £20 reward money for having been a state witness at a murder trial.[58] In 1873, Denis McDonnell, a baker, used a well-worn excuse when prosecuted for desertion, stating in

---

[55] Board of Guardian Minutes, Westport, 15 March 1906. (NLI, Westport Union. Minute Books of the Board of Guardians, July 1900 to Jan. 1909. MS 12,696).
[56] Board of Guardian Minutes, Westport, 24 June 1915 (NLI, Westport Union. Minute Books of the Board of Guardians, Jan. to Dec. 1915. MS 12,696).
[57] Board of Guardian Minutes, Westport, 1 July 1915 (NLI, Westport Union. Minute Books of the Board of Guardians, Jan. to Dec. 1915. MS 12,696).
[58] NAI, CSO/RP/1826/272.

court that his wife 'did not act properly as a wife towards him'. Andrew Lloyd said he deserted his wife and child because her mother 'was in the habit of drinking'. Although in 'good employment' he refused to support his family and was imprisoned for one month with hard labour.[59] A number of husbands claimed that their wives had deserted them and refused to return home. A man named Wilson told the court that the house was open to his wife but she would not live with him. He also declared to the court that he would not give her a separate allowance but if she preferred she could divorce him and he would cover the costs.[60] John Hughes was prosecuted for desertion a second time, and in court offered his wife the opportunity to return home, which she refused. He was a drunkard and the couple had been married for seven years. The court was sympathetic to his wife's situation and he was jailed for a month and told to keep sober.[61] In 1882, when William Bourke refused to support his wife and child he was sentenced to three months, the maximum allowed under the law. The apparent cause of his refusal to support his family was because his mother objected to his wife.[62]

Husbands also drew on patriarchal rhetoric to argue that their wives had usurped their authority and they used the courts to reassert that control. Indeed, this is a common theme throughout many of the chapters in this book as husbands claimed to be irritated, often leading to violent responses, by the perceived disobedience of their wives.[63] In 1873, Mary Meehan and her two children were discharged from the Limerick workhouse at the request of her husband.[64] The authority of the father/husband over his family/wife tended to hold sway in the guardians' meeting rooms. Honora Tuohy was also released from the Limerick workhouse when her husband informed the board of guardians that she had entered the institution without his knowledge and 'against his consent'.[65] In 1870, the husband of a woman who had entered the Limerick workhouse informed the relieving officer that he was willing to support her but that she was a 'terrible drunkard'. When the woman was brought before the board of guardians she stated she had entered the workhouse because of her 'bad treatment' though she admitted she was 'well

---

[59] *Freeman's Journal*, 19 Oct. 1853.
[60] *Freeman's Journal*, 27 June 1881. Legally a husband was obliged to pay the costs of a successful divorce petition. See p. 384.
[61] *Irish Times*, 31 Jan. 1873.   [62] NAI, CIF 1882 B42.
[63] See Chapters 9,11 and 12, for further examples.
[64] Board of Guardian Minutes, Limerick, 19 April 1873. BG/110 A/56. 2 April 1873–1 Oct. 1873.
[65] Board of Guardian Minutes, Limerick, 2 July 1864. BG/110 A/41. 23 March 1864–1 March 1865.

supported' by him. The board discharged her on the grounds that she was not destitute.[66] Violence in the home was one of the major reasons given by women for deserting their husbands.

Some women claimed that they had had a falling out with their husbands and with nowhere else to go turned to the workhouse for assistance. Anne Cody gave a dispute with her husband as the reason why she entered the workhouse and declared in a memorial to the Lord Lieutenant that her husband was now willing to support her again.[67] The fact of entering the workhouse was sometimes used by women as leverage against their husbands. These women, once in the workhouse, gave information against their husbands who were then threatened with prosecution by the boards of guardians. Unless they took their wives back, they were faced with a prison sentence or a bill for their maintenance in the workhouse. This may have been the basis of some form of negotiation within the household, a strategy used by a wife to improve her husband's behaviour or the distribution of household resources.

As we have seen, a number of deserting husbands did end up in prison, and their deserted wives sometimes addressed petitions to the Lord Lieutenant for their husband's release. Pressure may have been brought to bear on them by their husbands to do this. However, the interesting point is that the desertion had occurred, the husband had been prosecuted and then his wife sent a petition to secure his early release. Perhaps these wives trusted that the husbands had learned a lesson; the petitions tended to note that the husband had agreed to support his wife and family. The wife of Joseph Williams sent a petition to the Lord Lieutenant seeking his early release as she claimed that she and her children were in 'great distress' and needed his support to survive.[68] This was also, as we have seen in Chapter 10, a common reason given in petitions where husbands had assaulted their wives and ended up in prison. Many women noted the difficulty in maintaining their families without a husband's financial support.

Securing Relief

After 1840, relief for deserted women and families came primarily through the Poor Law system. However, there were other resources also open to deserted wives and children. Petitioning various members of the clergy for charitable relief, or, if the family lived as tenants on an estate, the landlord, was one strategy used to secure some financial support.[69] Among the

---

[66] *Limerick Reporter*, 22 July 1870.   [67] NAI, CIF, 1847 C1.
[68] NAI, CIF 1850 W15.
[69] R. A. Houston, *Peasant Petitions: Social Relations and Economic Life on Landed Estates, 1600–1850* (Basingstoke, 2014).

mid-nineteenth-century petitions to the landlord or his agent on the Shirley Estate in County Monaghan are requests from wives of tenant holders to compel their husbands to act in a particular way or to secure financial support on a spouse's desertion. In October 1849, Mary Gartlan wrote to the landlord, Evelyn John Shirley, outlining the circumstances of her husband's desertion. Gartlan married her first husband, 'a respectable shopkeeper', in Carrickmacross. He died in 1832 leaving her with three children. She then let their townhouse and went to live with her father. Both her parents had died by 1835 and she, being an only child, had inherited a large farm and a 'valuable stock of cattle'. She was not able to manage the farm and so married a young man from County Louth, by whom she had three more children. Initially the husband did well, but then his cattle died and this development, followed by the impact of the Famine, 'cramped his means'. He opened a public house in Carrickmacross 'which did not answer his expectations', and on 12 March 1848 he deserted his wife and children and went to America. Gartlan was left destitute and was fearful that unless the landlord helped her she would end up, with her children, in the workhouse. It is not known what became of her. Within the Shirley papers a later letter dated 15 November 1849 recorded that she 'found all the avenues of sympathy closed against me'.[70]

Mary McMahon deserted her husband Peter McCabe having, she noted, 'done all that human industry could to maintain the place [a farm], but unfortunately her husband's indolence and forced bad management, baffled all her exertions, and the place went to shameful desolation, till fear of starvation (or worse consequence), obliged her to seek shelter with her aged, infirm father'. She lived with her father for a year when her husband told her he was going to sell the property to maintain himself and 'she could do as she liked'.[71] In her letter to the land agent, George Morant, Alice Callan claimed that her husband was enticed away from her and kept another woman in a house provided by a neighbour. She further alleged that this neighbour 'has bought a meadow from the husband and she, Alice, is now destitute'. Her husband's nephew was providing her with shelter.[72] The responses of agents and landlords to these petitions do not survive. It is clear, however, that on some estates, women in small tenant farming families believed in the possibility of support from a landlord or land agent. The outlining of a strong case, which revealed a feckless husband wasting or unable to utilise resources, with a hardworking wife, may have brought some support in times of need.

[70] Petition of Mary Gartlan (PRONI, Shirley Papers, D/3531/P, Box 1).
[71] Petition of Mary McMahon 12 Feb. 1844 (PRONI, Shirley Papers, D/3531/P, Box 1).
[72] Alice Callan to George Morant, n.d. (PRONI, Shirley Papers, D/3531/P, Box 3).

In cases where petitions for clemency were sent to the Lord Lieutenant it was the practice to ask the relevant prosecuting board of guardians for their views. Boards of guardians generally declined to offer an opinion in such cases but noted the need to compel the husband to support his wife and family if he were to be released early.[73] How such a 'compulsion' might be ensured is not noted. There is nothing to tell us how many of those arrested or imprisoned for desertion under the Poor Law system were repeat offenders. Nor do we know how many deserting husbands and wives actually returned to their families.

Family Intervention

As we have seen, networks of knowledge existed within families, neighbours and communities that allowed deserting husbands and wives to be discovered. How the reward system worked for some of the Poor Law unions is not clear, though rewards must have been attractive to individuals who had knowledge of a deserting spouse. Families were sometimes aware of impending desertions. In 1864, Mary Sullivan's father informed the relieving officer of the Tralee workhouse that his daughter's husband was about to desert her and leave the country. The relieving officer, on receiving this information, spoke to the husband, who declared he was willing to support his wife. Three weeks later she was in the workhouse, and a warrant was issued for her husband's arrest that was effected by her father, as the husband was on his way to catch the boat to America. At the trial the defendant argued that he had no real intention of leaving the country but the evidence was against him. Finding that the defendant had left no money for the benefit of his wife and that he had tried to sneak out of the country the judge was determined to make 'an example' of the defendant. He sentenced him to three months' hard labour.[74] His wife, who might have seen a change in her husband's behaviour, may have informed her father of the impending desertion. Or her husband may even have hinted to her that he was about to leave, thinking she would do nothing about it.

There were other ways in which families sought to assist deserted women. If wives could not secure financial support from their husbands, family members sometimes sued for maintenance. Miss Lizzie Murphy sued her brother-in-law at Mullingar quarter sessions for £16 10s for the cost of board and lodging for his wife and child for twenty-two weeks. The women were sisters and Lizzie had sheltered her sister due to the ill-treatment of her husband, caused by his drinking. Mrs Julia Flood, said

---

[73] See, for instance, NAI, CIF 1846 C66.
[74] *Tralee Chronicle and Killarney Echo*, 7 Oct. 1864.

that her husband drank and beat her. Her husband wanted her to return to the family home but she refused.[75] Richard Allen was sued by his father-in-law for the cost of fifteen weeks' maintenance of his wife. The father-in-law claimed that his daughter had been so badly treated by Allen that she was forced to leave the marital home and live with her father. Her husband claimed that since she had left the home he had provided for her against his wishes as she had forfeited any claim to maintenance. The court suggested they come to some arrangement and the case was dismissed.[76]

One of the organisations that had an impact on family desertion was the Society for the Prevention of Cruelty to Children. As noted in Chapter 10, the SPCC was established in Ireland in the same year as the enactment of the 1889 Cruelty to Children Act. The Act gave inspectors legal powers to enter homes and investigate the conditions in which children were being cared for. From the 1890s the SPCC began to play a significant role in prosecuting husbands who deserted their families. William Campbell was prosecuted by the SPCC for deserting his family, while the guardians of the North Dublin Union charged him with leaving his family dependant on the rates. The prisoner was given a week to find a job and begin to support his family.[77] SPCC inspectors provided evidence of child neglect in courts; they commented on the characters of the parents and magistrates were clearly swayed by their evidence.

Changes in the Law

As we have seen in other chapters, the law played a pivotal role in regulating aspects of marriage. Many advantages accrued to wives from changes in the law, and as the nineteenth century advanced new laws gave deserted women the right to protect money or property that they had acquired through their own industry or had owned prior to marriage. As indicated in Chapter 7, some of these changes came about through the Married Women's Property Acts of 1865, 1870 and 1885. The 1870 Act also imposed on the wife the obligation of supporting a husband or children who were maintained in the workhouse, an obligation that had applied to men since the implementation of the Poor Law in 1838.[78]

As we have discussed in Chapter 7, the Married Women's Property (Ireland) Act 1865 gave some protection to women compelled to work

---

[75] *Irish Times*, 18 April 1911.   [76] *Irish Times*, 10 Nov. 1875.
[77] *Freeman's Journal*, 28 Oct. 1896.
[78] Lee Holcombe, *Wives and Property: Reform of the Married Women's Property Law in Nineteenth-Century* (Oxford, 1983), pp. 178–9. For the support of children born outside marriage see p. 356 above.

because they had been deserted by their husbands and whose husbands had returned to seize their property. The Act allowed deserted wives to petition justices for an order protecting their property. A penalty could be imposed on a husband who took his wife's possessions in breach of a protection order. Deserted wives were eager and able to utilise the law to ensure their economic wellbeing. A number of married women's protection orders survive. For instance, Mary Waring had been deserted by her husband on 1 May 1864 and she applied to the magistrate at the petty session in Belfast in December 1869 for a protection order. This was granted to her and was backdated to the first day of the desertion.[79] Between 1869 and 1923, seventy-two such protection orders were provided by the Belfast petty sessions. Between 1867 and 1886, nine such orders were made at Lisburn petty sessions. In 1897, Catherine Kennedy from Killiney petitioned for a protection order alleging that her husband was 'always drunk, and since his desertion he had twice forcibly broken into my place and took away my bedclothes and other property I am able to earn for myself'.[80] In 1892, Anne Murphy, who was supporting herself through her 'own industry', by carrying on the business of a green grocer in Ranelagh, deposed that her husband was of 'very intemperate habits … continually beating and ill-treating me'.[81]

Maintenance

Under the 1878 Matrimonial Causes Amendment Act, magistrates had the power to order a husband to pay maintenance to support his wife. If a husband was convicted of aggravated assault upon his wife then he could be forced to pay her maintenance, and if her life was considered to be in danger the court could order that she was no longer obliged to live with her husband. This legislation was in effect transferring to the civil court the powers formerly exercised by the ecclesiastical courts. As we have seen in domestic abuse cases, however, magistrates in the common law courts had imposed maintenance payments on some husbands who abused their wives long before this legislation was enacted. An order for the payment of maintenance did not necessarily mean a separation agreement had been made or agreed between the couple but it might be the precursor to such proceedings. From 1886, a married woman who had been deserted by her husband could summon him before the

---

[79] Married Women's Protection Orders (PRONI, Belf/7/4/1).
[80] Affidavit of Catherine Kennedy, 7 June 1897 (NAI, 1C/72/860).
[81] Affidavit of Anne Murphy, 17 May 1892 (NAI, 1C/72/860).

Illustration 11.1 This image of the petty sessions depicts the variety of people who attended the local courts, which were especially popular among the middle and lower classes in Ireland for settling often minor local disputes.

Table 11.1 *Orders for maintenance in cases of desertion, 1895–1914 (49 & 50 Vict. c.52. 1886)*

No. of applications		No. of orders made	Orders enforced by imprisonment
1895	135	106	11
1896	56	10	
1897	66		
1898	51	45	18
1899	76	59	14
1900	64	52	23
1901	74	68	13
1902	59	54	14
1903	71	58	12
1904	155	117	14
1905	185	147	29
1906	195	167	18
1907	231	203	18
1908	258	224	34
1909	274	176	21
1910	262	172	27
1911	340	228	32
1912	323	218	33
1913	398	258	31
1914	333	220	15

Source: *Criminal and Judicial Statistics for Ireland*, 1896–1915

magistrates at petty sessions. The onus was on the applicant to prove the desertion. The magistrates would then check to see if the husband could 'support his wife or his wife and family wholly or in part and if he does not do so, then he has deserted them'. They would then make an order that the husband was to pay his wife a weekly sum, not exceeding £2, and in accordance with his means. The order could be altered if the circumstances of either party changed. If the wife had committed adultery then no order was made; if she committed adultery after the order was made the money could be taken from her.[82] Figures for maintenance for women in cases of desertion are available from 1895. Table 11.1 identifies the number of maintenance requests pursued through the petty sessions courts, the numbers granted and those orders that were enforced by the imprisonment of the deserting husbands. The Summary

---

[82] Married Women (Maintenance in Cases of Desertion) Act (Ireland) 49 & 50 Vict. c.52. 1886. See also Married Women's (Ireland) Property Act, 28 & 29 Vict. c.43 1868; Married Women's Property Act, 45 & 46 Vict. c.75 1882; Married Women's Property Act, 47 & 48 Vict. c.14. 1884.

Jurisdiction (Married Women) Act, 1895, which gave further protection to deserted wives, did not extend to Ireland or Scotland, though the government was asked to consider extending its provisions to Ireland.[83]

The percentage of individuals imprisoned for non-payment of maintenance was relatively small, just over 10 per cent (11 cases) in 1895, and 24 per cent in 1900; about 20 per cent in 1905 and just 7 per cent by 1914. Deserted wives were, however, making use of the courts to secure support from their erring husbands. By that date there was also a general increase in the numbers of applications for maintenance. There was also a considerable decrease in the numbers of cases dealing with failure to pay maintenance. Had such payments become an acceptable way to arrange for marital separations without going to court? Or was it simply that such cases were pursued less and less through the courts? It is difficult to assess what was really happening from the statistical evidence.

Wives' entitlement to maintenance was strongly supported by the court system. Justices paid little attention to arguments of 'bad conduct' on the part of the wife without substantial proof. They usually upheld the principle that the husband had an obligation to provide for his wife and frequently issued interim maintenance orders while formal divorce proceedings were initiated. In 1892 a couple who were married for eleven years appeared in the Dublin Police court. He was a painter and decorator and the couple had five children. He had deserted them about three weeks before the court case, and had since failed to contribute to the family's support. He claimed that his wife had misconducted herself with a lodger and that he wanted a divorce. She claimed that he had treated her badly for at least two years, beating her and giving her black eyes. He was ordered to pay her 25s a week, pending the divorce.[84]

At the Waterford City petty sessions in 1922, John Fitzgerald, a corporation workman, was sued by his wife for desertion. They met a few days before they married on 30 April 1920. He did not live with her until early May 1920 and he claimed that from that day she was 'continually nagging, bullying, barking, and biting like a dog, and kicking like a young horse in a stable'. He was single when they married but he was his wife's third husband and 'she had great experience with the management of husbands'. He left her after a few days. The court recognised this as a clear case of desertion and awarded the wife 12s 6d for maintenance.[85]

Concerns over the difficulty in securing maintenance for deserted wives and children saw the introduction of legislation to assist in the collection of such payments in reciprocal arrangements throughout the

---

[83] Question from Maurice Healy, HC Debates, 22 Jan. 1897, 45, *c.* 291.
[84] *Irish Times*, 29 April 1892.   [85] *Irish Times*, 25 March 1922.

empire. The Maintenance Orders (Facilities for Enforcement) Act 1920 was implemented in Ireland and England. Under the Act a husband could resist an order on various grounds, including that the court had no jurisdiction; that there was no valid marriage; that a judicial separation was already in place; that the couple lived apart by mutual consent; that she deserted him; that she had committed adultery, which he had not condoned, connived at, or by wilful neglect and misconduct conduced to; that he had reasonable cause to leave; that she was already getting alimony; or that he had no means to pay.[86] It is difficult to know how successful the Act was in Ireland, given its introduction at a time of violent upheaval.

The belief that husbands were responsible for the maintenance of their wives was, however, sustained in the Dáil Courts.[87] Maintenance cases came before these courts and while most were related to the support of illegitimate children, there were also a smaller number that were concerned with the maintenance of a deserted wife. For instance, we find that in Bandon, in 1924, Helena Bowan sued her husband Cornelius for an increase of alimony (to maintain her and their child) from £2 to £2 15s. per week. The court agreed to an increase of £2 5s per week and ordered the husband not to interfere in any other way with the agreement drawn up between the parties.[88] We have no clear idea of the numbers of such cases that came before the Dáil Courts, but a perusal of the records reveals that men were generally willing to abide by the decisions of the courts.

Conclusion

In the absence of an affordable form of divorce, men and women developed their own solutions to leaving unhappy or unsatisfactory marriages. Deserted husbands sought to ensure their own economic survival in the face of possible legal claims for a wife's use of credit by warning creditors that they would not meet these debts. They did so in the most public forum of the newspaper. Women who deserted their husbands or families also needed to be sure that they too could survive economically and some, therefore, are recorded as taking domestic goods with them as they established new households. Desertion could upset the economic balance of poorer households. The introduction of the Poor Law mitigated to some extent a descent into absolute poverty by providing shelter

---

[86] Department of the Taoiseach (NAI, S2063).
[87] On the Dáil courts see pp. 152, 171–2.
[88] Dáil Éireann Court Register Book (NAI, fo. 86).

and other necessities to deserted wives and children within the institu-
tuon of the workhouse. Poor Law guardians and the minor courts had a
very clear sense of the duty of husbands to support their wives and
families. The authorities thus attempted to regulate and enforce this
fundamental principle of married life by coercion through imprisonment,
fines and forcing maintenance payments. How successful any courts
were in implementing maintenance orders is still an unanswered question. The workhouse remained the primary source of support for the
deserted wives and children of the poorer classes until the mid-1920s.[89]

From the evidence available, a man's ability to move around the
country to find work was an advantage when he decided to desert his wife
and family. Men were, unlike many women deserting, usually unencum-
bered by children. However, many men who did desert were caught,
particularly those targeted by the Poor Law guardians. The ease with
which Poor Law guardians could locate deserting husbands suggests that
neighbours and others were willing to provide the necessary information
to the authorities. This would suggest that desertion, particularly when
there were children involved, was not always an acceptable action.

Desertion was, among other things, a way out of domestic unhappiness, strife, poverty or economic distress. All courts generally looked on
deserted wives with some sympathy. The evolution of the law throughout
the period saw the removal of legal constraints placed upon women
granting them, for instance, greater property rights and economic auton-
omy. By the end of the nineteenth century the law provided more
substantial support to women who were deserted, or separated, particularly in the area of securing maintenance payments. The law gradually
allowed deserted women a degree of financial independence and safeguarded their earnings. What is evident also is that the authorities, aided
by the law, became much more interventionist in family life, though it is
clear that many individuals and couples resisted such intervention and
pursued their own agendas.

---

[89] A deserted wife's allowance was finally introduced in Ireland in 1970.

12   Divorce

In 1852, Charles O'Callaghan requested the dissolution of his marriage to Anne Dillon. O'Callaghan explained to Archbishop Paul Cullen that he had met Dillon in 1848, and after three meetings (during two of which they were both 'in a state of intoxication'), they ran way to get married. After about five weeks of marriage, Dillon left O'Callaghan's home and refused thereafter to live with him. She told him that her father and brother had secretly known about the marriage and that they had forced her to agree to it. Dillon also claimed that she felt compelled to go through with the marriage because having run away she was 'as bad as she could be in the voice of the country'. After she left O'Callaghan, Dillon gave birth to two children by a cousin. O'Callaghan pleaded for a dissolution of his marriage because he was 'left without a partner, left without one to take care of my place since my mother's decease, my soul wrought to agony, to think of her dereliction of duty'.[1] O'Callaghan noted in his correspondence that although he was anxious to fulfil his duty as a Roman Catholic, he did not want to have 'this drag chain upon my liberty'. He reminded the archbishop that he could 'take other proceedings' to solve his marriage problems, by which he presumably meant that he could go to the civil courts for a divorce.[2] In fact, Dillon, if she could convince the Catholic authorities that she had been forced into a marriage, also had a strong case for a dissolution of the marriage.[3]

The 'drag chain' of a marriage that could not be dissolved was a dilemma facing many married men and women in Ireland from the seventeenth through to the twentieth century. Yet, this chapter will argue that the period is also marked by creative legal solutions designed to undermine ecclesiastical control of marital dissolution. By 1900, the civil courts had begun to consider marriage cases that in 1660 would have

---

[1] Armagh Archdiocese Archive, Cardinal Tomás Ó Fiaich Library & Archive, Armagh.
[2] Ibid.
[3] See also Armagh Diocesan Archive, Cardinal Tomás Ó Fiaich Library & Archive, Armagh.

been deemed the business of the consistory courts. The canon law prohibition on remarriage after divorce was, as we shall see, undermined by private parliamentary acts that dissolved marriages and permitted those involved to remarry. The increasing use of formal and informal private deeds of separation in which spouses agreed to live apart also weakened strict adherence to church regulations. While these changes did not represent a complete secularisation of Irish marriage law and regulations, they do suggest that men and women were willing to be flexible in their interpretation of church guidelines, particularly when they were considering how to end a problematic union.

Divorce *a vinculo matrimonii*

According to canon law, which guided the ecclesiastical courts in determining marriage litigation, there were two types of divorce. The first, *a vinculo matrimonii* (i.e. from the chains of marriage) was, in effect, a judgment that the marriage was null and void because it had never existed in the first place. A formal dissolution of the marriage was granted if one of the partners was incapable, mentally or physically, of consummating the marriage, or if it could be proved that force was used to coerce an individual into marriage. Bigamy and marrying within the prohibited degrees of affinity and consanguinity were also valid reasons for voiding a marriage.

The documentary evidence for requests for divorce *a vinculo matrimonii* from Irish ecclesiastical courts is fragmentary. Two petitions for divorce survive in the records of the Killaloe consistory court dating to the early eighteenth century. Both were presented by women and both requested a divorce on the grounds of impotency.[4] We do not know the outcome of either request, but for the women involved the process of securing an annulment of their marriages could be a long, drawn out one. A woman wishing to have her marriage annulled because her husband could not consummate the union had to wait a minimum of three years before she could commence legal proceedings. In a request for a marriage annulment submitted to the Catholic authorities in mid-eighteenth century Galway, it was acknowledged that the woman involved, Margaret Joyce, 'can't be persuaded to agree' to wait for three years to have her

---

[4] For more details see Mary O'Dowd, 'Marriage breakdown in Ireland, c. 1660–1857' in Niamh Howlin and Kevin Costello (eds.), *Law and the Family in Ireland 1800–1950* (London, 2015), pp. 7–23. See also PRONI, D2107/4/7 for a copy of a petition filed by Margaret Walker to the Dublin consistory court for the dissolution of her marriage to Thomas Walker on grounds of impotency. They had married in 1788 and Margaret submitted her petition three years later in 1791.

marriage dissolved by an ecclesiastical court and, hence, had asked for an annulment from the Catholic authorities. Joyce also claimed that she had been compelled against her will to marry an older, impotent man. The Catholic church followed the same canon law concerning grounds for marriage annulment as the ecclesiastical court and the priest dealing with Joyce's request agreed that she had two grounds for a divorce: impotency and the absence of consent. He determined, however, to recommend annulment due to 'the defect of the consent on the part of the woman' because he was concerned that granting a divorce on grounds of impotency might lead others to make similar claims that were, by their nature, difficult to prove.[5] The implication of the priest's comments was that such cases were rare.

Requests for dissolution of marriage due to the absence of free consent on the part of the woman continued to be heard by Catholic clergymen in the nineteenth century. The prevalence of abductions and marriages agreed in haste or under family compulsion provided reasonable grounds for such requests, although few were seemingly sought or granted. Petitions for the dissolution of marriage based on the family connections of husband and wife were also submitted to Catholic clergy throughout the period covered by this volume.[6] Such requests had a long tradition in Ireland. In the medieval period, men from Gaelic families regularly appealed to church authorities for the dissolution of their marriages on the grounds of consanguinity. In the sixteenth and seventeenth centuries, clergymen colluded with Gaelic families to approve annulments based on the family relationship between husband and wife.[7] As noted in Chapter 3, most people, particularly in rural society, married someone from within their local community, which meant that it was not unusual for a couple to have a family link that breached the Roman Catholic law on consanguinity. This familiar connection could prove useful in the event of a marital breakdown. In the visitation book for the Catholic diocese of Ossory, for the years 1750–1774, four cases of divorce were recorded. Two dissolutions were requested on the grounds of impotency and two because the husband and wife were related within the prohibited degrees of consanguinity. In the latter cases, the couples were offered the opportunity to have their unions regularised through the granting of official dispensations to validate the union retrospectively. Both refused and clearly recognised that by insisting that the church consider their

---

[5] Galway Diocesan Archives, Box 8/file 1.
[6] See Chapter 1 on the law of consanguinity and affinity.
[7] Mary O'Dowd, 'Men, women and children in early modern Ireland' in Jane Ohlmeyer (ed.), *Cambridge History of Ireland* (4 vols., Cambridge, 2018), ii, pp. 337–63.

initial marriage as invalid, they were requesting a dissolution of the union.[8] Policing church laws on consanguinity and affinity was challenging for Catholic priests as they had to familiarise themselves with family relations going back four generations. Some agreed that when discovered the couple should be separated and be free to remarry. In 1816, Archbishop Richard Reilly advised a priest in his diocese that if he was sure that a married couple were related in the third and fourth degrees and had no dispensation to marry, then 'you will not hesitate to declare their marriage invalid, and to allow each to form a new connection'.[9] If the couple sought and were granted a post-marital dispensation, they were encouraged by the late eighteenth century to renew their marriage vows. In 1850, the ever pragmatic Dean John O'Sullivan of Kenmare warned priests to exercise caution in insisting on this practice because a renewal of vows could also lead some husbands and wives to question the validity of their marriages and use it as a means to separate. O'Sullivan described how he had, with some difficulty, acquired a retrospective dispensation for one couple. As he was about to begin the ceremony to renew their vows, the husband 'exclaimed "It must be the former marriage was no use when you are now going to marry us again", bolted out of the room and left the wife there and it was only after two years occasional denunciation of the vagabond that I compelled him to marry the woman'.[10] In O'Sullivan's view, it was often 'better not *quieta movere*'.[11]

With the appointment of Paul Cullen as Archbishop of Armagh in 1849, such a practical and flexible attitude to the implementation of church regulations was increasingly deemed unacceptable. Under Cullen's reforming regime, bishops and priests were directed to regularise marital relations in their respective localities and to make sure that marrying couples were aware of Catholic canon law on consanguinity and affinity. It was the priest's responsibility to ensure that the law was observed.[12]

As we have noted in earlier chapters, of the three main Christian denominations, Presbyterianism had the most flexible attitude towards the dissolution of marriage. According to the Westminster Confession of Faith (1646), it was permissible for a person to sue for divorce if their

---

[8] C. O'Dwyer (ed.), 'Archbishop Butler's visitation book', *Archivium Hibernicum*, 33 (1975), 15, 30.
[9] Armagh Diocesan Archive, Reilly Papers, Cardinal Tomás Ó Fiaich Library & Archive, Armagh.
[10] John O'Sullivan, 'Praxis Parochi', i, p. 694 (Kerry Diocesan Archives, Killarney).
[11] Ibid., i, p. 696. *Quieta movere*: not to disturb what is settled.
[12] See, for example, Armagh Diocesan Archive, Dixon Papers, Cardinal Tomás Ó Fiaich Library & Archive, Armagh.

partner committed adultery and 'after the divorce to marry another, as if the offending party were dead'. Divorce was also possible in the event of 'willful desertion as can no way be remedied by the church or civil magistrate'.[13] The power to permit a couple to divorce was vested in the Presbytery. A survey of the minutes of seven Presbyteries, 1739–1841, suggest that while requests for divorce were not common, they were viewed sympathetically by at least some congregations. The minute books recorded seventeen requests for divorce or permission to remarry even though a spouse from a previous marriage was still alive.[14] Eight of the cases were considered by the Seceder Presbytery of Down in the years 1786–1800 and three were heard in another Seceder Presbytery, that of Upper Tyrone, between 1802 and 1810. All of the requests for divorce were based on the desertion of a spouse rather than on adultery. In 1802, two women applied to the Presbytery of Upper Tyrone for divorces because their husbands had deserted them. Following an interrogation of the women and other witnesses by the members of the Presbytery, it was agreed that they 'were free from all obligation to their men and were divorced'.[15] The enquiry into a third woman's request for a divorce from the same Presbytery took a little longer, but she too was eventually pronounced 'freed from the love' of her husband and divorced.[16] A priority for the Presbytery was to establish that the person applying for the divorce had not provoked his or her spouse into leaving the marriage. In 1811, for example, Jane Gordin's request to the Burgher Presbytery of Upper Tyrone for a divorce was rejected because she had refused to live with her husband from shortly after the marriage had taken place. Although Gordin's husband had remarried, she was not given permission to do likewise or to rejoin the congregation.[17]

In addition to requests for divorce, Presbyteries were also asked to consider petitions from individuals who wished to be admitted or restored to the 'privileges of the church' but who had remarried without

[13] The Westminster Confession of Faith (1646), chapter xxiv, articles v, vi. See also Andrew Holmes, *The Shaping of Ulster Presbyterian Belief and Practice, 1770–1840* (Oxford, 2006), pp. 212, 223 and pp. 284–6 above.

[14] Minutes of the Presbytery of Upper Tyrone (Seceder), 1802–1810 (PHSIB); Minutes of the Burgher Presbytery of Upper Tyrone, 1810–1830 (PHSIB), pp. 21–4. Minutes of the Presbytery of Down (Seceder), 1837–1841 (PHSIB); Minutes of Down Presbytery, 1785–1842 (PHSIB); Minutes of Presbytery of Monaghan, 1800–1817 (PHSIB); Minutes of the Presbytery of Route, 1811–1834 (PHSIB); Minutes of the Reformed Presbytery of Ireland, 1803–1811 (PRONI, CR5/5A/1/2A). The authors are grateful to Dr Leanne Calvert and Dr Rachel Wilson for their research on the minute books.

[15] Minutes of the Presbytery of Upper Tyrone (Seceder), 1802–1810 (PHSIB).

[16] Ibid.

[17] Minutes of Burgher Presbytery of Upper Tyrone, 1810–1830, pp. 21–4 (PHSIB).

permission from the Presbytery when their former partner had eloped or deserted them. Between 1800 and 1817, the Presbytery in Monaghan considered seven referrals from the kirk session in which individuals had either remarried when their first spouse had eloped or had married someone whose spouse had left them. In 1804, for example, when James Hovy's first wife, Fanny Sharp, eloped, he married again and had eight children by his second wife. He told the Presbytery that Sharp had committed adultery and had gone to America. She was also reported to be dead. Hovy was clearly identifying for the Presbytery all the reasons why he should be granted a retrospective divorce. The Presbytery was, as in many similar cases, uncertain how to proceed and referred the matter back to the session for more information. One of the concerns of the Presbytery was that Hovy had married his second wife less than two years after his first wife's departure. The issue remained unresolved six years later when Hovy made another similar request.[18]

The number of requests for divorce seems to have declined in the nineteenth century. Presbyteries that had granted divorces in the late eighteenth and early nineteenth centuries did so rarely in later decades. In December 1840, the Seceder Presbytery of Down was asked whether a man from the congregation in Drumlee could remarry because his wife had deserted him. She had emigrated to America and, 'as was believed, had been married to another man'. The Presbytery did not know how to answer the query and the clerk was asked to look through the minutes of previous meetings to ascertain 'what had been the practice in similar cases'. At a later meeting of the Presbytery in July 1841, it was resolved that the man could be given permission to remarry as his wife had 'voluntarily and without cause deserted him'.[19]

More orthodox Presbyteries appear to have been reluctant to encourage applications for divorce as the records of meetings indicate that such requests were rarely, if ever, considered. The legal ambiguity of a marriage following a Presbyterian-style divorce was possibly one reason why this was the case. A divorce granted by a Presbytery had no legal status in common law. The latter permitted a person to remarry if their partner had been missing for seven years or more and was, therefore, deemed by law to be dead. If, as seems to have been the case, Presbyteries granted divorces and gave permission to remarry to individuals who had been deserted for shorter periods of time, then the second or subsequent marriages would have been deemed bigamous under statute law. Patrick

---

[18] Minutes of Presbytery of Monaghan, 1800–1817 (PHSIB). See entries for 29 May 1804, 4 Sept. 1804, 4 Sept. 1810.

[19] Minutes of the Presbytery of Down (Seceder), 1837–1841 (PHSIB).

Griffin has also suggested that Presbyterians with marital problems in the eighteenth century may have preferred to have them resolved through the discreet process of the consistorial court rather than through the more public enquiry conducted by the local sessions or Presbytery.[20]

In 1702, the Presbyterian minister and writer, John McBride, published a scathing critique of the Anglican view of marriage. He argued that it was unreasonable for the established church to oblige couples to take a vow to remain together 'til death them do part' even when one of the partners to the marriage had deserted. McBride was also critical of the ecclesiastical court's refusal to permit remarriage, even if a wife was proven to be 'a most gross and notorious adulteress'.[21] Later Presbyterian commentators were, however, more muted in their attitude to divorce. Few drew public attention to the distinct Presbyterian regulations on divorce and there was very little support within the Irish Presbyterian church for the extension of the English 1857 law on divorce to Ireland. The Presbyterian authorities shared with the other main religious denominations a view of marriage as a life commitment that could only be dissolved in exceptional circumstances.[22]

In Chapter 1, we noted the confused state of Irish marriage law as it related to the definition of a legally valid marriage. We can also identify a similar confusion concerning the annulment of marriage. Although only fragmentary records of the Irish ecclesiastical courts have survived, it is clear that Catholic and Presbyterian men and women appealed to them for annulment of their marriages. One of the women noted above, who petitioned the ecclesiastical court for an annulment, married in a Catholic service and was represented by a Catholic lawyer. As indicated already, Margaret Joyce only approached the Catholic authorities for an annulment because she was not prepared to wait the required three years to sue for one in the consistory court.[23] Nevertheless, there were legal problems attached to an annulment granted by the Catholic church. It would not have been recognised by the consistory court; and those involved, like Presbyterians in an analogous position, would have been liable to prosecution for bigamy in the civil courts if they remarried.

---

[20] Patrick Griffin, *The People with No Name: Ireland's Ulster Scots, America's Scots Irish, and the Creation of a British Atlantic World* (Princeton, 2001), pp. 41–2.

[21] John McBride, *A Vindication of Marriage, as Solemnized by Presbyterians in the North of Ireland Wherein, Their Principles, Practice, and Reasons Thereof, Are Candidly Shown, With the Causes of Their Non-conformity to the Form Prescribed in the Liturgy* (Belfast, 1702), pp. 29–30.

[22] Diane Urquhart, 'Ireland and the Divorce and Matrimonial Causes Act of 1857', *Journal of Family History*, 38, 3 (2013), 307. See also Urquhart, *Irish Divorce: A History*, pp. 70–5.

[23] O'Dowd, 'Marriage breakdown in Ireland, 1660–1857', p. 11.

Similarly, a Catholic marriage annulled by the consistory court would not have been automatically annulled by the Catholic church. The different regulations of the churches on consanguinity and affinity, in particular, meant that they did not agree on what were valid grounds for a dissolution *a vinculo matrimonii*. As we have demonstrated elsewhere in the volume, partnerships, although illegal under civil law, appear to have received community tolerance, particularly within the Presbyterian community. In other words, people were willing to participate in marriages that were considered illegal by the state but approved by their respective churches.

Divorce *A Mensa et Thoro*

The majority of people seeking a marital separation in the 265 years covered by this book did not apply for an annulment or dissolution of their union. Instead, they sought to end their marriage in other ways. Far more common in the consistory court and its secular successor than applications for divorces *a vinculo matrimonii* were petitions for divorce *a mensa et thoro* or from 'bed and board'. This was, in modern terms, a request for a judicial separation rather than a divorce. Unlike *a vinculo matrimonii*, a divorce *a mensa et thoro* did not permit either partner to remarry

Before the second half of the nineteenth century, the criteria by which a man or woman could apply for a divorce *a mensa et thoro* were gendered: a husband had to prove that his wife was an adulteress but a wife had to provide evidence that not only was her husband an adulterer but that he had treated her cruelly or was found guilty of incest or 'unnatural practices'. By the last decades of the nineteenth century, a woman could petition for divorce on the grounds of adultery *or* cruelty both or any other aggravating factors and was no longer required to prove more than one. This change was partly a consequence of the influence of the English Court for Divorce and Matrimonial Causes established under the Matrimonial Causes Act (1857). As noted already Ireland was excluded from the legislation, but by the late nineteenth century the Irish courts were following the English divorce court's simplified criteria for divorce, which enabled men and women to sue on the same grounds.[24]

Throughout the period covered by this book, more women than men submitted petitions for this type of divorce, mainly because it was a means of securing financial assistance to leave a violent marriage. As in the proceedings concerning desertion described in the last chapter, the

---

[24] William Duncan, 'Desertion and cruelty in Irish matrimonial law', *Irish Jurist*, 2 (1972), 213–40. See also Urquhart, *Irish Divorce: A History*, chapter 6.

courts hearing divorce petitions upheld the wife's claim to economic support from her husband for her 'necessities' or her bed and board. If the court granted the divorce, it would not only permit the woman to live apart from her husband but it would also compel him to pay her an annuity. In addition, the husband was obliged to pay the legal costs involved in the case. The official parliamentary statistics on divorce petitions that were recorded from 1863 to 1919 confirm the greater appeal of the legal action for women, with 86.2 per cent (213) of petitions lodged by wives.[25]

In determining the amount of alimony to be granted to the wife, the judge in the ecclesiastical court might include consideration of the number of children voluntarily left in her care by her husband. The ecclesiastical court had, however, no jurisdiction over the legal custody of the children of the marriage. Under common law, a father had an automatic right to the custody of a child in the event of marriage breakdown. A woman who wished to secure legal custody of her children had to initiate a separate legal action in chancery. In the course of the nineteenth century, successive parliamentary acts strengthened a mother's right to custody, but it was not until 1964 that Irish law recognised the equal rights of both parents to joint custody of their children.[26]

Although the ecclesiastical court system made provision for the poor to submit petitions to the court *in forma pauperi*, most of the people who sued for divorce *a mensa et thoro* (where their economic background can be ascertained) were from the middle class, with a scattering of more upper class or aristocratic individuals. Of the more than 400 cases reported in the *Irish Times*, 1869–1925, many of the petitioners and their spouses, not surprisingly, came from Dublin with the wealthy suburbs of Rathgar and Rathmines and the more affluent streets of the city centre predominating. The Protestant middle class of Dublin did not, however, monopolise the matrimonial and probate court. The cities of Belfast and Cork were also well represented. By the early twentieth century, an increasing number of Catholic farming families were also appearing in the Dublin court seeking marital separations. In the latter cases, it was occasionally noted that a clergyman had tried to reconcile the couple.[27] Public proceedings for divorce frequently

---

[25] The statistics refer to the cases presented in the marital court but do not include those dealt with in courts outside Dublin.

[26] Alan J. Shatter, *Family Law in the Republic of Ireland* (2nd ed., Dublin, 1981), pp. 343–54.

[27] See, for example, *Irish Times*, 2 May 1883; 3 June 1904; 17 Feb. 1905; 2 Dec. 1905; 21 July 1921.

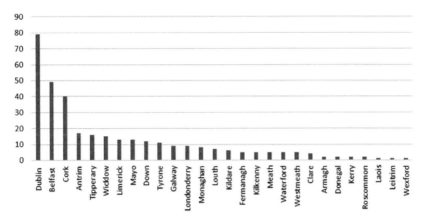

Figure 12.1 Number of divorce cases reported in the *Irish Times*, 1869–1925.
Source: Authors' database

followed a long period of unsuccessful attempts to resolve the marital problems outside of the court.

The relatively low numbers of petitions for divorce can be explained by the social stigma attached to the concept of divorce, particularly in middle-class families. Most couples preferred to deal with a marriage break up as discreetly as possible. In her memoir, Elizabeth McCulloch recalled the secrecy and her family's sense of shame when her parents divorced in 1928: 'I was told to explain that my father was abroad in India, or was it Africa? … He was in fact in Worthing …'[28]

The presentation of petitions for divorce *a mensa et thoro* was a public process in the nineteenth and early twentieth century, which often attracted considerable public attention. From the early decades of the nineteenth century, Irish newspapers regularly included detailed accounts of Irish divorce trials. While members of parliament and newspaper editors occasionally expressed concern over the level of prurient detail included in newspaper accounts of divorce trials, publications such as the *Irish Times* and the *Freeman's Journal,* as well as more Dublin-focussed newspapers like the *Dublin Daily Express,* continued until the 1910s to fill their law reports with many columns of print on selected divorce cases. Regional newspapers also copied material from the Dublin newspapers, particularly if the trial involved either a locally based couple or included salacious details about the private lives of respectable figures

---

[28] Elizabeth McCullogh, *A Square Peg: An Ulster Childhood* (Dublin, 1997), p. 62.

such as medical doctors or clergymen. One 'sensational' case that received widespread newspaper coverage was the divorce of Julia Taylor and Dean Conroy Taylor in 1870. Julia Taylor (*née* Parsons) was the daughter of a County Down landlord and justice of the peace, while her husband was the son of a Church of Ireland clergyman and served as a lieutenant in the South Down militia. Julia Taylor filed the petition on the grounds of cruelty, alleging that her husband was an alcoholic who physically and verbally abused her. She also accused him of infidelity. In response, Dean Conroy Taylor claimed that his wife had acted in a violent manner towards him and that she was guilty of adultery. The divorce case attracted considerable publicity as servants and relatives of the couple were summoned as witnesses and questioned, in particular, about what they knew of Julia Taylor's adultery. Servants in hotels and in the family home testified that they had seen Mrs Taylor kiss and behave in an intimate fashion with two men. For over a week, local and national newspapers in Ireland and many local English newspapers carried detailed reports of the proceedings. The reports also noted that, as the trial continued, the courtroom became increasingly crowded with an overflow into the corridor outside. Presumably, many of the people who attended the courthouse had read the newspaper reports and wanted to observe the proceedings for themselves. The presiding judge, George Battersby, granted Julia Taylor her petition for divorce *a mensa et thoro* and dismissed the evidence of her infidelity as not having been substantiated by credible evidence. Despite her legal victory, Julia Taylor's reputation was severely damaged by the court proceedings and the widespread publicity that they received.[29]

In addition to accounts of Irish court cases, the *Irish Times* and other Irish newspapers routinely included reports of the proceedings of the English divorce court, and cases involving an Irish partner were given particular prominence. Peter Kuch has suggested that the writer James

---

[29] For Irish newspaper reporting of the case see, for instance, *Belfast Morning News*, 23, 25, 28 Nov. 1870; *Cork Constitution*, 22, 24, 28, 29 Nov. 1870; *Cork Examiner*, 24, 26 Nov., 3 Dec. 1870; *Downpatrick Recorder*, 10 June, 7 Oct. 1871; *Dublin Evening Post*, 21, 25 Nov., 2 Dec. 1870; *Dublin Weekly Nation*, 26, 29 Nov. 1870; *Enniskillen Chronicle and Erne Packet*, 24 Nov. 1870; *Irish Times*, 13, 17, 23, 28 Nov. 1870; *Newry Examiner and Louth Advertiser*, 23, 26 Nov. 1870; *Newry Reporter*, 26 Nov., 8 Dec. 1870; *Newry Telegraph*, 22, 29 Nov. 1870; *Northern Whig*, 21, 24 Nov., 3 Dec. 1870; *Saunders's News-Letter*, 21, 25, 28 Nov. 1870. For English and Scottish newspaper reporting see *Glasgow Evening Post*, 26 Nov., 3 Dec. 1870; *Morning Post*, 24 Nov. 1870; *Sheffield Daily Telegraph*, 24 Nov. 1870; *Glasgow Evening Citizen*, 19, 25, 26 Nov. 1870; *Bradford Daily Telegraph*, 3 Dec. 1870. This represents only a sample of the newspapers that carried detailed reports of the proceedings.

Joyce might have read reports of up to 1,500 divorce cases reported in Irish and English newspapers.[30] In 1890, the newspapers eagerly awaited the London divorce proceedings of Captain John O'Shea, who had filed for divorce from his wife, Katherine, in late 1889. O'Shea's citation of Charles Stewart Parnell as his wife's lover led to newspaper editors expecting a long and, from their perspective, financially profitable, case. When the proceedings eventually began in November 1890, they lasted for just two days. Neither Parnell nor Mrs O'Shea appeared in court. Parnell offered no defence while Mrs O'Shea was represented by a barrister who had been instructed by his client not to cross-examine the witnesses. The proceedings were reported in detail in English newspapers, but the editors' disappointment at the curtailment of the trial was evident.

The reporting of the O'Shea divorce case may have been muted but the political scandal provoked by the citation of Parnell initiated a public discourse on divorce, which contributed to an increasingly anti-divorce rhetoric in Irish courts.[31] When two well-known figures in Irish nationalist circles, Maud Gonne and Major John MacBride, divorced in Paris, some newspapers in Ireland were initially reticent to publish lengthy accounts of the court proceedings. MacBride, however, drew more attention to the details revealed about his and Gonne's private life in court when he sued Independent Newspapers for reporting what he claimed were false allegations made against him by Gonne and her lawyers.[32]

Change in the Law

The changes in the Irish court system in the 1870s and 1880s increased the access of the public (and newspaper reporters) to cases involving marital disputes. In 1870, following the disestablishment of the Church of Ireland, the Irish ecclesiastical court system was abolished and the business of the courts transferred to the newly established Court for Matrimonial Causes and Matters. Although the new court was to follow the 'principle and rules' of the ecclesiastical courts, two innovations were

---

[30] Peter Kuch, *Irish Divorce/Joyce's Ulysses* (London, 2017), p. xi.

[31] See below for anti-divorce rhetoric in the Irish courts. For the O'Shea divorce trial, see, for example, *Birmingham Daily Post*, 17, 18 Nov. 1890; *Reynolds Sunday Newspaper*, 16 Nov. 1890; *Dublin Daily Express*, 17, 18 Nov. 1890; *Irish Times*, 17–19 Nov. 1890. In February 1890, O'Shea sued the *Freeman's Journal* and two other newspapers in a London court for their reporting on his initial filing of divorce proceedings. The judge dismissed the case against two of the newspapers but fined the London manager of the *Freeman's Journal*. See *Irish Times*, 19, 28 Feb. 1890.

[32] *Irish Independent*, 27 Feb. 1905; *Freeman's Journal*, 12 Dec. 1905; *Dublin Daily Express*, 18 Dec. 1906; *DIB*.

introduced.[33] Firstly, the judge was given the power to summon a jury to hear aspects of a case and the suitors to the court could also request that he do so.[34] Secondly, husbands and wives were regularly interrogated in court about their behaviour in the marriage and their responses to the accusations of their spouses. They could also be cross-examined orally by either side. In the ecclesiastical courts, the parties involved in the divorce petition provided evidence in writing but were not questioned in court. As noted in Chapter 1, the Court for Matrimonial Causes and Matters existed for only six years. In 1877, as part of a wider consolidation of the Irish judicial system, it was subsumed under the newly created Supreme Court.[35] From the 1880s, divorce proceedings could also be heard in local assizes. The impact of these reforms was to make the proceedings not only more public but also more adversarial, as barristers presented their arguments with an awareness that they would be reported in detail in the local newspapers.

Why Did Men and Women Petition for Divorce
A Mensa et Thoro?

The majority of men who petitioned the court for a divorce cited their wife's adultery as their reason for doing so. Evidence for adultery usually had to be supported, as in the Taylor case, by statements from witnesses such as domestic servants or the employees in a hotel where the adulterous couple lodged overnight. If the judge or jury were satisfied that the witnesses were telling the truth, the processing of a petition for divorce on grounds of adultery was straightforward and usually granted.[36]

The main reasons offered by women who petitioned the court for a judicial separation were the 'cruelty' and violence of their husbands, often triggered by alcohol. As indicated in Chapter 10, historians have traced the changing definitions of the term 'cruelty' in the English court system from the early modern period.[37] In the sixteenth and seventeenth centuries, cruelty administered by a spouse (in almost all cases the

---

[33] An Act to Provide for the Administration of the Law Relating to Matrimonial Causes and Matters, and to Amend the Law Relating to Marriage in Ireland. 33 & 34 Vict. c.10. 1870.

[34] Judges had the power to summon a special jury of professional men, allegedly qualified to determine particular aspects of the case or a common jury composed of those normally eligible for jury service. They could also determine to hear the case without a jury. By 1921, women were selected to sit as jurors for divorce trials. See, for example, *Irish Times,* 27 Oct. 1921.

[35] Supreme Court of Judicature Act (Ireland), 1877. The court was renamed the Court of Probate and Matrimonial Causes.

[36] Based on analysis of cases reported in the *Irish Times.*   [37] See pp. 314–15 above.

husband) was defined as life-threatening physical abuse, but by the late eighteenth century, the definition could also include the threat of violence or persistent verbal abuse. The Irish ecclesiastical court had, however, an ambiguous attitude towards following developments in English courts. In 1770, Ann Shea applied to the Dublin consistory court for a divorce from her husband, Robert, on grounds of cruelty. After less than two years of marriage, Robert had infected Ann with a venereal disease which, her defence advocates argued, constituted legal cruelty as defined by the court because she 'cannot, nor dare live or cohabit with him, with safety to her health or life'. The court refused Ann's request on the grounds that there was no precedent for widening the definition of legal cruelty in this way. Ann Shea's appeal had noted that the English courts had accepted infection with a venereal disease as constituting a form of cruelty, but this was rejected by the Irish consistory court.[38]

By contrast, in the early nineteenth century, the judge in the Dublin consistory court, John Radcliff seemed to be concerned that his court follow precedents set in the English consistory courts. In his definition of cruelty in 1827 Radcliff warned that the ecclesiastical court, unlike the common law courts, could not interfere in 'ordinary domestic quarrels and 'that there may be much unhappiness from unkind treatment, or violent and abusive language in which no relief can be had here'. As we indicated in Chapter 10, however, Radcliff acknowledged that the threat of violence could be considered within the understanding of 'cruelty' if the life of a spouse appeared to be at risk. 'Words of menace' could be defined as cruelty if the threat behind them appeared to be real.[39]

Radcliff's successors as judges in matrimonial cases in the nineteenth and early twentieth centuries returned to a narrower definition of legal cruelty, which had to include proof of behaviour on the part of either spouse that led to a 'reasonable apprehension of danger to life or health'. As Judge Dodgson Hamilton Madden told a jury in 1906 that there was conduct which might 'ordinarily' be called cruelty but for a judicial separation there must be a 'danger to life or health'.[40] By 1915, Irish

---

[38] Ann appealed this decision to the English court of delegates but her husband queried the jurisdiction of the English court to hear an Irish case and, consequently, the case was referred back to the Irish High court of delegates, which appears to have refused to consider the case due to its being out of time. See, *In His Majesty's High Court of Delegates in Ireland, Ann Shea Otherwise Wills v Robert Percy Shea* (Dublin, 1771).

[39] C. R. Milward, *Reports of Cases Argued and Determined in the Court of Prerogative in Ireland, and in the Consistory Court of Dublin, During the Time of the Right Honourable John Radcliff, LL. D* (Dublin, 1847), p. 159–61. See also pp. 314–15.

[40] *Irish Times*, 9 May 1906.

courts did, however, accept that a wife who contracted a venereal disease from her husband could sue for divorce on grounds of cruelty. In awarding a divorce decree to a woman who was 'suffering from a serious illness', the presiding judge, William Huston Dodd, asserted that the wife deserved the 'protection of the court in the extreme degree'.[41]

In 1917, the newly appointed Chief Justice, James Campbell (later Lord Glenavy) reintroduced mental cruelty as valid grounds for divorce. Campbell had practised in the English divorce court for a number of years and in one of his few judgments on an Irish divorce case, he drew on the more flexible definition of cruelty used in the English court:

if either husband or wife was guilty towards the other of acts of violence or of such a course of conduct as necessarily humiliated and degraded the other, and caused injury to health, or where the course of conduct adopted by a husband had been such as to cause a reasonable woman reasonable apprehension of her safety should she continue to live with him that constituted legal cruelty.[42]

In 1921, Campbell was appointed to the Irish Seanad where he expressed support for the introduction of divorce legislation.[43] Although divorces *a mensa et thoro* continued to be granted in the Irish Free State courts it does not appear that Glenavy's definition of legal cruelty set a precedent for later judgments. Court statements on divorce proceedings in the mid-twentieth century looked back to the Radcliff judgment of the 1820s rather than to Campbell's statement, to extend the definition of cruelty to include a possibility that a spouse could become mentally ill if he or she continued in the marriage.[44]

Changing Court Rhetoric on Divorce

In the decades after the enactment of the English divorce act, there were several attempts made to extend its jurisdiction to Ireland. This was firmly resisted by the Irish Catholic hierarchy and by members of the Irish Parliamentary Party. Increasingly, the inability of men and women to divorce and remarry through the Irish court system was presented as an indication of the civilised nature of Irish society by comparison with England. In 1906, William Redmond, the MP for the borough of Wexford, linked the absence of a divorce law in Ireland with its status as 'the most civilised country in the world'.[45] This might have been a slightly tongue in cheek remark but the core sentiment was shared by many in his

---

[41] *Irish Times*, 13 Feb. 1915.   [42] *Irish Times*, 29 June 1917.   [43] *DIB*.
[44] Shatter, *Family Law*, p. 112.
[45] Kuch, *Irish Divorce/Joyce's Ulysses*, pp. 2–3. More generally on the debate on extending the English divorce legislation to Ireland, see Urquhart, *Irish Divorce: A History*, chapter 4.

party, despite or perhaps because of the citation of their former party leader in a divorce case.

The fact that the English divorce act did not apply in Ireland also encouraged barristers to rely on anti-divorce sentiment to defend their clients against petitions for marital separation. This type of defence was undoubtedly strengthened in the aftermath of the political scandal provoked by the O'Shea divorce case in 1890. The lawyers' emphasis on the distinction between Ireland and England in relation to divorce law may also have led the judges in the Irish matrimonial court to adhere to a narrow definition of legal cruelty that did not reflect the more flexible position adopted in the English court. In 1894, for example, the barrister for William Jarvis appealed to the jury not to 'put in force the law of divorce in such a case – separating man and wife who had been joined for fifty years in a matrimonial bond'. The presiding judge, Robert Warren, was compelled to explain to the jury that the court had no power to dissolve marriages as suggested by the 'strong observations' of the defendant's counsel, but he too expressed his disapproval of any provision in Ireland that would make those 'who go through a religious ceremony in the nature of a sacrament cease to be man and wife'.[46] In 1901, when Margaret Donnellan from Cork applied for a divorce from her husband, Thomas, the defence barrister condemned the ease with which the 'sacred relations' of marriage could be so easily set aside. He also emphasised to the jury that the legal definition of cruelty had to include an acknowledgment that co-habitation was unsafe for the wife. Once again the judge had to emphasise to the jury that they were determining a judicial separation not a divorce as defined by the English legislation.[47] In 1912, the barrister for Delia Coyne presented compelling evidence of the physical violence committed against her by her husband, John. The latter's barrister, A. M. Sullivan, however, reminded the jurors that a separation could only be agreed if legal cruelty was proven, and not for what he referred to as 'nagging or scuffling'. He too noted the strong anti-divorce culture in Irish society. According to the report in the *Irish Times*, Sullivan said that in Ireland, 'people believed that a man and wife should stand by one another, compose their differences and accommodate themselves'.[48]

The barrister in the Donnellan case also drew on another rhetorical device evident in divorce proceedings and, as we have seen in other

---

[46] *Freeman's Journal*, 1 Feb. 1894. On changing definitions of cruelty in the English divorce court see Diane Urquhart, 'Irish divorce and domestic violence, 1857–1922', *Women's History Review*, 22, 5 (2013), 820–37.

[47] *Irish Times*, 29 Feb. 1901.   [48] *Irish Times*, 16 Feb. 1912.

chapters, in most legal proceedings relating to marriage in the late nineteenth and early twentieth centuries. He suggested that Thomas Donnellan's violent behaviour towards his wife was provoked by her failure to fulfil the role of a good wife: 'She had refused to get his breakfast leaving it to the servant to do, but lay in bed till a late hour ... all those little details a good wife should attend to were wholly unheeded'. Other barristers also referred to the negligence of a wife in the home and in the care of her husband and children.[49] Women in full-time employment outside the home were particularly vulnerable to unsympathetic treatment in the court room. In 1905, Johanna Hannan petitioned for a divorce from her husband, William, who was the manager of the creamery in the Glen of Aherlow, County Tipperary. Johanna was a school teacher in Lisronagh, near Clonmel, also in County Tipperary. The couple had met in Lisdoonvarnagh in the summer of 1899 and had married later the same year. Johanna kept her job as a teacher after the marriage and continued to live in Lisronagh while William worked in the Glen of Aherlow but came to stay with his wife at weekends. Within six months of the marriage, William began physically to abuse his wife, which included knocking her head against a door, dragging her by the hair across the bedroom a few days before she gave birth to their first child, hitting her in the face with a clenched fist and holding her by the arms and swinging her against a wall. Witnesses, including a policeman, testified to this violence in court. The defence lawyer, Mr Shaughnessy, argued that William's behaviour had been provoked by Johanna's refusal to adhere to her marriage vows of loving, honouring and obeying him 'until death do us part' and drawing on anti-divorce rhetoric, he suggested that the latter phrase had been dropped from American marriage services in favour of 'until death do us part, or until lawfully divorced'.[50]

The implication was that Johanna was at fault for refusing to live with a violent husband. A key piece of testimony provided by the defence was a letter that she had written to her husband asserting that he had no right to tell her how to manage her household as he would 'never enter this house or garden [again] while I live'. Johanna also queried her husband's mental stability and acknowledged that she would 'simply loathe and despise myself for putting up with your cruel treatment for so long'. Both the defence barrister and the judge in the case appear to be in agreement that this was 'a discreditable thing for a wife to write to her husband'. The closing speech of the defence barrister emphasised Johanna's 'most peculiar' ideas about her married duties:

[49] *Irish Times*, 29 Feb. 1901.   [50] *Irish Times*, 17 Feb. 1905.

All this from the supposed independence of this woman who had been earning her own bread. The jury would not, he hoped, lightly trifle with the bond and vow of marriage that death alone should sever. There were few married people who had not their little differences.[51]

Despite the clear evidence of physical cruelty, the jury failed to reach a verdict and a retrial was ordered.[52]

The anti-divorce rhetoric evident in the courts reflected the wider opinion of Irish society. Campaigns to reform Irish divorce laws received little support. In 1878, a woman petitioner for a divorce *a mensa et thoro*, Mrs Sarah Parker, claimed to be a campaigner for the reform of the divorce law and that in submitting her petition, she was acting not just for herself but 'for the hundreds of other enslaved women'. In a highly unusual case, Parker was permitted to represent herself in court. Much to the fascination of the barristers in the four courts, as well as to the members of the public who crowded into the court, Parker conducted her own questioning of her husband and members of her family about the state of her marriage. Her central argument was that she could no longer bear to live with her husband and that to compel her to do so was an act of cruelty. She also alleged that she had been forced to marry by her father and that her husband had a problem with alcohol. Parker's petition was rejected by the judge on the grounds that she had produced no evidence of acts of cruelty as defined by the marital court. Parker's defence that she was attempting to draw attention to the limited criteria for divorce in Ireland received little public support, with newspapers reporting the case in an amused or bemused manner.[53]

The decline in the number of divorces *a mensa et thoro* approved in the late nineteenth and early twentieth century reflected the strengthening of an anti-divorce rhetoric in the courts as well as the emergence of a public discourse that expressed concern at the notion of an 'independent' woman. At the same time, the increase in the number of women filing petitions for divorce led to a reluctance to grant even the modified form of legal marital separation available within the Irish court system.

---

[51] Ibid.
[52] *Irish Times*, 17 Feb. 1905. The couple may have agreed a settlement as there are no further newspaper references to the case. In the 1911 census, Johanna Hannan was recorded as still working as a school teacher and living with her two children and a sister. There is no reference to her husband, William Hannan (NAI, 1911 Census Online).
[53] *Irish Times*, 19 Jan. 1878.

Parliamentary Divorce

The Irish parliament passed its first divorce act in 1730 when it voted to dissolve the marriage of Joseph Austin, a Cork merchant, and Mary Mitchell, daughter of another merchant family in the city. The proceedings in the legislature were initiated by Austin, who accused his wife of adultery and of co-habiting with William Owgan, a business man who later served as mayor of Cork. In order to obtain his parliamentary divorce, Austin was obliged to undertake a cumbersome legal process. He had first to apply for a divorce *a mensa et thoro* in the ecclesiastical court and then sue his wife's lover in a civil court for 'criminal' damages (i.e. adultery). Following the success of both cases, Austin petitioned the Irish House of Lords for permission to present an act dissolving his marriage. The Lords examined the evidence that had been produced in the ecclesiastical and civil courts and gave permission for heads of bills to be prepared. They then appointed a committee that functioned as a third court, examining witnesses and hearing testimony from counsel. The final stage was the approval of the bill by the privy council in London and the passing of the act in both houses of the Irish parliament.[54]

The legal device of a private parliamentary act to dissolve a marriage was initiated in England in the late seventeenth century as men and their lawyers searched for ways around the canonical declaration that marriage was only dissolvable by God and, therefore, effectively, by death. The argument that a husband of an adulteress wife could not be certain that he and not his wife's lover had fathered his heir resonated with a parliament of property owners. In 1701, the English House of Lords approved the first act to dissolve a marriage and permit the husband to remarry legally. The act noted that if the marriage was not dissolved the husband was 'liable to have spurious issue forced upon him', a phrase that was to be repeated in subsequent divorce bills.[55]

Divorce by parliamentary statute was not only legally complicated, it was also expensive. The minimum cost in the mid-nineteenth century was £450–£500, which meant that it was out of the reach of the majority of people.[56] Unsurprisingly, therefore, the number of divorce petitions was small. There were eleven petitions for private divorce acts presented to the

---

[54] John Bergin, 'Irish private divorce bills and acts of the eighteenth century' in James Kelly, John McCafferty and Charles Ivar McGrath (eds.), *People, Politics and Power: Essays on Irish History in Honour of James I. McGuire* (Dublin, 2009), p. 97; James Roberts, *Divorce Bills in the Imperial Parliament* (Dublin, 1906), p. 9. Both Austen and Mitchell remarried.

[55] Roberts, *Divorce Bills in the Imperial Parliament*, p. 3.

[56] Urquhart, 'Ireland and the Divorce and Matrimonial Causes Act', 302, 309.

eighteenth-century Irish parliament and about another dozen Irish petitions presented to the Westminster parliament.[57] Between 1857 and 1910, thirty-nine petitions for divorce were submitted by Irish residents to the imperial parliament; between 1910 and 1922, the figure was fifty-three.[58] Diane Urquhart has pointed to one important change in the petitioners in the twentieth century. Prior to 1857, a total of four women had applied to Westminster for a parliamentary divorce. In the early twentieth century, however, Urquhart estimates that over half of the Irish petitioners were women.[59] The first Irish woman to present a petition for divorce to the House of Lords was Louisa Westropp who, in 1886, successfully applied for a divorce on the grounds of her husband's adultery and physical abuse of herself and her children. The Westropp divorce case also pioneered the widening of the criteria by which women could sue for a parliamentary divorce, bringing it into line with proceedings in the English divorce court. The acceptance of adultery without any aggravating circumstances as grounds for divorce by the House of Lords also helps to explain the increase in the number of women petitioning for divorce.[60]

Irish residents were not permitted to avail of the 1857 Matrimonial Causes Act which provided for the establishment of the London divorce court and had the power to dissolve marriages and permit those involved to remarry. The exclusion of Ireland from the Act meant that Irish men and women who wished to have their marriages dissolved were obliged to continue to apply for parliamentary divorces at Westminster until the establishment of the Irish Free State in 1922.[61] Temporary residence in England was, however, one way by which Irish people could take advantage of the English legislation. Two years after the 1857 Act was passed, there were three cases involving Irish residents being considered by the court. Subsequently, the judge in the divorce court attempted to tighten the regulations in order to prevent the issuing of decrees to Irish people who did not live permanently in England.[62]

---

[57] Bergin, 'Irish private divorce bills', pp. 94–5.

[58] Urquhart, 'Ireland and the Divorce and Matrimonial Causes Act of 1857', 313; David Fitzpatrick, 'Divorce and separation in modern Irish history', *Past and Present*, 114 (Feb. 1987), 174.

[59] Urquhart, 'Ireland and the Divorce and Matrimonial Causes Act of 1857', 313; 'Irish divorce and domestic violence, 1857–1922', 820–37.

[60] Ibid., 828–30; Diane Urquhart, 'A woman's response: Women and the divorce law reform in Victorian Ireland' in Brendan Walsh (ed.), *Knowing Their Place: The Intellectual Life of Women in Nineteenth-Century Ireland* (Dublin, 2014), pp. 128–47.

[61] Urquhart, 'Ireland and the Divorce and Matrimonial Causes Act', 301–20.

[62] Urquhart, 'Irish divorce and domestic violence, 1857–1922', 820–37; Roberts, *Divorce Bills in the Imperial Parliament*, pp. 11–4.

Securing a divorce outside the jurisdiction of the Irish courts remained, however, an option for those who could afford it into the twentieth century.[63]

Irish Free State and Divorce

The framers of the first constitution of the Irish Free State assumed that the Irish parliament would take on the responsibility of the House of Lords and hear private bills of divorce. The attorney general, Hugh Kennedy, declared that he was 'strongly of the opinion we should make provision for Divorce Bills for those who approve of that sort of thing'. Kennedy also noted that he was aware of a 'batch of cases' ready to be considered. Among them was a young Protestant English woman who married in England but her husband had since moved to Ireland. He had been 'thoroughly dishonourable' to her but because of his Irish residence, she could not commence divorce proceedings in the English divorce court. Her solicitor argued that it was very unfair that a young woman of twenty four should be 'tied' for life under legislation that had not existed when she married.[64]

A joint committee of the new Oireachtas met to discuss procedures for Standing Orders, which would review proposed legislation for the new parliament. The committee included Major Bryan Cooper, who had secured a parliamentary divorce in 1925. The members failed, however, to agree on the procedure to be followed for divorce bills. A Dáil proposal for Standing Orders to refuse to consider divorce bills was rejected by the Seanad as unconstitutional. A compromise solution proposed by the chairman of the joint committee, James Douglas, suggested that Standing Orders could approve proposals for divorce bills but it would be understood that when the bills were introduced to the Dáil they would be rejected by the overwhelming majority of members. Privately, however, the Catholic archbishop of Dublin, Edward Byrne, made it clear to the President of the Executive Council, W. T. Cosgrave, that he deemed even the consideration of a divorce bill by the Oireachtas unacceptable. The archbishop was determined to assert the control of the Catholic church over marriage in the new state. He told Cosgrave's legal advisor, Éamon Ó Dugáin, that

---

[63] Urquhart, *Irish Divorce: A History*, chapter 6.
[64] Hugh Kennedy to Éamon Ó Dugáin, 12 March 1923 and enclosures (NAI, Department of the Taoiseach files, S4127).

the Church regards Matrimony as a sacrament only and claims sole jurisdiction in regards to it ... they could not even sanction divorce for non-Catholics for the reason that all persons who had been baptised are members of the Church and under its jurisdiction.[65]

As indicated in Chapter 1, prior to the establishment of the Irish Free State, the Irish courts had refused to recognise the legal validity of Catholic canon law on marriage. Byrne's conversations with Cosgrave and Ó Dugáin seemed to have been aimed at asserting the pre-eminence of it. Byrne's efforts were successful. Cosgrave expressed his appreciation of the guidance on church law provided by the archbishop and agreed that any discussion in the Dáil of James Douglas's compromise would be unacceptable. Consequently, there was no further discussion on the issue. From 1922 until 1937, when Article 41.3.2 of the new constitution prohibited divorce in the Irish Free State, it was theoretically possible to submit a bill for a private divorce to the Dáil, but no one chose to do so. Any attempt would have been blocked by a predominantly Catholic cabinet following private lobbying from the Catholic hierarchy.[66]

By contrast, in 1921, the parliament in Northern Ireland agreed the establishment of a joint standing committee to review divorce bills. This facilitated the transfer from Westminster to Stormont of the responsibility for the consideration of bills that related to couples domiciled in Northern Ireland. The procedure for the submission of a divorce bill closely followed that which had prevailed at Westminster. The bill was read in the House of Commons and the Senate. It was then passed for consideration to a committee composed of members from both houses of parliament, which heard oral and written evidence and made a recommendation on passing or rejecting the bill. In 1939, this cumbersome procedure was abandoned and responsibility for granting divorces was transferred to the High Court of Northern Ireland. From then on, divorce law in Northern Ireland began to follow the same procedures and precedents that prevailed in the English divorce court.[67]

In the Irish Free State in the midst of the controversy on the introduction of divorce bills, a newly appointed judge in the Supreme Court, Gerald Fitzgibbon, suggested that the reform of the provision for child custody in divorce *a mensa et thoro* cases was a more urgent matter than the approval of parliamentary divorce bills. He echoed the argument of

---

[65] Éamon Ó Dugáin to W. T. Cosgrave, 20 March 1923 (NAI, Department of the Taoiseach files, S4127). See also W. T. Cosgrave to Bishop James Downey, 21 Sept. 1925 (ibid.).

[66] See file on 'Divorce in the Irish Free State, Jan. 1923–Aug. 1929' (NAI, Department of the Taoiseach files, S4127).

[67] Urquhart, *Irish Divorce: A History*, pp. 147–54.

lawyer and parliamentarian, Arthur Samuels, who almost forty years earlier in 1887 had advocated that the Irish marital court be given the same power as the English divorce court to determine the custody of children of separating spouses.[68] The public controversy provoked by the proposal to permit divorce bills to be considered by the Oireachtas meant, however, that no politician wanted to become embroiled in a conflict with the Catholic hierarchy concerning family law. Ironically, therefore, until the 1970s, the child custody laws in the Irish state remained frozen in the patriarchal principles that had been abandoned by the imperial parliament at Westminster many years before.

Criminal Conversation

As part of the process of securing a parliamentary divorce, a husband was obliged to sue his wife's sexual partner for damages in a civil court. This type of 'criminal conversation' case, as it was euphemistically described, appears in Ireland in the late eighteenth century. The legal argument behind 'crim con' cases involved an expansion of the law of trespass. The adulterer was prosecuted for trespassing on the husband's possession, his wife, and for depriving him of her company. The husband could seek financial damages for this act of trespass.[69] A legal basis for a wife to initiate a criminal conversation suit against her husband was never developed and, as a consequence, women who petitioned the Westminster parliament for divorce were exempt from the requirement to do so.

   Although integral to the legal process involved in securing a parliamentary divorce, an action for criminal conversation was legally separate from it. A man suing for criminal conversation was not obliged to follow his suit with a petition for a parliamentary divorce. Out of a sample of twenty criminal conversation cases reported in Irish newspapers, 1859–1917, less than a third can be linked to a divorce case listed in the *Irish Times* for the same period.[70] This would suggest that a desire for a legal separation was not the main reason why most husbands initiated criminal conversation cases. Financial gain or personal revenge and

---

[68] Gerald Fitzgibbon to President W. T. Cosgrave, 5 Feb. 1925 (NAI, Department of the Taoiseach files, S-4127); Arthur W. Samuels, 'The law of divorce in Ireland', *Journal of the Statistical and Social Inquiry Society of Ireland*, ix, part lxvi (1886–7), 188–90.

[69] For legal arguments involved in criminal conversation cases, see Niamh Howlin, 'Adultery in the courts: Criminal conversation in Ireland, 1791–1981' in Howlin and Costello (eds.), *Law and the Family in Ireland 1800–1950*, pp. 87–106.

[70] In the absence of court records, these figures are necessarily approximate. The absence of a newspaper report does not necessarily mean that divorce proceedings were not initiated.

anger seem to have been stronger motivating factors. In the eighteenth century, criminal conversation cases were mainly associated with wealthy landowners or aristocratic families, but by the middle decades of the nineteenth century plaintiffs included men from further down the social hierarchy including medical doctors, army personnel, civil servants and businessmen.[71]

As with other law suits involving sexual misdemeanours, the scandalous accounts of the intimate relations between a husband and wife and her alleged lover attracted crowds to the court for criminal conversation cases. Printers also recognised the commercial value of publishing the proceedings in pamphlet form and, later in the nineteenth century, of including detailed reports of the trial in newspapers. The publicity attached to 'crim con' cases and, particularly, the reporting of the damages awarded undoubtedly helped to persuade some husbands to try their luck in court. In the late eighteenth and early nineteenth century, large sums of money were extracted from wealthy landlords or members of the aristocracy accused of adultery with a married woman. In 1804, for example, when the Reverend Charles Massy sued Thomas Taylour, 1st Marquess of Headfort, in 1804 for eloping with his wife, the jury awarded him £10,000 (he had asked for £40,000).[72] The wealth of the plaintiff and his ability to pay the allocated sum was taken into consideration when damages were determined by the jury.[73] Six years later, when John Blachford sued a member of the La Touche family, the defendant's estimated wealth of £6,000 was noted in his trial. Blachford was awarded damages of £2,000.[74] Not surprisingly, given the sums of money involved, judges and juries were alert to the possibilities of collusion between husband and wife.

Most husbands were not, however, awarded such large sums and the tendency to make awards over £1,000 had diminished by the second half of the nineteenth century. By that time, the financial gain for many plaintiffs in 'crim con' cases was usually considerably smaller than the damages claimed. Husbands may have requested damages in excess of £1,000 but few received such a large amount. According to official statistics, between 1869 and 1919, awards of more than £1,000 were made in only 5 per cent of the fifty-four cases listed for that period. The

---

[71] Based on cases reported in *Freeman's Journal* and Howlin, 'Adultery in the courts'.

[72] *A Report of the Trial on an Action for Damages Brought by the Reverend Charles Massy against the Most Noble Marquis of Headfort for Criminal Conversation with Plaintiff's Wife* (Dublin, 1804).

[73] See Howlin, 'Adultery in the courts' for a discussion on the purpose of compensation awarded in 'crim con' cases.

[74] *Saunders's News-Letter*, 22 Dec. 1810.

most common award was considerably lower at between £100 and £200. Legal costs were almost always only nominally recognised by juries, with a token sum of six pence.[75] From his award, the plaintiff would not only have had to pay his legal team but also the expenses of witnesses summoned to appear as part of his defence. The net financial gain for many was, therefore, quite limited.

By the late nineteenth century, the majority of criminal conversation cases did not attract the sensational reporting of an earlier time. This was particularly the case if the proceedings were part of the requirements for a parliamentary divorce. The 'crim con' case was increasingly heard on the same day as the divorce petition with the same judge presiding. The newspaper reports suggest that the main business of the criminal conversation cases was to determine the damages to be awarded to the husband without the need to rehearse again the details of the adultery involved. This doubling up of the divorce proceedings with that of the criminal conversation case was intended to reduce the legal expenses involved in applying for a parliamentary divorce. It might also have led, as in England prior to the 1857 Divorce Act, to discreet collusion between all the parties involved, with the husband anxious to complete the legal process rather than extract a large sum of money from his wife's lover. Between 1879 and 1919, there were fifty-two criminal conversation cases recorded for the Irish courts and of these, 75 per cent were decided in favour of the plaintiff.[76]

While the husband and the alleged adulterer were the two parties involved in a criminal conversation case, they were not the main actors in court. It was initially rare for either to give testimony in court and, prior to the 1870s, the wife with whom the defendant allegedly had adulterous relations never appeared in court. Instead, the court and jury heard testimony from household servants and family members who related what they knew about the relationship between husband and wife and what they saw of the alleged adulterous affair. As we noted in Chapter 8, they told stories of locked doors, secret meetings and the exchange of clandestine messages and letters between the alleged lovers.[77]

For their part, the aim of the prosecution was to prove that husband and wife had participated in a legally valid marriage and had lived contently together, often for many years prior to the wife's indiscretion. The husband's barrister presented him as a loving and attentive spouse and the defendant as the person responsible for destroying a blissfully happy household. The defendant was frequently a family friend or relative and

[75] Compiled from *Judicial Statistics*.   [76] Compiled from *Judicial Statistics*.
[77] See, for example, pp. 265–6.

his actions were, consequently, denounced as a betrayal of the husband's trust. The defence, on the other hand, pointed to the husband's short-comings. They focused, in particular, on his failure to suspect the defendant's ill intentions towards his wife with often a suggestion that he may have implicitly condoned the adultery. The barristers for the defendant and, sometimes, the judges in their summing up, laid emphasis on the patriarchal principle that it was the responsibility of a husband to protect his wife, a task that included defending her from philandering men. If a jury decided that a husband had not done enough to prevent his wife committing adultery, then they would (usually with the encouragement of the presiding judge) reduce the damages awarded. In 1817, when Mark Brown sued Martin Joseph Blake for £30,000, the judge recommended to the jury that they not award any compensation to Brown because he believed that he had not guided his young wife well and that he had therefore 'connived at his own disgrace'.[78]

A strong belief in the patriarchal role of the husband frequently, therefore, protected a wife from explicit criticism. By the end of the nineteenth century, however, this form of polite gallantry had disap-peared and in a number of high profile cases the wife was depicted as the seducer rather than the seduced. In May 1890, Richard Watson Joynt, editor of the *Ballina Journal* sued James Jackson, manager of the Bank of Ireland, Ballina for damages of £5,000. The case attracted considerable publicity partly because of the social status of the men involved but also because Mrs Joynt admitted her adultery with Jackson and other men. It was, in the experience of the presiding judge, Baron Dowse, the first case 'in which a woman had been put into the witness-box to declare her own shame and by her own shame to carry the case in favour of her husband'.[79] Jackson denied that Charlotte Joynt was telling the truth and his defence focused on presenting her as an untrustworthy witness who led a drunken, immoral life and who 'never seemed to have felt a sense of shame, and never of the sacred influence of religion or morality'.[80] Richard Joynt was presented as unfortunate to have had such

---

[78] *Crim. Con. A Full, Faithful and Impartial Account of That Curious, Extraordinary and Interesting Trial with Speeches of Counsel and Judge's Charge, in the Case Wherein Mark Brown, Esq. Was Plaintiff and Martin Joseph Blake, Esq. Defendant in an Action of Damages for Crim. Con. against the Plaintiff's Wife* (Dublin, 1818). See also S. M. Waddams, 'English matrimonial law on the eve of reform (1828–57)', *Journal of Legal History*, 21, 2 (2000), 66.

[79] *Authentic Report of the Crim. Con. Trial of Joynt V. Jackson, in the Exchequer Court, Dublin, Commencing May 10th 1880* (Dublin, 1880), p. 28; Howlin, 'Adultery in the courts', pp. 87–106.

[80] *Authentic Report of the Crim. Con. Trial of Joynt V. Jackson*, p. 24; *Freeman's Journal*, 11 May 1880; *Irish Times*, 15 May, 29 June 1890.

a wife rather than, as might have been the case fifty years earlier, being criticised for not preventing her from falling on to the 'path of vice'.[81]

Lawrence Stone traced the changing attitudes to 'crim con' cases in England and argued that while such cases were initially linked to the concept of preserving a man's honour, by the 1830s many commentators viewed such cases as morally distasteful; they encouraged what were perceived as pornographic publications dressed in the guise of a serious law report. Others expressed their opposition to the 'treatment of female adultery as a public crime'.[82] Stone, thus, linked the widespread contempt for 'crim con' cases by the middle of the nineteenth century to changing moral values in society and the reforms in marriage law. It was for a combination of these reasons that the Matrimonial Causes Act of 1857 abolished the process in England and Wales.

There was never a large number of criminal conversation cases in the Irish courts. Official statistics from 1863 to 1919 suggest that there were on average one to two per year.[83] Criminal conversation cases could be heard in a number of central courts and, from the 1870s, in circuit courts. This meant that many judges and barristers in Dublin and elsewhere rarely, if ever, dealt with a criminal conversation case. When they did do so, some lauded their lack of experience in such cases with an implied suggestion that it reflected favourably on the sexual morality of Irish people.[84] The public discourse in Ireland on criminal conversation cases differed, therefore, from that in England. Criminal conversation actions continued to be heard in Ireland until they were abolished in the Republic of Ireland in 1981 and in Northern Ireland in 1939. One of the reasons for retaining 'crim con' on the Irish statute book before 1922 was that it was a requirement for men seeking a parliamentary divorce, but long after that possibility was ruled out by the Oireachtas, the legislation remained on the Irish statute book. Unlike parliamentary divorce or divorce *a mensa et thoro,* the moral justification for criminal conversation cases could be incorporated into the Catholic ethos that had begun to prevail in Irish society by the early twentieth century. Such cases facilitated the public condemnation of female adulterers and upheld the sanctity of marriage. A Working Party of the Law Reform Commission, established in the 1970s, noted how the moral justification for criminal conversation cases had changed. The concept of a wife as a chattel of her husband was no longer acceptable but, it argued, the prosecution of a

---

[81] *Authentic Report of the Crim. Con. Trial of Joynt V. Jackson,* p. 24.
[82] Lawrence Stone, *Road to Divorce: England 1530–1987* (Oxford, 1990), pp. 303–5.
[83] Based on *Judicial Statistics, 1863–1919.*
[84] *Authentic Report of the Crim. Con. Trial of Joynt V. Jackson,* p. 2.

spouse for adultery was a means of protecting the sanctity of the family. Rather than abolishing the legal concept of criminal conversation, the Working Party proposed that the action be expanded to permit either spouse to take an action in the interests of the family.[85] The proposal was not included in the Family Law Act (1981) but the recommendation of the Working Party is revealing of why the law on criminal conversation had a different history in Ireland than in England.

Private Deeds of Separation

Applying to a court to resolve marital disagreements involved public scrutiny of the intimate details of a couple's private life. Petitioners and defendants in divorce cases could ask for their case to be heard in private but, as one judge observed, newspaper editors were entitled to publish reports of proceedings that took place in open court. He did, however, urge solicitors not to release additional information about the divorcing couple to journalists, which many clearly did.[86]

A decision to petition for a divorce in a public courtroom was usually the last resort for anyone wishing to separate from their spouse. It frequently followed years of tension and conflict in the marriage as well as efforts to reconcile the couple on the part of family members and clergymen. As the figures indicate, only a small minority of predominantly middle-class men and women took their marital problems voluntarily to a Dublin court and even fewer proceeded to request a dissolution of their marriage through a parliamentary bill. The move to court might also be tactical, designed to force a spouse to agree to a private settlement. In the newspaper reporting of divorce cases in the Irish courts, it was regularly recorded that a petition had been withdrawn because a settlement had been agreed. Judges also acknowledged their approval of couples agreeing to resolve their differences in private.[87]

It is likely that the majority of feuding couples did just that. A privately agreed deed of separation could give both parties the means to leave the marriage and live independently. Although it could not sanction remarriage, a deed of separation could give a wife the legal status of a single woman (*femme sole*), which meant that her husband would no longer be economically responsible for his wife and that she could sign contracts and earn an income in her own name. The custody arrangements for any children of the marriage might also be detailed in

---

[85] Law Reform Commission, 'Working Paper No 5–1978'. https://publications.lawreform.ie.
[86] *Irish Times*, 28 June 1883.
[87] See, for example, *Irish Times*, 3 May 1899; 23 Dec. 1905; 23 Jan. 1921.

the separation deed and this too was an attractive feature of a private settlement for women who otherwise would have had to apply to the court of chancery for access to their children. In a settlement agreed in 1921, a Dublin public house manager agreed to give his wife £2 a week as alimony and full custody of their daughter until she was seven years of age. It was also agreed that the father could have access to the child at all times and that after her seventh birthday, both parents were to share equal rights.[88] In 1888, the wife of John M'Niffe admitted that she had initiated a divorce *a mensa et thoro* proceedings against her husband in order to force him to agree to a deed of separation granting her custody of the children. The tactic was successful and the court arranged for an agreement to be signed by both parties.[89]

A deed of separation could also dissolve the marriage settlement and arrange for the wife's future income from her husband. In 1897, a retired customs officer from Tinahely, County Wicklow signed a deed in which he agreed to release all his claims under his marriage settlement and that he would pay his wife an annual allowance of £300. In return, he was to be indemnified from any further legal action against him by his wife.[90] Other couples acknowledged that they would give each other freedom to live with whom they wished. In 1816, a deed of separation was signed by Henry Bell, a linen draper in Lambeg, County Antrim, and his wife Ann and her brother, James Moreland, a Belfast merchant.[91] Henry had requested the divorce because of the 'dissimilarity of taste, disposition and manners' between Ann and himself. The deed was, however, careful to absolve Ann of any impropriety or misconduct. Henry agreed to give Ann an annual allowance of £50 and permit her to live with whomsoever she thought fit 'wholly freed and discharged from [Henry's] control and authority as if she were a feme sole'. Both parties to the deed also undertook not to initiate a suit in the ecclesiastical court that queried their separate living arrangements. Finally, in her new status as a *feme sole*, Ann was given the right to make a will that Henry agreed could be proved in the ecclesiastical court. The signatories to the deed were, in effect, agreeing to bypass or ignore the legal requirements of the ecclesiastical court on marriage and property.

The Irish courts determined in 1824 that private deeds of separation were 'inveterate in the law, and cannot be questioned'.[92] Despite this

---

[88] *Irish Times*, 9 April 1921.
[89] *Irish Times*, 11 Feb. 1888; *Freeman's Journal*, 13 Feb. 1888.
[90] *Irish Times*, 19 July 1897.   [91] PRONI, D/577/74.
[92] *MacDonnell v Murphy* (1824). See Michael Charles Fox and Thomas Berry Cusack (eds.), *Reports of Cases Argued and Determined in the Court of King's Bench and Court of Error* (2 vols., Dublin, 1825), i, pp. 279–305. The authors are grateful to Dr Niamh Howlin for this reference. See also O'Dowd, 'Marriage breakdown in Ireland, 1660–1857', 14.

assurance, however, if divorce proceedings had been initiated prior to the agreement of a settlement, the terms of the deed were frequently read into the court record, presumably to strengthen its legal status.[93] If the couple reconciled even for a short period of time, the terms of the agreement could also be rendered invalid. When Sarah Parker petitioned for a divorce *a mensa et thoro* in 1878, she acknowledged that she had earlier made a private separation agreement with her husband but she argued that the terms had been broken as her husband had attempted a reconciliation. This breach of the agreement also enabled Parker, like other women in a similar situation, to ask for a higher financial settlement through her divorce petition.[94]

It is impossible to estimate how many Irish marriages ended in private separation agreements in the period covered by this volume. References to a tradition of a woman handing back her wedding ring to her husband when an agreement was reached suggests that it may have been more common than might be assumed. In 1921, a woman from County Tipperary agreed a deed of separation with her farmer husband. He agreed to give her £150, which he refused to hand over until she had returned her wedding ring. When she subsequently queried the terms of the settlement, she acknowledged that 'among country people ... the giving up of the ring [was] a sign that you have given up all claims as a wife'.[95] Other wives also reported that they had given their wedding ring back to their husbands.[96]

Conclusion

During the period covered by this volume, there was no major change in statute law on divorce. The existing laws were, however, stretched to facilitate new interpretations that undermined canon and civil law on marital separation and remarriage. Lawrence Stone argued that this flexibility led inexorably in England and Wales to the Matrimonial Causes Act of 1857. The exclusion of Ireland from that legislation prevented the same development. By contrast with England, the public discourse in late nineteenth-century Ireland became increasingly hostile to any form of marital separation. Women petitioners found it more difficult to acquire a divorce *a mensa et thoro* and the Irish Free State

---

[93] Prior to 1882, a wife could not act alone in signing a deed of separation. A male relative, often her brother or father, was obliged to act jointly with her in the agreement. See Deborah Wilson, *Women, Marriage and Property in Wealthy Landed Families in Ireland, 1750–1850* (Manchester, 2009), pp. 39–53; Fitzpatrick, 'Divorce and separation in modern Irish history', 176.

[94] *Irish Times*, 19 Jan. 1978.   [95] *Irish Times*, 21 July 1921.

[96] See, for example, *Irish Times*, 28 Jan. 1892.

rejected attempts to introduce the process of parliamentary divorce. Criminal conversation cases continued to be heard and were perceived as a morally acceptable means of condemning female adultery. In his famous speech in favour of retaining parliamentary divorce in the Irish Free State in 1925, W. B. Yeats optimistically compared opposition to the proposal as like an iceberg in warm water. He was convinced that the tolerant nature of Irish society would eventually overturn the hostility to divorce. Yeats's optimism may not have been misplaced but it took almost eighty years for the ice to melt and for the Irish parliament to pass legislation permitting divorce and remarriage.[97]

[97] *Seanad Éireann Debate*, 11 June 1925.

Conclusion

The aim of this book has been to understand the logistics of heterosexual marriage in Ireland, particularly among the lower and middle classes from 1660 to 1925. Our starting point was the establishment of a legal chronology of marriage in Ireland during the period, and the identification of the key developments in the regulation of marriage within the main Christian denominations of the Church of Ireland, Protestant Dissenters and Roman Catholicism. This was not a simple task as, throughout the period, there was considerable confusion and uncertainty in both church and state over the definition of a valid marriage. Parliamentary legislation reflected an ambivalent attitude towards marriage ceremonies not celebrated by Church of Ireland clergymen and this legal uncertainty was not fully removed until the later decades of the nineteenth century.

'Irregular' marriage, however it was defined, remained a social and political issue in Ireland until the mid-nineteenth century, and, as we document in the book, its implications and consequences were evident in a variety of legal contexts. Ignorance of the laws relating to marriage appeared to have been widespread even, at times, in the Dublin courts as barristers struggled to identify legal precedents from a very limited archive of former cases. Many relied on a mixture of printed reports of Irish and English cases and, consequently, confused Irish and English practices. Defendants accused of bigamy also claimed ignorance and pleaded that they were unaware that a marriage by a couple beggar was legally binding, however drunk they might have been when it was solemnised. They also told the courts that they had not realised that the couple beggar had no power to undo a marriage that he had conducted even if he deleted the couple's name from his register or tore up the marriage certificate that he had issued. Paradoxically, the fact that bigamous couples were keen to have a marriage ceremony suggests a belief in marriage as a social ritual and an act of social conformity. By the late nineteenth century, the civil law on marriage was more clearly articulated, although there remained some tension around the definition of a

Catholic marriage. It was not until the establishment of the Irish Free State that Catholic canon law on marriage was more fully recognised by the civil courts.

Laws passed in the Irish parliament before 1801 were frequently direct copies of English statute law. Not all English laws relating to marriage were, however, enacted in Ireland. There were two important absences from the Irish legal code. Firstly, the 1753 Act for the Better Preventing of Clandestine Marriage incorporated into English statute law the process involved in a legally valid marriage: where the ceremony should take place, the necessity for the proclamation of banns and the securing of the consent of both parties to the marriage and of their parents if they were under age. The so-called Hardwicke's Marriage Act clarified the law on marriage in England and eliminated irregular unions that did not follow the outlined procedure. The failure to pass similar legislation in Ireland was the most distinguishing difference between Irish and English marriage law in pre-Famine Ireland. The absence of an equivalent of the 1753 Act was also at the core of much of the legal confusion concerning marriage in Ireland.

The second important piece of English legislation that was not extended to Ireland was the Matrimonial Causes Act of 1857, which established the English divorce court and simplified the divorce process. It enabled relatively poor men and women to secure a divorce and remarry within a short period of time. The exemption of Ireland from this legislation meant that securing a divorce with permission to remarry continued to be cumbersome. Only a small minority of men and women could afford the lengthy and expensive process of a parliamentary divorce. It was the elimination of even this route to the dissolution of a marriage that was the subject of debate in the Irish parliament in 1925.

In addition to the state apparatus, all of the main Christian denominations had an infrastructure in place to supervise the choice of marriage partner by members of their respective congregations as well as the performance of the marriage ceremony and the behaviour of both partners during the marriage. There were, however, considerable differences between what was expected by church regulation and people's actual behaviour. The priorities of individual men and women did not always conform to the expectations of their respective churches. In England, most people, before the introduction of civil marriages in a registry office in 1836, married in their local Anglican church in a service solemnised by a Church of England clergyman. By contrast, Irish couples had a range of options from which to choose both a venue and a presiding minister for their marriage service. They could decide to marry in their local church before a clergyman of their own denomination; they could ask the cleric to come to one of their family homes for the service or for him to marry them in his own home; they could choose to marry in a Church of Ireland church; they could pay a couple beggar to perform the service or they might, particularly if they were members of a dissenting congregation, opt out of a formal marriage solemnisation and make a private promise of marriage to each other. It was not until after 1850 that marriage procedure in Ireland began to look more like that which had long prevailed in England: i.e. most people married in their local church, chapel or meeting house before a minister whose authority was fully recognised by their respective church.

In court, the legal strategies of barristers involved in marital cases of various kinds were based on carefully constructed gendered images of the perceived role of husband and wife. There was a discursive construction of the 'normal' or 'ordinary' woman or wife and how she should behave. The man's role in a marriage was less clearly defined but barristers in domestic abuse disputes often stressed the limitations of patriarchal power in the home. Barristers also challenged, when it was deemed appropriate, the model of the ideal woman and, in doing so, revealed a more realistic and nuanced understanding of the actual lived experiences of men and women in society. Judges and juries rewarded women who sued men for reneging on promises to marry or who petitioned for a separation from an abusive husband. By the 1900s, however, the rhetoric of the chaste Irish woman proliferated in the courts as divorce and, more generally, sexual promiscuity were increasingly identified as alien to the perceived sexual purity of Irish society.

In choosing a marriage partner, individuals and families were influenced by a number of criteria including, most importantly, the economic and social status of the potential partner. We have focussed attention on the process of courtship, and the extent to which parental and family approval could take precedence over individual wishes. Money and land were not the only forms of exchange and, as we have seen, at the lower end of the social hierarchy a woman might be valued for the labour she could bring to her husband's house or for her willingness to beg, if necessary.

It has been difficult to plot significant changes in attitudes towards dowries and the monetary arrangements for marriage. Since the publications of K. H. Connell, it has been generally assumed by historians that marriage became a more mercenary affair in post-Famine Ireland with many young people, particularly women, forced into marriages deemed to be in the family interest. Yet, no substantial evidence survives to document this change. Our analysis suggests that arranged marriages, and an emphasis on family priorities, formed a central part of marriage, particularly among the middling ranks of society throughout the period covered by this book. Eighteenth and early nineteenth century wills testify to the importance that fathers attached to providing adequate dowries or marriage partners for their daughters long before the social and economic disruption of the Famine. Fathers, and sometimes mothers, also made financial provision for their daughters' marriages conditional on their marrying with the approval of the surviving parent or the main heir to a man's estate.

The most challenging aspect of writing this book involved research into the intimate lives of married couples. Unlike the documentation preserved in family archives of wealthier families, few middle-class husbands or wives kept their letters to one another and few records survive of the poor giving their views on marriage. The small number of private letters and diaries that we have identified reveal expressions of sexual desire, the need for comfort and intimacy and the expectations that some couples had of married life, while also reminding us of the complexity of relationships between individuals.

Children only feature peripherally in this study. Here the children, rather than being objects of study in themselves, provide and invite external scrutiny of marital behaviour. Couples produced children, whether legitimate or not; married men had children outside marriage, and married women sometimes remarried bigamously and had children. Parents sometimes used institutions such as workhouses to provide care for their children. Children appear in cases of desertion by parents. There was violence towards children and they certainly witnessed violent parental and familial relationships. Attitudes towards adult children, especially in regard to controlling marriage choices, property and the ownership of goods and land caused fraught relationships in many homes. Sometimes this tension led to murder. There is still much work to be done on the emotional relationships that existed between parents and children and between siblings. We know little of how children were viewed as part of family life, or the effects of childlessness on couples and its familial and social meanings.

In the period of time in which this book was in gestation, we became aware, therefore, of areas for future research. The records with which we worked allowed us to capture instances of a moment in a family's history, but we have not followed any family's history over a period of time. Although beyond the scope of this study, a regional study of household formation over the centuries would provide us with a deeper understanding of both family and community life, particularly in rural Ireland.

Another fruitful area of research is an international comparative study of the history of marriage in Ireland. We have noted already some of the significant legal differences with English marriage law. The levels of violence tolerated in Irish society in Irish courtship practices and marriage also warrant a comparative analysis. As we note in Chapter 5, abductions of potential brides were not unique to Ireland but it would also be worth investigating if the level of domestic abuse was higher in Ireland than elsewhere. Edward Wakefield's claim that women in early nineteenth-century Ireland were treated like 'beasts of burden' may not withstand comparison with other rural societies. It is often implicitly assumed that Irish marital patterns differed from elsewhere due to a variety of factors: most notably the rapid growth in the Irish population before the Famine, the high levels of celibacy afterwards and the political complexities on the island for all of the period covered by this book. Yet, none of these assumptions have been tested by detailed comparative analysis. The work in this study opens the way for such comparative work.

Public rhetoric in twenty-first century Ireland lauds the new sexual freedoms of Irish society. Men and women wishing to live together may do so with or without a formal marriage service. If they opt for the former, they can choose from a wide range of religious and secular ceremonies. This is perceived as being in sharp contrast to the significance ascribed to marriage in Ireland's past, when a religious service was deemed essential and engaging in sexual activity outside marriage was denounced as sinful by a controlling Catholic church. Same-sex marriage, of course, did not exist. Marriage was 'for better or worse', for life and no reprieve was possible even in a union that both partners found unsatisfactory. Yet, we demonstrate that throughout the long time span covered by this book, subversive behaviour and side-stepping the laws of church and state in relation to personal and intimate relationships were common. The pursuit of love by Irish men and women, however that was understood in practical or romantic terms, their demand for personal attachment, their desire for sexual fulfilment and their assertion of economic agency, challenged social norms throughout the period. The narrowing of options for marriage and the social and legal repression of the practice of sexuality, was arguably at its height from the early years of the Free State through to the 1960s. Women and men rebelled then, too, but many of their stories have yet to be told.

Select Bibliography

Please note that this is a select bibliography. For other references consult the footnotes.

PRIMARY SOURCES

BRITISH LIBRARY, LONDON

Papers of the Consistory Court of Killaloe, 1671–1824 (Add. MS 31881–2).

BUREAU OF MILITARY HISTORY, DUBLIN

Witness Statement, Bridget Thornton, WSO259.

CARDINAL TOMÁS Ó FIAICH LIBRARY & ARCHIVE, ARMAGH

Richard Reilly Papers.
Joseph Dixon Papers.
Daniel McGettigan Papers.
Cardinal Michael Logue Papers.

CLONTARF AND SCOTS PRESBYTERIAN CHURCH, DUBLIN

Plunkett Street/Usher's Quay Session Book, 1726–1766.

CORK AND ROSS DIOCESAN ARCHIVES

Delaney Papers.
Moylan Papers.
Murphy Papers.
O'Callaghan Papers.

DUBLIN DIOCESAN ARCHIVES

Hamilton Papers.
Cullen Papers.
Troy Papers.

Carpenter Papers.
Murray Papers.
Walsh Papers.
Byrne Papers.

GALWAY DIOCESAN ARCHIVES

Boxes 5, 7, 8, 9, 15.

GENERAL REGISTRAR'S OFFICE, ROSCOMMON

Marriage Register of Johann Georg Schulz, 1806–37.

KERRY COUNTY LIBRARY, TRALEE

Board of Guardian Rough Minute Book, Tralee Union, 14 Dec. 1861–6
Dec. 1862. BG 1154 1 AA17.

KERRY DIOCESAN ARCHIVES, KILLARNEY

Moriarty Papers.
Mangan Papers.
Coffey Papers.
Higgins Papers.
McCarthy Papers.
O'Sullivan, John, *Praxis Parochi in Hibernia*. MS draft and two volumes,
1850–52.
Sugrue Papers.

KILDARE COUNTY LIBRARY, NAAS, COUNTY KILDARE

Workhouse Minutes, Naas Union, 10 Oct. 1863.

KILDARE AND LEIGHLIN DIOCESAN ARCHIVES

Keefe Papers, 1770–1785.
Delaney Papers, 1770–1807.
Corcoran Papers, 1815–1819.
Nolan Papers, 1825–1837.
Haly Papers, 1862–1888.

LAMBETH PALACE ARCHIVES

Davidson Papers.

NATIONAL ARCHIVES OF IRELAND

Chief Secretary's Office Registered Papers.
Chief Secretary Office, Registered Papers, Outrage Reports.

Convict Reference Files 1836–1924.
Criminal Index Files 1841–1922.
Crown and Peace Office Records.
Dáil Éireann Court Register Books.
Dáil Éireann Winding Up Commission 1922–1925.
Department of the Taoiseach Files, 1922–1925.
Dublin Consistory Court Cause Papers (4/271/37).
Board of Guardian Minutes, South Dublin Union.
Irish Crime Records, Returns of Outrages, 1848–1878 CSO/CR/1.
Killaloe Court and Register Book 1707–1868 (4/201/31).
Samuel Kingston, 'A Psychological Proposal' (21 June 1913) (PRIV1234/4/1/1(3)).
Limerick District Probate Registry Will Book, 1889–9 June 1893 (1A/15/131).
Petty Sessions Records, 1828–1915.
Probate and Matrimonial, 1865–1870, Dublin Provincial.
Probate and Matrimonial 1902–1904.
Printed Outrage Reports 1836–1912.
Prison Registers, 1799–1920.
Prisoners' Petitions and Cases, 1778–1836.
Settlement of the Intermarriage of Patrick Kain and Mary Kenny, 1841 (MS 999/22/20).
Tuam Consistory Court Book, 1740–42 (M 6833).
Will Books, Transcripts:
MFGS 41/041-2 Will Books Prerogative 1728–1729.
MFGS 41/8 Prerogative Connor 1853–1858; Down: 1850–1858.
MFGS 41/15 Ballina District 1892–1899.
MFGS 41/38B Galway/Roscommon District.
MFGS 41/42 Waterford District Registry, 17 Aug. 1885–10 Aug. 1894.
MFGS 41/47 Various Districts 1865–1881.
Marriage Settlements (MS 999/22/2; MS 999/30/3; MS 999/132/1; MS 999/138/4; MS 999/149/3).

NATIONAL LIBRARY OF IRELAND

Assize Records for Antrim, Carlow, King's County, Westmeath (MS807).
Calendar of the Papers of the Butler Archbishops of Cashel and Emly, 1712–1791.
Calendar of the Papers of Dr T. Bray, 1792–1829.
Calendar of the Papers of Dr M. Slattery, 1834–57.
Calendar of the Papers of Dr Croke, 1841–1902.
Calendar of the Papers of Dr Leahy, 1857–75.
Donegal Assizes (MS 12,911).
Ceannt and O'Brennan Papers, 1851–1953 (MS 13069).
Journal of Mary Shackleton Leadbeater, 1769–1826 (MSS 9292–9346).
Leadbeater Correspondence (MS 8003).
Parish Records (Dioceses of Dublin, Ferns, Kildare and Leghlin, Wexford).

Rosamond Jacob Diaries (MS 32,582).
Westport Union. Minute Books of the Board of Guardians, Aug. 1850–
March 1860 (MSS 12,613–12,625).

PRESBYTERIAN HISTORICAL SOCIETY OF IRELAND, BELFAST

Aghadowey Session Book, 1702–1761.
Cahans Session Books, 1751–1911.
Carnmoney Session Book, 1786–1821.
Down Presbytery Minute Book, 1785–1842.
Down Presbytery (Seceder) Minute Book, 1837–1841.
Dundonald Session and Committee Book, 1678.
Glascar Session Book, 1760–1818.
Moira and Lisburn Presbytery Minute Book, 1670–1830.
Monaghan Presbytery Minute Book, 1800–1817.
Route Presbytery Minute Book, 1811–1834.
Upper Tyrone (Seceder) Presbytery Minute Book, 1800–1830.

PUBLIC RECORD OFFICE, NORTHERN IRELAND

Black Papers (D4457/4).
Board of Guardian Minutes, Ballymoney Union.
Board of Guardian Minutes, Enniskillen.
Correspondence of William Drennan with Sarah Swanwick (T581).
Dunraven Papers (D3196).
Married Women's Protection Orders.
Minutes of the Lisburn Society of Friends Women's Meetings (MIC16/29).
Minutes of the Reformed Presbytery of Ireland, 1803–1811 (CR5/5A/1/2A).
Roman Catholic Diocese of Clogher Papers (DIORC/1).
Roman Catholic Diocese of Dromore Papers (DIORC/3).
Shirley Papers (D3531/P).
Templepatrick Presbytery Minute Books, 1795–1915 (PRONI, MIC1P/85/1).
Tennent Papers (D1748).
Transcripts of Wills by Genealogical Society (T581).

REPRESENTATIVE CHURCH BODY LIBRARY, DUBLIN

MS 512. St John's Watch Record (P328.3.1–7).

REGISTRY OF DEEDS, DUBLIN

Transcript Books.

SOCIETY OF FRIENDS LIBRARY, DUBLIN

Diary of Elizabeth Clibborn (1780–1861).
Cork Meeting Minute Books.
Munster Quarterly Meeting Minutes.
Waterford Meeting Minute Books.

THE NATIONAL ARCHIVES, KEW

Court of Delegate Records: FitzMaurice alias Leeson versus FitzMaurice, 1730–34 (DEL 2/27).

TIPPERARY STUDIES, THE SOURCE, THURLES, COUNTY TIPPERARY

The O'Carroll Diaries (typescript edited by Rev. James Feehan).

UNIVERSITY COLLEGE DUBLIN

National Folklore Collection
Volume 2028, Marriage Customs Questionnaire.

UCD Archives
Papers of Daniel O'Connell (1775–1847), IE UCDA P12.

UNIVERSITY OF HULL

Marie Stopes Papers, DX/66/2, Brynmor Jones Library.

NEWSPAPERS

Full details of the newspapers used have been provided in the footnotes. We made extensive use of The British Newspaper Archive (britishnewspaperarchive.co.uk), the Irish Newspaper Archive (Irishnewsarchive.com) and The Irish Times (irishtimes.com). We also looked at many newspapers that have not yet been digitised and are held in the National Library of Ireland, the Gilbert Library, Pearse Street, Dublin, and many local records offices around the country.

EDITED MANUSCRIPT SOURCES

Agnew, J. (ed.), *The Drennan–McTier Letters, 1776–1819* (3 vols., Dublin, 1998–2001).
Boulter, H. *Letters Written by His Excellency, Hugh Boulter, D.D., Lord Primate of All Ireland, Etc.* (2 vols., Dublin, 1770).
Brady, J., 'Archbishop Troy's Pastoral on Clandestine Marriages, 1789', *Reportorium Novum*, 1, 2 (1956), 481–5.
 Catholics and Catholicism in the Eighteenth Century Press (Maynooth, 1965).
Brady, W. M. (ed.), *The McGillicuddy Papers: A Selection from the Family Archives of the McGillicuddy of the Reeks with an Introductory Memoir: Being a Contribution to the History of the County of Kerry* (London, 1867).
Calvert, L. (ed.), 'Carnmoney Kirk Session Minute Chapter Book, January 1786–March 1804' (unpublished transcript of original in PHSIB).
Daniell, F. H. B. (ed.), *Calendar of State Papers Domestic: Charles II, 1683 January–June* (London, 1933).

Day, A. and P. McWilliams (eds.), *Ordnance Survey Memoirs of Ireland* (40 vols., Belfast, 1995).

Derr, E. A. and M. MacKenna (eds.), 'Episcopal visitations of the diocese of Cloyne and Ross, 1785–1828 [with index]', *Archivium Hibernicum*, 66 (2013), 261–393.

Ellison, C. C. (ed.), 'Bishop Dopping's visitation book 1682–1685', *Ríocht na Midhe*, 5, 1 (1971), 28–39; 5, 2 (1972), 3–13; 5, 3 (1973), 3–11.

Eustace, P. B. (ed.), *Registry of Deeds. Dublin. Abstracts of Wills, 1708–1832* (3 vols., Dublin, 1956–1984).

Farrell, E. (ed.), *Infanticide in the Irish Crown Files at Assizes, 1883–1900* (Dublin, 2012).

Flanagan, P. J., 'The Diocese of Clogher in 1714', *Clogher Record*, 2 (1954), 39–42; 3 (1955), 125–30.

Goodbody, O., *Guide to Irish Quaker Records, 1654–1860*. With contribution on Northern Ireland records by B. G. Hutton (Dublin, 1967).

Hanly, J. (ed.), *The Letters of Saint Oliver Plunkett 1625–1681; Archbishop of Armagh and Primate of all Ireland* (Dublin, 1979).

Herbert, D., *Retrospections of Dorothea Herbert, 1770–1806* (Dublin, 1988).

Kelly, J. and M. A. Lyons (eds.), *The Proclamations of Ireland 1660–1820* (5 vols., Dublin, 2015).

King, Sir C. S., *A Great Archbishop of Dublin: William King, D.D., 1650–1729: His Autobiography, Family, and a Selection from His Correspondence* (London, 1906).

Latimer, W. T., 'The old session–book of Templepatrick Presbyterian Church, Co. Antrim', *Journal of Royal Society of Antiquaries of Ireland*, 5, 2 (1895), 130–4; 31, 2 (1901), 162–75; 31, 3 (1901), 259–72.

Legg, M. L. (ed.), *The Diary of Nicholas Peacock, 1740–51: The Worlds of a County Limerick Farmer and Agent* (Dublin, 2005).

Linn, R. (ed.), 'Marriage register of the Presbyterian congregation of Banbridge, County Down, 1756–1794', *Journal of the Royal Society of Antiquaries of Ireland*, 39 (1909), 75–84.

Mahaffy, R. P. (ed.), *Calendar of State Papers Ireland, 1666–1669* (London, 1908).

McDowell, H. (ed.), *Irregular Marriages in Dublin before 1837* (Dundalk, 2015).

McGrath, M. (ed.), *Cinnlae Amhlaoibh Uí Shúileabháin: The Diary of Humphrey O'Sullivan* (4 vols., Dublin, 1936–37).

O'Connell, M. R. (ed.), *The Correspondence of Daniel O'Connell, 1775–1847* (8 vols., Dublin, 1972–1977).

Power, P. (ed.), *A Bishop of the Penal Times: Being Letters and Reports of John Brenan, Bishop of Waterford (1671–93) and Archbishop of Cashel (1677–93)* (Cork, 1932).

Raughter, R. (ed.), '"Your own for ever, sis": Letters to Parsonstown, 1898–1903', *Bulletin of the Methodist Historical Society of Ireland*, 22, 1 (2017), 36–116.

Records of the General Synod of Ulster: From 1691 to 1820. Published by the Authority of the General Assembly of the Presbyterian Church in Ireland, with the Sanction of the General Synod (3 vols., Belfast, 1898).

Refaussé, R., 'Marriage licences from the Diocese of Ossory 1739–1804', *Irish Genealogist*, 8 (1990), 122–44; (1991), 239–67; (1992), 393–428.

Renehan, L. F., *Collections on Irish Church History*. Edited by D. McCarthy (Dublin, 1861).

Walsh, H. D., 'Ossory marriage license bonds', *Irish Genealogist*, 4 (1971), 331–41.

CONTEMPORARY PRINTED MATERIAL

Authentic Report of the Crim. Con. Trial of Joynt V. Jackson, in the Exchequer Court, Dublin, Commencing May 10th 1880 (Dublin, 1880).

Barrington, J., *Personal Sketches of His Own Times* (3rd ed., 2 vols., London, 1869).

Blackstone, W., *Commentaries on the Laws of England* (13th ed., 4 vols., London, 1800).

Browne, A., *A Compendious View of the Civil Law and of the Law Admiralty, Being the Substance of a Course of Lectures Read in the University of Dublin* (2 vols., Dublin, 1802).

   A Compendious View of the Ecclesiastical Law of Ireland: Being the Substance of a Course of Lectures Read in the University of Dublin. To Which Is Added, a Sketch of the Practice of the Ecclesiastical Courts, with Some Cases Determined Therein, In Ireland (Dublin, 1803).

Bullinbrooke, E., *Ecclesiastical Law; or, the Statutes, Constitutions, Canons, Rubricks, and Articles, of the Church of Ireland …* (2 vols., Dublin, 1770).

Burke, O. J., *Anecdotes of the Connaught Circuit* (Dublin, 1885).

Butler, James A., *Justification of the Tenets of the Roman Catholic Religion and a Refutation of the Charges Brought against Its Clergy* (Dublin, 1787).

Constitutions and Canons Ecclesiastical, Treated upon by the Archbishops and Bishops and the Rest of the Clergy of Ireland: And Agreed by the King's Majesty's License in Their Synod, Begun and Holden at Dublin, Anno Domini, 1634…. To Which Is Added Constitutions and Canons Ecclesiastical, Treated upon by the Archbishops and Bishops, and the Rest of the Clergy of Ireland: And Agreed upon by the Queen's Majesty's License in Their Synod, Begun and Holden at Dublin, Anno Domini, 1711 … (Dublin, 1767).

Capp, C., *Memoirs of the Life of the Late Mrs Catharine Capp Written by Herself* (Boston, 1824).

Carleton, W., *Traits and Stories of the Irish Peasantry* (London, 1890).

A Concise Guide to the Practice (Contentious and Non-Contentious) in the Probate (and Matrimonial) Division of the High Court of Justice, Ireland: And in Its District Registries and in the County Courts (Testamentary Cases): With an Appendix, Containing the Acts of Parliament and the New Rules and Forms under the Code of January, 1891 and Also Schedules of Court and Professional Fees (5th ed., Dublin, 1891).

Cornwall Lewis, G., *Local Disturbances in Ireland* (London, 1836; reprinted Cork, 1977).

A Correct and Full Report of the Trial of Sir J. B. Piers for Criminal Conversation with Lady Cloncurry (Dublin, 1807).

Cousins, J. H. and M. E., *We Two Together* (Madras, 1950).

Crawford, George and Edward Spencer Dix, *Reports of Cases Argued and Ruled in the Circuits, in Ireland: During the Years 1839–1846. Together with Cases Decided at the Nisi Prius Sittings, and in the Courts of Criminal Jurisdiction at Dublin* (3 vols., Dublin, 1841–47).

Crim. Con.; A Full, Faithful and Impartial Account of That Curious, Extraordinary and Interesting Trial with Speeches of Counsel and Judge's Charge, in the Case Wherein Mark Brown, Esq. Was Plaintiff and Martin Joseph Blake, Esq. Defendant in an Action of Damages for Crim. Con. Against the Plaintiff's Wife (Dublin, 1818).

Crim Con.: A Full, Faithful and Impartial Report of the Trial Wherein Sir John M. Doyle, KCB & KTS, Was Plaintiff and George Peter Brown, Esq, Defendant (Dublin, 1820).

Dallas, M., *A Second Letter from the Reverend Marmaduke Dallas, A.M. to the Right Reverend Jemmet Lord Bishop of Cork and Ross: In Answer to His Lordship's Letter, Dated Nov. 20, 1740* (Dublin, 1750).

A Fourth Letter from the Reverend Marmaduke Dallas, A.M. to the Right Reverend Jemmet, Lord Bishop of Cork and Ross. To be Continued, 'Till the Bishop of Cork's Whole Letter Is Examined (Dublin, 1750).

A Short and True State of the Affair Betwixt the Rt. Revd. J–m–t, Lord Bishop of C–rk and R—ss and the Revd, M–rm–duke Dallas, A.M. (Dublin, 1750).

Directory for the Publicke Worship of God throughout the Three Kingdoms of Scotland, England and Ireland (Edinburgh, 1645).

Faloon, W. H., *The Marriage Law of Ireland. With an Introduction and Notes* (Dublin, 1881).

A Full and Correct Report of a Trial for Seduction, Wherein Nicholas Kavanagh, of Kilcullen in the County of Kildare, Was Plaintiff and Edward Kelly, of New Abbey in Said County, Defendant … (Dublin, 1827).

Full Report of the Extraordinary Divorce Case, Grady v Grady, Co–Respondent, Michael Monahan (Dublin, 1880).

The Genuine Declaration of Edward Shuel a Degraded Clergyman of the Church of Ireland, Who Is to be Executed Near St. Stephens Green, This Present Saturday Being the 29th of This Instant November 1740… (Dublin, 1740).

A Guardian of the Poor, The Irish Peasant: A Sociological Study (London, 1892).

Instructions for the Guidance of Resident Magistrates (Dublin, 1837).

Hamilton, S. and R. Bourke, *Report of Two Cases upon the Marriage Law of Ireland, Argued and Determined in the Court of Queen's Bench* (Dublin, 1842).

Hayes, E., *Crimes and Punishments: Or, An Analytical Digest of the Criminal Statute Law in Ireland* (Dublin, 1837).

In His Majesty's High Court of Delegates in Ireland, Ann Shea Otherwise Wills v Robert Percy Shea (Dublin, 1771).

Inglis, H. D., *A Journey Throughout Ireland* (London, 1838).

Ingram, E. D. (ed.), *Reports of Cases Argued and Determined in the English Ecclesiastical Courts, with Tables of the Cases and Principal Matters* (2 vols., Philadelphia, 1831).

Jebb, R., *Cases Chiefly Relating to the Criminal and Presentment Law, Reserved for Consideration, and Decided by the Twelve Judges of Ireland, From May 1822, to November 1840* (Dublin, 1841).

Kisbey, W. H., *The Law and Practice of the Court for Matrimonial Causes and Matters* (Dublin, 1871).

Lambert, R., *An Answer to a Late Pamphlet, Entitl'd a Vindication of Marriage, as Solemniz'd by Presbyterians in the North of Ireland* (Dublin, 1704).

Leadbeater, M., *Cottage Dialogues among the Irish Peasantry* (London, 1811).

A Letter from a Clergyman in Dublin, to a Clergyman in Cork. In Answer to a Letter Published in Dublin, Dec. 8th, 1749. Vindicating the Conduct of the Bishop of Cork, in the Degradation of Mr. Dallas (Dublin, 1749).

A Letter from a Clergyman of the Dioceses of Corke, to His Friend in Dublin, Relating the Conduct of the Bishop of Corke, in the Degradation of Mr. Dallas (Dublin, 1749).

Levinge, E. P., *The Justice of the Peace for Ireland* (3rd ed. updated by L.S. Montgomery, Dublin, 1872).

Loftus, D., *The Case of Ware and Sherley as It Was Set Forth in Matter of Fact and Argued in Several Points of Law in the Consistory Court of Dublin, in Michael Term 1668* (Dublin, 1669).

Love without Artifice: Or, the Disappointed Peer. A History of the Amour between Lord Mauritio and Emilia. Being the Case of Elizabeth Fitz-Maurice, Alias Leeson, and the Lord William Fitz-Maurice, Relating to a Marriage-Contract between Them; Which Was Confirmed by a Court of Delegates, in the Lady's Behalf, on Wednesday, March 14th 1732–3, at Serjeant's-Inn, in Chancery-Lane (London, 1733).

Love without Artifice: Or, the Disappointed Peer. A History of the Amour between Lord Mauritio and Emilia. Being the Case of Elizabeth Fitz–Maurice, Alias Leeson, and the Lord William Fitz-Maurice, Relating to a Marriage-Contract between Them; Which Was Confirmed by a Court of Decreta Synodi Plenariae Episcoporum Hiberniae Apud Thurles Habitae, Anno MDCCCL (Dublin, 1851).

MacBride, J., *A Vindication of Marriage: As Solemnized by Presbyterians, in the North of Ireland* (1702).

Margaret Dawes, Widow, Plaintiff, Richard O'Connor, Attorney, Defendant, Trial for the Seduction of Margaret Dawes, the Plaintiff's Daughter (Dublin, 1828).

Matheson, R. E., *Digest of the Irish Marriage Law* (5th ed., Dublin, 1896).

Miller, G., *Judgement in the Consistorial Court of Armagh, Involving the Question of the Law of Marriage in Ireland* (Armagh, 1840).

Milward, C. R., *Reports of Cases Argued and Determined in the Court of Prerogative in Ireland, and in the Consistory Court of Dublin, During the Time of the Right Honourable John Radcliff, LL. D* (Dublin, 1847).

O'Donoghue, D. J., *The Life of William Carleton: Being His Autobiography and Letters; and an Account of His Life and Writings, from the Point at Which the Autobiography Breaks Off* (2 vols., London, 1896).

Observations on the Case of the Right Honourable the Lord Fitzmaurice, and Mrs Elizabeth Leeson, Concerning a Pretended Contract of Marriage (London, 1733).

Oulton, A. N., *Index to the Statutes, at Present in Force or Affecting Ireland, from the Year 1310 to 1838, Inclusive: Continued by Annual Supplements* (2nd ed., Dublin, 1839).

Index to the Statutes in Force in, or Affecting Ireland: Passed in the Years 1839 to 1849 and Continuation of the Chronological Table (Dublin, 1849).

Philadelphicus's Second Letter in Answer to the Vindication of the Conduct of the B—p of C—k in a Letter Dated November 20, 1749 (Cork, 1749(?)).

Proceedings of the Trial of Capt J Caulfield for Criminal Conversation with the Wife of Capt George Chambers (1804).

Report of the Trial of an Action, Wherein John Birch, an Englishman, Was Plaintiff, and Joshua Paul Meredith, Esq… for Seduction … of Sarah Birch (Dublin, 1819).

Report of the Trial in the Cause of Henrietta Anne Head v Simon George Purdon, Esq. (Dublin, [1837]).

A Report of the Trial of Robert Robinson, for Bigamy; Tried in the Sessions House, Green Street at the Commission of Oyer and Terminer (Dublin, 1812).

Revans, J., *Evils of the State of Ireland; Their Cause and Their Remedy: A Poor Law* (London, 1835).

Ryan, E. and W. Moody, *Reports of Cases Determined at Nisi Prius, in the Courts of King's Bench and Common Pleas, and on the Oxford and Western Circuits from the Sittings after Michaelmas Term, 4 George IV, 1823 …* (London, 1827).

Sayers, P. and M. Ní Chinnéide, *Peig* (Dublin, 1936).

Seduction. A Full and Correct Report of a Trial for Seduction Wherein Nicholas Kavanagh … Plaintiff and Edward Kelly… Defendant (Dublin, 1821).

Selection of Parochial Examinations Relative to the Destitute Classes in Ireland (Dublin, 1835).

Shaw Mason, W., *A Statistical Account or Parochial Survey of Ireland Drawn up from the Communication of the Clergy* (3 vols., Dublin, 1814–1819).

Smith, G. H., *Practice of the Court for Matrimonial Causes and Matters, Ireland* (Dublin, 1871).

Spence Dix, E., *Report on the Cases of Regina v Millis et Regina v Carroll in the Queen's Bench in Ireland in Easter and Trinity Terms, 1842* (Dublin, 1842).

Stopford, E. A., *A Handbook of Ecclesiastical Law and Duty: For the Use of the Irish Clergy* (Dublin, 1861).

Synge, E., *A Defence of the Establish'd Church and Laws, in Answer to a Book Entitul'd, A Vindication of Marriage, as Solemniz'd by Presbyterians in the North of Ireland* (Dublin, 1705).

The Assembly's Shorter Catechism Explained. By Way of Question and Answer … (Belfast, 1764).

The Constitution and Discipline of the Presbyterian Church; with a Directory for the Celebration of Ordinances, and the Performance of Ministerial Duties (Belfast, 1825).

The Humble Advice of the Assembly of Divines, Now by Authority of Parliament Sitting at Westminster, Concerning a Confession of Faith, Presented by Them Lately to Both Houses of Parliament (London, 1647).

The Statutes at Large Passed in the Parliaments Held in Ireland (20 vols., Dublin, 1786–1801).

Townsend, H., *A Statistical Survey of the County of Cork* (Dublin, 1810).

The Trial of Mrs Ellen Byrne for the Murder of Mr Augustine Byrne, Her Husband; at the Commission Court Dublin (Dublin, 1842).

The Trial of Sir Henry Browne Hayes, Knt. for Forcibly and Feloniously Taking Away Miss Mary Pike on the 22nd Day of July, 1797 (Cork, 1797).

Trial of William Grace, esq ... for Breach of Promise of Marriage to Miss Mary Anne McCarthy, of Killarney (Cork, 1816).

Vane, C. (ed.), *Memoirs and Correspondence of Viscount Castlereagh, Second Marquess of Londonderry* (4 vols., London, 1849).

Warburton, J., J. Whitelaw and R. Walsh, *History of the City of Dublin, from the Earliest Accounts to the Present Time* (3 vols., Dublin, 1818).

Wakefield, E., *An Account of Ireland, Statistical and Political* (2 vols., London, 1812).

Whately, R., *Extract From a Letter on the Marriage Laws: Addressed By the Late Archbishop of Dublin (Dr. Whately) to the Late Bishop of Norwich (Dr. Hinds)* (Dublin?, 1851).

Young, A., *A Tour in Ireland* (2nd ed., 2 vols., London, 1780).

PARLIAMENTARY PAPERS

[Below are listed those parliamentary papers used most frequently in this study. Other papers are detailed in the footnotes. We have made use of EPPI (Enhanced Parliamentary Papers on Ireland) available at dippam.ac.uk and ProQuest UK Parliamentary Papers.

Abstract of the Answers and Returns Made Pursuant to an Act of the United Parliament, Passed in the 55th Year of the Reign of His Late Majesty George The Third, Intituled, 'An Act to Provide for Taking an Account of the Population of Ireland, And for Ascertaining the Increase or Diminution Thereof.' Preliminary Observations. Enumeration Abstract. Appendix. M. DCCC. XXI. (House of Commons, 1823).

Annual Reports of the Directors of Convict Prisons in Ireland, with Appendices: First to Twenty-Fourth Report, 1854–1877, HC 1854–1878.

Assaults on Women and Children (Dublin): Return of the Number of Men Charged at or Summoned to the Different Police Offices in Dublin, During the Past Year, for Assaults on Women and Children; Stating How Many Have Been Sent for Trial, and how Many Have Been Summarily Convicted. HC 1854–55 (221).

Census of Ireland: A Comparative View of the Census of Ireland in 1841 and 1851; Distinguishing the Several Unions and Electoral Divisions, and Showing the Area and Population of Those Districts Respectively (House of Commons, 1852).

Commitments, Trials, Convictions, &c. Ireland (House of Commons, 1814–1818).

Commitments. Returns from the Clerks of the Crown and Clerks of the Peace of the Several Counties, &C. In Ireland (House of Commons, 1824).

Criminal and Judicial Statistics (Ireland), 1864–1919.

Dáil Éireann Debates, 1922–1925.

Journals of the Irish House of Lords.

Judicial Statistics. Ireland. Part I. Police—Criminal Proceedings—Prisons. Part II. Common Law—Equity—Civil and Canon Law (Dublin, 1866–1921).

Outrages (Ireland): A Return of Outrages Reported to the Constabulary Office, Dublin Castle (Dublin, 1836–1912).

Papers Relating to the State of Ireland (House of Commons, 1834).

Poor Inquiry (Ireland): Appendix (H), Part ii. Remarks on the Evidence Taken in the Poor Inquiry (Ireland), Contained in the Appendices (D) (E) (F) By One of the Commissioners.

Population, Ireland: Abstract of Answers and Returns under the Population Acts, 55 Geo. III. Chap. 120. 3 Geo. IV. Chap. 5. 2 Geo. IV. Chap. 30. 1 Will. IV. Chap. 19. Enumeration 1831 (House of Commons, 1833).

Prisons of Ireland: Reports of the Inspectors General on the General State of the Prisons of Ireland (Dublin, 1805–1856).

Report of the Commissioners Appointed to Take the Census of Ireland, for the Year 1841 (Dublin, 1843).

Reports and Summary, Select Committee on the State of the Poor in Ireland 1830, HC 1830 (589, 654, 665, 667), vii.

Reports of the Commissioners for Inquiring into the Conditions of the Poorer Classes in Ireland: First Report, HC 1835 (369), xxxii, pts. 1&2; *Second Report*, HC 1837 (68), xxxi; *Third Report*, HC 1836 (43), xxx.

Reports of the Registrar-General of Marriages in Ireland, under the Provisions of the Act 7 & 8 Vic., chap. 81 (Dublin, 1849–1921).

Report of the Royal Commission on the Laws of Marriage (London, 1868).

Royal Commission on Labour: The Agricultural Labourer (London, 1893–4).

Royal Commission on Venereal Diseases, Reports and Minutes of Evidence, HC (Cd 7475) 1917–1918, xvi.

State of Ireland Minutes of Evidence Taken before the Select Committee Appointed to Inquire into the Disturbances in Ireland, in the Last Session of Parliament, 13th May–18th June 1824. HC 1825 (20).

Statistical Tables of the Dublin Metropolitan Police for the Year (Dublin, 1838–1918).

Censi of Ireland for the years 1851, 1861, 1871, 1881, 1891, 1901, 1911, 1912–1913 (Dublin, 1852–1913).

The Registrar General's Report Containing General Abstracts of Marriages, Births and Deaths, Registered in Northern Ireland (Belfast, 1922–1925).

SECONDARY LITERATURE

Agnew, J., *Belfast Merchant Families in the Seventeenth Century* (Dublin, 1996).

Ahern, M., *The Quakers of County Tipperary, 1655–1924* (Clonmel, 2009).

Akenson, D. H., *Small Differences: Irish Catholics and Irish Protestants, 1815–1922: An International Perspective* (Montreal, 1991).

Andrews, C. S., *Man of No Property* (Dublin, 1982).

Bailey, J., *Unquiet Lives: Marriage and Marriage Breakdown in England, 1660–1800* (Cambridge, 2003).

Ballard, L., *Forgetting Frolic: Marriage Traditions in Ireland* (Belfast, 1998).

'Matchmaking and marriage revisited', *Heart of Breifne*, 2, 4 (1985), 75–81.

'Wedding pranks', *Archaeology Ireland*, 5, 4 (1991), 21–2.

Barclay, K., 'Farmwives, domesticity and work in late nineteenth-century Ireland', *Rural History*, 24, 2 (2013), 143–60.

'Place and power in Irish farms at the end of the nineteenth century', *Women's History Review*, 21, 4 (2012), 571–88.

Barnard, T., *The Abduction of a Limerick Heiress* (Dublin, 1998).

Barry, P. C., 'The legislation of the Synod of Thurles, 1850', *Irish Theological Quarterly* (1 June 1969), 131–66.

Beckett, J. C., *Protestant Dissent in Ireland, 1687–1780* (London, 1948).

Bergin, J. 'Irish private divorce bills and acts of the eighteenth century' in J. Kelly, J. McCafferty and C. McGrath (eds.), *People, Politics and Power: Essays on Irish History 1660–1850 in Honour of James I. McGuire* (Dublin, 2009), pp. 94–121.

Berry, H. and E. Foyster (eds.), *The Family in Early Modern England* (Cambridge, 2007).

Bishop, E., *The World of Mary O'Connell, 1778–1836* (Dublin, 1999).

(ed.), *My Darling Danny: Letters from Mary O'Connell to Her Daniel, 1830–1832* (Cork, 1998).

Boyle, D., *Half–Hanged MacNaghten* (Derry, 1993).

Brack, A., *Irregular Marriages at Portpatrick, Wigtownshire 1759–1826* (Dumfries, 1997).

Calvert, L., '"Do not forget your bit wife": Love, marriage and the negotiation of patriarchy in Irish Presbyterian marriages, c. 1780–1850', *Women's History Review*, 26, 3 (2017), 433–54.

'"He came to her bed pretending courtship" Sex, courtship and the making of marriage in Ulster, 1750–1844', *Irish Historical Studies*, 42 (162) (2018), 244–64.

Calvert, L. (ed.), 'The journal of John Tennent, 1786–90', *Analecta Hibernica*, 43 (2012), 91, 117.

Capp, B., 'Bigamous marriage in early modern England', *Historical Journal*, 52, 3 (2009), 537–56.

Carbery, M., *The Farm by Lough Gur* (Cork, 1973).

Christensen-Nugues, C. 'Parental authority and freedom of choice: The debate on clandestinity and parental consent at the Council of Trent (1545–63)', *Sixteenth Century Journal*, 45, 1 (2014), 51–72.

Clarkson, L. A., 'Irish population revisited, 1687–1821' in J. M. Goldstrom and L. A. Clarkson (eds.), *Irish Population, Economy, and Society: Essays in Honour of the Late K.H. Connell* (Oxford, 1981), pp. 13–35.

'Marriage and fertility in nineteenth–century Ireland' in R. B Outhwaite (ed.), *Marriage and Society: Studies in the Social History of Marriage* (New York, 1982), pp. 237–55.

'Love, labour and life: Women in Carrick–On–Suir in the late eighteenth century', *Irish Economic and Social History*, 20 (1993), 18–34.

'The demography of Carrick–on–Suir, 1799', *Proceedings of Royal Irish Academy*, Section C, 87 (1987), 13–36.

Clear, C., *Social Change and Everyday Life in Ireland, 1850–1922* (Manchester, 2007).

Coghlan, D., 'The Church and Christian marriage: Or Mrs McCann and the decree "Ne Temere"', *Catholic Bulletin*, 1, 1, 3 (March 1911), 139–47.

Conley, C., *Certain Other Countries: Homicide, Gender and National Identity in Late Nineteenth Century England, Ireland, Scotland and Wales* (Ohio, 2007).

Melancholy Accidents: The Meaning of Violence in Post–Famine Ireland (Kentucky, 1999).

Connell, K. H., *Irish Peasant Society* (Oxford, 1968).

The Population of Ireland, 1750–1845 (Oxford, 1950).

'Marriage in Ireland after the famine: The diffusion of the match', *Journal of the Statistical & Social Inquiry Society of Ireland*, 19 (1957), 82–103.

'Peasant marriage in Ireland after the Great Famine', *Past and Present*, 12 (1957), 76–91.

'Peasant marriage in Ireland: Its structure and development since the famine', *Economic History Review*, 14, 3 (1962), 502–23.

Connick, A. J., 'Canonical doctrine concerning mixed marriages – before Trent and during the seventeenth and early eighteenth centuries', *Jurist*, 20 (1960), 295–326; 398–418.

Connolly, S. J., *Priests and People in Pre-famine Ireland, 1780–1845* (Dublin, 1982).

'Illegitimacy and pre-nuptial pregnancy in Ireland before 1864: The evidence of some Catholic parish registers', *Irish Economic and Social History*, 6 (1979), 5–23.

'Marriage in pre-Famine Ireland' in A. Cosgrove (ed.), *Marriage in Ireland* (Dublin, 1985), pp. 78–98.

'Patterns of marriage in nineteenth and twentieth-century Ireland', *Familia*, 2, 8 (1992), 87–93.

Conway, W., 'Marriage in Ireland: Church and state', *Irish Ecclesiastical Record*, 68 (1946), 361–6.

Corish, P. J., *The Irish Catholic Experience. A Historical Survey* (Dublin, 1985).

'Catholic marriage under the penal code' in A. Cosgrove (ed.), *Marriage in Ireland* (Dublin, 1985), pp. 67–77.

Cosgrove, A., 'Marrying and marriage litigation in medieval Ireland' in P. L. Reynolds and J. Witte, Jr. (eds.), *To Have and to Hold: Marrying and Its Documentation in Western Christendom, 400–1600* (Cambridge, 2007), pp. 332–59.

Costello, K., 'Married women's property in Ireland, 1800–1900' in N. Howlin and K. Costello (eds.), *Law and the Family in Ireland, 1800–1950* (London, 2017), pp. 66–86.

Crossman, V., *Poverty and the Poor Law in Ireland, 1850–1914* (Liverpool, 2013).

Cullen, L. M., *Economy, Trade and Irish Merchants at Home and Abroad, 1600–1988* (Dublin, 2012).

'Irish history without the potato', *Past and Present*, 40 (1968), 72–83.

Cunningham, T. P., 'Mixed marriages in Ireland before *Ne Temere* decree', *Irish Ecclesiastical Review*, 101 (1964), 53–6.

Daly, M. E., *Dublin: The Deposed Capital: A Social and Economic History, 1860–1914* (Cork, 1985).

'Marriage, fertility and women's lives in twentieth-century Ireland (*c*. 1900–*c*. 1970)', *Women's History Review*, 15, 4 (2006), 571–85.

Daultrey, S., D. Dickson and C. Ó Gráda, 'Eighteenth-century Irish population: New perspectives from old sources', *The Journal of Economic History*, 41, 3 (Sept. 1981), 601–28.

De Bháldraithe, E., 'Mixed marriages and Irish politics: The effect of "Ne Temere"', *Studies: An Irish Quarterly Review*, 77, 307 (Autumn 1988), 284–99.

'Mixed marriages in the new code: Can we now implement the Anglican–Roman Catholic recommendations?', *Jurist*, 46 (1986), 419–51.

De Val, S., 'Robert Phaire and Elizabeth Grogan: An eighteenth century bigamy case', *The Past*, 8 (1970), 36–42.

Dickson, D., C. Ó Gráda and S. Daultrey, 'Hearth tax, household size and Irish population change, 1672–1821', *Proceedings of the Royal Irish Academy*, 82 C (1982), 125–81.

Doggett, M. E., *Marriage, Wife-Beating and the Law in Victorian England* (Columbia, 1993).

Donnelly Jr., J. S., *The Land and the People of Nineteenth-Century Cork: The Rural Economy and the Land Question* (London, 1975).

Duncan, W., 'Desertion and cruelty in Irish matrimonial law', *The Irish Jurist*, 2 (1972), 213–40.

Dwyer, P., *The Diocese of Killaloe: From the Reformation to the Close of the Eighteenth Century* (Dublin, 1878).

Earner–Byrne, L., '"Behind closed doors": Society, law and familial violence in Ireland, 1922–1990' in N. Howlin and K. Costello (eds.), *Law and the Family in Ireland, 1800–1950* (London, 2017), pp. 142–59.

Earner-Byrne, L., 'The family in Ireland, 1880–2015' in T. Bartlett (ed.), *The Cambridge History of Ireland, vol. 4, 1880 to the Present* (Cambridge, 2018), pp. 641–72.

Erickson, A. B., and Fr. J. R. McCarthy, 'The Yelverton case: Civil legislation and marriage', *Victorian Studies*, 14, 3 (March, 1971), 275–91.

Fallon, R., *A County Roscommon Wedding, 1892: The Marriage of John Hughes and Mary Gavin* (Dublin, 2004).

Farrell, E., *'A Most Diabolical Deed': Infanticide and Irish Society, 1850–1900* (Manchester, 2013).

Fernihough, A., C. Ó Gráda and B. M. Walsh, 'Mixed marriages in Ireland a century ago' (University College Dublin Centre for Economic Research Working Paper Series; WP14/07). http://hdl.handle.net/10197/5480. Accessed 25 January 2019.

Fitzgerald, J., 'Irish demography since 1740' in E. F. Biagini and M. E. Daly (eds.), *The Cambridge Social History of Modern Ireland* (Cambridge, 2017), pp. 7–24.

Fitzpatrick, D., 'Divorce and separation in modern Irish history', *Past and Present*, 114 (1987), 172–96.

Forrestal, A., *Catholic Synods in Ireland, 1600–1690* (Dublin 1998).

Foster, R. F., *Vivid Faces: The Revolutionary Generation in Ireland 1890–1923* (London, 2014).

Foyster, E., *Marital Violence: An English Family History, 1660–1857* (Cambridge, 2005).

Freeman, T. W., *Pre-famine Ireland: A Study in Historical Geography* (Manchester, 1957).

'Land and people, *c.* 1841' in W. E. Vaughan (ed.), *A New History of Ireland: Ireland under the Union, 1801–70* (Oxford, 1989).

Frost, G. S., *Living in Sin: Cohabiting as Husband and Wife in Nineteenth-Century England* (Manchester, 2008).

Gamble, J., *A View of Society and Manners in the North of Ireland: In the Summer and Autumn of 1812* (London, 1813).

Garnham, N., *The Courts, Crime and the Criminal Law in Ireland, 1692–1760* (Dublin, 1996).

Gillis, J. R., *For Better, For Worse: British Marriages, 1600 to the Present* (New York, 1985).

Goodbody, O., 'Seventeenth century Quaker marriages in Ireland', *Journal of the Friends' Historical Society*, 50, 4 (1964), 248–9.

Grace, D., 'The income of Catholic priests in pre-Famine Ireland: Some evidence from the Diocese of Killaloe', *Tipperary Historical Journal*, 30 (2017), 75–90.

Grace, P., *The Middle Class of Callan, Co. Kilkenny, 1825–45* (Dublin, 2015).

Grattan, S., 'Of pin-money and paraphernalia, the widow's shilling and a free ride to mass: One hundred and fifty years of property for the Irish wife' in N. Dawson, D. Greer and P. Ingram (eds.), *One Hundred and Fifty Years of Irish Law* (Belfast, 1996), pp. 213–38.

Greaves, R. L., *God's Other Children: Protestant Nonconformists and the Emergence of Denominational Churches in Ireland, 1660–1700* (Stanford, 1997).

Guinnane, T. W., *The Vanishing Irish: Households, Migration, and the Rural Economy in Ireland, 1850–1914* (Princeton, 1997).

Gurrin, B., 'Population and emigration, 1730–1845' in J. Kelly (ed.), *Cambridge History of Ireland* (4 vols., Cambridge, 2018), iii, pp. 204–27.

Häiring, B., *Marriage in the Modern World* (Cork, 1965).

Hanawalt, B. A., *The Ties That Bound: Peasant Families in Medieval England* (Oxford, 1986).

Harding, M., 'The curious incident of the Marriage Act (No 2) 1537 and the Irish statute book', *Legal Studies*, 32, 1 (2012), 78–108.

Helmholz, R. H., 'Local ecclesiastical courts in England' in W. Hartmann and K. Pennington (eds.), *The History of Courts and Procedure in Medieval Canon Law* (Washington, 2016), pp. 344–91.

Henry, B., *Dublin Hanged: Crime, Law Enforcement and Punishment in Late Eighteenth-Century Dublin* (Dublin, 1994).

Hepburn, A. C., *A Past Apart: Studies in the History of Catholic Belfast, 1850–1950* (Belfast, 1996).

Holcombe, L., *Wives and Property: Reform of the Married Women's Property law in Nineteenth-Century* (Oxford, 1983).

Holmes, A. R., *The Shaping of Ulster Presbyterian Belief and Practice, 1770–1840* (Oxford, 2006).

Howlin, N., *Juries in Ireland: Laypersons and Law in the Long Nineteenth Century* (Dublin, 2017).

Howlin, N. and K. Costello (eds.), *Law and the Family in Ireland, 1800–1950* (London, 2017).

Huggins, M., *Social Conflict in Pre-famine Ireland: The Case of County Roscommon* (Dublin, 2007).

Jameson, D., 'The religious upbringing of children in "mixed marriages": The evolution of Irish law', *New Hibernia Review*, 18, 2 (Summer 2014), 65–72.

Keenan, D., *The Catholic Church in Nineteenth-Century Ireland: A Sociological Study* (Dublin, 1983).

Kelly, J., *Gallows Speeches from Eighteenth-Century Ireland* (Dublin, 2001).
   'Infanticide in eighteenth-century Ireland', *Irish Economic and Social History*, 19 (1992), 5–26.
   'The abduction of women of fortune in eighteenth-century Ireland', *Eighteenth-Century Ireland*, 9 (1994), 7–43.

Kennedy, L., K. A. Miller and B. Gurrin, 'People and population change, 1600–1914' in L. Kennedy and P. Ollerenshaw (eds.), *Ulster Since 1600: Politics, Economy, and Society* (Oxford, 2013), pp. 58–73.

Kilroy, P., *Protestant Dissent and Controversy in Ireland, 1660–1714* (Cork, 1994).

Kinmonth, C., *Irish Country Furniture, 1700–1950* (New Haven, 1993).
   Irish Rural Interiors in Art (New Haven, 2006).

Lane, L., *Rosamund Jacob: Third Person Singular* (Dublin, 2010).

Larkin, E., 'The devotional revolution in Ireland, 1850–1875', *American Historical Review*, 77, 3 (June 1972), 625–52.

Lawrenson Swanson, D., *Emerging from the Shadow: The Lives of Sarah Anne Lawrenson and Lucy Olive Kingston* (Dublin, 1994).

Lee, G. A., 'Canon and civil marriage laws in Ireland', *Irish Ecclesiastical Record*, 67 (1946), 154–8.

Lee, J., 'Marriage and population growth in Ireland, 1750–1845', *Economic History Review*, 16, 2 (1963), 301–13.
   'Marriage and population in pre-Famine Ireland', *Economic History Review*, 21 (1968), 283–95.

Lee, R. M., 'Intermarriage, conflict and social control in Ireland: The decree "Ne Temere"', *Economic and Social Review*, 17, 2(1985), 11–27.

Leneman, L., *Promises, Promises: Marriage Litigation in Scotland, 1698–1830* (Edinburgh, 2003).

Lettmaier, S., *Broken Engagements: The Action for Breach of Promise of Marriage and the Feminine Ideal, 1800–1940* (Oxford, 2010).

Lindsey, K., '"The absolute distress of females": Irish abduction and British newspapers, 1800–1850', *Journal of Imperial and Commonwealth History*, 42, 2 (2014), 625–44.

Luddy, M., *Matters of Deceit: Breach of Promise to Marry Cases in Nineteenth and Early Twentieth Century Limerick* (Dublin, 2011).
   Prostitution and Irish Society, 1800–1940 (Cambridge, 2007).
   'Abduction in nineteenth-century Ireland', *New Hibernia Review*, 17, 2 (Summer 2013), 17–44.

'Moral rescue and unmarried mothers in Ireland in the 1920s', *Women's Studies*, 30, 6 (2001), 797–817.

'The early years of the NSPCC in Ireland', *Eire/Ireland*, 44, 1&2 (Spring/Summer 2009), 62–90.

'Unmarried mothers in Ireland', *Women's History Review*, 21, 1 (2011), 109–26.

Macafee, W., 'The demographic history of Ulster, 1750–1841' in H. T. Blethen and C. W. Wood, Jr. (eds.), *Ulster and North America: Transatlantic Perspectives on the Scotch-Irish* (Chapel Hill, 1991), pp. 41–60.

MacLysaght, E. and H. F. Berry, 'Report on documents relating to the wardenship of Galway', *Analecta Hibernica*, 14 (December 1944), 189–250.

MacPherson, D. A. J., '"Exploited with fury on a thousand platforms": Women, unionism and the *Ne Temere* decree in Ireland, 1908–1913' in J. Allen and R. Allen (eds.), *Faith of Our Fathers: Popular Culture and Belief in Post-Reformation England, Ireland and Wales* (Newcastle upon Tyne, 2009), pp. 157–75.

Malcolmson, A. P. W., *The Pursuit of the Heiress: Aristocratic Marriage in Ireland 1740–1840* (2nd ed., Belfast, 2006).

Manning, M., 'Dr Nicholas Madgett's Constitutio Ecclesiastica', *Journal of Kerry Archaeological and Historical Society*, 9 (1976), 68–91.

Marnane, D. G., *Land and Violence: A History of West Tipperary from 1660* (Tipperary, 1985).

McClintock, B., 'The 1844 Marriage Act: Politico-religious agitation and its consequence for Ulster genealogy', *Familia. Ulster Genealogical Review*, 1, 2 (1986), 33–58.

McCoole, S., *Easter Widows: Seven Irish Women Who Lived in the Shadow of the 1916 Rising* (London, 2014).

McDiarmid, L., *At Home in the Revolution: What Women Said and Did in 1916* (Dublin, 2015).

McGoff McCann, M., *Melancholy Madness, a Coroner's Casebook* (Cork, 2003).

McKenna, E. E., 'Marriage and fertility in post-Famine Ireland: A multivariate analysis', *American Journal of Sociology*, 80 (1974), 688–705.

McMahon, R., *Homicide in Pre-famine and Famine Ireland* (Liverpool, 2013).

Mhic Giobuin, M., 'Sir Henry Browne Hayes, abductor' in L. Clare and M. N. Chearbhaill (eds.), *Trouble with the Law: Crimes and Trials from Ireland's Past* (Dublin, 2007), pp. 37–54.

Nic Eoin, M., *B'ait Leo Bean. Gnéithe den Idé-eolaíocht Inscne I dTradisiún Liteartha na Gaeilge* (Dundalk, 1998).

Ó Danachair, C., 'Some marriage customs and their regional distribution', *Béaloideas*, 42–44, 1 (1976), 35–175.

'Marriage in Irish folk tradition' in A. Cosgrove (ed.), *Marriage in Ireland* (Dublin, 1985), pp. 99–115.

O'Dowd, A., 'Women in rural Ireland in the nineteenth century and early twentieth centuries: How the daughters, wives and sisters of small farmers and landless labourers fared', *Rural History*, 5, 2 (1994), 171–83.

O'Dowd, M., 'Adolescent girlhood in eighteenth-century Ireland' in M. O'Dowd and J. Purvis (eds.), *A History of the Girl: Formation, Identity and Education* (London, 2018), pp. 53–73.

A History of Women in Ireland, 1500–1800 (Harlow, 2005).

'Marriage breakdown in Ireland, *c.* 1660–1857' in N. Howlin and K. Costello (eds.), *Law and the Family in Ireland 1800–1950* (London, 2017), pp. 7–23.

'Mary Leadbeater: Modern woman and Irish Quaker' in D. Hayton and A. Holmes (eds.), *Ourselves Alone? Religion, Society and Politics in Eighteenth- and Nineteenth-century Ireland: Essays Presented to S. J. Connolly* (Dublin, 2016), pp. 137–53.

'Men, women, children and the family, 1550–1730' in J. Ohlmeyer (ed.), *Cambridge History of Ireland* (4 vols., Cambridge, 2018), ii, pp. 298–320.

'Ware versus Shirley' in M. Lyons (ed.), *Mystery Stories from Early Modern Ireland* (forthcoming).

'Women litigants in early eighteenth-century Ireland' in Teresa Phipps and Deborah Youngs (eds.), *Litigating women* (forthcoming).

Ó Grada, C., *Ireland: A New Economic History 1780–1939* (Oxford, 1995).

'Fertility control early in marriage in Ireland a century ago', *Journal of Population Economics*, 8, 4 (1995), 423–31.

Ó Gráda, C., T. Guinnane and C. M. Moehling, 'Fertility in South Dublin a Century Ago: First Look' (University College Dublin Centre for Economic Research Working Paper Series; WP01/26, 2001–11). http://hdl.handle.net/10197/503. Accessed 25 January 2019.

O'Neill, K., *Family and Farm in Pre-famine Ireland: The Parish of Killashandra* (Madison, 1984).

'Almost a gentlewoman: Gender and adolescence in the diary of Mary Shackleton' in M. O'Dowd and S. Wichert (eds.), *Chattel, Servant or Citizen: Women's Status in Church and State* (Belfast, 1995), pp. 91–102.

'"Pale and dejected, exhausted by the waste of sorrow": Courtship and the expression of emotion, Mary Shackleton, 1783–1791' in W. Ruberg and K. Steenbergh (eds.), *Sexed Sentiments: Interdisciplinary Perspectives on Gender and Emotion* (Amsterdam, 2011), pp. 47–73.

O'Shea, K., 'Three early nineteenth-century diocesan reports', *Journal of Kerry Archaeological Historical Society*, 10 (1977), 55–76.

Pollock, L., 'Rethinking patriarchy and the family in seventeenth-century England', *Journal of Family History*, 23 (1998), 3–27.

Power, T. P., *Forcibly without Her Consent: Abductions in Ireland, 1700–1850* (New York, 2010).

Probert, R., *Marriage Law and Practice in the Long Eighteenth Century: A Reassessment* (Cambridge, 2009).

'R v Millis reconsidered: Binding contracts and bigamous marriages', *Legal Studies*, 28, 3 (Sept. 2008), 337–55.

'The impact of the Marriage Act of 1753: Was it really "a most cruel law for the fair sex"?' *Eighteenth-Century Studies*, 38, 2 (2005), 247–62.

'The judicial interpretation of Lord Hardwicke's Act 1753', *Journal of Legal History*, 23, 2 (2002), 129–51.

Quinlan, C., *Genteel Revolutionaries: Anna and Thomas Haslam and the Irish Women's Movement* (Cork, 2002).

'"Dark and obscure to the average wife": Maria Stopes, Anna and Thomas Haslam, and the birth control question', *Women's Studies*, 30, 6 (2001), 779–96.

Rattigan, C., *'What Else Could I Do?" Single Mothers and Infanticide, Ireland 1900–1950* (Dublin, 2012).

Reynolds, P. L., 'Marrying and its documentation in pre-modern Europe: Consent, celebration and property' in P. L. Reynolds and J. Witte, Jr. (eds.), *To Have and to Hold: Marrying and Its Documentation in Western Christendom, 400–1600* (Cambridge, 2007), pp. 1–42.

Rhodes, R. M., *Women and the Family in Post-Famine Ireland: Status and Opportunity in a Patriarchal Society* (New York, 1992).

Roberts, J., *Divorce Bills in the Imperial Parliament* (Dublin, 1906).

Ryan, S. (ed.), *Marriage and the Irish: A Miscellany* (Dublin, 2019).

Shatter, A. J., *Family Law in the Republic of Ireland* (2nd ed., Dublin, 1981).

Smout, T. C., 'Scottish marriage, regular and irregular 1500–1940' in R. B. Outhwaite (ed.), *Marriage and Society: Studies in the Social History of Marriage* (London, 1981), pp. 204–36.

Staves, S., *Married Women's Separate Property in England, 1660–1833* (Cambridge, MA, 1990).

'Money for honour: Damages for criminal conversation', *Studies in Eighteenth-Century Culture*, 11 (1982), 279–97.

'"Pin money"', *Studies in Eighteenth-Century Culture*, 14 (1985), 47–77.

'Separate maintenance contracts', *Eighteenth Century Life*, 11, 2 (1987), 78–101.

Steiner-Scott, L., '"To bounce a boot off her now and then...": Domestic violence in post-Famine Ireland' in M. G. Valiulis and M. O'Dowd (eds.), *Women and Irish History* (Dublin, 1997), pp. 124–43.

Stone, L., *The Family, Sex and Marriage in England, 1500–1800* (New York, 1977).

Road to Divorce: England, 1530–1987 (Oxford, 1990).

Uncertain Unions: Marriage in England, 1660–1753 (Oxford, 1992).

Urquhart, D., 'Ireland and the Divorce and Matrimonial Causes Act of 1857' *Journal of Family History*, 38, 3 (2013), 301–20.

'Irish divorce and domestic violence, 1857–1922', *Women's History Review*, 22, 5 (2013), 820–37.

'A woman's reply: Women and divorce law reform in Victorian Ireland' in B. Walsh (ed.), *Knowing Their Place? The Intellectual and Professional Life of Women in the 19th-Century* (Dublin, 2014), pp. 128–47.

Irish Divorce: A History (Cambridge, 2020).

Vaughan, W. E., *Murder Trials in Ireland, 1836–1914* (Dublin, 2009).

Weiner, M., *Matters of Felony: A Reconstruction* (London, 1967).

Wiener, M. J., *Men of Blood: Violence, Manliness, and Criminal Justice in Victorian England* (Cambridge, 2006).

Wilson, D., *Women Marriage and Property in Wealthy Landed Families in Ireland, 1750–1850* (Manchester, 2009).

Wilson, J. C., *Conor: 1881–1968: The Life and Work of an Ulster Artist* (Belfast, 1981).

Wilson, R., *Elite Women in Ascendancy Ireland, 1690–1745: Imitation and Innovation* (Woodbridge, 2015).

Wood, H., 'Registration of marriages in Ireland', *The New Irish Jurist and Local Government Review*, 12 (Sept. 1902), 379–80; 19 (Sept. 1902), 386–7; 26 (Sept. 1902), 392–4.

'Report by Mr Herbert Wood on certain registers of irregular marriages, celebrated by unlicensed clergymen, known as couple beggars', *Thirty-Third Report of the Deputy Keeper of the Public Records and Keeper of the State Papers in Ireland*. HC 1902 [1176] 49 779 (Dublin, 1902).

Wright, J. J., 'Love, loss and learning in late Georgian Belfast' in D. W. Hayton and A. R. Holmes (eds.), *Ourselves Alone? Religion, Society and Politics in Eighteenth- and Nineteenth-Century Ireland* (Dublin, 2016), pp. 169–91.

'Robert Hyndman's toe: Romanticism, schoolboy politics and the affective revolution in late Georgian Belfast' in C. Cox and S. Riordan (eds.), *Adolescence in Modern Irish History* (Basingstoke, 2015), pp. 15–41.

UNPUBLISHED THESES

Barkley, J. M., 'A history of the ruling eldership in Irish Presbyterianism' (2 vols., unpublished MA thesis, Queen's University Belfast, 1952).

Calvert, L., 'Love, life and the family in the Ulster Presbyterian community, 1780–1844' (unpublished PhD thesis, Queen's University Belfast, 2015).

Gray, W. P., 'A social history of illegitimacy in Ireland from the late eighteenth to the early twentieth century' (unpublished PhD thesis, Queen's University Belfast, 2000).

Gurrin, B. F., 'Land and people in Wicklow, 1660–1840' (2 vols., unpublished PhD thesis, NUI Maynooth, 2006).

McGarry, J. G., 'The statutes of Tuam from the Council of Trent to the nineteenth century' (unpublished MA thesis, University College Galway, 1932).

Thomas Smith, G., 'The state and the culture of violence in London, 1760–1840' (unpublished PhD thesis, University of Toronto, 1999).

ONLINE SOURCES

Board of Guardian Minutes: https://www.limerick.ie/discover/explore/historical-resources/limerick-archives/archive-collections/limerick-union-board. Accessed January 2017.

Catholic Encyclopedia: www.newadvent.org/cathen/14441b.htm. Accessed September 2019.

Central Statistics Office: www.cso.ie. Accessed 9 March 2020.

Dictionary of Irish Biography Online: http://dib.cambridge.org.

Early English Books Online: http://eebo.chadwyck.com.

Eighteenth Century Collections Online: http://find.galegroup.com.

Find My Past: www.findmypast.co.uk.

Irish Legislation Database: www.qub.ac.uk/ild/?func=help&section=sources. Accessed 28 January 2019.

Moxhams of Ireland: https://moxhamireland.wordpress.com/2016/07/21/charl tons–endowment–charitable–trust–fund–marriage–certificates/. Accessed 6 February 2020.

Oxford Dictionary of National Biography Online: www.oxforddnb.com.

Studies in Scarlet Marriage and Sexuality in the U.S. & U.K., 1815–1914 https:// curiosity.lib.harvard.edu/studies–in–scarlet. Accessed 29 January 2019.

Index